Inside Active Directory

Inside Active Directory

A System Administrator's Guide

Sakari Kouti

Mika Seitsonen

✦✦ Addison-Wesley

BOSTON • SAN FRANCISCO • NEW YORK • TORONTO • MONTREAL
LONDON • MUNICH • PARIS • MADRID
CAPETOWN • SYDNEY • TOKYO • SINGAPORE • MEXICO CITY

Many of the designations used by manufacturers and sellers to distinguish their products are claimed as trademarks. Where those designations appear in this book, and Addison-Wesley was aware of a trademark claim, the designations have been printed with initial capital letters or in all capitals.

The authors and publisher have taken care in the preparation of this book, but make no expressed or implied warranty of any kind and assume no responsibility for errors or omissions. No liability is assumed for incidental or consequential damages in connection with or arising out of the use of the information or programs contained herein.

The publisher offers discounts on this book when ordered in quantity for bulk purchases and special sales. For more information, please contact:

U.S. Corporate and Government Sales
(800) 382-3419
corpsales@pearsontechgroup.com

For sales outside of the U.S., please contact:

International Sales
(317) 581-3793
international@pearsontechgroup.com

Visit Addison-Wesley on the Web: www.awprofessional.com

Library of Congress Cataloging-in-Publication Data

Kouti, Sakari.
   Inside Active Directory : a system administrator's guide / Sakari Kouti, Mika Seitsonen.
        p.   cm.
   Includes bibliographical references and index.
   ISBN 0-201-61621-1 (alk. paper)
   1. Directory services (Computer network technology) 2. Microsoft Windows (Computer file) I. Seitsonen, Mika. II. Title.

TK5105.595 .K68 2002
005.7'13769—dc21   2001045733

ISBN: 0-201-61621-1
Text printed on recycled and acid-free paper.
ISBN 0201616211
3 4 5 6 7 8 MA   06 05 04
3rd Printing   January 2004

To my son, Miika
—Sakari

To my parents, who rest in peace
—Mika

Contents

Chapter 4   **Securing Active Directory**   **203**

Preface

During the seven years that Windows NT was sold before Windows 2000 shipped, administrators didn't need to learn practically anything new, at least about the core operating system features. User and group management, domains and domain models, and resource management had been the same in all Windows NT versions.

With the introduction of Windows 2000 and Active Directory, that all changed. There is a huge difference in managing Windows networks over the old NT administration model. Therefore, Active Directory will require quite a lot of study on the part of NT professionals.

Despite some administrative wizards in the user interface and the new Microsoft Management Console (MMC) administration interface, implementing and administering Active Directory requires probably more learning, testing, piloting, and planning than Windows NT required.

ABOUT THIS BOOK

This book is an implementer and administrator's guide to Active Directory. Throughout the book, you will learn the workings, architecture, administration, and planning of Active Directory. Depending on your needs, however, you don't have to read this book from cover to cover, as we describe later in this preface.

The following list evaluates the appropriateness of this book for a number of potential audiences.

- *A current NT professional.* You are the target audience for this book. However, you may want to browse relatively fast through the introductory pages that we have in the beginning of many chapters.

- *A current NetWare or UNIX professional.* Prior knowledge of Windows NT is not required to successfully learn from this book. Your earlier networking skills will most likely enable you to pick up each topic quite fast. However, you probably shouldn't skip any introductory topics.

- *A network operating systems novice.* Because we tend to start each chapter with the very basics, at least in theory you can use this book to effectively learn Active Directory. Obviously, you need to invest more time reading than an experienced IT professional. You should also have a test PC that you can use to try out the different tasks and experiments that the book describes.

- *A current Windows 2000 professional.* Even if you are already familiar with Active Directory, we trust that you will learn more than a few things from this book.

- *A developer.* This book is an administrator's guide and not a programmer's guide. However, the book contains more architectural topics than the average book for an administrator, so you may find this book valuable to you in addition to a programmer's guide.

For all target audiences, it is possible that you are not interested in all the advanced topics in this book, so you are free to skip any of them.

We believe that this book has the following strengths.

- We present well-thought-out diagrams that help you easily comprehend the various key concepts and other topics related to Active Directory.

- At worst, a book just shows screen shots and shortly explains what is already evident from the user interface or the online Help. In contrast, this book contains thorough and accurate information on the topics it covers.

- We claim that this book contains very few errors.

- Even though this book is not a reference guide, we present many extensive reference tables.

- If you install Active Directory on a test PC, you can try out most of the tasks and experiments described in this book, whether they are written to be walk-throughs or not.

We have divided the book into three parts.

- *Part I: Background Skills* (Chapters 1 and 2) gives the big picture of Active Directory so you can successfully plan and implement an Active Directory network. This part also discusses the installation of Windows 2000 and Active Directory.

- *Part II: Core Skills* (Chapters 3 through 7) describes the concepts, planning, and administration of both the physical and the logical structure of Active

Directory. The topics presented in this part include user and group management, access control, and Group Policy. Even though Part III covers advanced skills, most chapters in this part discuss related advanced topics.

- *Part III: Advanced Skills* (Chapters 8 through 11) looks at advanced techniques, including the schema and scripting. Along with these topics we also uncover many aspects of Active Directory architecture. You can probably live without the information in these chapters, but by reading them you can greatly deepen your knowledge and understanding of Active Directory and make use of it when implementing and administering Active Directory networks.

We'll now present a short summary of each chapter. Mika wrote Chapter 2 and Chapter 7, and Sakari wrote the remaining chapters.

Chapter 1: Active Directory: The Big Picture

Before going into detail, we give you a general picture of Active Directory. After you learn the concepts introduced in this chapter, you can freely skip some later chapters that you might not be interested in. However, we encourage you to browse through the table of contents of any such chapter to make sure that you are not going to unintentionally miss anything important.

Chapter 2: Installation of Windows 2000 and Active Directory

In this chapter, we explain how to install both Windows 2000 and Active Directory. We also describe the post-installation tasks, as well as how to automate and troubleshoot installation.

Chapter 3: Managing OUs, Users, and Groups

Once you have an Active Directory domain up and running, one obvious task is to create a user account for each user and plan how to enhance user administration by using groups and organizational units (OUs). This chapter looks at managing OUs, users, contacts, groups, and computer objects, and covers some related topics.

Chapter 4: Securing Active Directory

Active Directory has an access control mechanism that enables you to define who can read or modify what information in Active Directory. In this chapter, we explain the concepts and architecture of access control, as well as how to manage permissions in various scenarios.

Chapter 5: Sites and Replication

For Active Directory to work efficiently when your network spans multiple geographic locations, you must plan and implement the physical structure and define it in Active Directory itself. In this chapter, we describe the concepts, management, and advanced topics of the physical structure. Some of the content is also relevant for a company with just one site.

Chapter 6: Domains and Forests

Active Directory has several levels of hierarchies that you can use to implement an effective logical structure for your company network. In this chapter, we discuss whether you should use one or many domains and one or many forests, and how you should plan and manage that logical structure. We also revisit the physical structure, because it somewhat overlaps with the logical structure. In addition, we explain the anatomy of LDAP searches.

Chapter 7: Group Policy

Active Directory has an extensive management architecture called "Group Policy." You can use Group Policy to manage user desktops and server settings, as we describe in this chapter. You learn the architecture, inheritance, and processing of Group Policy in this chapter.

Chapter 8: Active Directory Schema

This chapter examines the Active Directory data model and how it is enforced by the rules of the schema. After reading this chapter, you'll better understand how Active Directory works behind the scenes and you'll also gain knowledge that you can use if you are going to extend the schema.

Chapter 9: Extending the Schema

One of Active Directory's advantages over Windows NT is that you can extend Active Directory schema, either to accommodate directory-enabled applications or for some administrative purpose. In this chapter, we explain the considerations for extensions and describe the process itself.

Chapter 10: Administration Scripts: Concepts

By downloading scripts from the Internet or writing your own scripts and executing them you can greatly enhance and automate administration. In this chapter we explain how to get started with technologies such as Windows Script Host (WSH), VBScript, and Active Directory Service Interfaces (ADSI).

Chapter 11: Administration Scripts: Examples

In this chapter, we present over 50 sample scripts along with their explanations. Outputs of many of the scripts provide some architectural information about Active Directory and you can run those scripts without understanding what they do on each line. Therefore, you can use these scripts not only for various administrative tasks, but also to gain more knowledge about Active Directory. This chapter also introduces some additional scripting concepts, such as ActiveX Data Objects (ADO), between the sample scripts.

About the Authors

Both authors of this book are Finnish. Even though Finland is a small country, you may be familiar with something that came from here—for example, the Linux operating system, Nokia cell phones, and the IRC protocol for Internet chatting.

Sakari has worked with microcomputers for 19 years and with PC networks for 15 years. The last 12 years he has instructed courses on network operating systems, such as LAN Manager, NetWare, and Windows NT. Because he has always enjoyed learning new technologies thoroughly and explaining and teaching them to others, it was quite natural for Sakari to write first technical articles and later this book. While still a student back in the 1980s, Sakari worked part-time as a programmer, which helped him write the scripting chapters in this book.

Mika's network experience also spans over 10 years. After spending 5 years in implementing networks, he became a network trainer. Consequently, Mika shares Sakari's background in continually learning new technologies and passing that information on to others.

This book has a companion Web site: `http://www.kouti.com/`. This site contains all the sample scripts presented in the book as downloadable files, as well as some other tables and files relating to the book's contents.

Acknowledgments

We would like to thank Gary Clarke of Addison-Wesley, who originally hired us to write this book. We would also like to thank Rebecca Bence, Jenie Pak, Michael Slaughter, and Stephane Thomas from Addison-Wesley, as well as the entire production team for their cooperation and assistance (including Joan M. Flaherty, Tyrrell Albaugh, Amy Fleischer, Nicole LeClerc, and Kathy Glidden).

We are deeply grateful to our Addison-Wesley reviewers, Jeff Dunkelberger, Scott Lewandowski, and Erik Olson, who read the manuscript and gave us valuable feedback. Our special thanks go to Keith Walls for his great reviews.

Our thanks also go to Pertti Pellonpoika and our other colleagues at Knowledge-Pool Tieturi for discussions that helped in creating this book. We also appreciate the patience of KnowledgePool Tieturi personnel when we were sometimes absent, or at least absentminded, because of the writing process. We acknowledge KnowledgePool Tieturi as a fine training organization and as a working environment that stimulates learning. The company also gave us the opportunity to use 200 PCs as a lab if we needed to run any tests for a large Active Directory environment. However, usually fewer than 10 PCs were quite enough.

Andreas Luther and Richard Ault of Microsoft answered many of our questions, for which we are grateful.

Sakari would like to personally thank Dina Ralston, who hired him to write some articles for *Windows NT Magazine* (nowadays *Windows 2000 Magazine*) and as a member of the magazine's editorial review board. This started the series of events that led to writing this book. Sakari would also like to thank Reino Korpela, who taught Sakari computers at school back in 1977 and who later gave him his first summer job in microcomputers in 1982; Ilkka Liedes, who hired him in 1986 to work with personal computers and who soon after assigned him his first project with PC networks; and Risto Linturi and Veikko Kanerva, who hired him in

1989 to instruct courses on PC operating systems and network operating systems. And finally, Sakari would like to express special thanks to Satu. His first son, Miika, was born 12 months before the manuscript deadline, and Satu took care of Miika so that Sakari could concentrate (well, mostly anyway) on writing and finishing the book.

Mika first and foremost thanks Sakari for asking him to join this project, which Mika regards as yet another great learning experience. Mika also appreciates his wonderful girlfriend, Päivi, for having the patience for Mika's book writing, which seemed to always be on the to-do list. Mika's thanks are also due to Peter Ting, who gave him great confidence and advice for the walk of life.

Sakari Kouti
Espoo, Finland

Mika Seitsonen
Helsinki, Finland
September 2001

BACKGROUND SKILLS

Active Directory: The Big Picture

In this chapter we introduce the major concepts, definitions, building blocks, and features of Active Directory. This overview provides a frame of reference so that as you read the later chapters, you can see where each topic fits into the big picture. Topics in this chapter include

- A brief comparison of Active Directory to Windows NT and to Novell's NDS (Novell Directory Services)
- Basic building blocks, such as domains, domain controllers, trust relationships, organizational units, groups, objects, sites, replication, and global catalog
- Active Directory hierarchies: OU trees, which are built of organizational units (OUs); domain trees; and forests
- An explanation of the way Active Directory uses the Domain Name System (DNS) and its dynamic updates, Group Policy, access control with inheritance, and delegation
- Architecture, including the data model, the schema, container and leaf objects, partitions, object naming, X.500, the Lightweight Directory Access Protocol (LDAP), programmatic access, the Kerberos authentication protocol, and public key infrastructure (PKI)
- Other features of interest, such as virtual containers and publishing
- Active Directory's limitations

The presentation of these topics is brief because we address most of them in depth in later chapters. We discuss the following topics, however, only in this chapter: a comparison of Active Directory to Windows NT and NDS, object naming, X.500, the Kerberos protocol, PKI, and Active Directory's limitations.

INTRODUCTION TO ACTIVE DIRECTORY

Active Directory is a *directory service* and, like any directory service, its ultimate purpose is to store information about users, resources, and other network entities, and to provide that information to anyone or anything that has access to the directory, according to access permissions. This information helps administrators to manage the network and users to find people and resources.

Active Directory replaces the user account database and domain models that were used in Windows NT. It also adds a wealth of features that qualify it as a directory service, rather than a simple user account database.

Even though Active Directory has a database of information, it is not a relational database like SQL Server. The information in Active Directory is represented as *objects* that you create for each user, group, and computer. There are also objects for contact people, printers, shared folders, application services, other resources, and configuration information.

A Brief Description

We can describe Active Directory from three points of view. From each point, we view one of the three "faces" of Active Directory:

- *The Windows NT face.* Administrators can create user accounts to control how each user can use the network. Users log on using these accounts and act according to the settings that administrators have specified (such as having to change the password every month).

- *The enterprise services face.* Active Directory provides a scalable and hierarchical infrastructure for managing enterprise-sized distributed networks. For example, administration of various parts can be delegated to lower levels. If desired or necessary, the head office administrators can set policies that affect desktops of some or every satellite office.

- *The directory face.* An organization can store its address book of users and customers, as well as other relevant information about anything they want. For example, it can use Active Directory to search users by name or printers by features. This directory need not be for internal use only. If an organization desires, it can publish part of the directory on the Internet. Because permissions specify granular access to the information, the organization can publish some information (such as phone number extensions and e-mail addresses) to its partner companies on the Internet, other information (such as office numbers and manager names) only to its employees, and yet other information (such as more sensitive human-resources data) only to privileged managers in the company.

We can also characterize Active Directory by three types of users.

- *Administrators* manage and configure the network, including the user accounts, services, and devices. They do this by creating specific objects and storing appropriate configuration and other information in them. All administration can be done through Active Directory, and doing so should result in efficient administration, as well as a secure and consistent network environment.

- *Users* log on to Active Directory (i.e., "to the network") using a password or a smart card, and then use the configured resources and possibly search for people, resources, or other useful information. If permitted, users can also modify information in Active Directory. Active Directory group policies can provide users with certain desktop settings and restrictions, as well as offer company applications for them to use. Group policies are applied during logon and periodically refreshed afterward.

- *Applications, services, and computing devices* can read their configuration information from Active Directory and act accordingly. They can also write information to Active Directory, if so programmed. Consequently, we can talk about *directory-enabled applications (DEAs)* and *directory-enabled networking (DEN)*. In addition to configuration information, an application (for example, a faxing application) can use Active Directory in ways it would use an address book. The server services of client/server applications (using such technologies as RPC, WinSock, and COM) may publish their connection points in Active Directory for users and client applications to find them.

In general, the information in Active Directory falls into one of two categories.

- Certain information in certain objects is *significant* (as we call it), which means that it affects how some aspects of Windows 2000 work. For example, significant information controls when and how network users can log on or which services they can use.

- The remaining information is *informational* (e.g., Jack's postal address). It may be interesting and useful to people or directory-enabled applications, but Windows 2000 doesn't use this information itself. Consequently, informational data doesn't have the controlling aspect of significant information.

Given these definitions, informational information can still control users' lives, even though Windows 2000 doesn't use that information. For example, a device to control the main door of a company could use Active Directory to store information such as the access codes. In this example, when a user types a key code at the door, the device can check Active Directory for approval of the code and open the door only if the code is verified.

NOTE
We use the terms *significant* and *informational* to help you understand the two categories of information that Active Directory contains. You can use the categories as a reference, but it is not important to try to place each piece of information into one of the categories.

Finally, Active Directory has the following technical features:

- The information in Active Directory is highly available because identical information is on several servers (called *domain controllers*). As administrators design the network, they can choose the location of each server. This provides both fault tolerance and, in the case of a geographically dispersed network, proximity of information.

- A change in one domain controller is guaranteed to reach the other domain controllers, even though this will take a while. Consequently, some domain controllers may be out-of-date at any given time. This concept is called *loose consistency*. Inside a local area network (LAN), each change in one domain controller should reach any other domain controller within 15 minutes (or up to 20 minutes in some large networks with tens of domain controllers).

- Because all changes (are likely to) need to be copied to several domain controllers, both in the same building as well as perhaps to offices located on other continents, the information put in Active Directory should be "globally" useful and relatively static, and each piece should not be very large. If an organization needs to store information that doesn't fit these criteria, it should consider storing that information somewhere else, such as the SQL Server or file system.

- Hierarchies and permissions allow distributed management of the data. Network administrators can delegate tasks so that assisting administrators and even end users can maintain part of the information. Also, Active Directory is one of the foundations of the Windows 2000 security model.

- Permissions allow control over which users will see what information.

- Optimization for a high number of reads.

- The information is highly typed, which means that Active Directory enforces rules for the structure and content of the information.

- Distributed security allows companies to build intranets and extranets and to use distributed applications in this environment.

- Allowance of standards-based read and write access using the LDAP protocol. Additionally, LDAP allows effective searches on the information in Active Directory.

The First Look at Active Directory

Figure 1.1 and Figure 1.2 show two basic views of Active Directory. The screen shot in Figure 1.1 shows an administrator's view of the objects for users, groups, and contacts. The screen shot in Figure 1.2 shows the view an end user sees when she opens My Network Places. In this case, the two views show exactly the same objects, but this may not be the case every time.

NOTE   As Figure 1.1 and Figure 1.2 show, the administrator's and end user's views of the directory are quite similar. In practice, however, end users typically use a search user interface instead of a navigation tree.

History

Windows 2000 and Active Directory are the latest in a long line of Microsoft operating systems and network operating systems (NOS). In this section, we review

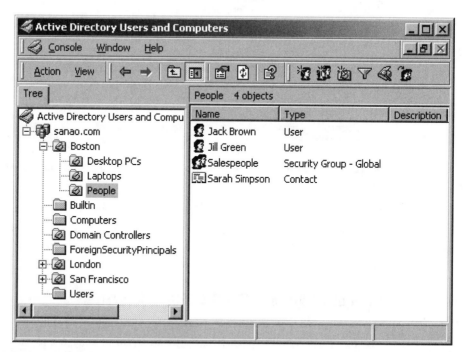

FIGURE 1.1 An administrator can create a tree of folders, like the tree in the left pane. Each folder may contain user, group, and contact objects, among others. Note that this figure shows only a small part of Active Directory's contents.

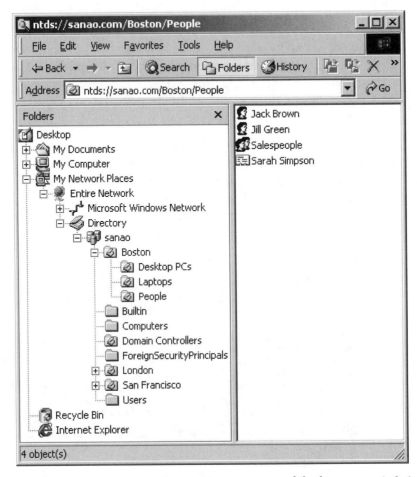

FIGURE 1.2 An end user can open My Network Places to see part of the directory tree in Active Directory.

Microsoft's previous NOS products, explore the history of directories, including some products from other vendors, and look at the development of Windows 2000.

PREVIOUS MICROSOFT NETWORK OPERATING SYSTEMS

Microsoft's first network operating system was MS-NET, which was used in the 1980s with Microsoft's disk operating system (MS-DOS). Microsoft's next NOS was LAN Manager, which first shipped in 1988 to be used with Operating System/2 (OS/2) version 1.1. OS/2 was developed jointly by Microsoft and IBM. With either MS-NET plus MS-DOS or LAN Manager plus OS/2, there was a separate NOS and an operating system, but the subsequent version, Windows NT, integrated the two. Microsoft and IBM had agreed that IBM would develop OS/2 version 2 while Microsoft would simultaneously work on OS/2 version 3. Microsoft started this development in early 1989.

In 1990, the launch of Windows 3.0 was a huge success. Microsoft changed the user and programming interfaces of the version it was developing from OS/2 Presentation Manager to Windows and changed the product name from OS/2 to Windows NT. Understandably, the cooperation between Microsoft and IBM ended, so Microsoft became the sole owner and developer of Windows NT. Since 1993, Microsoft has published the following versions of Windows NT:

- 1993: Windows NT 3.1
- 1994: Windows NT 3.5
- 1995: Windows NT 3.51
- 1996: Windows NT 4.0
- 1997: Windows NT 4.0 Service Pack 3
- 1998: Windows NT 4.0 Service Pack 4

Although not truly new versions, the two service packs are in the list because they brought a number of new features to Windows NT. For a few years there was no new version of Windows NT because Microsoft focused all its efforts on the next major version of its operating system, Windows 2000.

THE HISTORY OF DIRECTORIES

Telephone directories as well as other directories and catalogs on paper existed long before any computer systems. Now in the computer era, we have new kinds of directories, including

- *E-mail systems* such as Lotus (currently owned by IBM) Notes, Novell Group-Wise, and Microsoft Exchange. Each has a directory of the e-mail users of the system and the contact people outside the organization.
- Practically all *network operating systems* have had some kind of directory to contain the usernames and passwords of the users of that network. Examples are Microsoft LAN Manager and Windows NT with their user account databases, as well as Novell NetWare 3 with its Bindery.
- There have been also *real directory services in network operating systems.* The most notable are StreetTalk and NDS. Banyan started selling StreetTalk for its VINES network operating system in 1980s, and Novell shipped NDS with NetWare 4.0 in 1993.
- *Internet directories* are offered by companies such as Yahoo, Switchboard, and WhoWhere. If you open the Windows 2000 Address Book, you will see a longer list of these companies.

All the directories listed (short of NDS) concentrate on storing contact information about users or information that allows users to log on. However, a directory doesn't have to be only for these purposes. For example, Active Directory allows storing information about practically anything, although its foremost use is to store information about people.

Directory standards—the most important being X.500 and LDAP—are part of directory history. X.500 is an international standard for directories and LDAP is a popular protocol for accessing directories. (We will discuss both standards at the end of this chapter.) The following chronology indicates the major milestones in the history of directories.

- 1988: The first version of X.500 was finalized.
- 1992: Developers from the University of Michigan released the first LDAP software.
- 1993: The first version of LDAP (LDAPv1) was published as RFC (Request For Comments) 1487.
- 1995: LDAPv2 was published as RFC 1777 (and other RFCs).
- 1996: About 40 companies, including Microsoft, Netscape, and Novell, announced that they would support LDAP in their directory services products.
- 1997: LDAPv3 was published as RFC 2251 (and others).
- 1998: Netscape shipped the first commercial LDAPv3 server.

Finally, as you know, Windows 2000 with Active Directory shipped in 2000.

THE HISTORY OF WINDOWS 2000

The development of Windows NT's successor, code-named Windows "Cairo," started early in the 1990s, even though Windows NT wasn't published until 1993. Cairo's roots might be in the keynote speech of the Comdex trade show in 1990. In that speech Microsoft's Bill Gates introduced a vision called "information at your fingertips," and demonstrated some of its possible technologies accompanied by music and themes from the TV series *Twin Peaks.*

In 1991 the project for Cairo was launched, and Jim Allchin was appointed to be the project lead. Before joining Microsoft, Allchin was a technology officer at Banyan, the maker of StreetTalk. Allchin was a suitable choice for the Cairo project because he was a professor-type guy who could understand and develop new technologies that many people in the industry or at Microsoft couldn't even imagine.

Originally Cairo was planned to contain, among other things, an object-oriented file system, a distributed file system, and Kerberos security. The last two features made it to Windows 2000, but the object-oriented file system did not. A directory service was also part of the picture, but at that time X.500 was too complex and resource-intensive to be used in personal computers. Only some years later, when the lighter LDAP was born, could Microsoft start incorporating it to Cairo.

Cairo was a parallel project to Windows NT development. The two had separate project teams; however, some Cairo technologies were used already in Windows NT. Also, during the years the definition of Cairo evolved, and at some point it began to refer to a vision of a future Windows version instead of a specific forthcoming product.

In 1996 Microsoft demonstrated Cairo technologies to the public and named the forthcoming product "Windows NT 5.0." Although it was anticipated that Windows NT 5.0 would ship in 1997, a few more years passed before the launch.

In 1998 Microsoft renamed Windows NT 5.0 to "Windows 2000" for at least two reasons. People often called Windows NT simply "NT," which was a trademark of Northern Telecom (currently Nortel Networks). However, Microsoft does own the trademark "Windows." Also, Microsoft was planning to consolidate all Windows versions to the NT platform, in which case the designation "NT" would no longer be needed.

Windows 2000 had quite a long beta-testing phase, as the following chronology illustrates:

- 1996: Technology preview to run on Windows NT 4.0
- 1997: Windows NT 5.0 beta 1
- 1998: Windows NT 5.0 beta 2
- 1999: Windows 2000 beta 3
- 2000: Windows 2000

The main new feature of Windows 2000 is its directory service (Active Directory). When Microsoft launched Windows NT 4.0 in 1996, its marketing actually renamed Windows NT domain models "directory services," but the change was in the name only, not in the features.

Because Novell NDS shipped in 1993 and Windows 2000 shipped in 2000, Microsoft could be considered 7 years behind Novell. However, in its first version, Active Directory is already an enterprise-class directory service, but of course it could benefit from some maturing. An advantage over Novell, however, is that Microsoft got a fresh start to build its directory service for the needs of the current intranet and Internet era. The only old burden Microsoft carries is the old Windows NT domain concept, which introduces some rigidity to Active Directory.

Active Directory Compared to Windows NT

Table 1.1 lists some technical changes from Windows NT to Active Directory. If you are not familiar with the previous version, you probably will want to skip this table. We explain each item later in the chapter.

TABLE 1.1 Windows NT versus Active Directory

Feature	Windows NT*	Active Directory
Group types	Only security groups	Security groups and distribution groups
Group scopes	Global and local groups	Global, universal, and domain local groups
Group nesting	Global groups may be members of local groups	Free nesting within each scope
Trust relationships	Intransitive, one way (although you can create one trust to either direction)	Transitive, bidirectional
Replication type	Single master from PDC to BDC	Multimaster from any domain controller to another, except in some special cases
Replication in WAN	Needs to replicate the same data multiple times over a WAN link (to different BDCs)	Replicates the data only once over a given WAN link
Replication amount	Whole object at a time	Only changed properties of an object
Replication amount for a new user account	About 1KB	At least about 4KB (however, this is compressed up to over 10:1 when replicated between sites)
Member server may be changed to domain controller without reinstalling	No	Yes
Per-domain controller administration privileges	No	Some
Object hierarchy	No	In folders called organizational units (OUs) (and in other container objects)
Delegation of administration	Only per domain (also some "delegation" with operator privileges)	Per OU, per object, or per attribute (and also operator privileges)
Policies	System Policy	Group Policy
Extensible schema	No	Yes, may add new object classes and properties

(*continued*)

TABLE 1.1 (*continued*)

Feature	Windows NT*	Active Directory
User object properties	About 32	Over 200 (in the base schema)
TCP/IP	May be used	Must be used
NetBIOS	Always present	May be used if needed for downward compatibility
Database	SAM, part of the registry	Extensible Storage Engine (ESE), developed from the Jet database
Authentication	NTLM	Kerberos (also NTLM supported)

* When we refer to Windows NT without a version number, we mean the latest version, 4.0. However, in most cases the information also applies to earlier versions.

Active Directory Compared to NDS

Some differences between NDS and Active Directory are listed in Table 1.2. If you are familiar with NDS, you can use the table to relate your knowledge to Active Directory. If you are not familiar with NDS, you will probably want to skip this table.

NOTE   Despite the plus and minus column, the purpose of Table 1.2 is not to be a competitive comparison of all pros and cons. It is included merely to help you learn Active Directory on the basis of your existing NDS knowledge.

Table 1.2 mainly covers the legacy NDS version that is shipping with NetWare 4, although NetWare 5 is also mentioned once. As NDS is continually developed, the information may not apply to the newest NDS versions.

NOTE   As of this writing, a newer version of NDS eDirectory (formerly called NDS 8) is shipping. One of its new features is native LDAP support.

A Sample Company

Throughout this book, we use Sanao Corporation as our sample company. Its registered DNS name is `sanao.com`. Depending on our demonstrational needs, we may present slightly different Sanao Corporations in different chapters. Thus, Sanao Corporation may have just one domain in one example and three domains in another example.

TABLE 1.2 NDS Compared to Active Directory

Feature	NDS	Active Directory	Active Directory versus NDS*
Group types	One type, can be used for security and distribution	Security groups and distribution groups	+
Group scopes	One scope, about the same as universal in Active Directory	Global, universal, and domain local groups	+
Group nesting	No	Free nesting within each scope	+
Replication type	Multimaster	Multimaster, except some special cases	
Replication criteria	Time, which must be synchronized for all servers	Universal Sequence Numbers, no great need to synchronize time	+
Site	No (WAN replication not so effective)	Yes (allows effective WAN replication)	+
A server can host replicas of multiple partitions	Yes	No	−
Per-server administration privileges	Yes	Some	−
Object hierarchy	Yes, one big OU tree	Yes, a domain tree or forest and a separate OU tree in each domain	
Can give permissions to OUs for other objects	Yes	No	−
Country, Locality, Organization object types	Yes	Exist in the schema but are not used	
May merge trees	Yes	No	−
Partitions	OU tree-based; may be split and merged	Domains; changing is difficult or impossible	−

(continued)

TABLE 1.2 *(continued)*

Feature	NDS	Active Directory	Active Directory versus NDS*
Partition is also administrative boundary	No	Yes	−
Global catalog	Catalog Services starting from NetWare 5; has drawbacks compared to Active Directory	Yes	+
Delegation of administration	Per OU, per object, or per attribute	Per OU, per object, or per attribute	
Policies	Z.E.N.works add-on	Group Policy	
Administration tools	One "big" tool to the whole directory (NwAdmin)	Several "small" tools for various aspects of the directory (MMC snap-ins)	
Extensible schema	Yes	Yes	
TCP/IP	May be used	Must be used	
LDAP support	Through a gateway	Native	+
Alias objects	Yes	No; however, the functionality is rarely needed	
Security equivalence	Yes	No	
RDN and current context	Yes	Not in the relative sense, but the object-naming attribute is also called RDN	
Tree visibility to end users	Visible, which is somewhat distracting to users	Mostly invisible, which should result in easier use	+
Typeless naming of objects	Yes	No, although canonical names get close	

* A plus sign (+) indicates that Active Directory has an advantage over NDS. A minus sign (−) indicates that Active Directory is at a disadvantage compared to NDS. If neither sign appears in the column, the feature is not, in our opinion, better or worse; it is just different.

BASIC BUILDING BLOCKS

Active Directory has a number of building blocks, beginning with *domains,* which you create by installing *domain controller* servers. Domains have *trust relationships* between them. Active Directory information must be *replicated* between domain controllers, whether they are located in the same or different *sites.* You can organize the objects in Active Directory in *organizational units (OUs).* Figure 1.3 shows the logical and physical structure of Active Directory.

The following sections introduce these basic building blocks of Active Directory. In addition, they briefly explain how you can use different kinds of *groups* to help in administration and how the *global catalog* knows every object in your Active Directory.

Domain Controllers

When you install Active Directory on a Windows 2000 server computer (Windows 2000 Server, Advanced Server, or Datacenter Server), you *promote* it to a *domain controller (DC).* Usually you perform this installation right after you install Windows 2000 itself by running a utility called DCPromo.

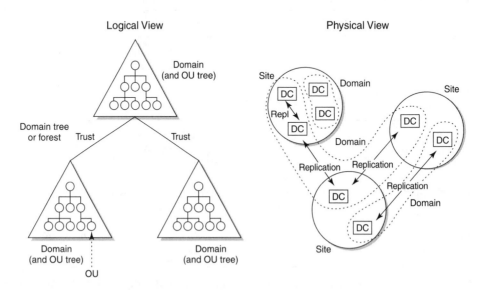

FIGURE 1.3 Active Directory has a logical and a physical structure, which are mostly independent from each other. "DC" stands for "domain controller."

During the Active Directory installation, you have the option to create a new domain or to join the server to an existing domain. Each domain controller belongs to exactly one domain.

Domains

A *domain* is maintained by one or (preferably) more domain controllers. The domain controllers of one domain may reside in one or more physical locations. An organization may choose to have one or more domains. Each domain is three things at the same time.

- *A unit of replication.* When you add a user or other object to an Active Directory server (i.e., a domain controller), that object is replicated to all other domain controllers in that domain. The outcome is that all the domain controllers in one domain contain the same Active Directory information (except when there has just been a change that hasn't yet reached the other domain controllers).
- *Part of the DNS namespace.* Therefore, the domain has a DNS name, such as `sales.sanao.com`. In other words, each Active Directory domain is also a DNS domain.
- *An administrative unit.* The people who create a domain usually have control over its domain controllers and Active Directory information. The groups Domain Admins, Account Operators, and Administrators have various administrative rights to the domain controllers of the domain and permissions to Active Directory information of the domain, and these rights and permissions are domainwide. A domain also acts as a security policy boundary, so there are some security settings (password policy, account lockout policy, and Kerberos policy) that affect the whole domain.

IF YOU KNOW NT   Like Windows NT, Active Directory uses domains and trusts between the domains as basic building blocks. However, both of these basic items in Active Directory include new features.

Trust Relationships

If an organization has more than one domain, its domains might be totally separate. More likely, though, they are connected with trust relationships.

The advantage of having trusts between domains is that you can give a user or group in one domain permission to access a resource in another domain. Thus, if a user needs to access the resources in two domains, there is no need to make two user accounts for him or her. Two other benefits are that groups can have members from other domains, and you can use the group policies of one domain in other domains (although group policies applied from foreign domains are less efficient than local ones).

Normal trusts between Active Directory domains are *transitive* and *bidirectional.* Transitive trusts allow access to go across domains ("trans" means "across" or "through"); that is, if you have a trust between domains A and B, and another one between domains B and C, you can give a user from domain A access to a resource in domain C, even though there is no direct trust between A and C. The trust in this case goes through domain B. Transitive trusts greatly reduce the number of necessary trusts because there is no need to explicitly define a trust between every pair of domains.

A bidirectional trust is a trust that works both ways ("bi" means "two"). Not only can you give users in domain A access to resources in domain C, but you can also give users in domain C access to resources in domain A.

IF YOU KNOW NT   Trusts in Windows NT are neither transitive nor bidirectional (although you could create two unidirectional trusts to look like one bidirectional trust). This architecture often required a large number of trusts and complex domain models. Each domain with user accounts needed to be trusted by all other domains. For this reason, it usually made sense to have the user accounts in one or few domains to keep the number of trusts smaller than they would be without this arrangement. This, in turn, led to two tiers of domains: First-tier domains contained user accounts and second-tier domains were created for resources. There are no tiers in Active Directory; everything is symmetrical and you can have user accounts in any domain.

Figure 1.4a shows six Windows NT domains in a complete trust domain model. All six domains contain user accounts. Because the trusts are unidirectional and intransitive, there must be two of them between each pair of domains (symbolized with two-headed arrows). In other words, each domain must have one trust with each of the five other domains. This makes 6 × 5 = 30 trusts, or 15 lines. (Actually, if you have six circles on paper, 15 is the maximum number of lines that you can draw between them.) Figure 1.4b shows six Active Directory domains in a domain tree. Because these trusts are transitive and bidirectional, you need only five trusts, or five lines (the minimum number to connect the six triangles on paper), to establish the same functionality as in Figure 1.4a. Finally, Figure 1.4c shows Active Directory rotated to emphasize that, unlike Windows NT, Active Directory doesn't have first-tier and second-tier domains. The users in all Active Directory domains are equal and all of them can access the resources in all

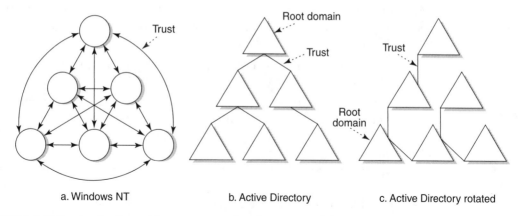

a. Windows NT b. Active Directory c. Active Directory rotated

FIGURE 1.4 Bidirectional and transitive trusts streamline the structure of domain relationships.

domains (with proper permissions, of course). Thus, an Active Directory domain tree (and forest) is comparable to a Windows NT complete trust model, with far fewer trusts. The formula for Windows NT is $n \times (n - 1)$, while for Active Directory it is just $n - 1$.

Organizational Units and Other Objects

An administrator using Active Directory creates a user object for each user, a printer object for each printer, and so on. Other object types include computer, group, and shared folder. The administrator does not create all objects—some are created automatically by Active Directory or some other software, especially during installation.

You can create organizational units (OUs) in Active Directory domains just like you create folders in a file system. You can store objects in different OUs just like you store files in different folders in a file system. This way, you can store them in logical groupings in a tree structure, which is especially useful if you have many objects.

In addition to this logical grouping of objects, you can use OUs for the following purposes.

- You can delegate the administration of each OU (including users and other objects there) to a different administrator. For example, in a geographically dispersed network, perhaps covering several time zones, it is probably easier to give the local administrators permission to create user objects, reset forgotten passwords, and so on. Delegation of administration is implemented with permissions.

- You can control how end users see, read, and modify the objects and their properties in each OU by specifying various permissions to users to access the OU contents.
- You can assign different group policies to the users and computers in each OU.

NOTE   You can assign permissions (to read, write, create, and so on) per object, not just per OU. However, this is usually impractical and a better choice is to stick to the per-OU permissions.

Unfortunately you cannot assign permissions to OUs. This means that if you have an OU that contains 30 users, you probably need to create a security group and put those users in this group in order to give them permissions for specific folders or other resources.

IF YOU KNOW NDS   In NDS you can give permissions to OUs, so there is no need to create a group to correspond to each OU.

You can create OUs to match administrative units, physical locations, or object types (e.g., users in one OU and printers in another). You can even create OUs based on your organizational structure. For example, the top-level OUs could be Human Resources, Finance, and Marketing.

Groups

You can use groups in Active Directory for at least two purposes. It is easier and more efficient to give access permissions to groups than it is to give them to a large number of individual users or computers. You can also use groups as e-mail distribution lists, given that your e-mail application can read the lists from Active Directory. This leads to two *group types:*

- *Distribution groups* can be used as distribution lists in Active Directory–capable e-mail applications, but also for any other Active Directory–capable application. For example, an application could control the doors of your company and let only people in a certain distribution group go through a certain door. This may sound like a security-related function, but the point is that there is an application that uses this distribution group for something, but Windows 2000 doesn't use the group for anything.

- *Security groups* are everything that distribution groups are. Additionally, you can assign Windows 2000 access permissions to a security group, while you cannot do so to a distribution group. That is, a security group can be given permissions for various parts of the operating system, such as Active Directory or a file system.

NOTE   Windows 2000 uses only security groups; it does not use distribution groups.

Every group, whether a distribution or a security group, has a defined scope. There are three *group scopes:*

- Global
- Universal
- Domain local

The group scope defines how a group can be used across domain boundaries. Depending on its scope, the group may be valid in other domains, so that it can be assigned as a member of a group in another domain, or assigned permissions for resources in that domain. The scope also dictates whether the group can have members from other domains.

In addition, the group scope determines which group can be a member of which other group. A global group can be a member of a universal group and a universal group can be a member of a domain local group. Also, a global group can be a member of a domain local group. The remaining combinations are not possible, such as a universal group being a member of a global group. Figure 1.5 illustrates the possible memberships and permissions assignments for global and domain local security groups.

Instead of giving permissions for resources directly to users or computers, you can put them in groups and give the access permissions to these groups. This approach greatly facilitates permission management. As Figure 1.5 indicates, a global group can be used in another domain and a domain local group can take members from other domains, but not vice versa. Figure 1.5 also shows the recommended path, which the thicker line represents. You will normally save time and energy in administration if you follow the recommended path and avoid the others.

In addition to *nesting* groups of the different scopes that we have described, you can freely nest groups of the same scope. For example, group A can be a member of group B, which is a member of group C, which is a member of group D, and so on. You shouldn't nest more than a few groups, however, because you would quickly lose track of who is a member of which group. However, being

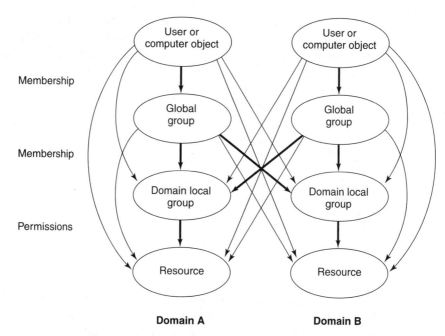

FIGURE 1.5 Grouping users and computers and assigning permissions to the groups facilitates management of access.

able to nest groups should help you create a selection of groups, the members of which can be easily managed.

The easiest strategy for group usage is to use only universal groups because they have no membership limitations. However, there is a penalty attached to them when you have both multiple domains and multiple sites. The members of universal groups are stored in the global catalog, which contains some information about every object in the entire Active Directory. The more you use these groups, the more replication traffic there is between sites and the slower user logons become.

IF YOU KNOW NT The groups in Windows NT correspond to security groups in Active Directory. Windows NT's old global and local groups are about the same as global and domain local groups in Active Directory. Universal groups and free group nesting are new features.

IF YOU KNOW NDS NDS has only one type of group, and it does not allow nesting.

Sites

Administrators create *sites* as areas with "good connectivity." Typically, each LAN would be a site, and the wide area network (WAN) connections between these sites (i.e., LANs) would be called *site links*. Technically, you define a site as one or more TCP/IP subnets.

Why do we need sites? They help Active Directory to understand what the world and physical network is like. When Active Directory knows which servers are on the same site, it knows whether there is a fast or slow communications link between any two servers. For slow links (i.e., intersite), domain controllers compress the replicated data, but for fast links (i.e., intrasite LANs), they save processor cycles and send the data uncompressed. You can also define for each site link a cost parameter that determines the route Active Directory will use to replicate between multiple sites.

NOTE The cost parameter determines only which domain controllers will communicate when replicating. It doesn't affect the physical IP routing (unless some router vendor makes a router that would understand the costs of Active Directory site links).

Based on this information, Active Directory and Windows 2000 use sites mainly for the following purposes.

- Active Directory can decide how to replicate information between domain controllers.
- Active Directory clients find logon servers (i.e., domain controllers) based on sites.
- The Distributed File System (DFS) of Windows 2000 can use site information to make intelligent decisions about which server gives users the files they requested.
- Windows 2000's File Replication Service (FRS) uses sites to know how to replicate SysVol and other folders that you assign to be replicated.
- An administrator using Active Directory can assign group policies to sites.
- Active Directory-aware applications may use site information for their own purposes.

NOTE In addition to the site functions listed, knowledge about the physical network is used when users locate printers. When a user queries Active Directory for a printer, she will be offered printers first from her TCP/IP subnet. If she wants, she can search for printers from other locations also.

Replication

Active Directory information should reside on more than one domain controller. This setup provides fault tolerance against a server failure. Another benefit is load balancing when many workstations are accessing Active Directory simultaneously. The third advantage is proximity of information—when a domain controller is placed on the same site with users and Active Directory information is replicated to that domain controller, workstations get the information from a local server instead of across a WAN link.

For the information to reside on several domain controllers, it must be *replicated* from one server to another. In other words, the information is kept up-to-date by periodically copying the changes in one domain controller across the network to the other domain controllers of that domain.

NOTE   Not all Active Directory information is replicated. For example, each domain controller tracks when a user last logged on using that domain controller. This information is part of the user objects, but it is a nonreplicating property. Also, the Active Directory database contains indexes of the properties that are marked (either in the base configuration or by an administrator) to be indexed. Each domain controller builds these indexes locally.

Remember that domains are units of replication, but sites tell when and how to replicate. Inside a site, domain controllers initiate replication after having waited 5 minutes after a change. In this case, they use direct remote procedure call (RPC) connections.

When you add more than one domain controller to a site, Active Directory builds a certain replication topology. If there were ten domain controllers, a bad topology would be one long chain. This would mean that domain controller A would replicate to B (one hop), which would replicate to C (a second hop), which would replicate to D (a third hop), and so on up until domain controller J (a total of nine hops). The chain would be so long that replicating changes from A to J would take too much time and J would fall behind. For this reason, Active Directory takes care that the replication chain is on the average not more than three hops from one domain controller to another. Active Directory achieves this by arranging the domain controllers in a ring topology and adding shortcuts across the ring (unless you turn off the shortcut creation).

Between sites, Active Directory compresses the replicated data. The replication takes place by default every 3 hours, but an administrator can change that to another interval (e.g., once an hour or every 30 minutes). RPC is usually used, as in the intrasite case, but you can also choose SMTP messaging (automated e-mail).

The SMTP option uses the Intersite Messaging service, which is part of Windows 2000. However, you can use SMTP instead of RPC to replicate only the enterprise forest information between domains. Normal domain replication must always use RPC.

Active Directory uses *multimaster* replication. This means that you can make changes, such as adding users, to any domain controller (of the appropriate domain). Your changes are then replicated to all other domain controllers in the same domain. Windows NT used *single-master* replication, which allowed changes to only one server, the *primary domain controller (PDC)*. These changes were then replicated to other domain controllers, called *backup domain controllers (BDCs)*. This made making changes sometimes a bit difficult, especially in WAN environments and failure situations. If the PDC was on a remote site, to make any changes you had to communicate with it over a WAN link, and if the PDC or the WAN link was down, changes were not possible.

Active Directory replicates only changed properties, not entire user accounts as in Windows NT. Unlike Novell NDS, Active Directory replication does not rely on synchronized time in different servers. To determine what to replicate, Active Directory uses *update sequence numbers (USN)* and version numbers. This removes the need to maintain a time synchronization service.

NOTE   There is a time synchronization service under Active Directory. It is needed mainly because the Kerberos authentication protocol requires the workstation clock to be within 5 minutes (by default) of the server clock.

Although normal Active Directory replication is multimaster, all domain controllers are not equal. There are two forestwide and three domainwide roles, which are held by only one (per forest or per domain) domain controller at a time.

The five roles are called *operations masters,* or *flexible single-master operations (FSMOs)*. As the name implies, they work in a single-master fashion, meaning that a particular domain controller is needed for a particular operation.

The two forestwide roles are

- Schema master
- Domain naming master

    The three domainwide roles are

- RID master (where "RID" stands for "relative identifier")
- PDC master (or PDC emulator)
- Infrastructure master

Describing the functions of these operations masters is not feasible in this introductory chapter. We address them in Chapter 5.

Global Catalog

In a large network with many sites, all Active Directory domain information is probably not replicated to all sites. This means that only part of the information is at the same site as the user. If that user searched the Active Directory for other users or for resources such as printers, the user's query would travel from site to site across many WAN links to collect all the requested information, which is not efficient. Also, if the result were a list of 1,000 user names, it would be slow to transfer back to the user who performed the search.

To avoid such time-consuming and costly steps, the *global catalog (GC)* helps to do all searches in your entire enterprise forest locally, which should dramatically increase their efficiency. The global catalog contains some basic information about every object in the whole Active Directory forest. It contains properties that are likely to be used in search operations, such as a user's first and last name.

One of the global catalog properties is the distinguished name of each object. It specifies the domain name and complete path to the object, which makes it easy to locate the object. To read properties that are not in the global catalog, your workstation must contact a domain controller of the domain where the object is; the distinguished name will be needed in this location process.

Out of the box, the global catalog contains 138 of all 863 properties. If you want, you can define additional properties to be included in the global catalog.

Administrators designate which domain controllers host a copy of the global catalog. After that, replication of the global catalog occurs with the normal replication of the Active Directory, so any changes will be replicated as soon as any other changes. By contrast, the Catalog Services in NetWare 5 use a separate process to copy the information to the catalog, perhaps once a day.

Information in the global catalog is subject to the same per-object and per-property permissions as normal domain data. Additionally, the global catalog is read-only.

Normally, there should be at least one global catalog server on each site, but sometimes it is better to leave some sites without a global catalog server, in which case the users of those sites have to read the information in the global catalog over a WAN link. Alternatively, those users do not use the global catalog at all, as we explain in Chapter 6.

HIERARCHIES

Depending on the size of the network, an administrator will probably build some kind of structure and hierarchy into Active Directory. The four models from the simplest and smallest to the largest are as follows:

- Single domain with no OU structure
- OU tree in a single domain
- Domain tree (with an OU tree in each domain)
- Forest of domain trees (with an OU tree in each domain)

As you might guess, a small company with centralized administration might choose a simple model with just one domain and no OU tree, whereas a large enterprise with decentralized administration would do better with a multidomain forest model.

The following sections introduce these four models and discuss the situations in which they would be most appropriate. These sections also summarize some concepts introduced earlier in this chapter.

NOTE   In Chapter 6 we discuss this topic further and give additional considerations for which model to select.

NOTE   In addition to the four models listed here, an organization can choose to create several forests. This is the most decentralized approach, but because it is not an actual hierarchy, we don't discuss it here. Instead, we cover it in Chapter 6.

Single Domain with No OU Structure

The first model, one domain with no OU structure (see Figure 1.6), is suitable for small companies with centralized administration. They could either put all users and groups in the predefined Users container, or they could actually create a couple of OUs. However, we still call this a "no structure" model because there are not enough OUs to talk about an OU tree.

In this model, one company could even be in several locations, as long as the company's WAN links could handle the amount of replication (which depends on the size of the Active Directory database and the frequency of changes). In single-domain environments, the whole database is replicated automatically to all domain controllers on all sites.

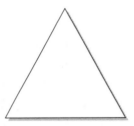

FIGURE 1.6 The simplest form of hierarchy is no hierarchy, such as this single domain with no internal structure. Active Directory domains are usually represented with triangles.

IF YOU KNOW NT   One domain with no OUs in Active Directory is quite similar to one domain in Windows NT. If you currently have just one domain, chances are that you will have one domain with Windows 2000.

Fortunately, Active Directory also has some improvement over Windows NT. There should be less data to be replicated, because you will replicate only the changed properties, not entire user accounts. On the other hand, you will have more information in your Active Directory to replicate than you had in Windows NT. You can store more information about each user, such as fax numbers, addresses, and so on in Active Directory. In addition, you are not limited to storing just users and groups: Active Directory can host information about printers, services, applications, and other resources or data.

In Active Directory, you can assign some administrative *privileges* for domain controllers even on a per-server basis. This helps if you have three remote sites with one domain controller and one administrator on each. You can allow each site administrator to "log on locally" via the server keyboard and perform some administrative tasks on his or her "own" domain controller, and at the same time you can disallow these privileges on the domain controllers of the other sites. For example, you could create a group called London Local Administrators and give this group the right to log on locally, as well as other appropriate user rights.

Unfortunately, you cannot assign all privileges this way. For example, the right to share folders or format hard disks is always assigned per domain, applying to none or all domain controllers.

IF YOU KNOW NT   In Windows NT, the administrative privileges apply to all domain controllers in a domain.

OU Tree in a Single Domain

As explained earlier, administrators create OUs to group objects, delegate administration, control what users can see and modify, and assign group policies. When you create a number of OUs for any of these reasons, you get an OU tree, which is our second model. Because our first model had no hierarchy, this second model is the first level of hierarchy. Figure 1.7 shows an OU tree inside a domain.

NOTE   The top object in an OU tree is not an OU, but rather the same domain that we represent with a triangle. We draw it as part of the tree to get a complete tree. See Figure 1.7 for an example.

An administrator should have a specific reason to create each OU and he should not just create them because it feels nice. Obviously, a tree's naming and structure should be logical. Also, the tree should be no larger or deeper than necessary.

End users will see the OU tree if they open My Network Places and double-click Entire Network and then Directory. Otherwise, they don't usually see the tree.

Because a domain is a unit of replication and there is just one domain in this model, all information is replicated to all domain controllers on all sites (as in the previous model). This is a good thing if your WAN links can handle the resulting (compressed) amount of replication of all the changes. If not, you should evaluate using multiple domains, so that you would have one of the remaining two models, a domain tree or a forest.

IF YOU   When you migrate from Windows NT 4.0 or 3.51 to Windows 2000, you might
KNOW NT   elect to use a single domain with an OU tree, even if you currently run a master domain model with several resource domains. With Windows NT, resource domains were created to decentralize administration, but given the per-OU and

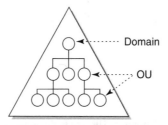

FIGURE 1.7 The first level of hierarchy is a tree of OUs inside a domain. When you place users and other objects in this tree, you can delegate their administration on a per-OU basis.

(limited) per-server administration capabilities of Windows 2000, you might achieve the same goal with just one domain. Therefore, you might no longer need separate resource domains.

Domain Trees

When it becomes impractical to replicate everything to everywhere, you need to create several domains. You will most likely organize them as a *domain tree*. Because domains are more independent than OUs inside a domain, this also means a step toward decentralization in the administrative model.

For example, password and lockout policies are domainwide and can be different in each domain, but not in each OU. Similarly, each domain has groups called Administrators and Server Operators, who can share folders on domain controllers and format their hard disks. If you want to give someone these privileges for domain controller A but not for domain controller B, these two domain controllers must be in different domains.

When you create several domains and put them in one tree, you get a model like the tree in Figure 1.8. The first domain you create becomes the *root domain* of its tree. When you place each subsequent domain in the tree, you select some existing domain as the *parent domain* for it. A transitive and bidirectional trust is automatically established between a domain and its parent.

The trust relationships make all the domains in the tree one big happy family. As stated earlier, you can give any user in any domain permissions for any resource

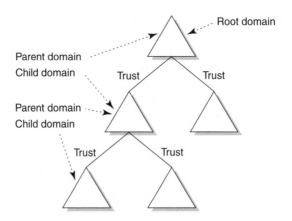

FIGURE 1.8 Whereas an OU tree is the lower-level hierarchy, a domain tree, such as the one in this figure (or a forest), is the higher-level hierarchy. Each domain has a transitive trust to its parent domain. The top domain with no parents is the root domain.

or object in any domain, either directly or via group memberships. The domains in a tree also share a common schema (explained later in the chapter) and global catalog.

If the domain tree grows large, the path from one subdomain to another can become quite long. In this case, you can create extra unidirectional *shortcut trusts* between distant domains. They speed up authentication from one domain to another.

Each domain in the tree has its own OU tree, which is totally separate from all others. By contrast, in NDS all OUs form one big tree.

With a domain tree (and a forest), your organization needs to agree on who will own and maintain the root domain. You might consider implementing your business units as second-level domains below the root domain. These units would have their independent OU structures and possibly some child domains. Because you may not want higher-level domains to change often, an even better choice might be to base them on continents and locations.

DOMAIN NAMES

Every Active Directory domain must match a DNS domain so that Active Directory domains use DNS names. The root domain of our sample company's Active Directory domain tree is called `sanao.com` and the two next-level Active Directory child domains are `sales.sanao.com` and `rd.sanao.com`.

Each of these domains also has an LDAP name, such as `DC=rd, DC=sanao, DC=com`. (More on LDAP later in this chapter.)

The DNS namespace of a domain tree is *contiguous*. You create a child's domain name by prepending a part to the parent's domain name, as Figure 1.9 shows.

- `Sanao.com` is the registered DNS name of our sample company, so it is the root domain name in this example.
- When we add "sales," we get `sales.sanao.com`.
- When we add "largecust," we get `largecust.sales.sanao.com`.

If the namespace is not contiguous, the domains cannot be in the same tree, but they can be in the same forest. In addition to the preceding example, you could have another domain tree with the two domains `sales.sanaoint.com` and `sanaoint.com`. The two trees would be in the same forest.

Surprisingly, the DNS names of workstations, member servers, and domain controllers don't have to be in the same DNS domain as the Active Directory domain they belong to. Therefore, computer `ws1.eastcost.sanao.com` can be a member of the `sales.sanao.com` Active Directory domain. This arrangement is not recommended, however, because it is normally more difficult to use and maintain.

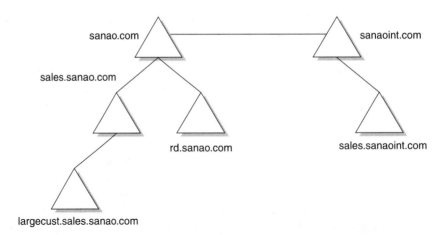

FIGURE 1.9 Active Directory domains use DNS names. The Active Directory domains in a tree must have a contiguous namespace. If this is not the case, you must have a forest with more than one domain tree. Here `sanao.com` is one tree and `sanaoint.com` is another tree.

Forest of Domain Trees

If you must or want to use more than one DNS name on the top level, such as `sanao.com` and `sanaoint.com` in our previous example, you will end up with more than one domain tree, and thus have a *forest*. Remember, all domain trees in the forest have contiguous DNS namespaces.

There are only two differences between a domain tree and a forest of several domain trees.

- The DNS namespace is not contiguous in a forest.
- When you perform a search on objects of a subtree, the search's scope includes just one domain tree at a time. (For more information on this subject, see Chapter 6.)

As one domain tree, a forest of domain trees has the transitive and bidirectional trusts for access permissions and group assignments, as well as a common schema and global catalog. Figure 1.10 shows a forest of domain trees.

The layout in Figure 1.10 of a two-tree forest gives the impression that the root domains of both trees are on one level. This is true only from the DNS naming point of view. From the administrative point of view, the root domain of the second tree is below the root domain of the first tree, as Figure 1.11 illustrates. Only the first domain of the forest (forest root domain) contains such groups as Enterprise Admins and Schema Admins, which give control to some forestwide administration.

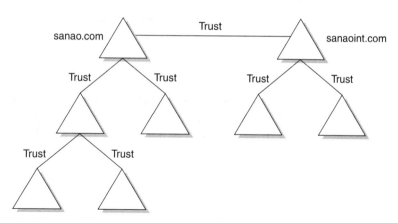

FIGURE 1.10 A forest of domain trees. The main difference between one domain tree and a forest is that the domain DNS names in a forest are not contiguous.

If independent business units have their own domain trees in a forest, they are no more independent than if they had child domains right below the root domain of the first domain tree (i.e., the forest root domain).

As Figure 1.11 shows, the second domain tree is not on par with the first one. However, the problem is that now it looks like there is just one domain tree rather than a forest of two domain trees. The only slight difference between Figure 1.8 (single domain tree) and Figure 1.11 is that the intertree trust (called a *tree root trust*) is drawn on the sides of the two top triangles instead of starting from the bottom of the first triangle and ending at the top of the other.

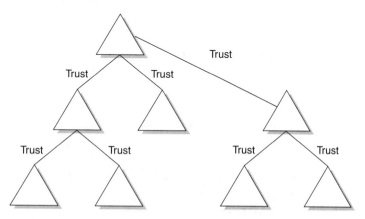

FIGURE 1.11 These two domain trees are not equal, as they may seem to be in Figure 1.10. However, placing one tree lower in the figure, as shown here, might incorrectly make it look like a branch of the first tree.

NOTE   Figure 1.10, with the two domain trees drawn on the same level, is the normal way to represent a forest.

Even though in this section we call only this fourth model a forest, you would of course have a forest even when you have just one domain with just one domain controller. From here on, we use the term "forest" whether one or several domain trees are in that forest, unless we specifically need to address a single domain tree. After all, there are only two differences between them, as described in the beginning of this subsection.

DNS INTEGRATION

Active Directory has a close relationship with DNS, the naming system used for the Internet and many intranets. Active Directory uses DNS for two related purposes: naming domains and computers and locating servers and (Active Directory) services. Therefore, to use Active Directory, the DNS service must be running on the network. The foremost choice is to use the DNS service included in Windows 2000. Another possibility for companies is to continue using their existing DNS infrastructure.

The most common existing DNS product is the Berkeley Internet Name Domain service, or BIND, which runs on UNIX. For BIND to work with Active Directory, the former must support a feature called *service* (or *SRV*) *records* to be able to locate services and not just computers. Your life will also be easier if it supports dynamic updates of DNS information. BIND version 8.2.2 and later fulfill both requirements.

The best choice is probably to use the Windows 2000 DNS service. It naturally supports service records and dynamic updates. Also, you can store the DNS information (i.e., *zone*) in Active Directory instead of a text file. This allows secure updates. If you select this option, only authenticated domain members can perform dynamic DNS updates.

Another benefit of storing the information in Active Directory is multimaster replication-traditional DNS uses single-master replication. In multimaster replication, any domain controller that has the DNS service installed and running can serve as the primary DNS server. Consequently, the dynamic DNS updates that client computers perform do not depend on only one server.

If a UNIX-based DNS service is used with Active Directory, it is best to stick to the standard character set of A through Z, 0 through 9, and the dash. With the DNS service included in Windows 2000, you may use the Unicode character set, which offers you a much broader selection of characters. However, to ensure interoperability with various systems, even with Windows 2000, it may be wise to use the basic character set.

NOTE   Even if your organization chooses to use Windows 2000 DNS for Active Directory services, you can continue to use a UNIX-based DNS implementation as your main DNS service.

Locating Computers and Services

The job of a DNS service is to know which computer name or service name corresponds to which IP address and to tell this information to anyone who asks for it.

To be able to communicate with a server called `dc1.sanao.com`, a workstation first needs to request that server's IP address from a DNS server. The answer looks something like this: 192.168.15.14.

For a user to be able to log on to Active Directory, the workstation needs an IP address of any domain controller in that domain. Therefore, the workstation doesn't query the DNS for a particular server name, but rather for a specific service name. The process may involve several queries and, because the site information is also used, the workstation can find a domain controller on its own site, or secondarily, a domain controller on the closest site.

When querying a service name, DNS might return the IP addresses of more than one server, along with some priority and weight information. This way, the workstation can choose the best server among those that offer the desired service.

Dynamic DNS Updates

The DNS service in Windows 2000 supports dynamic DNS updates, as defined in RFC 2136 (Request For Comments, meaning an "Internet standard"). It relieves the administrator from manually adding and editing the DNS records for computers and services.

NOTE   Quite a few Web sites contain RFC documents for you to read and download. The "original" RFC site is `http://www.ietf.org/rfc`.

Each workstation and server has an IP address, which is either configured statically in the computer or retrieved from a Dynamic Host Configuration Protocol (DHCP) server at start-up. As each Windows 2000 computer boots up, it automatically registers this IP address with the dynamic DNS. Domain controllers also register the necessary service names so that other computers can find Active Directory services.

Dynamic DNS will make Windows Internet Naming Service (WINS) obsolete eventually. However, this will not happen until organizations eliminate existing legacy Windows computers. Until all machines are Windows 2000 or later, these companies will be forced to use WINS or some other form of NetBIOS name resolution.

SECURITY AND POLICIES

Active Directory is part of the trusted computing base of Windows 2000. This means that information in Active Directory is protected, as are the files in the Windows 2000 file system. Anyone who wants to access information in Active Directory or the file system must be authenticated, usually with a username and password, and then subjected to discretionary access control.

Access Control

There is a *security descriptor (SD)* attached to each object in Active Directory. Both OUs and objects inside OUs have security descriptors. A security descriptor contains the owner of the object, the *discretionary access control list (DACL)*, and the *system access control list (SACL)*. The DACL contains a list of *access control entries (ACEs)*, which define who can access the object and in what way (read, write, and so on). If necessary, you can set read and write access on individual properties, such as a certain user's last name or fax number.

You can give an OU object any of five *standard permissions*. Each of the standard permissions maps to a set of *special permissions*. Usually the standard permissions are enough, but if necessary, you can go to a more detailed level and use the special permissions. Figures 1.12 and 1.13 show the lists of the permission options for an OU object, although in the latter figure all the special permissions don't fit in the window.

Active Directory permissions and old NTFS permissions in Windows NT are very similar because both use SDs, DACLs, and ACEs. However, there are three major differences. First, Active Directory uses a different inheritance model (which is explained in the next section). Second, you can set permissions on individual properties. And third, the user interface in Active Directory enables you to deny individual permissions—in Windows NT you can only deny all access.

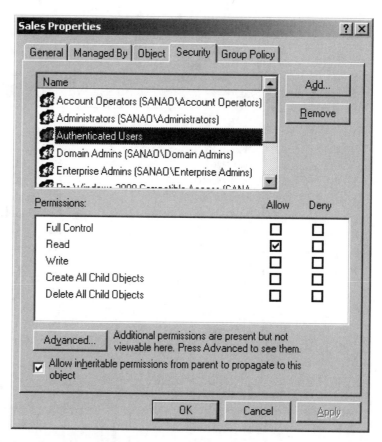

FIGURE 1.12 For every Active Directory object, you can define who can access it and in what way.

IF YOU KNOW NT	Actually, the first and third changes (inheritance and allow/deny individual permissions) are also true for NTFS 5.0, which is included in Windows 2000.

Inheritance

Active Directory uses *static inheritance* for object permissions. The word "inheritance" means that when you add permissions for some OU or other container, you can specify that these new permissions apply also to the child objects. You can choose to which type of children they apply and whether the permissions apply only to immediate children or to the whole tree beneath the object. Also, for each object you can choose whether it will allow inheriting permissions from above.

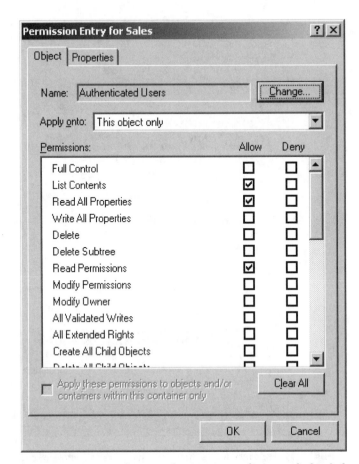

FIGURE 1.13 If necessary, you can select special permissions to fine-tune the level of access to an object in Active Directory.

Static inheritance means that Active Directory copies the new permissions to the access control list of each appropriate child object. This copying takes some processor power, as well as space in the Active Directory database, but the advantage is that when the objects are later accessed, Active Directory doesn't need to walk up the tree to check for inheritable permissions.

IF YOU KNOW NDS   NDS uses dynamic inheritance, which has exactly the opposite pros and cons of Active Directory. That is, it doesn't take any processing power when applying the permissions, but when objects are later accessed, NDS needs to walk up the tree to check for inheritable permissions. Also, disk space is saved because there are no copied permissions in the child objects.

IF YOU KNOW NT

Active Directory has a couple of significant improvements over Windows NT NTFS. First, when you apply new permissions to child objects, these permissions won't completely replace the old permissions; they just add new ACEs to the list. Second, the new ACEs carry a flag, which indicates that they are inherited. This way, both people and machines recognize which permissions are inherited and which are assigned directly to an object.

NOTE

If you add a permission that affects a thousand objects, only the security descriptor of the one parent object needs to be replicated to the other domain controllers. When they receive a new inheritable permission, they will copy it locally to the child objects.

Delegation of Administration

Because you can set access control by the OU, by the object, and even by the property, you can delegate administration of all or part of your OU tree. For example, if you create three OUs, different administrators can manage users and other objects in each of them. You can also set permissions so that a certain user can edit the e-mail and postal addresses of all users, but can do nothing else.

The Delegation of Control wizard helps in delegation. Ultimately the wizard just assigns permissions, so you can do the same delegation with the dialog boxes shown in Figures 1.12 and 1.13. The wizard interface, however, may be less intimidating, especially in the beginning of the learning process.

Group Policy

You can use *Group Policy* to control users' working environment and workstations. Group Policy also affects servers, and administrators use it to define, apply, and enforce the following:

- Automated application installation (either forced or optional)
- Forced registry settings to users or computers
- Security settings
- Logon/logoff scripts and startup/shutdown scripts
- Folder redirection of the Start Menu, Desktop, My Documents, and Application Data folders so that they can be located on a network server instead of the normal user profile folder
- Some settings for Remote Installation Services (RIS)

Some of the Group Policy settings affect computers and some affect users. You store the settings in *Group Policy objects,* or *GPOs,* that you create for chosen sites, domains, and OUs. The locations of the user objects and computer objects determine which GPOs apply to each user and computer. Figure 1.14 shows the contents of a Group Policy object.

IF YOU KNOW NT   Group Policy replaces System Policy and user rights. However, Group Policy includes additional settings.

Several GPOs may affect a user and a computer simultaneously. There could be one GPO assigned to the site, one to the domain, one to an upper-level OU, and yet another to the lower-level OU where the user or computer object resides. A nearer GPO in this chain overrides settings in a farther GPO, unless you have blocked this inheritance. You can also force inheritance on the upper level, which takes precedence over blocking.

Despite the name, you cannot assign GPOs directly to groups, nor can you assign GPOs to individual users or computers. You can get the same result, however,

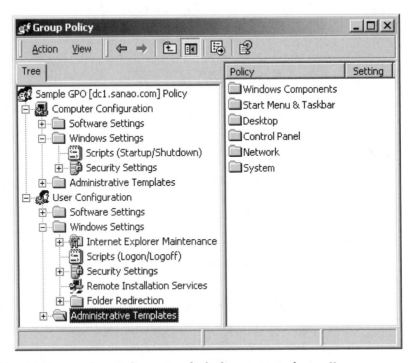

FIGURE 1.14 There are Group Policy settings for both computers and users. However, you can disable either.

by giving the read and apply permissions only to some of the users or computers in an OU where the GPO applies.

Because group policies may contain hundreds of settings, it may be tedious to set them correctly manually. Fortunately, at least for the security settings, you can avoid this burden somewhat by using *security templates,* which are predefined text files that list the appropriate choice of settings (e.g., for a "secure workstation").

ARCHITECTURE

This section introduces the Active Directory data model and other architecture-related issues. The schema, object naming, X.500, and LDAP are covered, as well as the physical architecture, Kerberos, public key infrastructure, and programmatic access to Active Directory.

Data Model

Active Directory stores information about users, resources, and other network entities. The stored information is represented as objects, so there is an object for each user, computer, printer, and so on.

Objects of the same type belong to the same *class,* such as (again) user, computer, and printQueue. Out of the box, Active Directory currently supports 142 classes. However, if you use the basic administrative tool, the Users and Computers snap-in, you can directly create objects in only 7 of the classes.

Every class defines a set of *mandatory* and *optional properties* that the objects belonging to the class must or may have, respectively. A property is often called an *attribute.* Out of the box, Active Directory has a total of 863 properties and the user class uses 207 of them. Fortunately, you don't need to enter data in all of the properties when you create a user account. Examples of user properties are sn (surname) and homePhone.

In Chapter 3, we list about 60 user properties that you can set with the Users and Computers snap-in. In Chapter 11, we present a script that lists all properties of a given class.

Figure 1.15 shows the relationship between a class and an object of that class.

The Users and Computers snap-in doesn't always seem to match the underlying data model. For example, you cannot create a user account using the snap-in unless you enter a "User logon name." However, the corresponding property (called userPrincipalName) is actually optional, not mandatory.

Each property uses one of 23 *syntaxes,* such as integer 14, string "abc," or time 04/26/2000 2:59:01 PM. The property may be *single-valued* (having just one value), such as homePhone, or *multivalued* (having a list of values), such as

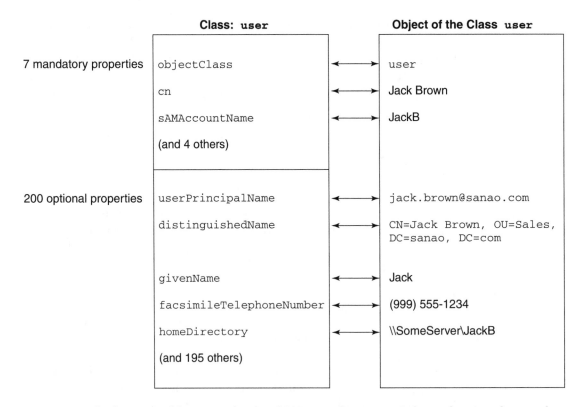

FIGURE 1.15 The class user defines 7 mandatory and 200 optional properties. Each user object must have a value for all mandatory properties and it may have a value for any optional property.

otherHomePhone. Because Active Directory is also a database, some of the properties are indexed, as in any decent database implementation. Searching for objects is faster if the search criteria use an indexed property.

The Schema

The *schema* is a set of rules that dictate which object classes a directory can contain, the object relationships, and the possible content of each object. This is true for Active Directory, as well as other directory services. In other words, the schema governs the structure and content of Active Directory. For example, the schema states which object classes, attributes, and syntaxes your Active Directory can contain. It specifies the mandatory and optional attributes of each class and indicates whether an attribute is indexed. In addition, it defines which attributes are replicated to the global catalog.

Classes can *inherit* from one another. For example, there is a class called `person` that has, among other attributes, `sn` (surname) and `telephoneNumber`. Another class, `organizationalPerson`, inherits all attributes in `person`, and adds `title` and `facsimileTelephoneNumber`. Finally, class `user` inherits all attributes in `organizationalPerson` and adds attributes such as `homeDirectory` and `badPwdCount`.

In addition to the inheritance chain, the user class gets a number of attributes from the *auxiliary* classes `mailRecipient` and `securityPrincipal`.

NOTE   You may wonder about the strange names of some attributes. Many of them come from the X.500 standard (discussed a little later in this chapter).

Extending the Schema

When you create a forest, it uses the base schema that Microsoft has defined as a default for all installations. Microsoft chose to store the Active Directory schema as objects in Active Directory itself. You may thus query the schema to find out what it supports. You (or your applications) can also extend the schema—that is, you can create new classes or attributes or add new attributes to existing classes. When creating classes, you would probably use the class inheritance described in the preceding section.

Adding attributes such as `userSalaryInformation` allows the use of *directory-enabled applications* in areas such as messaging or human resource management. For example, Exchange 2000 uses Active Directory and extends the schema for its purposes.

In a global network, the organization must agree on the centralized administration of the schema. For example, the Australian administrators cannot just install their own directory-enabled application, such as a human-resources application, and the Canadians install some other directory-enabled application. Because the schema is common for the whole forest, only those who belong to the Schema Admins security group are able to extend the schema.

Schema changes require careful planning and testing because many of the changes have implications for the whole enterprise, and they are often irreversible (at least without reinstalling the forest). Fortunately, Active Directory has many restrictions and guarding mechanisms to prevent disastrous changes.

Container and Leaf Objects

Objects of some classes are *container objects,* which means that they can contain other objects, just as folders can contain files. The rest are *leaf objects.* They cannot contain other objects, no more than files can contain other files. We call these two types of classes *container classes* and *leaf classes.*

One obvious example of a container class is `organizationalUnit` and an example of a leaf class is `contact`. However, there are many others: A total of 56 classes of Active Directory's base schema are container classes and 86 are leaf classes.

A class that seems to be a leaf class in the user interface could actually be a container class under the hood. An example of this is the `user` class. `User` objects may contain `nTFRSSubscriptions` and `classStore` objects, so the `user` class is actually a container class.

NOTE   In addition to referring to a type of class, the words "container" and "leaf" can also refer to two specific classes. One of the 56 container classes is a class called `container` and one of the 86 leaf classes is a class called `leaf`.

NOTE   The X.500 standard defines such container classes as `country`, `locality`, and `organization`, but Active Directory doesn't normally use them.

Partitions

As mentioned earlier, an Active Directory domain is a unit of replication. A unit of replication is called a *partition,* or sometimes a *naming context.* This means that a domain is a partition. However, domain is not the only type of partition. Every domain controller holds a copy of the following three partitions:

- The *domain partition,* where users, groups, OUs, and such reside
- The *schema partition,* where schema classes and attributes reside
- The *configuration partition,* where information on the forest structure resides, such as the sites and domains

Information in the first partition (i.e., users, groups, and so on) is replicated among the domain controllers of one domain, whereas the schema and configuration partitions are replicated among all domain controllers in the forest. A copy of a partition in a given domain controller is called a *replica.*

In addition to the three partitions listed here, the domain controllers that are designated as global catalog servers hold a partial copy of all other domain partitions of the forest. A partial copy contains all objects, but it contains only those attributes that are part of the global catalog.

Figure 1.16 shows the partitions of one sample forest. The two rightmost partitions exist in every domain controller, whereas the `sales.sanao.com` and `sanao.com` partitions exist only in the domain controllers of the corresponding domain.

You can manage the two leftmost partitions using the Users and Computers snap-in. Most of the configuration partition you manage with the Sites and Services snap-in and the schema partition (at least partly) with the Schema Manager snap-in.

Naming Objects

Just as each file in the file system needs a name, each object in Active Directory needs a name. Actually, there are quite a few names for an object in Active Directory, as Table 1.3 shows.

Using the examples in Table 1.3, following is a brief discussion on each naming syntax:

- *Distinguished name (DN)*. Because every object resides in an OU tree, which in turn resides in a domain tree, a distinguished name specifies the path to the object in both trees. `CN=Jack Brown, OU=Sales` specifies the object's name and location inside one domain's OU tree, and `DC=sanao, DC=com` identifies the domain. Each component of the name has a naming attribute

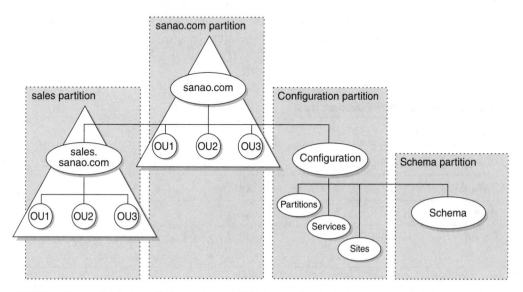

FIGURE 1.16 Configuration, schema, and every child domain is an independent partition, but together they form a logical tree, where each one is a child to some other partition.

prefix. CN stands for common name, OU for organizational unit, and DC for domain component. There are also prefixes C (country), O (organization), and L (locality), but they are usually not used in Active Directory.

- *Relative distinguished name (RDN).* This is the first component (i.e., the "least significant") of the distinguished name and it must be unique among its *sibling objects* (i.e., objects in the same container). In other words, the RDN is the name of an object in its parent container. The RDN of a user, group, computer, and almost all other objects is the same as its common name. The RDN of an OU is the same as its OU attribute and the RDN of a domain is the same as its DC attribute. CN, OU, and DC are also called *naming attributes.* Our example in Table 1.3 shows just `Jack Brown`, but with some utilities you may need to include the prefix, such as `CN=Jack Brown`.

- *Common name (CN).* Our sample names are for a user object; therefore, the object has a common name, which is the same as its RDN.

- *Canonical name.* This is an alternative format (or actually two formats) for a distinguished name. The first format uses slashes as separators where a distinguished name uses commas. Also, as we go through the name from left to right, the first format lists the name components from top to bottom, while a distinguished name lists them from bottom to top. The second format is quite similar to a Web page's Uniform Resource Locator (URL), such as `www.microsoft.com/windows2000`.

- *User principal name (UPN).* You can define a UPN for each user, who then uses it to log on and to enter in other places that require a username. Because a UPN looks like an e-mail address, it should be easy for users to remember and type.

TABLE 1.3 Syntaxes of Active Directory Names

Type	Example
LDAP distinguished name (DN)	`CN=Jack Brown, OU=Sales, DC=sanao, DC=com`
LDAP relative distinguished name (RDN)	Jack Brown
Common name (CN)	Jack Brown
Canonical name, two versions	`DC=com/DC=sanao/OU=Sales/CN=Jack Brown` or `sanao.com/Sales/Jack Brown`
User principal name (UPN)	`Jack.Brown@sanao.com`
Downlevel name (SAM name)	SANAO\JackB

- *Downlevel (SAM) name.* Each user (and some other objects such as groups and computers) must have a downlevel name, which is similar to the user account names in Windows NT. The downlevel name can also be used for logon and in many other places where a username is required. Depending on the place, the user types either "SANAO\JackB" or just "JackB."

NOTE   All Active Directory objects have a DN, an RDN, and a canonical name, but objects of only some classes have a UPN or downlevel name. For example, a user object *may* have a UPN (an optional attribute) and *must* have a downlevel name (a mandatory attribute). A CN exists for most object classes.

NOTE   None of the names are case-sensitive.

Fortunately, you don't have to type all of these long names every time you want to access an object. For example, the GUI relieves end users from typing names other than sometimes UPNs and downlevel names. Also, administrators can survive without typing the names, at least as long as they use the graphical MMC snap-ins shipping with Windows 2000. However, if they start using the utilities in the Support Tools package (included in Windows 2000 CD) or the Resource Kit (sold separately), they need to learn to type those long names (mostly the distinguished names).

The X.500 Standards

"X.500" refers to a series of international standards that define the features and aspects of a directory service, including its information model, functional model, namespace, and authentication framework. Table 1.4 lists some of these standards.

The standards were prepared collaboratively by the International Organization for Standardization/International Electrotechnical Commission (ISO/IEC) (http://www.iso.ch/) and the International Telecommunication Union, Telecommunications Standardization Sector (ITU-T) (http://www.itu.int/).

ITU-T is one of the United Nations organizations and it publishes standards, called Recommendations, in series designated by letters. The X series, including X.500, concerns "data networks and open system communications." The V series concerns "data communication over the telephone network." If you have used a V.34 modem, you have been using a device that conforms to one of these recommendations.

TABLE 1.4 X.500 Standards

ITU-T Recommendation	ISO/IEC Standard	Name
X.500 (8/1997)	9594-1:1999	The Directory: Overview of concepts, models, and services
X.501 (8/1997)	9594-2:1999	The Directory: Models
X.509 (8/1997)	9594-8:1999	The Directory: Authentication framework
X.511 (8/1997)	9594-3:1999	The Directory: Abstract service definition
X.518 (8/1997)	9594-4:1999	The Directory: Procedures for distributed operation
X.519 (8/1997)	9594-5:1999	The Directory: Protocol specifications
X.520 (8/1997)	9594-6:1999	The Directory: Selected attribute types
X.521 (8/1997)	9594-7:1999	The Directory: Selected object classes
X.525 (8/1997)	9594-9:1999	The Directory: Replication
X.530 (8/1997)	9594-10:1999	The Directory: Use of systems management for administration of the Directory

ITU-T has traditionally approved of new recommendations in a World Tele-communication Standardization Conference held every four years. The first version of X.500 appeared in 1988 and is often called X.500 (88). Similarly, the next two versions are X.500 (93) and X.500 (96).

The Active Directory data model (classes and so on) is derived from the X.500 data model, and Active Directory implements many X.500 features. Examples are a subset of the 1993 version of Directory Access Protocol (DAP), Directory System Protocol (DSP), and Directory Information Shadowing Protocol (DISP). However, Active Directory is not a full X.500 directory service. Microsoft has stripped away more complex and unnecessary features. Also, Active Directory uses LDAP, which makes some difference.

X.500 is also referred to as an "OSI directory service," where "OSI" stands for "Open Systems Interconnection." OSI hasn't had a particularly good reputation in the telecommunications area. OSI protocols and other OSI standards have been considered slow, complex, and resource-intensive. For these reasons, most of them have not been widely adopted. LDAP made X.500 viable by taking the best parts of it and streamlining it.

The bad reputation is also true for DAP, which we just mentioned. X.500 clients use it to access directory information on directory servers (also called *Directory System Agents,* or *DSAs*). DAP and other X.500 protocols run over ISO/OSI transport protocols, so there are two protocols with bad reputations that run on top of each other. For these reasons, a lightweight version of DAP (LDAP) was developed.

LDAP

The Lightweight Directory Access Protocol (LDAP) is a simplified version of the more complex DAP, and it runs on the more popular and light TCP/IP, rather than ISO/OSI. Clients can use LDAP to connect to and be authenticated to directories and to search and modify information in them either over the Internet or inside an organization. Active Directory is also a directory and Windows 2000 clients access Active Directory using LDAP. In other words, clients "talk LDAP" when they read or write information to Active Directory domain controllers.

NOTE   Although in the next section we list the other access methods, we want to emphasize that almost all access to Active Directory takes place with LDAP.

LDAP version 1 was published as RFC 1487 in 1993 and was made obsolete by LDAP version 2 (LDAPv2), RFC 1777, in 1995. The next year about 40 companies, including Microsoft, Netscape, and Novell, announced that they would support LDAP in their directory services products. Finally, in 1997 LDAP version 3 (LDAPv3) was published as RFC 2251.

As of this writing, RFC 1777 still has a "draft" status and RFC 2251 has a "proposed" status. However, you shouldn't worry that they don't carry an actual "standard" status. They are still widely supported, and many other Internet technologies still have a "proposed" status. For example, RFC 977, which defines the NNTP protocol to be used to distribute news articles (or discussions and junk ads in practice) on Internet news areas and query news servers, has been on the "proposed" status list since 1986, and yet tens of millions of people use it every day.

NOTE   When people wanted a lighter version of DAP back in 1993, the average PC was dramatically slower than it is nowadays. Compared to the other services that Windows 2000 is running, DAP would be a piece of cake with the current microcomputers. However, LDAP has already taken over DAP, so it is *probably* too late for a DAP era.

LDAPV3 SPECIFICATIONS

Although we earlier indicated just one RFC number per LDAP version, a number of specifications actually make up each LDAP version. To give you an idea of the kind of things the LDAP specification family includes, Table 1.5 lists them for LDAPv3.

The RFCs in the table carry a "proposed" status except for RFC 1823, which is "informational." Informational RFCs are not on the normal RFC standards track. Some other standards organization or vendor has perhaps developed them, but they are published as RFCs because they may be of general interest

TABLE 1.5 LDAPv3 Specifications

RFC Number	Title
RFC 2251*	Lightweight Directory Access Protocol (v3)
RFC 2252	Lightweight Directory Access Protocol (v3): Attribute Syntax Definitions
RFC 2253	Lightweight Directory Access Protocol (v3): UTF-8 String Representation of Distinguished Names
RFC 2254	The String Representation of LDAP Search Filters
RFC 2255	The LDAP URL Format
RFC 2256	A Summary of the X.500(96) User Schema for use with LDAPv3
RFC 1823	The LDAP Application Program Interface (an "informational" RFC)
RFC 2164	Use of an X.500/LDAP directory to support MIXER address mapping
RFC 2247	Using Domains in LDAP/X.500 Distinguished Names
RFC 2589	Lightweight Directory Access Protocol (v3): Extensions for Dynamic Directory Services
RFC 2596	Use of Language Codes in LDAP
RFC 2739	Calendar Attributes for vCard and LDAP
RFC 2829	Authentication Methods for LDAP
RFC 2830	Lightweight Directory Access Protocol (v3): Extension for Transport Layer Security
RFC 2849	The LDAP Data Interchange Format (LDIF)—Technical Specification
RFC 2891	LDAP Control Extension for Server Side Sorting of Search Results

* The first six RFCs (2251 through 2256) are the "core" specifications for LDAPv3 and the others define additional features.

or may be recommended for use on the Internet. The following LDAP RFCs are informational:

- RFC 2044: UTF-8, a transformation format of Unicode and ISO 10646
- RFC 2696: LDAP Control Extension for Simple Paged Results Manipulation
- RFC 2713: Schema for Representing Java(tm) Objects in an LDAP Directory
- RFC 2714: Schema for Representing CORBA Object References in an LDAP Directory
- RFC 2798: Definition of the inetOrgPerson LDAP Object Class
- RFC 2820: Access Control Requirements for LDAP

Active Directory supports LDAPv2 and LDAPv3. Each domain controller is an LDAPv3 directory server, but it can also communicate with LDAPv2 clients.

Each application protocol over TCP/IP must use a port number. LDAP's port number is by default 389. Web browsing would use by default port 80 and DNS lookups port 53.

LDAPV3 OPERATIONS

RFC 2251 defines 11 LDAPv3 operations, which are described in Table 1.6.

A client can send most requests either *synchronously* or *asynchronously*. The former choice means that the client application won't do anything else while it waits for a response; the latter choice indicates just the opposite situation.

One of the ways DAP was lightened to become LDAP was by the exclusion of Read or Move operations. They were unnecessary because the Search and Modify DN operations provide the functionality.

Physical Architecture

In X.500 a directory server is called a *Directory System Agent (DSA)* and each Active Directory domain controller is also a DSA. In Windows 2000 the DSA feature "lives" in a process called LSASS.EXE (Local Security Authority Subsystem) and there is a file, NTDSA.DLL (NT Directory System Agent), that implements most of the functionality. Figure 1.17 shows NTDSA.DLL, as well as the other physical components of a domain controller.

NOTE   Obviously the files NTDSA.DLL and ESENT.DLL reside also on disk (permanent storage), but in Figure 1.17 we have drawn them in RAM. In this context, they are only meaningful when they are loaded in RAM and their functions are executed there.

TABLE 1.6 LDAPv3 Operations

Operation	Description
Bind	This operation connects* and authenticates (perhaps anonymously) the client to a directory server.
Unbind	This operation terminates a session to a directory server.
Unsolicited Notification	This is an advisory message that a directory server sends to the client in the event of an extraordinary event (i.e., an error). This message is not a response to any client request.
Search	This operation retrieves the selected attributes of one or more directory objects. You can either do a genuine search on some criteria or just "search" with a certain distinguished name. The latter case is actually a normal read, because you exactly specify the object to read.
Modify	This operation applies a list of modifications to a given directory object.
Add	This operation adds a given object to the directory, with the included attribute values.
Delete	This operation deletes a given object from the directory.
Modify DN	This operation renames a given object or moves a given subtree to a new location.
Compare	This operation compares a given object and a given attribute value. For example, you could ask if Jack's phone number is "555-1234." The LDAP server would answer either yes or no.
Abandon	This operation abandons a designated previous operation.
Extended	This operation allows extending existing operations and adding operations.

* Although in the table we say that the operations do this and that, to be exact, they just send a request to a server. Insufficient permissions, some other restrictions, or an error condition will prevent the server from fulfilling the request.

Whenever Active Directory modifies some information, it does so through *transactions.* This means that the requested modify operation is atomic—that is, it either completes in full or it is not applied at all. Each transaction is first written to a transaction log and, if this succeeds, the information is also stored in the actual database (NTDS.DIT). This protects the database from corruption, and any decent database product, such as SQL Server, uses a similar technique. Generally, directory information is mostly searched and read; the transaction logs are needed only when the information is modified.

The Extensible Storage Engine (ESE) handles the storage files, and the DB layer above it handles the database tables on a logical level. Active Directory uses only two database tables, while a typical customer-tracking application uses tens of tables, created perhaps in SQL Server. The *object table* contains the information of

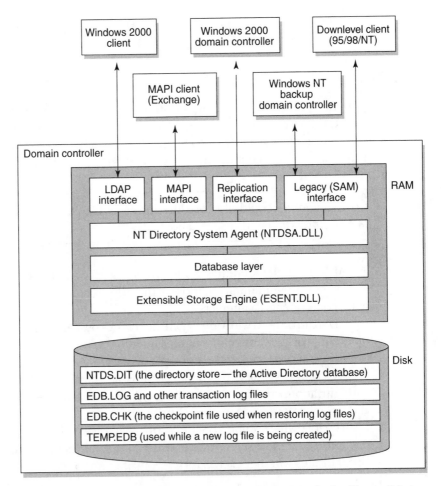

FIGURE 1.17 Each Active Directory domain controller has NTDS.DIT and other files on disk that contain Active Directory information. Through a selection of interfaces, the DSA component offers this information to others who need it.

all Active Directory objects and the *link table* implements the object relationships. You can think of the object table as a large Excel spreadsheet, where each row corresponds to one object and each column corresponds to one attribute.

ESE uses the Indexed Sequential Access Method (ISAM) technology, which Microsoft called Jet previously. Microsoft uses an ISAM table manager in Access, Exchange, WINS, and FRS, among others.

The DB layer handles data using a flat model; in other words, there is no hierarchy. The Directory System Agent (DSA) above it creates the hierarchical namespace where OUs and other containers form a tree of objects. You could also call the DSA a directory layer.

Most of the directory access takes place using the LDAP protocol. Normal Windows 2000 clients use it, as do other LDAP clients.

ADSI

Whether you write simple administration scripts with VBScript or applications with C/C++, you will use *Active Directory Service Interfaces (ADSI)* to programmatically access Active Directory. ADSI is a strategic API for Microsoft: All Active Directory management utilities included in Windows 2000 use ADSI.

NOTE   C programmers could also use the low-level LDAP C API instead of ADSI, but Microsoft recommends using ADSI.

ADSI is implemented as *Component Object Model (COM)* objects. COM is Microsoft's programming technology that allows, among other things, binary program components to interact.

ADSI can be used with other LDAP directories besides Active Directory and, using different providers, with Internet Information Server, NetWare, and Windows NT.

Figure 1.18 illustrates the principle of ADSI.

As LDAP does as a protocol, ADSI as an interface includes operations for authentication, creating, and deleting objects in Active Directory and for reading and writing information in object attributes.

The following six-line VBScript script will give you an idea of what ADSI scripts might look like. The sample script lists all class names that exist in the schema. It also indicates whether each class is a container or not.

```
Set objSchema = GetObject("LDAP://Schema")
For Each objChild In objSchema
  If (objChild.Class = "Class") Then
     WScript.Echo objChild.Name & " - Cont: " & objChild.Container
  End If
Next
```

Use Notepad to save the lines with the filename Classes.vbs. Start the command prompt and change to the folder where you saved the file. Then type "cscript classes.vbs" (without quotes) and press Enter.

The first lines of the output you get should look like the following (the first line is the command line):

```
C:\MyTests>cscript classes.vbs
remoteMailRecipient - Cont: False
packageRegistration - Cont: False
```

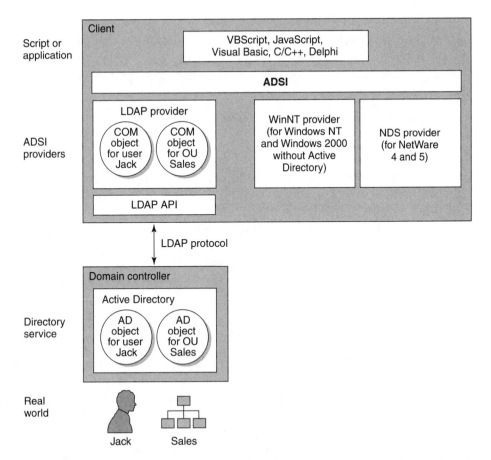

FIGURE 1.18 Active Directory objects abstract real-world users and resources. ADSI COM objects in turn abstract Active Directory objects. When your script manipulates the COM objects, it eventually affects the corresponding Active Directory objects.

```
mSMQQueue - Cont: True
rpcServer - Cont: True
samServer - Cont: False
rRASAdministrationDictionary - Cont: False
```

The six lines after the command line each contain a class name and indicate whether the class is a container.

When searching a number of objects using some search criteria, you can use *ActiveX Data Objects (ADO)*. ADO is a general Microsoft database interface on top of ADSI, among other data providers, so you can make simultaneous queries for information from more than one data source—for example, in Active Directory and SQL Server or Oracle database.

NOTE   The WinNT provider is not just for Windows NT. You use it to manage users and groups in Windows 2000 workstations and member servers. You also use the WinNT provider when you manage file shares and so on, on any Windows 2000 computer, including domain controllers.

Kerberos Authentication

Active Directory uses Kerberos version 5 (RFC 1510) as its primary authentication method instead of Windows NT/LAN Manager (NTLM), which was used in Windows NT.

Kerberos is based on tickets. When a workstation starts up, it contacts a Kerberos *key distribution center (KDC)*, which is basically any domain controller. The KDC returns a *ticket-granting ticket (TGT)*, which the workstation caches for later use. The user needs the TGT when she wants to start a session with some server. In this case, her workstation acquires a *session ticket* from the KDC for that server. Figure 1.19 illustrates the computers and the tickets.

Kerberos has three advantages over NTLM that are worth mentioning.

- *Faster session authentication.* When a client connects to a member server in a domain (such as server B operating as a file server in Figure 1.19), the client offers its session key. The key has enough information for authentication, so the server does not need to contact its domain controller to check the user's validity. This speeds up client connections, especially when many clients are accessing one server.

- *Impersonation.* If a client makes a request to a server (server B in Figure 1.19), and in order to fulfill it the server makes a request to another server (server C in Figure 1.19), the first server can impersonate the client to the second server. That is, it gets the data using the client's credentials, not using some fixed account for all users.

- *Mutual authentication.* Not only does the server know that it is talking to the correct client, but the client knows that it is communicating with the correct server.

NOTE   Active Directory still supports NTLM for downlevel clients and when authenticating from one forest to another.

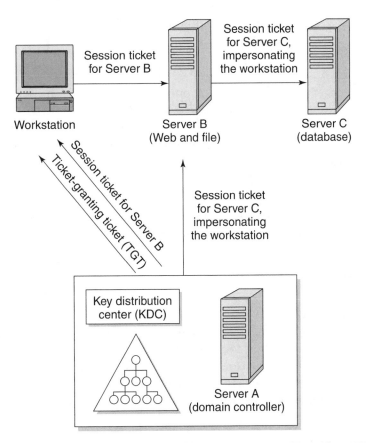

FIGURE 1.19 A Kerberos key distribution center (KDC) issues ticket-granting tickets (TGT) and session tickets to workstations and servers for authentication.

Public Key Infrastructure

Active Directory and Windows 2000 support *public key technology.* In other words, they can use X.509 version 3 certificates with private/public-key pairs. This is referred to as *public key infrastructure (PKI).* You can choose to buy certificates from a commercial *certificate authority (CA),* for example VeriSign, or you can create certificates yourself using the Certificate Services included in Windows 2000. In either case, the certificates are stored in Active Directory, so you and your users can use them for the following purposes:

- File encryption with Encrypting File System (EFS)
- E-mail encryption
- Web browser traffic encryption (i.e., HTTPS)

- TCP/IP traffic encryption (i.e., IPSEC)
- Logon and authentication
- Use of digitally signed drivers and system files (AuthentiCode)

Windows 2000 also supports *smart cards,* which could be described as "credit cards with processor and memory." They are a very secure place to store users' private keys. You can use a smart card and a personal identification number (PIN) for logon instead of a traditional username and password, which increases logon security dramatically.

If you have an extranet for customers and business partners, you can create user accounts for them and store their public keys in your Active Directory. They can then authenticate to your network using their own private keys and gain access to resources you have assigned to them.

OTHER FEATURES

Active Directory has many features—far too many to delve into in this introductory chapter, but we will mention two more that we haven't already covered. You can create virtual containers for external directories and you can publish certain services in Active Directory. Also in this section, we will say a few words about special considerations that Active Directory adds when connecting your network to the Internet, and we'll list the current limitations of Active Directory.

Virtual Containers

You can make another LDAP directory look like part of your Active Directory by creating a *virtual container.* To make this happen, you create an external cross-reference and define three things:

- The common name for the cross-reference object
- The DNS name of the server holding a copy of the foreign directory
- The DN of the "starting point" in the foreign directory

Publishing

Publishing is making information available in Active Directory so users can find it. The information can be interesting by itself, such as another user's phone number, or it can be a reference to something interesting, such as a printer, a shared folder, or an application service.

Whenever you create a user or printer object, publishing happens automatically at the same time. When developing applications, however, you can choose what to publish in Active Directory and what to store elsewhere, most likely in the file system.

As you know, the information in Active Directory is replicated to all domain controllers in a domain. For this reason, it pays to put in Active Directory information that doesn't change often and that is of interest to a large number of people. For example, a printer object is static, but a print job is not.

The following application information is probably well suited for storage in Active Directory:

- *Application configuration.* This information would help provide consistent settings to all users in your company.

- *Connection points for client-server applications.* With connection points, a client can find server services and connect to them, whether they are provided with the RPC, WinSock, or COM technology. The client doesn't need to know the name or address of the server computer beforehand, because the client can find this information in Active Directory. The connection points are standard Active Directory objects and they can be separate for end users and administrators. (To be exact, COM-based services advertise themselves a little differently. They use the class store instead of connection point objects.)

- *Application data.* If the data is relatively static, of interest to a number of people, and suitable for Active Directory object-attribute structure, that data could be stored in Active Directory instead of the file system.

We mentioned the term "directory-enabled application" (or DEA) when we covered extending the schema. If an application is using any of the three items in the previous list, it will also have to be directory enabled.

Connecting to the Internet

Windows 2000 and Active Directory use pretty much the same TCP/IP protocols in an internal network that are being used on the public Internet. If you connect your network to the Internet, you may need to install a firewall to control what information (such as computer names) is displayed on the Internet as well as control incoming and outgoing traffic.

IF YOU KNOW NT Windows NT networks are based on NetBIOS names and NetBIOS communications. A small- or medium-sized company using Windows NT could easily get some sort of protection for its network by filtering the NetBIOS ports 137 through

139 in its Internet router. Many such companies neither need nor want the hassle of installing and configuring firewalls.

Outside the firewall is a *demilitarized zone (DMZ)*. The servers on this zone are made to be visible to the Internet, even though there is usually another firewall between the DMZ and the Internet. Figure 1.20 shows the two firewalls and the servers.

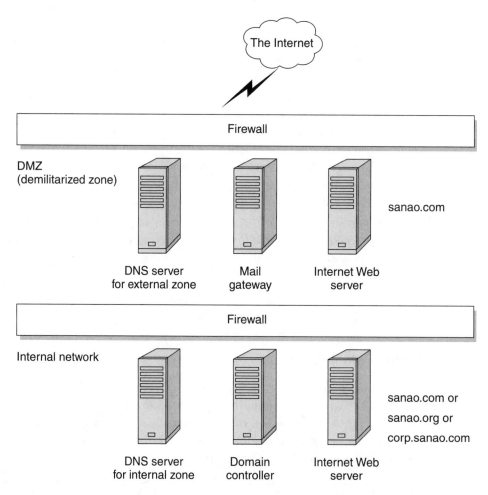

FIGURE 1.20 An organization that has Internet presence usually has a DNS server, a mail gateway, and a Web server that are accessible from the Internet. Here they are placed on the DMZ between the two firewalls. Note that there are no Active Directory servers (i.e., domain controllers) in this zone.

NOTE   In practice there are several ways to implement firewalls, but in this context we are interested only in what is and is not visible to the Internet (e.g., the DMZ is visible, but the internal network is not).

There are separate DNS zones (DNS information database) for the outside world and internal use. This means that people on the Internet don't see the same computer and domain names and IP addresses that the company employees see.

Because the servers in the DMZ are made visible to the Internet, Internet users can see www.sanao.com and send e-mail to some.one@sanao.com. Note that the Internet service provider could also host any of the three servers on the DMZ.

There are no Active Directory servers (i.e., domain controllers) outside the inner firewall, so they should be safe from hackers and crackers.

There are three ways to pick up the Active Directory forest name that is in use internally (see Figure 1.20).

- Use the same DNS name (e.g., sanao.com) internally and externally. This choice is logical, because the employees can use the same domain name whether they are accessing resources from the internal network or the Internet. However, it may be confusing for both administrators and users to comprehend and remember which resources are on the internal Web servers and which are on the servers for the public Internet.

- Use different DNS names internally and externally. In Figure 1.20 we have sanao.org, but you could have something else, such as sanaoint.com or sanao.local. Unless you use the "local" top-level domain, you should register the internal name with a registration authority (a company or organization that issues registered DNS names—for more information, visit The Internet Corporation for Assigned Names and Numbers at http://www.icann. org/).

- Use a DNS name internally that is delegated from the external name (e.g., corp.sanao.com).

Active Directory's Current Limitations

This chapter has introduced Active Directory's features and concepts. In the real world, nothing is perfect. So, to give you a full picture, we must address some of Active Directory's limitations and shortcomings. We mentioned some of them earlier in this chapter, so this section serves also as a summary and indicates what is expected to appear in Active Directory in the next versions over the next few years.

NO FOREST CHANGES

Active Directory offers many choices, but it does not always allow you to change them after installation. Thus, you must make some things right the first time.

A domain can join a forest only when you create the domain. You cannot rename a domain or move it to another place in the forest. However, removing a domain is possible. If the domain to be removed has child domains, they are also removed.

In addition, you cannot rename a domain controller, although you can remove it and reinstall it with another name.

You cannot merge two domain trees or forests, nor can you merge two trees to form a forest.

The partition concept is not transparent, because it is tied to domains. For example, you cannot split a domain into two partitions or merge two domains into one—you cannot change partition boundaries. This difficulty is somewhat relieved by the fact that you can move objects from one domain to another. However, even if you remove all objects from a domain, you cannot eliminate the domain without eliminating its child domains.

IF YOU KNOW NDS   In Novell NDS you can freely create (split) and merge partitions to control what to replicate to which locations (although you cannot differentiate local and remote replication).

Because research and development are constantly under way, future versions of Active Directory will probably not have many of the current limitations.

DOMAIN NATURE

An Active Directory domain is three things at the same time that you could claim shouldn't have anything to do with each other:

- A partition (i.e., a replication unit)
- Part of the DNS namespace, so that an Active Directory domain must match a DNS domain
- An administrative unit and a security boundary

This means that when you choose your domain structure and boundaries, even though the three are independent, you must consider all three at the same time and make them coincide. Fortunately, these three planning criteria often match quite easily.

In NDS, partitions and administrative units are independent.

OTHER LIMITATIONS

The two preceding sections, as well as this one, list Active Directory's shortcomings when it is compared to NDS. This is not to say that NDS is better. Active Directory also has many advantages over NDS. It is not useful, however, to focus on them here.

One NDS server can host replicas of multiple partitions, which is something an Active Directory server cannot do. If you have 20 small branch offices, and each office has one server with its own domain, Active Directory does not allow you to place replicas of those directory databases in one server in your main office. Instead, you need 20 extra servers (one for each domain) to host the replicas. On the other hand, if you put those branch offices in the headquarters domain, they would unnecessarily replicate all the user and object information from the headquarters and other offices. One thing you can do, however, is create a common domain for the 20 branch offices. This way you avoid having 20 domains or the need to replicate all headquarters users to the branch offices.

As mentioned previously, you cannot give permissions to OUs. This means that if you have 30 users in an OU, you probably need to create a group and put the same 30 users in it to be able to give them permissions for certain folders or objects.

SOME DIFFERENCES FROM NDS

Active Directory is missing two non-necessary features, which we obviously don't consider a shortcoming. We mention them here so that you can see other possibilities.

In NDS you can move around the directory tree using the workstation command line (command CX), and your current location is called the *current context*. If you refer to an object with a relative path (*relative distinguished name,* or *RDN* in NDS), this path depends on your current context like a relative filename depends on your current directory (i.e., ..\SomeFolder\SomeFile). Active Directory does not have the concept of current context. It does have the concept of RDN, but Active Directory RDN is always relative to the parent object name.

Unlike NDS, Active Directory does not support creating *alias objects.* An alias object would point to another object—this way, a user could refer to an object either directly or through its alias. The need for alias objects in Active Directory is not great, however. Extensive search capability, UPNs, shared folder objects, and other techniques are used instead.

The Next Version of Active Directory

As of this writing, Microsoft expects to ship the next version of Active Directory in 2002. It is part of the Windows .NET Server product that was code-named "Whistler." (Whistler also referred to the workstation version, which became Windows XP.) According to the preliminary information and beta versions, the Whistler version of Active Directory will have the following improvements (among others):

- *Larger groups.* The current version of Active Directory has a limit of 850 values for normal multivalued attributes and 5,000 values for linked multivalued attributes. Whistler will remove the latter limit and because each group membership list is stored in a linked multivalued attribute, there will no longer be a 5,000-member maximum.

- *Optimized group membership replication.* With the current version, when you add a member to a group, the list of all group members is replicated to other domain controllers. With Whistler, only the changes need to be replicated, saving network bandwidth.

- *No group membership conflicts.* Because the current version replicates multivalued attributes as one entity, you may lose some group member changes. This happens if you add a member to a group and then, using a different domain controller, add another member to the same group without waiting for the first change to replicate to the second domain controller (which may take 5 minutes or more, depending on the network). Because Whistler replicates the values independently, this conflict is not possible.

- *The global catalog not required for logon.* Universal group memberships are stored in the global catalog, which means that when a user logs on to a native-mode domain, the authenticating domain controller needs to check those memberships from the global catalog (unless the checking is disabled). With Whistler this information can be cached, which helps in branch offices without global catalog servers. Users there can still log on, even if the link to a global catalog server is down.

- *Full sync not required when adding properties to the global catalog.* When an administrator adds a new property to the global catalog in the current version of Active Directory, the whole global catalog must be replicated (i.e., full sync). With Whistler, this costly requirement is removed.

- *Less resource-intensive automatic intersite topology creation.* Whistler uses improved algorithms when calculating automatic replication connection between domain controllers on different sites (i.e., the intersite topology). The current version of Active Directory requires manual creation of this intersite topology when there are more than roughly 200 sites (depending on the number of domains). With Whistler's better algorithms, this number will be higher.

- *Application partitions.* Whistler will support application partitions, which help administrators define better which information will be replicated to which domain controllers, independent of domain membership. This feature can be used for applications and services that want to store dynamic volatile data in Active Directory. It cannot be used to store user and group objects separately from domains.

- *Ability to install a domain controller from media.* When you install an additional domain controller to a domain, Whistler allows taking most of the domain partition data from a tape, CD-R disk, or other file source. The data on any of these media is a normal Active Directory backup taken on an existing domain controller of the same domain. Only the recent changes to the domain data need to be replicated over the network.

- *Ability to edit multiple users.* The Users and Computers snap-in included in Whistler enables editing the properties of multiple users at once. However, this doesn't cover all user properties that are available through the Users and Computers snap-in.

- *Forest trusts.* Whistler will include a new trust type: forest trust. It can be one-way or two-way and because it is transitive, all domains in the trusting forest effectively trust all domains in the trusted forest. However, a forest trust is not transitive among more than two forests—there must be a forest trust between every pair of forests that needs the functionality. The trusting forest can specify which users and groups in the other forest it trusts. Forest trusts allow better cooperation among forests while maintaining most of the independence of each forest. Users from other forests can be taken as members in the local forest and granted permissions in the local forest.

- *Cross-forest authentication.* The current version of Active Directory allows a user of any domain in a forest to log on to any computer in the forest. Whistler will extend this to also between forests. In other words, a forest user can log on with her account on a computer that is part of another forest.

- *InetOrgPerson objects.* RFC 2798 defines the inetOrgPerson class that companies such as Novell and Netscape use. Whistler supports this class for better interoperability between Active Directory and other LDAP directories.

- *Objects of any class as group members.* The current version of Active Directory allows only users, contacts, computers, and other groups as group members. Whistler will allow objects of any class as group members. Third-party applications can use this feature for enhanced management.

The version after Whistler is code-named "Blackcomb."

CONCLUSION

This chapter introduced the concepts on which Active Directory is based and the features it offers. Understanding these elements now forms the base of your knowledge of Active Directory. The next chapter explains the installation process. You will soon have your server up and running so you can start exploring Active Directory.

Chapter 2

Installation of Windows 2000 and Active Directory

Many phases of installing Windows 2000 have been automated so well that it is usually quite easy to set up, even for a person who is not technologically skilled. However, there are some complex issues involved in a Windows 2000 installation, which we cover in this chapter.

The installation is separated into two parts: installing Windows 2000 and installing Active Directory. We have separated this chapter according to these two tasks followed by automation, troubleshooting, and uninstallation. The chapter is divided into the following sections:

- The "Before You Install Windows 2000" section discusses procedures and decisions that have to be handled properly prior to installation. It also presents considerations for dual booting with other Windows operating systems and states the requirements and recommendations for a successful Windows 2000 installation.

- The "Installing Windows 2000" section goes through the various stages involved in the installation as well as the decisions you have to make during those stages.

- The "Installing Active Directory" section discusses a number of far-reaching decisions related to Active Directory and DNS designs. Using the sample configuration described in this chapter, you might consider installing Active Directory on a test computer first. For Windows 2000, changes in domain structure design are not possible without demoting domain controllers first and then promoting them again.

- The "Automating Installation" section briefly introduces various ways to automate the installation of both Windows 2000 and Active Directory. However, discussing matters such as how to manually modify answer files is beyond the scope of this book.

- The "Troubleshooting Installation" section presents some scenarios you might come across when implementing Windows 2000. The most common recovery tools are also introduced.

- The "Uninstalling Windows 2000 and Active Directory" section provides you with the information you need to uninstall Windows 2000 and Active Directory.

**IF YOU
KNOW NT**   When you installed Windows NT, you had to know whether to install it as a stand-alone server, or as a primary or backup domain controller. After setup, the only way to change the role between stand-alone and domain controller was to rein-stall the operating system.

BEFORE YOU INSTALL WINDOWS 2000

The Windows 2000 installation process is rather straightforward; however, you must consider several issues before you begin the setup. First, you must decide whether to upgrade an existing installation or start with a completely new one. We recommend installing a fresh copy whenever possible. Of course, if you're upgrading a working network and its servers, it may be more feasible to upgrade your servers in order to preserve the settings for existing applications. When you upgrade, you also retain existing users, groups, rights, and permissions.

Before you start the actual installation, you should know the answers to the following questions:

- Which decisions make permanent changes that cannot be reversed?
- Should I keep another operating system and dual boot with Windows 2000?
- What are the requirements and recommendations?

Decisions That Cannot Be Reversed

You must consider the following question before you start the installation: What has to be done right the first time? Some decisions that cannot be reversed and their effects include the following.

- First, you create the installation partition. Then, you must set the file system for this partition correctly. To install Active Directory, NT file system (NTFS) must be on at least one partition—specifically, the System Volume folder (by default WINNT\SYSVOL). The content of the System Volume (SysVol) folder is replicated among Windows 2000 domain controllers. It is always advisable to use NTFS if possible.

IF YOU KNOW NT   The SysVol folder is somewhat similar for Windows 2000 domain controllers to what was the NETLOGON share in Windows NT (i.e., %windir%\system32\repl\import\scripts). In Windows 2000 domain controllers, in addition to scripts, SysVol also contains other data such as Group Policies. The folder that is shared as NETLOGON for pre-Windows 2000 clients is actually %windir%\SysVol\sysvol\<*domain*>\scripts.

- You must carefully determine the sufficient space for the boot partition. Although it is possible to increase the size of other partitions later by creating spanned volumes, this isn't possible for boot and system partitions. Third-party products, such as PowerQuest PartitionMagic, do exist but using them without first backing up the system is risky. Our recommendation for the boot partition—in other words, the partition where Windows 2000 system files and the WINNT folder are located—is at least 2GB. The recommended file system is NTFS, but before you start the installation, you should read the "Dual Booting" section in this chapter to help you decide which file system to use.

TIP   See the "Installing Active Directory" section later in this chapter to help you determine the sufficient amount of space for your Active Directory database.

NOTE   Microsoft's naming convention for partitions is somewhat misleading. The partition that contains the files (BOOT.INI, NTDETECT.COM, and NTLDR) required to boot the operating system is called the *primary,* or *system, partition.* The partition that contains the Windows NT/2000 system files (and by default the WINNT folder) is called the *boot partition.*

- Another issue that cannot be changed later is the installation folder. The default folder is WINNT, and we recommend that you use the default. Nothing prevents you from using a different directory name, but remember that this is a permanent decision.
- If the computer is about to become a domain controller, its name must be set up correctly. After you promote a computer to a domain controller, you cannot change its name unless you first demote it to a member or stand-alone server. The same limitation applies to a server with certificate services

installed—that is, its name cannot be changed without first uninstalling the service.

- Another issue to consider carefully is the choice of correct licensing mode. The Windows 2000 server supports two licensing modes: per seat and per server. Per-seat licensing requires a separate client access license (CAL) for each computer that accesses a Windows 2000 server, whereas per-server mode requires a CAL for each concurrent connection to this server. When you purchase a per-server licensed Windows 2000 box, it includes a number of CALs. Per-server licensing is more common in small companies that have only one Windows 2000 server, as well as in situations where a server is acting as a remote access server or Internet server. The licensing mode can be changed once from per server to per seat at no cost.

In contrast to these issues, most network settings can be changed after installation and often even without rebooting. The default networking protocol in Windows 2000 is TCP/IP. Therefore, you must determine the IP (Internet Protocol) settings, such as IP address, subnet mask, and default gateway, to be used during the installation. You must also consider how to handle name resolution. Options to consider include implementing Dynamic Host Configuration Protocol (DHCP), Domain Name System (DNS), and Windows Internet Naming Service (WINS) services. DNS is compulsory in Windows 2000 networks.

NOTE   The number of events that require rebooting has been drastically reduced in Windows 2000 from Windows NT 4.0.

NOTE   You can find additional information on installation in read1st.txt, setup.txt, and the release notes (\setuptxt\srv*.txt and advsrv*.txt) on the Windows 2000 CD.

Dual Booting

If possible, you should install Windows 2000 on a computer dedicated for Windows 2000. However, while you learn Windows 2000 and Active Directory, you may want to keep your existing operating system. In addition, you may have applications or hardware that do not work on Windows 2000, in which case you have to use other operating systems on the same computer. These are just some of the situations that require an administrator to understand the issues involved with dual booting.

IF YOU KNOW NT   With Windows NT, installing another operating system in a file allocation table (FAT) partition allowed you to at least start the computer and edit the start-up files in that partition in case NT had problems. In Windows 2000, this is not as important a consideration because Windows 2000 includes better disaster-recovery features such as Safe Mode and the Recovery Console. We discuss these features toward the end of this chapter in the "Troubleshooting Installation" section.

There are several differences among the file systems supported by Windows 2000. Table 2.1 compares the features of three file systems.

NOTE   Windows 2000 introduces a new version of the NTFS file system, version 5. Only Windows NT 4.0 versions equipped with Service Pack 4 or later are able to read a partition formatted with NTFS version 5 on the same computer. Note also that if a computer has both Windows NT 4.0 and Windows 2000, the NTFS version 4–formatted partitions are automatically converted to NTFS version 5 during Windows 2000 setup or when the partition is accessed by Windows 2000 for the first time.

Most often, dual booting takes place with Windows 98 or Windows NT 4.0. In order to use Windows 98 on the same computer, the Windows 2000 primary, or system, partition must be formatted as either FAT or FAT32. Similarly, the partition where Windows 98 is installed must be formatted as either FAT or FAT32. We recommend installing Windows 98 prior to installing Windows 2000, although you can install them in reverse order. If you dual boot with Windows 95, you must always install it prior to installing Windows 2000; otherwise, the master boot record (MBR) will be overwritten and repair becomes necessary.

TIP   If you accidentally overwrite the MBR, you can use the Recovery Console command FIXMBR. See the "Recovery Options" section later in this chapter for more information. Alternatively, you can start the computer with setup disks or directly with a Windows 2000 setup CD, select Repair instead of Install, select Manual Repair, and finally select the "Inspect boot sector" and "Inspect startup environment" options.

If you prefer to use Windows NT 4.0, the matter of dual booting becomes slightly complicated. Windows 2000 uses a new version of NTFS and some of the more advanced features are not available to Windows NT 4.0, no matter what you

TABLE 2.1 File Systems Supported by Windows 2000

	FAT	**FAT32**	**NTFS (ver. 5)**
Supported by Windows 98	Yes	Yes	No
Supported by Windows NT 4.0	Yes	No	Partially, but only with Service Pack 4 or later. New features, such as disk quotas and encrypting file system, are not supported.
Minimum volume	Diskette or 8MB	39MB	8MB
Maximum volume	4GB	Windows 2000 supports 2TB. However, only 32GB can be formatted with Windows 2000.	Recommended practical maximum is 2TB.
Maximum file	2GB	4GB	Limited by volume.
Restrictions for the number of clusters (allocation units)	Maximum is 65,526.	Between 65,526 and 268,435,446.	N/A
Cluster size	Depends on the partition size.	Depends on the partition size; smaller than in FAT.	Can be set for 512, 1024, 2048, 4096, or 8192 bytes, 16KB, 32KB, or 64KB. Compression is not supported for cluster sizes above 4,096 bytes.
Supports local permissions	No	No	Yes
Supports disk quotas	No	No	Yes
Supports encryption	No	No	Yes
Conversion to NTFS	Possible with convert. exe; however, NTFS permissions for system files are left with Everyone with Full Control.	Possible with convert. exe; however, NTFS permissions for system files are left with Everyone with Full Control.	N/A

(continued)

TABLE 2.1 *(continued)*

	FAT	FAT32	NTFS (ver. 5)
Other	Not recommended on partitions larger than 2GB.	If the installation partition is larger than 2GB and you choose FAT, Setup automatically formats partition as FAT32.	Cannot be used on floppies. If volume was formatted as NTFS with Windows NT, the upgrade to NTFS version 5 takes place automatically.

do. In addition, when you install Windows 2000, all NTFS partitions are automatically converted to NTFS version 5. For these reasons, Microsoft doesn't recommend using NTFS as the only file system on a computer that dual boots Windows 2000 and Windows NT 4.0.

If you are using Windows NT 4.0 and want to be able to access the files stored on an NTFS partition, you must be using Windows NT 4.0 with Service Pack 4 or later. Also, if you want to install Windows NT 4.0 on a hard disk that contains any NTFS version 5 partitions, you must use WINNT32.EXE, which is located in the SUPPORT\ WINNT32\I386 folder on the Windows NT 4.0 Service Pack CD. If you don't have the CD, you can download the files from `ftp://ftp.microsoft.com/bussys/ winnt/winnt-public/fixes/usa/nt40/ussp4/additional/`.

If, after all that has been mentioned, you decide to dual boot, make sure that you install different operating systems along with their applications on separate partitions. If several operating systems are installed onto the same partition, some directories, such as Program Files, are shared and can cause conflicts in application settings.

Some other points worth mentioning are as follows:

- When you install Windows 2000, it is installed by default on a partition on which no other operating system is located.

- If the dual-boot computer participates in a Windows NT or Windows 2000 domain, each installation of Windows NT 4.0 and Windows 2000 must have a different computer name.

TIP We have found an excellent way to experiment with various operating systems without reboots. A company called VMware (`http://www.vmware.com/`) has a product called VMware Workstation. The product enables you to run various operating systems simultaneously in virtual boxes with very few limitations.

Requirements and Recommendations

To install Windows 2000, you must ensure that several requirements are met. Although Microsoft has set certain absolute minimums, to work comfortably you should go beyond the minimum requirements. Table 2.2 lists the requirements and our recommendations.

HARDWARE COMPATIBILITY

To check the compatibility of hardware components, read the HCL.TXT document located in the SUPPORT folder of the Windows 2000 CD. If you have Internet access, point your browser to `http://www.microsoft.com/hcl` for the latest version of the document. In addition, the Windows 2000 Setup program automatically checks your hardware and software and reports possible conflicts. Another way to verify that your hardware will support Windows 2000 is to use the `checkupgradeonly` switch of the Winnt32 command (as explained later in this chapter).

You should also check that you have updated drivers for your hardware devices and the latest system BIOS. You can obtain these from the device manufacturers.

TIP   You must update your BIOS prior to installing Windows 2000. This is especially important for laptop computers because Advanced Configuration and Power Interface (ACPI) support is required for more advanced power management, including Standby. Your computer might support ACPI only with the most recent BIOS version. The operating system does not upgrade from Advanced Power Management (APM) to ACPI support when you install the latest BIOS; instead, you will have to reinstall the operating system.

Preparation

You must complete several operations before you start the setup.

- If you are upgrading a computer, always back up all files that are stored on the hard disk.
- If the partition into which you are going to install Windows 2000 is compressed with either DriveSpace or DoubleSpace, you must uncompress it prior to the installation.
- If disk mirroring is used, you must disable it before running the Setup program.
- If you have an uninterruptible power supply (UPS) device connected to your computer, disconnect its serial cable prior to running the Setup program. It

TABLE 2.2 Hardware Requirements and Recommendations for Windows 2000 Server

Component	Microsoft Requirement	Our Recommendation
Processor	Pentium 166	At least Pentium II 300, although Windows 2000 will run on a Pentium 166–equipped computer.
RAM	128MB minimum; 256MB recommended; 4GB maximum	At least 196MB to prevent unnecessary paging because after installing Active Directory, the total memory consumption is almost 100MB.
Free hard disk space	850MB plus 2MB for each MB of RAM	1GB for setup but use at least 2GB to accommodate future growth. If you are upgrading a Windows NT 4.0 domain controller, the size of the user account database may expand by as much as a factor of ten. Using FAT or installing from a network requires at least 100MB to 200MB more space.
Monitor	VGA or higher resolution	At least a 17" XGA monitor with a high refresh frequency. More is better when you use MMC-based administration tools.
Keyboard	Yes	Essential, although you can do without it after the installation because the server can be administered remotely (for example, with Terminal Services).
Mouse or other pointing device (optional)	Yes	Yes, because although it is possible to use Windows 2000 without a mouse, a lot of administration tools have a GUI, so not using a mouse becomes quickly infeasible.
CD-ROM drive	A CD-ROM drive (12x or faster recommended); high-density 3.5-inch floppy disk drive (unless your CD-ROM drive is bootable and supports starting the Setup program from a CD)	Yes, to install new software, although a CD-ROM drive is required only for CD-ROM installation. If your CD-ROM doesn't support booting, you can prepare setup disks as instructed in the "Starting Installation" section.
Network adapter card	Windows 2000–compatible	Yes, a network card is required only for network installation. However, even for the purposes of learning Active Directory, a computer without network connectivity is not of much use.

might cause problems because Windows 2000 attempts to automatically detect devices connected to serial ports.

Now you are ready to start the installation.

INSTALLING WINDOWS 2000

The Windows 2000 setup includes two or three phases separated by computer restarts. If something goes wrong with the installation, you have to return only to the beginning of that phase. Once a phase is completed, you cannot redo it. For example, if the power supply is interrupted during the setup, you can restart from the beginning of the phase that was interrupted. After the setup is completed, the Configure Your Server screen is displayed, enabling you to configure the server to your specific needs. Figure 2.1 illustrates the basic installation phases.

Starting Installation

As Figure 2.1 shows, there are several methods you can use to start the Windows 2000 installation.

If your CD-ROM drive is of the so-called El Torito type, you can boot the computer from the CD and proceed from there. Another way to start is to boot the computer with an existing operating system such as DOS, Windows 3.*x*, Windows 9*x*, or Windows NT 4.0. Then, you install Windows 2000 from a CD.

TIP   To be able to start from the CD, you might have to change the BIOS start-up options. See your computer manual for further information.

Alternatively, you can start the installation from the traditional setup floppy disks and let Setup copy the installation files from a CD. You can create the setup disks by running the MAKEBOOT command in the BOOTDISK folder of the CD.

NOTE   Windows 2000 Professional and Server setup disks are different and are not interchangeable.

IF YOU KNOW NT   There are four start-up disks in Windows 2000. In Windows NT, there were three disks.

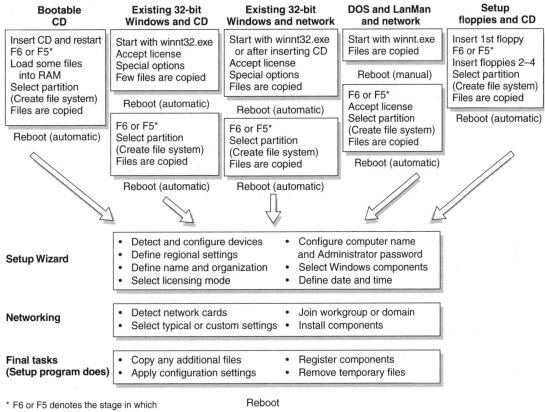

FIGURE 2.1 The initial stages of Windows 2000 installation vary depending on the system you have. For example, if you start a new installation from within Windows NT 4.0, you accept the license in a very early stage. The last three phases are similar with very minor differences.

The last way to start the setup is with a start-up floppy disk to load DOS and some network client software (such as LAN Manager) and to access the setup files from a shared folder on a network server.

No matter which method you use, you can either upgrade the existing operating system or install Windows 2000 to a different folder or partition.

NOTE   The operating systems that can be directly upgraded to Windows 2000 Server are NT 3.51 and 4.0 Server. See the "Upgrading Your Operating System" section later in this chapter for further details.

The commands for starting the installation from an existing operating system or from the network are WINNT and WINNT32. Both programs are located in the i386 folder of the Windows 2000 CD. Alternatively, they could be located in a shared folder on your file server. If you are starting the installation process from DOS, Windows 3.1, or Windows for Workgroups 3.11, use the WINNT command. If you are starting the installation from DOS or Windows 3.x, you should enable disk caching with the command SMARTDRIVE. The file-copying stage will take a long time if you do not start SMARTDRIVE before starting the setup. If you are starting the installation from Windows 95/98/ME, Windows NT 3.51 or 4.0, or Windows 2000, use the WINNT32 command. You can modify the operation of the setup program by defining additional switches for the WINNT and WINNT32 commands. Table 2.3 and Table 2.4 list the most important switches and their actions.

| **IF YOU KNOW NT** | You no longer need to use the /b switch to indicate that start-up diskettes are not used when you start the setup with WINNT. |

TABLE 2.3 Important WINNT Switches

Switch	Action
/e	Specifies a command to be executed at the end of GUI-mode setup.
/i:inf_file	Specifies the filename (no path) of the Setup information file, which controls the files that are copied during the first part of the setup phase. The default is Dosnet.inf.
/r:folder	Specifies an optional folder to be installed. The folder remains after Setup finishes. Use additional /r switches to install additional folders.
/s:sourcepath	Location of the Windows 2000 source files. The location must be a full path of the form x:\[path] or \\server\share[\path]. The default is the folder where you gave the WINNT command.
/t:drive_letter	Temporary setup files are copied to this drive. If you don't use the /t switch, Setup uses the partition with the most free space. Use this switch also to define the partition into which the operating system is installed when installing Windows 2000 automatically with an answer file.
/u[:answer file]	Performs an unattended setup using an answer file (requires /s). The answer file provides answers to some or all of the prompts that the person performing the setup normally responds to.

TABLE 2.4 Important WINNT32 Switches

Switch	Action
/checkupgradeonly	Checks your computer for upgrade compatibility with Windows 2000. Reports are located in Windows\Upgrade.txt in Windows 95/98 and in %Systemroot%\Winnt32.log in Windows NT 3.51 or 4.0.
/cmd:command_line	Executes a specific command before the final Setup program phase.
/cmdcons	Adds a Recovery Console option to boot.ini; can be used only after Windows 2000 has been installed.
/copydir: folder_name and /copysource: folder_name	Creates an additional folder(s) within the folder in which the Windows 2000 files are installed. You can use both options to create as many folders as you want. /copysource removes the folders after Setup completes.
/makelocalsource	Copies installation source files to your hard disk. Use it to ensure that the setup CD or a network access to your file server is not needed when adding components.
/noreboot	The computer won't restart automatically after the file-copying phase of WINNT32 is completed.
/s:sourcepath	Location of the Windows 2000 source files. You can specify multiple /s sources in order to copy files from several file servers simultaneously. If you use multiple /s switches, the first specified server must be available or Setup will fail.
/syspart: drive_letter	You can copy Setup files to a hard drive, mark the drive as active, and then install the drive in another computer. When you start that computer, Setup automatically starts with the next phase. You must always use the /tempdrive switch with the /syspart switch.
/tempdrive: drive_letter	Directs Setup to place temporary files on the specified partition and to install Windows 2000 on that partition.
/unattend	Silently upgrades your previous version of Windows 2000.
/unattend[num]: [answer_file]	Installs a new Windows 2000 version in unattended setup mode with the settings specified in the answer file. "Num" is the number of seconds between the time that Setup finishes copying the files and when it restarts. You can use the num option only on a computer running Windows 2000.

The Setup Program

The initial phases of the installation process vary slightly depending on whether you are copying the installation files from a CD or downloading the files from a file server. You can choose to read only one of the two following sections depending on the media you use.

INSTALLING WINDOWS 2000 FROM THE CD

If your existing operating system supports running CDs automatically, you can insert the Windows 2000 CD into your CD-ROM drive and allow Setup to display the setup screen. If the version of the Windows operating system you are using is upgradeable to Windows 2000, Setup will suggest you upgrade it. You can select No and start performing a new installation. Even if you select Yes, you can still choose either to upgrade or to install a new copy. Alternatively, if you are performing a new installation, you can insert the CD into the drive and reboot the computer, provided that your computer supports booting from the CD.

If you use the setup floppy disks, you must boot the computer with the first floppy. You must then continue to insert all floppies until the Setup program informs you that it is starting Windows 2000.

INSTALLING WINDOWS 2000 FROM A NETWORK

To install Windows 2000 from a network, the installation files must be available on that network. Although the CD itself can be shared, it is advisable to copy the files onto a file server and share the folder. This is especially true if a number of users are using the same installation files. Installation starts with either the WINNT or the WINNT32 command. If you are using a 32-bit Windows operating system, Setup asks you whether you want to upgrade the current operating system or install a new copy. You will learn more about upgrading in the "Upgrading Your Operating System" section later in this chapter.

TIP   In Windows 2000 you can include service pack files in the installation folder with the command `\<servicepacklocation>\update\update -s:X:\i386`, where X is mapped to the installation directory of the original (SP0) Windows 2000. This technique is called service pack *slipstreaming*.

If you start with the WINNT command: When you select Clean Install, you must have enough (at least 300MB) free formatted disk space for the temporary files. You must also specify the location of the Windows 2000 installation files. After the MS-DOS portion of the setup is complete, you have to restart the computer manually.

The default installation folder for system files is WINNT, which you cannot change when you start with WINNT.

TIP   There is actually a complicated way to change the installation folder in this case. You have to create an answer file and save it as winnt.sif on a floppy disk, which you have to have in the drive while performing the setup.

If you start with the WINNT32 command: The first screen enables you to upgrade your operating system or install a new copy of Windows 2000. The next screen displays the licensing agreement and asks for your approval. After you have read the agreement and approved it, you can set language, advanced, and accessibility options (see Figure 2.2). Language options determine the default settings for dates, times, currency, numbers, character sets, and keyboard layout. Advanced options enable you to define the location of the Windows 2000 installation files and the target installation folder. You can also set an option to choose the installation partition later during the setup. Accessibility options enable you to select magnifier and narrator tools for users with vision limitations.

NOTE   The keyboard setting you define in the Language Options dialog box becomes the default keyboard setting for the system—that is, the layout that is effective during logon.

Next, you have the option to upgrade your existing FAT or FAT32 partition(s) to NTFS. You shouldn't upgrade the drive, however, if you intend to dual boot with another operating system later. Finally, Setup copies the installation files from the file server, after which the computer restarts automatically.

NOTE   All NTFS version 4 partitions are automatically converted to NTFS version 5 during setup or when you mount the disk.

USING ALTERNATIVE DRIVERS

When "Press F6 if you need to install a third party SCSI or RAID driver" is displayed on the line at the bottom of the screen, you can press F6 to use a driver on the floppy disk that came with your hardware. The Setup program copies several files after which it asks you to provide the necessary drivers on a floppy disk. After you have provided the appropriate driver or if the device was compatible without

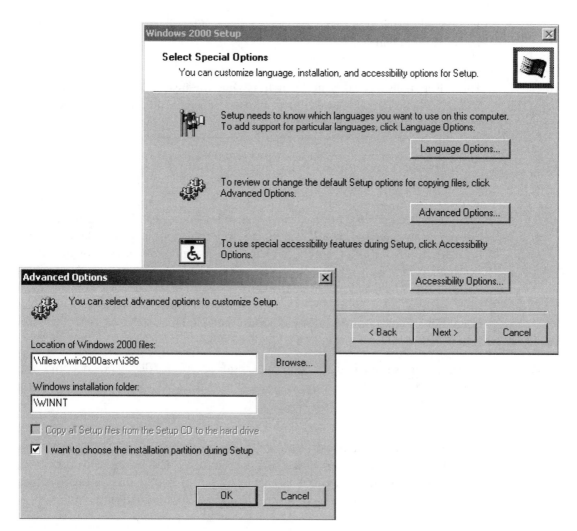

FIGURE 2.2 **Special options for WINNT32 installation enable you to define default language, advanced, and accessibility options.**

additional drivers, Setup continues to copy the files necessary for various common adapters. If your mass storage controller is not compatible with Windows 2000 or if you fail to provide a separate driver file, Setup will end with an error message indicating an inaccessible boot device.

NOTE   If the driver for your adapter didn't come with the device, you can probably find it on the manufacturer's Web site.

Instead of pressing F6, you can press F5 (which is not indicated in any way) to select an appropriate hardware abstraction layer (HAL) for your hardware. HAL enables Windows 2000 to run on computers with different motherboard designs. The HALs currently included with Windows 2000 are MPS Multiprocessor PC, Standard PC, and Standard PC with C-Step i486.

SELECTING AN INSTALLATION PARTITION

Depending on the method you used to start the setup, the computer might restart once. When the blue screen appears, you have the option to start a new installation ("Setup Windows 2000 now") or to repair an existing Windows 2000 installation. If you started Setup from floppy disks, now is the time to insert the Windows 2000 CD into the drive.

Read and accept the license agreement. Press F8 to continue.

Next, select an existing partition or create a new one to install Windows 2000 onto. If not enough space is available, you can delete a partition. If you are installing Windows 2000 onto a computer with a Windows operating system prior to Windows NT 4.0 with Service Pack 4 and with some partitions formatted as NTFS, you get a warning that some of your files might not be accessible from those older operating systems.

After you've chosen the installation partition, you must choose the file system if you didn't earlier choose to upgrade your drive to NTFS. If the partition already exists and is formatted with a file system other than NTFS, you can choose to format it with NTFS. Be careful here if you have data stored on the hard disk because it will be erased during formatting. The files are copied from temporary installation folders (WIN_NT.~BT and WIN_NT.~LS) onto the setup folder (WINNT by default) and the computer is restarted. The temporary folders are removed when the setup is complete.

The Setup Wizard

After the computer has restarted, the Setup Wizard starts. After you click the Next button or you wait for a while, the Setup Wizard starts detecting and configuring devices. This stage can take quite a while and the screen might also blink while the Setup Wizard detects the video adapter.

NOTE   Windows 2000 supports Plug and Play (PnP) technology, which is used to detect and configure devices automatically. Thus, you could set your devices to PnP mode instead of using static settings and define in BIOS that PnP is controlled by the operating system.

Next, you define regional settings. You can use multiple languages and regional settings. The system locale enables applications to display menus and dialog boxes in a user's native language. Windows 2000 uses the code page and font settings of this language. The menus and dialog boxes of Windows 2000 are not affected.

NOTE   You shouldn't mix system locale with the default settings for keyboard layout. If you defined it incorrectly earlier, you have to change it directly in the Windows 2000 registry.

User locale refers to the locality of the computer—that is, the formatting of numbers, currencies, times, and dates. Windows 2000 also supports multiple languages, which are selected here, too. At this stage, you also define the keyboard layout(s) that you want to use.

NOTE   There are a number of language versions of Windows 2000. Especially for multinational corporations, it is useful to standardize one language version and install support for other languages with Microsoft's MultiLanguage version. In this manner, even one PC can support users understanding multiple languages. For additional information, visit `http://www.microsoft.com/globaldev/faqs/multilang.asp`.

The next stage includes defining your name and organization (optional) and choosing the licensing mode. If you are not sure which mode to select, choose Per Server because according to the licensing conditions you can change it later to Per Seat. The opposite is not true.

Next, you must define the computer's name (to be used as both host and NetBIOS names) and the administrator's password. The computer's name must be unique in your network and must not exceed 63 characters. If the computer's name is longer than 15 characters, any Windows operating system prior to Windows 2000 will recognize this computer by only the first 15 characters of the name. In addition, if the computer dual boots and belongs to a domain, each operating system must have a unique name. We don't recommend using the name that the Setup Wizard suggests (derived from the licensing organization—for example, SANAO-PFS0L4O7), unless your network is very small.

IF YOU   A Windows NT computer had two names: a NetBIOS name and a DNS host name.
KNOW NT   In Windows 2000, the NetBIOS and host names are the same.

The administrator is the default user for administering Windows 2000 computers. Thus, the Setup Wizard creates this user account automatically. It is a good idea to set the password for this user during the setup, although you can change it later. You should use at least eight characters for the administrator's password and make it complex by including different types of characters, such as lowercase and uppercase letters, numbers, and special characters. The maximum length for the administrator's password is 127 characters.

COMPONENTS TO INSTALL

Next, you must decide which Windows 2000 components to install. Every additional component consumes disk space and because most services are configured to start automatically, they consequently consume memory. The Setup Wizard automatically installs a number of core components; the other components that are installed are most of the subcomponents of the Internet Information Services (IIS) and Script Debugger. You can always install additional components, or remove components after the installation is complete, by selecting Add/Remove Programs, Add/Remove Windows components from the Control Panel. Table 2.5 presents the additional components from which you can choose.

The only necessary component at this point might be the DNS service, although even that can be installed automatically during the Active Directory installation. You might also consider installing Network Monitor (under Management and Monitoring Tools) because it is very useful when learning different network protocols and analyzing network traffic.

If your operational server has roles other than being a domain controller, you have to select components carefully. For example, if you want to improve the remote administration capability of your server, you might want to install Terminal Services in Remote Administration mode.

TIP   Have you ever wondered how to uninstall certain components, such as games? You can get them visible and selectable in the Add/Remove Windows Components dialog box by locating SYSOC.INF with Windows Explorer in the WINNT\INF folder and by removing "HIDE" from the corresponding lines—that is, `Games=ocgen.dll,OcEntry,games.inf,`~~`HIDE`~~`,7 AccessUtil=ocgen.dll,OcEntry,accessor.inf,`~~`HIDE`~~`,7`.

TIP   You can perform automated installation or removal of Windows 2000 components with command SYSOCMGR. See Microsoft Knowledgebase article Q222444 for more information.

TABLE 2.5 Windows 2000 Server Components

Component	Note
Accessories and Utilities	Includes the Accessibility Wizard, accessories, communications, games, and multimedia.
Certificate Services	Enables you to set a Certification Authority capable of issuing and distributing X.509v3 digital certificates. Certificates are used for secure e-mail, authentication of WWW servers and clients, and during smart card logons.
Cluster Service	Enables two or more servers to be grouped to increase fault tolerance. This option appears only if you're installing Windows 2000 Advanced Server or Datacenter Server.
Indexing Service	Enables full-text or attribute searches of documents stored on the disk or on virtual directories of WWW servers.
Internet Information Services (IIS)	Includes several services such as World Wide Web (WWW) publishing service, File Transfer Protocol (FTP), Simple Mail Transfer Protocol (SMTP), and Network News Transfer Protocol (NNTP) services.
Management and Monitoring Tools	Includes tools such as Network Monitor, which can be used to analyze network traffic. Connection Manager components are also in this folder together with Simple Network Management Protocol (SNMP) service.
Message Queuing Services	Provides services for distributed applications that are used in heterogeneous or unreliable networks.
Networking Services	Includes numerous networking services, such as Domain Name System (DNS), Dynamic Host Configuration Protocol (DHCP), and Windows Internet Name Service (WINS).
Other Network File and Print Services	Services for integrating file and print services with Macintosh and UNIX computers.
Remote Installation Services	Enables remote and automated installation of Windows 2000 Professional from a designated server. Requires a separate NTFS partition on the server as well as clients that can reboot remotely. Active Directory and DHCP are also required.
Remote Storage	Provides an extension to your hard disk by enabling the use of Hierarchical Storage. Less frequently accessed files are transferred automatically to removable media such as tape, and they are retrieved when necessary.
Script Debugger	For debugging both client-side and server-side ActiveX Script Engines such as VBScript and JScript.

(continued)

TABLE 2.5 (*continued*)

Component	Note
Terminal Services	Enables Windows 95/98/ME, Windows NT, Windows-based terminals (WBT), and Windows 2000 clients to access a virtual Windows 2000 Server desktop session and to run Windows applications on the server. Two modes are available: Remote Administration mode, which requires no additional licenses and by default allows two administrators to access the server simultaneously, and Application Server mode, which enables a larger number of users to run applications centrally. If you choose Application Server mode, you must also install Terminal Services Licensing in either this or another Windows 2000 server. Also, a server in Application Server mode must be licensed within 90 days of installation at Microsoft's Web site.
Terminal Services Licensing	Enables registering and tracking of Terminal Services client licenses.
Windows Media Services	Helps you create and publish streaming multimedia presentations to your intranet or to the Internet.

DATE AND TIME SETTINGS

The last task to do before you go into networking settings is to define the current date, time, and time zone settings.

Installing and Configuring a Network

The next phase of installation starts when Setup detects the network adapters. You can then choose the easy way to install the networking components. So-called typical settings include Client for Microsoft Networks, File and Print Sharing for Microsoft Networks, and the TCP/IP protocol with automatic addressing. Automatic addressing uses IP settings obtained from a DHCP server if one is available. Otherwise, the settings are determined with Microsoft Automatic Private Internet Protocol Addressing (APIPA).

NOTE   You may see your DHCP configured IP address as 169.254.x.x. This is an indication that DHCP server was not available or could not be contacted and thus an IP address was assigned automatically by Windows 2000. Use the command `ipconfig /renew` to try to obtain a new IP address from the DHCP server.

If you want to define the settings yourself, or if your network requires additional services or protocols to be installed, you can choose Custom Settings. This option enables you to install Gateway (and Client) services for NetWare, QoS Packet Scheduler, or various protocols. If the component you require is not listed, you can install it after the setup is complete.

The minimum network settings you should define include the IP address and subnet mask. If you want to communicate with computers outside your subnet, you must define the default gateway. To have some means of name resolution, you might also want to define IP addresses for a DNS or a WINS server, or both.

NOTE   If you intend to let the Active Directory Installation Wizard install and configure the DNS service, you can leave the IP address for DNS server empty at this point.

The last networking issue to define is whether the computer belongs to a workgroup or a domain. If the computer belongs to a workgroup, it is called a *stand-alone server,* and if it becomes a member of a domain, it is called a *member server.* Read the options carefully because the dialog box is not very clearly laid out, as you can see in Figure 2.3.

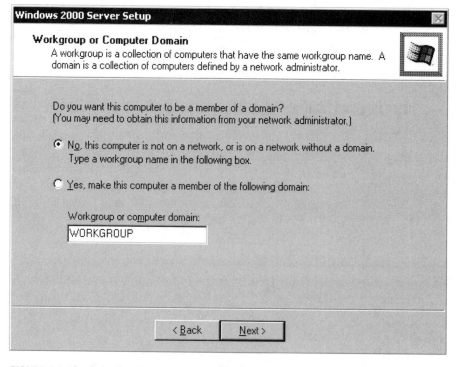

FIGURE 2.3 The dialog box for leaving the computer in a workgroup or joining a domain is not very clear. As a result, you should read it carefully.

Finalizing the Setup

From here on, the rest is automatically carried out by the Setup wizard, which performs some final tasks such as installing components, installing Start menu items, registering components, saving settings, and removing temporary files. The installation phase usually takes a few minutes and the component registration might last slightly longer. When all of these tasks are finished, you are prompted to restart the computer.

Upgrading Your Operating System

The procedure for upgrading your operating system (Windows 3.1 or Windows for Workgroups 3.11, Windows 95 or 98, Windows NT 3.51 or 4.0) to Windows 2000 doesn't differ much from the procedure (presented earlier) for installing a new system. The main difference is that you don't have to answer so many questions. As Table 2.6 illustrates, there are certain restrictions for upgrading.

As an example, we'll present the steps involved in upgrading a Windows NT 4.0 Primary Domain Controller to Windows 2000. You must first accept the licensing agreement, after which you might be asked to upgrade your file system to NTFS. For upgrading to proceed, your Windows boot partition must have 604MB of free space.

After Setup has copied the necessary files onto the hard disk, the computer restarts and continues copying files. This stage takes several minutes, depending on the speed of your system and especially the CD-ROM drive. After the copying is finished, the configuration is saved and the computer restarts automatically.

TABLE 2.6 Windows 2000 Server Upgrade Considerations

Existing Operating System	Compatibility
Windows NT 4.0 Workstation or Windows 2000 Professional	Cannot be upgraded to Windows 2000 Server
Windows NT 3.1 or 3.5	Must be upgraded to Windows NT 3.51 or 4.0 prior to upgrading to Windows 2000
Windows NT 3.51 or 4.0 Server	Can be upgraded to Windows 2000 Server or Advanced Server
Windows NT 4.0 Server, Enterprise Edition	Can be upgraded to only Windows 2000 Advanced Server or Datacenter Server
Windows NT 4.0 Server, Terminal Server Edition	Can be upgraded to any Windows 2000 Server version

If you opted to upgrade your drive to NTFS, the upgrade is performed, after which the computer restarts again. There might be a considerable length of time after the computer restarts in which nothing seems to happen. Just stay calm.

After the computer restarts again, Setup detects and configures devices, installs networking components, installs other Windows components, performs final tasks, and restarts the computer for the last time. Now your computer is finally upgraded—unless the computer was a domain controller, in which case you can click Next to start the automated Active Directory installation.

NOTE   You have to change the domain NetBIOS name prior to upgrade because changing the Windows 2000 domain name is impossible without removing and reinstalling Active Directory.

After You've Installed Windows 2000 Server

After you have successfully installed Windows 2000 Server, the Configure Your Server dialog box displays. It asks whether the computer onto which you've just installed Windows 2000 is the only server in the network or if other servers exist. If there are other servers in your network, the next screen appears with a check box, which you can clear in order to prevent this dialog box from appearing at every start-up.

If your computer is the only server on your network, you can start installing Active Directory directly from this Configure Your Server dialog box. You are first presented an option to learn something about Active Directory and DHCP and DNS. Installing Active Directory this way makes the computer a new domain controller in a new forest. After you fill in a few fields, Active Directory is automatically installed using unattended installation. See Figure 2.4.

If necessary, you can always start the Configure Your Server program again from Administrative Tools in the Start menu. We do not recommend that you plan to administer your Windows 2000 server through this screen—there are faster and more efficient ways to accomplish administrative tasks, which you will have learned by the time you have finished reading this book.

WARNING   If you define that your computer is the only one on the network and let the Configure Your Server program install Active Directory, DNS, and DHCP, you will end up having 10.10.1.1 as your computer's IP address and an active DHCP server serving clients with IP addresses from the 10.0.0.x class.

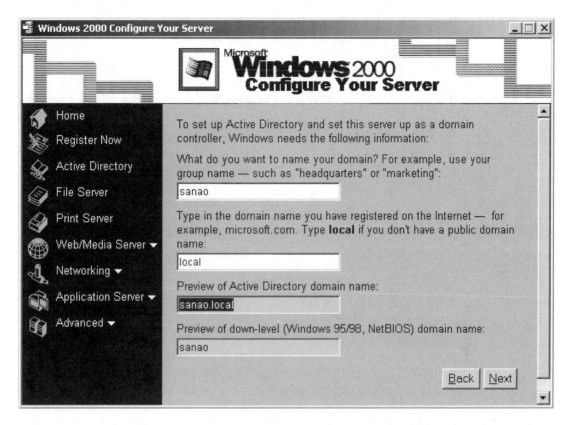

FIGURE 2.4 Using the Configure Your Server screen, you can install Active Directory to the only (or first) Windows 2000 server on the network.

Some of the common tasks to complete after the installation include the following:

- Install the latest service pack and consider whether any hot fixes are necessary.
- Use Windows Update on the Start menu to update components.

TIP It is not very economical for every user in an organization to download updates individually. Thus, Microsoft has created the Windows Update Corporate Site (http://corporate.windowsupdate.microsoft.com/).

- Register your computer through the Windows 2000 Registration Wizard. You can start the wizard from the Configure Your Server screen.

- If you are using disk mirroring and you disabled it before you started the installation, you may want to enable it again.

- Reconnect the UPS serial cable to your computer.

- Rename the Administrator user account to improve security. You can change the name through Computer Management, System Tools, Local Users and Groups. Alternatively, you can wait until Active Directory is installed and then use the Active Directory Users and Computers snap-in.

- If you live in a country outside the United States and Canada, install the high encryption pack to enable 128-bit encryption to increase security. It is available at `http://www.microsoft.com/windows2000/downloads`.

NOTE   128-bit encryption is included in Windows 2000 Service Pack 2.

- Because various Windows 2000 settings are targeted toward the end user, an administrator may want to modify many settings. For example, he or she might want to enable showing all files and file extensions (in any Windows Explorer folder window, select Tools, Folder Options).

- Unless you are dual booting with another operating system, you may want to upgrade your disks to dynamic type, which is more flexible because it enables you to create different types of volumes (for example, spanned volume). For dynamic disks, the partition configuration data is stored on the disk rather than in the registry.

NOTE   Dynamic disks are not available on laptop computers.

- If you intend to install certificate services on your server and want this computer to become the Enterprise Root CA (Certification Authority), you must install Active Directory first.

IF YOU KNOW NT   You might want to read the "New Ways to Do Familiar Tasks" section in the Windows 2000 Help.

Installing Windows 2000 Professional

This chapter has mainly dealt with installing the Windows 2000 Server. However, you can perform the same steps to install Windows 2000 Professional that you did to install Windows 2000 Server, with only a few minor differences. These differences include the following:

- Lower hardware requirements—64MB of RAM is enough unless you intend to run a large number of applications simultaneously.
- There is no need to define a licensing option.
- There are no additional components to choose during setup.
- IIS is not installed by default.
- Terminal Services are not available.
- Obviously, there is no way to install Active Directory.

INSTALLING ACTIVE DIRECTORY

The installation of Active Directory is completely separate from the Windows 2000 setup. It is usually started with the command DCPROMO. Alternatively, you could start it from the Active Directory section in the Configure Your Server screen.

When Active Directory is installed onto a computer, the computer is promoted to a domain controller. The same command, DCPROMO, can be used to uninstall Active Directory—that is, to demote the computer to a stand-alone or member server.

IF YOU KNOW NT It was important to select the server role right the first time when installing Windows NT because you *could not* change the roles of stand-alone/member server and domain controller after installation.

Requirements and Recommendations

In order to install Active Directory, you must have the following:

- A computer running Windows 2000 Server, Advanced Server, or Datacenter Server
- A partition or volume formatted as NTFS, because SysVol needs NTFS
- Adequate disk space (200MB for the Active Directory database and 50MB for the Active Directory log files)
- TCP/IP installed
- A DNS server that supports service (SRV) resource records

TIP   In order to estimate the space requirement for the Active Directory database, you might want to use Active Directory Sizer, which comes with the Windows 2000 Resource Kit Supplement 1 in the apps\adsizer folder. You can download the Sizer from `http://www.microsoft.com/windows2000/downloads`.

The following features are also recommended for the DNS service:

- Support for the dynamic update protocol (RFC 2136), because it reduces administrative effort considerably.
- Support for incremental zone transfers (RFC 1995). Only new or updated resource records are replicated between DNS servers.

TIP   You can find the RFC Internet standards at `http://www.ietf.org/`.

TIP   A working TCP/IP stack must be available when Active Directory Installation Wizard is running. Although the wizard will start, it won't complete. You might come across this situation when you install a laptop with the network cable disconnected. To get around this problem, you can install the Microsoft Loopback Adapter, which is a virtual network adapter installable using the Hardware Wizard. Alternatively, see Microsoft Knowledge Base article Q239924 for instructions on disabling technology known as "Media Sense," Windows 2000's ability to detect network connection status.

If you do not want to install your own DNS server, you must define the IP address of an existing DNS server. If you are using a BIND DNS server, you should use at least version 8.1.2.

Creating Domains, Trees, and Forests

As mentioned, installing Active Directory is initiated with the DCPROMO command, which starts the Active Directory Installation Wizard. Although only a few steps are involved in using the Installation Wizard, the decisions that you make during those few steps have far-reaching consequences.

BEFORE INSTALLATION

Before you install Active Directory, you must choose the Active Directory domain name. The domain name should conform to DNS standards and it could even be the same name that you or your company is known by on the Internet. If possible, select a name that represents your entire organization, because an Active Directory tree can accommodate only one DNS root name. If one DNS root name cannot be used (for example, if your company has acquired another company with a strong DNS identity), you can join these two domains to form a forest.

If your network is connected to the Internet and you are not using firewalls or proxy servers, the root domain name must be unique in the Internet DNS namespace. You can ensure its uniqueness by registering your root domain name with an Internet domain name registering authority.

In addition, if the connection to the Internet exists, your DNS naming scheme must conform to the Internet's domain-naming rules. For additional information, see RFCs 1034, 1035, 1036, and 2052.

As you will notice while learning Active Directory, thorough knowledge of DNS is essential. Active Directory and DNS are tightly integrated.

Next, you must decide where in the Active Directory namespace to locate your new domain controller. Your options include

- A new forest
- A new domain tree in an existing forest
- A new domain in an existing tree
- A new domain controller for an existing domain

If you are installing your first Windows 2000 domain controller, the domain becomes a forest root domain (FRD) and forms a new Active Directory forest.

The Installation Process

The flowchart in Figure 2.5 shows the steps you need to perform to install the computer in the preferred position.

The common steps for most options include the following:

- Define the NetBIOS name of the domain to be used by the clients of an earlier Windows version. If a domain with that same name already exists in your network, the wizard suggests you use that name suffixed by a sequence number starting from zero.
- Define the location for the database that stores Active Directory. The default location is %systemroot%\NTDS.
- Define the location for the log files. The log files temporarily store the changes to Active Directory. To optimize performance, place the database and log files on separate physical disks. The default location is %systemroot%\ NTDS.

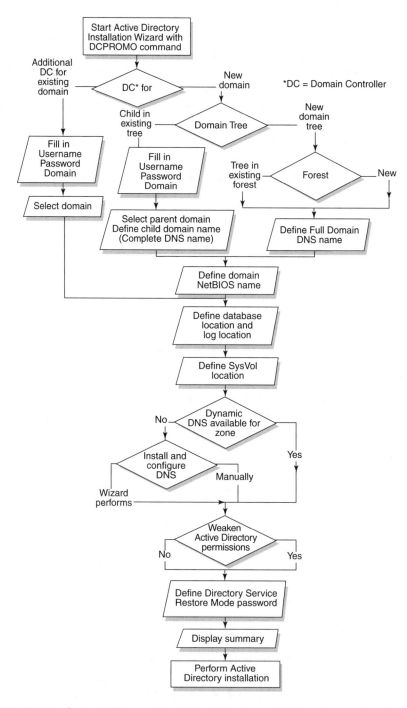

FIGURE 2.5 Using the Active Directory Installation Wizard, an administrator goes through these steps to define Active Directory settings.

- Define the location for System Volume (SysVol). The shared system volume is a folder tree that stores Group Policies and some other files. SysVol is replicated among domain controllers. SysVol must be located on a partition or volume formatted as NTFS. The default location is %systemroot%\SYSVOL.

- Define the password for the administrator in Active Directory Restore Mode. You can access the restore mode from the start-up screen by pressing F8, and because Active Directory is not running in this option, another administrator user account (along with the password) is stored in the registry.

- Decide whether to weaken the permissions for users accessing the network through NT 4.0 RAS servers. If you decide to weaken the permissions, the Everyone group is added to the Builtin group Pre-Windows 2000 Compatible Access. This group has permission to read any attribute of any user object in Active Directory. Thus, you should consider the security implications twice before enabling this option.

NOTE   The membership of the Pre-Windows 2000 Compatible Access group is obviously per domain, and as such, it only appears when installing the first domain controller for a new domain.

TIP   If you want to remove the Everyone group after installation, use Active Directory Users and Computers snap-in. To add the Everyone group into the Pre-Windows 2000 Compatible Access group, use the following command: `net localgroup "Pre-Windows 2000 Compatible Access" /add everyone`.

In addition to the steps you perform, certain events take place behind the scenes.

- First, the Installation Wizard verifies the existence of a properly configured TCP/IP stack. If the TCP/IP protocol is not installed properly, the wizard will stop and enable you to install and configure it.

- Next, the wizard verifies the operation of the DNS service. If the DNS client is not running on the first domain controller, if its DNS server IP address is improperly configured, or if the DNS cannot be found, you might see the following message: "The wizard cannot contact the DNS server that handles the name 'sanao.com' to determine if it supports dynamic update. Confirm your DNS configuration, or install and configure a DNS server on this computer." After this message is displayed and you have clicked OK, you choose whether to install and configure the DNS service yourself or to let the wizard do it.

- The wizard checks that the DNS name is unique in the forest. The wizard will not continue without a valid name. Similarly, after you have entered the NetBIOS name, its uniqueness is verified within your network. If the name already exists, the Installation Wizard suggests a name suffixed by a number zero.

- The wizard verifies the user's credentials. The account used to create new domains must have the appropriate access privileges. By default, only members of the Enterprise Admins group have this permission.

The actual installation starts after you've completed all steps in the Installation Wizard and accepted the settings displayed on the Summary screen shown in Figure 2.6.

There are a number of steps included in the creation of Active Directory. These steps differ significantly depending on the role of the new domain controller. Table 2.7 lists the common steps for promoting the domain controller for a new forest—that is, for creating a new forest.

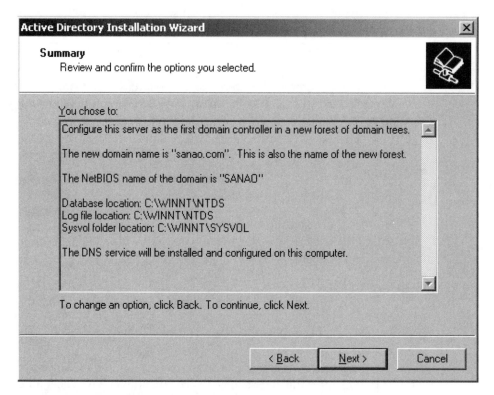

FIGURE 2.6 The Active Directory Installation Wizard lets you review the settings before it starts the promotion.

TABLE 2.7 Steps during Active Directory Installation

Step	Notes
Stop service NETLOGON.	Nobody can log on to the domain using this computer.
Create the System Volume C:\WINNT\SYSVOL.	
Prepare for system volume replication using root C:\WINNT\SYSVOL.	
Copy initial Directory Service database file C:\WINNT\system32\ntds.dit to C:\WINNT\NTDS\ntds.dit.	
Install the Directory Service.	
Configure service RPCLOCATOR.	
Configure service NETLOGON.	
Set the LSA policy information from policy (null).	
Configure service kdc.	KDC service generates session keys and grants service tickets for mutual client-server authentication.
Configure service IsmServ.	InterSite messaging service allows the sending and receiving of replication messages between domain controllers in different sites.
Configure service TrkSvr.	Distributed Link Tracking Server service stores information so that files moved among volumes can be tracked for each volume in the domain.
Configure service w32time.	Windows Time service synchronizes the computer clock with an external source as well as among the computers in Active Directory.
Set the computer's DNS computer name root to sanao.com.	
Set security on the domain controller and Directory Service files and registry keys.	NTFS and registry ACLs are updated.

While the Installation Wizard configures Active Directory, it displays its progress in a window, as shown in Figure 2.7.

To work with our sample company Sanao as you progress through this book, create a new forest with the settings in Table 2.8.

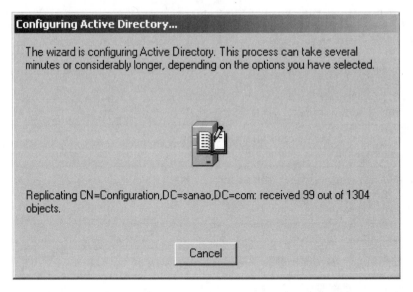

FIGURE 2.7 When you install a child domain, certain objects are replicated from the parent domain.

TABLE 2.8 Sample Configuration Used in This Book

Setting	Value
Type of domain	New forest (i.e., a new domain in a new tree in a new forest)
Complete DNS name	sanao.com
NetBIOS name	SANAO
Location of database and log files	C:\WINNT\NTDS
Location of SysVol folder	C:\WINNT\SYSVOL
Permissions compatible with pre-Windows 2000 servers	No (in other words, select "Permissions compatible only with Windows 2000 servers")

After Active Directory Installation

After the Active Directory installation is complete, you have to restart your computer (see Figure 2.8). Now you will have to determine if everything went well.

VERIFYING THE INSTALLATION

You can verify that the Active Directory installation was successful by checking that the following items are present.

FIGURE 2.8 When the Active Directory installation is finished, the Installation Wizard displays information about the created domain and site. You can now restart your computer.

- Database file ntds.dit is stored in %Systemroot%\NTDS.
- Shared system volume is located in %Systemroot%\SYSVOL.
- A site called Default-First-Site-Name has been created. You can check this with the Active Directory Sites and Services snap-in in the Administrative Tools.
- The first domain controller in the forest is a GC server. You can verify this by checking the properties of Sites, Default-First-Site-Name, Servers, <*Yourservername*>, NTDS Settings in Active Directory Sites and Services.
- Domain Controllers OU and default containers Builtin, Computers, and Users have been created in Active Directory. Check this with the Active Directory Users and Computers snap-in.
- Five new shortcuts for MMC snap-ins have been created in the Start menu under Administrative Tools: Active Directory Domains and Trusts, Active Directory Sites and Services, Active Directory Users and Computers, Domain Security Policy, and Domain Controller Security Policy.

The database file and the shared SysVol may be located elsewhere if you used locations different from the defaults provided during the installation.

TIP   You can change the location of the directory database and the log files afterwards with the NTDSUtil tool.

In addition, you may want to check the Active Directory installation log files dcpromo.log and dcpromoui.log, which are stored in the %Systemroot%\Debug folder. To ensure that the DNS service (SRV) resource records were created during the promotion, make sure you see them in the %Systemroot%\System32\Config\netlogon.dns file. You can copy them from this file to an alternative DNS server that doesn't support dynamic updates. However, if you're using Windows 2000, you should see the four subdomains (_msdcs, _sites, _tcp, _udp) containing the SRV records within the MMC as displayed in Figure 2.9. If you cannot see the subdomains, you can try restarting the Netlogon service (select Administrative Tools, Services) and refreshing DNS thereafter. Another place you might want to check is the IP address of the DNS server that your DNS client (resolver) uses.

REMOVING THE DNS ROOT DOMAIN AND CONFIGURING A FORWARDING ADDRESS

If your computer doesn't have an IP address, when you started the installation the Installation Wizard assumed that you were not connected to the Internet or that you were using a network address translation (NAT) and possibly a firewall. As a result, the wizard created a zone for a DNS root domain (.). If you later connect your computer to the Internet through your company or an ISP, you might want to remove the root domain from the Forward Lookup Zones in order to enable name resolution for the clients. You do this by starting the DNS snap-in from Administrative Tools. Then double-click Forward Lookup Zones and delete the root zone. Restart the snap-in or click the computer icon and refresh by pressing F5. This enables you to configure your DNS server as a *forwarder*—that is, it forwards the DNS queries that it cannot answer by itself to another defined name server. To configure the IP address of the DNS server to which you want to forward the queries, go to the Forwarders tab in DNS Server Properties.

CREATING A FORWARD LOOKUP ZONE AND ENABLING DYNAMIC UPDATES

If you decided not to let the Active Directory Installation Wizard install and configure DNS service, you must first install the DNS service and then configure a Forward Lookup Zone for the DNS service. You can install the service from the Control Panel by selecting Add/Remove Programs, Add/Remove Windows Components, Networking. Perform the following steps to create the Forward Lookup Zone:

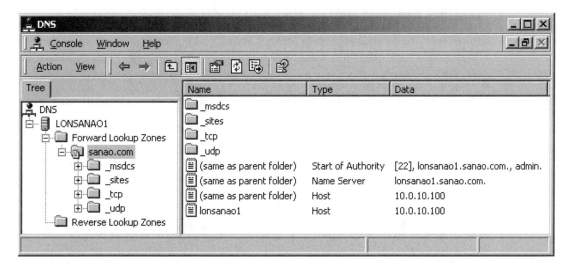

Figure 2.9 A DNS snap-in contains subdomains, _msdcs, _sites, _tcp, and _udp that contain the SRV records after Active Directory has been installed.

1. Start the DNS Service snap-in from the Start menu if it isn't already running.

2. Double-click your computer icon.

3. Double-click Forward Lookup Zones.

4. Right-click Forward Lookup Zones and select Create a New Zone from the context menu. Click Next.

5. Select Standard Primary or Active Directory Integrated. If you select Standard Primary, the zone file is stored in %windir%\System32\Dns and replicated to other DNS servers with zone transfers (that you must manually configure). An Active Directory integrated zone is stored in Active Directory and replicated automatically through Active Directory replication.

6. Type the name for the zone. It is probably the same as your Active Directory forest root (i.e., sanao.com). Then click Next twice and click Finish once.

7. Right-click the newly created zone (sanao.com). Select Properties from the context menu. If Properties doesn't appear, you might want to double-click the zone first.

8. Select Yes in the "Allow dynamic updates" field and click OK.

9. Enter the command ipconfig /registerdns on the command line in order to register the record.

10. Restart Netlogon service (select Administrative Tools, Services or enter the following commands: net stop netlogon followed by net start netlogon).

CREATING A REVERSE LOOKUP ZONE AND ENABLING DYNAMIC UPDATES

In order to test the DNS service with either its own monitoring tool or the DNS diagnostics tool, nslookup, you should first configure a Reverse Lookup Zone for the DNS service. Perform the following steps to create the Reverse Lookup Zone:

1. Start the DNS service snap-in from the Start menu if it isn't already running.
2. Double-click your computer icon.
3. Double-click Reverse Lookup Zones.
4. Right-click Reverse Lookup Zones and select Create a New Zone from the context menu. Click Next.
5. Select Standard Primary or Active Directory Integrated.
6. Type the first three octets of your network ID (for example, 10.0.10), and then click Next twice and click Finish once.
7. Right-click the newly created zone (for example, 10.0.10.in-addr.arpa). Select Properties from the context menu. If Properties doesn't appear, you might want to double-click the zone first.
8. Select Yes in the "Allow dynamic updates" field and click OK.
9. Enter the command `ipconfig /registerdns` on the command line to register the record.

When you start nslookup in the interactive mode, the first thing it does is try to find the name corresponding to the IP address. If you do not create the Reverse Lookup Zone or if the DNS computer does not have its record there, you'll see an error like the following:

```
C:\>nslookup
DNS request timed out.
    timeout was 2 seconds.
*** Can't find server name for address 10.0.10.100: Timed out
*** Default servers are not available
Default Server:  UnKnown
Address:  10.0.10.100
```

OTHER DNS-RELATED TASKS

Other tasks that you might want to perform after installing Active Directory include configuring a DNS zone as Active Directory Integrated. If you let the Active Directory Installation Wizard install and configure the DNS service, the zone would already be Active Directory integrated—that is, records would be stored in Active Directory and also replicated within it. Active Directory Integrated zones also support Secure Dynamic updates as per RFCs 2137 and 2078. This means that permissions defined for records stored in Active Directory are checked before updates are possible. You can change a zone to only allow secure dynamic updates by selecting Only secure updates in Allow dynamic updates field of zone properties.

OTHER POST-INSTALLATION TASKS

In order to increase fault tolerance, it's a good idea to have at least two domain controllers per domain.

Another task is to change your domain to native mode. By doing this, you can start using all the features, such as universal groups, provided by Active Directory and Windows 2000. On the other hand, changing a domain to native mode prevents installation of new Windows NT backup domain controllers to this domain and removes the option to roll back an unsuccessful upgrade. You can find the button to change a domain into native mode in Active Directory Users and Computers by right-clicking the domain and selecting Properties.

WARNING Changing a domain into native mode is a one-way operation and it cannot be reversed!

AUTOMATING INSTALLATION

When you are installing Windows 2000 onto several computers, it becomes worthwhile to consider automated installation. It can save you a considerable amount of effort and time. Several methods are available for automation, some of them are for installing only the operating system and some are for installing applications, too.

Automating Windows 2000 Installation

Methods to automate installation of Windows 2000 include the following:

- Use an answer file created with Setup Manager Wizard.
- Duplicate disk images with the System Preparation Tool and a third-party product.
- Use SysPart for computers with dissimilar hardware.
- Use a bootable CD.

In addition, you can use Remote Installation Services (RIS) to install Windows 2000 Professional and applications on client computers from a designated RIS server.

ANSWER FILES AND THE SETUP MANAGER WIZARD

Instead of manually answering every question that is presented during the manual installation, you can prepare files that include these answers (see Figure 2.10). These answer files can be created easily with a new version of the Setup Manager Wizard. Not only does Setup Manager Wizard enable you to create new answer files from scratch or edit an existing file, but it also makes it possible to install and configure a master machine and create an answer file for installing other computers with similar settings. Using the Setup Manager Wizard greatly reduces the possibility of errors compared with modifying the answer files manually with a text editor such as Notepad. You can install the Setup Manager Wizard by extracting it from the file Support\Tools\Deploy.cab on the Windows 2000 CD. It is also available in the Windows 2000 Resource Kit.

After you have created the answer file, you modify the unattended installation with various other files. To define computer-specific settings, such as computer name, you use the Uniqueness Database File (UDF). You can also customize the system by indicating which files and components are installed by modifying the DOSNET.INF, TXTSETUP.SIF, and LAYOUT.INF files. These files are located in the Windows 2000 installation folder.

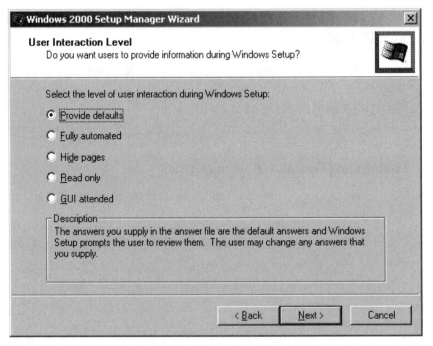

FIGURE 2.10 When you create the answer file with the Setup Manager Wizard, you can define the level of user interaction during Windows 2000 setup.

In addition to modifying the unattended installation of Windows 2000, you can automate the setup of applications. The tool provided to do so is called SYSDIFF.

TIP   For further information on using answer files and SysPrep, see Unattend.doc in the Docs folder of the uncompressed SysPrep 1.1 package.

DUPLICATING DISK IMAGES

Using disk duplication might be the most efficient deployment method if you have a number of computers with reasonably similar hardware and identical configurations (see Figure 2.11). You first install Windows 2000 and the required

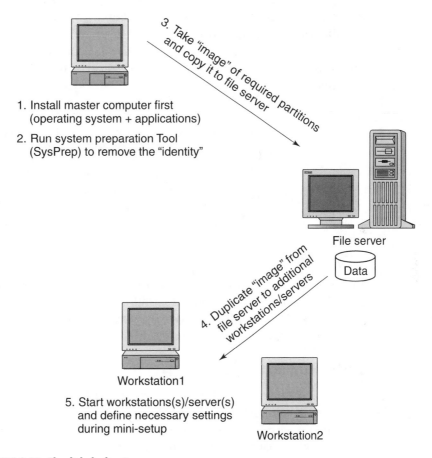

3. Take "image" of required partitions and copy it to file server

1. Install master computer first
   (operating system + applications)

2. Run system preparation Tool
   (SysPrep) to remove the "identity"

File server

Data

4. Duplicate "image" from file server to additional workstations/servers

Workstation1

5. Start workstations(s)/server(s)
   and define necessary settings
   during mini-setup

Workstation2

FIGURE 2.11 The disk duplication process

applications on a master machine and then run the System Preparation Tool (SysPrep). SysPrep prepares the installation to be duplicated to other computers by means of third-party disk duplication software such as Norton Ghost, Micro-House ImageCast, and PowerQuest Drive Image. The preparation includes removing machine-specific settings and security IDs (SIDs). As the last step, SysPrep shuts down the computer.

NOTE   You can download SysPrep 1.1 from Microsoft's Web site (`http://www.microsoft.com/windows2000/download`). It enhances the usability of disk duplication to machines with different types of disk controllers (for example, IDE and SCSI).

The duplication software copies the "image" of required partitions to a file server from which you can copy it to additional workstations/servers. After you start the copied workstation/server for the first time, you are prompted to provide certain computer-specific settings, such as the computer name, administrator password, and network settings during the so-called mini-setup, which only takes a few minutes.

NOTE   Duplicating domain controllers with this method is not possible!

IF YOU KNOW NT   Microsoft didn't support disk duplication for NT computers until late 1998 when duplicating workstations and stand-alone/member servers became supported.

USING SYSPART

Preparing the installation with WINNT32 /SysPart enables you to copy the Windows 2000 installation files onto a partition on a hard disk, after which the partition is marked active. You can move the hard disk to another computer, and after that computer boots up, setup starts automatically.

USING A BOOTABLE CD

A bootable CD carries all the information necessary to start a computer, such as the operation system files. The easiest way to create a bootable CD is to copy it from an original operating system CD. Otherwise, you will have to use a CD burning application that supports creating such CDs.

Although a computer is usually booted from a hard disk, a bootable CD is useful for installing Windows 2000 onto individual systems or for when it is installed in remote locations with slow WAN links. The computers onto which Windows 2000 is to be installed must have El Torito support for bootable CDs. You can find this out from the BIOS settings of the computers. To automatically install Windows 2000 with a bootable CD, you must provide an answer file called Winnt.sif on a floppy disk during the installation.

Automating Active Directory Installation

Just like the Windows 2000 installation, the Active Directory installation can be automated. So far, there are no tools to create an answer file for Active Directory installation. It is reasonably simple, however, and you can use the following example as a template and modify the files with a text editor (Notepad, for example).

Let's say you want to create a new Active Directory forest with the root domain called `sanao.com`. You assume Windows 2000 has been installed with default settings. Here are the contents of a sample answer file for Active Directory installation:

```
[DCInstall]
RebootOnSuccess=Yes
DatabasePath=c:\winnt\ntds
LogPath=c:\winnt\ntds
SysVolPath=c:\winnt\sysvol
SiteName=Default-First-Site-Name
ReplicaOrNewDomain=Domain
TreeOrChild=Tree
CreateOrJoin=Create
DomainNetbiosName=sanao
NewDomainDNSName=sanao.com
DNSOnNetwork=No
AdministratorPassword=password
AutoConfigDNS=Yes
```

You start automated Active Directory installation with a command switch /answer—for example, `DCPROMO /answer:c:\dcpromo.txt`. Alternatively, you could include the preceding lines in the Windows 2000 answer file in order to automate installation of Windows 2000 and, subsequently, Active Directory.

TIP   For further information on using answer files to automate Active Directory installation, read Unattend.doc in the Docs folder of the uncompressed SysPrep 1.1 package.

TROUBLESHOOTING INSTALLATION

Usually the installation of Windows 2000 and Active Directory goes smoothly. However, sometimes you may run into problems, so in this section we describe some of the more common problems.

Incompatible Devices

If the computer doesn't start after you have selected the installation partition and the Setup program has copied files and restarted the computer, check that all your devices are on the Hardware Compatibility List (HCL). For information on checking compatibility, review the "Hardware Compatibility" section earlier this chapter.

Problems with ACPI

Windows 2000 tries to install ACPI (ACPI supports advanced power-saving options such as standby) support for any computer with BIOS dated after January 1, 1999. You might have updated your BIOS and for some reason Setup freezes when it displays Starting Windows 2000 at the bottom of the screen. You might be able to get Windows 2000 installed by editing txtsetup.sif to read ACPIEnable=0.

Incorrectly Detected Devices

Sometimes a computer has a combination of devices that prevents Windows 2000 device detection from working properly. For example, a network card might not work due to a conflict with IRQ (Interrupt) settings. In this situation, you may try removing some of your device(s) for the setup and installing them again after setup is complete. Alternatively, you may take an optional device inventory either by using an existing operating system or by checking through the device configurations. The device inventory (i.e., the IRQs, memory addresses, and so on) for all devices can help in troubleshooting setup problems. Some programs that may help you in this task are Windows NT Diagnostics and Windows 95/98 Device Manager.

You may try to install Windows 2000 without peripheral devices first and insert those devices after installation. This approach can also be used if two devices are causing a resource conflict.

Problems with Active Directory Installation

The most common problems with Active Directory are related to name resolution (that is, DNS). These include the inability to find a parent domain, problems with simple DNS queries, and so on.

You can try to sort out the name-resolution problems by testing the DNS service with the DNS snap-in or nslookup. To use the snap-in, open it from the Start menu, right-click your server, and select Properties. You can test the operation of the service by checking the Simple Query and Recursive Query box and clicking Test Now. Alternatively, you can check whether the DNS service replies to queries by using the command-line tool nslookup, as follows:

1. Start the command prompt by clicking the Start button, selecting Run, cmd, and then pressing Enter.

2. At the command prompt, type "nslookup" (without quotes) and press Enter.

3. Type "set type=SRV" (without quotes) and press Enter. This filters the SRV-type records only.

4. Type "_ldap._tcp.Active_Directory_Domain_Name" (without quotes) and press Enter.

5. You should see a response that looks like this:

```
C:\>nslookup
Default Server:  lonsanao1.sanao.com
Address:  10.0.10.100
> set type=srv
> _ldap._tcp.sanao.com
Server:  lonsanao1.sanao.com
Address:  10.0.10.100
_ldap._tcp.sanao.com      SRV service location:
          priority      = 0
          weight        = 100
          port          = 389
          svr hostname  = lonsanao1.sanao.com
lonsanao1.sanao.com        internet address = 10.0.10.100
```

Recovery Options

Windows 2000 includes a number of recovery options. We briefly discuss the most important of them in the following sections. For further information on recovery, see the Windows 2000 online Help and Resource Kit.

SAFE MODE

Safe Mode is familiar to everyone who has used Windows 95 or 98. It enables you to start a computer with minimal drivers and services loaded. If a newly installed driver causes Windows 2000 to stop working, the Last Known Good option might be the cure. Table 2.9 presents the various Safe Mode options and their uses.

TABLE 2.9 Windows 2000 Safe Mode Options

Option	Purpose
Safe Mode	Starts Windows 2000 using basic files and drivers only, without networking. The drivers and files used are for mouse, monitor, keyboard, mass storage, base video, and default system services. A boot log file is also saved.
Safe Mode with Networking	Starts Windows 2000 using basic files and drivers only (Safe Mode), but includes network support. Does not support PCMCIA networking. A boot log file is also saved.
Safe Mode with Command Prompt	Starts Windows 2000 using basic files and drivers only, without networking, and displays only the command prompt. A boot log file is also saved.
Enable Boot Logging	Creates a boot log of devices and services that are loading. The log is saved to a file named Ntbtlog.txt in the %systemroot% directory.
Enable VGA Mode	Starts Windows 2000 using the basic VGA (video) driver. This mode is useful when a newly installed driver for your video card is preventing Windows 2000 from starting properly. The basic video driver is always used when you start Windows 2000 in any Safe Mode.
Last Known Good Configuration	Starts Windows 2000 using the settings (registry information) that Windows saved at the last shutdown. Use only in cases of incorrect configuration, as it does not solve problems caused by corrupted or missing drivers or files.*
Directory Services Restore Mode	Starts a domain controller without Active Directory. You must know the Restore Mode administrator password that you defined during Active Directory installation. This option is only for Windows 2000 domain controllers.
Debugging Mode	Starts Windows 2000 while sending debug information through a serial cable to another computer.

*Note: When you use Last Known Good Configuration, any system setting changes made after the last successful start-up are lost.

RECOVERY CONSOLE

The Recovery Console is a utility that many Windows NT administrators have looked forward to for a long time. The Recovery Console enables you to start Windows 2000 into a command-line console where certain operations, such as replacing damaged files or disabling services, are possible. Earlier this kind of functionality existed only with third-party products such as ERD Commander from Sysinternals (http://www.sysinternals.com/).

Table 2.10 lists the console commands and their purposes. Most file- or folder-related commands work only in the system directories of the Windows installation, removable media, the root folder of any hard disk partition, or the local installation sources. Most commands are restricted versions of the equivalent Windows 2000 or earlier commands.

INSTALLING AND STARTING THE RECOVERY CONSOLE

You can install the Recovery Console using the WINNT32 /CMDCONS command. The installation takes 7MB of disk space from the system partition (i.e., the partition where the necessary files to load the operating system are stored). After you've installed the Recovery Console, it appears on the Windows 2000 boot-up menu. From there, you can start it any time you boot up the computer.

Alternatively, you can use the setup floppy disks or the Windows 2000 setup CD to boot up the computer and select Repair instead of Install. On the next screen, you have the option to use the traditional ERD process or to start the Recovery Console.

IF YOU KNOW NT The Recovery Console is new to Windows 2000. You can also use it to try to repair NT 4.0, although this is not supported.

USING THE RECOVERY CONSOLE

After the Recovery Console starts, it scans the hard disk for existing Windows 2000 installations. You select from a list the installation that you want to repair, after which you have to type the local administrator's password.

NOTE The Recovery Console does not use country settings—that is, the keyboard layout configuration is set to U.S. (English).

UNINSTALLING WINDOWS 2000 AND ACTIVE DIRECTORY

Sometimes it is necessary to uninstall Windows 2000 or Active Directory. Such occasions include when you want to remove the secondary operating system used for testing purposes or you want to remove Active Directory because it is incorrectly configured. The following sections present the ways to perform uninstallations efficiently.

Uninstalling Windows 2000

Uninstalling Windows 2000 includes deleting the files and folders. The problem appears when you start installing an older operating system onto a disk with a partition formatted as NTFS. Because other operating systems don't recognize

TABLE 2.10 Windows 2000 Recovery Console Commands

Command	Purpose
ATTRIB	Changes file or folder (directory) attributes.
BATCH	Executes a command specified in a text file.
CD/CHDIR	Changes the current folder or displays its name. Use quotation marks around a folder name that contains spaces.
CHKDSK	Checks disk and displays a status report. Requires AUTOCHK.EXE file.
CLS	Clears the screen.
COPY	Copies a single file to a new location. Doesn't support wildcards. Compressed files from installation source are extracted automatically.
DEL/DELETE	Deletes one or more files.
DIR	Lists files and folders, also with various attributes such as hidden, system, and so on.
DISABLE	Disables a specified Windows system service or driver.
DISKPART	Used for managing disk partitions. Displays a similar partition-management interface to the one used during setup if you start it without parameters.
ENABLE	Enables a specified Windows system service or driver.
EXIT	Exits the recovery console and restarts the computer.
EXTRACT	Extracts a file from a compressed cabinet (.cab) file. Works only if the system was booted from the original installation media. Doesn't support wildcards.
FIXBOOT	Writes a new boot sector onto the system partition. Supports only Intel platform.
FIXMBR	Repairs the MBR of the disk from where the system starts booting (system partition).
FORMAT	Formats a partition or volume with FAT, FAT32, or NTFS.
HELP	Displays a list of Recovery Console commands.
LISTSVC	Lists all available services and drivers.
LOGON	Lists available Windows 2000 installations and requests the password for the local administrator.
MAP	Lists active mappings between drive letters and physical devices. Displays ARC paths (that are used in BOOT.INI) with Arc parameter.
MD/MKDIR	Creates a folder (directory).

(continued)

TABLE 2.10 (*continued*)

Command	Purpose
MORE	Displays the contents of a text file.
RD/RMDIR	Removes a folder (directory).
REN/RENAME	Renames a single file.
SET	Displays and sets system variables.
SYSTEMROOT	Sets the current directory to systemroot.
TYPE	Displays the contents of a text file.

the NTFS version 5, you must use another program to delete partitions. The most obvious way is to try to use the Recovery Console and its DISKPART command. Another choice is to use a third-party product that can delete NTFS version 5 partitions, such as PowerQuest PartitionMagic.

If you are dual booting and want to get rid of Windows 2000 and retain the earlier operating system's boot menu, you can use the FDISK/MBR command.

Uninstalling Active Directory

There are situations in which you might want to uninstall Active Directory. For example, a software developer might have created an application that updates the schema. You cannot currently remove added attributes or classes from an Active Directory schema; you can only disable them. Thus, it might become necessary to uninstall Active Directory from a computer to clean up the schema, after which you can reinstall Active Directory. Another situation would be if you have been experimenting with Active Directory and you want to install the computer to an existing domain.

Uninstalling Active Directory couldn't be much easier. You start by demoting a domain controller into a stand-alone/member server with the DCPROMO command. If the domain controller in question is also a GC server and other domain controllers will remain in the forest, you should ensure that some other domain controller is defined as a GC server. Otherwise, the users might not be able to log on to a domain.

Next, you are asked whether the domain controller in question is the last domain controller in a domain. If this is the case, the computer becomes a stand-alone server and the domain no longer exists. If it isn't, it will be demoted to a member server. Next, you must enter the Enterprise Admin credentials in order to be able to complete the removal and finally define a new password for the local administrator.

As Figure 2.12 shows, a number of things happen when Active Directory is removed from the last domain controller in a domain.

- Member computers in the domain cannot log on to the domain, nor can they access any services in it.
- All user, group, computer, and other objects are removed.
- All cryptographic keys are deleted. Thus, they should be exported with the Certificate Export Wizard before the uninstallation continues.

TIP   Search the Windows 2000 online Help with the keywords "certificate export" for further instructions on exporting certificates along with private keys.

- All encrypted data should be decrypted, although it is possible to access the data if the keys were exported.

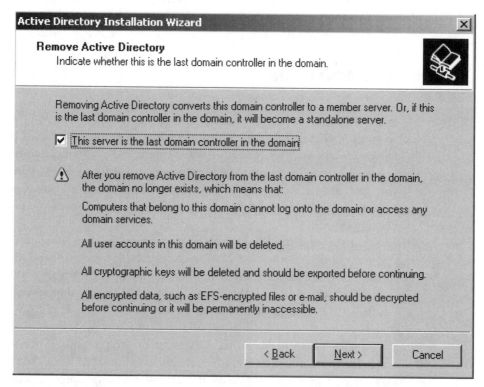

FIGURE 2.12 Removing Active Directory from the last domain controller in the domain has a number of consequences.

- DNS subdomains and SRV records are deleted upon restarting the computer. If the computer is the last domain of the Active Directory root domain, the Forward Lookup Zone is also removed.

WARNING   If you select "This server is the last domain controller in the domain" for the server you are going to demote, make sure that the server is actually the last one in the domain. Otherwise, you will end up with a major problem because data in Active Directory will become inconsistent with the actual situation.

AUTOMATING ACTIVE DIRECTORY UNINSTALLATION

Uninstalling Active Directory can be automated in the same way Active Directory installation can be automated. Obviously, the answer file differs because there are not so many questions to be answered and the questions are somewhat different.

Here's a sample answer file called UNINST.TXT for uninstalling Active Directory:

```
[DCInstall]
RebootOnSuccess=Yes
IsLastDCInDomain=No
AdministratorPassword=password
Password=password
UserName=Administrator
```

This file can be used with the command dcpromo /answer:c:\uninst.txt.

CONCLUSION

In this chapter, you have learned how to install Windows 2000 Server and promote it to a domain controller. Now you have at least a small Active Directory network up and running, so you are ready to explore various aspects of Active Directory. Chapter 3 begins this exploration with the management of OUs, users, and groups, which make up the core content of Active Directory.

CORE SKILLS

Managing OUs, Users, and Groups

The most visible part of Active Directory administration is managing objects with the Users and Computers snap-in. This snap-in enables you to create organizational units (OUs) to set up an OU tree in a domain. You also use this snap-in to populate the OU tree by creating objects of the following six classes in the OUs you want:

- Users
- Contacts
- Computers
- Groups
- Shared folders
- Printers

This chapter covers managing OUs and the first four classes in the list. We will proceed as follows:

- First, we describe the contents of your Active Directory domain right after installation.
- Second, we explore how to manage OUs and objects of each of the four other classes (i.e., users, contacts, computers, and groups).
- Finally, we discuss some additional features of the Users and Computers snap-in, and we list additional tools for managing objects.

This chapter focuses on the Users and Computers snap-in. If you have to create many objects, other tools you can use include LDIFDE, CSVDE, scripting, or some Resource Kit tools. Although listed at the end of this chapter, these tools are covered later in the book.

NOTE   Behind the scenes, a domain object can contain objects of 23 classes and an OU can contain objects of 35 classes. However, with the Users and Computers snap-in, you can normally create and see objects of only the 7 classes just listed.

ACTIVE DIRECTORY AFTER INSTALLATION

After you have created your first domain by installing Active Directory on a server (i.e., promoting it to a domain controller), there are certain users, computers, groups, and containers already in place (see Figure 3.1). You see these objects with the Users and Computers snap-in, which you start by clicking the Start button and selecting Programs, Administrative Tools, Active Directory Users and Computers.

TIP   Another way to start the Users and Computers snap-in is to click the Start button, select Run, type "dsa.msc," and press Enter.

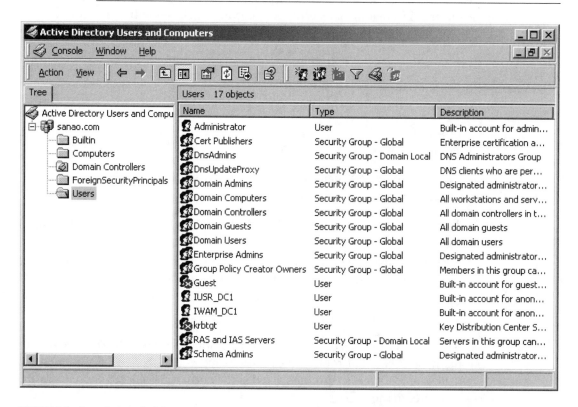

FIGURE 3.1 A newly installed domain (sanao.com in the figure), which is the root domain of a forest

You will see the following predefined objects in the snap-in:

- Five containers, one of which is an OU
- Some user objects (or user accounts)
- Some group objects (or group accounts)
- One computer object (or computer account) for your domain controller

NOTE   Active Directory contains only objects. Users, groups, and computers, however, are often called *accounts* instead of objects.

NOTE   If you upgrade a Windows NT 4.0 or 3.51 domain, you will see the users, groups, and computers of that domain in Active Directory.

Predefined OUs and Other Containers

The objects in a domain should reside in containers instead of at the domain level, just as files on disk should reside in folders instead of in the root folder. Accordingly, the predefined objects are stored in containers below the domain level. Table 3.1 describes the five predefined containers. You cannot rename or delete them—they are always there.

NOTE   In Table 3.1, the Possible Contents column lists the object types (that is, classes) that you can create in the corresponding container using the Users and Computers snap-in. With an "under-the-hood" tool, such as ADSI Edit, you could create other types of objects. However, there is no need to use the predefined containers for anything but what is described in the table.

You shouldn't use the Builtin container for anything, even though it is possible to create computers, groups, and users in it. Likewise, you could create users in the Computers container or computers in the Users container, but there is no point in doing so. Putting such things together is comparable to placing your cookbooks and music CDs on the same shelf. It is possible, but why do it?

If you want, you can keep your users in the Users container and computers in the Computers container. If you do so, however, you can neither create OUs in them nor assign Group Policy for them because these containers are not OUs. If you have more than 20 users, for example, and you want to delegate some

TABLE 3.1 The Predefined Containers in Active Directory

Container	OU	Purpose	Possible Contents
Builtin	No	This is a container for the predefined built-in local security groups (you cannot create them yourself).	Computer, group, user
Computers	No	This is a default container for computer objects corresponding to Windows NT/2000 workstations and member servers in this domain.	Computer, contact, group, printer, user, shared folder
Domain Controllers	Yes	This is a default container for computer objects corresponding to domain controllers of this domain.	Computer, contact, group, OU, printer, user, shared folder
ForeignSecurity-Principals	No	This is a container for placeholders that represent group members from domains external to the forest. This includes well-known security principals, such as Authenticated Users, if they are members of some group in the domain.* Objects in this container are visible only when the snap-in's Advanced Features are turned on.	Computer, contact, group, printer, user, shared folder
Users	No	This is a default container for users and groups.	Computer, contact, group, printer, user, shared folder

* We discuss well-known security principals in Chapter 4 and foreign security principals in Chapter 6.

administration, you will probably end up creating new OUs for your users and computers (i.e., outside the Users or Computers containers). We will come back to this issue in the "Administering OUs" section later in this chapter.

The Domain Controllers container is an OU and, therefore, you can create OUs in it and assign Group Policy(ies) for it. This OU already has a Default Domain Controllers Policy Group Policy object (GPO) assigned, which affects the security and other settings of your domain controllers. You are likely to keep the computer objects for your domain controllers in this container and other OUs that you create below it.

WHY THESE CONTAINERS?

It may seem that the way these predefined containers were chosen is odd. Why are most of them not OUs? Some explanation is given by the fact that these containers ease the upgrade from Windows NT 4.0 or 3.51 to Active Directory. During the upgrade process, the old user and group accounts are migrated to the Users container, old workstation and member server accounts are migrated to the Computers container, and old domain controller accounts are migrated to the Domain Controllers container.

In Windows NT, built-in local groups were internally stored separately from other groups, users, and computer accounts. This separation was brought over to Active Directory in the form of the Builtin container.

So why are these three containers not OUs? One explanation could be that this way you are intentionally discouraged from using them in the long run and you must create new OUs instead.

Predefined Users

Two user objects are always present: Administrator and Guest. You cannot delete either of them, but you can rename them at will. Renaming Administrator offers some extra protection because a potential network intruder would need to guess the new name in addition to the password. However, if you have a large network and many administrative personnel, it may be confusing for the Administrator account to have a different name.

NOTE　　The default permissions of Active Directory allow any user of the forest to see the names of administrative accounts, so renaming them is really minimal "protection." You can think of it as adding a small extra hurdle in a potential intruder's path. If you chose permissions compatible with pre–Windows 2000 servers, anonymous users can also see this information.

Active Directory has predefined user accounts besides Administrator and Guest, depending on what services you installed in your server. Table 3.2 lists the predefined user accounts in Active Directory.

If you enable the Guest account, be careful about the permissions you give to it. After all, anyone who "walks in the door" can use it. There are two ways to use the Guest account.

- If your workstation is a member of a domain of the forest where the Guest account is enabled (in some of its domains), you just type "guest" in the logon dialog box, select the correct domain, and start using the workstation and the network.

- If your workstation is in a workgroup or in a different forest from the one in which the Guest account is enabled (in some of its domains), you first need to log on with some other user account. When you connect to the resources of

TABLE 3.2 The Predefined User Accounts in Active Directory

Name	Present	Description
Administrator	Always (although could be renamed); cannot be disabled	The only user account you can use when you log on for the first time. The Administrator account of the first domain in a forest has the widest possible administrative permissions on Active Directory and the domain controllers in the same forest. You can create other user accounts with permissions as wide. The Administrator accounts of the later domains in a forest have the widest possible administrative permissions for their own domains.
Guest	Always (although could be renamed); disabled by default	If someone doesn't have a user account, he can use the Guest account (if the account is enabled). (See the discussion in the text.)
IUSR_*servername*	One for each domain controller that has IIS installed	If IIS allows anonymous access (e.g., by Web browsers), anonymous users use permissions of this user account.
IWAM_*servername*	One for each domain controller that has IIS installed	IWAM stands for IIS Web Application Manager. The IISWAM.OutofProcessPool component (part of IIS) uses this user account.
krbtgt	Always; disabled by default; cannot be enabled or renamed	The Kerberos key distribution center (KDC) uses this account. "Krbtgt" is part of the KDC's service principal name (SPN). Also, a symmetric key is derived from the password of krbtgt, and this key is used to encrypt and decrypt TGTs. Only the KDC knows this password and it changes the password periodically.
TsInternetUser		When an optional Internet Connector license is enabled, Terminal Services clients are not prompted with a logon dialog box. Instead, they are logged on automatically with the TsInternetUser account.

the domain where the Guest account is enabled, you are granted access based on that Guest account's permissions. You never type "guest" anywhere—you just use "Jack," for example. When the server doesn't recognize "Jack," it switches to use "Guest" automatically. The catch is that if there is another Jack, who most likely uses a different password, you are denied access. The server just thinks that someone is trying to crack Jack's account and doesn't use Guest at all.

Predefined Groups

Active Directory includes predefined security groups. Some of them reside in the Builtin container and the rest reside in the Users container, as follows:

- *Builtin:* Built-in local security groups
- *Users:* Mostly global security groups

The primary purpose of most of these predefined groups is to be the means by which administrative rights and permissions are assigned. To be anything more than an end user in the network, a user needs one or more of the following types of permission or rights:

- User rights, such as permission to change the system time or log on locally. These rights are controlled with Group Policy settings and/or local policy settings. There are also some fixed rights. For example, only members of the Administrators group can format hard drives, and you cannot give this right to anyone else.
- Administrative permissions (i.e., the ability to create, delete, change, and so on) for Active Directory objects.
- Administrative permissions for registry keys.
- Administrative permissions for folders and files.
- Administrative permissions for other resources (printers, for example).

Most of the predefined groups have specific administrative rights or permissions associated with them, so you can give some users the appropriate rights and permissions by adding their names to the corresponding groups. Instead of worrying about all of the items in the list individually, it is far easier to just put Jack in the Account Operators group and Jill in the DNS Admins group, for example. They will get suitable permissions in one package.

Sticking just to "predefined" doesn't get you through life, though—at least not with Windows 2000. You often need to assign individual rights and permissions, probably not using the predefined groups. But that's a story for another chapter (Chapter 4, to be exact).

Figure 3.2 shows the relationship among the groups in the Builtin and Users containers in an Active Directory domain. It also shows the corresponding relationships that existed in Windows NT.

NOTE   In addition to the permissions and rights shown in Figure 3.2, built-in local (security) groups have permissions for system files and registry keys.

NOTE   In Windows NT it was easy to make a user of another domain a domain administrator in a local domain. It only required making him a member of the Administrators group in the local domain. Because of the difference in how global groups get permissions, as illustrated in Figure 3.2, this is more difficult in Active Directory. If you make the foreign user a member of Administrators in Active Directory, he won't get the permissions of Domain Admins, so he will be only a partial administrator. You cannot make him a member of Domain Admins because that group accepts members only from the same domain.

PREDEFINED BUILT-IN LOCAL SECURITY GROUPS

Table 3.3 describes the predefined groups in the Builtin container. You cannot delete, rename, or move any of them. Note that each group in the table is always present in all domains. They have rights and/or permissions to their local domain only.

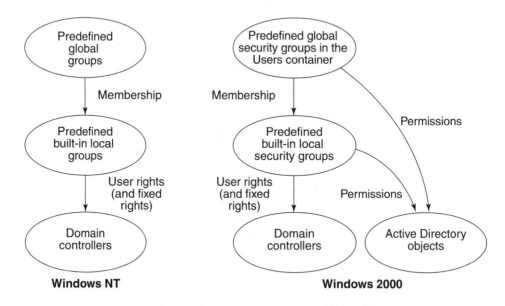

FIGURE 3.2 In Windows NT, the only meaning of predefined global groups (Domain Admins, Domain Users, and Domain Guests) was that they were members of some built-in local groups, which in turn had rights to administer the system. This is true also for Windows 2000, but in addition both group categories have certain direct permissions to Active Directory objects.

TABLE 3.3 The Predefined Built-in Local Security Groups

Name	Predefined Members	Abilities
Administrators	Administrator, Domain Admins, Enterprise Admins	By default, members of this group have almost total control of the domain controllers of the domain, including formatting hard drives and all the rights that the following four "operators" have. For Active Directory, this group has by default "Full Control except Delete Subtree" permission for almost all objects in the domain.
Account Operators	None	By default, members of this group can create, delete, and manage user, group, and computer objects in the Active Directory domain.
Server Operators	None	Members of this group can create, delete, and manage file shares, printers, and services in the domain controllers of the domain.
Backup Operators	None	By default, members of this group can back up and restore files and folders in the domain controllers of the domain, even if the member user doesn't have permissions for those files and folders.
Print Operators	None	Members of this group can create, delete, manage, and share printers in domain controllers of the domain, and by default they can create, delete, and manage printer objects in the Active Directory domain.
Users	Domain Users, Authenticated Users, Interactive	By default, this group has no user rights or permissions. You can just ignore this group.* If you want to give permissions to all forest users, you can use Authenticated Users. You can also create groups such as SanaoUsers or SanaoBostonUsers and use them instead of the predefined Users group.
Guests	Guest, Domain Guests, IUSR_*servername*, IWAM *servername*, TsInternetUser	By default, this group has no rights or permissions. You can just ignore this group.
Pre-Windows 2000 Compatible Access	Everyone**, if you selected "Permissions compatible with pre-	By default, this group has permission to see all the objects in a domain and all the properties of all users and groups. You need these permissions if you have

(continued)

TABLE 3.3 The Predefined Built-in Local Security Groups (*continued*)

Name	Predefined Members	Abilities
	Windows 2000 servers when you installed the domain; otherwise, no members	certain server services (e.g., Remote Access Service) running on Windows NT servers in your Active Directory domain.
Replicator	None	Windows NT servers and workstations use this group for the Directory Replicator service.

* Note that being able to ignore the Users group refers to the Users group in Active Directory, which is visible only on domain controllers. Each member server and workstation has a separate Users group, and each of them has some permissions for the corresponding local computer. Therefore, you probably need to use that latter Users group when managing permissions of the workstations and member servers in your organization.

** This refers to the well-known security principal Everyone.

By default, members of the Administrators and four "operators" groups can log on locally to domain controllers.

NOTE   In the next chapter, we describe in more detail the default user rights and default Active Directory permissions of the groups in Table 3.3.

PREDEFINED GROUPS IN THE USERS CONTAINER

The remaining predefined groups are in the Users container. They are mostly global security groups, but there are also some domain local security groups. Table 3.4 describes the predefined groups in the Users container of a domain.

NOTE   When you install the first domain of the forest, Enterprise Admins and Schema Admins are global groups. When you later change this domain to *native mode* (as discussed later in this chapter), those groups will change to universal groups, which allows them to have members from other domains.

Enterprise Admins and Schema Admins are present only in the first domain of the forest. The remaining groups are present in each domain, although the DNS groups are missing if there is no DNS service in the domain.

By default, Domain Admins is a member of the Administrators group of all workstations and member servers. Similarly, Domain Users is a member of the Users group of those computers.

TABLE 3.4 The Predefined Groups in the Users Container

Name	Predefined Members	Description
Enterprise Admins	Administrator of the first domain of the forest	Members of this group can administer all the domains in the enterprise. By default, this group is a member of Administrators in all domains of the forest. Enterprise Admins has Full Control to practically all objects in all domains of the forest. In addition, membership in this group is necessary to create child domains or sites.
Schema Admins	Administrator of the first domain of the forest	Members of this group can modify the schema of the forest.
Domain Admins	Administrator	Members of this group can administer this domain. By default, this group is a member of Administrators in this domain and all joined workstations/member servers. Domain Admins has Full Control to most objects of the domain.
Group Policy Creator Owners	Administrator	Members of this group can create Group Policy objects (GPOs) if they also have appropriate permissions for the the OU for which they are creating the GPO. In addition, they can manage the GPOs they have created.
Domain Users	Every user account of the same domain	By default, this group has no rights or permissions. You can use it if you need to give permissions to all users of the domain.
Domain Guests	Guest	By default, this group has no rights or permissions. You probably don't need this group.
Domain Controllers	Each domain controller of the same domain	By default, this group has no rights or permissions. You can use it if you need to give permissions to all domain controllers of the domain.
Domain Computers	Each workstation and member server of the same domain	By default, this group has no rights or permissions. You can use it if you need to give permissions to all workstations and member servers of the domain.
Cert Publishers	Each computer that is running an enterprise certificate authority	By default, this group has permission to read and write the `userCertificate` property of the users and computers in the domain. Therefore, members of this group can publish certificates for users and computers.

(continued)

TABLE 3.4 The Predefined Groups in the Users Container (*continued*)

Name	Predefined Members	Description
DnsUpdateProxy	None	DHCP servers may dynamically register DNS resource records on behalf of DHCP clients. In this case, the DHCP servers become the owners of those records. This is a problem if the client or some other DHCP server later wants to start maintaining those records. By placing the computer objects of the DHCP servers as members in this group, the servers won't become record owners, so the problem described here is resolved.
DnsAdmins	None	Members of this group can administer the DNS service.
RAS and IAS Servers	Each computer that is running the Routing and Remote Access Services (RRAS)	By default, this group has permission to read Logon Information, Remote Access Information, and Account Restrictions of all users of the domain. RRAS servers need those permissions.

Figure 3.3 illustrates the memberships of some predefined users, global groups, and built-in local groups that are listed in Tables 3.2 through 3.4.

In Chapter 4, we discuss the well-known security principals. Many of them are like groups, and you can assign permissions to them. They are not real groups, however, because the operating system, not a network administrator, controls their "membership."

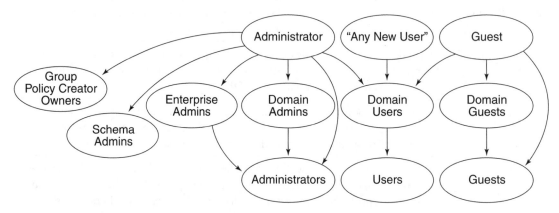

FIGURE 3.3 The predefined users and groups have several predefined memberships. In addition, any new user is a member of Domain Users.

Well-known security principals include Authenticated Users and Everyone, which you already saw as group members in Table 3.3 and Table 3.4. Therefore, we have included Figure 3.4 to illustrate those memberships here, even though the remaining discussion is in the next chapter.

Figure 3.4 reveals the memberships for the various end-user groups. Table 3.5 lists the end users (users of the group's domain, users of the whole forest, and so on) that are members of each user group.

Typically, an administrator uses Authenticated Users to assign permissions to all users of a forest and Domain Users to assign permissions only to the users of one domain.

Predefined Computer Objects

In the beginning, there is just one computer object. It is for your first (and at that point, only) domain controller in the Domain Controllers container.

Changing the Domain Mode

An Active Directory domain is in one of two modes.

- *Mixed mode:* This mode enables you to have Windows NT 4.0 and 3.51 backup domain controllers (BDCs) in the domain and to install new ones.

- *Native mode:* In this mode, all current and future domain controllers must be running Windows 2000.

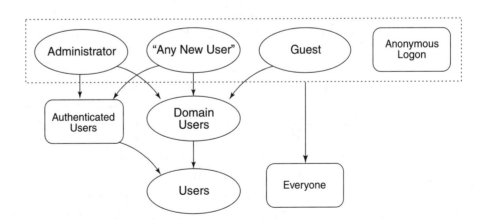

FIGURE 3.4 The well-known security principals Authenticated Users, Everyone, and Anonymous Logon can be seen as part of the membership hierarchy. However, their "membership" is controlled by the operating system, not by a network administrator.

TABLE 3.5 End-User Memberships

Group	Type	Group's Domain	All Forest Users	Guest	Anonymous
Everyone	Well-known	X	X	X	X
Users	Built-in local	X	X	X	
Authenticated Users	Well-known	X	X		
Domain Users	Global	X		X	

When you install a new domain, it first runs in mixed mode. You can change the domain's mode to native mode when you don't have old BDCs and you know for sure that you are not going to add any. The mode change is irreversible. Native mode is better, so when you start straight with Windows 2000, there is normally no reason not to change the mode right after you install each new domain.

While a domain is in mixed mode, you are subject to the following restrictions:

- You cannot have universal security groups.

- You cannot change the type or scope of any group.

- You cannot nest groups, except that you can make a global group a member of a domain local group.

- Domain local groups are not available in member servers or workstations.

- If a Windows NT workstation is joined in a mixed-mode domain, it cannot fully benefit from the transitivity of trusts between domains. The domain list in the logon dialog box contains only the workstation's host domain and the domains that are directly trusted. Consequently, users from indirectly trusted domains (i.e., using transitive trusts) cannot log on to that workstation. The same indirectly trusted domains are missing also from the List Names From list of the User Manager and permission dialog boxes. Therefore, users of those domains cannot be members or have permissions in this workstation. However, a user on this workstation can access resources from indirectly trusting domains with the help of transitive trusts.

- You cannot use per-user remote access policies.

- You can have "only" 40,000 objects in your domain.

- The SID History feature is not available. When SID History becomes available in native mode, you can move users from one domain to another so that they retain their old permissions for folders and other resources.

- A global catalog server is not very "important." Once in native mode, a global catalog server must be contacted during each logon; otherwise, the logon will fail.

| **IF YOU** | In mixed mode, you have the same groups as in Windows NT and they work |
| **KNOW NT** | exactly the same way. |

If you don't want to test how things work in mixed mode, you can change your test domain to native mode at this point. To do so, perform the following steps.

1. Open the Users and Computers snap-in.
2. Right-click your domain object and choose Properties.
3. Click the Change Mode button on the General tab and confirm your selection by clicking the Yes button.

| **NOTE** | If you are familiar with Windows NT, you might want to postpone changing the domain mode. This will help you learn in steps, because later in this chapter we explain how groups work in mixed mode. At that point, if your test domain is still in mixed mode, you will have an opportunity to try the familiar groups in a new environment. After that, you can switch to native mode and try the groups again, this time with the new features enabled. |

If there is more than one domain controller in your domain, all other domain controllers will know about the new mode once the information has replicated to them. You will know that this replication has occurred when you see the text "Domain operation mode: Native Mode" in the domain properties dialog box. Note that you must connect to a specific domain controller with the Users and Computers snap-in to see the status of that domain controller.

ADMINISTERING OUs

As you know, it is more efficient to organize your disk files in folders than to keep them in the root directory of a disk. Similarly, you are usually better off when you store Active Directory users, groups, and other objects in "folders" called OUs (organizational units). These OUs form an OU tree (also referred to as a domain structure) inside your domain. Figure 3.5 illustrates this.

| **NOTE** | In Figure 3.5, the uppermost circle (the root of the tree) is not an OU but rather the domain object that represents the domain (the triangle). We could drop the domain object out of the image, but it's more natural to have the tree as a whole. Also, in many ways the domain object behaves like an OU, so you can think of it as part of the tree. |

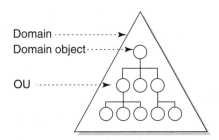

FIGURE 3.5 OUs inside a domain form an OU tree

Features of OUs

Besides providing a logical structure through the OU tree, OUs offer the following benefits:

- An OU is a Group Policy target, so you can assign a different Group Policy to each OU.
- If you want to delegate administration of some Active Directory objects, the most convenient way to do so is to put them in one OU and delegate administration of that OU. You could delegate administration of even single users and other objects, but the outcome would be difficult to manage. If you stick to only per-OU permissions, it is easier for you to track what you are doing.
- Using per-OU permissions, you can control object visibility—that is, which objects and object properties various users may see.

Unfortunately, even though you can assign permissions *for* OUs, you cannot assign permissions *to* OUs. In other words, you cannot define that all users in a certain OU get access to a certain folder or other resource. This will probably result in extra work for you, because you need to create a security group and put all the users in this group to give them access.

IF YOU KNOW NDS   In NDS you can give permissions to OUs, so there is no need to create a group to correspond to each OU.

NOTE   In Active Directory, OUs are not related to partitioning the directory database. They are purely logical units inside a domain. The domain in turn is the partition unit.

If there are several domains in your forest, each has a totally independent OU tree. The OU tree of an upper domain does not "continue" to a tree in a lower domain. However, when you look at the tree by selecting My Network Places, Entire Network, Directory, you will see the child domains as siblings of the first-level OUs, as Figure 3.6 illustrates.

IF YOU KNOW NDS	In NDS, all OUs form one big tree.

OUs are created primarily for administrators' use—end users don't usually see OUs. For example, when an end user performs a search operation for other people in Active Directory (by clicking the Start button and selecting Search, For People), the user doesn't see the found users' OUs at all, and he couldn't even if he wanted to. For example, if there is a Jack Brown in OU Sales and another Jack Brown in OU Production, the person doing the search cannot tell the difference between them from the search dialog box. This is also true if a user is searching for a certain printer.

On the other hand, if the user selects My Network Places, Entire Network, Directory, he will be able to browse the OU tree and see which user or printer is in which OU.

It is a matter of opinion whether hiding the OU tree from users is a good or bad thing.

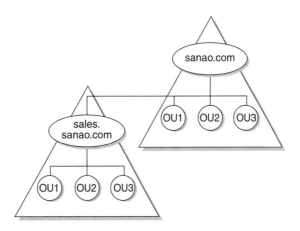

FIGURE 3.6 The Sales domain is a child of the Sanao domain. If you look at the tree via My Network Places, you will see Sales as a sibling of the first-level OUs of Sanao.

Managing OUs

Managing OUs includes the following tasks:

- Creating OUs
- Setting OU properties
- Moving, renaming, and deleting OUs
- Setting Group Policy, assigning permissions, and delegating administrative tasks

In this chapter, we focus on the first three items in the list. The last item is discussed in later chapters.

As you read on, we encourage you to try these management tasks in your domain. You cannot do any irreversible harm to your domain.

CREATING OUs

Creating an OU is as easy as creating a disk folder. Just follow these steps:

1. Launch the Users and Computers snap-in.
2. Right-click the parent OU you want (or the domain object) and choose New, Organizational Unit.
3. Type in the name you want and press Enter.

IF YOU KNOW NDS   Unfortunately, the Insert key doesn't do the trick here like it does with the NwAdmin software for NDS.

The maximum number of characters in an OU's name is 64, which is usually more than enough. After all, it is best to use short (but descriptive) names. The OU name is a Unicode character string, so at least in theory you could have some Gurmukhi characters in an OU name. You could also put all the possible punctuation characters in an OU name, but this would make your life harder if every now and then you had to type the distinguished name of such an OU.

SETTING OU PROPERTIES

After you have created an OU, you can set its properties by right-clicking the OU and choosing Properties. The dialog box in Figure 3.7 will appear.

Table 3.6 lists the property choices. None of them affects the way Windows 2000 works. They just provide information for human beings.

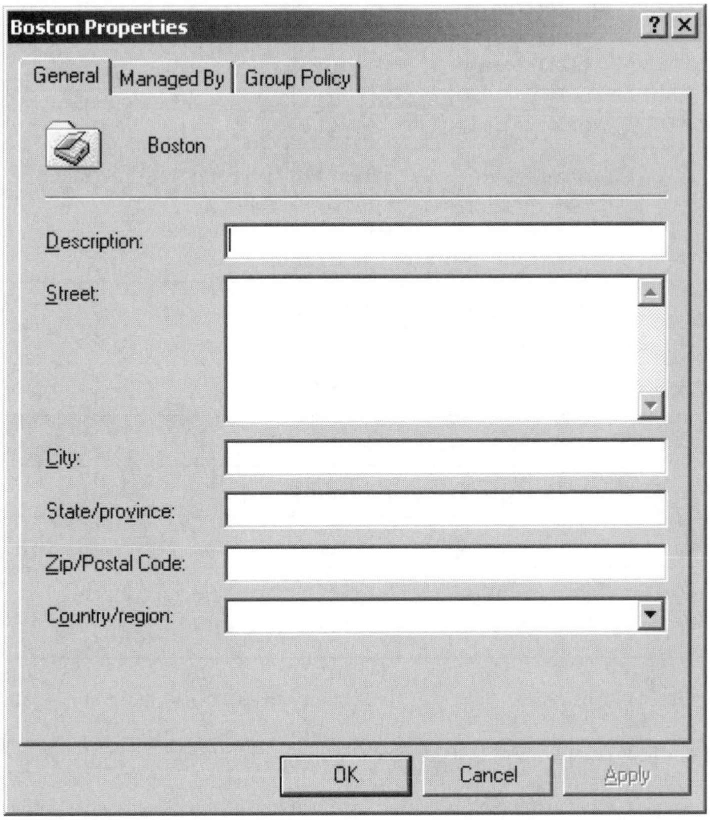

FIGURE 3.7 Some of the properties that you can enter for an OU include address-related information.

Table 3.6 shows the property LDAP names, which you will need if you use certain Resource Kit utilities or scripting or if you set per-property permissions. One of the properties in the table is indexed and five are part of the global catalog. Indexing makes searches faster, and the global catalog makes reading properties faster if you have multiple domains and sites.

NOTE   When you set properties for an OU, if you add a user in the Managed By tab as the "manager" of an OU, that user doesn't get any permissions for the OU. This setting is purely informational. The other fields on that tab are the manager's properties, not the OU's.

TABLE 3.6 Properties of an OU Object

Property	LDAP Name*	Syntax	Indexed	In GC
Description	`description`	Text (1024)**		X
Street	`street` (Street-Address)	Text (1024) (Each new line takes two characters.)		X
City	`l` (Locality-Name)	Text (128)	X	X
State/province	`st` (State-Or-Province-Name)	Text (128)		X
Zip/Postal Code	`postalCode`	Text (40)		
Country/region***	`co` (Text-Country)	Text (128)		
	`c` (Country-Name)	Text (3)		X
	`countryCode`	Integer		
Managed By	`managedBy`	DN**** (You select a user or contact from a list.)		

* In addition to the LDAP name, each property has a common name. It is included in parentheses if it is different from the LDAP name.
** If the syntax is Text (i.e., a string of Unicode characters), we indicate also the maximum number of characters in the property (e.g., 1024).
*** Country/region is stored in three properties: `co` contains the country's name (e.g., UNITED STATES), `c` contains the country's abbreviation (e.g., US), and `countryCode` contains the numeric ISO country code (e.g., 840).
**** DN = distinguished name

NOTE   Behind the scenes, the base schema lists 104 possible properties for an OU. Most of them are not used, so it doesn't matter that you can set only a few of them using the Users and Computers snap-in.

If you have advanced features turned on in the Users and Computers snap-in, you will see also the Security and Object tabs in the properties dialog box. The information in the former tab is discussed in Chapter 4 and the information in the latter tab is discussed in Chapter 5.

MOVING, RENAMING, AND DELETING OUs IN A TREE

You may find that your original OU tree is no longer optimal as a result of either insufficient planning or changed circumstances. If you need to rearrange your OU tree, you can easily move, rename, and delete OUs.

To move an OU inside a domain, right-click it and select Move. Then choose the destination from the OU tree that opens up and click OK. Note that not all of the OU's group policies and permissions move with it.

- Group policies and permissions that are assigned for the object being moved move with the object.
- Group policies and permissions that are inherited from above do not move with the object being moved. Instead, the OU will inherit new ones in its new location.

You can move several sibling OUs at once. Select them in the right-hand pane of the snap-in by using the Shift and/or Ctrl keys. Then proceed as previously described.

NOTE   If you want to move an OU to another domain in your forest, you need to use the Support Tools command-line tool MoveTree. It is discussed further in Chapter 6.

You can rename an OU either by right-clicking the OU and selecting Rename or by selecting the OU and pressing F2. After you type the new name, press Enter.

Similarly, you delete an OU by right-clicking it and selecting Delete or by selecting the OU and pressing the Delete key. If the OU being deleted contains other objects, you are prompted to accept deleting them, too.

Planning OUs

Even though "OU" stands for "organizational unit," you don't necessarily create OUs to match the organizational units of your company. You create OUs for administrative units, physical locations, and object types (e.g., an OU for users, an OU for printers, and so on), or you can create OUs based on corporate structure.

OU trees are like folder trees on disk: There isn't just one "right" way to create them. When planning your OUs, keep in mind the following aspects of OUs:

- OUs are purely logical entities: They are not related to physical partitions or replication.
- OUs are for delegation of administration.
- OUs are for Group Policy (including application publishing and assignment).
- OUs are for controlling object visibility.
- OUs are easy to reorganize. However, reorganizing them may confuse some users if they have learned a certain structure.
- OUs are mainly administrative units; users do not need to see them.

If you have more than one domain, you might want the OU trees in all domains to be planned according to similar principles.

ADMINISTERING USERS AND CONTACTS

The traditional reason for creating user accounts is to give your users a means to log on to the network. The properties of a user's account control the user's access to the network, and the properties can define some network services for the user in question. Examples of these properties are the password, the account expiration date, a requirement for a smart card logon, and the network path of the user's home folder.

Directory services such as Active Directory have brought a second aspect to user accounts. At this point, we tend to refer to them as "user objects" instead of "accounts." In addition to being a means of access to the network and its services, a user object can store additional information about the user. Some of this information is meant for other human beings—for example, the user's fax number, title, or Web home page address. As a container of such "contact" properties, a user object can function much like an address book entry. A user object can also include properties for use by directory-enabled applications (e.g., Exchange e-mail, a faxing application, personnel-management software, and so on).

In addition to user objects, you can create *contact objects.* Typically you create a user object for each employee of your organization and a contact object for each person outside your organization whose contact information you want to store. A contact object can contain a subset of the properties that a user object can contain, as you can see in Figure 3.8 and Table 3.7.

The Users and Computers snap-in shows the properties of a contact and user object in a number of tabs in the properties dialog box, as shown in Figure 3.8.

Table 3.7 lists the tabs shown in Figure 3.8, except for the tabs Remote control, Terminal Services Profile, Environment, and Sessions, which are related to Terminal Services. (We don't cover them in this book about Active Directory.) Table 3.7 introduces the terms *significant properties* and *informational properties* and shows that a user object can contain both types of properties, but a contact object can contain only the latter.

The Users and Computers snap-in contains tabs for user and/or contact objects that are not shown in Figure 3.8.

- The Published Certificates tab is visible only when you turn on Advanced Features from the View menu.

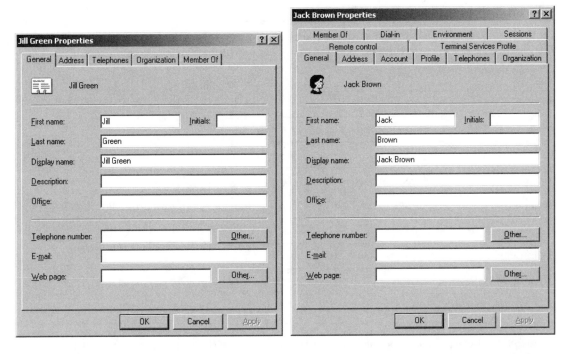

FIGURE 3.8 Contact object properties on the left are shown in five tabs. User object on the right has the same five tabs of a contact object and seven additional tabs. The five tabs that appear in both screen shots (General, Address, Telephones, Organization, and Member Of) contain the same properties except that the Member Of tab contains a Primary Group setting only for user objects.

- Turning on Advanced Features also makes the Object and Security tabs visible. Because they are common to all object types, we don't include them in this discussion of user and contact objects.

- Applications can add tabs. For example, if you install Exchange 2000, it will add some tabs, such as Exchange General and Exchange Features.

To summarize the functions for user objects (and to add a couple of functions):

- A user object is an account that a user can log on with (using the corresponding significant properties).

- A user object is a placeholder for a collection of informational properties.

- A user object is a *security principal.* This means that you can give permissions to the user for resources and assign security group memberships to the user.

- The location of a user object in Active Directory dictates which group policies apply to the corresponding user.

TABLE 3.7 The Nature of User and Contact Objects

Tab Name	User Object	Contact Object	Category*
Account	X		*Significant properties:* Properties that control user access to the network or define network services for the user
Profile	X		
Published Certificates	X		
Member Of**	X		
Dial-in	X		
General	X	X	*Informational properties:* Properties that contain information for human beings or are meant for some applications to use
Address	X	X	
Telephones	X	X	
Organization	X	X	
Member Of	X	X	

* The terms "significant properties" and "informational properties" are not official. They are introduced in this book to distinguish these two types of properties.
** The Member Of tab is shown twice because it has two natures: security and distribution list. The first nature applies only to user objects, but the second nature applies to both user and contact objects.

A contact object (actually, the person who corresponds to the object) can never log on to the network. Also, a contact object is not a security principal, so it cannot have any permissions. Of course, even if a contact object had permissions, no one would be able to use them, because a contact object cannot be used to log on.

When you start to manage users and contacts, your tasks will include some or all of the following.

- Create users and contacts.
- Set user and contact properties.
- Copy users, and move, rename, and delete users and contacts.
- Assign Group Policy and permissions, and delegate administration.

The next sections cover the first three items, but as mentioned earlier, the last item will be discussed in later chapters (Chapter 7 and Chapter 4).

If you want to try the management tasks discussed in this section, create a test OU where you can create test users.

Creating Users

When you choose to create a user with the Users and Computers snap-in, you use a three-page wizard to do so. Figure 3.9 shows the first page of the wizard, where you enter the various names of the new user. Figure 3.10 shows the second page of the wizard, where you can specify a password and some password settings. For example, you can require that a new user change her password at first logon so that only the user knows it and only she can legitimately log on with that account. Alternatively, you can specify that the user cannot change the password. This capability is useful, for example, when several users use the same account. With this setting, you can prevent any of the users from changing the common password. The third page of the wizard displays a summary of what you have selected.

Table 3.8 describes the different name properties shown in the first page of the user creation wizard. All the name properties in the table are Unicode strings, and all, except Initials, are indexed and part of the global catalog.

WARNING   Experience with Windows NT shows that using even common European characters, such as ä, in names may cause problems. Even though they are supported in principle, many command-line and graphical utilities can't handle them.

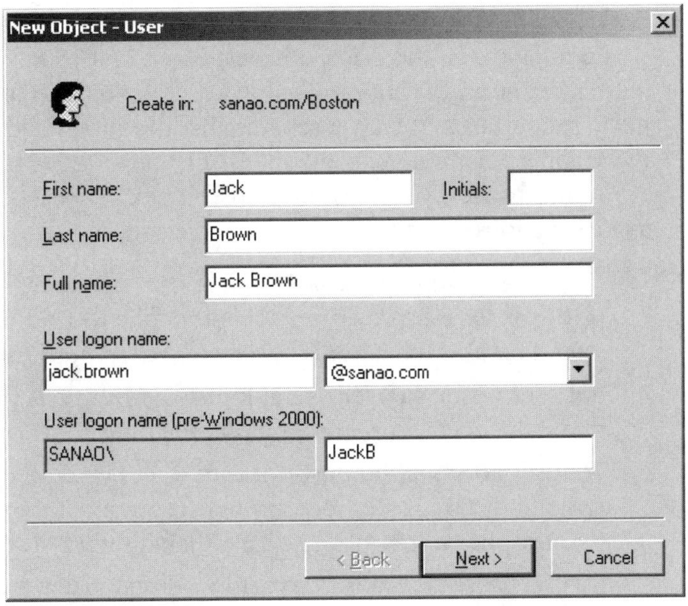

FIGURE 3.9 On the first page of the user creation wizard, you enter the various names of the new user.

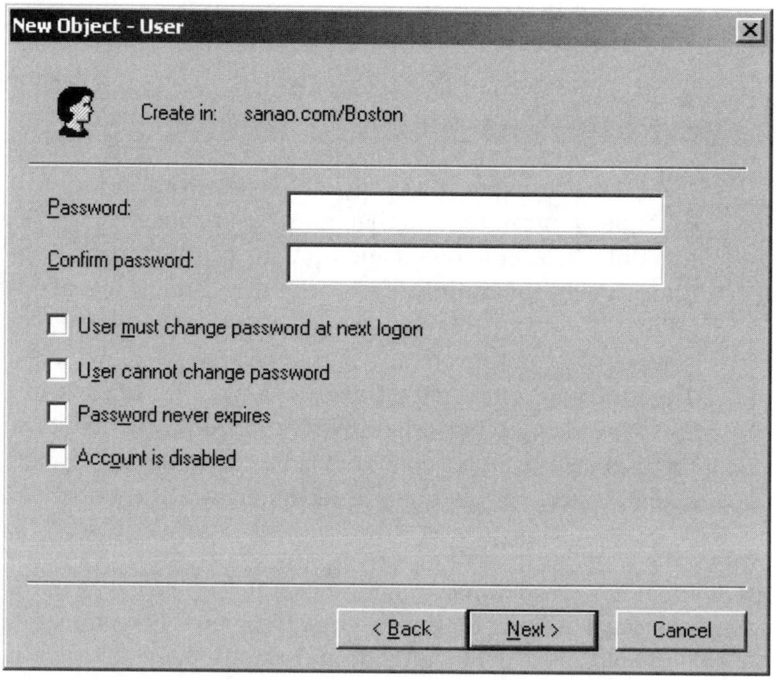

FIGURE 3.10 On the second page of the user creation wizard, you can specify a password and the way it will be used.

In addition to the name properties in Table 3.8, each object has a distinguished name and a canonical name (see Chapter 1). Furthermore, there are two name properties in the base schema that the snap-in doesn't display: the middle name and generation qualifier (Jr., Sr., III, and so on).

In most cases, you create one user object for each network user. However, some situations call for a second user account.

- If a user is an administrator, he might have two user accounts: one with normal privileges for everyday use and another one with administrative privileges. It is safer if he uses the latter account only when performing administrative tasks.

- If a user needs to use several forests and there is no explicit trust between them, she needs a user account in each forest.

- If a user accesses the network with a mobile device through the Mobile Information 2001 Server, he may have a second account with fewer rights and permissions for this mobile access than his normal account has.

- If a user has a stand-alone server or workstation that is in a workgroup instead of a domain, he will need a *local* user account in that machine. Active Directory user accounts cannot be used when the computer hasn't joined a domain.

TABLE 3.8 Name Properties of a User Object

Property	LDAP Name	Maximum Length (Characters)	Required	Unique	Description
First name	givenName	64		No	Purely informational
Initials*	initials	6**		No	Purely informational
Last name	sn (Surname)	64		No	Purely informational
Full name	name (RDN) and cn (Common-Name)	64	X	Within OU	This becomes the object's common name in the OU tree. The wizard suggests "firstname. initials. lastname".***
Display name	displayName	256		No	Purely informational, initially the same as Full name. You can change it later, independently of Full name.
User logon name	userPrincipal-Name	"Without" limit	X	Within forest	User can log on using this name on a Windows 2000 computer. This name is often the same as the user's e-mail address.
User logon name (pre-Windows 2000)	sAMAccount-Name	256 (schema rule), 20 (SAM rule)	X	Within domain	User can log on using this name on any old or new Windows machine. Despite its label, this name can be used throughout Windows 2000. This name also becomes the name of the user's profile folder when she logs on for the first time.

* The user creation wizard treats Initials as the middle-name initial and not the first- and last-name initials (for example, "JB" for "Jack Brown").

** Even though the maximum length for initials is six characters, the user creation wizard in the Users and Computers snap-in allows only four characters.

*** You can modify the forest configuration so that the default full name is "lastname, firstname" instead of the normal "firstname lastname." We explain how to do this in Table 9.8 in Chapter 9.

UPN SUFFIXES

User logon names consist of two parts: the actual user name (e.g., `jack.brown`) and a *UPN suffix* (e.g., `@sanao.com`). For the first part you can enter any text, but for the second part you must choose the UPN suffix from a fixed list. By default, the list contains the name of the domain (e.g., `sales.sanao.com`) and the name of the root domain (e.g., `sanao.com`).

An enterprise administrator of a forest can add UPN suffixes to the list using the Domains and Trusts snap-in (click the Start button and then select Programs, Administrative Tools, Active Directory Domains and Trusts). Once the snap-in has started, the enterprise administrator right-clicks the uppermost line of the left pane (i.e., Active Directory Domains and Trusts) and selects Properties. The dialog box that appears enables the administrator to define additional UPN suffixes.

If the root domain is `corp.sanao.com`, for example, the administrator can add a UPN suffix `sanao.com`, so the users in the forest can have logon names such as `jack.brown@sanao.com` instead of `jack.brown@corp.sanao.com`.

Creating Contacts

To create a contact, you use the contact creation wizard in the Users and Computers snap-in. The wizard has only one page, which is shown in Figure 3.11. A contact object is like an address book entry for e-mail and other applications and it contains only informational properties. It usually represents a person who is not working for your company, and a contact cannot log on to your network. Therefore, you don't specify a logon name for a contact object. The "Full name" entry becomes the common name of the object in the OU tree.

Setting User and Contact Properties

You can define more than 50 settings for each user and more than 30 settings for each contact. Behind the scenes, a user object can have 207 properties and a contact object can have 138 properties. Fortunately, the only *required* properties are a few names (which we mentioned in our discussion of creating users).

NOTE   Although we mention exact counts here and in many other places, you don't have to know the exact numbers. We use exact counts because it is simply easier to express "138 properties" than "well over 100 properties." It is not always possible to be precise, however. We say that you can define "more than 50" settings. In this case, there is more than one way to count the settings in the user interface.

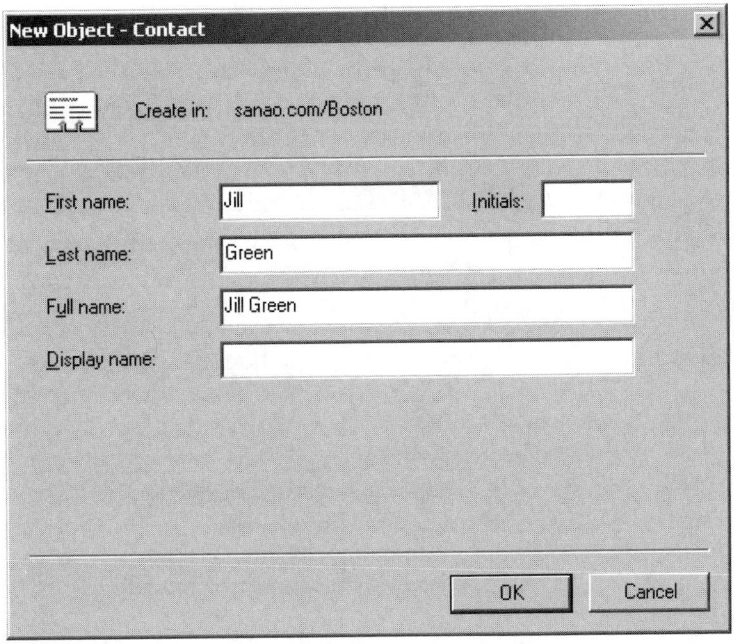

FIGURE 3.11 **When you create a contact, you don't specify logon names. Also, there is no second page, which would have the password settings (i.e., significant properties) that you saw when creating a user object.**

Of the many possible settings, the major significant properties of a user object are set in the Account, Profile, and Dial-in tabs. The major informational properties of user and contact objects are set in the General, Address, Telephones, and Organization tabs. The Member Of tab is covered in the "Administering Groups" section of this chapter.

NOTE   Windows 2000 provides context-sensitive help for each of the settings. In addition, many of the setting names are self-explanatory.

Unfortunately, you can only edit properties for one user or contact at a time. A future version of the snap-in may enable you to edit several users at once.

SIGNIFICANT PROPERTIES OF A USER OBJECT: THE ACCOUNT TAB

Figure 3.12 shows the contents of the Account tab, which sets significant properties of a user. It includes settings that control how and when the user can log on,

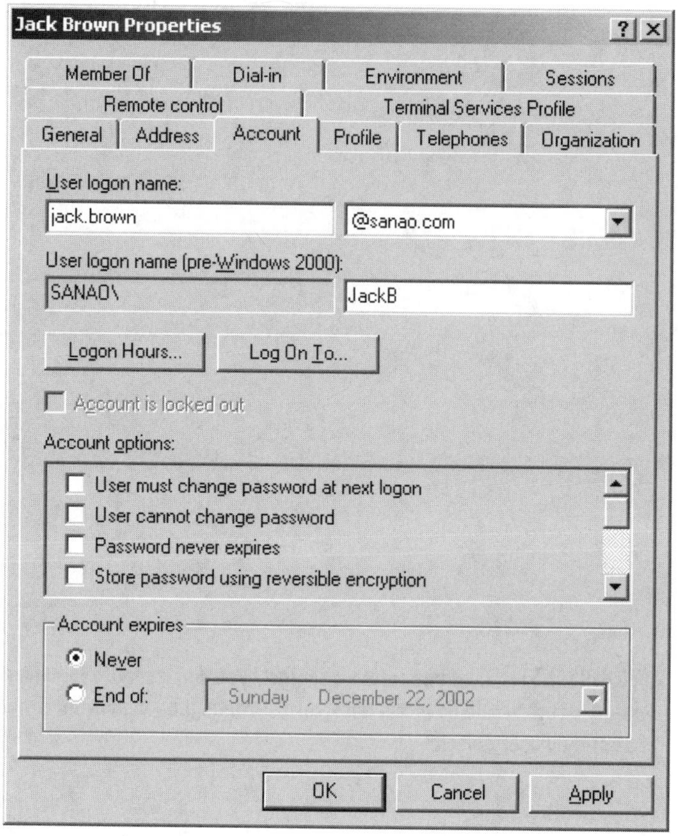

FIGURE 3.12 The Account tab of the user Jack Brown

as well as a few settings that control passwords. Table 3.9 lists other settings, except the 11 yes/no check boxes, which appear in Table 3.10.

NOTE Because Logon Hours is internally stored as GMT/UTC, an administrator who looks at a user's settings will see the hours as local to the administrator's time zone, regardless of where that is. For example, if a Boston administrator allows a user in Boston to log on between 8:00 AM and 3:00 PM, an administrator in Belgium (6 hours ahead of Boston) who checks that user's setting for logon hours would see times between 2:00 PM and 9:00 PM. There are no adjustments for daylight saving time, however. This is good because this way the allowed logon hours won't change twice a year, when daylight saving time and standard time start.

TABLE 3.9 Significant Properties of a User Object: The Account Tab

Property/Setting	LDAP Name	Syntax	Description
User logon name	`userPrincipalName`	Text	User can log on using this name on a Windows 2000 computer. This name is often the same as user's e-mail address.
User logon name (pre-Windows 2000)	`sAMAccountName`	Text (256 [schema rule], 20 [SAM rule])*	User can log on using this name on any old or new Windows machine. Despite its label, this name can be used throughout Windows 2000. Also, this name becomes the name of user's profile folder when she logs on to each Windows NT/2000 computer for the first time.
Logon Hours**	`logonHours`	(Binary)	Weekdays and hours in one-hour increments during which the user is allowed to log on.
Log On To/Logon Workstations	`userWorkstations`	Text (1024)	A list of computer NetBIOS names that the user is allowed to log on to.
Account options	`userAccountControl`	Yes/No	These 11 settings are described in Table 3.10.
Account expires	`accountExpires`	Date	The date after which the user account is no longer usable (although it doesn't vanish then). You can use this for temporary users.

* If the syntax is Text (i.e., a string of Unicode characters), we indicate also the maximum number of characters in the property (e.g., 256).
** The Logon Hours property is set and shown in local time but internally stored as GMT/UTC. The amount of time zone correction is taken from the local computer configuration.

Table 3.10 lists the yes/no settings in the Account tab. You cannot set the first setting—you can only clear it. The other 10 settings you can either set or clear. Eight of the 11 settings are stored in a property called `userAccountControl` so that one bit represents each setting.

The setting "Account is locked out" is stored in the `lockoutTime` property, the setting "User must change password at next logon" is stored in the `pwdLastSet` property, and the setting "User cannot change password" is determined by permissions. You can learn more about the way settings are stored in Chapter 11.

TABLE 3.10 Significant Properties of a User Object: The Account Options

Setting	Description
Account is locked out	If someone tries to log on and enters a wrong password too many times, the account is locked either for a specified time or until the administrator unlocks it. You define the acceptable number of wrong attempts and associated time periods using Group Policy.
User must change password at next logon	After you assign a password to a user, it is a good practice to require the user to change it as soon as he logs on. Then you won't know it anymore.
User cannot change password	This is useful, for example, if several users use one account. You can use this setting to prevent them from changing the password.
Password never expires	You can force users to change their passwords periodically (e.g., every 30 days), but then use this setting to exempt some users from this policy. This is useful, for example, when defining passwords for service accounts. In that case, there is no human being to change the password every month.
Store password using reversible encryption	Normally Active Directory stores passwords using irreversible encryption, meaning that user's clear-text password cannot be calculated (except through a special "dictionary attack"). You must enable this setting if the corresponding user is using a Macintosh workstation or if she wants to use IIS digest authentication to be able to pass a firewall.
Account is disabled	If a user is away a long time, you can "freeze" the user's account for that time but still not delete it.
Smart card is required for interactive logon	Self-explanatory
Account is trusted for delegation	This setting is described in Chapter 4 in the "Impersonation and Delegation" section.
Account is sensitive and cannot be delegated	This setting is described in Chapter 4 in the "Impersonation and Delegation" section.
Use DES encryption types for this account	This setting causes Windows 2000 to use Kerberos DES-CBC-MD5 instead of the default RSADSI RC4-HMAC for this user account. The setting affects how Kerberos ticket-granting tickets (TGTs) are encrypted. Data

(continued)

TABLE 3.10 *(continued)*

Setting	Description
	Encryption Standard (DES) is used to encrypt both the ticket and the key of the initial TGT, and DES is also used to encrypt the key of the forwarded TGT. However, RSA is used to encrypt the ticket of the forwarded TGT.
Do not require Kerberos preauthentication	Normally Windows 2000 uses preauthentication with Kerberos authentication, but it is not compatible with all implementations of Kerberos. Consequently, you must not require preauthentication if the corresponding user account is going to use such an implementation. Selecting this option may expose the user account to denial of service attacks.

There is one password setting that is not visible in the Users and Computers snap-in. You could type the following command on the command line when sitting at a domain controller:

```
NET USER JackB /PasswordReq:No
```

This command relieves JackB of having a password. For example, even though other users of the domain would be required to use at least a six-character password, he would not. Note that you must use the pre–Windows 2000 name of the user in this command.

Even though this command relieves Jack from having a password, he cannot clear his password—an administrator must do this. If Jack later changes his password to "abcdef," he cannot change it back to empty.

You can see the current setting for Jack using the following command:

```
NET USER JackB
```

NOTE   The minimum length of a password for domain users is set using Group Policy, which is discussed in Chapter 7.

NOTE   If you test the settings in Table 3.10, the Users and Computers snap-in doesn't always keep up with you. For example, if you select "User must change password at next logon," click Apply, then deselect it, click Apply again, and finally click OK, the setting will remain in the selected state, even though you deselected it and clicked both Apply and OK.

SIGNIFICANT PROPERTIES OF A USER OBJECT: THE PROFILE TAB

Figure 3.13 shows the contents of the Profile tab. The Profile tab is not about control as the Account tab is—it's about providing services to users. Table 3.11 lists the Profile tab's four significant properties. They all may contain an "unlimited" number of Unicode characters.

You may use the `%username%` environment variable in the "Profile path" and "Home folder: To" fields. Its value will be the user's logon name (pre–Windows

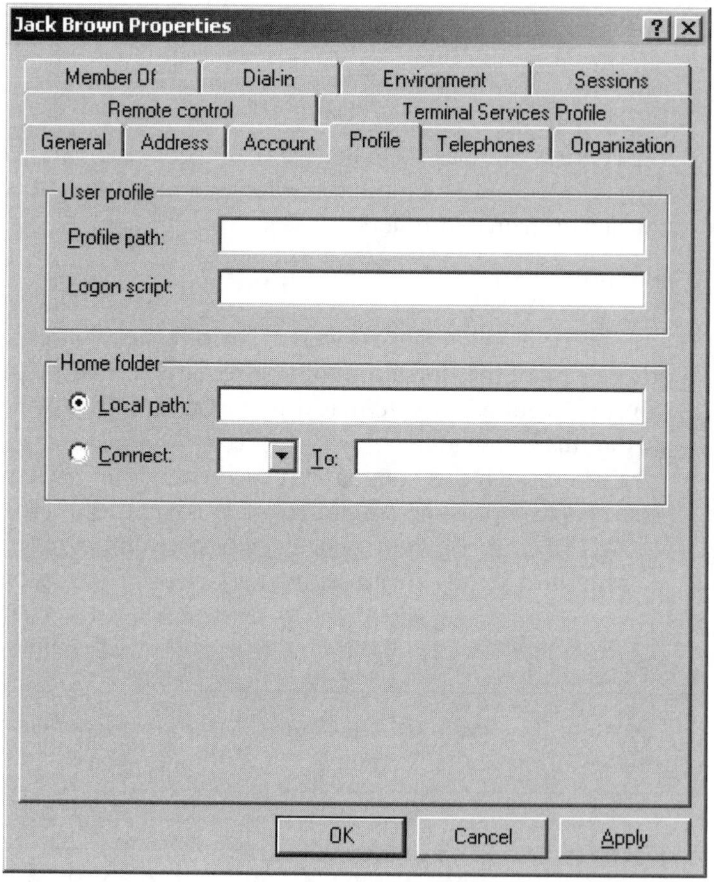

FIGURE 3.13 The Profile tab of the user Jack Brown

TABLE 3.11 Significant Properties of a User Object: The Profile Tab

Property	LDAP Name	Description
Profile path	`profilePath`	This specifies a Uniform Naming Convention (UNC) name, such as \\Server\Prof$\JackB, to be the network folder where the user's roaming profile is stored. This way, Jack's roaming profile is downloaded to whichever Windows NT/2000 workstation he logs onto and it is uploaded back to the server when he logs off. The dollar sign ($) in the Prof$ sharename makes it invisible so that users don't browse it.
Logon script	`scriptPath`	This field is the old (i.e., Windows NT) way to define a logon script for a user. The new way (i.e., Active Directory) is to use Group Policy. An example of this path is Logon.Bat. The name is relative to the UNC path *anydomaincontroller*\Netlogon.
Home folder: Local path/To	`homeDirectory`	You can assign each user a private or shared folder on some server. The To field defines the path—for example, \\Server\Users\JackB. If possible, the snap-in creates the folder for you. It also removes all permissions from the folder and gives Administrators and the user Full Control. A home folder is an alternative to the My Documents folder, which you can also store on a server using Group Policy. When saving documents, newer applications usually default to My Documents, whereas some may use the %homedrive% and %homepath% environment variables. The "Local path" field defines a path such as D:\JackB, but that path exists on only one local machine.
Home folder: Connect	`homeDrive`	A drive letter that connects (or maps) to the user's home folder.

2000)—that is, his "downlevel logon name." For example, the path \\Server\Prof$\%username% actually means \\Server\Prof$\JackB. This variable will become handy when Microsoft adds support to edit several users at once. At that time, for example, you will be able to set the home folder for several users at once.

SIGNIFICANT PROPERTIES OF A USER OBJECT: THE DIAL-IN TAB

The settings in the Dial-in tab define whether the user may use dial-in or virtual private network (VPN) connections, and if so, in what way. These significant properties apply more to managing communication settings than to managing user settings. Therefore, this tab is outside the scope of this book. The screen shot in Figure 3.14 is provided here for reference.

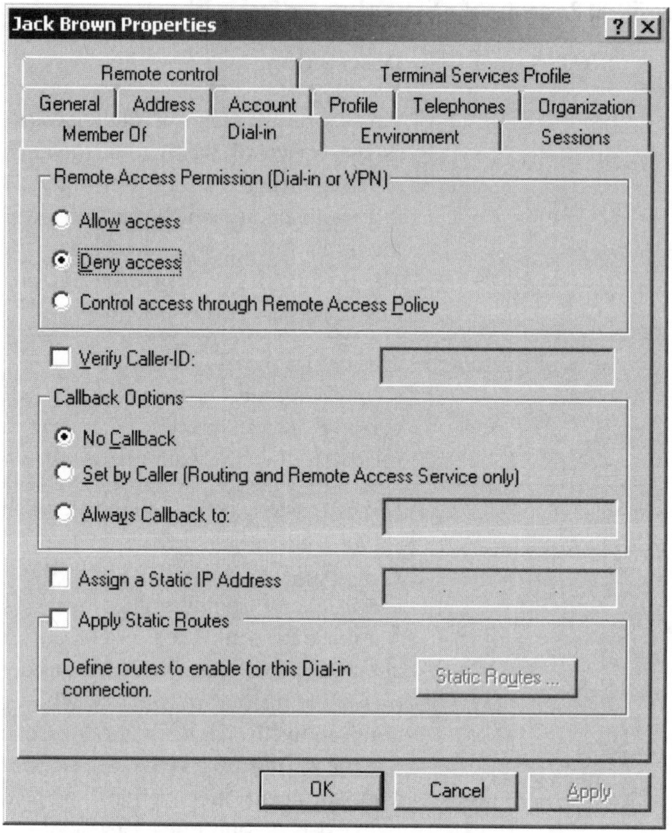

FIGURE 3.14 The Dial-in tab defines whether the user may use dial-in or VPN connections.

INFORMATIONAL PROPERTIES OF USERS AND CONTACTS

As previously stated, the informational properties don't affect the network user. They provide information for other people and for applications that use them. Consequently, these two criteria dictate how you use each of the informational properties. We cannot tell you here the rules to use each informational property, but we can offer a few general guidelines.

If you or any of your users are not interested in these properties, and if you don't have applications to take advantage of them, you can simply leave all the informational properties blank.

Except for Country/region and Manager, both of which you select from a list, you edit all the informational properties in text fields that have very little format checking. These fields have no stringent requirements for acceptable entries. This means that you could fill in the property fields with just about anything, such as your favorite recipes or the hair color of each user, even though the property label indicates a phone number.

Although you have free reign in determining informational properties, the following are some guidelines to keep in mind.

- Use each property consistently. Ideally, you have a written document that describes which properties are in use in your company and in what format the information should be entered.

- Some of the properties can be used in search operations. Here, consistency is especially important.

- By default, each user can see all of his or her properties. Each user can also change those properties that are categorized as Personal Information and Web Information (together consisting of 43 properties).

- By default, every logged-on user can see certain properties of all other users. These properties are categorized as General Information, Public Information, Personal Information, and Web Information, and they consist of a total of 89 properties.

NOTE   The information categories mentioned here (Personal Information, General Information, and so on) are used in the management of permissions. Therefore, they are covered in detail in the next chapter, which deals with securing Active Directory. Unfortunately, the categories are quite different from the tabs in user properties. For example, General Information doesn't have anything to do with the General tab.

Table 3.12 lists the properties in the four tabs containing informational properties. We don't include screen shots, because they would show just a number of text boxes.

The "Country/region" field has a fixed set of options from which you choose. The result is stored in three properties, as described in the table.

Other Operations to Manage Users and Contacts

After you have created a number of users and contacts and packed them full of properties, you are ready to perform other operations. Open the context menu by

TABLE 3.12 Informational Properties of User and Contact Objects

Property	LDAP Name	Syntax (Characters)	Index	GC	Comments
General Tab					
First name	givenName	Text (64)	X	X	
Initials	initials	Text (6)			Even though the creation wizard treats this as a middle-name initial, you can enter "JB" for an existing Jack Brown.
Last name	sn (Surname)	Text (64)	X	X	
Display name	displayName	Text (256)	X	X	This is not the common name (cn) you see in the OU tree. The user's display name is shown in the Computer Locked dialog box, for example.
Description	description	Text (1024)		X	
Office	physical-DeliveryOffice-Name	Text (128)	X		
Telephone number	telephoneNumber	Text (64)		X	This is the primary office phone number.
Phone Number (Others)	otherTelephone	Text (64)			These are the other office phone numbers.
E-mail	mail	Text (256)	X	X	
Web page	wWWHomePage	Text (2048)			http://something, ftp://something, file://something.
Web Page Address (Others)	url	Text			A list of multiple values.
Address Tab					
Street	streetAddress	Text (1024)			
P.O. Box	postOfficeBox	Text (40)			

(continued)

TABLE 3.12 (*continued*)

Property	LDAP Name	Syntax (Characters)	Index	GC	Comments
Address Tab					
City	l (Locality-Name)	Text (128)	X	X	
State/province	st (State-Or-Province-Name)	Text (128)		X	
Zip/Postal Code	postalCode	Text (40)			
Country/region	co (Text-Country)	Text (128)			For example, "UNITED STATES."
	c (Country-Name)	Text (3)		X	For example, "US."
	countryCode	Integer			For example, "840."
Telephones Tab					
Home	homePhone	Text (64)		X	
Home Phone (Others)	otherHome-Phone	Text (64)			A list of multiple values.
Pager	pager	Text (64)			
Pager Number (Others)	otherPager	Text (64)			A list of multiple values.
Mobile	mobile	Text (64)			
Mobile Number (Others)	otherMobile	Text (64)			A list of multiple values.
Fax	facsimile-TelephoneNumber	Text (64)			
Fax Number (Others)	otherFacsimile-TelephoneNumber	Text (64)			A list of multiple values.
IP phone	ipPhone	Text		X	
IP Phone Number (Others)	otherIpPhone	Text		X	A list of multiple values.
Notes	info	Text (1024)			

(continued)

TABLE 3.12 Informational Properties of User and Contact Objects (*continued*)

Property	LDAP Name	Syntax (Characters)	Index	GC	Comments
Organization Tab					
Title	`title`	Text (64)			
Department	`department`	Text (64)			
Company	`company`	Text (64)			
Manager	`manager`	DN; you select a user or contact from list	X		Setting this doesn't give the manager any permissions.
Direct reports	`directReports`	DN			The current snap-in doesn't allow you to set this.

right-clicking with your mouse or press a shortcut key to manipulate existing users and contacts in the following ways:

- Copy (only users, not contacts)
- Move
- Rename
- Delete
- Disable an account (only users, not contacts)
- Reset a password (only users, not contacts)
- Open a home page
- Send e-mail

COPYING USERS

You can copy an existing user to create a new user. You do this by right-clicking the user object and then selecting Copy. This launches a wizard similar to the one that enables you to create users from scratch.

Copying a user saves time if the new user will have many of the same properties as an existing one. When you copy the user, by default 32 properties of the existing user are copied to the new one. However, only 20 of these properties are visible in the Users and Computers snap-in. Table 3.13 lists these properties, as well as some other categories.

The remaining 12 properties may have values to copy if you have set them programmatically with ADSI Edit or with some other means. However, it's not likely that you have done so.

Obviously, several properties (e.g., names and phone numbers) are personal and therefore not meaningful to copy. On the other hand, there are properties that would be nice to copy, but which are by default not included in the 32 copied properties. Table 3.13 lists six such properties.

NOTE   One of the properties defined to be copied when copying a user, the `employee Type` property, is not a user property at all.

If you anticipate needing to create several similar user objects, you can create user templates. A user template is a normal user object that represents a typical user of some department. When you need a new user for that department, you can copy the user template to be the new user and modify it as necessary.

The copied properties are defined in the schema. You can add attributes (e.g., `streetAddress`) to the list, as Chapter 9 will explain.

TABLE 3.13 Properties That Are Copied When Users Are Copied

Category	Properties
Copied and visible in the snap-in (20 properties)	`accountExpires`, `c` (Country/region)*, `co` (Country/region), `company`, `countryCode` (Country/region), `department`, `homeDirectory`, `homeDrive`, `l` (City), `logonHours`, `manager`, `memberOf`, `postalCode` (Zip/Postal Code), `postOfficeBox`, `primaryGroupID`, `profilePath`, `scriptPath` (Logon script), `st` (State/province), `userAccountControl` (Account options), and `userWorkstations` (Logon Workstations)
Copied but not visible in the snap-in (12 properties)	`Assistant`, `codePage`, `division`, `localeID`, `logonWorkstation`, `maxStorage`, `otherLoginWorkstations`, `postalAddress`, `preferredOU`, `showInAddressBook`, `showInAdvancedViewOnly`, and `street`
Not copied but visible in the snap-in and would be nice to be copied (6 properties)	`description`, `directReports`, `facsimileTelephoneNumber` (Fax), `otherFacsimileTelephoneNumber` (Fax Number (Others)), `physicalDeliveryOfficeName` (Office), and `streetAddress` (Street)
Not a user property	`employeeType`

* We have included in parentheses the property names that you see in the Users and Computers snap-in if those names are quite different from the LDAP names in the table.

MOVING USERS AND CONTACTS

Every now and then you may want to move some users or contacts from one OU to another. You move them within a domain by right-clicking the object and then selecting Move. Then you choose the destination from the OU tree that appears and click OK. Note that

- Permissions that are assigned for the user object being moved move with the object.
- Group policies and permissions that are inherited by the user object from above do not move with the object being moved. Instead, the moved object inherits the new group policies and permissions in its new location.

You can move several sibling objects at once. Select them in the right-hand pane of the snap-in by using the Shift and/or Ctrl keys. Then proceed as usual.

It is possible to move objects to another domain in your forest. To do so, you need to use the Support Tools command-line tool MoveTree, which is discussed in Chapter 6.

RENAMING USERS AND CONTACTS

You can rename a user or contact by right-clicking the object and selecting Rename or by selecting the object and pressing F2. A third way is to click an already selected object. After you type the new name, press Enter. Because these objects have many names, you have a chance to change one or all of the names in a dialog box, as Figures 3.15 and 3.16 show.

After you rename a user, the old name still appears in the following properties: E-mail, Web page, Profile path, Logon script (if using personal), and Home folder. Also, the corresponding physical folders, as well as the local copy of the user's profile (i.e., C:\Documents and Settings*username*), will keep the old name. If you want all of these to reflect the new name, you must change each of them manually.

DELETING USERS AND CONTACTS

You delete an object by right-clicking it and selecting Delete or by selecting the object and pressing the Delete key. As a safety mechanism, you need to confirm the delete but you cannot undo it.

A user object is a security principal: It may have security group memberships and permissions for resources. Each user object has a security ID (SID), which is the identifier to be used in these assignments. A SID is a long number and a SID is never reused. If you delete a user object and then recreate it, it will have a new SID, so the new user has none of the memberships or permissions of the old user. You must assign memberships and permissions specifically to the new user.

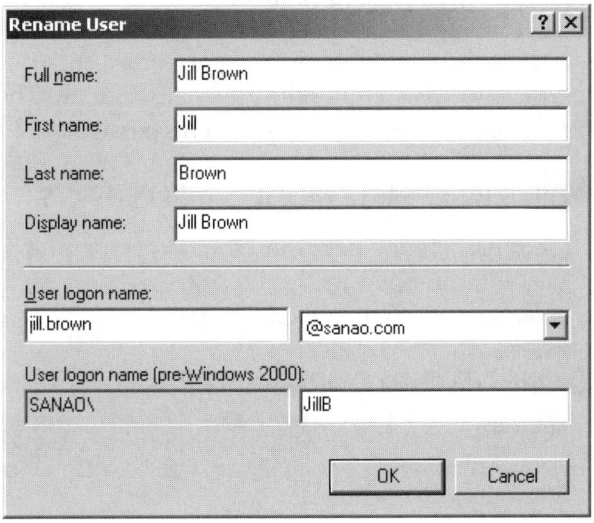

FIGURE 3.15 When you rename a user, you are prompted with a dialog box that enables you to change a number of names at once. The first field, Full name, refers to the common name of the object.

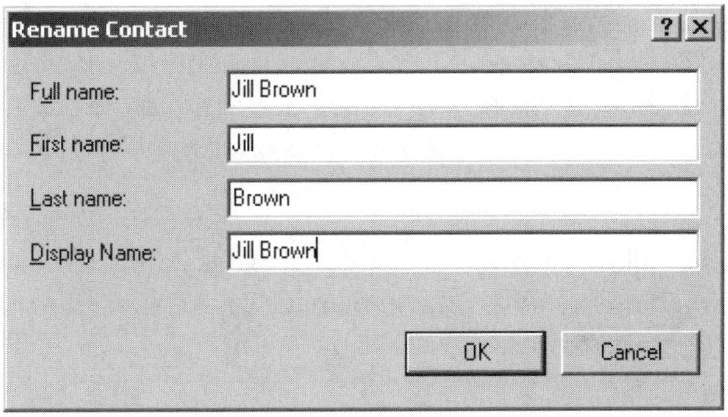

FIGURE 3.16 When you rename a contact, you are prompted with a dialog box that enables you to change a number of names at once. The first field, Full name, refers to the common name of the object.

DISABLING USER ACCOUNTS

The context menu for a user object contains an operation called "Disable Account." It has the same effect as the "Account is disabled" check box in the Account tab of the properties dialog box. This operation is usually used for a limited time. For example, if someone is out of the company for 6 months, you could freeze his user account but still not delete it.

When you see a red *X* icon on the user, the account is already disabled. In this case the context menu has an operation called "Enable Account."

RESETTING USER PASSWORDS

You will never see your users' passwords, but you can change them using the Reset Password operation in the context menu. The most obvious reason to do this is because a user has forgotten his password.

OPENING HOME PAGES OF USERS AND CONTACTS

If a user has a home page, and the corresponding property is defined in his user object, you can open the home page in a browser using the "Open home page" operation in the context menu.

SENDING E-MAIL TO USERS AND CONTACTS

If a user has an e-mail address, and the corresponding property is defined in her user object, you can send her e-mail with the "Send mail" operation in the context menu.

ADMINISTERING COMPUTER OBJECTS

Just as Active Directory has a user object for each network user, it has a computer object for each computer in the domain. However, this applies "only" to Windows 2000 and Windows NT computers. Other workstations (e.g., Windows 95 and 98 and non-Microsoft operating systems) that are not using the NT-based integrated security cannot have a computer object.

IF YOU KNOW NDS NDS allows a broader range of workstation types than does Active Directory, which means that you can manage more types of workstations with the help of the directory service.

Also, computer objects are used only for computers that join a domain. If a stand-alone server or workstation will be in a workgroup instead of a domain, it will not be assigned a computer object in Active Directory.

You could categorize computer object properties as either significant or informational, just as we did with user objects. However, the distinction among computer objects is not as clear as it is among user objects, so we don't use these terms with computer objects in this book (short of a couple of exceptions).

The purposes of computer objects are as follows:

- As inherited from the very first version of Windows NT back in 1993, a computer account ties the workstation or server to the Windows NT/2000 security model.

- A computer object is a placeholder for properties that help you when you are remotely installing and managing workstations.
- A computer object is a placeholder for properties that are purely informational.
- A computer object is a security principal. This means that just as with a user, you can give permissions for resources and assign security group memberships to the computer.
- The location of a computer object in Active Directory dictates which group policies apply to the corresponding computer.

Computer objects are treated slightly differently, depending on whether they are for domain controllers or for workstations and member servers. Table 3.14 compares the two.

When you start to manage computer objects, your tasks will include the following:

- Create computer objects.
- Set computer object properties.
- Move, rename, disable, reset, and delete computer objects.
- Assign Group Policy and permissions, and delegate administrative tasks.

In this chapter, we focus on the first three items in the list. The last item is discussed in later chapters. If you want to try the management tasks discussed in this

TABLE 3.14 Comparing Domain Controllers and Other Computer Objects

Feature	Domain Controller	Workstation and Member Server
Creation of the object	Automatically while installing Active Directory on the server (using DCPromo)	• Semiautomatically while joining the computer to the domain • Manually with the Users and Computers snap-in
Default container of the object	Domain Controllers	Computers
Use of the default location	Probably yes	Probably not (place the computer objects in OUs instead)
Computer GUID	You cannot set this property.	You may set this property, which helps when using Remote Installation Services and signifies a managed computer.

section, you can create some test computer objects in your test OU. To test all the features, however, you will need some test workstations.

Creating Computer Objects

As Table 3.14 in the previous section implies, computer objects are created in three ways.

- A computer object for a domain controller is created automatically in the Domain Controllers OU when you install Active Directory on that server by running the Active Directory Installation Wizard (i.e., DCPromo).

- When you join a stand-alone server or workstation to a domain, either during computer installation or afterward, you have the option to create the computer object. An object created in this way goes to the Computers container.

- You precreate the computer object manually using the Users and Computers snap-in. This choice is explained next.

NOTE   The second and third items in the list require appropriate permissions or user rights, which are explained in Chapter 4. In short, any forest user can by default join ten workstations to a domain.

You can store the computer objects either in the Computers container or in various OUs in the domain. The latter option allows different OU-based group policies for different computers.

When you right-click the appropriate target OU and select New, Computer, you will see the dialog box shown in Figure 3.17. Here you specify the name for the object, the downlevel name for the computer, and the user or group who can later join the computer to the domain.

If you use Remote Installation Services (RIS) to install Windows 2000 Professional computers, there will be one or two additional pages in the creation wizard. Figure 3.18 shows the first of these pages.

NOTE   Whether you get the two additional wizard pages or not depends on which computer you are sitting at. For example, if there are two domain controllers in your domain (DC1 and DC2) and you have installed RIS on DC2, you will see the two additional pages if you are sitting at DC2 or any workstation. However, if you are sitting at DC1, you won't see the pages.

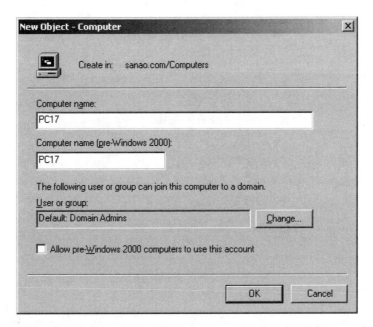

FIGURE 3.17 When you create a computer object, you are prompted to specify the name for the object, the downlevel name for the computer, and the user or group who can later join the computer to the domain. If the joining computer is running Windows NT, you must select the bottom check box.

Computer manufacturers assign a unique GUID to each computer they sell. If you enter this GUID into Active Directory, it will help RIS match a certain computer system to a certain computer object.

After you have bought a computer and turned it on for the first time to install Windows 2000 Professional onto it, the RIS service sends the computer's GUID to a RIS server. This way, RIS can locate the correct computer object in Active Directory.

If you selected the "This is a managed computer" option on the wizard's second page, you will see one more page, which is shown in Figure 3.19.

NOTE The computer GUID shown in Figure 3.18 is not the same as the GUID that each Active Directory object has. Chapter 8 offers more in-depth treatment of object GUIDs.

NOTE You cannot specify the computer GUID or RIS server name for an existing computer object using the Users and Computers snap-in if you didn't specify

FIGURE 3.18 If you use RIS, you will see a second page in the creation wizard. You can specify that this is a "managed computer" and enter the computer's GUID.

"managed computer" when you first created the object. To edit properties directly, you need to use ADSI Edit or some other means. The aforementioned information is stored in the properties `netbootGUID` and `netbootMachine-FilePath`.

A computer object has several names, which are listed in Table 3.15.

Setting Computer Object Properties

The Users and Computers snap-in shows you about 15 computer object properties, and you can set about 8 of them. Behind the scenes, a computer object may have 228 properties.

Table 3.16 lists the properties in five of the six tabs. We discuss the sixth tab, Member Of, later in this chapter in the "Administering Groups" section. We don't include screen shots, because they would show just a number of text boxes. Many of the setting names are self-explanatory. Note that Windows 2000 also provides context-sensitive help for each of the settings.

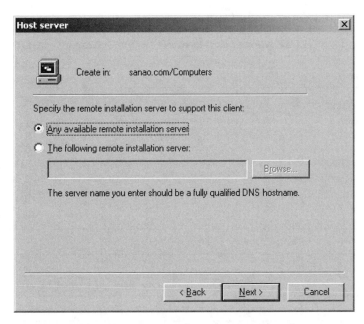

FIGURE 3.19 If you selected the "This is a managed computer" option in the creation wizard's second page (Figure 3.18), you will see another page that enables you to specify a certain remote installation server. You can use this for load balancing, so that certain client computers (identified by the GUID) install Windows 2000 Professional from a certain server.

TABLE 3.15 Name Properties of a Computer Object

Property	LDAP Name	Maximum Length	Required	Unique	Comments
Computer name	name (RDN) and cn (Common-Name)	64	X	Within OU	This becomes the object common name in the tree.
DNS name	dNSHostName	2048		In the world	The target computer updates this property automatically.
Computer name (pre-Windows 2000)	sAMAccountName	256 (schema rule), 20 (SAM rule)	X	Within the enterprise	This is the downlevel name of the computer, which is also the same as the computer NetBIOS name. Internally, Active Directory stores a dollar sign ($) at the end of the name.

TABLE 3.16 Properties of a Computer Object

Property	LDAP Name	Syntax*	Index	GC	Comments
General Tab					
Computer name (pre-Windows 2000)	sAMAccountName	Text (256 [schema rule], 20 [SAM rule])	X	X	This is the downlevel name of the computer, which is also the same as the computer NetBIOS name. Internally, Active Directory stores a dollar sign ($) at the end of the name.
DNS name	dNSHostName	Text (2048)		X	
Role					"Domain controller" or "Workstation or server"
Description	description	Text (1024)		X	
Trust computer for delegation	userAccount-Control	Yes/no	X	X	This setting is described in Chapter 4 in the "Impersonation and Delegation" section.
Operating System Tab					
Name	operating-System	Text			A read-only text such as "Windows 2000 Server."
Version	operating-SystemVersion	Text			A read-only text to indicate the normal version, such as "5.0" (i.e., Windows 2000), and the more precise version (i.e., build number), such as "2195."
Service Pack	operating-System-ServicePack	Text			A read-only text to indicate whether or not you have installed any Windows 2000 service packs on the machine, such as "Service Pack 1."

(continued)

TABLE 3.16 (*continued*)

Property	LDAP Name	Syntax*	Index	GC	Comments
Location Tab					
Location	`location`	Text (1024)	X	X	
Managed By Tab					
Managed By	`managedBy`	DN; you select a user or contact from list			The user or contact you select gets no permissions for the computer. This setting is purely informational. The other fields on the tab are the manager's properties.
Remote Install Tab*					
Computer's unique ID	`netbootGUID`	Binary (text in the user interface)	X	X	Same as the computer's GUID. It helps when using RIS, and it signifies a managed computer.
Remote Installation server	`netboot-Machine-FilePath`	Text		X	This property specifies the DNS name of the selected installation server.
Server settings	N/A	N/A	N/A	N/A	This button takes you to the properties of the server object.

* If the syntax is Text (i.e., a string of Unicode characters), we indicate also the maximum number of characters in the property (e.g., 1024).

** The Remote Install tab is present only if you created the object for a "managed computer" by checking the box on the second page of the creation wizard. Even then, it is present only when you are sitting at the correct computer, as explained in the preceding section, "Creating Computer Objects."

Other Operations to Manage Computer Objects

Other operations you can do to manipulate computer objects are move, delete, disable, and reset. You can also rename computers or start computer management to manage the computer corresponding to the object.

MOVING COMPUTER OBJECTS

If you need to move a computer object from one OU to another, you do it in the same way you move users. When you are moving a computer within a domain, you right-click the computer object and select Move. Then you choose the destination and click OK. Between domains in a forest you use the Support Tools command-line tool MoveTree, which is discussed in Chapter 6.

You can move several sibling objects at once by selecting them in the right-hand pane of the snap-in by using the Shift and/or the Ctrl key.

When you move computer objects

- Permissions that are assigned for the object being moved move with the object.
- Group policies and permissions that are inherited from above do not move with the object being moved. Instead, the moved object inherits the policies and permissions from its new location.

DELETING COMPUTER OBJECTS

You delete an object by right-clicking it and selecting Delete or by selecting the object and pressing the Delete key. Because there is no Undo option, a safety mechanism asks you to confirm the deletion.

A computer object is a security principal like a user object. Therefore, if you delete a computer object and then recreate it, the new object doesn't have the memberships or permissions of the old one.

If you delete a computer object, the corresponding computer is no longer part of the domain. Therefore, no one can log on to the computer using a domain user account.

DISABLING COMPUTER ACCOUNTS

You can disable the computer account by right-clicking the computer object and selecting Disable Account. Doing so will prevent users sitting at that computer from logging on using a domain user account.

You cannot disable a domain controller.

RESETTING COMPUTER ACCOUNTS

When a Windows 2000 (or Windows NT) computer that is a member of a domain starts, the computer logs on to the domain using the computer account and some password known to the machine. After this, a user sitting at the computer can enter his username and password to log on to the domain.

The aforementioned machine logon sets up a *secure channel,* which enables the member computer to communicate with a domain controller to exchange user and password information. For example, if the computer account password stored in the local computer (called *LSA secret*) doesn't match the one stored in Active Directory, authentication to the domain is not possible and the user will receive an error like the one shown in Figure 3.20.

An administrator can solve the problem by using the Reset Account context menu item on the corresponding computer object. Resetting a computer account resets its password to the initial value, which is "computername$" (without quotes). In addition, the member computer must be joined to a workgroup and then joined to the domain again.

NOTE   Support Tools includes two command-line utilities, NetDom and NLTest, which you can also use to reset computer accounts, among other things.

MANAGING COMPUTERS

When you right-click the computer object and select Manage, the Computer Management snap-in starts and sets the focus to the corresponding computer. This way you can manage its system tools, storage, server applications, and services.

RENAMING COMPUTERS

You rename a Windows 2000 workstation or member server using the Control Panel of that computer. Select System, then the Network Identification tab, and finally the Properties button. Once you enter a new name and click OK, you are prompted for the name of a domain user who has permission to change the name of the workstation or member server, as well as that user's password.

FIGURE 3.20 If the member computer cannot establish a secure channel with a domain controller, the user receives an error message and is not able to log on using a domain user account.

This operation renames the computer (i.e., the NetBIOS name and DNS name) and changes the pre–Windows 2000 name of the computer object. However, the object's common name doesn't change and you cannot change it using the Users and Computers snap-in. Instead, you must use ADSI Edit, which is part of Support Tools.

NOTE   You cannot rename domain controllers.

ADMINISTERING GROUPS

Managing users, contacts, and computer objects is usually much more effective when you treat them in groups than when you treat them individually. Whether you need to send e-mail or assign permissions for a printer, you most often want the target to be several users instead of just one. When you need the same group again, the fact that you already have it created will save you work. Of course, there is no laborsaving benefit if you create a group and then use it only once.

Groups are extremely handy and you really cannot manage a network without them. However, you use them mainly for assigning permissions and group policies. Specifically, you cannot use groups for the following purposes:

- Setting properties of several users, contacts, or computer objects, or applying properties for them
- Moving or deleting several users, contacts, or computer objects

In addition to administrators, end users can use Active Directory groups, usually as distribution lists. Table 3.17 describes in more detail the purposes for which you can use groups.

Group Types

You can create two types of groups in Active Directory, *security groups* and *distribution groups*. Both types can have users, contacts, and computer objects as members.

Table 3.17 illustrates that security groups have two natures, but distribution groups have only one. Thus, distribution groups have a subset of security group features.

NOTE   Even though labeled "application nature," an application could use the distribution feature also for some security use. For example, you could have an application that controls the doors of your company. The application could open a certain door for a user if he is a member of a certain distribution group. The Note is related to Table 3.17.

TABLE 3.17 The Nature of Security and Distribution Groups

Nature	Security	Distribution	Purpose
Security nature	X		Assign permissions, and possibly audit settings, for folders, files, and Active Directory objects
Group is a security principal, which Windows 2000 uses to determine permissions.			Assign group policies (not directly, but by assigning permissions for a certain Group Policy only to some group)
			Other miscellaneous uses, such as check the group membership in a logon script and then apply some commands, in case the user was in that group
Application nature	X	X	Send e-mail (i.e., the group operates as a distribution list)
Group is available to directory-enabled applications. Windows 2000 doesn't use it but any application may use it.			When using a directory-enabled application, use the group for whatever purpose the application needs

IF YOU KNOW NT   Security groups are the traditional groups that existed in Windows NT. Distribution groups are new.

As Table 3.17 indicates, a security group has all the features of a distribution group, and it can also be used for assigning permissions. This leads to the following question: Why do we use distribution groups at all, if they are less capable? The reason is that they are a little "cheaper" than security groups in terms of logon process.

When a user logs on to the network or accesses the resources of a server for the first time, Windows 2000 builds an *access token* for that user. An access token is a list in RAM that contains the user's identity and the groups that the user belongs to. But it doesn't contain any distribution groups. Because distribution groups are not needed when determining access, they are not needed in the access tokens. This, in turn, leads to a somewhat faster logon process and a smaller access token in memory. Of course, you probably won't notice the difference in a small network.

On the other hand, as long as you don't have any directory-enabled applications, you cannot use distribution groups, even though you can create them. Remember that Windows 2000 doesn't use them. This means that it's quite possible that you need to create only security groups, even though they are a little more "expensive."

Figure 3.21 summarizes the features of the two group types.

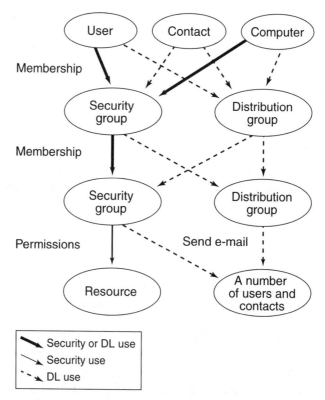

FIGURE 3.21 The solid lines in this figure represent the security nature of groups. All lines except the thin solid line in the lower-left corner represent the application nature of groups.

NOTE   A contact is never able to log on, so it never gets an access token, and it cannot access resources. Therefore, it is not part of the security nature of groups, even though it can be a member of a security group.

NOTE   Figure 3.21 shows groups as members of other groups. Depending on the domain mode (mixed/native) and group scopes (discussed in the next section), not all groups can be members of all other groups.

Group Scopes

In addition to the two group types (security and distribution), groups are divided into three scopes: *global groups, universal groups,* and *domain local groups.* The group scope indicates if the group can accept members from other domains and if it can be used in other domains.

Group scopes are not very important if you have only one domain. In that case, you can do just fine with only universal groups, unless you anticipate having several domains at some later time.

Group scopes and nesting behave differently depending on whether your domain is in mixed mode or native mode. We will first explain the mixed-mode case. Even if you have already changed your domain to native mode and/or plan to use only native mode, you should read the section about mixed mode. In the next section we explain many principles of how to use groups in administration, regardless of the mode.

GROUP SCOPES IN MIXED MODE

Distribution groups in mixed mode work just like distribution groups in native mode. Consequently, we'll discuss distribution groups in the next section, which is about native mode.

NOTE   Contact objects don't quite follow the containment rules that we will present from this point on. A global group can have user and computer object members only from its own domain, but it can have contact object members also from other domains.

Security groups in mixed mode work like the groups in Windows NT. You can have global and domain local security groups, but you can't have universal security groups.

You cannot freely nest security groups in mixed mode, but you can put global groups as members into domain local groups, as Figure 3.22 illustrates.

NOTE   We don't include contact objects in the figures from now on because we are concentrating on the security nature of the groups.

In the one-domain case in Figure 3.22, you can draw an arrow from any circle to any other, as long as you move downward. In the two-domain case, only the two upper circles are visible in the other domain, and only the two lower circles accept arrows from the other domain.

Remember that normal trust relationships in Active Directory are bidirectional. In the case of two domains, domain A trusts domain B and vice versa. Consequently, a domain A global group can be a member of a domain B domain local group, and a domain B global group can be a member of a domain A domain local group. In other words, if you looked at Figure 3.22 in a mirror, you would see a similar figure.

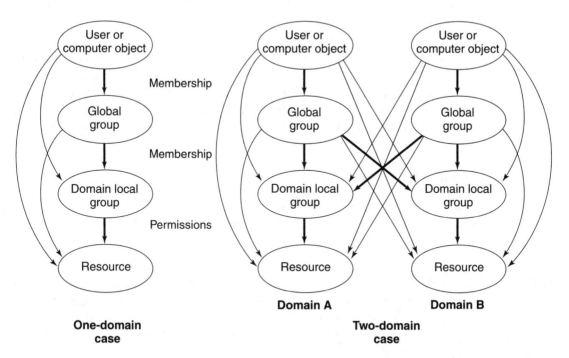

FIGURE 3.22 In mixed mode you can put users and computer objects in global groups, put global groups in domain local groups, and then give permissions to domain local groups. This preferred arrangement is indicated in the image by thick lines. You can also use the shortcuts indicated by the thin lines.

Because Figure 3.22 has quite a few arrows, to simplify the two-domain case, Figure 3.23 shows only the preferred (thick) arrows.

The thin lines (shortcuts) are less desirable for the following reasons:

- By giving permissions to one group instead of 200 users, you get dramatically shorter permission lists. This saves disk space, speeds up permission evaluation, and is easier to manage. For example, when your organization hires a new employee, she will get all the needed permissions when you add her to a few groups. The worse alternative would be to go through all server folders and add permissions to this new user.

- You should use global groups to group users (and computer objects). These groups are also a level of isolation. If the user list changes, the groups stay the same, and therefore hide the changes from the lower levels. This is especially valuable in a multidomain situation. If one domain gets a new user, the administrators in other domains don't have to do anything, because they already have the appropriate global groups as members in the appropriate domain local groups.

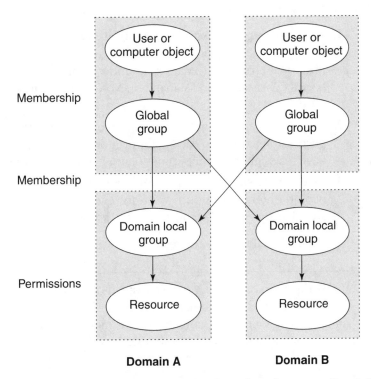

FIGURE 3.23 Global groups are usually associated with people (and computer objects). Domain local groups are resource oriented. The dotted boxes symbolize this division.

- You should use domain local groups for resource-oriented purposes. You often create a domain local group either for one resource or for a certain type of resource, such as all color printers. This way, if a new group of users needs access to all the color printers, you can just make this group a member of the rColorPrintersPrint domain local group, instead of giving permissions for 17 color printers individually.

NOTE The first *r* in the rColorPrintersPrint domain local group name indicates that it is a resource-oriented group. *Print* indicates that this group has the print permission for the corresponding printers. You can use these kinds of naming conventions at will.

EXAMPLE OF GROUP USAGE

We present in this section a basic example of group usage. We want to limit the number of people who can print on the color printers in our domain, so we perform the following steps.

1. When we deployed Active Directory, we established certain global groups to group the users in our domain. We put the users in groups based on the organizational structure (oMarketing and oFinance), as well as functional categories (fAssistants and fManagers). Note that we cannot use OUs for anything here.

2. Now we create a new local group, rColorPrintersPrint, and give that group permission to print to each color printer. We have three color printers and we have to assign the Print permission for each printer individually.

3. As the final step, we assign appropriate global groups as members of the rColorPrintersPrint group. We want everyone in the marketing department and all managers to be able to print in color.

   Figure 3.24 illustrates the result.

NOTE If a workstation or member server, instead of a domain controller, handles one of the color printers, the domain local group cannot be used while we are still in mixed mode. Once we change to native mode, we can start using domain local groups in workstations and member servers.

If you have only one domain and you feel that you don't need two levels of groups, you may skip either level. Either you can make users (and computer

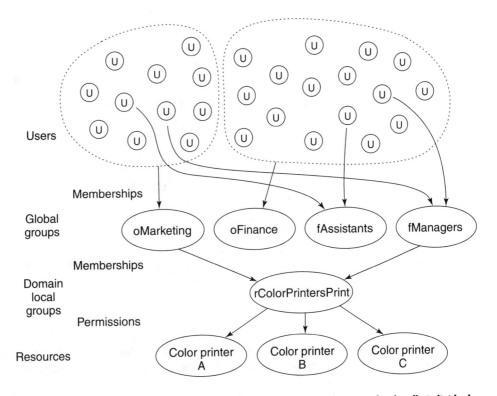

FIGURE 3.24 We have grouped our users into global groups, so we don't need to handle individual users. We give the actual Print permission to a domain local group and then assign appropriate global groups as members of this domain local group.

objects) members of domain local groups, or you can give permissions directly to global groups.

The domain local group in Figure 3.24 may seem unnecessary. However, imagine that you have 17 color printers and, along with marketing personnel and managers, you want to allow assistants to print to them. With the domain local group you can do this quickly: You only need to put fAssistants as a member in rColor PrintersPrint. Without the domain local group, you would need to open the properties dialog box of 17 printers in quite a few servers and assign permissions to fAssistants individually in each dialog box.

GROUP SCOPES IN NATIVE MODE

In native mode you can have any of the three group scopes in either of the two group types—that is, there are six possible combinations. Unlike in mixed mode, in native mode you can have universal security groups.

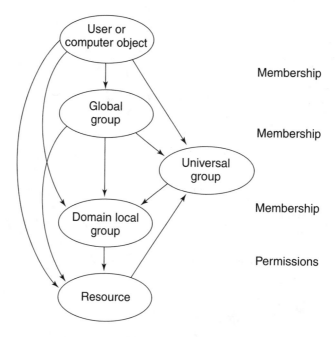

FIGURE 3.25 In native mode you have three levels of groups. Any upper-level object can be a member of any lower-level object. This figure illustrates the situation in one domain.

Security groups and distribution groups work the same way in native mode. Therefore, we don't need to make a distinction between them and we don't discuss them separately here.

In mixed mode, global groups are the upper level and domain local groups are the lower level. In native mode, universal groups are a third level between the two earlier levels. A group from a higher level can be a member in a group from a lower level, as Figure 3.25 illustrates.

NOTE   Figure 3.26, Figure 3.27, and Figure 3.28 are more complex than earlier images. To be as clear as possible, we don't show users and computer objects on the top or resources on the bottom in those three figures. You can still imagine them to be there.

Deciding on how to use all these groups in native mode is more complicated than in mixed mode. We delve into this discussion in the "Planning Groups" section later in the chapter. We'll just mention the three basic strategies here:

- Forget universal groups and use only global and domain local groups, as described in the preceding section about mixed mode.

- Use only universal groups.
- Use all three levels (and pray that you know what is going on in Active Directory). If you have several domains and sites, you will probably need all three levels.

NOTE   Because there are three possible strategies for using groups in native mode, Figure 3.25 does not indicate (with thick lines) a preferred path.

Figure 3.26 introduces a second domain. It illustrates that global groups cannot accept members from other domains (except contacts), and domain local groups cannot be used in other domains, but universal groups don't have either of these restrictions.

NOTE   As you may remember from the mixed-mode section, the arrows between domains should be symmetrical. To keep Figure 3.26 uncluttered, we do not show the arrows from domain A to domain B.

If one of the domains in Figure 3.26 were in mixed mode and the other were in native mode, the image would still be accurate. Obviously, one of the domains couldn't have universal security groups, but after having removed that, all the remaining arrows would be valid. For example, if domain A were in mixed mode

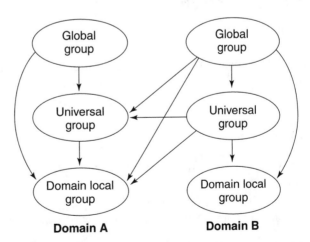

FIGURE 3.26 When crossing domain boundaries, global groups cannot accept members from other domains, and domain local groups cannot be used in other domains. Universal groups, however, have no such restrictions.

and domain B were in native mode, the domain local groups in domain A would accept both global and universal groups as members from domain B.

The figures so far have shown only one group of each scope in each domain. In reality, you will have many groups of each scope. In native mode you can freely nest groups of the same scope. Global group A can be a member of global group B, which is a member of global group C, which is a member of global group D, and so on. In other words, any group can be a member of any other group of the same scope in the same domain.

Building on Figure 3.26, Figure 3.27 shows five groups of each scope in each domain.

NOTE   In Figure 3.27, the arrow from the global groups in domain A to the universal groups in domain A symbolizes that any of the upper five groups can be a member of any of the lower five groups. An actual representation would have 25 arrows, but we use just one. These 25 arrows would be needed 14 times, between each scope of groups in each domain. To give you a clear image, we use only 10 arrows instead of 350.

NOTE   Again, in Figure 3.27, arrows from domain A to domain B were left out to make the image clear.

BUILT-IN LOCAL GROUPS

The last aspect of group scopes concerns the built-in local security groups (Administrators, Account Operators, and so on) that reside in the Builtin container. Technically, they belong to a different "domain"—the Built-in domain—therefore, you cannot nest domain local groups with built-in local security groups or vice versa. Figure 3.28 illustrates this concept.

Managing Groups

Now you are ready to create and manage groups. Before you implement the groups in your production environment, you should first read the "Planning Groups" section of this chapter.

Managing groups includes the following tasks:

• Creating groups of different types and scopes
• Changing the type or scope of a group
• Managing group memberships

- Setting the primary group of a user
- Setting group properties
- Moving, renaming, and deleting groups
- Sending e-mail to groups

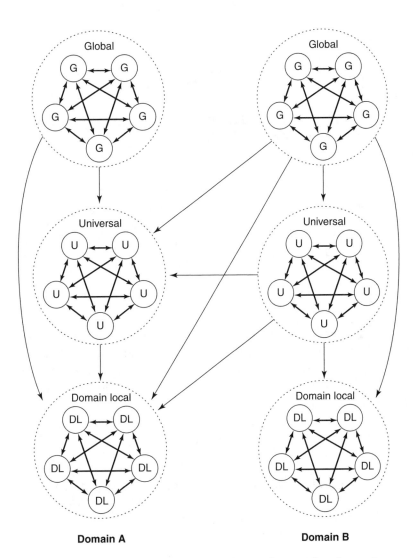

FIGURE 3.27 Within each scope in each domain, any group can be a member of any other group. From one scope or domain to another, groups that can be a member of other groups are indicated with an arrow.

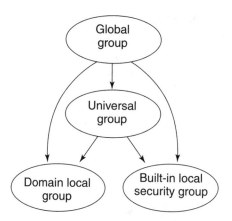

FIGURE 3.28 Built-in local security groups belong technically to a different "domain." Therefore, you cannot nest them with domain local groups.

When you create and manage groups, we suggest that you visualize your groups in the way that we have presented groups in the figures in this book. Having a clear visual image of them in your head, or even on paper, will help. The user interface of the Users and Computers snap-in doesn't indicate graphically that you should put users in global groups, global groups (perhaps) in universal groups, and so on.

CREATING GROUPS

You create groups with the Users and Computers snap-in just like you create any other object. Right-click the target OU and select New, Group. Figure 3.29 is a screen shot of the dialog box that appears. Because you cannot assign permissions to an OU, the first group you create is probably a global security group with the same name as the OU. When you add each user of the OU to this group, you can give him or her permissions with the help of this group.

Table 3.18 describes the two names shown in Figure 3.29.

NOTE   Distribution groups are created for directory-enabled applications. It is unlikely that those applications use the pre–Windows 2000 name. However, you must define it for every distribution group.

Many of the dialog boxes in the Users and Computers snap-in give no hint of the scope or type of existing groups. Therefore, you might consider adding your own hint—for example, add "gs" to the name, with "g" standing for "global" and

TABLE 3.18 Name Properties of a Group Object

Property	LDAP Name	Maximum Length	Required	Unique	Description
Group name	name (RDN) and cn (Common-Name)	64	X	Within OU	This becomes the object common name in the tree.
Group name (pre–Windows 2000)	sAMAccountName	256	X	Within domain	This name appears on non–Active Directory computers and software, such as the old User Manager. Despite its label, this name can be used throughout Windows 2000.

"s" standing for "security" group. With domain local groups you could use "l" instead of "d" to not confuse them with distribution groups.

You could also use letters to indicate whether the group was created by organization, by functionality, by resource, or by some other criteria. Table 3.19 gives some suggestions on how to use these symbol letters.

In addition to making names more descriptive, these symbols sort similar groups sequentially when the user interface is using an alphabetical list.

Table 3.19 presents examples of letters that indicate scope and type, such as "gs," and letters that indicate logical grouping, such as "o." Of course, you can use both types, but be aware that confusion can arise if you use too many identifiers like these.

CHANGING GROUP TYPE OR SCOPE

Mixed mode doesn't enable you to change group type or scope. Native mode enables these changes, with two restrictions (see Figure 3.30).

- If the new type or scope would lead to an illegal situation in terms of memberships, the change is obviously forbidden. For example, if your domain local group has other domain local groups as members, you cannot change it to a universal group. Universal groups cannot have domain local groups as members.

- You cannot change a domain local group to a global group or vice versa, except via a universal group.

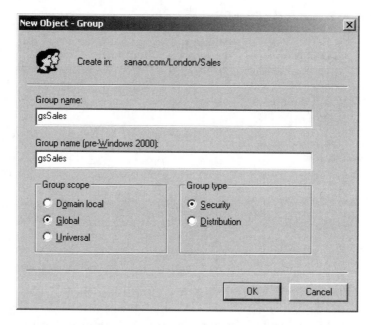

FIGURE 3.29 When you create a group, the first dialog box that appears calls for naming the group and assigning its scope and type. The first group is likely to have the same name as the OU.

NOTE   The Users and Computers snap-in actually allows you to change a global group to universal, even if the group-to-be-changed is a member of another global group. Because the result is illegal, however, the corresponding membership is not effective.

MANAGING GROUP MEMBERSHIPS

Each user, contact, computer, and group is a "member" of only one OU. At the same time, each can be a member of several groups, because a group membership is just a group property; it is not part of the tree structure.

The Users and Computers snap-in allows you to manage group membership in three ways:

- The Members tab of the group
- The Member Of tab of the (incoming) member
- The "Add members to a group" function

TABLE 3.19 Symbol Letters for Group Names

Letter(s)	Examples	Meaning
gs	gsSales	Global security groups
us	usSAPUsers	Universal security groups
ls	lsSAPUse lsColorPrint	Domain local security groups. The first group has permissions to use SAP software and the second group has permissions to print in color.
o	oDirectSales oChannelSales	Groups created according to the organizational structure (which don't match OUs).
ou	ouSales	Groups created to match OUs
f	fSalesmen fAssistants	Groups created according to function (for example, salesmen from all OUs)
r	rSAPUser ColorPrint	Groups created for resources. Because these are usually domain local groups, this example has the same group names as the "ls" example.

One of the Active Directory design goals was drag-and-drop administration. In the first version of Windows 2000, however, you cannot drag objects over groups to become members of them.

WARNING   If you delegate group management to assistant administrators, you should advise them to modify group memberships only on one domain controller (perhaps the PDC emulator). All members of a group are stored in one multivalued property. If that member list is modified on two domain controllers simultaneously (within replication latency), one of the two changes will be lost.

FIGURE 3.30 You can change a group scope to and from a universal group, but you can't change scope directly from a domain local group to a global group or vice versa.

WARNING   You could give users the permission to "Add/Remove self as member" of some group. For the reason given in the previous warning, some changes could be lost, and the risk would be quite great if all users could modify membership themselves.

NOTE   Because all members of a group are stored in one multivalued property, there is a limit of 5,000 members in one group.

The Members Tab of the Group

The first way to manage groups is through the Members tab. When you right-click a group, select Properties, and then click the Members tab, you'll see a list of the members of the group, as Figure 3.31 shows.

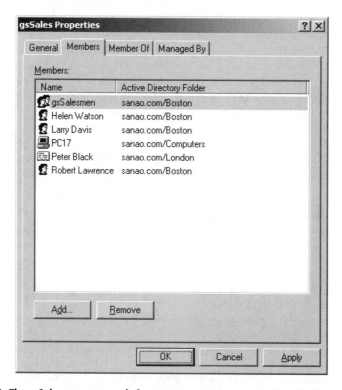

FIGURE 3.31   **The gsSales group currently has users, contacts, computers, and other groups as members.**

As you would guess, you remove members by selecting them and clicking the Remove button.

To add members to a list, click Add. Another dialog box opens where you can select objects to be added as members. To select members for a group, in the "Look in" field choose the domain (or Entire Directory), select objects from the list, and click Add. The selected objects then appear in the lower box and you click OK (see Figure 3.32).

NOTE   You can select several members simultaneously by holding down the Shift and/or Ctrl key.

Instead of selecting objects from the list, you can type their names in the lower list. Then you can check whether they are valid with the Check Names button. If you want to type several names, you must separate them with semicolons. If more than one object matches the name you typed, clicking Check Names brings up dialog box in Figure 3.33.

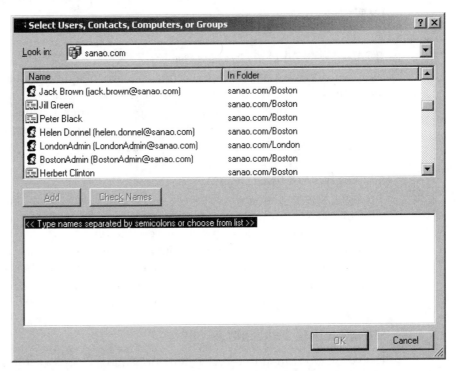

FIGURE 3.32 To select members for a group, first choose the domain (or Entire Directory) in the "Look in" field, select the members from the list, click Add to copy the selected objects to the lower list, and then click OK.

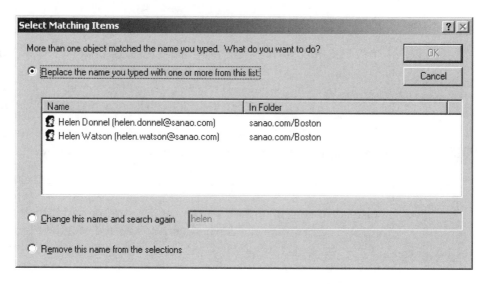

FIGURE 3.33 If you type a name that matches several objects, you are prompted to select the name you intended.

The Member Of Tab of the Incoming Member

User, contact, computer, and group objects have a Member Of tab, which shows the groups that the object belongs to. If you have several domains in the forest, however, the tab shows just universal groups from other domains.

The Members Of tab and consequent dialog boxes work in the same way as the Members tab and consequent dialog boxes.

Add Members to a Group Function

The context menu of each user and contact (accessed with a right-click) has an "Add members to a group" option. When you select this menu item, you can choose the group in which to place the selected object.

The "Add members to a group" option is a menu item for each OU, also. In this case, you can make all users and contacts in the OU members of the group. If the OU has child OUs, you can choose for each one whether to include users and contacts in them as well.

SETTING A USER'S PRIMARY GROUP

Each user and computer object's Member Of tab includes a setting for a *primary group*. You probably won't need this setting, because it is used only by the POSIX subsystem (i.e., when running a kind of UNIX application in Windows 2000) or by Apple Macintosh workstations.

The default primary group of a user is Domain Users and the default primary group of a computer is Domain Computers. If needed, you can change this setting to some other global or universal security group.

You cannot remove an object from its primary group. Therefore, if you want to move a user out of Domain Users, you first must change that user's primary group to something else.

NOTE   The primary group of a user is not stored in the members property of the group, but rather in the `primaryGroupID` property of the user. Consequently, the 5,000-member maximum doesn't apply to primary groups, which means that you could have 100,000 users (or more) in your domain and they could all be members of Domain Users.

SETTING GROUP PROPERTIES

Behind the scenes a group object may, by default, have 107 properties. However, many of them are not needed, so the user interface displays only a few of them, as shown in Figure 3.34.

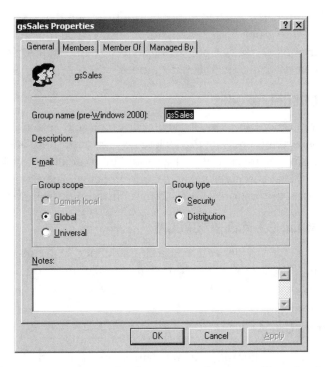

FIGURE 3.34 There are not many properties that you can set for a group object using the user interface.

Table 3.20 lists the properties of group objects that are visible in the Users and Computers snap-in other than group type, scope, and members, which we discussed in the previous sections. The settings are mostly self-explanatory. Note that Windows 2000 also provides context-sensitive help for each of the settings.

MOVING GROUPS

You move groups between OUs just like you move other objects. When moving them within a domain, you right-click the group, select Move, choose the destination, and click OK. To move groups between domains in your forest, you use the Support Tools command-line tool MoveTree. It is discussed in Chapter 6.

You move several sibling objects at once by selecting them in the right-hand pane of the snap-in and using the Shift and/or Ctrl key.

When you move groups

- Permissions that are assigned for the object being moved move with the object.
- Permissions that are inherited from above do not move with the object being moved. Instead, the object inherits new permissions in its new location.

RENAMING GROUPS

You rename a group either by right-clicking it and selecting Rename or by selecting the group and pressing F2. After you type the new name, press Enter. Because groups also have a pre–Windows 2000 name, a dialog box appears that gives you a chance to change that name, too.

DELETING GROUPS

You delete an object by right-clicking it and selecting Delete or by selecting the object and pressing the Delete key. Because there is no Undo, as a safety mechanism, you must confirm that you want to delete the object.

Like a user, a group is a security principal. Therefore, if you delete and then recreate it, the new object doesn't have the memberships or permissions of the old one.

SENDING E-MAIL TO GROUPS

If the group has an e-mail address defined, you can send it e-mail with the "Send mail" operation in the context menu. Naturally, you need an e-mail application for this feature to work.

Planning Groups

Now you know group mechanics and properties, so you can use this knowledge to decide what the best way is to use groups effectively for a specific

TABLE 3.20 Properties of a Group Object

Property	LDAP Name	Syntax*	Index	GC	Comments
General Tab					
Description	description	Text (1024)		X	
Group name (pre–Windows 2000)	sAMAccountName	Text (256)	X	X	This name appears on non–Active Directory computers and software, such as the old User Manager. Despite its label, this name can be used throughout Windows 2000.
E-Mail	mail	Text (256)	X	X	
Comments	info	Text (1024)			
Managed By Tab					
Managed By	managedBy	DN** (you select a user or contact from list)			The user or contact you select doesn't get permission for the group. This setting is purely informational. The other fields on the tab are the manager's properties.

* In the Syntax column, Text (256) means a text field with a maximum of 256 Unicode characters.
** DN = distinguished name.

network in terms of manageability, administrative burden, and cost to network efficiency.

Planning groups involves deciding on group names, types, and scopes.

- It often pays to use letters in group names that indicate the kind of group it is, as explained earlier in this chapter.

- As explained earlier, because of access tokens, you should use distribution groups when you don't need the security feature but intend just to use the group with some directory-enabled application.

- This section concentrates on group scopes and describes three strategies for using them.

Before we discuss the three strategies, we need to study universal groups a little more.

UNIVERSAL GROUPS REVISITED

Recall that universal groups don't have the limitations of global or domain local groups. This prompts the following question: Why not use only the most feasible (i.e., universal) groups? Actually, Microsoft originally planned Active Directory to have only universal groups, not global or domain local groups. But the universal groups introduce extra cost, so Microsoft brought along the other two scopes.

Universal groups are more expensive in two ways. The first is related to the global catalog and the second is related to access tokens. Table 3.21 explains both.

The outcome of the rightmost column in Table 3.21 is that if you have only one domain, neither cost in the table is an issue, so you can use universal groups with confidence.

The reason to have universal group members in the global catalog is to provide an efficient means to effectively implement groups in a WAN environment with multiple sites. The global catalog takes care that the membership information is present on all sites (provided each site has a global catalog server). Therefore, checking a user's membership (needed to determine his access to resources) doesn't require crossing WAN links to other sites.

TABLE 3.21 The Extra Costs Related to Universal Groups

Cost	Explanation	Is an Issue
Global catalog	All membership information of universal groups is replicated to the global catalog. This means that every time the members change, this information has to be replicated to all sites of the enterprise throughout the world (provided that they all have a global catalog server). To minimize changes, have only groups as members of universal groups. This way, changes in membership don't occur as often as when users are members.	If you have both multiple domains and multiple sites
Access tokens	Global and domain local groups come only from the applicable domain into the user's access tokens. Universal groups, however, come to the user's access tokens from all domains of the enterprise forest. Thus, using universal groups leads to larger access tokens (consuming some memory) and to slower logon times.	If you have multiple domains and a fairly large number of groups

NOTE   If you test universal groups, you may run into the following "problem": You create a test universal group on a domain controller that is not a global catalog server.

Then you test the new group and find out that it doesn't work (yet). The reason is that, because the universal group membership is read from a global catalog server, it doesn't work until the group and the membership information have been replicated to the global catalog server, where your domain controller reads this information. You may even be sitting at a domain controller that contains this information, but still it must be read from elsewhere.

To summarize, we can make two claims that may sound contradictory at first:

- Universal groups are suitable for small networks.
- Universal groups are suitable for large networks.

The rationale behind the two claims comes from the three benefits of universal groups.

- *For small networks:* Cost is not an issue, and universal groups are easy to learn because there is only one scope with free nesting.
- *For large networks:* Universal groups provide an effective way to create groups with members from multiple sites.
- *For large networks:* Only universal groups have the scope to take members from different domains and to be assigned permissions for resources in different domains (see Figure 3.35).

The first benefit (for small networks) means that you would use only universal groups. The other two benefits (for large networks) means that you would use universal groups occasionally in addition to global and domain local groups.

NOTE   If you removed the universal group from Figure 3.35, you could achieve the same networking result. It would be very cumbersome to do so, however. You would need 9 (3 × 3) direct memberships from the global groups to the domain local groups. Or, with 17 domains, you would need 289 (17 × 17) direct memberships.

THREE GROUP STRATEGIES

There are three basic approaches to organizing groups according to scope, as Figure 3.36 illustrates.

- *Use only global and domain local groups.* If you feel comfortable with the two levels of groups that global and domain local groups provide (most likely from earlier Windows NT experience), you could use this as your group strategy. You either have just one domain or maybe a few of them.

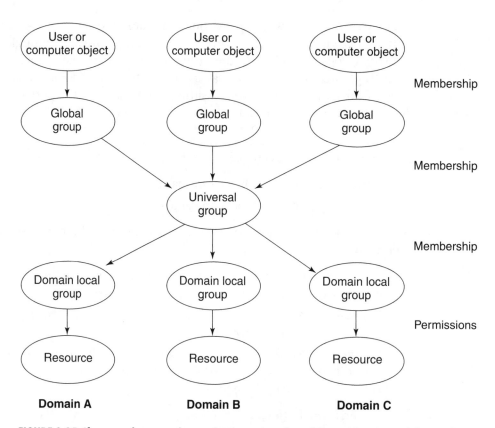

FIGURE 3.35 If you need a group that can have members from different domains and that can be given permissions for resources in different domains, your only choice is a universal group.

- *Use only universal groups.* If you have only one domain and you don't want to learn and think about different group scopes or levels, you will do fine with using just universal groups. You can use one level of groups between users and resources, without group nesting. Or you can put some groups in other groups to have a little nesting. Whether or not you develop logical levels for your groups is your choice. Of course, there are always some predefined global and local groups.

- *Use all three scopes.* If you have multiple domains (and perhaps sites), you probably need all three group scopes. You'll mostly use global and domain local groups because they don't have the extra "cost." In this strategy, you use universal groups only when you need a group with members from different domains (perhaps in different sites) and when you want to assign permissions for resources in different domains.

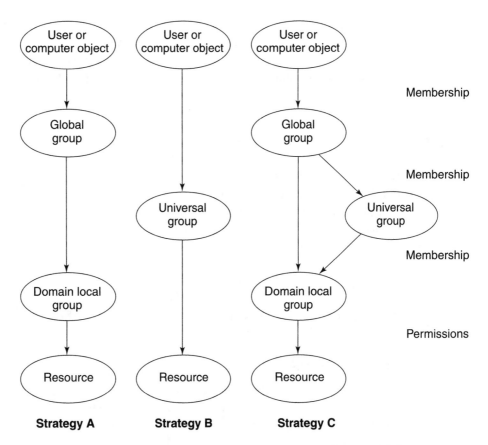

FIGURE 3.36 Depending on your network's size and needs, you can choose one of three group scope use strategies.

We have a few final comments about group usage before we move on to the next section.

- Don't get carried away with group nesting. If you have more than three levels, you might lose track of your group hierarchy. Too much nesting could easily confuse, rather than simplify, network administration.

- You might want to create a group containing only one person. Active Directory doesn't have a role object class like Novell NDS has, but you could use groups in this sense. Usually one person at a time holds a role, so the group has only one member. For example, if some user is taking care of backups this month, you could put her in a group and give that group the appropriate permissions. When someone else takes over the role, you change the group membership by removing the first user and adding the new user.

- You may want to offer your security groups for users to be used in e-mail, but the names have symbol letters and other conventions that might trouble your users. In this case, you can create a corresponding distribution group with a user-friendly name and make the distribution group a member of the security group.

TIPS ON TOOLS

We use the Users and Computers snap-in often, as a main tool, and there are some helpful tips that we haven't yet covered. In addition, the snap-in is not the only tool available to manage Active Directory objects. Before we conclude this chapter, we'll say a few words about the Users and Computers snap-in, as well as about other means to manage objects.

The Users and Computers Snap-In

We have been using the Users and Computers snap-in throughout the chapter. Here we'll briefly fill in some last few holes.

CHOOSING A DOMAIN

You can connect to another domain by right-clicking the uppermost line of the left pane (Active Directory Users and Computers . . .), selecting Connect to Domain, and then specifying a new domain either by typing its name or selecting it from a list.

CHOOSING A DOMAIN CONTROLLER

Sometimes you want to communicate with a certain domain controller. You can choose one by right-clicking the uppermost line of the left pane (Active Directory Users and Computers . . .), selecting Connect to Domain Controller, and then selecting a new domain controller or typing in a new domain controller's name in the dialog box shown in Figure 3.37.

FINDING OBJECTS AND INFORMATION

The item list of the context menu of the domain object and each OU has a Find item. You can use it to find objects that match certain criteria.

FILTER OPTIONS

The item list of the View menu of the snap-in includes Filter Options. This feature enables you to specify the objects you want to see when you browse various

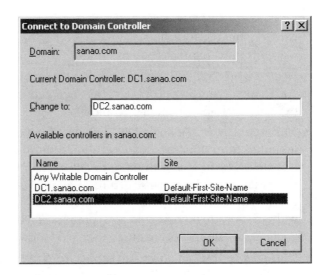

FIGURE 3.37 You can specify a domain controller to communicate with in the Connect to Domain Controller dialog box.

container objects. (For more information about finding and filtering objects, see Chapter 6.)

VIEWING ADVANCED FEATURES

The item list of the View menu of the snap-in includes Advanced Features. If you turn on those features, the user interface will make the following adaptations:

- Each object will show additional tabs in the property pages. We discuss the Security tab in Chapter 4 and the information in the Object tab in Chapter 5.
- You will see additional containers and objects. The System container includes miscellaneous domain-specific objects, such as the DNS records of Active Directory's integrated zones and Group Policy containers. The LostAndFound container includes objects that lost their parent container due to a replication conflict. This is explained in Chapter 5.

Alternative Means to Manage Users and Other Objects

In addition to the Users and Computers snap-in, you also have the following means available to you to manage users and other objects:

- *ADSI Edit:* This tool is part of Windows 2000 Support Tools. While the Users and Computers snap-in shows only some objects and some of their properties, ADSI Edit shows everything. It is not practical for everyday administration, but occasionally you might need it. We use ADSI Edit in quite a few places in later chapters.

- *LDIFDE and CSVDE:* These two tools are part of Windows 2000. They enable you to import and export objects between Active Directory and a text file. We explain how to use them in Chapter 6.

- *NET commands:* Windows 2000 includes about 20 NET commands that were inherited from Windows NT, which inherited them from LAN Manager. You can create batch files with them to automate administration, but they don't understand the directory structure of Active Directory. You can get a list of these commands by typing "NET HELP" (without quotes), and you get help with an individual command by typing "NET HELP *command*." Chapter 11 includes an example of creating a user account with these commands.

- *WSH scripts:* You can download scripts from the Internet or write scripts that will do "anything," including manage Active Directory objects. Chapter 10 and Chapter 11 provide further information.

CONCLUSION

At this point you should have a pretty good understanding of users, computers, and groups in Active Directory and how to manage them. Later chapters address designing Active Directory and give practical examples of how to use the objects discussed in this chapter.

This chapter focused on one tool: the Users and Computers snap-in. Later chapters introduce some Resource Kit tools and explain how to use scripting in user and group management.

This chapter assumed that you have full control over all objects in Active Directory. The next chapter explains how to control access and administrative rights to Active Directory by assigning permissions and user rights.

Chapter 4

Securing Active Directory

The previous chapter's discussion of managing OUs, users, and groups in Active Directory assumes that you always have a right to do what you want. In fact, Active Directory has access control features that facilitate the management of access to various elements in the directory. In this chapter we examine how Active Directory's access control works.

First we briefly review Windows 2000 security in general. Then we give some background for Active Directory access control. After that we move to the main topic, which is how permissions work to protect each Active Directory object.

You have three ways to manage permissions, and we describe each of them in separate sections of the chapter:

- You can manage the permissions manually. In our explanation, we don't just describe how to manage permissions, we also explore the permission mechanisms behind the administrative user interface.
- You can use the Delegation of Control wizard.
- You can accept the default permissions, which we list in a number of tables.

After we describe the mechanisms and user interface, we introduce scenarios to illustrate the kinds of permissions you can use in different practical situations and the way to implement these permissions.

As a final step to discussing permissions, we delve into the underlying architecture. This information is normally presented only to programmers, but administrators can also benefit from it.

At the end of the chapter we introduce *user rights*. They don't control access to individual objects—they control access to the system as a whole.

INTRODUCTION TO WINDOWS 2000 SECURITY

From the very beginning, Windows NT, and consequently Windows 2000, was designed with security in mind. Windows 2000 enhances the security features of Windows NT and introduces new security technologies to accommodate the needs of the current intranet and Internet era. Securing data so that only those who are supposed to see it do see it is a major concern of businesses. Windows 2000 has "A A A" security as a result of the following features:

- *Authentication* checks the user's identity when he starts to use the network. A user tells who he is by typing a logon name and proves this by typing the correct password. Alternatively, a user can be required to insert a smart card in a reader and type a personal identification number (PIN). Authentication may be *interactive* when it takes place in the computer that the user is sitting at. Otherwise, a *network* authentication occurs when the target resource is in a different computer from the one the user is using. There are various underlying authentication protocols such as Kerberos version 5 and Windows NT/LAN Manager (NTLM).

- *Authorization* protects the objects and resources in the network. This process determines whether the user has permission to read, modify, create, or delete a certain object or resource.

- *Auditing* enables administrators to log the usage of objects and resources. This allows administrators to see who has been gaining access to each object and what he has been doing with it.

This chapter focuses on authorization with respect to objects in Active Directory. We also briefly discuss auditing.

Some other features of Windows 2000 security include the following.

- Windows 2000 supports *single sign-on,* which means that a user must enter her logon name and password only once, and then she can use objects and resources in different servers and workstations, even in different domains.

- *Public key infrastructure (PKI)* provides data protection by encrypting the data on disk (Encrypting File System, or EFS) and on the wire (SSL and IPSec) so that unauthorized users on a network cannot read the data. PKI also allows digital signing of documents and software components to ensure they are not tampered with. Another application of PKI is to authenticate users who have digital certificates.

- An administrator can assign and enforce the security settings he chooses to a number of workstations and servers by using *Group Policy* and *security templates.* He can also analyze whether the current security settings of those computers are acceptable. (See Chapter 7 for more information about Group Policy.)

Whether you are administering or simply using a Windows 2000 network, you must have appropriate rights and permissions to do the things you need to do. Table 4.1 lists the typical areas of rights and permissions.

Merely putting people in correct security groups often gives them all the rights and permissions they need. Unfortunately, there are cases that require setting them manually. Therefore, Table 4.1 mentions which utility you can use in each case to control the rights and permissions.

NOTE   User rights may override permissions. For example, if a user has the right to make backups, she can do so even though she doesn't have permission to read the files she is backing up.

TABLE 4.1 Rights and Permissions Needed to Administer and Use Windows 2000

Rights or Permissions	Explanation	Utility to Control
User rights	Control systemwide things such as who can back up the system, log on locally to a computer, or change computer time	Group Policy Editor (accessed via Site, Domain, and OU Properties) or the Local Security Policy snap-in
Permissions for Active Directory objects	Control who can create, delete, or modify Active Directory objects, or even just see their names and properties	The Users and Computers snap-in
Permissions for registry keys	Control querying and setting values in the registry (which includes most of the computer and application settings)	Registry Editor (RegEdt32.Exe)
Permissions for folders, files, and shares	Control the use and modification of files	Folder and file properties in Windows Explorer or any folder window
Permissions for other resources (e.g., printers)	Control the usage and administration of the corresponding resources	Printer properties in Printers folder
Permissions for services	Control service-related operations such as who can start and stop a service or change its configuration	Group Policy Editor or the Security Configuration and Analysis snap-in

NOTE	The utilities mentioned are the typical ones, but there may be other choices. Also, you can control rights and permissions with scripting.

NOTE	Table 4.1 lists rights and permissions that you can assign to users and groups (the latter is usually preferable). In addition, a number of security settings affect the whole computer and are not user- or group-specific. For example, you can disable the Ctrl-Alt-Delete requirement for logon if you don't need the protection it offers against malicious password-capturing programs.

BACKGROUND FOR ACTIVE DIRECTORY ACCESS CONTROL

When any user tries to access any Active Directory object, the system first checks if that user has permission for the access he requested. Depending on the result, the user is either granted or denied access.

Active Directory permissions are used to control access to Active Directory. Administrators obviously need permission to create users and other objects, as well as modify existing objects. End users need permission to read the proper-ties of their own objects and perhaps modify some of those properties. They also benefit from being able to see other users' e-mail addresses, fax numbers, and so on.

Between a full-powered administrator and an ordinary end user, there may be various levels of assistant administrators with partial administrative permissions and rights. There may also be a person who is otherwise an end user, but who can modify some information, such as the address information of all the users in her department.

In the previous chapter about OUs, users, and groups, you operated with full access. In this chapter you will learn and study what the world looks like when access is controlled and limited.

Controlling Access

The permissions that determine who can access an object and in which way (read, modify, create, delete, and so on) are stored as a property (called nTSecurity-Descriptor) in every Active Directory object. That property also identifies the *owner* of the object.

The permissions are defined as a list of individual permission entries. It is up to the owner to specify appropriate permissions for the objects she owns. One of the permissions the owner can give to someone else is Modify Permissions. As the name implies, this allows the other party (in addition to the owner) to modify the permission list. Figure 4.1 illustrates these concepts.

NOTE   A developer could create an object without an access control list. In that case, everyone would have full access to the object. In reality, however, there is always an access control list. If (and when) the list exists but is empty, no one has access to the object.

NTSecurityDescriptor is part of the global catalog. This means that when users search for other users or resources, they can search only on the properties that they are allowed to read, and they are shown only the objects and properties they are allowed to read.

Security Principals

You assign permissions to *security principals,* which are users, computer objects, security groups and well-known security principals. Figure 4.2 shows them on the left. You cannot give permissions to OUs; however, we include it (unattached) in Figure 4.2 in anticipation of Microsoft making this possible in the future. You can give permissions for any Active directory object, as shown on the right side of Figure 4.2.

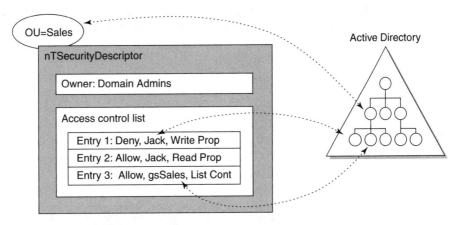

FIGURE 4.1 Each Active Directory object contains the nTSecurityDescriptor property, which identifies the owner of the object and specifies the permissions given to various users and groups. These users and groups are also objects in Active Directory.

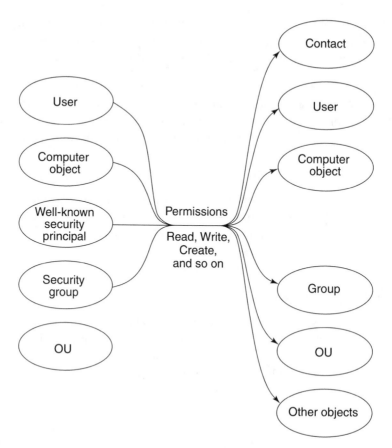

FIGURE 4.2 You can give permissions to four different security principals, shown on the left side of the image, and you can give them for any Active Directory object, like those shown on the right side of the image.

**IF YOU
KNOW NDS**   In Active Directory, only the four types on the left side of Figure 4.2 can have permissions for objects and resources, while in NDS any directory object can have permissions for objects and resources.

As Figure 4.2 shows, you can assign user Jack permissions for group gsSales, group gsSales permissions for user Jack, user Jack permissions for user Jill, or user Jill permissions for user Jack.

NOTE   Remember that the best choice is to assign permissions to domain local groups, the second best choice is to use global or universal groups, and the last choice is to assign permissions directly to users.

No matter which type of security principal gets the permissions, it's always the logged-on user (or a background process running under some user account) who is actually using them. Table 4.2 lists when a user can leverage the permissions given to one of the four security principal types.

IF YOU   There is no concept of security equivalence in Active Directory.
KNOW NDS

Well-Known Security Principals

The term *well-known security principal* refers to fixed accounts that are kind of like users or groups. However, you cannot delete or rename them. Actually, you don't even see them in the list of users and groups (except in the dialog boxes where you give permissions).

A well-known security principal may include a number of users, but you cannot designate who these "members" are. For example, whether a user is a "member" of Interactive depends on the circumstances—he is a "member" if he is sitting at the computer where the resource being accessed resides. Table 4.3 explains Interactive and the other well-known security principals.

TABLE 4.2 Security Principal Types

Security Principal Type	When a User Can Leverage
User	Obviously, when the user is the user himself
Computer object	When the process is using the local System account (more on this in the "Access Control Architecture" section)
Well-known security principal (e.g., Interactive)	When the user meets the condition (e.g., when he is an interactive user)
Security group	When the user is a member of the group, either directly or via other groups

TABLE 4.3 Well-Known Security Principals

Security Principal	Explanation
Anonymous Logon	This account represents anyone who just came to the network and started accessing a server without a username (if anonymous logon is allowed). This is sometimes referred to as *null session*. Note that Windows clients don't let users choose whether or not to use a username. This choice depends on the operation (most operations use the username, but some operations use a null session) and is made automatically in the background.
Authenticated Users	This account includes anyone* who has been authenticated by a valid username and, usually, a valid password. This includes all users that have a valid user account in the forest or any trusted external domain. However, the Guest account is not included.
Batch	This account includes anyone who did the authentication using a special Batch logon type (e.g., the task scheduler jobs).
Creator Owner	Permissions given to Creator Owner are inherited by child objects so that the owner of each existing and new child object (usually the one who created the child object) gets permissions for the child object. If you later change some Creator Owner permissions, the change will affect the existing objects as well. Also, if the owner changes, the new owner will get these permissions. (For more information, see the "Creator Owner" section later in this chapter.)
Creator Group	This choice is the same as the preceding one, except that instead of the owner himself, his primary group is used. Only POSIX applications and Macintosh clients use primary groups.
Dialup	This account includes anyone who logged on using a dial-up or virtual private network (VPN) connection.
Enterprise Domain Controllers	This account includes the Active Directory domain controllers of the forest.
Everyone	This account includes everyone, with or without a username. Anyone can use permissions given to Everyone, even without logging on to the network (if anonymous logon is allowed). Everyone = Authenticated Users + Anonymous Logon + Guest.
Interactive	This account includes anyone who authenticated from the same (local) computer. In other words, the user must be sitting at the keyboard of the computer where the resource is.
Network	This account includes anyone whose authentication request came from some other computer.

(continued)

TABLE 4.3 (*continued*)

Security Principal	Explanation
Proxy	Not used in Windows 2000.
Restricted	Reserved for future use.
Self	This account is a placeholder for the object itself. Giving Self some permission for Jack is the same as giving Jack that permission for Jack. Using Self is especially helpful when giving some permission to all users in an OU for themselves (i.e., giving the permission for the OU and specifying that it is inherited by all child user objects).
Service	This account includes anyone who did the authentication using a special Service logon type. Examples of this are the services running in a computer.
System	This is a fixed account that services in Windows 2000 run with, unless they are assigned to use some other account (see also the "Access Control Architecture" section). This account is also known as LocalSystem.
Terminal Server User	This account includes users that logged on using Terminal Services.

* Here "anyone" could mean either a real user (person) or some process in the computer.

Well-known security principals are referred to as *special identities* in Windows 2000 Help. The reason for well-known security principals to exist is that they allow administrators to assign permissions to these special identities, so that appropriate users can use those permissions. You can also think of well-known security principals as "dynamic groups," because their "member" lists are dynamically determined.

NOTE   You shouldn't use the System account to run third-party services in domain controllers, because that account has so many rights. It is safer to use some other account. However, in member servers and workstations, it's fine to use System for services.

IF YOU   In Windows NT it was quite common to run services with the System account. If
KNOW NT   you got into this habit, now is a good time to get out of it.

NOTE   You cannot extend the list of well-known security principals. For example, you cannot add a "Those who logged on using a smart card" principal.

You can put a well-known security principal as a member in a domain local or built-in group, but you cannot do this using the Users and Computers snap-in. Instead, you must use a command such as

```
NET LOCALGROUP "Print Operators" Interactive /ADD
```

This command would put Interactive as a member in the Print Operators built-in group, allowing any locally logged-on user to create a print queue, for example.

NOTE   You can put Interactive in a domain local or built-in group, or assign permissions to Interactive. However, Active Directory doesn't honor either of these settings—that is, a user logged on at a domain controller cannot use those permissions to access Active Directory. For example, if Interactive is a member of Print Operators, a user who is logged on at a domain controller cannot create a printer object. However, he can create a printer (i.e., print queue) because it is outside Active Directory.

MANAGING ACTIVE DIRECTORY PERMISSIONS

To manage permissions in your Active Directory, you can use the following means (in order of preference):

- *Default settings.* If you can cope with per-domain permissions, and you don't need per-OU (or even more granular) permissions, you will probably do fine with the default permissions. All you need to do is put users in appropriate, predefined administrative groups, such as Account Operators.
- *Wizard.* Use the Delegation of Control wizard to give additional permissions that the defaults won't cover.
- *ACL Editor.* Turn on Advanced Features in the Users and Computers snap-in and start using the Security tab (i.e., ACL Editor) to assign permissions manually.

In this chapter we discuss the three choices in just the opposite order. First we explore ACL Editor and the mechanisms behind it. Then we talk about the Delegation of Control wizard. Last, we list the default permissions for various Active Directory objects. The reason for the opposite order is that if you want to understand the Delegation of Control wizard or the defaults, you need to understand the permissions mechanisms. Those in turn can best be explained with the manual user interface, so we start with it.

Remember that to be able to manage permissions for some object, you need to either be the owner of that object or have Modify Permissions permission for it.

When you start to use ACL Editor, we recommend you proceed in the following order:

- Don't change anything.
- Don't click OK or Apply.
- Learn how the permissions work.
- Learn some more.
- First use a small test network.
- When you finally start making changes in the production network, explore the results after each change.

If you make unwanted changes, permissions may become either too loose or too tight. The former case is a security risk if someone accidentally or deliberately makes use of the excess permissions. The latter case may result in a loss of some functionality.

To correct the wrong permissions, you first need to discover the problem and then know which permissions to restore. To determine the latter, you can see what kind of permissions other similar objects have and proceed on the assumption that those permissions are appropriate to restore.

NOTE   If you remove all administrative permissions for an object (usually by blocking inheritance to it and removing some permission entries), the owner of the object can restore the permissions.

Permission Concepts

Before we look at the user interface for permission management, we'll introduce a few concepts.

- By *special permissions* we mean individual "atomic" permissions. A *standard permission* is a group of special permissions; that is, one standard permission maps to a group of special permissions. The goal is to define standard permissions so that you seldom need to assign individual special permissions. This is analogous to file and folder permissions; however, the distinction between standard and special permissions is not as clear in the case of Active Directory as in the case of files and folders.

- Permission may be for access to the whole object *(object permissions)*, or it may be for access to one or several of the properties of the object *(property permissions)*.

- Permissions can be *inherited* (or they can propagate) so that a permission assigned in an upper level affects all the lower levels.

IF YOU KNOW NT   Active Directory permissions are in many ways similar to the old NTFS permissions in Windows NT because both build on security descriptors, owners, DACLs, and ACEs. However, there are three major differences. First, Active Directory uses a different inheritance model, which is explained later in this chapter. Second, in Active Directory you can set permissions on individual properties. Third, the user interface in Active Directory enables you to deny individual permissions, rather than deny everything, as you must in Windows NT.

NOTE   When you change any permissions, they take effect immediately after the change has replicated to the user's target domain controller. The user doesn't need to log off and log on again for the changes to take effect.

Table 4.4 shows an overview of standard and special permissions, as well as object and property permissions.

TABLE 4.4 Overview of Permissions

	Standard Permissions	**Special Permissions**
Object Permissions	Full Control, Read, Write (each of which maps to several special permissions)	Eleven individual permissions for any object class (e.g., List Contents, Delete Subtree, and Modify Owner) and two more for parent classes (Create All Child Objects and Delete All Child Objects); also numerous individual permissions for one object class (e.g., Manage Replication Topology for domain or Reset Password for user)
Property Permissions	Read or Write permission for a *property set* (i.e., a certain group of properties)	Read or Write permission for an individual property

With these few basic concepts in mind, we turn to the user interface for permissions management.

Anatomy of ACL Editor Dialog Boxes

You can assign permissions via four dialog boxes. You may not need to use them all, however.

- *Dialog box A:* A view of standard and some special permissions for an object and standard permissions for its properties ("Basic")
- *Dialog box B:* A view of individual permission entries, either standard or special ("Advanced")
- *Dialog box C:* A view of special permissions for an object
- *Dialog box D:* A view of standard and special permissions for object properties

Figure 4.3 illustrates how these four dialog boxes cover standard and special permissions for objects and properties.

The four dialog boxes may seem a little complicated at first. After all, you have to select Advanced Features and click the Advanced button to see them. To help

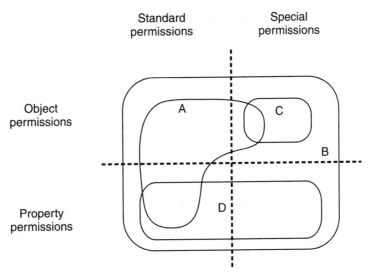

FIGURE 4.3 The four dialog boxes of ACL Editor (A, B, C, and D) cover standard and special permissions, as well as object and property permissions in different ways.

you understand the dialog boxes, we discuss each one and show a screen shot of it in the sections that follow.

We'll mention the inheritance features here, but we'll study them in more detail a little later in the "Inheritance" section.

DIALOG BOX A

Dialog box A consists of four parts, which we have separated with thick lines, as shown in Figure 4.4. Table 4.5 describes each part.

WARNING   There are two cases where dialog box A adds check marks (and consequently, permissions) automatically. First, if you add a name to the list, it probably gets a number of check marks right away. Second, if you check the Read box, for

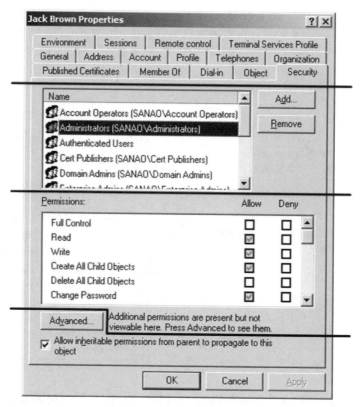

FIGURE 4.4 Dialog box A ("Basic") shows standard and some special permissions for an object and standard permissions for its properties.

TABLE 4.5 Parts of Dialog Box A ("Basic")

Part	Description
Uppermost part	Indicates that you are looking at permissions for Jack Brown.
Second part	Shows all the names (i.e., security principals) that have some permissions for Jack Brown. Each name appears just once on the list. This part also enables you to add and remove names from the list.
Third part	Lists the standard permissions and some special permissions that this class of object may have and standard permissions that its properties may have. (The check marks indicate which permissions the *selected name* is granted or denied.) Obviously, you can check and uncheck the Allow and Deny boxes to change the permissions of the selected name. If a check box is grayed out, it means that the permission in question was inherited from an upper level—you cannot change the setting here. If the permissions include something that cannot be shown in these lines, you will see the "Additional permissions are present . . ." message.
Lowermost part	Neither option in this part is related to any name on the list. Instead, they apply to the target object as a whole (i.e., Jack Brown). The "Allow inheritable permissions . . ." check box dictates whether this object can inherit permissions from upper levels. Clicking the Advanced button takes you to dialog box B.

example, a number of other boxes get checked automatically. If you now clear that Read box, the other boxes won't clear. Unfortunately, there is no Clear All button. Before you click OK or Apply, be sure that only appropriate boxes have check marks.

WARNING   In some cases there are additional permissions present, even though the dialog box doesn't show the "Additional permissions are present . . ." message, so you cannot be sure that the information it shows is always accurate.

WARNING   Some of the permissions are passed on to child objects by inheritance and some are not. Dialog box A may look exactly the same for both cases, so you cannot tell the difference without opening dialog box B.

DIALOG BOX B

Figure 4.5 shows dialog box B. The box displays a list of entries to indicate who has permissions, the type of permissions, and whether each applies to the target object and/or child objects. Table 4.6 describes the elements in this box.

WARNING   If you click OK or Apply in dialog box B, your changes are saved, even if you subsequently click Cancel in dialog box A.

TIP   You can sort the entries by any column by clicking that column header. When you sort by the Name column, you can make sure that you see all the entries of a given security principal.

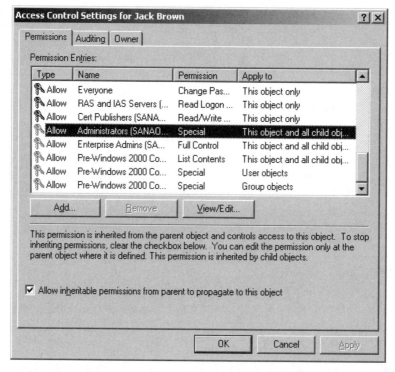

FIGURE 4.5   Dialog box B ("Advanced") shows the individual permission entries as either standard or special permissions. However, the text might display just "Special" without further information.

TABLE 4.6 Elements of Dialog Box B ("Advanced")

Element	Description
Permission Entries	There is one line for each entry. (You may be familiar with the term *access control entry* [ACE] from Windows NT. A "permission entry" here is the same as an ACE.) Note that sometimes one entry is multiplied to several entries (and consequently, lines in the dialog box). This takes place if you check a combination of permissions that Active Directory cannot store in a single entry. For example, if Jack has Full Control and you modify this entry by removing one property permission (using dialog box D), Jack will have at least 50 permission entries after that. They list all other permissions, except the one removed property permission.
Type column	This column is either Allow or Deny, depending on whether you are giving or prohibiting the associated permission(s). The corresponding icon displays either keys or a lock. If the permission entry is inherited, the icon is dimmed to indicate that you cannot make changes on this level. (You can actually edit an inherited permission entry to include more permissions. However, this results in the creation of a new entry.)
Name column	This column contains the security principal that has the permission(s). The same name can appear on the list several times to cover all the different permission elements this security principal has.
Permission column	This column briefly describes the permission(s) given with this entry. If it displays just "Special" or "Read Property," you need to click the View/Edit button to see the actual permission(s). Note that one permission entry may correspond to one or several permissions. In the latter case, however, the permissions must have similar characteristics so that Active Directory can store them in a single permission entry.
Apply to column	This column shows the scope of the permission(s). (For more information, see the "Inheritance" section later in this chapter.)
Description text	This text indicates three things about the *selected permission entry*: if it is inherited; if it controls this object (or just children); and if it controls some child objects.
Allow inheritable permissions . . .	This check box, which is identical to the check box in dialog box A, dictates whether this object can inherit permissions from upper levels.
Buttons	The Add and Remove buttons enable you to add and remove entries. Clicking the Add or View/Edit button takes you to dialog box C. Note that unlike the Advanced button in dialog box A, this button is related to the selected entry.

DIALOG BOX C

Figure 4.6 shows dialog box C, which displays the special permissions for an object. Table 4.7 describes the elements in this dialog box.

DIALOG BOX D

Figure 4.7 shows dialog box D. The elements (fields) in dialog box D are the same as in dialog box C. The difference is that instead of special object permissions, the list contains standard and special permissions for object properties. (We'll study the list in the "Permissions for Object Properties" section later in this chapter.) In the visible area of the list in Figure 4.7, Logon Information and Web Information are standard permissions, and the remaining items are special permissions.

SUMMARY OF THE DIALOG BOXES

As a summary, Table 4.8 lists how dialog boxes A, C, and D show the various standard/special and object/property permissions. Also, this time we have divided

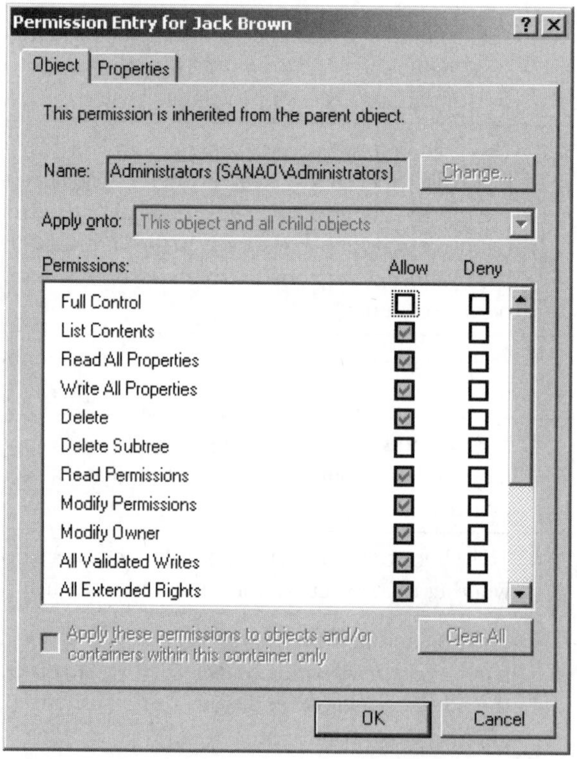

FIGURE 4.6 Dialog box C shows the special permissions for an object.

TABLE 4.7 Elements of Dialog Box C

Element	Description
Name/Change	The "Name" field shows which security principal has the permission(s) shown in the dialog box. If you need to change the owner of this (these) permission(s), you can click the Change button. Note, however, that the original security principal loses its permission(s) and the change you make applies to the selected permission entry only.
Apply onto	This field determines the scope of the permission(s).
Permissions	This field lists all the special object permissions that this class of object can have. The check marks indicate the current permissions, and if the box is grayed out, the permission is inherited and you cannot change it here.
Apply these permissions . . .	If the "Apply onto" field defines that the permissions apply to children also, then by default they apply to the whole OU tree beneath. By checking this box you limit the scope to the first level only.
Clear All	Clicking this button clears all the check boxes.

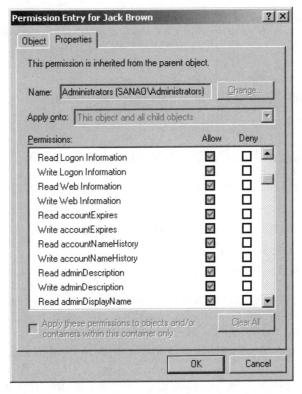

FIGURE 4.7 Dialog box D shows the standard and special permissions for object properties.

TABLE 4.8 Permissions for a User Object by Categories

Type	For	Permissions	A	C**	D**
Standard	Objects	Full Control, Read, Write	X		
Special	Objects	Eleven individual permissions for any object class (such as List Contents, Delete Subtree, and Modify Owner) and two more for parent classes (Create All Child Objects and Delete All Child Objects)	(X)*	X	
Special	Objects	"Extended rights" (e.g., Manage Replication Topology for domain objects or Reset Password for user objects)	X	X	
Special	Objects	Create or delete objects of a certain class		X	
Standard	Properties	Read or Write permission for a property set (i.e., a certain group of properties)	X		X
Special	Properties	Read or Write permission for an individual property			X

* Of the 13 first special object permissions, dialog box A shows only two (Create/Delete All Child Objects). Consequently, we have put the X in parentheses.
** In addition to the X marks in the table, dialog box C shows Full Control and dialog box D contains Read/Write All Properties.

special object permissions into three categories. We don't include dialog box B because it shows all permissions that are specified for an object.

Standard and Special Object Permissions

As Table 4.8 indicates, in addition to standard object permissions there are three categories of special object permissions:

- Thirteen (or 11) individual permissions
- Extended rights
- Create/delete objects of a certain class

We suggested earlier that you first try to use standard permissions, and only if they are not enough, use the more granular special permissions. Even though the "basic" dialog box A already shows some special permissions, you should keep in mind that dialog box A shows only an approximation of permissions, while dialog boxes B, C, and D describe them accurately. Therefore, if you start to define special permissions, it is a good idea to switch to use dialog boxes B, C, and D.

In this section we delve into the permissions that you see on the lists of the dialog boxes and the relationship between standard and special permissions, or among dialog boxes.

We start by categorizing dialog box A permissions for a user object. Remember that each object class may have a slightly different list (see Table 4.9).

The six special object permissions listed in Table 4.9 exist in dialog boxes A and C.

STANDARD OBJECT PERMISSIONS

There are three standard object permissions: Full Control, Read, and Write. You see them in dialog box A and each of them maps to a number of special permissions that you see in dialog box C. Table 4.10 lists these mappings.

When you check some permissions in dialog box A, you will see the corresponding permissions checked in dialog box C. Likewise, if in dialog box C you check a combination that matches a permission in dialog box A, you will see that permission checked when you go back to dialog box A.

NOTE   Some check boxes automatically check others outside Table 4.10. For example, checking All Extended Rights autochecks Change Password. The autochecked permissions are actually a subset of the first checked permission.

TABLE 4.9 Dialog Box A Permissions for a User Object by Category

Type	For	Permissions	Comments
Standard	Objects	Full Control Read Write	You'll see these three permissions for practically any object class.
Special	Objects	Create All Child Objects Delete All Child Objects	You'll see these two permissions for any container object class. Note that user and computer objects are internally containers, but a contact is not.
Special	Objects	Change Password Receive As Reset Password Send As	These listed extended rights are for user objects (and computer objects).
Standard	Properties	Read/Write Phone and Mail Options and so on	These permissions are for user objects (and maybe also for some others).

TABLE 4.10 Dialog Box A Permission Mappings to Dialog Box C

Special Permission	Full Control*	Read	Write
List Contents	X	X	
List Object**	X		
Read All Properties	X	X	
Write All Properties	X		X
Delete	X		
Delete Subtree	X		
Read Permissions	X	X	
Modify Permissions	X		
Modify Owner	X		
All Validated Writes	X		X
All Extended Rights	X		
Create All Child Objects	X		
Delete All Child Objects	X		

* Dialog box C contains Full Control also. It is not a special permission: It shows on the list as a shortcut to quickly give all permissions.
** By default, the List Object functionality is not enabled and the permission is not visible in dialog box C.

THIRTEEN (OR 11) INDIVIDUAL PERMISSIONS

This category of special object permissions doesn't have a name, but each time you see 13 or 11 in this chapter, it most likely refers to this category. Each of the 13 permissions corresponds to one bit in the AccessMask field of a permission entry. This set of 13 permissions may apply to any Active Directory object except two (Create/Delete All Child Objects) that apply only to container objects.

Table 4.11 lists the same permissions as Table 4.10, but now we include an explanation of each permission.

Enabling and Using the List Object Permission

The three visible "read" permissions (i.e., List Contents, Read All Properties, and Read Permissions) are usually enough to cover various read-related scenarios. The fourth (normally invisible) "read" permission is List Object.

TABLE 4.11 Special Object Permissions for Any Object Class

Special Permission	Explanation
List Contents	The right to list names of the immediate children of this object but not their properties or even types (i.e., classes).
List Object	By default, this functionality is not enabled and the permission is not visible in the list of dialog box C. If you add this permission programmatically, however, it will show in dialog box B. You can enable the functionality and make the permission visible in dialog box C (see the explanation of this permission in the text).
Read All Properties*	The permission to read all properties (except the owner and permissions) of the object.
Write All Properties	The permission to write to all properties (except the owner and permissions) of the object.
Delete	The permission to delete the object.
Delete Subtree	The permission to delete a subtree as one operation. However, this only works if the user also has the Delete permission for the root object of the subtree.
Read Permissions	The permission to see the owner and permissions for the object but not its auditing settings.
Modify Permissions	The permission to modify the permissions for the object.
Modify Owner	The permission to take ownership of the object. Giving the ownership to someone else is not possible.
All Validated Writes	The permission to perform any validated write. Active Directory can validate that writes to certain properties are of the correct syntax. Examples of such properties are the DNS host name and service principal name.
All Extended Rights	As the name implies, this permission is equal to all extended rights.
Create All Child Objects	The permission to create child objects for the object.
Delete All Child Objects	The permission to delete immediate child objects of the object.

* You could claim that some of the permissions in the table, such as Read All Properties and Write All Properties, are for properties, not for the object. Also, permissions and owner are technically stored in one property, so being able to modify them is actually being able to modify a property. However, we count them all as object permissions.

To enable the List Object functionality and make the permission visible in dialog box C, you must modify the `dSHeuristics` property (using ADSI Edit, for example) of the object `CN=Directory Service, CN=Windows NT, CN=Services, CN=Configuration, DC=sanao, DC=com`. The property uses string syntax and by default the value is not set. Each character in the value corresponds to one setting, so that "0" indicates a default setting and "1" indicates the alternate setting. The third character from left controls the List Object functionality. In other words, to enable it, you must write "001" (without quotes) into the `dSHeuristics` property.

NOTE   If `dSHeuristics` already contains a value, you should only change the third character from "0" to "1." If the first character of the property is "1," the first/last name functionality of Ambiguous Name Resolution (ANR) is suppressed, and if the second character is "1," the last/first name functionality is suppressed. For more information on ANR, see Chapter 8.

While the List Contents permission allows viewing of all immediate child objects, using List Object allows hiding some of them. If someone doesn't have List Contents to the parent object, List Object can be used to grant him permission to see the existence of individual child objects. That user sees only those child objects for which he has the List Object permission and the remaining child objects are invisible to him.

NOTE   For the List Object permission to work, you must grant it also for the parent object. Consequently, you must block permission inheritance of those child objects that you want to make invisible by removing List Object from them.

The List Object Permission Peculiarity

In a prerelease version of Windows 2000, the standard permission Read corresponded to four special permissions: List Contents, List Object, Read All Properties, and Read Permissions. In the final release, however, Microsoft dropped List Object, so Read now corresponds to three special permissions.

Quite a few Active Directory default permission entries are still based on the old definition of Read, so with the new definition, those entries actually are "standard permission Read + special permission List Object." This will show in the following ways in the dialog boxes:

- *Dialog box A:* Read and "Additional permissions are present . . ."
- *Dialog box B:* Special
- *Dialog box C:* List Contents, Read All Properties, and Read Permissions

NOTE   Dialog box C's display of the "standard permission Read + special permission List Object" entry is incorrect, or incomplete, because it doesn't include List Object (unless you have enabled the functionality with the dSHeuristics property).

Consider the following example. When you create a new group object, Authenticated Users gets Read + List Object default permissions for the group, and this shows in dialog boxes A, B, and C as just listed. If you next give Jack a Read permission for the group, the permission will, of course, show as Read in dialog boxes A and B. In dialog box C, however, Jack's permission (i.e., Read) maps to the same three permissions (List Contents, Read All Properties, and Read Permissions) as the default permission (i.e., Read + List Object) seems to map. The fact that the latter contains a fourth permission is invisible.

NOTE   This peculiarity in the user interface doesn't hurt your permission management by causing any wrong permissions. After all, as List Object is invisible by default, it is also inactive. It is just a slight inconvenience that instead of seeing Read in dialog boxes A and B, you see "Additional permissions are present . . ." or Special.

EXTENDED RIGHTS

Active Directory defines 39 extended rights out of the box. Each of them has a corresponding Active Directory object to define it (as discussed in more detail in the "Access Control Architecture" section).

Extended rights apply to one or more object classes, and consequently, you will see a different list of these permissions in different object classes. Table 4.12 describes the four extended rights that apply to user objects.

Table 4.13 lists the extended rights that apply to each class (excluding the user class).

Contact or shared folder objects have no extended rights of their own.

NOTE   Shared folders have, of course, share permissions and folder permissions, but those are outside Active Directory.

We won't try to describe the meaning of the permissions in Table 4.12 because each of them relates to a certain service or function. To understand the meaning of the permission, you must be familiar with that service or function. Also, the permission names are more or less self-explanatory.

TABLE 4.12 Extended Rights for User Objects

Special Permission	Explanation
Change Password	Allows the password to be changed if the old password is known. In other words, the user can change her own password.
Reset Password	Allows a new password to be set even if the old password is not known. In other words, an administrator can change a user's forgotten password.
Receive As	Not used by Windows 2000.
Send As	Not used by Windows 2000.

TABLE 4.13 Extended Rights for Other Classes

Object Class	Exists As	Extended Rights
computer	Trivial	Validated write to DNS host name, Validated write to service principal name, Receive As, Send As, Change Password, Reset Password
group	Trivial	Add/Remove self as member, Send To
domain	DC=sanao, DC=com	Domain Password & Lockout Policies
domainDNS	DC=sanao, DC=com	Add GUID, Change PDC, Add/Remove Replica In Domain
dMD	CN=Schema, CN=Configuration, DC=sanao, DC=com	Change Schema Master, Update Schema Cache
dMD, configuration, domainDNS	Two previous (DC=sanao and CN=Schema), and CN=Configuration, DC=sanao, DC=com	Replicating Directory Changes, Manage Replication Topology, Replication Synchronization
addressBookContainer	Doesn't exist by default	Open Address List
crossRefContainer	CN=Partitions, CN=Configuration, DC=sanao, DC=com	Change Domain Master
groupPolicyContainer	CN={31B2...}, CN=Policies, CN=System, DC=sanao, DC=com	Apply Group Policy

(continued)

TABLE 4.13 (*continued*)

Object Class	Exists As	Extended Rights
infrastructureUpdate	CN=Infrastructure, DC=sanao, DC=com	Change Infrastructure Master
mSMQConfiguration	Doesn't exist by default	Peek Computer Journal, Peek Dead Letter, Receive Computer Journal, Receive Dead Letter
mSMQQueue	Doesn't exist by default	Peek Message, Receive Message, Receive Journal, Send Message
nTDSDSA	CN=NTDS Settings	Abandon Replication, Allocate Rids, Do Garbage Collection, Check Stale Phantoms, Recalculate Hierarchy, Recalculate Security Inheritance
pKICertificateTemplate	Doesn't exist by default	Enroll
rIDManager	CN=RID Manager$, CN=System, DC=sanao, DC=com	Change Rid Master
samServer	CN=Server, CN=System, DC=sanao, DC=com	Domain Administer Server
site	Trivial	Open Connector Queue

CREATE/DELETE OBJECTS OF A CERTAIN CLASS

In addition to giving permission to create and delete child objects of any class, you can give the permission for each applicable object class separately. For example, you could give permission to create just user objects.

Permissions for Object Properties

In addition to object permissions, you can control who can read and write Active Directory information on a per-property basis.

The permission list in dialog box D (i.e., the Properties tab in Advanced, View/Edit) has the following types of permissions, although the second one may not be present with all object classes:

- Read/Write all properties
- Read/Write various property sets (i.e., groups of properties)
- Read/Write individual properties

The first item on the list (Read/Write all) is actually one of the special object permissions. We will discuss the other two, permissions for property sets and individual properties, in the following subsections.

NOTE Technically, object permissions and owner are stored in one property. However, even if you have write permission to all properties, you cannot modify permissions or owner.

PERMISSIONS FOR PROPERTY SETS

In addition to extended rights, property sets are defined in corresponding Active Directory objects. Table 4.14 lists the ten property sets that exist in Active Directory out of the box. The table also lists the classes to which each property set applies and the common name of each corresponding object.

As mentioned earlier, each property set includes a number of properties. For example, giving the permission Read Public Information is equivalent to giving Read permissions for 34 corresponding properties.

TABLE 4.14 Base Schema Property Sets

Property Set	Object Common Name	User	Computer	Contact	Group	Domain
Phone and Mail Options	Email-Information	X			X	
General Information	General-Information	X				
Group Membership	Membership	X				
Personal Information	Personal-Information	X	X	X		
Public Information	Public-Information	X	X			
Remote Access Information	RAS-Information	X				
Account Restrictions	User-Account-Restrictions	X	X			
Logon Information	User-Logon	X				
Web Information	Web-Information	X		X		
Domain Password & Lockout Policies	Domain-Password					X

Of the ten property sets in Table 4.14, you cannot use the following:

- *Phone and Mail Options.* This property set doesn't include any properties, so checking it has no meaning.

- *Group Membership.* This property set includes one property (member) and it gives permission to add and modify members. However, this property set applies only to users and users cannot have members, so you never need that property set. It doesn't give permission to make the user a member in a group. Once we told Microsoft about this bug, they promised that it will be fixed in Windows .NET Server.

- *Domain Password & Lockout Policies.* This property set applies to class domain, which is an abstract class that cannot have objects in the directory. (The domain objects that you do see are of class domainDNS.) Consequently, this property set is never visible in ACL Editor.

The following seven tables (Tables 4.15 through 4.21) list the properties that are included in each of the remaining property sets. The tables have the following three columns:

- *Snap-in Tab:* Because the property sets are quite user oriented, we list in which tab of a user object you can see the corresponding property when using the Users and Computers snap-in. "N/A" (not applicable) indicates the properties that are not visible in the snap-in. As you will notice, the property sets have nothing in common with the tabs of the snap-in.

- *Snap-in Name:* The field name you see in that tab.

- *LDAP Name:* The attribute name that you use with ADSI and LDAP. If the attribute common name is quite different from the LDAP name, we include the common name in parentheses.

Table 4.15 lists the properties that are included in the General Information property set.

TABLE 4.15 Property Sets: General Information

Snap-in Tab	Snap-in Name	LDAP Name
General	Display name	displayName
Member Of	Primary group	primaryGroupID
Account	User logon name (pre-Windows 2000)	sAMAccountName
N/A	N/A	adminDescription, codePage, countryCode, objectSid, sAMAccountType, sDRightsEffective, showInAdvancedViewOnly, sIDHistory, comment (User-Comment)*

* The last property, comment, is not the same as Comments in the Telephones tab.

Table 4.16 lists the properties that are included in the Personal Information property set.

TABLE 4.16 Property Sets: Personal Information

Snap-in Tab	Snap-in Name	LDAP Name
General	Office	physicalDeliveryOfficeName
General	Telephone number	telephoneNumber
General	Phone Number (Others)	otherTelephone (Phone-Office-Other)
Address	Street	streetAddress (Address)
Address	P.O. Box	postOfficeBox
Address	City	l (Locality-Name)
Address	State/province	st (State-Or-Province-Name)
Address	Zip/Postal Code	postalCode
Address	Country/region	c (Country-Name)
Telephones	Home	homePhone (Phone-Home-Primary)
Telephones	Home Phone (Others)	otherHomePhone (Phone-Home-Other)
Telephones	Pager	pager (Phone-Pager-Primary)

(continued)

TABLE 4.16 (*continued*)

Snap-in Tab	Snap-in Name	LDAP Name
Telephones	Pager Number (Others)	`otherPager` (Phone-Pager-Other)
Telephones	Mobile	`mobile` (Phone-Mobile-Primary)
Telephones	Mobile Number (Others)	`otherMobile` (Phone-Mobile-Other)
Telephones	Fax	`facsimileTelephoneNumber`
Telephones	Fax Number (Others)	`otherFacsimileTelephoneNumber` (Phone-Fax-Other)
Telephones	IP phone	`ipPhone` (Phone-Ip-Primary)
Telephones	IP Phone Number (Others)	`otherIpPhone` (Phone-Ip-Other)
Telephones	Notes	`info` (Comment)
Published Certificates	List of X509 certificates published for the user account	`userCertificate` (X509-Cert)
N/A	N/A	`assistant, homePostalAddress` (Address-Home), `internationalISDNNumber, mSMQDigests, mSMQSignCertificates, personalTitle, postalAddress, preferredDeliveryMethod, primaryInternationalISDNNumber` (Phone-ISDN-Primary), `primaryTelexNumber` (Telex-Primary), `registeredAddress, street` (Street-Address), `teletexTerminalIdentifier, telexNumber, thumbnailPhoto` (Picture), `userCert, userSharedFolder, userSharedFolderOther, userSMIMECertificate, x121Address`

NOTE   The Personal Information property set includes all properties of the Address and Telephones tabs.

Table 4.17 lists the properties that are included in the Public Information property set.

TABLE 4.17 Property Sets: Public Information

Snap-in Tab	Snap-in Name	LDAP Name
General	N/A	cn (Common-Name)
General	N/A	name (RDN)
General	First name	givenName
General	Initials	initials
General	Last name	sn (Surname)
General	Description	description
General	E-mail	mail (E-mail-Addresses)
Account	User logon name	userPrincipalName
Organization	Title	title
Organization	Department	department
Organization	Company	company
Organization	Manager	manager
Organization	Direct reports	directReports (Reports)
Object	Object class	objectClass
N/A	N/A	allowedAttributes, allowedAttributesEffective, allowedChildClasses, allowedChildClassesEffective, altSecurityIdentities, co (Text-Country), displayNamePrintable, distinguishedName (Obj-Dist-Name), division, legacyExchangeDN, notes (Additional-Information), o (Organization-Name), objectCategory, objectGUID, otherMailbox, ou (Organizational-Unit-Name), proxyAddresses, servicePrincipalName, showInAddressBook, systemFlags

NOTE   The Public Information property set includes all properties of the Organization tab.

Table 4.18 lists the properties that are included in the Remote Access Information property set.

TABLE 4.18 Property Sets: Remote Access Information

LDAP Name

msNPAllowDialin, msNPCallingStationID, msRADIUSCallbackNumber,
msRADIUSFramedIPAddress, msRADIUSFramedRoute, msRADIUSServiceType,
tokenGroups, tokenGroupsGlobalAndUniversal, tokenGroupsNoGCAcceptable

Table 4.19 lists the properties that are included in the Account Restrictions property set.

Table 4.20 lists the properties that are included in the Logon Information property set.

Table 4.21 lists the properties that are included in the Web Information property set.

If you have write permission for only some of the properties, the Users and Computers snap-in displays those properties as editable, while other properties are grayed out.

TABLE 4.19 Property Sets: Account Restrictions

Snap-in Tab	Snap-in Name	LDAP Name
Account	Account options	userAccountControl
Account	Account expires	accountExpires
N/A	N/A	pwdLastSet, userParameters

TABLE 4.20 Property Sets: Logon Information

Snap-in Tab	Snap-in Name	LDAP Name
Account	Logon Hours	logonHours
Account	Log On To/Logon Workstations	logonWorkstation
Profile	Profile path	profilePath
Profile	Home folder: Local path/To	homeDirectory
Profile	Home folder: Connect	homeDrive
N/A	N/A	badPwdCount, lastLogoff, lastLogon, logonCount

TABLE 4.21 Property Sets: Web Information

Snap-in Tab	Snap-in Name	LDAP Name
General	Web page	wWWHomePage
General	Web Page Address (Others)	url (WWW-Page-Other)

NOTE   The screen shot in Figure 4.8 doesn't imply that the writable properties shown would make a sensible combination.

PERMISSIONS FOR INDIVIDUAL PROPERTIES

Dialog box D shows a list of properties from which you select read and write permissions for individual properties. Normally only some of the properties of a

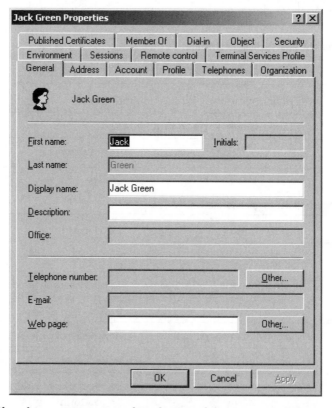

FIGURE 4.8 If you have write permission for only some of the properties, the Users and Computers snap-in displays those properties as editable (white background), while other properties are grayed out.

given class are visible in the dialog box. For user objects, you see about 65 properties of the 207 possible properties.

Each property in the list is shown using one of two names:

- *Display name (such as First Name).* A display name is used if one is specified for the property in the container such as CN=409, CN=Display Specifiers, CN=Configuration, DC=sanao, DC=com. Display names are explained in Chapter 9.
- *LDAP name (such as* givenName). An LDAP name is used if there is no display name for the property.

NOTE   The display name is often the same as the descriptive name that you see in the user property pages of the Users and Computers snap-in, but it can also be different. For example, the display name could be E-Mail Address while the descriptive name is E-mail.

You may find the default list of properties to be unsatisfactory for you. For example, there are First Name and E-Mail Address (Others) in the list, but Last Name and the ordinary E-mail are missing. Also, the default list contains many properties (such as userSharedFolder) that are not visible in the Users and Computers snap-in.

You can modify the property list by editing the file DSSec.Dat, which is in the Winnt\System32 folder. The file is about 12,000 lines of text—it lists the attributes of each class that should be filtered out of the list in dialog box D.

NOTE   You must edit DSSec.Dat on the computer that you use to run the Users and Computers snap-in and ACL Editor.

The following lines show some of the contents of DSSec.Dat (although not consecutive lines):

```
[user]
aCSPolicyName=7
dSCorePropagationData=7
mail=7
mhsORAddress=7
ou=7
siteObjectBL=7
sn=7
```

The header line in brackets (`[user]`) specifies the LDAP name of the class, and each subsequent line gives an LDAP name of the property to be filtered out. You have the following choices to specify values:

- *Property=7:* The property is not included in dialog box D.
- *Property=6:* "Read property" is included.
- *Property=5:* "Write property" is included.
- *Property=0:* Both "Read property" and "Write property" are included.
- *The property is not included in DSSec.Dat:* Both "Read property" and "Write property" are included in dialog box D.

If you want to give permission to read or write e-mail address or last name properties individually, perform the following steps:

1. Make a backup copy of the file DSSec.Dat.
2. Open the file and locate the line `[user]`.
3. After that header line, locate the line `mail=7`. Either remove the line or change the value to 0.
4. After that header line, locate the line `sn=7`. Either remove the line or change the value to 0.
5. Restart the Users and Computers snap-in. Now you should see E-Mail Address and Last Name in dialog box D.

Most of the classes in the file have the following line after the class header:

```
@=7
```

This line specifies that the corresponding class shouldn't be visible in the ACL Editor list of possible "Apply onto" classes. By default, 120 classes are invisible and 22 are visible.

If you once modify DSSec.Dat to your needs, you can copy the new version to the other workstations and servers on which you are going to run the Users and Computers snap-in and ACL Editor.

RENAMING OBJECTS

There is no single Rename permission in Active Directory. Instead, you have permission to rename an object if you have permission to write to certain of its properties.

Recall from Chapter 1 that the name of the object in its parent container is its RDN. Depending on the object class, the RDN is exactly the same as the CN, OU, or DC property (or one of the more rare alternatives). Consequently, if you want to rename an object, you must have write permission to both its RDN property and this other property, such as CN. Also, if you have the Write All Properties permission, you can rename an object.

Giving permission to write to all properties is easy, but giving permission to write to only the CN and RDN properties (to be able to rename an object) is trickier. We explain the process and use contact objects as an example. Contact objects use CN as their naming property, so to rename them you must be able to write to the CN and RDN properties.

Remember that all properties have an LDAP name and some properties also have a display name. Table 4.22 lists both of these names for the CN and RDN properties.

The ACL Editor dialog box D for contact objects has a "Write name" line. You allow writing to the RDN property by checking the Allow column in that line.

The CN property is not visible in dialog box D until you edit the file DSSec.Dat. Because that property has a display name defined, that name will be used in dialog box D, and (after editing DSSec.Dat) you will see the "Write Name" line. Once you have checked it, you have allowed writing to the CN property. Now, anyone to whom you gave permission to write both Name and name can rename the object.

NOTE   If you rename a contact object with ADSI Edit, you only need permission to write to the CN and RDN properties. If you use the Users and Computers snap-in, you also need permission to write to the First Name property. That snap-in tries to write to the First Name property, even if you are changing only the last name.

The preceding example applies to user objects, too. The only difference between contact objects and user objects is that the RDN property for user objects does not appear in dialog box D unless you edit DSSec.Dat.

TABLE 4.22 Names of Object-Naming Properties

Naming Property	Display Name	LDAP Name
CN	Name	cn
RDN	N/A	name

Permissions in Applications

Application developers can write applications that add extended rights to Active Directory. If your company develops or buys such applications, you may see additional permissions not listed in the previous section. For example, an application could add a new "Can decide own salary" permission, which would apply to user objects. Windows 2000 wouldn't use this permission for anything, but the application in question could make use of it.

If the application adds properties to the schema of a forest, those properties will be visible in dialog box D. It is also possible to create new property sets. (For an example of creating a property set, see Chapter 9.)

Applications can launch the four permission dialog boxes (A, B, C, and D), so you may see them as part of some application on your system.

Inheritance

Active Directory uses *static inheritance* for permissions. The word "inheritance" means that when you add permissions for some OU or other container, you can specify that these new permissions apply also to the child objects—that is, the children inherit the permissions from the parent object. You can choose to which types of children the permissions apply and whether they apply only to immediate children or to the whole tree beneath the object.

Static inheritance means that Active Directory copies the permissions to the access control list of each appropriate child object. This takes some processor power while copying, as well as space in the Active Directory database, but the advantage is that when the objects are later accessed, Active Directory only has to check the permissions of the object itself. With *dynamic inheritance,* each opening of an object requires checking the permissions of that object and all its parent objects.

IF YOU KNOW NDS   While Active Directory uses static inheritance, NDS uses dynamic inheritance.

IF YOU KNOW NT   Active Directory has two significant improvements over Windows NT NTFS. First, when you apply new permissions to child objects in Active Directory, these permissions won't completely replace the old permissions (as was the case with Windows NT's "Copy to subdirectories" option)—they just add ACEs to the list. Second, the new ACEs carry a flag that indicates they are inherited. This way, both humans and machines will recognize which permissions are inherited and which are assigned directly to an object.

NOTE   If you add a permission that affects a thousand objects, only the security descriptor of the one parent object needs to be replicated to the other domain controllers. When the other domain controllers receive a new inheritable permission, they copy it locally to the child objects.

You can control inheritance in two ways.

- You can choose per object whether or not an object will inherit permissions. If you choose that the object declines to inherit, there is no way to force inheritance from the upper level.

- When you add permissions, you can choose whether they apply also to child objects, and if so, to which type of children. You can apply the permissions only to immediate children or to the whole OU tree subordinate to the object.

IF YOU KNOW NDS   Active Directory has no inheritance filters. An object inherits either all or nothing.

CHOOSING IF A CHILD ALLOWS INHERITANCE

At the bottom of dialog boxes A (Figure 4.4) and B (Figure 4.5), there is a check box with the text "Allow inheritable permissions from parent to propagate to this object." The default is checked—that is, inheritance is on for that object. If you clear the check box to turn inheritance off, you have to select whether to copy or remove the permissions that were previously inherited, as shown in Figure 4.9.

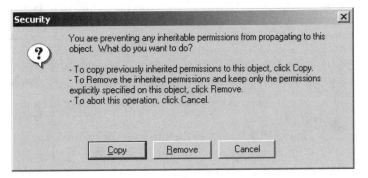

FIGURE 4.9 If you clear the "Allow inheritable permissions . . ." check box, you have to select whether to copy or remove the permissions that were previously inherited.

Normally it's best to click Copy. Then it is easy to browse through the list to remove unnecessary permissions. If you click Remove, you must remember to add administrative permissions for someone before you click OK or Apply.

NOTE   If the result is that no one has administrative permissions, the owner of the object can still restore the permissions.

If you deny inheritance to an object, the permissions above that object in the hierarchy won't pass on to children below that object either.

If you stop inheritance and click Copy and then allow inheritance again, you'll see all the permission entries twice: once for the copy created when you stopped inheritance and once for the permission that is now inherited again.

CHOOSING IF A PARENT WANTS A CHILD TO INHERIT

Each time you define a permission entry for an object, you also decide if it will affect children (provided, of course, that the children allow it to affect). You have four choices for the scope of the entry (in parentheses is the text that you see in the user interface).

- It will affect the object only ("This object only").
- It will affect the children only ("Child objects only").
- It will affect both the object and children ("This object and all child objects").
- It will affect one type of child only (e.g., "User objects").

NOTE   When setting permissions for a user object, for example, you could choose inheritance of permissions by 20 child classes, such as Site Link object or Printer object. However, none of those classes can be a child of a user, so choosing them has no meaning.

By default, inheritance in the last three cases is for the whole tree beneath. If you want to limit the inheritance to the immediate children only, you can check the "Apply these permissions to objects and/or containers within this container only" box.

Figure 4.10 illustrates the inheritance choices.

When you add permissions in dialog box A, they default to "This object only." Also, you cannot see or control inheritance in that dialog box. When you add permissions in dialog box B, the default is "This object and all child objects."

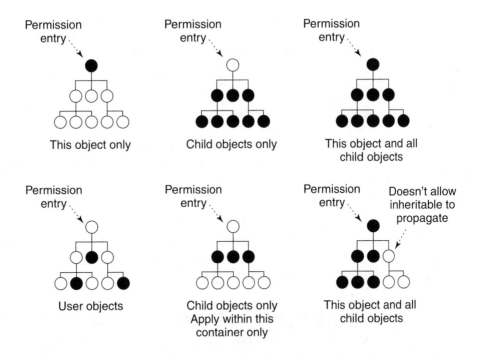

FIGURE 4.10 Various inheritance options enable you to define which objects (filled circles) inherit a permission entry.

NOTE   As soon as permissions are something other than "This object only," they might not show in dialog box A. There is perhaps just the text "Additional permissions are present . . .".

Ownership

Each Active Directory object has an owner. She can always control the permissions for her object. That is, she can decide who can access that object and in what way. Of course, anyone who has the Modify Permissions permission can control permissions, too.

By default, the owner is the user who created the object. However

- If the creator is a member of Domain Admins, that group is the owner.

- If the creator is not a member of Domain Admins, but is a member of Administrators, the latter group is the owner.

You may take ownership of an object if either of the following is true:

- You have the Modify Owner permission (which is also part of Full Control).
- You have the user right to "Take ownership of files or other objects," which by default the Administrators group has.

NOTE   It is possible that different domain controllers have different settings for user rights. If this is the case, whether you can take ownership or not depends on which domain controller you are connected to.

When a normal user changes ownership of an object, he becomes the new owner (i.e., he "takes ownership"), but an administrator can choose whether he or the group Administrators becomes the new owner (see Figure 4.11).

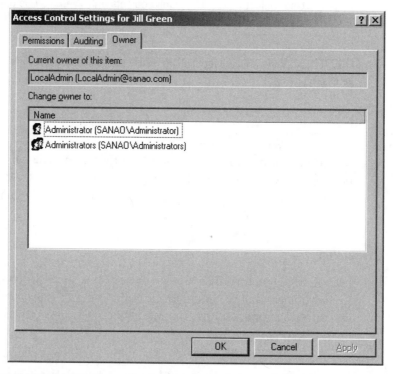

FIGURE 4.11 An administrator can choose whether to take ownership himself or to give it to the group Administrators.

Giving the ownership to someone else is not possible (except for an administrator to the group Administrators). This ensures that an administrator cannot take ownership from some user, access the object, and then give the ownership back before the original owner notices anything.

CREATOR OWNER

One of the well-known security principals is Creator Owner. If you assign permissions to this security principal, those permissions will be inherited in a special way. That is, any present or future owner of a present or future child object can use those permissions on that child object. Figure 4.12 illustrates the following example:

- First you assign the Write All Properties permission to Creator Owner for OU=Sales, DC=sanao, DC=com.

- If you specify that the permission should apply to "This object only" or "This object and all child objects," Active Directory will change that to "Child objects only." However, you could specify that the permissions apply only to some objects, such as users, or only to immediate children.

- Now Jack creates a user called CN=Helen, OU=Sales, DC=sanao, DC=com. Jack is not an administrator, so he becomes the owner of Helen.

- The Creator Owner entry that was created three steps earlier will cause two inherited permission entries for the Helen object. The first entry is the Write All Properties permission to Jack, applying to "This object only." The second entry is the Write All Properties permission to Creator Owner, applying to "Child objects only."

If the ownership changes, the new owner will get the Creator Owner permissions and the old owner will lose them.

How Permissions Accumulate

Active Directory permissions are cumulative. For a given user, Windows 2000 sums up all the permissions granted to him directly, permission granted to the groups he belongs to (either directly or indirectly), and permissions granted to the well-known security principals that apply to him.

For a target object, Windows 2000 sums up permissions assigned for that object, as well as all the permissions that affect the object by inheritance. The exception to this normal rule of accumulation is the set of Deny permissions. They usually take precedence over Allow permissions, as described in the following section.

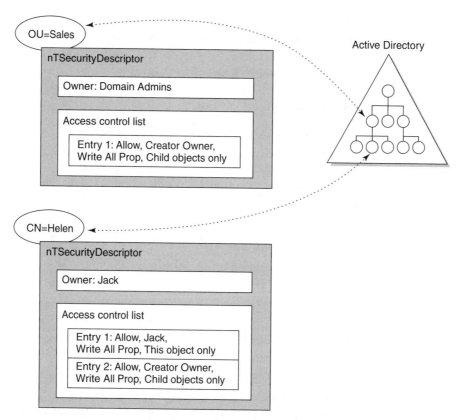

FIGURE 4.12 Permissions given to Creator Owner (for `OU=Sales`) cause two inherited permission entries to appear for child objects (`CN=Helen`).

Deny Permissions and the Ordering of Permission Entries

When someone tries to access an Active Directory object (or another protected object such as a file on disk), a Windows 2000 component called the security reference monitor (SRM) evaluates whether the requested access should be allowed or denied. As the SRM performs its duty, it steps through the list of permission entries starting from the beginning. As soon as it finds enough entries to determine that the access should be denied or allowed, it stops walking the list and returns the result. This means that the order of the permission entries dictates what the effective permissions actually are.

The order of the entries in the list is as follows:

1. Noninherited Deny entries

2. Noninherited Allow entries

3. Inherited Deny entries

4. Inherited Allow entries

Consequently, Deny permissions take precedence over Allow permissions, except that inherited Deny permissions don't take precedence over noninherited Allow permissions.

You can use Deny entries for two main purposes.

- You can allow certain permissions to a broad set of users (i.e., a group) and then exclude a narrower set of users (i.e., another group or an individual user) from getting those permissions.

- You can allow "almost all permissions." For example, if you need to allow writing almost all properties, you can "allow all" in one permission entry and then "deny one or two" in another entry.

If you tried to implement the latter scenario without Deny entries, you might get quite a few permission entries. For example, if you first give Write All Properties

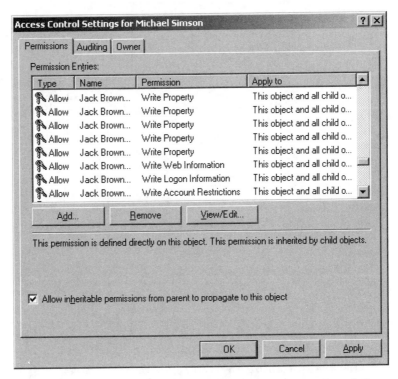

FIGURE 4.13 Deselecting a permission for one property generates a separate permission entry for all remaining properties.

to Jack and then deselect one of the properties, ACL Editor would generate over 60 Write Property entries and 9 property set entries (see Figure 4.13).

Using Deny entries for either of the aforementioned purposes leads to a smaller number of permission entries than not using Deny entries. This has the following two advantages:

- Permission management is easier.
- Performance is better because Active Directory has fewer entries to evaluate (see the next section about permission performance).

Figure 4.14 shows how to allow "all but one property." The fifth entry on the list grants Jack permission to write to any property, but the first entry denies writing to one of the properties. Deny entries are ordered to be the first in the list. That way they (except the inherited Deny entries) override any Allow entries when the permissions are evaluated.

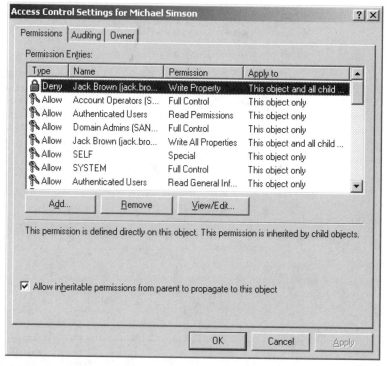

FIGURE 4.14 The better way to deny permission to a single property is to use a Deny permission entry. The first entry in the figure overrides the fifth entry.

NOTE   You can sort the entries freely in the user interface by clicking any of the column headers. This doesn't affect the internal storage order, which causes Deny permissions to override Allow permissions.

Permission Performance

You should avoid a large number of permission entries for an object. Having fewer entries has three advantages.

- The directory database requires less space.
- Accessing Active Directory is faster, because it needs to evaluate fewer entries when determining whether to allow access to a user.
- Accessing Active Directory is faster because more objects fit in the domain controller cache, so fewer objects need to be read from disk.

Microsoft Knowledge Base article Q271876 lists several ways to reduce the number of permission entries. At this point in the chapter, they should all be quite obvious. We include them here (although expressed a little differently) because they nicely sum up this discussion of permissions.

We listed the 13 (or 11) individual permissions earlier in this chapter. Any combination of them can be stored in one 32-bit number and, consequently, in a single permission entry. This includes the standard permissions Full Control, Read, and Write, as well as any custom combination you select.

The number of permission entries will be larger if you specify certain properties, child object types, or extended rights instead of just granting permissions to all of them.

- When granting read and/or write permission to all properties, you can cover all properties with one permission entry (along with the other 11 or 9 individual permissions). If this is not viable, using a property set is better than using individual properties (if there is a property set to match your need).
- Similarly, granting create and/or delete permission to all child objects fits in one permission entry. If you need to specify three object types, that will take three permission entries.
- Each individual extended right requires one permission entry, while All Extended Rights is just one entry.

If a permission entry is passed on to child objects by inheritance, it will need space and slow down the permission evaluation of those objects also.

Therefore, you should avoid inheritance of a large number of permission entries in a large OU tree. (The "Access Control Architecture" section later in this chapter offers more background information about what a single permission entry can store.)

NOTE   It is easy to monitor the number of permission entries, because they all show on separate lines in ACL Editor dialog box B.

DSACLS

Windows 2000 Support Tools includes a command-line tool, DSACLS, that allows you to display and modify permission entries. You can list the permission entries of an object using a command such as

```
dsacls ou=boston,dc=sanao,dc=com
```

That object would probably contain about 17 permission entries. The output of the first three entries would look like the following:

```
Access list:
Effective Permissions on this object are:
Allow NT AUTHORITY\SYSTEM                    FULL CONTROL
Allow SANAO\Domain Admins                    FULL CONTROL
Allow NT AUTHORITY\Authenticated Users       SPECIAL ACCESS
                                             READ PERMISSONS
                                             LIST CONTENTS
                                             READ PROPERTY
                                             LIST OBJECT
```

Note that in the third permission entry, SPECIAL ACCESS is the heading and the following four lines list the individual permissions of that entry.

NOTE   In Chapter 11 we present some scripts that list detailed information of permission entries, either on the command line or in Excel. You can also check two other permission-related command-line tools in Support Tools: ACLDiag and SDCheck. ACLDiag enables you to check if a given object's permissions include any of the Delegation of Control wizard's common tasks (discussed later in the chapter) or if the permissions include the schema defaults (also discussed later in the chapter). SDCheck enables you to compare object permissions in different domain controllers to verify that they are replicated correctly.

AdminSDHolder Object

Active Directory contains a mechanism to protect the user accounts that are members of the Administrators or Domain Admins groups. Every hour, the domain controller that holds the PDC emulator role in the domain checks that the permission lists of these user accounts are identical to the permission list of a special AdminSDHolder object. The PDC emulator modifies any differing permission list, so that it will be again identical to the permission list of AdminSDHolder.

The AdminSDHolder object resides in the System container of the domain. By default, this object doesn't allow inheritance and its permission list is somewhat stricter than those in normal user accounts. This way, a lower-level administrator cannot make unwanted changes on the most powerful administrative user accounts.

You can modify the permission list of AdminSDHolder, which will reflect in a while the permission lists of the administrative user accounts. However, we don't recommend you do so.

DELEGATION OF CONTROL WIZARD

The previous section explains how to control permissions manually with ACL Editor dialog boxes, which we designated A, B, C, and D, as well as the permission mechanisms behind them. In this section we introduce an alternative user interface, the Delegation of Control wizard. The Delegation of Control wizard is a shortcut to assigning permissions. With it you can quickly assign permissions for some typical cases, but naturally the wizard offers only a small subset of possibilities compared to ACL Editor.

As mentioned earlier, Microsoft recommends using the wizard as the primary tool for managing permissions and delegating administrative tasks because it is easier to learn than ACL Editor and it is straightforward to use. However, if you are comfortable with ACL Editor, there is no reason why you shouldn't use it.

You can also first use the wizard to get things approximately right and then fine-tune the permissions with ACL Editor.

In short, "delegation" means that you give someone else permission to make changes to some of the objects in an Active Directory domain. Because you can do this either manually or using the wizard, we discuss the various delegation scenarios in a separate section, "Usage Scenarios for Active Directory Permissions." There we introduce a number of delegation scenarios and how to implement them using either the wizard or ACL Editor.

Common Tasks

When you use the wizard, the target for delegation is normally either at the OU or domain level. Consequently, you start the wizard by right-clicking an OU or domain object and selecting Delegate Control. You can use the wizard to delegate either "common" or "custom" tasks. With the first option, you have to define only the following:

- Which group, or perhaps user, will get the permissions.
- Which of the predefined common tasks you want to select. An OU has six pre-defined tasks and a domain has two.

The screen shots in Figure 4.15 and Figure 4.16 illustrate these two selections. Three characteristics are common to all common tasks:

- The resulting permissions apply to the whole tree beneath, not just one object or one level.
- The wizard doesn't stop inheritance—that is, it doesn't create an independent tree.
- All six choices of common tasks for an OU delegate administration only for one type of object.

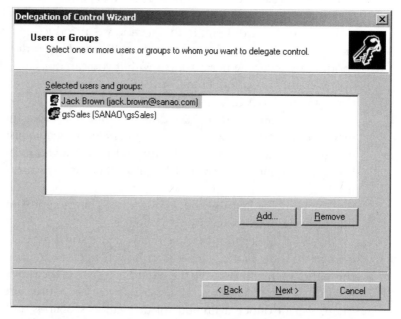

FIGURE 4.15 Your first task with the Delegation of Control wizard is to choose which users or groups will get the permissions.

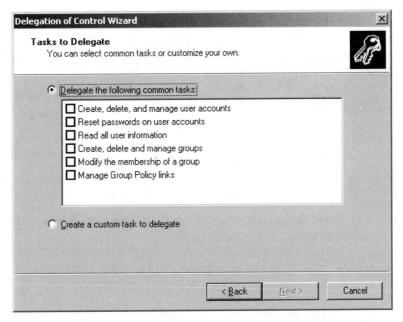

FIGURE 4.16 The Delegation of Control wizard offers six predefined common tasks for an OU. If one (or more) of them is right for you, you don't need to specify anything else.

Table 4.23 lists the permissions that result from delegating each common task.

WARNING   If you delegate group management to some assistant administrators, it's a good idea to advise them to modify group memberships on only one domain controller (e.g., the PDC emulator). All members of a group are stored in one multivalued property. If that member list is modified on two domain controllers simultaneously (within replication latency), one of the two changes will be lost.

If you use the Delegation of Control wizard for a class of container that is not listed in Table 4.23, such as the Users container, there are no common tasks available. Consequently, the wizard skips the common tasks page and goes straight to the custom tasks (see the "Custom Tasks" section).

TABLE 4.23 Delegation of Control Wizard Common Tasks

Present For	Common Task	Resulting Permission Entries	Apply To
OUs	Create, delete and manage user accounts	Create/Delete User Objects	This object and all child objects
		Full Control	User objects
OUs	Reset passwords on user accounts	Reset Password	User objects
OUs	Read all user information	Read All Properties	User objects
OUs	Create, delete and manage groups	Create/Delete Group Objects	This object and all child objects
		Full Control	Group objects
OUs	Modify the membership of a group	Read/Write Members	Group objects
Domains	Join a computer to the domain	Create Computer Objects	This object and all child objects
OUs, domains, sites	Manage Group Policy links	Read/Write gPLink	This object and all child objects
		Read/Write gPOptions	This object and all child objects

CUSTOMIZING THE LIST OF COMMON TASKS

The list of common tasks is defined in the file DelegWiz.Inf, which is in the Winnt\Inf folder. The file is about 110 lines of text—it lists three features of each common task:

- For which container classes the common task is available
- The descriptive text of the common task
- Which permissions are granted if the common task is delegated

The file syntax is relatively straightforward, and once you have finished reading this chapter, you should be able to modify the file to your needs. The following lines show the definition of the first common task that was described in Table 4.23:

```
[template1]
AppliesToClasses=domainDns,organizationalUnit

Description = "Create, delete, and manage user accounts"

ObjectTypes = SCOPE, user

[template1.SCOPE]
user=CC,DC

[template1.user]
@=GA
```

The first two lines after the `[template1]` section heading are easy to interpret.

- The `AppliesToClasses` line lists the classes for which the template is present.
- The `Description` line includes the descriptive text of the common task.

NOTE   The `AppliesToClasses` line in the sample does *not* specify that the common task would be present for domain objects. Microsoft has specified domainDns on the line, while the LDAP name of the domain class is domainDNS. This small difference in uppercase/lowercase causes the common task (as well as three others in the default DelegWiz.Inf) not to be present for domain objects.

The remaining lines specify the permissions that this common task induces and these lines are slightly trickier.

- The `ObjectTypes` line lists the permission entries (two, in this case): `SCOPE` indicates that the first entry will apply to "this object and all child objects" and `user` indicates the class to which the second entry will apply.
- The `user=CC,DC` line means "create children, delete children, where children are user objects."
- On the `@=GA` line, `GA` stands for "Generic All" (which is the same as Full Control) and `@` indicates that the permission entry should apply to the class listed on the `ObjectTypes` line. In other words, the line defines that the delegate gets Full Control to user objects.

The acronyms CC, DC, and GA are defined in Security Descriptor Definition Language (SDDL). See Chapter 9 for more information on SDDL and Chapter 11 for more information on Generic All.

Next, we show two examples of how to add new common tasks. The first sample task enables the delegate not only to reset user passwords (which is a predefined common task), but also to require users to change their password at the next logon. This possible requirement is stored in the `pwdLastSet` property of each user, as further explained in Chapter 11.

```
[template8]
AppliesToClasses=organizationalUnit

Description = "Reset passwords on users and require to change them at
next logon"

ObjectTypes = user

[template8.user]
CONTROLRIGHT= "Reset Password"
pwdLastSet=RP,WP
```

`RP` and `WP` stand for "read property" and "write property," respectively.

The other sample task enables the delegate to unlock locked user accounts. The possible lock state is stored in the `lockoutTime` property of each user, as (again) explained in Chapter 11.

```
[template9]
AppliesToClasses=organizationalUnit

Description = "Unlock locked user accounts"

ObjectTypes = user

[template9.user]
lockoutTime=RP,WP
```

In addition to inserting the preceding lines in DelegWiz.Inf, you must also add the template names (`template8` and `template9`) at the beginning of the file on the `Templates` line.

NOTE You must edit DelegWiz.Inf on the computer that you use to run the Delegation of Control wizard.

Custom Tasks

An alternative to selecting from the list of common tasks is creating a custom task. Again, you start by right-clicking the target object and selecting Delegate Control. Then you perform the following steps:

1. In the first screen, select the group, or perhaps user, who will get the permissions (see Figure 4.15).

2. In the second screen, select "Create a custom task to delegate" (see Figure 4.16).

3. Select that the resulting permissions will apply to all objects or that they will apply to certain object types from a list of 22 object types (see Figure 4.17).

4. Select the permissions to grant (see Figure 4.18).

NOTE DSSec.Dat, which we discussed earlier in the section on per-property permissions, affects also the classes and properties that are visible in the Delegation of Control wizard.

NOTE One permission, Write All Properties, didn't fit in the visible area of the permission list in Figure 4.18.

NOTE The list in Figure 4.18 is different for different object types (classes) that you selected in the previous step.

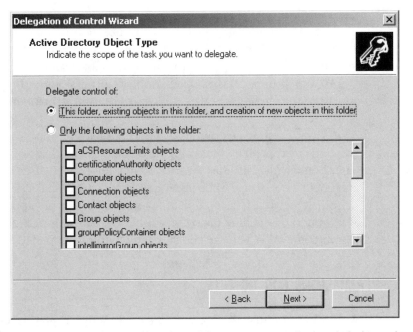

FIGURE 4.17 When you create custom tasks to delegate, you must select to which objects the resulting permissions will apply.

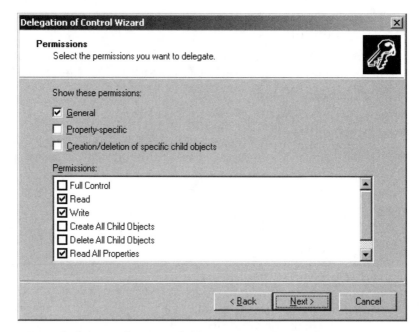

FIGURE 4.18 As the last step of custom task delegation, you select the permissions to grant.

Note that the dialog box to customize permissions to delegate does not include most of the "11/13" special object permissions (List Contents, Delete Subtree, and so on) that appear in dialog boxes A, B, C, and D.

As with common tasks, delegation of permissions with custom tasks always applies to the whole tree. Also, the wizard doesn't stop inheritance in this branch of the tree.

Clearly, creating custom tasks with the Delegation of Control wizard doesn't give you any capability that dialog boxes A, B, C, and D do not offer. The wizard's main benefit (as with any wizard) is the step-by-step user interface, which is a great help when you are performing tasks you are not accustomed to.

After the wizard has completed, you can check which permissions were actually granted by opening dialog box B of ACL Editor. It may be educational to see the outcome. Also, you can check that everything happened as you wished.

DEFAULT PERMISSIONS FOR OBJECTS

We said earlier that it's preferable to use Active Directory default permissions unless you specifically need something different. For this reason, you should know what the defaults are and where they come from.

Sources of Default Permissions

The predefined objects in Active Directory (such as the Users container or Domain Admins group) have the default permissions that Microsoft decided would be most appropriate. Any new objects that are created in your forest after the installation will have default permissions from the following two sources:

- *Inherited permissions.* New objects (except Group Policy containers) allow inheritance, so any inheritable permissions from the parent object apply to them.

- *Class-specific defaults from the schema.* The schema contains definitions for all object types (i.e., classes). Part of that definition is the default access control list for a new object.

Because Active Directory permissions accumulate, the effect of both sources is combined.

Common Features of Default Permissions

The default permissions for objects that are visible in the Users and Computers snap-in when Advanced Features are not turned on have some features in common.

- Almost all objects allow inheritance. The only exceptions are the predefined objects Enterprise Admins, Schema Admins, Domain Admins, and Administrator.

- The only objects that add inheritable permission entries are the domain object and Builtin container. All other objects have "This object only" permission entries (except that they will pass on what was inherited from the domain object).

- The only objects that have any Deny entries are Guest, IUSR_server, and IWAM_server. They deny permission to change the password from Everyone and (redundantly) SELF.

- Authenticated Users (i.e., all users of the forest and trusted external domains) have Read + List Object permission for all other objects except Guest, IUSR_server, IWAM_server, Administrators, Backup Operators, krbtgt, and new users. For the first five of these seven exceptions, Authenticated Users has permission to read all properties, and for the remaining two they have permission to Read Permissions as well as to read General, Personal, Web, and Public Information.

NOTE   The last item on the list of common features of default permissions means that, by default, all users can see who the members of Schema Admins and Enterprise Admins are. It also means that all users can see the permissions for Administrator, but they cannot see the permissions for Guest.

Pre-Windows 2000 Compatible Access

One of the well-known security principals is Pre-Windows 2000 Compatible Access. By default, this group has permissions for most of the objects in a domain.

The member list of Pre-Windows 2000 Compatible Access was determined when you installed Active Directory to create a new domain and chose the option for Permission.

- If you selected "Permissions compatible with pre-Windows 2000 servers," Everyone will be a member.

- If you selected "Permissions compatible with only Windows 2000 servers," there will be no members.

Remember that Everyone includes all authenticated and anonymous users.

If you want to change the choice you made at the time of installation, you can use one of the following commands (deletion is possible also with the Users and Computers snap-in):

```
NET LOCALGROUP "Pre-Windows 2000 Compatible Access" Everyone /ADD
NET LOCALGROUP "Pre-Windows 2000 Compatible Access" Everyone /DELETE
```

Listing Default Permissions

You can use ACL Editor anytime to see what the permissions are for any object. Some other means are DSACLS, described earlier in this chapter, and the VBS scripts shown in Chapter 11.

To give you an overview of the default permissions, we include Tables 4.24 through 4.32, which list the default permissions for the following predefined and new objects:

- Domain object (Table 4.24 and Table 4.25)
- Users container and Computers container (Table 4.26)
- Domain Controllers OU (Table 4.27)
- First domain controller in Domain Controllers OU and workstation in Computers container (Table 4.28)
- New OU in domain (Table 4.29)
- New contact or new shared folder in new OU (Table 4.30)
- New group in new OU (Table 4.31)
- New user in new OU (Table 4.32)

There is a more comprehensive Excel table of default permissions on the Web at http://www.kouti.com/.

TABLE 4.24 Inheritable Default Permissions for the Domain Object

Security Principal	Permissions	Apply To
Administrators	Full Control except Delete All Child Objects and Delete Subtree	
Enterprise Admins	Full Control	
Pre-Windows 2000 Compatible Access	List Contents	
Pre-Windows 2000 Compatible Access	Read Remote Access Information	User
Pre-Windows 2000 Compatible Access	Read General Information	User
Pre-Windows 2000 Compatible Access	Read Group Membership	User
Pre-Windows 2000 Compatible Access	Read Account Restrictions	User
Pre-Windows 2000 Compatible Access	Read Logon Information	User
Pre-Windows 2000 Compatible Access	Read, List Object	Group
Pre-Windows 2000 Compatible Access	Read, List Object	User

TABLE 4.25 Noninheritable Default Permissions for the Domain Object

Security Principal	Permissions
Everyone	Read All Properties
Enterprise Domain Controllers	Replicating Directory Changes
Enterprise Domain Controllers	Replication Synchronization
Enterprise Domain Controllers	Manage Replication Topology
Administrators	Replicating Directory Changes
Administrators	Replication Synchronization
Administrators	Manage Replication Topology
Authenticated Users	Read, List Object
Domain Admins	Full Control except Delete, Delete Subtree, and Delete All Child Objects
LocalSystem	Full Control
Pre-Windows 2000 Compatible Access	Read Permissions

We have divided the domain object permission entries in two tables. The first table (Table 4.24) lists the inheritable permission entries. They affect all objects that allow inheritance and that are of applicable type.

Table 4.25 lists the domain object permission entries for "This object only."

Table 4.28 lists the default permissions for the first domain controller in your forest. The same default permissions apply also to workstations that you add in the Computers container, with the difference described in the table note.

NOTE Even though Administrators is not on the permission list, remember that they have most permissions to every object by inheritance. However, if you block inheritance to some OU and you don't copy Administrators' inherited permissions there, they cannot manage shared folder objects in that OU.

TABLE 4.26 Default Permissions for the Users and Computers Containers

Security Principal	Permissions
LocalSystem	Full Control
Domain Admins	Full Control except Delete and Delete Subtree
Account Operators	Create/Delete Computer Objects*
Account Operators	Create/Delete User Objects
Account Operators	Create/Delete Group Objects
Print Operators	Create/Delete Printer Objects
Authenticated Users	Read, List Object

* This permission is only for the Computers container, not for the Users container.

TABLE 4.27 Default Permissions for the Domain Controllers OU

Security Principal	Permissions
Authenticated Users	Read, List Object
Domain Admins	Full Control except Delete, Delete Subtree, and Delete All Child Objects
LocalSystem	Full Control

TABLE 4.28 Default Permissions for the First Domain Controller in the Domain Controllers OU

Security Principal	Permissions
Domain Admins	Full Control
Account Operators	Full Control
LocalSystem	Full Control
Authenticated Users	Read, List Object
Everyone	Change Password
SELF	Create/Delete All Child Objects
Print Operators	Create/Delete Printer Objects
Cert Publishers	Read/Write userCertificate
SELF	Validated write to service principal name
SELF	Read/Write Personal Information
SELF	Validated write to DNS host name
Administrators*	Read, List Object, Delete, Delete Subtree, All Extended Rights
Administrators*	Write Account Restrictions
Administrators	Validated write to DNS host name
Administrators*	Validated write to service principal name

* In the case of workstation objects in the Computers container, these entries may have a different security principal (such as Domain Admins), depending on who you allow to install the corresponding workstation.

TABLE 4.29 Default Permissions for a New OU in a Domain

Security Principal	Permissions
LocalSystem	Full Control
Domain Admins	Full Control
Account Operators	Create/Delete Computer Objects
Account Operators	Create/Delete User Objects
Account Operators	Create/Delete Group Objects
Print Operators	Create/Delete Printer Objects
Authenticated Users	Read, List Object

TABLE 4.30 Default Permissions for a New Contact or a New Shared Folder in a New OU

Security Principal	Permissions
Domain Admins	Full Control
LocalSystem	Full Control
Authenticated Users	Read, List Object

TABLE 4.31 Default Permissions for a New Group in a New OU

Security Principal	Permissions
Domain Admins	Full Control
LocalSystem	Full Control
Authenticated Users	Read, List Object
Account Operators	Full Control
SELF	Read, List Object
Authenticated Users	Send To

TABLE 4.32 Default Permissions for a New User in a New OU

Security Principal	Permissions
Domain Admins	Full Control
LocalSystem	Full Control
Account Operators	Full Control
SELF	Read, List Object
SELF	Change Password
SELF	Send As
SELF	Receive As
SELF	Read/Write Personal Information
SELF	Read/Write Phone and Mail Options
SELF	Read/Write Web Information

(continued)

TABLE 4.32 (*continued*)

Security Principal	Permissions
RAS and IAS Servers	Read Remote Access Information
RAS and IAS Servers	Read Account Restrictions
RAS and IAS Servers	Read Group Membership
RAS and IAS Servers	Read Logon Information
Authenticated Users	Read Permissions
Authenticated Users	Read General Information
Authenticated Users	Read Personal Information
Authenticated Users	Read Web Information
Authenticated Users	Read Public Information
Everyone	Change Password
Cert Publishers	Read/Write userCertificate

NOTE Phone and Mail Options doesn't map to any properties, so that permission is meaningless. Also, Group Membership has no effect, because a user cannot have members.

NOTE There are three delete permissions: Delete, Delete Subtree, and Delete All Child Objects. Many of the tables mention "Full Control except Delete . . .". Note that there are various combinations of two or three delete permissions in the tables.

Where Security Principals Have Permissions

The preceding tables list which security principals have permissions for each target object. Table 4.33 takes a different perspective and shows where some of the most typical security principals have permissions. It serves as a brief summary and helps you see what it means to be a person, such as a domain administrator or account operator.

TABLE 4.33 Permissions of Typical Security Principals

Target	Account Operators	Administrators	Authenticated Users	Domain Admins
Domain object, Builtin		Three replication rights, Full Control except two deletes	Read + List Object	Full Control except three deletes
Domain controllers (OU)		Full Control except two deletes	Read + List Object	Full Control except three deletes
Computers (container), Users (container), new OU	Create/Delete User, Group, Computer (last one not in Users)	Full Control except two deletes	Read + List Object	Full Control except two deletes (in Computers and Users), Full Control (in new OU)
First DC	Full Control	Full Control except Delete All Child Objects	Read + List Object	Full Control
Administrators, Backup Operators		Full Control	Read + List Object	
Server Operators, Account Operators, Print Operators, Users (group), Guests, Replicator, Group Policy Creator Owners, Cert Publishers, RAS and IAS Servers, Domain Users, Domain Guests, Domain Controllers (group), Domain Computers, and new group	Full Control	Full Control except two deletes	Read + List Object, Send To	Full Control
krbtgt, new user	Full Control	Full Control except two deletes	Read some properties, Read Permissions	Full Control
IUSR_*yourserver*, IWAM_*yourserver*	Full Control	Full Control	Read All Properties	

(continued)

TABLE 4.33 *(continued)*

Target	Account Operators	Administrators	Authenticated Users	Domain Admins
Enterprise Admins, Schema Admins, Domain Admins, Administrator (these four don't allow inheritance)		Full Control except Delete Subtree	Read + List Object	Full Control except two deletes
New computer	Full Control	Full Control except two deletes	Read + List Object	Full Control
New contact, new shared folder		Full Control except two deletes	Read + List Object	Full Control

Changing Default ACLs

The default access control list for each type of new object is part of the class definitions in the schema. If some of the defaults don't meet your needs, you can change them.

In Chapter 8 we explain how the `defaultSecurityDescriptor` property specifies the default for each class using Security Descriptor Definition Language (SDDL). In Chapter 9 we explain how you can modify the class definitions.

You can list all default security descriptors with the following command (replacing `dc=sanao,dc=com` for your forest name):

```
ldifde -f defaults.txt -d cn=schema,cn=configuration,dc=sanao,dc=com -r
(objectCategory=classSchema) -l defaultSecurityDescriptor
```

NOTE   The command shows on two lines because of wrapping, but it is one command.

USAGE SCENARIOS FOR ACTIVE DIRECTORY PERMISSIONS

Generally speaking, you can have two goals when you modify Active Directory permissions:

- *To allow changes to be made.* You give someone permission(s) (i.e., delegate) to make certain changes, so he can manage some objects or properties in the objects.
- *To allow properties to be seen.* You give some end user permission(s) to see certain properties in certain objects, which allows her to use the corresponding information.

For both goals, we describe scenarios and their implementation. However, almost all scenarios relate to the first goal.

In addition to using default permissions, you have two ways to delegate administration:

- Use the Delegation of Control wizard.
- Assign permissions manually with ACL Editor.

You can use the methods independently or you can combine them. You can first use the Delegation of Control wizard to set some permissions and then adjust the permissions by hand with ACL Editor.

General Practices

Before we get to the actual scenarios, we list some general practices.

- It is usually best to assign permissions to a group instead of an individual user. This is true even if only one user would be a member of that group. For example, if you want to give someone permissions to manage the Sales OU, you could create a group gsSalesAdministrator, give it the permissions, and assign that one user as a member. This group would act as a role. It is more self-documenting to use this role in the permission lists instead of a username. Also, if the role owner changes, it is easy to put a new user in the group.
- If you delegate the administration of an OU to some role group, you might want to create that group in some OU other than the one being delegated. This makes sure that the assistant administrator cannot put other people in that group or accidentally delete it.
- Microsoft recommends that you establish comprehensive security groups and assign permissions to the groups before creating users.
- You can delegate administration of some groups to the managers of those groups.
- Remember that someone should have full control for every object.

- Because you cannot force inheritance, as soon as you give someone permission to modify permissions, he can block your access to that object. This is also true for any OU or other object that someone else has created. Fortunately, you can still take ownership and then restore your own permissions.

Delegation Scenarios (to Make Changes)

Because you can set permissions per OU, per object, and even per property, you may delegate administration of all or part of your OU tree. This means that you give total or partial control of all or some objects in all or some of your OUs to (an) assistant administrator(s). Such delegation can have the following benefits:

- It reduces your workload.
- Often people who are close to end users and resources have more information about them and are thus better able to manage them.
- End users probably get better service when they can turn to someone who is near them (and in the same time zone, if your network spans time zones).

When delegating, you need to implement proper naming and other standards as well as give enough information about the task, the technology, and the company policies to whomever you delegate something.

To make the possibilities clear, we offer several scenarios of delegation, followed by an example of each.

- *Scenario A: Delegating an OU Tree with Possible Blocking.* An assistant administrator gets total control over some OU and the whole tree beneath it. He could block you out (or maybe he did already).
- *Scenario B: Delegating an OU Tree without Blocking.* An assistant administrator gets total control over some OU and the whole tree beneath it. She cannot block you out.
- *Scenario C: Delegating Administration of Group Policy.* Even if you delegate the administration of an OU to an assistant administrator, he cannot create or manage group policies. Assigning permission to create or manage group policies is a separate task.
- *Scenario D: Delegating Administration of Certain Objects (Such as Users).* An assistant administrator gets total control over some object type, either in one OU or in the whole domain. For example, he could be responsible for managing user objects or printers.
- *Scenario E: Delegating Control over Noninformational Aspects.* An assistant administrator gets control over some noninformational aspects of users or other objects. For example, she could manage the members of some group or reset user passwords when needed.

- *Scenario F: Delegating Cross-Object Permissions to Carry Out a Function.* Some support people manage users' workstations. They may need cross-object type permissions to carry out their job functions, possibly for computer objects and group policies.

- *Scenario G: Delegating Administration of Informational Properties.* An assistant administrator gets partial control over user objects. For example, a secretary maintains some informational properties, such as address and organization information (e.g., title), for the employees of her department.

- *Scenario H: Delegating Permission to a User's Own Informational Properties.* A user (or several users) is given a permission to maintain all or most of his informational properties. You don't want to give him permission to modify any significant properties.

SCENARIO A: DELEGATING AN OU TREE WITH POSSIBLE BLOCKING

In this scenario you want to give an assistant administrator total control over an OU, including any objects beneath it (i.e., the whole OU tree). With total control, he could remove any permissions that you had for the OU—that is, he could block you out.

First, create a group such as gsSalesAdministrator and assign the appropriate user as a member of this group. He would become an "OU administrator." If you want to control gsSalesAdministrator and the user object of the OU administrator, you can create these two objects outside the OU being delegated.

Then, use the Delegation of Control wizard on the OU to create a "custom task to delegate," select "This folder, . . ." as the target, and specify Full Control.

An alternative way to accomplish the same goal is to use ACL Editor to create the following permission entry for the OU object:

- Allow / gsSalesAdministrator / Full Control / This object and all child objects

After these steps, the OU administrator should use ACL Editor to perform one or more of the following steps, depending on how independent he wants to be (because you gave him Full Control, you cannot control the level of independence anymore):

- *Take ownership of the OU.* When the assistant administrator takes ownership of the OU, the domain administrators can no longer control permissions for it (unless the assistant administrator lets them have Full Control).

- *Disallow inheritable permissions from parent.* The assistant administrator stops inheritance from the parent container. When ACL Editor asks whether to Copy or Remove the previously inherited permissions, the OU administrator should choose Copy and go on to the next step.

- *Remove unnecessary administrative permissions.* Because the OU administrator didn't remove permissions in the previous step, Enterprise Admins, Domain Admins, Administrators, and Account Operators probably still have various administrative permissions for the OU. The OU administrator should evaluate them and remove unnecessary permissions.

NOTE   The OU administrator might want to keep some permissions that were inherited and remove some permissions that were directly assigned for the OU object. Therefore, he cannot simply choose Remove when he is disallowing inheritance.

WARNING   By default, when a new user object is created, Domain Admins and Account Operators get Full Control for that object. This is defined in the base schema and it will happen even if the OU administrator disallows inheritance and removes all "unnecessary" administrative permissions.

If the OU administrator wants to be really independent and wants to disallow even the automatic permissions of Domain Admins and Account Operators (see the Warning), he has two options.

- Talk to the people who manage the enterprise forest to modify the base schema, so that Domain Admins and Account Operators wouldn't get Full Control by default to new user objects (as well as many other object types). (We explain default permissions in Chapter 8 and modification of the schema in Chapter 9.) If a change is made, it affects all OUs in all domains of the forest, not just the one OU being delegated.
- Modify the permissions of each new object after its creation.

Neither of the proposed solutions is very practical, so the OU administrator probably has to accept that he cannot be completely independent.

NOTE   By default, members of the Administrators group can take ownership of any object. Therefore, you can take the OU back from the OU administrator by taking the ownership, giving yourself Full Control, and removing the administrative permissions of the OU administrator.

The OU administrator cannot create Group Policy objects (GPOs) for his OU because GPOs are stored outside the OU. However, he can create links to existing GPOs.

SCENARIO B: DELEGATING AN OU TREE WITHOUT BLOCKING

This scenario is similar to scenario A in that you want to delegate the administration of an OU tree to an assistant administrator. The difference is that this time you don't want him to block you out. Therefore, you don't want to let him take ownership of the OU object or give permission to Modify Permissions. To achieve your goal, you use ACL Editor to create the following permission entries:

- Allow / gsSalesAdministrator / Full Control / Child objects only
- Allow / gsSalesAdministrator / all permissions except Delete, Modify Permissions, and Modify Owner / This object only

NOTE   Even though the assistant administrator cannot block you out of the base OU, he can create a sub-OU and block you out of there. He can also block your access to any other child object so that, for example, you cannot manage some user account in that OU. If that happens, remember that you can make yourself the owner of that object, after which you can give yourself permissions for it.

SCENARIO C: DELEGATING ADMINISTRATION OF GROUP POLICY

Even if an assistant administrator has Full Control for an OU, he cannot create Group Policy objects (GPOs) for it. You can change this by delegating the administration of GPOs using one of the following two methods:

- *Put the assistant administrator as a member in the Group Policy Creator Owners group.* This way, he can create GPOs for those OUs that he has the Write Property permission for the `gPLink` property. Most likely he will have this permission only for the OU that was delegated to him.
- *Create a GPO for the OU and assign administrative permissions to the assistant administrator for that GPO.* To do this, select Properties in the OU context menu, select the Group Policy tab, and click the New button. Once you have given the GPO a name and pressed Enter, click the Properties button, select the Security tab, and give the assistant administrator the appropriate permissions (as discussed in the next list).

The first option, making the assistant administrator a member of the Group Policy Creator Owners group, is probably easier if you don't want to control how many (and which) GPOs he creates. If you choose the second option, creating a

GPO and assigning the assistant administrator permissions for that GPO, you can give permissions to him in one of three ways:

- *Full Control.* The assistant administrator could manage the GPO, he could manage the permissions for the GPO, and the GPO would apply to him (given that his user account would reside in the scope of the GPO).

- *Full Control except Apply Group Policy.* First select Full Control, and then deselect Apply Group Policy. The assistant administrator could still manage everything, but restrictions or policies in the GPO wouldn't apply to him (see Figure 4.19).

- *Read and Write.* The assistant administrator can see the contents of the GPO and modify them, but he cannot modify permissions for the GPO. In addition, the GPO does not apply to him.

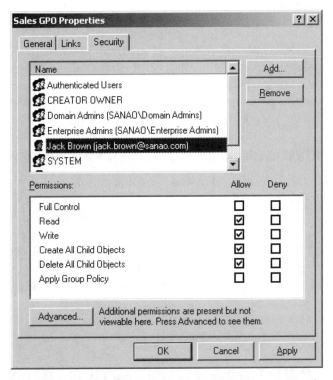

FIGURE 4.19 To give an assistant administrator (Jack) the indicated permissions, first select Full Control (which automatically selects the other five permissions) and then deselect Apply Group Policy. If you just select the four check boxes (Read, Write, Create, and Delete), you don't get the "additional permissions," such as Modify Permissions. You can see the difference in these two methods if you open dialog box C.

You can select any of the three options for giving permissions in dialog box A of ACL Editor.

SCENARIO D: DELEGATING ADMINISTRATION OF CERTAIN OBJECTS (SUCH AS USERS)

In this scenario, an assistant administrator gets total control over some object type, either in one OU or in the whole domain. For example, if you want to delegate administration of user objects in some OU tree to gsSalesUserAdmins, create the following permission entries for the OU:

- Allow / gsSalesUserAdmins / Create/Delete User Objects / This object and all child objects
- Allow / gsSalesUserAdmins / Full Control / User objects

Delegation of administration of user and group objects is one of the common tasks in the Delegation of Control wizard, but you can also do this with ACL Editor. If the delegation is to cover the whole domain, you can just make the assistant administrator a member of Account Operators (if it doesn't hurt that this way he will get permissions for computer and group objects, too).

SCENARIO E: CONTROL OVER NONINFORMATIONAL ASPECTS

In this scenario, an assistant administrator gets control over some noninformational aspects of users or other objects. For example, she could manage the members of some group or reset user passwords when needed. Both tasks are on the list of common tasks of the Delegation of Control wizard.

When we discussed the Delegation of Control wizard earlier in this chapter, we also showed how to add two new tasks on the list of its common tasks: require a user to change password at next logon and unlock a locked user account.

If you would like to delegate administration of some "normal" noninformational properties, you can follow the instructions in scenario G, which explains the task for informational properties.

SCENARIO F: CROSS-OBJECT PERMISSIONS TO CARRY OUT A FUNCTION

In this scenario, some support people need cross-object permissions to carry out some function. For example, they manage users' workstations and thus need permissions for computer objects and group policies. We have covered this, because in scenario C we explained how to delegate Group Policy administration and in scenario D we explained how to delegate administration of a certain object type.

Another example is the need to manage home folders. You would need the following permission entries for the base OU:

- Allow / gsHomeFolderAdmins / Write Property (Home Folder) / User objects
- Allow / gsHomeFolderAdmins / Write Property (Home Drive) / User objects

In addition, you would need to give Full Control to the folder on disk where the home folders would reside. This way, the home folder administrators could create home folders and give permissions to users for the folders.

NOTE You cannot delegate the permission to share folders. Only Administrators and Server Operators (and Power Users in member servers and workstations) can share folders.

SCENARIO G: ADMINISTERING INFORMATIONAL PROPERTIES

You can store address book information and other information properties in Active Directory. It is often easiest to delegate administration of at least some of these properties to non-IT personnel such as a secretary or assistant, whose task would be to maintain this information for the employees of his department. The permission entries that you create to delegate this task resemble the following:

- Allow / gsInfoAdmins / Write Property (Fax Number) / User objects

You could also consider using a property set, such as Public Information, instead of individual properties if you find a set that suits your needs.

SCENARIO H: USER'S OWN INFORMATIONAL PROPERTIES

In this scenario, you give a user (or several users) permission to maintain all or most of her informational properties. You don't want to give her permission to modify any significant properties, such as the logon name or password expiration settings.

Any user can modify her Personal Information and Web Information (Phone and Mail Options is also on the list of permission entries but it doesn't map to any properties). Personal Information includes all properties of the Address and Telephones tabs, so the user might already have all the permissions she needs.

If you need to add permissions, you would create the following permission entry for the base OU specifying the appropriate property:

- Allow / Self / Write Property / User objects

By using the well-known security principal Self, you can get the job done quite easily. An alternative would be much more tedious. You would have to assign Jack permissions for Jack, Jill permissions for Jill, Sarah permission for Sarah, and so on for all the remaining users.

NOTE   You can use Self nicely with OUs but not sensibly with groups.

User Scenarios (to See Properties)

End users can see by default the properties included in the General Information, Public Information, Private Information, and Web Information property sets of other users in the forest. Consequently, you probably don't need to add Read Property permissions to and for them. However, if the need arises—for example, when your organization adds user properties to the schema and wants other users to see them—you can use an almost similar permission entry as in the delegation scenarios:

- Allow / Authenticated Users / Read Property / User objects

If your organization has added some properties to the schema, you may have also created a property set for them. Obviously, you can use this property set in the permission entry shown here.

AUDITING ACTIVE DIRECTORY ACCESS

If you want to see who has done what in Active Directory, you can enable auditing. You may do it for both security and troubleshooting. Enabling auditing consists of two operations:

- Adding appropriate auditing entries, which you do in almost the same way as you create permission entries
- Turning on auditing for all or some domain controllers

Adding Auditing Entries

There is no wizard for adding auditing entries, so your only option is to use ACL Editor dialog boxes B, C, and D. (Dialog box A is not useful in this case, except that you need to use its Advanced button to get to dialog box B.) In dialog box B you select the Auditing tab. Clicking Add or View/Edit takes you to dialog boxes C and D.

NOTE   The Permissions and Auditing tabs both have an "Allow inheritable permissions . . ."
check box. These two check boxes work independently.

Although we call the three dialog boxes by the same names as the dialog
boxes for permissions, they are slightly different. The difference is that with permissions you have Allow and Deny entries, but with auditing you have Success and
Fail entries. An All entry means both Success and Fail. The list of possible permissions (Delete, Delete Subtree, and so on) is the same in both types of dialog
boxes.

Figure 4.20 shows dialog box B with some auditing entries.

Success and Fail entries cause Active Directory to generate an audit record
each time an object is accessed successfully or unsuccessfully, respectively. Different entries define whose access and what kind of access are logged.

By default, the domain object (as well as the root objects of schema and configuration partitions) has an auditing entry that applies to the domain object and

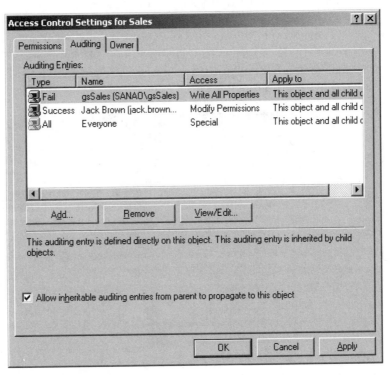

**FIGURE 4.20 In ACL Editor's dialog box B, you can add entries to audit successful access to an
object, failed access, or both.**

all child objects. The entry specifies that all modifications made by anyone (i.e., the well-known security principal Everyone) be logged.

The aforementioned default auditing entries would mean that all modifications to Active Directory would be logged. However, this doesn't happen because by default auditing is not turned on for any domain controller (nor any other computer). In the next section we turn on auditing, which actually starts the logging.

Turning On Auditing

If you want Active Directory to generate audit records, you need to turn on auditing. That setting could be different for every computer, but because you can access Active Directory objects using any domain controller, it makes sense to turn on auditing for all domain controllers of a domain, if any. The easiest way to do so is to edit the Domain Controller Security Policy. You do this by clicking the Start button and selecting Programs, Administrative Tools, Domain Controller Security Policy. This opens a security settings editor. In the left pane, navigate to Security Settings, Local Policies, Audit Policy. The resulting screen, shown in Figure 4.21, offers a list of policy options in the right pane. Here you double-click "Audit directory service access," and then check Success, Failure, or both.

Once you have specified the setting, it will eventually affect all domain controllers of the domain. The Windows 2000 File Replication Service replicates the change to other domain controllers and each of them refreshes the security policy settings every 5 minutes.

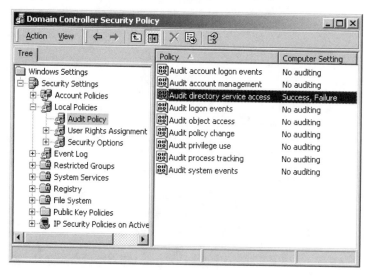

FIGURE 4.21 To audit Active Directory access, you must turn on auditing by specifying Success, Failure, or both to the "Audit directory service access" policy.

NOTE In addition to the Audit Policy node in the left pane of Figure 4.21, there is an Event Log node three lines below it. Event Log contains the log file settings, such as the maximum size for each log file.

NOTE Audit policy is part of Group Policy, which is a complex mechanism to control computer and user settings. In addition to this brief introduction, we discuss the subject a little more in the "User Rights" section at the end of this chapter. Also, Chapter 7 is dedicated to Group Policy.

Viewing Audit Records

Audit records that Active Directory generates are stored in a C:\Winnt\System32\ Config\SecEvent.Evt file on each domain controller. You can view them using the Event Viewer snap-in. One way to launch it is to click the Start button and select Programs, Administrative Tools, Event Viewer. When you select Security Log in the left pane, you see audit records that have been recorded on the local computer. You can see the audits recorded on another computer by right-clicking "Event Viewer (Local)" and selecting a new server name. Figure 4.22 shows some sample records.

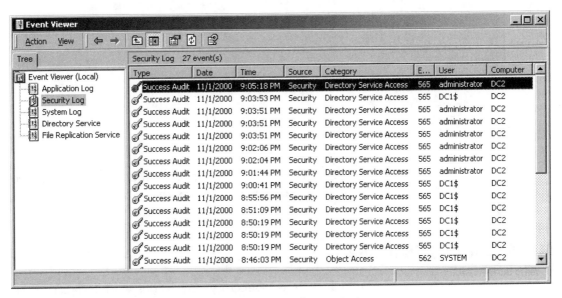

FIGURE 4.22 In the Event Viewer, audit records are shown under Security Log.

NOTE   Each domain controller generates audit records only for events that were originally performed on that domain controller. For example, an administrator (perhaps sitting at a workstation) connected to DC1 creates a user, and that user is replicated to DC2. Only DC1 will have corresponding audit records.

NOTE   When you create a user with the Users and Computers snap-in, the snap-in performs several operations, so there will be several audit records.

In addition to the header information shown in Figure 4.22, you can see a detailed description of each record. The following lines show a description of a record that was generated when Administrator modified the Initials property of Herbert.

```
Object Open:
        Object Server:        DS
        Object Type:   contact
        Object Name:   CN=Herbert Clinton,OU=London,DC=sanao,DC=com
        New Handle ID:        0
        Operation ID: {0,453878}
        Process ID:    244
        Primary User Name:    DC2$
        Primary Domain:       SANAO
        Primary Logon ID:     (0x0,0x3E7)
        Client User Name:     Administrator
        Client Domain:        SANAO
        Client Logon ID:      (0x0,0x6D4D4)
        Accesses              Write Property

        Privileges            -

 Properties:
Write Property
            Public Information
                initials
```

In the preceding lines, "Client User Name" specifies the user who requested the operation, and "Primary User Name" specifies the user who actually performed the operation (by impersonation, as explained in the next section).

ACCESS CONTROL ARCHITECTURE

Now that you know how Active Directory permissions work in practice, we take a further look "under the hood" in this section. Knowing the architecture of access control will help you understand better how permissions work in Active Directory. The basic elements are as follows:

- Each process runs in the *security context* of some user account; that is, the process is using the rights and permissions of that account.

- *SIDs* and *access tokens* help to identify each user and the security context of a process.

- Access to each object is controlled by a *security descriptor.* It contains, among other fields, a *discretionary access control list (DACL),* which in turn contains a number of *access control entries (ACEs).*

- Some ACEs are linked to *extended rights* and *property sets,* each ACE being linked to one extended right or property set.

Processes and User Accounts

Each process in a Windows 2000 computer runs with some user account (see Figure 4.23). In technical terms, the process runs in the *security context* of the

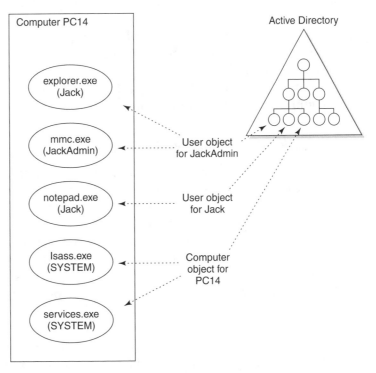

FIGURE 4.23 Each process in a computer runs with a user account and thus is using the rights and permissions of that account. An Active Directory computer object represents the local System account.

account. Most of the processes that correspond to the user's applications run naturally with his account. Many of the background processes, including *services,* run under a special account called *System,* or *LocalSystem.*

NOTE   Services in Windows 2000 can run in their own process, or several services can run in one process. Either way, all services run in the background—you don't see any windows for them onscreen.

A user may start an application with the Run As feature (see Windows 2000 Help for instructions), in which case she assigns some other user account for the application process. Services usually run with the System account, but you can define also for them that they run with some Active Directory user account.

The System account is a local "built-in" user account. It is not recognized outside that computer and thus cannot have rights outside that computer. If you want it to access something in the outside world, you can give the appropriate permissions to the computer object corresponding to that computer. The local System account can then use the permissions assigned to that computer object.

Because each user account can have different rights and permissions, each process in a computer can have different rights and permissions. Often, background services (running in the background processes) have more rights and permissions than the person sitting at the computer. Also, the user can start some programs (such as administrative utilities) with more rights and permissions using the Run As feature if she has an administrative account and password.

IMPERSONATION AND DELEGATION

A process that is serving others can *impersonate* them. This means that when a serving process starts doing work for a client process, a thread in the serving process first switches to use the security context of the client. This way the access check (for authorization) is done against the originating client's rights and permissions, not the powerful rights and permissions of the serving process.

When impersonating a client that is on a different computer than the server, the serving process and the resource being accessed must reside in the same computer. In other words, impersonation can take place only on two computers at the most.

Delegation takes authentication a step further, because now the target of access can be on a separate server, adding a third computer. A typical example is a configuration of a workstation with a Web browser, a Web server, and a database server. The Web browser requests a page from the Web server. In order to construct the page, the Web server needs to get some information from the database server. Because the Web server can make the query to the database with the (delegated) identity of the workstation user, every user can see on his Web page just the database information to which he has legitimate access.

IF YOU KNOW NT   Windows NT supported impersonation but not delegation. The Kerberos authentication protocol in Windows 2000 allows Windows 2000 to support delegation as well. The preceding three-computer scenario is possible if all three are running Windows 2000.

As Figure 4.24 shows, administrators can control if delegation is possible by using the following settings in the user and computer objects:

- *User account of the client.* The setting "Account is sensitive and cannot be delegated" must not be checked (as is the case by default).
- *Service account of the first service.* If the service is running as LocalSystem, the corresponding computer object must have the setting "Trust computer for delegation" checked (as is the case by default with domain controllers). If the service is running as some other user account, that account must have the setting "Account is trusted for delegation" checked.

NOTE   By default, domain controllers are trusted for delegation. If you enable delegation also for a member server, all the present and future services in that computer that use LocalSystem can start impersonating clients when accessing services in other servers. Therefore, it is safer to only enable delegation for a specific user account rather than the computer. A service that would need delegation would run as that user account.

SIDs

Windows 2000 identifies each security principal with a unique *security ID (SID)*. Thus every user, computer object, security group, and well-known security principal has a SID.

In the first three cases, the SID is stored in the `objectSid` property in each object. In the fourth case, the SIDs are "well known," meaning that the values are fixed. Well-known security principals are listed as objects in `CN=WellKnown Security Principals, CN=Configuration, DC=<forest_name>` and each of those objects contains an `objectSid` property to store the corresponding well-known SID.

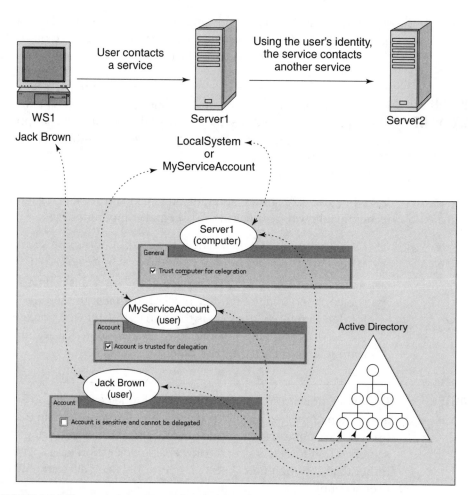

FIGURE 4.24 The service can run as either some user account or LocalSystem. Depending on the choice, the user account or the computer account must have the setting "Account is trusted for delegation"/"Trust computer for delegation" (respectively) checked. The client's user account must not have the "Account is sensitive and cannot be delegated" setting checked.

All access control in both Active Directory and the NTFS file system, as well as other security areas, is based on the fact that those who will access secured objects are identified with SIDs.

SIDs are internally stored as binary structures but they are usually represented as strings that start with an S followed by a string of numbers. A SID of a user account could look like the following:

```
S-1-5-21-1718597718-1078345429-1030254238-1207
```

We can cut the string to the parts listed in Table 4.34.

TABLE 4.34 Parts of a SID

Part	Description
1	Revision level. It doesn't change very often, because it has been the same the whole decade (i.e., for all Windows NT and 2000 versions).
5	Identifier authority. There are six options defined (see Table 4.35). However, there is plenty of room for more: The 48 bits of this part allow 281,474,976,710,656 choices.
21	A subauthority identifier. "21" indicates that this is a normal SID for some account in some domain.
1718597718- 1078345429- 1030254238	These three 32-bit numbers (a total of 96 bits) identify the domain. When a domain is installed, the installation process creates these numbers to be *statistically unique* (based on installation time and domain name). This should ensure that there are no two identical domain SIDs in the world.
1207	*Relative ID (RID),* a 32-bit number. For predefined users and groups, the RID is predefined (its value being less than 1000). For every user, group, and computer object that you create, Active Directory assigns a RID, starting from 1000. It never uses the same RID twice, so if you create a Jack, delete Jack, then create a new Jack, the latter Jack gets a new RID and thus a different SID.

Table 4.35 lists the six options for the identifier authority.

TABLE 4.35 Identifier Authorities

Value	Name	Comments
0	Null SID Authority	You don't need this.
1	World SID Authority	Contains "group" Everyone (S-1-1-0).
2	Local SID Authority	You don't need this.
3	Creator SID Authority	Contains "groups" Creator Owner and Creator Group (S-1-3-0 and S-1-3-1).
4	Nonunique Authority	You don't need this.
5	NT Authority	Contains all other well-known security principals (S-1-5-x), users, groups, and so on (see Table 4.36).

NOTE   Values 0 through 4 are universal well-known SID authorities. In theory they are meaningful also in operating systems other than Windows NT and Windows 2000, if those operating systems only used the same security model.

Table 4.36 lists the SIDs in the "NT Authority" category.

As you can see in Table 4.36, the built-in groups such as Administrators use the same SID in all domains. However, ACL Editor shows them belonging to different domains. Therefore, if you assign SANAO\Administrators some permissions for any object in the schema or configuration partitions and then check the result on a DC of another domain, it would seem that the permissions were assigned to a group such as SALES\Administrators. It would look like the permissions were not for the same trustee, when in reality the SID is S-1-5-32-544 on both domain controllers.

You can inspect different SIDs with the Resource Kit utility GetSID. At the command prompt, type the following:

```
GETSID \\MYSERVER "Domain Admins" \\MYSERVER "Domain Admins"
```

The utility will print the SID of Domain Admins on screen. You need to type everything twice, because GetSID wants to compare two accounts on two servers.

TABLE 4.36 NT Authority SIDs

SID	Description
S-1-5-1 . . . 18	Thirteen well-known security principals (Dialup, Network, Batch, Interactive, Service, Anonymous Logon, Proxy, Enterprise Domain Controllers, Self, Authenticated Users, Restricted, Terminal Server User, and System).*
S-1-5-21-x-x-x-x	Normal SID for some account in some domain. This includes three predefined user accounts (Administrator, Guest, and krbtgt) and ten predefined global groups (Domain Admins, Domain Users, Domain Guests, Domain Computers, Domain Controllers, Cert Publishers, Schema Admins, Enterprise Admins, Group Policy Creator Owners, and RAS and IAS Servers).
S-1-5-32-x	SIDs for "BUILTIN domain," also called *aliases*** (Administrators, Users, Guests, Power Users, Account Operators, Server Operators, Print Operators, Backup Operators, Replicator, and Pre-Windows 2000 Compatible Access). Power Users is not in Active Directory but is in member server and workstation local user databases.

* The meanings of the well-known security principals are explained in Table 4.3 in the "Well-Known Security Principals" section earlier in this chapter.
** Aliases in the BUILTIN domain also use well-known SIDs. However, in this book we call them groups instead of well-known security principals. You can assign members to them, after all.

GetSID is included in the Windows 2000 Resource Kit. If you have the utility from the Windows NT 4.0 Resource Kit, it works, except it may show the second number in a SID as 2, even though the right number is 5.

Access Tokens

Each time a user or background process authenticates itself to some computer (e.g., when a user logs on), Windows 2000 in that target computer builds an access token for that user for that session. An access token contains the following:

- SID for the user account
- SIDs for the groups the user is a member of (either directly or via other groups), including any well-known security principals, such as Interactive, the user "is a member of"
- List of the user rights held by the user or his groups
- Default permissions (default DACL) for newly created objects
- Owner SID—that is, the default owner for newly created objects (it must be one of the user or group SIDs in this access token)
- Primary group SID—that is, the default primary group for newly created objects (it must be one of the group SIDs in this access token)
- Access token source, which is an eight-character string that distinguishes sources such as Session Manager, LAN Manager, and RPC Server
- Indication whether the access token is a normal ("primary") or impersonation access token

An access token describes the security context of a process. Especially the first three items identify "who" this process is and which rights it has. When the process tries to perform various operations in the computer, Windows 2000 uses access token information to determine whether to allow or disallow each operation.

Each process has a *primary access token*. When a thread in a serving process impersonates a client, it has another access token called an *impersonation token,* or sometimes a *client access token.*

An access token is either built or copied. As mentioned previously, the access token is built during logon or authentication to a new server. If the user then starts new processes without specifying a different username, the access token of the starting process is copied more or less identically to the new process.

You may know that changes in group memberships are not effective until the user in question logs off and then logs on again. The reason is that the access token with the group information is generated only at logon time or when authenticating to a new server.

You can see the basic access token information (user, groups, and privileges) with the Resource Kit command WhoAmI. Figure 4.25 shows an example of the command output when user LocalAdmin executes the command.

NOTE Sometimes WhoAmI displays only some of the desired results. For example, it may display the username and first three groups and then quit.

Security Descriptors

Each object in Active Directory is protected with a *security descriptor,* which describes who is allowed to access the object and in what way. A security descriptor contains the *owner* of the object, the *discretionary access control list (DACL),* and the *system access control list (SACL).* DACLs and SACLs in turn contain a number of *access control entries (ACEs)* (see Figure 4.26). ACEs are the permission

```
C:\WINNT\System32\cmd.exe

C:\>whoami /all
[User]      = "SANAO\localadmin"  S-1-5-21-1547161642-1606980848-842925246-1112

[Group  1] = "SANAO\Domain Users"  S-1-5-21-1547161642-1606980848-842925246-513
[Group  2] = "Everyone"  S-1-1-0
[Group  3] = "BUILTIN\Administrators"  S-1-5-32-544
[Group  4] = "BUILTIN\Users"  S-1-5-32-545
[Group  5] = "BUILTIN\Pre-Windows 2000 Compatible Access"  S-1-5-32-554
[Group  6] = "LOCAL"  S-1-2-0
[Group  7] = "NT AUTHORITY\INTERACTIVE"  S-1-5-4
[Group  8] = "NT AUTHORITY\Authenticated Users"  S-1-5-11

(X) SeChangeNotifyPrivilege          = Bypass traverse checking
(O) SeSecurityPrivilege              = Manage auditing and security log
(O) SeBackupPrivilege                = Back up files and directories
(O) SeRestorePrivilege               = Restore files and directories
(O) SeSystemtimePrivilege            = Change the system time
(O) SeShutdownPrivilege              = Shut down the system
(O) SeRemoteShutdownPrivilege        = Force shutdown from a remote system
(O) SeDebugPrivilege                 = Debug programs
(O) SeSystemEnvironmentPrivilege     = Modify firmware environment values
(O) SeSystemProfilePrivilege         = Profile system performance
(O) SeProfileSingleProcessPrivilege  = Profile single process
(O) SeIncreaseBasePriorityPrivilege  = Increase scheduling priority
(X) SeLoadDriverPrivilege            = Load and unload device drivers
(O) SeCreatePagefilePrivilege        = Create a pagefile
(O) SeIncreaseQuotaPrivilege         = Increase quotas
(X) SeUndockPrivilege                = Remove computer from docking station
(O) gation                  = Enable computer and user accounts to be trusted for
 delegation
(O) SeMachineAccountPrivilege        = Add workstations to domain

C:\>_
```

FIGURE 4.25 WhoAmI allows the logged-on user to see her username, groups, and privileges, along with SIDs.

and auditing entries that you have seen throughout this chapter that determine which users and groups may access the object and in what way or whose usage is recorded in audit log, respectively. A DACL contains permission entries and a SACL contains auditing entries.

The security descriptor is stored with each object in the attribute `ntSecurity-Descriptor`. Table 4.37 describes most parts of a security descriptor.

NOTE   As you read about the contents and settings of a security descriptor, you will notice that they correspond to various check boxes and settings in the user interface. If the correspondence is obvious, we don't expressly describe it.

ACE CONTENTS

Because most access control information resides in ACEs, we describe each ACE field and its possible values in Tables 4.38 through 4.42. We start with a summary table (Table 4.38).

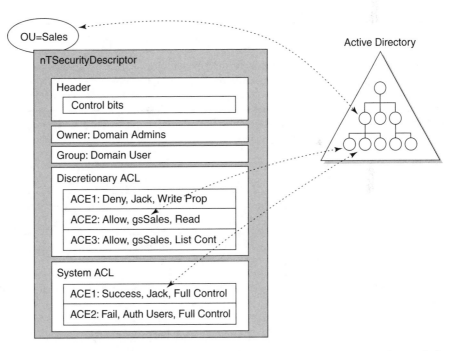

FIGURE 4.26 Each Active Directory object has an `ntSecurityDescriptor` attribute, which is where the security descriptor is stored. The discretionary ACL and the system ACL contain ACEs.

TABLE 4.37 Parts of a Security Descriptor

Part	Description
Header	Contains, among others, the flags SE_DACL_PROTECTED and SE_SACL_PROTECTED. Setting the former flag prevents this object from inheriting permission entries. Setting the latter flag does the same for auditing entries.
Owner	Owner of the object. This identity can control permissions for the object.
Group	Primary group of the owner. Active Directory doesn't use this information.
Discretionary ACL	Contains ACEs, and each ACE is one permission entry. ACEs in a DACL determine who may access the object and in what way. Some of the ACEs may be inherited from above, and some are assigned directly to the object.
System ACL	Contains ACEs, and each ACE is one auditing entry. ACEs in a SACL determine whose usage, and what kind, will be recorded in the audit log. Some of the ACEs may be inherited from above, and some are assigned directly to the object.

TABLE 4.38 Fields of an ACE

Field	Description
Trustee	The security principal to which this entry applies.
AccessMask	A 32-bit number (bitfield), each bit of which represents one permission mostly corresponding to special object permissions of the user interface (see Table 4.39).
AceFlags	A 32-bit number (bitfield) whose bits represent mostly different inheritance options (see Table 4.40).
AceType	A 32-bit number that indicates if this is an Allow, Deny, or auditing entry (see Table 4.42).
Flags	A 32-bit number (bitfield) whose two first bits tell whether ObjectType or InheritedObjectType are present (i.e., not empty) (see Table 4.41).
ObjectType	If the ACE applies to only one object class, property, property set, or extended right, this field identifies which one.
InheritedObjectType	If only one child object class can inherit the ACE, this field identifies which one.

The AccessMask, AceFlags, and Flags fields consist of bits, and each bit has some meaning (although perhaps not all 32 bits have assigned meanings). The idea of these *bitfields* is that you can pack several on/off settings into one field, each of them in one bit.

Tables 4.39 through 4.42 list the meanings of the bits. The hexadecimal values in the tables indicate in which bit each setting is. For example, a hex value 4 in binary is 0100. It is thus the third bit from the right (the rightmost bit is called the *least significant* bit).

TIP   You can try different values with Calculator. For example, choose the Scientific view, select Hex, enter "80," click Bin, and notice that the display shows "1000 0000" (with the space if you have Digit grouping on).

NOTE   The AceType field described in Table 4.42 isn't a bitfield. It's just one of six possible values.

TABLE 4.39 ACE AccessMask Bits

Name	Hex	Permission in User Interface
ADS_RIGHT_DS_CREATE_CHILD	1	Create All Child Objects, Create *certain* Objects
ADS_RIGHT_DS_DELETE_CHILD	2	Delete All Child Objects, Delete *certain* Objects
ADS_RIGHT_ACTRL_DS_LIST	4	List Contents
ADS_RIGHT_DS_SELF	8	All Validated Writes, Validated write to service principal name, and so on
ADS_RIGHT_DS_READ_PROP	10	Read All Properties, Read *property set*, Read *property*
ADS_RIGHT_DS_WRITE_PROP	20	Write All Properties, Write *property set*, Write *property*
ADS_RIGHT_DS_DELETE_TREE	40	Delete Subtree
ADS_RIGHT_DS_LIST_OBJECT	80	List Object (normally not visible in the UI)
ADS_RIGHT_DS_CONTROL_ACCESS	100	All Extended Rights, Change Password, Receive As, and so on
ADS_RIGHT_DELETE	10000	Delete
ADS_RIGHT_READ_CONTROL	20000	Read Permissions
ADS_RIGHT_WRITE_DAC	40000	Modify Permissions
ADS_RIGHT_WRITE_OWNER	80000	Modify Owner

TABLE 4.40 ACE AceFlags Bits

Name	Hex	Explanation
ADS_ACEFLAG_INHERIT_ACE	2	Child objects can inherit this ACE.
ADS_ACEFLAG_NO_PROPAGATE_ INHERIT_ACE	4	Only immediate child objects can inherit this ACE.
ADS_ACEFLAG_INHERIT_ONLY_ACE	8	This ACE doesn't apply to the object itself. The ACE is only for inheritance for children.
ADS_ACEFLAG_INHERITED_ACE	10	The system sets this flag if the ACE was inherited instead of assigned directly to the object.
ADS_ACEFLAG_SUCCESSFUL_ACCESS	40	If this flag is set in SACL, the system generates audit messages for successful accesses.
ADS_ACEFLAG_FAILED_ACCESS	80	If this flag is set in SACL, the system generates audit messages for failed access attempts.

TABLE 4.41 ACE Flags Bits

Name	Hex	Explanation
ADS_FLAG_OBJECT_TYPE_PRESENT	1	The ObjectType field is not empty.
ADS_FLAG_INHERITED_OBJECT_ TYPE_PRESENT	2	The InheritedObjectType field is not empty.

OBJECTTYPE FIELD

Many ACEs apply to only one object class, property, property set, or extended right. In this case, the ObjectType field contains a *globally unique identifier (GUID),* which identifies the target. A GUID is a 128-bit number that is usually represented as a series of 32 hexadecimal characters with some delimiting dashes and curly braces. For example, the schemaIDGUID for user objects class looks like the following:

```
{BF967ABA-0DE6-11D0-A285-00AA003049E2}
```

NOTE   Active Directory identifies each object with an `objectGUID` property. It is not used in this context.

TABLE 4.42 ACE AceType Bits

Name	Value	Explanation
ADS_ACETYPE_ACCESS_ALLOWED	0	This ACE allows access. ObjectType and InheritedObjectType are both empty, so this ACE isn't for a particular object class, property, property set, or extended right.
ADS_ACETYPE_ACCESS_DENIED	1	Same as previous, except this ACE denies access.
ADS_ACETYPE_SYSTEM_AUDIT	2	Same as previous, except this is an auditing ACE.
ADS_ACETYPE_ACCESS_ALLOWED_ OBJECT	5	This ACE allows access. Either ObjectType or InheritedObjectType is not empty, so this ACE is for some particular object class, property, property set, or extended right.
ADS_ACETYPE_ACCESS_DENIED_OBJECT	6	Same as previous, except this ACE denies access.
ADS_ACETYPE_SYSTEM_AUDIT_OBJECT	7	Same as previous, except this is an auditing ACE.

Table 4.43 lists the four cases: object class, property, property set, and extended right. It mentions which property the ObjectType GUID refers to and in which object this property resides. It also gives an example of each case (see also Figure 4.27).

Table 4.43 mentions `controlAccessRight` objects. There is one object for each property set and one for each extended right, so when granting either permission type, the corresponding ACE needs to be linked to one of these objects. They are stored in the configuration partition of Active Directory under the `CN=Extended-Rights` container.

ADDING EXTENDED RIGHTS

Active Directory contains a number of extended rights, such as Change Password, Reset Password, Receive As, and Send As. Software developers may add extended rights to be used with their applications. To be exact, they can write an installation program that adds these extended rights objects (`controlAccessRight` objects) once their customer runs it.

The new extended rights appear automatically in the permission user interfaces of the relevant objects.

Windows 2000 does not use the new extended rights for anything; they are only for the purposes of the application whose installation program created them.

TABLE 4.43 How the ObjectType Field Identifies a Permission Target

Target	Property to Refer	In Object	Example
Object class	schemaIDGUID	Some classSchema object	If a DS_CREATE_CHILD ACE applies only to user objects (i.e., Create User Objects), ObjectType field contains the schemaIDGUID of the user class.
Property	schemaIDGUID	Some attributeSchema object	If someone has permission to read only the Zip/Postal Code of some user, the ObjectType field of the ACE contains the schemaIDGUID of the postalCode attribute.
Property set	rightsGuid	Some controlAccessRight object	If someone has permission to read only the Personal Information of some user, the ObjectType field of the ACE contains the rightsGuid of the Personal-Information control access right.
Extended right	rightsGuid	Some controlAccessRight object	If someone has permission to Reset Password of some user, the ObjectType field contains the rightsGuid of the User-Force-Change-Password control access right. Also, a permission ADS_RIGHT_DS_CONTROL_ACCESS must be included in the AccessMask.

In Chapter 9 we present a detailed example of how to create a new property set. You can use that example also to create a new extended right if you make one modification: You must use the value "256" for the validAccesses property. That value corresponds to ADS_RIGHT_DS_CONTROL_ACCESS, which you saw in Table 4.39, AccessMask bits.

PROPERTY SETS

Some property sets are General Information and Personal Information. Developers may add property sets just like extended rights (Chapter 9 shows how to do this). Typically, a common installation program creates a property set and the properties it contains, and the installation program is included with the application that will use these new properties and property set(s). Many of the base schema properties already exist in some set and each property can belong to only one property set. Consequently, you probably don't create any property sets for base schema properties.

A property belongs to a property set if the `attributeSecurityGUID` property of the corresponding `attributeSchema` object contains the same GUID as the `rightsGuid` property of the `controlAccessRight` object corresponding to the property set. When an ACE applies to only one object class, property, property set, or extended right, the GUID in the ObjectType field links the ACE to the appropriate target. The target is either a certain class or attribute object or a `controlAccessRight` object corresponding to a property set or extended right. In Figure 4.27, the Postal-Code property belongs to the Personal-Information property set because of the `attributeSecurityGUID` link.

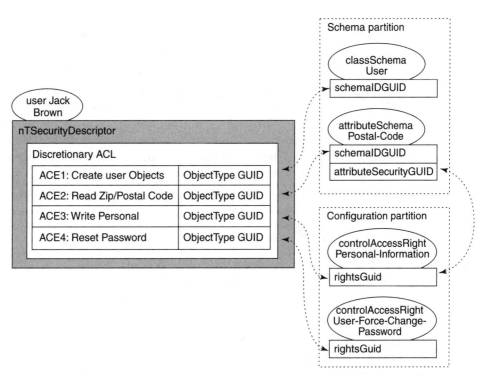

FIGURE 4.27 The arrows in the image represent matching GUIDs. For example, ACE2 applies only to one property, Postal-Code, and this is denoted by including Postal-Code's `schemaIDGUID` in ACE2. In addition, the rightmost arrow between `attributeSecurityGUID` and `rightsGuid` defines that the Postal-Code property belongs to the Personal Information property set. (This rightmost arrow is part of the base schema that Microsoft has defined. It's not part of the security settings that you would define.)

NOTE   One hundred twenty properties (i.e., `attributeSchema` objects) of the base schema belong to some property set. In addition, eight properties have `attribute-SecurityGUID` defined to a value that doesn't match to any property set.

This concludes our discussion about access control architecture and also access control. In Chapter 11 we will present a few scripts that you can use to list or manage ACEs using scripts. Even if you are not interested in scripting, we recommend that you read that section and try out the scripts that list ACEs without changing anything. Doing so will deepen your knowledge of the access control architecture.

USER RIGHTS

Permissions are properties relating to (and attached to) objects such as files, folders, and Active Directory objects. User rights are assignments relating to the system as a whole. An example of this is the right to change a computer's clock setting.

As with permissions, it is best to assign user rights to groups instead of individual users. Also, you might not want to change the user rights of a predefined group such as Backup Operators, but instead create a new group and assign it the needed rights. For example, if your goal is to assign some users rights that they might need to use a certain computer (e.g., "log on locally" and "change the time"), you could create a UsersOfThisComputer group and then assign the two corresponding user rights (and perhaps some others) to that group. Any user that you put in this group obviously gets the rights you want her to get.

User Rights Categories

There are 34 user rights that you can assign to security principals, except computer objects (i.e., users, security groups, and well-known security principals).

NOTE   Computer objects do not need user rights. Each computer object corresponds to the local System account of the computer, and those accounts have all the user rights they need anyway.

Some of the rights can be called "logon rights" and some can be called "privileges." We categorize them as follows:

- Four logon rights
- Four deny logon "rights" to correspond to each logon right

- Seventeen "normal" privileges (i.e., you might actually need these)
- Nine advanced privileges (i.e., you probably won't need these)

In addition to these settable rights, there are some fixed user rights. For example, the right to format hard drives is built into the Windows 2000 program code, so you cannot assign that right to any user or group. If you are a member of Administrators or Server Operators, you can format hard drives.

In the subsequent sections we list the user rights and which groups have them by default for a domain controller. There are also some user rights with the special users TsInternetUser, IURS_server, and IWAM_server, but we don't list them because they are related to specific services and not to Active Directory in general.

For a member server or workstation, the defaults are somewhat different from those of a domain controller. One reason for this is that those computers have the group Power Users instead of Server Operators, Print Operators, and Account Operators. We briefly list these user rights also.

The names of the rights are partly self-explanatory. Also, the Windows 2000 Help system has a description of each, so we don't repeat those descriptions here. Next to each right, we mention in parentheses the application programming interface (API) name for the user right. You may need the API name with some Resource Kit utilities (NTRights and ShowPriv).

IF YOU KNOW NT   The default user rights in Windows 2000 are somewhat stricter than the ones in Windows NT. The Power User level in Windows 2000 corresponds to the User level in Windows NT. In other words, the new User level gives fewer rights than the previous User level.

LOGON RIGHTS

Each time an authentication occurs, it is one of four types: Interactive, Network, Batch, or Service. The four logon rights define who can authenticate using which logon type. Table 4.44 lists these logon rights and their "deny" counterparts and the groups to which they are assigned.

TABLE 4.44 Logon Rights: Default Assignments for Domain Controllers

Logon Right	Admin*	SO	AO	PO	BO	AU	EO
Access this computer from the network (`SeNetworkLogonRight`)	X					X	X
Log on locally (`SeInteractiveLogonRight`)	X	X	X	X	X		
Log on as a batch job (`SeBatchLogonRight`)							
Log on as a service (`SeServiceLogonRight`)							
Deny access to this computer from the network (`SeDenyNetworkLogonRight`)							
Deny logon locally (`SeDenyInteractiveLogonRight`)							
Deny logon as a batch job (`SeDenyBatchLogonRight`)							
Deny logon as a service (`SeDenyServiceLogonRight`)							

* Admin = Administrators, SO = Server Operators, AO = Account Operators, PO = Printer Operators, BO = Backup Operators, AU = Authenticated Users, and EO = Everyone

The "deny logon" rights override the "allow logon" rights. Therefore, you can allow something to a broader set of users (i.e., a group) and then, if needed, exclude some of the rights from a narrower set of users (i.e., another group or individual user).

The first two logon rights in Table 4.44 have, by default, different assignments for a workstation and a member server. They are as follows:

- *Access this computer from the network:* Administrators, Power Users, Backup Operators, Users, Everyone
- *Log on locally:* Administrators, Power Users, Backup Operators, Users, Guest

In addition, for a member server the user Administrator has the "Log on as a service" right.

WARNING   Typically you don't want end users or guests to be able to log on at the keyboard of your member servers. To prevent them from doing so, remove Users and Guest from the "Log on locally" list.

NORMAL PRIVILEGES

This category includes the privileges that you might need at some point when administering Windows 2000 networks. Table 4.45 lists the 17 normal privileges along with their default assignments.

NOTE   We mentioned that there are some fixed rights, such as the right to format hard drives. "Take ownership of files or other objects" is listed in Table 4.45 as a user right that can be assigned. In addition, Administrators have that user right as a fixed right for objects outside Active Directory (such as files). In other words, even if you remove that right from Administrators, they still can take ownership of elements such as files and registry keys. However, they cannot take ownership of Active Directory objects anymore.

The default assignments of seven of the privileges are the same for member servers and workstations as those for domain controllers. Table 4.46 lists the remaining ten privileges that are assigned differently for member servers. These privileges apply to workstations too, except that the group Users also has the right "Shut down the system."

TABLE 4.45 Normal Privileges: Default Assignments for Domain Controllers

Privilege	Admin*	SO	AO	PO	BO	AU	EO
Add workstations to domain** (SeMachineAccountPrivilege)						X	
Back up files and directories (SeBackupPrivilege)	X	X			X		
Bypass traverse checking (SeChangeNotifyPrivilege)***	X					X	X
Change the system time (SeSystemtimePrivilege)	X	X					
Create a pagefile (SeCreatePagefilePrivilege)	X						
Enable computer and user accounts to be trusted for delegation (SeEnableDelegationPrivilege)	X						
Force shutdown from a remote system (SeRemoteShutdownPrivilege)	X	X					
Increase scheduling priority (SeIncreaseBasePriorityPrivilege)	X						

(continued)

TABLE 4.45 Normal Privileges: Default Assignments for Domain Controllers (*continued*)

Privilege	Admin*	SO	AO	PO	BO	AU	EO
Load and unload device drivers (`SeLoadDriverPrivilege`)	X						
Manage auditing and security log (`SeSecurityPrivilege`)	X						
Modify firmware environment values (`SeSystemEnvironmentPrivilege`)	X						
Profile single process (`SeProfileSingleProcessPrivilege`)	X						
Profile system performance (`SeSystemProfilePrivilege`)	X						
Remove computer from docking station (`SeUndockPrivilege`)	X						
Restore files and directories (`SeRestorePrivilege`)	X	X			X		
Shut down the system (`SeShutdownPrivilege`)	X	X	X	X	X		
Take ownership of files or other objects (`SeTakeOwnershipPrivilege`)	X						

* Admin = Administrators, SO = Server Operators, AO = Account Operators, PO = Printer Operators, BO = Backup Operators, AU = Authenticated Users, and EO = Everyone.
** This rights assignment means that by default, any user of the forest can add workstations and member servers to this domain—up to ten computers per user. This ten-computer limit is stored in the `ms-DS-MachineAccountQuota` property of each domain object. If the need arises, a domain administrator can change the value using a tool such as ADSI Edit.
*** This right has "ChangeNotify" in the API name because the same privilege is required to receive notifications of changes to files or directories.

ADVANCED PRIVILEGES

Table 4.47 lists the advanced user rights. By "advanced" we mean that you probably don't need to modify them or care about them. The default assignments for domain controllers are identical for workstations and member servers.

Fixed Rights

Table 4.48 lists some rights that are built into Windows 2000. The assignments are fixed, so you cannot modify them. There are also other operations an administrator can perform that a normal user cannot, so the list is not exhaustive. Those other operations are scattered throughout the operating system and listing them doesn't serve the purpose of this Active Directory book.

TABLE 4.46 Normal Privileges: Differing Default Assignments for Member Servers

Privilege	Admin*	PU	BO	Us	EO
Add workstations to domain (SeMachineAccountPrivilege)					
Back up files and directories (SeBackupPrivilege)	X		X		
Bypass traverse checking (SeChangeNotifyPrivilege)**	X	X	X	X	X
Change the system time (SeSystemtimePrivilege)	X	X			
Enable computer and user accounts to be trusted for delegation (SeEnableDelegationPrivilege)					
Force shutdown from a remote system (SeRemoteShutdownPrivilege)	X				
Profile single process (SeProfileSingleProcessPrivilege)	X	X			
Remove computer from docking station (SeUndockPrivilege)	X	X		X	
Restore files and directories (SeRestorePrivilege)	X		X		
Shut down the system (SeShutdownPrivilege)	X	X	X		

* Admin = Administrators, PU = Power Users, BO = Backup Operators, Us = Users, and EO = Everyone.
** This right has "ChangeNotify" in the API name because the same privilege is required to receive notifications of changes to files or directories.

NOTE   Because the rights in Table 4.48 are assigned only by the membership of certain groups, you cannot assign them to different domain controllers in one domain. For example, if you have a domain that has one domain controller in Boston and another domain controller in London, anyone who can format a hard drive in the Boston domain controller is allowed to do it also in the London domain controller.

Active Directory Permissions Instead of Rights

Having certain Active Directory permissions is effectively equivalent to having the following rights:

- *Fixed right:* Assign user rights (see Table 4.48)
- *User right:* Add workstations to domain (see Table 4.45)

TABLE 4.47 Advanced Privileges: Default Assignments for Domain Controllers

Privilege	Admin*	SO	AO	PO	BO	AU	EO
Act as part of the operating system (`SeTcbPrivilege`)**							
Create a token object (`SeCreateTokenPrivilege`)							
Create permanent shared objects (`SeCreatePermanentPrivilege`)							
Debug programs (`SeDebugPrivilege`)	X						
Generate security audits (`SeAuditPrivilege`)							
Increase quotas (`SeIncreaseQuotaPrivilege`)	X						
Lock pages in memory (`SeLockMemoryPrivilege`)							
Replace a process-level token (`SeAssignPrimaryTokenPrivilege`)							
Synchronize directory service data (`SeSyncAgentPrivilege`)							

* Admin = Administrators, SO = Server Operators, AO = Account Operators, PO = Printer Operators, BO = Backup Operators, AU = Authenticated Users, and EO = Everyone
** Tcb = trusted computer base

ASSIGN USER RIGHTS

If you have a Write permission to some Group Policy object, you can modify the user rights assignments that it contains, and the outcome is very similar to the "Assign user rights" fixed right. The two are not quite equal, however, because the Write permission doesn't allow using the NTRights command, which we describe shortly.

ADD WORKSTATIONS TO DOMAIN

Having the permissions Create Computer Objects and Delete Computer Objects for the Computers container is equal to having the "Add workstations to domain" user right (except for the ten-computer limit). Assigning these two permissions to a group such as gsWorkstationInstallers allows its members to join workstations and member servers to that domain.

The two permissions can also be assigned for any OU in the domain. In this case the joining process is a little different: The workstation installer must create the computer account in the appropriate OU before joining the workstation.

TABLE 4.48 Some Fixed Rights Assignments for Domain Controllers

Fixed Right	Admin*	SO	AO	PO	BO	AU
Assign user rights	X					
Unlock a locked computer	X					
Format hard drives	X					
Run CHKDSK	X					
Take ownership of files or other objects, excluding Active Directory objects	X					
Share folders and delete shares	X	X				
Create, manage, delete, and share printers	X	X	X			
Stop and start services	X	X				
Configure services	X	X				

* Admin = Administrators, SO = Server Operators, AO = Account Operators, PO = Printer Operators, BO = Backup Operators, and AU = Authenticated Users

Applying User Rights

User rights are applied using the Group Policy infrastructure and/or local security policy. Both are described in Chapter 7, so we don't go into the details in this chapter. This section, however, provides a brief introduction.

BRIEF INTRODUCTION TO GROUP POLICY

Group Policy affects a computer depending on where the corresponding computer object is located in Active Directory. The computer object of each domain controller is by default in an OU called Domain Controllers. To that OU is linked a Group Policy object (GPO) called Default Domain Controllers Policy. By default, the settings in that object affect every domain controller of that domain.

The computer object of each member server and workstation is by default in a container called Computers. It is not possible to link any Group Policy to this container, so what affects those computers by default is a GPO called Default Domain Policy. It is linked to the domain object.

If you place computer objects in some other OUs or you create new Group Policy objects, the defaults might no longer be in use. For example, you can create OUs Boston and London and then move all Boston domain controller objects to the Boston OU and all London domain controller objects to the London OU. This way, you can assign different user rights for the domain controllers of Boston and London.

If different GPOs apply to different domain controllers of the same domain, those domain controllers will have different user right assignments. This is a good thing when you control the right to log on locally, but it is a bad thing when you control the right to take ownership. It is not logical that your ability to take ownership of Active Directory objects depends on which domain controller you are connected to.

By default, the settings in a GPO linked to an object higher in the tree also affect objects on a lower level. Therefore, the settings defined in the Default Domain Policy also affect domain controllers unless the Default Domain Controllers Policy has conflicting settings, in which case the latter settings prevail.

Any Group Policy setting overrides the corresponding setting in the local security policy. However, the settings that are "not defined" in Group Policy can be set in the local security policy.

Group Policy settings are applied to a computer when it starts and afterward to a domain controller by default every 5 minutes. With member servers and workstations, that default interval is 90 minutes, give or take 30 minutes.

MODIFYING USER RIGHTS FOR DOMAIN CONTROLLERS

In this subsection we briefly describe the basic choices for modifying user rights for domain controllers. Because we are sticking to the basics, you would modify only the Default Domain Controllers Policy GPO. The most common ways to modify domain controller user rights (i.e., that GPO) are the following:

- *Edit the Default Domain Controllers Policy.* Right-click the Domain Controllers OU (in the Users and Computers snap-in), select Properties, select the Group Policy tab, select Default Domain Controllers Policy, and click Edit. This opens the Group Policy Editor. In the left pane, navigate to Computer Configuration, Windows Settings, Security Settings, Local Policies, User Rights Assignment.

- *Edit the Domain Controller Security Policy directly.* Click the Start button and select Programs, Administrative Tools, Domain Controller Security Policy. This opens a "subset" of the Group Policy Editor. In the left pane, navigate to Security Settings, Local Policies, User Rights Assignment.

- *Use the Resource Kit command NTRights.* For example, if you want to assign the right to log on locally to all users (not for a production network but perhaps for a test network), you use the following command:

```
ntrights +r SeInteractiveLogonRight -u Users
```

Figure 4.28 shows the contents of the Domain Controller Security Policy. In the left pane, User Rights Assignments is selected. The right pane shows the current user rights assignments for domain controllers. Note the exceptions to the default configuration: "Log on locally" is assigned also to the group Users (just for testing purposes—this is not good for a production network); and "Create a token object" is "Not defined" (being originally empty), which means that setting can be taken from the lower-priority local security policy. Some user rights are deliberately empty, which is different from "Not defined." An empty setting means that no one has the right, and it cannot be granted to anyone in the local security policy.

MODIFYING USER RIGHTS FOR MEMBER SERVERS AND WORKSTATIONS

Still sticking to the basics, the following are two strategies for modifying user rights for member servers and workstations:

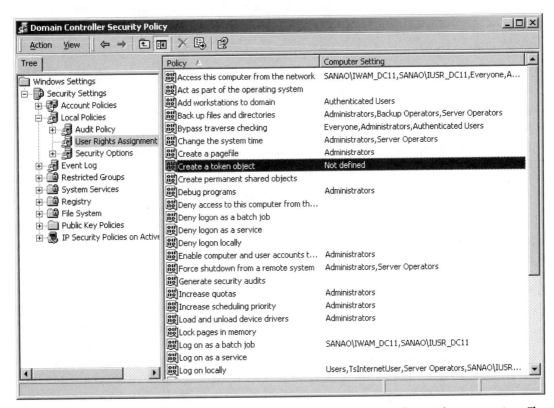

FIGURE 4.28 This figure shows the default user right assignments for domain controllers, with two exceptions. The right to "Log on locally" is assigned also to Users. "Create a token object" was changed to be "Not defined" (being originally empty), so that setting can be taken from the local security policy. The empty settings (such as "Create permanent shared objects") are specifically defined to be empty. In other words, they are not "Not defined."

- *Modify the Default Domain Policy GPO.* This affects all workstations and member servers in the domain.
- *Modify local security settings.* This affects only one computer.

To modify the Default Domain Policy GPO, you have the following two basic choices:

- *Edit the Default Domain Policy.* Right-click the domain object, select Properties, select the Group Policy tab, select Default Domain Policy, and click Edit. This opens the Group Policy Editor. In the left pane, navigate to Computer Configuration, Windows Settings, Security Settings, Local Policies, User Rights Assignment.
- *Edit the Domain Security Policy.* Click the Start button and select Programs, Administrative Tools, Domain Security Policy. This opens a "subset" of the Group Policy Editor. In the left pane, navigate to Security Settings, Local Policies, User Rights Assignment.

To modify local security settings, again you have two basic choices:

- *Edit the Local Security Policy.* Click the Start button and select Programs, Administrative Tools, Local Security Policy. This opens a "subset" of the Group Policy Editor. In the left pane, navigate to Security Settings, Local Policies, User Rights Assignment.
- *Use the Resource Kit command NTRights.* For example, if you want to assign the right to change system time to all users, you use the following command:

```
ntrights +r SeSystemTimePrivilege -u Users -m \\PC17
```

If you don't include the machine's name, the command will apply to the local computer.

CONCLUSION

In this chapter you learned how to control access to Active Directory objects by assigning permissions to them. With this information, along with the information presented in the previous chapter about managing users and other objects, you now have the knowledge and the skills to plan and administer the contents of Active Directory.

In the next two chapters we will explain the physical and logical structure of Active Directory. These structures make up the infrastructure that hosts Active Directory's contents.

Chapter 5

Sites and Replication

This chapter describes how Active Directory can keep identical information on several domain controllers by replicating a change of information in one domain controller to the other appropriate domain controllers. We also cover some other aspects of the physical communication between domain controllers.

To help Active Directory in its task, you must describe your physical network to it, such as which LANs you have and what kind of WAN links are between the LANs. You will do this by creating appropriate site objects and other objects in Active Directory.

We have divided the chapter into three sections.

- We start by introducing the concepts of the Active Directory physical structure. As we explain the terms and features, we try to keep the discussion at an introductory level. Regardless of the size of your network, you should read this section.

- The second section explains the administrative user interface and the various management tasks you should or may do. It covers setting things up step by step and administering the physical structure of an established network.

- In the third section we return to topics discussed in the first two sections, but this time we cover them in detail. As a result, this section contains information that not all readers will need. Here we describe such things as the replication process and the formation of replication topologies in different cases. The information in this advanced section explains the architecture of replication, which you can use when diagnosing replication problems. Also, if you plan replication for a large network, you should read this section.

There are also some replication-related topics in Chapter 6. In that chapter, we discuss Active Directory network traffic, which includes replication traffic. Also in Chapter 6, as we discuss planning domains and forests, we cover some physical aspects, such as how to place domain controllers on different sites.

CONCEPTS OF THE PHYSICAL STRUCTURE

Most of this book is about the logical aspects of Active Directory. In this chapter, however, it is time to get physical. Here we talk about *sites, replication, replicas, partitions, domain controllers,* and the *global catalog.* These elements make up the physical structure of Active Directory.

The logical and physical structures of Active Directory are independent of each other for the most part. However, as you may remember from Chapter 1, a domain is part of both structures. On the logical side, a domain is an administrative and security boundary, and part of the DNS namespace. On the physical side, a domain is the replication unit, or partition. In LDAP terminology, partitions are called *naming contexts (NCs).*

Why Replication?

Each section of Active Directory information resides in at least one domain controller. However, there should be redundancy—that is, all information should reside in more than one domain controller. The major time- and money-saving reasons for this are as follows:

- *Fault tolerance.* If one domain controller fails, the information is available from other domain controllers, which store the same information. Note that as with fault tolerance in general, redundancy with Active Directory doesn't eliminate the need to make backups.
- *Load balancing.* When many workstations are accessing Active Directory, the information they are requesting is retrieved faster when there is more than one domain controller to provide it.
- *Proximity of information.* Workstations get the information from a local domain controller instead across a slow WAN link.

Nature of Active Directory Replication

Active Directory is a *loosely consistent* database. The information in different domain controllers is not necessarily consistent (the same) at any given time. However, when there are no changes for a while, the information will tend toward consistency—that is, all the domain controllers of one domain will have the same information. This is called *convergence*.

For the information to be the same in several domain controllers, any changes must be *replicated* from one domain controller to another. Active Directory notices if an object is created, deleted, or moved/renamed, or if an attribute is added, changed, or deleted. All these operations are consequently replicated from the originating domain controller to the other appropriate domain controllers. This causes replication traffic in LANs in physical locations and in WAN links between physical locations.

There are two trade-offs associated with replication.

- *High replication load versus latency.* The more frequently you replicate changed information, the more load this puts on domain controllers and the network. On the other hand, the less frequently you replicate, the older the information will be in some domain controllers. In any case, there is always *latency;* that is, the changed information is not instantly available in all domain controllers.

- *Replication in WAN versus user access in WAN.* If the information source is in Boston and the consumer is in London, either the information needs to be replicated to London or the consumer needs to access it across a WAN link from Boston. An administrator makes this choice by either placing a remote domain controller in London or not. The decision must be made separately for each domain, because each domain contains different information.

These trade-offs are affected by how often the information is changed and how often it is read. If the information rarely changes, latency is not much of an issue. If that were the case, it would also be easier to put a domain controller in London, because few changes mean little replication. Also, if the London personnel read the information frequently, it would pay to put a domain controller there, so that the information is replicated once over the WAN link instead of several people reading it all the time over that link.

NOTE   We return to the topic of how to place domain controllers in Chapter 6. In that chapter we also explain the number of bytes that replication (and clients accessing domain controllers) puts on network traffic.

Active Directory mostly uses *multimaster* replication. This means that you can make changes (e.g., you can add users) to any domain controller of the domain, and then your changes are replicated to other domain controllers in the same domain.

As a contrast, with Windows NT you could make changes to only one server, which was called a *primary domain controller* (PDC). The changes were replicated to all other servers, which were called *backup domain controllers* (BDCs). The Windows NT approach (i.e., *single-master* replication) was a little more difficult than the Active Directory approach, especially in WAN environments and failure situations because you always had to communicate with the PDC when making a change.

If you have Windows NT backup domain controllers in an Active Directory domain, they will need to replicate the part of Active Directory information that is recognized by or compatible with the Windows NT world. The backup domain controllers use downlevel replication to get this information.

In addition to replicating information among Windows 2000 domain controllers, it is possible to synchronize objects in disparate systems, such as Novell NDS and Microsoft Exchange 5.5. The Windows 2000 Server CD includes Active Directory Connector (ADC), which enables you to synchronize Active Directory with Exchange 5.5. Microsoft Services for NetWare version 5 (SFNW5) includes the Microsoft Directory Synchronization Services (MSDSS) component, which enables you to synchronize among Novell NDS and Active Directory. Finally, Microsoft Metadirectory Services (MMS) enables you to use Active Directory to manage identity information stored in heterogeneous directory services.

Partitions and Replicas

When we talk about replication, we also need to talk about *partitions* and *replicas*. Partitions are the units of replication; that is, they dictate what is replicated to which domain controllers. Replicas are the identical copies of a given partition in different domain controllers.

NOTE   Remember that replicas of a partition are truly identical only when there have been no changes for a while. Otherwise, some replicas may have recent changes that haven't yet replicated to all other replicas of the same partition.

The vast majority of Active Directory information is in per-domain domain partitions. That is, most information is replicated among the domain controllers of one domain. There are also two forestwide partitions called *schema* and *configuration*. We often call them *enterprise partitions*.

Table 5.1 describes the three kinds of partitions in Active Directory. A domain partition has full replicas in normal domain controllers and partial replicas in global catalog servers.

TABLE 5.1 Active Directory Partition Types

Partition Name	Number	Domain Controller Used to Modify	Contains
Schema partition	One per forest	Schema master	The schema—the definitions of the classes and attributes supported in the forest
Configuration partition	One per forest	Any DC in the forest (some information, however, requires the domain naming master)	Knowledge about sites, partitions, extended rights, and some other per-forest information
Domain partition (full replica)	One per domain	Any DC of the corresponding domain	Per-domain objects such as users, OUs, and groups
Domain partition (partial replica for global catalog)		Replica is read-only, it is replicated from other domain partitions	Some attributes of every object in the corresponding domain partition

We mention in Table 5.1 that the global catalog is using partial replicas, because it contains only some of the attributes. Of the 863 attributes in the Active Directory base schema, 138 are included in the global catalog. We don't list them here, but in Chapter 11 we present a script that can list them for you.

Table 5.2 shows an example of the replicas of an enterprise forest that has three domains and five domain controllers.

The example in Table 5.2 has five partitions:

- One schema partition (one for the forest)
- One configuration partition (one for the forest)
- Three domain partitions (one for each domain)

As you can see in Table 5.2, every domain controller has a replica of at least three partitions (schema, configuration, and its own domain). Those that we have designated as global catalog servers (DC1 and DC4) also have partial replicas of all other domain partitions.

You can see too that in the sample forest there are 15 full replicas (3 × *number of domain controllers*) and four partial replicas ([*number of domains* – 1] × *number of global catalog servers*).

TABLE 5.2 Replicas of an Active Directory Sample Forest

	DC1 (in domain A)	DC2 (in domain A)	DC3 (in domain B)	DC4 (in domain C)	DC5 (in domain C)
Schema partition	Full replica	Full replica	Full replica	Full replica	Full replica
Configuration partition	Full replica	Full replica	Full replica	Full replica	Full replica
Domain partition of domain A	Full replica	Full replica		Partial replica	
Domain partition of domain B	Partial replica		Full replica	Partial replica	
Domain partition of domain C	Partial replica			Full replica	Full replica

NOTE   As discussed in Chapter 1, a domain controller cannot host full replicas of other domains. You must have separate server computers (i.e., domain controllers) to host full replicas of different domains.

Table 5.2 shows which replicas of which partitions are on which domain controllers. Figure 5.1 shows two domain partitions and configuration and schema partitions drawn in the logical namespace.

Overview of the Replication Process

Unlike Windows NT, Active Directory replicates only changed properties, not entire user accounts or other objects. This has two advantages.

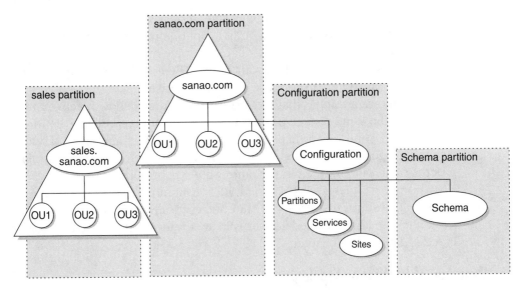

FIGURE 5.1 Configuration, schema, and every child domain is an independent partition, but together they form a logical tree where each partition is a child to another one.

- There is less data to be replicated.
- Replication conflicts are less frequent. If someone changes Jack's phone number in a Boston domain controller and someone else changes his fax number in a London domain controller, there is no conflict. Even though the changes are for the same object, they are for different properties.

Unlike Novell NDS, Active Directory replication does not rely on synchronized time among servers. Instead, Active Directory uses *update sequence numbers (USNs)* and version numbers to determine what to replicate.

However, Windows 2000 has a time service to synchronize time on all computers in a forest. The primary reason for this service is that the Kerberos authentication protocol requires the clocks in different computers to be approximately synchronized (within 5 minutes, by default). Also, Active Directory uses timestamps of changes in conflict resolution. One type of conflict is a situation where the same property of the same object has been changed in two domain controllers. If the time of the two domain controllers is not synchronized, regardless of time service, the "wrong" change could prevail, or win the conflict.

Consider the following example. Someone changes Jack's phone number in a Boston domain controller and then someone else changes it 10 seconds later in a London domain controller. The clock of the Boston domain controller is 15 seconds fast, so even if the change there were older, it would eventually prevail because the clock would indicate that it's the more recent change. Is this bad? No, because if two administrators change Jack's phone number to different values in Boston and London almost simultaneously, it only means that you haven't organized administration very well in your forest. There really isn't a sensible way to tell which phone number should be saved in that case.

The important thing is that the result is consistent, and with Active Directory replication, the same change prevails in every domain controller, even though it could be 10 seconds older than some other change. The timestamps of both conflicting changes are replicated with the change, so each domain controller will pick the same winner, whether the times were synchronized or not.

You may wonder how USNs and version numbers work in the replication process. The short answer is that they automatically work so that they get the job done. The long, detailed answer is in an advanced section, "The Replication Process," later in this chapter.

Overview of Replication Topologies

When you have more than one domain controller, Active Directory automatically builds a certain replication topology. That topology dictates from which domain controller (or controllers) every other domain controller will get the changes.

The component that creates the topology is the *Knowledge Consistency Checker (KCC)*. It wakes up every 15 minutes in each domain controller to check if there are changes in the selection of domain controllers or in any replication objects that would require changes in the replication topology.

The intrasite replication topology is by default a bidirectional ring. For example, with four domain controllers, A replicates to B, B to C, C to D, and D to A, and it's the same in the opposite direction. Figure 5.2 shows a ring with eight domain controllers.

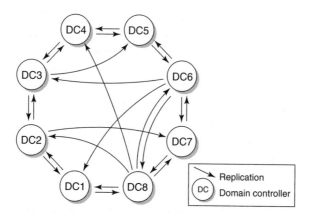

FIGURE 5.2 An intrasite replication topology forms a bidirectional ring, with possible shortcut connections to prevent chains from becoming too long.

As the number of domain controllers increases, the KCCs add shortcut connections to the ring to prevent the chain from becoming too long. The shortcut connections take care that the path between any two domain controllers (which replicate the same partition) is almost never more than three hops. Because the replication latency from one domain controller to another is 5 minutes, a maximum of three hops means a maximum of 15 minutes before the change is replicated to all appropriate domain controllers in a site.

The intersite replication topology is based on *bridgehead servers.* They are the only domain controllers that replicate to and from other sites. A bridgehead server collects all changes on its site in the partitions it is responsible for, and then replicates the changes to bridgehead servers on other appropriate sites. Those bridgehead servers in turn replicate the changes further on their sites. This way, any change needs to travel a WAN link only once.

In most cases the automatically generated intrasite topology is fine, and there is no need to adjust it manually, not to mention create the topology manually from the ground up. This applies also to the intersite topology with two exceptions: First, you must provide background information for Active Directory (and this requires planning), and second, there are cases where you might create at least some of the intersite connections manually.

Sites

Active Directory can replicate more efficiently if it knows which domain controllers are connected with a fast network (usually a LAN) and which are connected over a slower network (usually a WAN link). You can describe this to Active Directory by creating appropriate site objects and other objects in Active Directory.

In addition to Active Directory replication, sites serve a number of other uses.

- Active Directory clients find logon servers (i.e., domain controllers) based on sites. They will use a domain controller on the same site, but if none is available, they will use a domain controller on the closest site.

- Windows 2000 Distributed File System (DFS) uses site information to decide which server sends the user the files she requested.

- Windows 2000 File Replication Service (FRS) uses site information to know how to replicate SysVol and other folders.

- You may assign group policies to sites, in which case they by default apply to all users and computers on that site.

- Active Directory–aware applications may use site information for their own purposes.

Each site corresponds to one or more TCP/IP subnets. For example, one site could correspond to subnet 10.0.14.0/23 and another to subnet 10.0.17.0/24, or one site could correspond to both subnets.

The main function of subnets in Active Directory is to serve as building blocks to sites and operate as a link to the physical IP network. In addition, once you have described the subnets to Active Directory by creating appropriate subnet objects, you can enable users to find the printers closest to them using this subnet-based location information.

If you want to test intersite replication in a small test network, you can place domain controllers on different sites, even though they are physically in the same subnet. However, this doesn't work for a production network. In that case, you need correct subnet information because it determines on which site the client computers are assumed to be.

When you plan whether to have a site for a certain office or not, you can use the following considerations.

- There is no exact speed that indicates a network is fast or slow. If you have a T-1 or a 2Mbps link to some office, you could decide that the link is fast enough for the office not to be a separate site. Or you could decide the link is too slow and you need to create a new site for that office. The latter choice is more likely.

- Active Directory employs various techniques to use bandwidth sparingly when communicating among sites. One technique is data compression, and we list the other techniques in the next section. Consequently, speed is not the only criterion in your decision to create a separate site. If the link is fast but expensive, unreliable, or congested, you should create a separate site for the corresponding office.

- Most uses for sites that we list require that there is (or will be) at least one server at the physical location for which the site is being created. For example, DFS cannot offer files from a local server unless there is a local server. However, one of the items, assigning group policies, doesn't require an on-site server.

- If you create a site for an office, the domain controllers that replicate intersite (i.e., the bridgehead servers) need to use some CPU power to compress data and you will have a few more objects to manage. You also need to watch that these bridgehead servers are operational. Beyond these considerations, adding an extra site doesn't cost anything.

- If you create a site for an office or a neighboring building on a campus area, the replication latency to that office or building will be longer. If this is not tolerable, you can shorten the latency and even enable change notifications, in which case the intersite replication latency is as short as intrasite replication latency. The procedure is explained in an advanced section, "Using Change Notifications in Intersite Replication," later in this chapter.

- Inside a site, all domain controllers should be able to communicate freely with all others; you cannot (reasonably) limit this. If a firewall or some other aspect of the physical network doesn't allow free communication, you should create several sites, even though these domain controllers would be in the same LAN.

- If you have many domain controllers (e.g., more than 20) in a physical location, you will have quite a large replica ring with numerous shortcuts. You may consider creating several sites for that physical location, as long as you have several IP subnets there.

Each domain controller of every domain in a forest belongs to some site. If you don't create sites, all domain controllers go to a site called Default-First-Site-Name. On the other hand, if you create sites to match the physical locations of your network, the number and distribution of domain controllers would be arranged as they are in Table 5.3, and the layout would look something like Figure 5.3.

Sanao Corporation, our sample company, has headquarters in Boston and offices in San Francisco and London. In addition to the root domain, there are two child domains (Sales and RD). There are five domain controllers in Boston, three in San Francisco, and two in London.

Three cells in Table 5.3 are marked Simulated. There is no domain controller of the corresponding domain on the corresponding site. However, a domain controller from some other site (the closest possible) is pretending to be there by having registered the appropriate DNS service records. This way, a client can

TABLE 5.3 Number of Domain Controllers in Each Domain and Site of a Forest

	Boston	**San Francisco**	**London**
`sanao.com`	3 DCs	Simulated*	1 DC
`sales.sanao.com`	2 DCs	1 DC	1 DC
`rd.sanao.com`	Simulated*	2 DCs	Simulated*

* There is no domain controller (DC) of the corresponding domain on the corresponding site. A DC from the closest site registers itself in DNS to appear on the "empty" site, so clients on that site can find a DC.

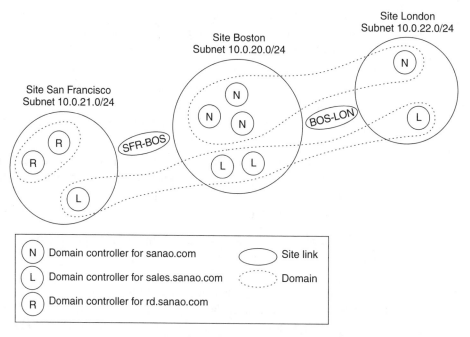

FIGURE 5.3 Each domain controller is on an Active Directory site, which usually matches a physical site. For example, you could create in Active Directory the London site for your London office.

always easily find a domain controller for logons and other similar domain communication. For example, there could be a workstation of the RD domain in London. When that client needs logon services, it can find a domain controller for this, even though that server is located in San Francisco. The domain controller in San Francisco is said to *cover* the London site.

You can control site coverage by using registry parameters located in HKEY_ LOCAL_MACHINE, SYSTEM, CurrentControlSet, Services, Netlogon, Parameters. To stop a domain controller from covering other sites, you should set the AutoSiteCoverage parameter (of type REG_DWORD) to 0. To add a specific site to be covered by a domain controller, add the site name in the SiteCoverage parameter (of type REG_MULTI_SZ). For more information on these parameters, see the Registry Reference included in the Resource Kit.

Links between sites are called *site links*. Site links represent networks, so each site link may correspond to one WAN link between two sites or to a network that connects several sites. Examples of the latter case are a frame relay, an ATM, or another kind of "cloud" network (meaning that you either don't know or don't care which route the network packets take to reach another site).

Overview of Intrasite and Intersite Replication

As mentioned, intrasite and intersite replication processes are different. Table 5.4 compares their features.

By default, replication is *transitive*. This means that domain controller B can pass on to domain controller C the changes it received from domain controller A. Domain controller A and domain controller C don't need to communicate directly. This is an advantage even in intrasite replication, but it pays off especially in intersite replication. The data needs to be replicated only once to the next city, and from the bridgehead server on the destination city it then spreads locally to other domain controllers.

TABLE 5.4 Comparison of Intrasite and Intersite Replication

Feature	Intrasite	Intersite
Transport protocol	RPC (Remote Procedure Call)	RPC (although called IP) or SMTP. The latter can be used only for the two enterprise partitions (schema, configuration) and the global catalog but not for the normal domain partitions.
Default topology	Ring (with possible shortcuts)	Minimum cost spanning tree.
Connections	Between any two domain controllers on the site	Between bridgehead servers on each site.
Approximate latency	By default, 5 minutes from one domain controller to the next (hop), almost always a maximum of 15 minutes from any domain controller to any other domain controller	By default, 3 hours from one site to the next, but you could change it to, for example, every 15 minutes or once a day.
Replication model	Notify and pull (via RPC), and pull with a schedule as a backup mechanism	Either pull with a schedule (via RPC) or store and forward (via SMTP).
Compression	No	Yes, compresses down to between 10 percent and 15 percent (or even less). However, if there is less than 32KB data to be replicated, there is no compression.

CHANGE NOTIFICATION

As mentioned in Table 5.4, intrasite replication uses the "notify and pull" method, which works as follows:

1. A domain controller has some new changes, which either originated on that domain controller or were replicated from another domain controller.

2. After waiting 5 minutes (by default), the domain controller sends a *change notification* to the domain controllers that are its direct replication partners (to that direction) on the same site. We can call them the source domain controller and the target domain controllers, respectively. To be exact, the change notifications are sent only to those replication partners that are interested in the corresponding partition. If the change is in some user object (i.e., the domain partition), the change notification is not sent to partners that replicate only the enterprise partitions from that source domain controller.

3. Each target domain controller requests the changes from the source domain controller, which sends the changes to the target.

If the change notifications were sent to all targets at the same time, they would "attack" the source simultaneously, causing a load peak. Therefore, the source domain controller actually sends the change notifications at slightly different times, using by default a 30-second delay. Both the 5-minute delay and 30-second delay can be changed by modifying the registry.

SCHEDULED REPLICATION

While intrasite replication is based on notifications, intersite replication is based on schedules. A target domain controller requests changes from the source domain controller according to a schedule.

By default, the schedule specifies that the target will request changes every 3 hours, day and night. Administrators can change the schedule either per site link or per server-to-server connection and specify the allowed hours and weekdays to request changes, as well as how often in these specified time periods the requests should be made. An example schedule would be once an hour between 1:00 AM and 7:00 AM. Certain weekdays can also be specified, but typically replication occurs at least daily.

Increasing the frequency from 3 hours has the effect of consuming more bandwidth; if we had 40KB to replicate every 15 minutes, the compression would be less efficient than if we combined the data to a 480KB chunk to be replicated every 3 hours. The obvious benefit of a higher frequency is that changes get to other sites sooner.

NOTE   You can enable change notification also for intersite replication. We explain this in the "Using Change Notifications in Intersite Replication" section later in this chapter.

NOTE   Intrasite replication uses change notification as the primary method. However, in case a notification is lost, there is a schedule-based replication as a backup mechanism. Each target domain controller requests changes from the source by default once an hour.

SITE LINK BRIDGES

It is possible to combine two or more site links as a *site link bridge*. You need to do this only in rare cases (e.g., when your WAN is not fully routed). You will probably never need site link bridges—in this introductory section we mention them only so that when you see them in the administrative interface, you will recognize them and know that you probably don't need them.

Urgent Replication

Active Directory may use three urgency levels for replication, as described in Table 5.5.

TABLE 5.5 Urgency Levels of Active Directory Replication

Urgency Level	Time Table	Examples of Events
Normal replication	After waiting 5 minutes from the first change (default) for intrasite, or according to a schedule (e.g., every 3 hours) for intersite	Almost all changes
Urgent replication	Immediately for intrasite; by default not used for intersite (i.e., normal intersite schedule is used)	Replicating a newly locked-out user object
No replication	Never replicated	`lastLogon` and `lastLogoff` properties of user objects

NOTE   Because the `lastLogon` property is never replicated from one domain controller to another, you will get different dates and times depending on where you read that property. On the other hand, if the `lastLogon` property were replicated, it would create large amounts of replication traffic, mostly in vain.

Like normal replication, urgent replication is based on change notifications, except that the source domain controller sends the notification immediately instead of waiting 5 minutes.

If you enable change notification on a per–site link basis for intersite replication, you will get urgent replication also between sites.

The following events trigger an urgent replication between Windows 2000 domain controllers.

- A user or computer account (i.e., object) is locked out as a result of too many failed logon attempts with a wrong password.
- A Local Security Authority (LSA) secret is changed. (An LSA secret is used by secure channels, trust relationships, and service passwords.)
- The RID master state is changed.

If the domain is in mixed mode when urgently replicating to Windows NT backup domain controllers, the first two items from the preceding list still apply (lockout and LSA secret). There is also one new event.

- An interdomain trust password is changed. Each trusting domain has an account in the trusted domain and the password for that account is automatically changed once a week (by default).

Password changes are not urgently replicated. However, if a user tries to access other servers immediately after changing her password, Active Directory can still allow the access by communicating the change to one central place (the PDC master), where the others can check it.

Nonreplicating Properties

As mentioned in Table 5.5, some properties are not replicated at all. There are 39 such properties in the base schema:

```
badPasswordTime              memberOf
badPwdCount                  isPrivilegeHolder
bridgeheadServerListBL       lastLogoff
dSCorePropagationData        lastLogon
frsComputerReferenceBL       logonCount
fRSMemberReferenceBL         managedObjects
```

```
masteredBy                          repsFrom
modifiedCount                       repsTo
netbootSCPBL                        rIDNextRID
nonSecurityMemberBL                 rIDPreviousAllocationPool
distinguishedName                   schemaUpdate
objectGUID                          serverReferenceBL
partialAttributeDeletionList        serverState
partialAttributeSet                 siteObjectBL
pekList                             subRefs
prefixMap                           uSNChanged
queryPolicyBL                       uSNCreated
replPropertyMetaData                uSNLastObjRem
replUpToDateVector                  whenChanged
directReports
```

NOTE   In addition to nonreplicating properties, the directory database of a domain controller (i.e., the NTDS.DIT file) contains other information that is not replicated. One large portion of such information consists of the database indexes that are created locally on each domain controller instead of being replicated across the network.

Global Catalog

In a large forest with many sites, not all Active Directory information is normally replicated to all sites. This means that only part of the information is on the site where the user is. Consequently, if that user searches Active Directory for other users or resources such as printers, her query needs to travel from site to site across many WAN links, which is not efficient. Also, if the result of the search is a list of 1,000 user names, it takes a long time for the result to transfer back to the user who performed the search.

The global catalog (GC) enables you to perform all searches locally from your enterprise forest, which should make them dramatically more efficient. The global catalog includes all the objects of a forest but only part of their properties. In other words, the global catalog contains a partial replica of all domain partitions in the forest. The global catalog includes especially properties that are likely to be used in search operations, such as a user's first and last name. The Active Directory base schema defines 863 properties, and by default 138 of them are in the global catalog. Originally, only the first domain controller of your forest is a global catalog server. Your responsibility is to assign additional domain controllers for the job. As a rule of thumb, each site should have (at least) one global catalog server. This allows users on all sites to search locally.

Overview of Operations Masters

Although Active Directory replication is mostly multimaster, there are five cases in which a special single-master role is attached to only one domain controller in a domain or the enterprise forest. These five roles are called *operations masters*. The old name was *flexible single-master operation,* and you may see *FSMO* (pronounced "fizmo") in a few places in the user interface and various documents. Table 5.6 describes the five roles.

The first domain controller in a forest will get the two forestwide roles, and the first domain controller in each domain will get the three domainwide roles. The first domain controller in the forest is also a global catalog server.

In a multidomain forest, the infrastructure master shouldn't be in a computer that is also a global catalog server, so for a root domain you should change the default configuration by transferring one of those roles to another domain controller.

TABLE 5.6 Operations Masters

Role	Number	Main Functions
Schema master	One per forest	When an administrator changes the schema (which he probably does rarely) this operations master performs the actual change.
Domain naming master	One per forest	When an administrator adds domains to or deletes domains from a forest, or he adds or removes cross-references to domains in external directories (which he probably does rarely), this operations master performs the actual additions or deletions.
RID master	One per domain	This operations master gives a number of RIDs to other domain controllers, so that the latter can use them for SIDs when creating security principals such as users and security groups.
PDC master (or PDC emulator)	One per domain	This operations master acts as a primary domain controller for any pre–Windows 2000 servers and workstations. It also serves as a center for password changes, account lockout, and time synchronization for Windows 2000 computers.
Infrastructure master	One per domain	This operations master maintains references to objects in other domains, such as group members.

MANAGING THE PHYSICAL STRUCTURE

You describe your physical network for Active Directory by creating and configuring a number of objects in the configuration partition of your enterprise forest. The tool you use for this is the Sites and Services snap-in. In the following sections, we describe the objects and the snap-in, as well as the various tasks you may need to perform. If you have only one physical location, you might not need to do anything. However, we do list some tasks even for a single-site case in the "Setting Up a Single Site" section.

Active Directory Objects for Sites and Replication

There are ten types of objects that you can use to define the physical structure and four types of container objects that help in building the object tree. Figure 5.4 shows these as an object tree. Table 5.7 briefly describes each object in Figure 5.4.

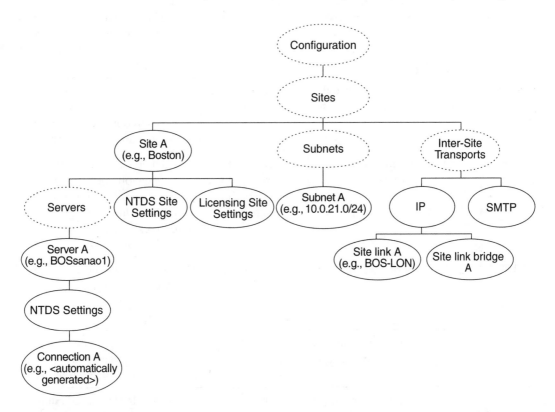

FIGURE 5.4 The solid line around an object indicates that the object is defining the physical structure of Active Directory. The objects with dotted lines are containers for other objects—they don't have meaningful properties. An A in an object's name (e.g., Site A) indicates that there may be more than one such object (e.g., Site A, Site B, and so on). In those cases, we also include a sample name, such as Boston.

TABLE 5.7 Active Directory Objects for Sites and Replication

Name	Type (and Class)	Number	Description
Boston*	Site (`site`)	1 per site	Enables you to divide your network into "islands" of fast connections and place each server on some "island."
NTDS Site Settings	Site Settings (`nTDSSiteSettings`)	1 per site	Contains some site properties. You probably don't need to modify them, however.
Licensing Site Settings	Licensing Site Settings (`licensingSite-Settings`)	1 per site	Defines the licensing computer for the licensing service. You probably don't need to modify the setting, however.
BOSsanao1*	Server (`server`)	1 per server	Enables you to define on which "island" the server is located, so various services will know what is local and what is not.
NTDS Settings	Domain Controller Settings (`nTDSDSA`)	1 per domain controller	The existence of this object symbolizes that the server is a domain controller. It also contains some domain controller settings.
<automatically generated>*	Connection (`nTDSConnection`)	1 per DC-to-DC replication link for each direction	Each domain controller has one connection object for every other domain controller it will replicate from. The object defines how and when replication occurs.
10.0.21.0/24*	Subnet (`subnet`)	1 per IP subnet	Enables you to describe the subnets of which a site consists and to which site a new server belongs.
IP	Inter-Site Transport (`interSiteTransport`)	1	Hosts all RPC over IP-based intersite links and site link bridges and contains some settings.
SMTP	Inter-Site Transport (`interSiteTransport`)	1	Hosts all SMTP-based intersite links and site link bridges and contains some settings.

(continued)

TABLE 5.7 (*continued*)

Name	Type (and Class)	Number	Description
BOS-LON*	Site Link (`siteLink`)	1 per link between sites	Enables you to define which and what kind of WAN links you have between your sites.
Whatever	Site Link Bridge (`siteLinkBridge`)	1 per collection of site links	Needed only in some special cases.

* These names correspond to items in Figure 5.4. Of course, the names of objects change according to each physical setup.

NOTE   Figure 5.4 shows object names, not types. For example, an object called NTDS Settings is actually of type Domain Controller Settings (meaning class `nTDSDSA`). Also, because object names IP and SMTP are the same type, there are 11, not 10, solid-line objects in the figure.

The Big Picture of Objects

We mentioned earlier that sites have functions besides controlling replication. If we focus only on this main function, and simplify things a bit, we can make the following related claims.

- Connection objects affect directly how, when, and where replication takes place.
- All other object types only exist to affect which and what kind of connection objects exist. Either they give hints to the KCCs that create the connection objects, or they enable you to create the connection objects you want under certain NTDS Settings objects for certain domain controllers.

Figure 5.5 illustrates these claims.

NOTE   NTDS stands for "NT Directory Service." Windows 2000 was called Windows NT 5.0 until it was renamed in 1998.

NOTE   There is no arrow from the Licensing Site Settings object because it is the only one that doesn't affect replication.

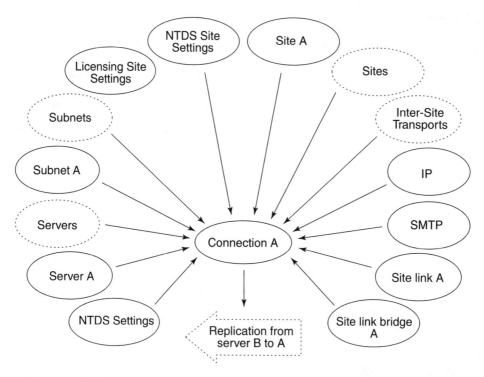

FIGURE 5.5 If we simplify things, connection objects dictate how, when, and where replication takes place. All other objects exist just to affect which and what kind of connection objects exist.

The aforementioned claims and consequently the diagram in Figure 5.5 are something of a simplification of the ways things work in reality. Next we show the object relationships (almost) without simplification.

The solid-line objects in Figure 5.4 and Figure 5.5 have properties that link them to other objects or control the replication topology and process. Figure 5.6 shows these relationships and functions and gives the big picture of the objects that define the physical structure of Active Directory.

NOTE   In Figure 5.6, the solid-line arrows (to represent an effect) that point to the connection object reflect how the other objects affect the automatically created connection objects. If you created some of the connection objects manually, these arrows wouldn't apply to them.

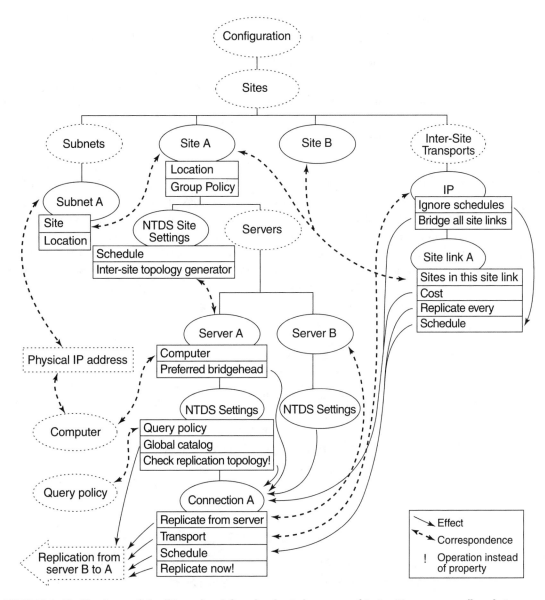

FIGURE 5.6 The big picture of the objects that define the physical structure of Active Directory as well as their relationships.

NOTE   When you create intersite connection objects, all arrows in Figure 5.6 apply. When you create intrasite connection objects, the arrows from the IP and site link objects, as well as those from the Preferred Bridgehead property, don't apply.

Figure 5.6 shows 8 of the 11 solid-line objects of Figure 5.4. We dropped the following three objects to make the figure a little more focused and clear:

- *SMTP.* It is mostly analogous to IP.

- *License Site Settings.* They are used for the awkward License Logging service. It is much easier to turn off the service and manage client access licenses by hand.

- *Site link bridges.* They are part of advanced topics and, consequently, we discuss them later in the "Creating and Managing Site Link Bridges" section.

There is actually one arrow missing from Figure 5.6. We could have drawn one from the Schedule property of NTDS Site Settings to the Schedule property of the connection object. We give a reason for this omission along with Figure 5.7, which shows a subset of the big picture that focuses on an automatically created (by a KCC) connection object. As Figure 5.7 illustrates, when a KCC determines which intersite connection objects to create and what properties to use for them, it uses (among others) two pieces of information: the selection of domain controllers (represented by NTDS Settings objects) and the selection of site links (along with their costs). The schedule and "Replicate every" frequency of the site link object

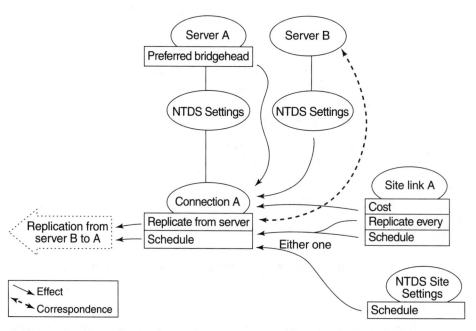

FIGURE 5.7 When a KCC determines which intersite connection objects to create and what properties to use for them, it uses a number of other objects as its information source. For intrasite connection objects, NTDS Site Settings properties are used instead of site link properties.

are combined to be the schedule of the connection object. If the connection object is for intrasite replication, the schedule in NTDS Site Settings is used instead of the one in the site link.

NOTE   The schedule in NTDS Site Settings is by default once an hour. As explained earlier, it is only a backup mechanism in case a notification gets lost. Normally the 5-minute delay of change notifications dictates the intrasite replication latency.

The Sites and Services Snap-In

You open the Sites and Services snap-in by clicking the Start button and selecting Programs, Administrative Tools, Active Directory Sites and Services. Alternatively, you can click the Start button, select Run, type "dssite.msc", and press Enter. A fully configured forest of our sample company Sanao Corporation could look like the one in Figure 5.8.

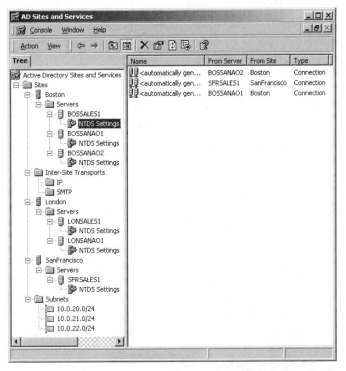

FIGURE 5.8 Here are the physical structure objects of Sanao Corporation. Compared to the preceding big picture, you can see six of eight objects. Site link and NTDS Site Settings are not visible, because you can't see the leaf objects of different containers at the same time.

You use the Sites and Services snap-in in pretty much the same way you use the Users and Computers snap-in to view, create, and manipulate objects. By default, the Sites and Services snap-in connects to "Any Writable Domain Controller." If you happen to sit at a domain controller, it will be that target. On the other hand, if you are at a workstation, the target is whatever domain controller your workstation has found. In either case, you can select a specific target by right-clicking the first node in the tree (Active Directory Sites and Services), selecting Connect to Domain Controller, and then selecting the target you want. You will see the currently selected domain controller in brackets in the first node in the tree.

NOTE   You can create and modify replication objects using any domain controller of the forest. However, there would be at least a 5-minute delay before any change would be replicated to other domain controllers. Consequently, it is often necessary to specify a certain domain controller as the snap-in target and also to change the target to various domain controllers to check if they already know about the change.

As an alternative to changing the target of the snap-in (see the corresponding Note), you could take the following steps:

1. Modify objects on the domain controller you already have as the target.
2. Initiate immediate replication of those objects to the domain controller that needs them.
3. Initiate immediate checking of replication topology on the latter domain controller, which generates some changes on the connection objects.
4. Initiate immediate replication back to your target domain controller.
5. Refresh the view.

These steps illustrate that because replication includes delays and several domain controllers, it takes quite a few mouse clicks to test things. When applying settings in production, you can either take the same steps to make sure that the result is what you wanted, or you can just perform step 1 and trust that in a while Active Directory will react as you want it to.

Because the name of the snap-in is "Sites and Services," you might wonder where the services are. You can access the Services node by right-clicking some object and selecting View, Show Services Node. However, the objects in the Services node don't have anything to do with the physical structure of Active Directory.

TEST ENVIRONMENT

Using just one computer, you can test-drive many of the things described in this chapter. That computer will be the first and only domain controller in your enterprise forest. If you also have a second computer available, you can test-drive even more things. Depending on what you want to test, you can promote the second computer to the following roles:

- Another domain controller in the same domain
- A domain controller in a child domain
- A member server in the domain
- A domain controller in another forest

The last two items are actually not related to this chapter, but we mention them here for completeness.

Tasks in Managing the Physical Structure

In this section we introduce the tasks you may or must do when managing the physical structure of Active Directory. We divide the tasks as follows:

- Setting up a single site
- Setting up multiple sites
- Administering sites

If your network spans multiple geographical locations, you should create and configure the appropriate Active Directory objects to model the physical network. On the other hand, if your entire network is in a single location and on a single LAN, everything happens fairly automatically. Setting up the physical structure of Active Directory is much easier in the latter case. Only Enterprise Admins can perform forestwide operations such as creating new sites and child domains. Per-domain administrators can perform domainwide operations such as adding a domain controller or initiating immediate domain replication from one domain controller to another. Tables 5.8 through 5.12 in the following sections list the tasks. The tables include references to pages in the later sections where we describe each task in more detail.

SETTING UP A SINGLE SITE

As mentioned, to set up a single site everything is quite automatic. About all you need to do is to install the domain controllers for the domains you want. (To review installation, see Chapter 2.) After you install domain controllers, you might need to perform only the three tasks in Table 5.8.

TABLE 5.8 Tasks for Setting Up a Single Site

Task	Background	See Page
Perhaps assign some additional domain controllers as global catalog servers.	The first domain controller you install in the enterprise forest automatically becomes a global catalog server. In a large environment, you may want more than one of them.	346
Change the infrastructure master role or the first global catalog server of the root domain to another domain controller if the forest contains several domains.	The first domain controller of a forest is both an infrastructure master and a global catalog server. However, these two roles shouldn't be in the same domain controller (unless you have only one domain in the forest).	411 or 346
In some cases, adjust the replication topology by creating appropriate connection objects.	The replication topology is created and maintained automatically.	380 in the "Advanced Topics" section

SETTING UP MULTIPLE SITES

To set up the physical structure for a multisite Active Directory network, you must first perform the tasks to set up a single site. Obviously, there are a number of additional tasks, which Table 5.9 and Table 5.10 list in their typical order.

NOTE   Table 5.9 and Table 5.10 assume that the physical network is up and running. To "create a subnet" just means that you need to create a certain Active Directory object. You must already have sufficient routers configured for the correct physical subnets and operational WAN links between the routers.

First, let's do a couple of simple things with your default site, which is probably your main site, and your default IP site link.

After performing the tasks in Table 5.9, your main site is configured. Of course, it can take 15 minutes (3 hops of 5 minutes each) for these changes to replicate to all domain controllers in the site.

TABLE 5.9 Tasks for the Default Site and Site Link

Task	Background	See Page
Rename Default-First-Site-Name to something else, such as "Boston."	When you install a new forest, a site called Default-First-Site-Name is created by default. All domain controllers that you install will first belong to this site (until you create additional sites and define their subnets). Because you will have several sites, this first site should have a descriptive name.	338
Create a subnet or subnets for this default site and associate this site with each of the subnets.	Each site should be assigned the correct subnets. This way, additional domain controllers that you install will belong to the appropriate site straight away. This also helps clients find a domain controller for logon and other needs.	339
Define the replication schedule and cost for DEFAULTIPSITELINK.	DEFAULTIPSITELINK is the only site link at this point. You'll probably start using it soon, so it's good to set the schedule now. The cost is relative to costs in other site links; you only need to set the cost if you will have other site links.	348 and 369

NOTE   If at this point your forest already has domain controllers in multiple physical locations, they all belong to one site anyway. The consequence is that they replicate using the intrasite replication mechanisms. Similarly, if you now install new domain controllers, they will go to your main (and only) site.

Next you perform the steps in Table 5.10 for each additional physical location (for which you have decided to create a site).

The tasks in Table 5.9 and Table 5.10 are more or less the normal things that you need to do when setting up the physical structure of Active Directory. In addition, there are a couple of tasks that we consider "advanced" that we list in Table 5.11 and discuss later in the "Advanced Topics" section.

TABLE 5.10 Tasks for Additional Sites and Site Links

Task	Background	See Page
Create a new site, such as "London." Select that it will use DEFAULTIPSITELINK.	Each site must use at least one site link. You can select just the default link at this point. When you create another link, you can attach this site to the new link at that time.	340
Create a subnet or subnets for the newly created site and associate this site with each of the subnets.	Each site should be assigned the correct subnets. This way, additional domain controllers that you install will belong to the appropriate site straight away. This helps clients find a domain controller for logon and other needs.	339
Perhaps create a site link and select sites that will use it. Set the schedule and cost of this site link.	Depending on your physical WAN and domain structure, you may want to create site links in addition to DEFAULTIPSITELINK. The site links are either RPC- ("normal") or SMTP-based.	348 (normal), 386 (SMTP)
Install new domain controllers for the new site and move the ones from your main site that belong here.	For the replication to work efficiently, each domain controller object must belong to the correct site.	341
Select the global catalog servers for the site.	Each site should usually contain at least one global catalog server. They must be assigned manually (except for the first one in a forest).	346

TABLE 5.11 Advanced Tasks for Setting Up Multiple Sites

Task	Background	See Page
If your TCP/IP network is not fully routed or has well over 100 sites, you may need to create site link bridges.	By default, all site links are bridged together. Sometimes you need to break this and create site link bridges for site links manually.	378

(continued)

TABLE 5.11 (*continued*)

Task	Background	See Page
Adjust the replication topology by creating appropriate connection objects and assigning preferred bridgehead servers.	The replication topology is created and maintained automatically (based on the sites and site links you have created). If you are not happy with the default, you can make changes manually. A bridgehead server is the domain controller that will replicate to and from other sites.	371 and 380

ADMINISTERING SITES

After you have set up your site or sites, you can perform the administrative tasks listed in Table 5.12.

TABLE 5.12 Tasks for Administering Sites

Task	Background	See Page
Change some operations master role to another domain controller, especially if the previous one fails.	Although Active Directory replication is mostly multimaster, there are five cases in which a special single-master role is attached to only one domain controller in a domain or the enterprise forest. These five roles are called "operations masters."	411
Use the Replicate Now option to initiate immediate replication.	Occasionally, you may not want to wait 5 minutes (intrasite) or longer (intersite) for the replication to take place. You can select the Replicate Now menu option to initiate immediate replication from one domain controller to another.	343
Use the Check Replication Topology option to initiate an immediate replication topology check.	The KCCs check every 15 minutes (by default) if the replication topology is still optimal. If you change domain controllers, site links, or other background information that affects replication, you can wake up the KCC to perform this check immediately by selecting Check Replication Topology from the menu.	343

(continued)

TABLE 5.12 Tasks for Administering Sites (continued)

Task	Background	See Page
Remove a domain controller.	There are obviously instances when you want to take a domain controller offline or remove it permanently	352
Monitor replication.	You can use various tools to monitor and diagnose replication.	354

If there are changes in your network, in addition to performing the administrative tasks listed in Table 5.12, you must revisit the earlier tasks of setting things up. For example, if you upgrade a WAN link to use a greater speed, you may want to modify some site link costs.

Using the Default-First-Site-Name Site

When you install a new forest, a site called Default-First-Site-Name is created automatically. Until you create more sites, all domain controllers that you install belong to this site. If you will have several sites, this first site should have a descriptive name, so you will want to rename it. If this will be your only site, you may leave the name unchanged. You rename the site like you would rename any other object by pressing F2 or right-clicking the object and selecting Rename. Figure 5.9 shows

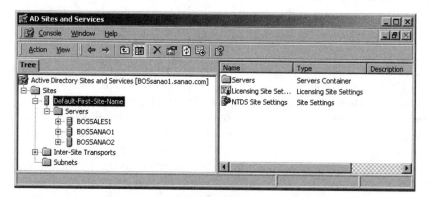

FIGURE 5.9 Default-First-Site-Name is waiting to be renamed to Boston. We include the location in the domain controller names, so the three installed domain controller names start with "BOS."

our sample company Sanao in a phase where the first site is not yet renamed to Boston and the other two sites for San Francisco and London are missing.

After you have created other sites, you can actually move all your domain controllers to them and then delete the Default-First-Site-Name site. However, you gain nothing by doing it this way—it is easier simply to rename the site.

Creating and Managing Subnet Objects

Each site consists of one or more subnets. One of the administrator's tasks is to create an object for each subnet and attach it to the appropriate site object. Figure 5.10 shows the creation of a subnet object.

Once the site's subnet infrastructure is in place, it makes installing domain controllers easier. When you promote a server to a domain controller, it will know by its IP address to which subnet, and thus to which site, it belongs. Otherwise, the domain controller would go to the site of its source domain controller and you might need to move it to the correct site manually. The source domain controller is the domain controller that is contacted by the server being promoted. The latter must be able to communicate with an existing forest during the promotion process.

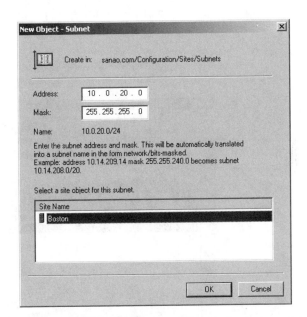

FIGURE 5.10 When creating a subnet object, you must select its site. Our sample company Sanao uses the address 10.0.20.0 for its Boston headquarters.

After you have created a subnet, you can make the following changes:

- *Rename a subnet.* When you rename a subnet, such as 10.0.20.0/24, you actually change either the network address or mask of the subnet.
- *Change the site.* You can select a new site for the subnet if needed.
- *Delete a subnet.*
- *Set the description and location texts.* The location text helps users to locate printers.
- *Change permissions, auditing entries, or ownership of the object.* In practice, you don't do this because the default permissions are fine.

Creating and Managing Site Objects

You define a site for Active Directory by creating an object for the site, as Figure 5.11 illustrates.

If you create a site before you create its site link or links, you must select DEFAULTIPSITELINK. Later when you create the correct site link or links, you can attach them to this site.

If the site link or links for the new site already exist(s), you can select one of them when creating the site object. If you want to attach several site links to the new site, you need to attach the other site links after you have created the site object.

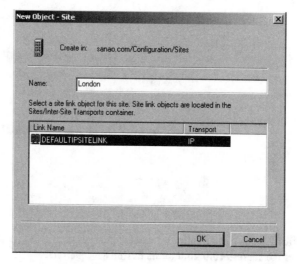

FIGURE 5.11 To create a site object, enter a name for it and select the site link to use.

You can also choose to have the site use DEFAULTIPSITELINK permanently. Other operations you can perform on sites are as follows:

- *Rename a site.* A site name is purely informational, so renaming it doesn't affect anything. Remember, though, that other software may use Active Directory sites.
- *Delete a site.* Before you delete a site, move all its domain controllers to other sites. Otherwise, those server objects will be deleted with the site object, in which event your forest won't have information on all its domain controllers anymore.
- *Set the description and location texts.*
- *Assign Group Policy.* This is discussed in Chapter 7.
- *Change permissions, auditing entries, or ownership of the object.* You can usually get by without doing this, because the default permissions are fine.
- *Set the replication schedule in NTDS Site Settings.* Intrasite replication is notification based (with a default delay of 5 minutes), so this schedule is used only as a backup mechanism in case a notification message gets lost. If you think you'll lose sleep worrying about lost notifications, you could change this backup schedule from 60 minutes to a lower value, such as 30 or 15 minutes.

Moving and Managing Server Objects

Each domain controller in an Active Directory forest is represented by a server object, which contains an NTDS Settings object. As mentioned earlier, the server object may already belong to the appropriate site or you may need to move it there. The location of the server objects tells Active Directory which domain controllers are on the same site so it can decide, for example, whether to use intrasite or intersite replication mechanisms and how to build the replication topology.

The object type is Server, not Domain Controller, because it could also represent member servers of the forest. This enables you to define, for example, on which sites the member servers that are running your DFS services will reside.

Server objects for domain controllers contain an NTDS Settings object, but server objects for member servers don't. Server objects for domain controllers are created automatically, but server objects for member servers must be created manually (only if you need to define a location of a member server).

NOTE   In this chapter we often refer to a domain controller object (or just domain controller) when we mean the server object that corresponds to a domain controller. This occurs most of the time, actually, because we don't talk much about member servers.

Figure 5.12 shows the Sanao configuration after the London site has been created but before the two corresponding domain controller objects were moved there. Subnet 10.0.22.0 is for London, but you don't need the subnet when you move domain controllers.

NOTE   Because of replication latency, it may take a while until you can see a moved server in the new site.

Now that the London site exists and the subnet 10.0.22.0 has been defined for it, any new domain controller that is using a corresponding IP address (10.0.22.x) will appear in the London site right after it has been promoted.

In addition to moving domain controller objects between locations, you can also perform the following operations on the server objects:

- *Delete a server object.* We discuss this operation in the "Removing Domain Controllers" section.

- *Set the description text.* This text is purely informational.

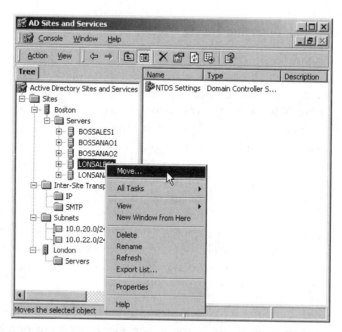

FIGURE 5.12 The London site was just created so the two "LON" domain controllers are still under the Boston site object. Now we move them to the correct location, the London site.

- *Set a domain controller as a preferred bridgehead.* This setting causes the domain controller to be the "only one" to communicate with domain controllers on other sites. We discuss this later in this chapter in the "Intersite Replication Topologies" section.

- *Change the computer object associated with a server object.* You could use this operation when you have created a server object for a member server.

- *Change permissions, auditing entries, or ownership of the object.* You probably won't perform any of these operations, because the default permissions are fine.

NOTE   You cannot rename a domain controller.

Managing NTDS Settings

As mentioned earlier, every server object corresponding to a domain controller contains an NTDS Settings child object. This child object hosts the domain controller–specific properties, which control replication to that domain controller. The existence of the NTDS Settings object also indicates that the corresponding server is a domain controller.

The NTDS Settings object in turn contains connection objects that dictate where the domain controller pulls its replication data from. The KCCs in each domain controller create connection objects automatically when building up the replication topology. You can also create and manage the connection objects manually, which we discuss in the "Intersite Replication Topologies" section later in the chapter.

The associated operations are as follows:

- *Check the replication topology.* If you make changes that could affect the optimal replication topology, such as when you add domain controllers or change site links, you can either wait up to 15 minutes for the KCC to wake up or you can initiate the check immediately by right-clicking NTDS Settings and selecting Check Replication Topology. For intersite topologies, this function takes effect only if the corresponding domain controller is an *inter-site topology generator.*

- *Replicate now.* If you don't want to wait 5 minutes for the intrasite replication to take place (or longer for the intersite replication), you can right-click a connection object and select Replicate Now.

- *Set the description text for NTDS Settings.* This text is purely informational.

- *Set the query policy.* Query policies enable administrators to set certain maximums for the resources a domain controller may use when answering LDAP queries of LDAP clients. The maximums can be used to prevent denial of service attacks, for example. The NTDSUtil tool allows definition of the default policy values. You can also programmatically (using ADSI) create query policy objects and then select one of them for a certain domain controller or site. The Windows 2000 Resource Kit includes a script, ModifyLDAP.vbs, that enables you to create and manage query policies. Because query policies are related to the LDAP protocol and not the physical structure of Active Directory, we don't cover them here.

- *Set a domain controller to be a global catalog server.*

Figures 5.13 through 5.16 show how to use an NTDS Settings object and the connection objects in it.

NOTE   You can check the replication topology for BOSsanao1 even though your Sites and Services snap-in is connected to BOSsanao2. This will adjust the connection objects of BOSsanao1 immediately. However, these adjustments won't show until they have replicated from BOSsanao1 to BOSsanao2 and you have selected Refresh.

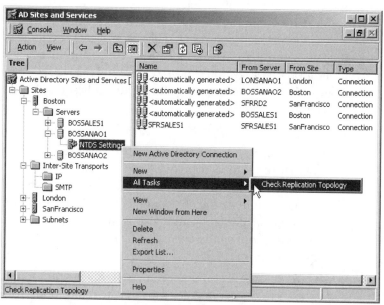

FIGURE 5.13 You can manually check if the automatically generated connection objects are still optimal. In addition, the KCC performs the check automatically every 15 minutes.

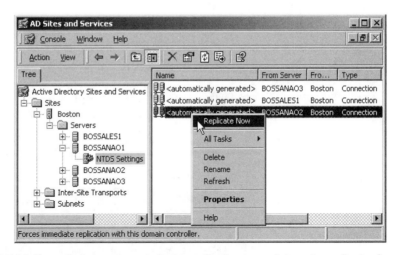

FIGURE 5.14 If you don't want to wait 5 minutes for the automatic intrasite replication from BOSSANAO2 to BOSSANAO1, you can start it immediately.

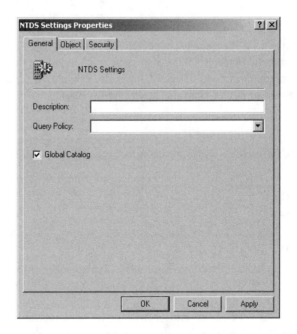

FIGURE 5.15 NTDS Settings properties include an indication of whether or not the corresponding domain controller is a global catalog server.

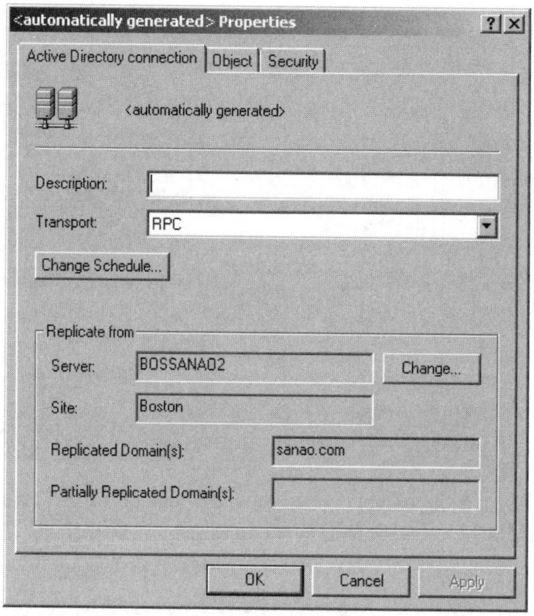

FIGURE 5.16 The property page of a connection object defines where to replicate from and what to replicate. "Replicated Domain(s): sanao.com" means that this domain controller replicates the domain partition from BOSsanao2. It will also replicate the schema and configuration partitions, even though this isn't indicated on the property page.

PROMOTING A DOMAIN CONTROLLER TO BE A GLOBAL CATALOG SERVER

If you implement Active Directory in a new remote office, you will probably have at least one domain controller there, and at least one of the domain controllers would be a global catalog server.

If you have a large network and a lot of objects in Active Directory, you may want to perform the implementation in steps. You can first install a domain controller to the remote office, let it replicate the domain partition, and let the local administrators get acquainted with the new environment.

After a few days, or perhaps a week, when you can see that everything is OK, you can set the domain controller to be a global catalog server also. If there was 500MB to replicate for the domain partition, the global catalog might now need another 500MB.

When you check Global Catalog in the NTDS Settings properties and click OK or Apply, the corresponding domain controller starts replicating in the partial replicas of other domains in the forest (depending on the schedule settings). It doesn't yet advertise itself to be a global catalog server.

By default, advertising starts when the domain controller has received a partial replica of all other domains that have a domain controller on the same site. Advertising means that the domain controller dynamically registers the appropriate SRV records in DNS.

Once the global catalog promotion is complete and the advertising starts, the advertising doesn't stop, even if there is to be a new domain that the global catalog server doesn't have yet. You can check to see if a domain controller is a global catalog server (i.e., the promotion is complete) in the following ways.

- There is a registry entry `Global Catalog Promotion Complete` with the value "1" in the key `HKEY_LOCAL_MACHINE, SYSTEM, CurrentControl- Set, Services, NTDS, Parameters`.

- The `rootDSE` object contains an attribute `isGlobalCatalogReady` with the value TRUE. You can see this by starting the LDP utility, opening the Connection menu, selecting Connect, typing the domain controller name, and clicking OK. The attribute should now be visible in the right-hand pane. (In addition, Chapter 11 contains a script to display the `rootDSE` attributes.)

- Go to the command prompt and enter a command such as `nltest /dsgetdc:sanao /server:dc1`. You should see eight lines of information about the domain controller. If the promotion is complete, the last line (`Flags`) contains "GC."

NOTE   LDP and NLTest are included in Windows 2000 Support Tools.

If you uncheck Global Catalog in the NTDS Settings properties and click OK or Apply, the KCC in the corresponding domain controller starts tearing down the partial replicas of that domain controller. It removes 500 objects every 15 minutes as long as there are objects to remove. At this pace, the KCC removes 2,000 objects in an hour, or 48,000 objects in 24 hours. Depending on the number of objects in your forest, it may take a while for the KCC to complete its mission. In the next version of Active Directory included in Windows .NET Server, the teardown pace will be faster.

If during the teardown process you recheck the domain controller to be a global catalog server again, the KCC is not allowed to add partial replicas that are currently being removed. Consequently, only when the last partial replica has been removed can the last partial replica be added again and the domain controller start advertising itself as a global catalog server.

Creating and Managing Site Links

A site link connects two or more sites. As you create each site, you must associate it with at least one site link. As Figure 5.17 shows, site link objects reside under Inter-Site Transports in either the IP or SMTP container depending on whether they apply to RPC or SMTP replication, respectively.

If you have only two sites, you don't need more than one site link: DEFAULT-IPSITELINK. If you have a few sites, say three or four, you may still do fine with no additional site links. This is true if the network among the sites is like a cloud or a mesh (e.g., a frame relay network). That is, it doesn't matter which route the packets take as they travel from one site to another.

Knowing which site links to create requires familiarity with the intersite topologies of Active Directory. We address topologies and planning site links in the advanced section of this chapter.

You usually create site links in the IP container. The process to create STMP site links is similar, but there are some special considerations. We discuss SMTP site links later in the "Configuring SMTP Replication" section.

Besides the descriptive text and the list of sites, a site link has three properties you can set: cost, replication interval, and schedule (see Figure 5.18).

- Cost is a number between 1 and 32,767, with the default being 100. It doesn't represent actual money—it is just a number that Active Directory compares with costs in other site links. When building the intersite replication topology, Active Directory favors site links with lower cost over links with higher cost. Because a site link's cost is relative to the costs of other site links, the cost doesn't matter when you have only one site link. We discuss assignment of costs in the "Site Link Costs" section later in this chapter.

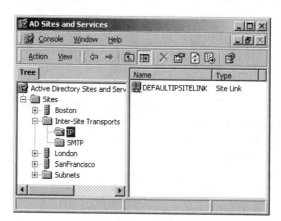

FIGURE 5.17 The first site link is the predefined DEFAULTIPSITELINK. As you need them, you can create more site links in the containers IP and SMTP.

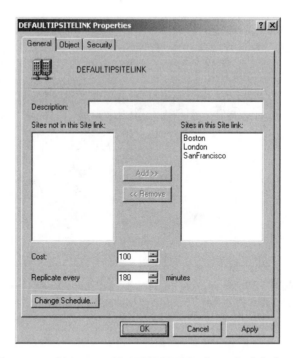

FIGURE 5.18 All three sites of Sanao use DEFAULTIPSITELINK first. The default relative cost is 100 and default replication interval is 180 minutes, or 3 hours.

- The "Replicate every" field indicates the replication interval in minutes. By default, intersite replication takes place every 3 hours (180 minutes). The possible range is 15 to 10,080 minutes (1 week).

- The Change Schedule button enables you to list the weekdays and hours when this site link is available—that is, when replication can occur using the interval indicated in the "Replicate every" property field. By default, a site link is always available. Figure 5.19 shows the dialog box that appears when you click the Change Schedule button.

As illustrated in Figure 5.6, the replication properties of a site link object don't affect replication directly. Instead, they act as a template for automatically generated connection objects. When a connection object is generated, the effect of the site link's interval and availability properties is combined. For example, if the interval for a site link is 30 minutes and the link is available from 5:00 PM to 7:00 AM daily, the resulting connection object's schedule will be "twice per hour, but only from 5:00 PM to 7:00 AM."

The IP and SMTP containers have two check boxes that affect all site link objects under the corresponding container (see Figure 5.20).

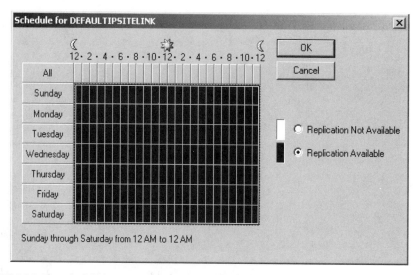

FIGURE 5.19 The schedule for a site link indicates the hours and days of the week that the site link is available. By default, it is always available.

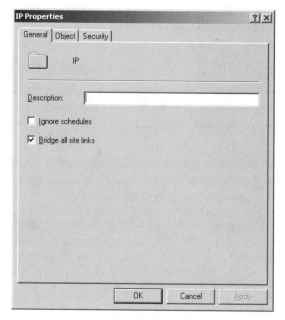

FIGURE 5.20 The IP and SMTP containers have two settings that affect all the site links under the corresponding container.

If you check the "Ignore schedules" box, replication will be always available to the corresponding protocol, using the interval specified in the "Replicate every" field. SMTP ignores schedules by default. The "Bridge all site links" check box is discussed in the advanced section "Intersite Replication Topologies"—for now, don't touch it.

Managing Licensing Computers

Each site has one server designated as a licensing computer. By default, it is the first domain controller on the site, but you can change the role to another server. The licensing computer does not have to be a domain controller. Figure 5.21 shows one of the property pages of the Licensing Site Settings object.

A licensing computer stores licensing information in three files in the %Systemroot%\System32 folder (often C:\Winnt\System32). The file LLS\LlsUser.LLS (user and usage information) is always present. Files CPL.CFG (purchase history) and LLS\LlsMap.LLS (license groups) are present depending on the licensing configuration and group mappings you selected. If you want to move the information in these files to the new server when you change a licensing computer, you need to do the following:

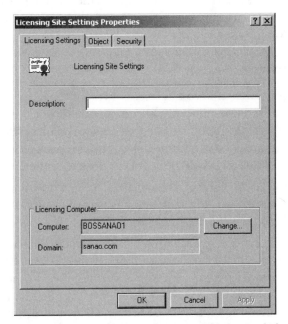

FIGURE 5.21 Each site object has Licensing Site Settings as a child object, which enables you to select the licensing computer for the site.

1. Change the licensing computer to be a new server.

2. Stop the License Logging service on the new server.

3. Copy the three files from the old server to the new server to the same locations as on the old server.

4. Start the License Logging service on the new server.

NOTE   The level of sophistication (or rather, the lack of it) of the Windows 2000 License Logging service and the administrative user interface is about the same as that contained in Windows NT.

Removing Domain Controllers

From time to time, you may want to take a domain controller offline, either temporarily or permanently. It is best to do this in a planned and organized way.

First, consider how the downtime of the domain controller will affect your network. This obviously depends on the current functions of the domain controller, the length of the downtime, your network size, your network configuration, and so on.

The domain controller may offer the following Active Directory–related services:

- *Normal domain services.* Even if the target domain controller is a plain domain controller with no special services, it should offer logon and LDAP services (among others) to network clients. Each domain probably has other domain controllers to offer these services as well, but the one you are taking offline might be the only one close to some users.

- *Global catalog server.* If the target domain controller is a global catalog server, will you have enough global catalog servers (in suitable locations) if you remove this one?

- *Operations master roles.* If the target domain controller holds some operations master roles, depending on the roles and length of the downtime, you should perhaps transfer the roles to another domain controller(s). If you demote the domain controller by running DCPromo, the roles will be transferred automatically. However, Microsoft recommends that you do not rely on this automatic role transfer feature. We discuss the five operations master roles, including the impact of the downtime of each, in the "Managing Operations Masters" section later in this chapter.

- *Bridgehead server.* The target domain controller may be a bridgehead server, meaning that intersite replication goes through that domain controller. If you haven't assigned preferred bridgehead servers, Active Directory will select a new bridgehead server if the original goes offline.

NOTE   Remember to check whether the target domain controller hosts any services that are not related to Active Directory, such as normal file services, Web services, and application services.

Once you have made sure that you can take the domain controller offline without undesirable consequences, you can do so with the following instructions. (Remember that "temporary" tends to become "permanent.")

- Shut down the domain controller and do whatever maintenance you need to do. This is probably OK for a short downtime. Note, however, that your domain controller doesn't replicate any changes to other domain controllers before shutdown. Therefore, if you can't get the domain controller back online for any reason, you lose the recent changes to Active Directory (the ones that weren't replicated). You can reduce the risk if you use the Replicate Now function just before shutting down. Because that operation initiates only incoming replication, you must select some other domain controller of the same domain for which you perform the Replicate Now operation.

- If the downtime extends to days or you cannot get the domain controller online at all, you can delete the corresponding NTDS Settings object. This way, the KCCs will know that this domain controller doesn't exist and they will adapt the replication topology accordingly. Note, however, that even if you don't delete the NTDS Settings, the other domain controllers will notice that one is missing and they will create temporary connections to bypass the missing domain controller. It is not possible to delete the NTDS Settings object while the domain controller is still online. If you bring the domain controller back online, it will recreate the NTDS Settings object and things will get back to normal. Even though you could delete the NTDS Settings object manually, Microsoft Knowledge Base article Q216498 ("How to Remove Data in the Active Directory after an Unsuccessful Domain Controller Demotion") describes the steps to delete the object using the NTDSUtil command-line tool. The advantage of using NTDSUtil is that it performs a more complete cleanup of obsolete objects and DNS records.

- If you are permanently removing a domain controller, you must first demote it to a member server (or to a stand-alone server, if it is the last domain controller in the domain) by running DCPromo. This will delete the NTDS Settings object automatically and has the benefit of replicating all the recent changes out from the domain controller. The process also automatically transfers any operations master roles (but not global catalogs) to other domain controllers. After you have shut the server down permanently, you can delete the corresponding server and computer objects.

NOTE   The server object and NTDS Settings object will be recreated if you restart the corresponding domain controller. However, once you delete the computer object, it's difficult, if not impossible, to get the domain controller back into your domain (except by reinstalling it or by authoritatively restoring the computer object from a backup).

NOTE   If you delete the computer object for a running domain controller, it cannot replicate with other domain controllers anymore. Note that even though it is isolated from the rest of the domain, it may still accept changes and logons from workstations, which don't suspect that there is anything wrong. If you add a workstation to the domain, it may create its object in this isolated domain controller and you will be in trouble, because you now have two versions of your domain.

When you demote a domain controller to a member server, the corresponding computer object is moved from Domain Controllers (or whatever container it was in) to the Computers container and the membership of the object is changed from the Domain Controllers group to Domain Computers. If you change a member server from a domain to a workgroup, the corresponding computer object will be disabled, but not deleted. You may delete it if you wish.

Monitoring and Diagnosing the Physical Structure

A number of tools help you monitor and diagnose the physical structure of Active Directory. The *Distributed Systems Guide* of the Windows 2000 Server Resource Kit contains about 200 pages about monitoring and diagnosing Active Directory. We recommend it as a source of information and for detailed instructions on how to solve a certain problem or use a certain tool. Table 5.13 lists the names of the tools, along with brief descriptions.

TIP   The contents of the *Distributed Systems Guide* of the Windows 2000 Server
            Resource Kit are available on Microsoft's Web site (`http://www.microsoft.`
            `com/`), so you can point your Web browser there and perform a search using
            words that relate to your problem.

TABLE 5.13 Tools to Diagnose Replication

Tool	Type	Description
Sites and Services	Snap-in	We described this tool earlier in this chapter.
Replication Monitor* (ReplMon.exe)	Graphical	A feature-rich but not very polished tool to show and log various aspects of the physical structure.
Event Viewer	Snap-in	One of the Windows 2000 logs is Directory Service. Event sources NTDS Replication and NTDS KCC generate information, warnings, or error messages related to replication.
Performance Monitor	Snap-in	The NTDS performance object includes more than 100 counters. The names of quite a few start with *DRA* (Directory Replication Agent). You can use them, for example, to show a graph over time of replicated incoming and outgoing bytes.
Network Monitor (NetMon.exe)	Graphical	You can use Network Monitor to capture and analyze network packets (called frames). The version included in Windows 2000 has some restrictions. For example, you can capture only packets that are sent to or from the local computer (including multicasts and broadcasts). The full version is included in Microsoft Systems Management Server (SMS).
Registry Editor (RegEdt32.exe)	Graphical	You can use Registry Editor to specify some settings or to check existing settings.
RepAdmin.exe*	Command	Includes about 20 command-line switches that enable you to show replication data or manage replication.
DCDiag.exe*	Command	Tests to see if all is OK in one domain controller or all domain controllers of a site or forest.

(continued)

TABLE 5.13 Tools to Diagnose Replication (*continued*)

Tool	Type	Description
NetDiag.exe*	Command	Performs a number of network connectivity tests and is also able to fix minor problems.
NLTest.exe*	Command	Includes about 30 command-line switches that enable you to show, as well as manage, domain and replication-related information.
DSAStat.exe*	Command	Compares replicas on different domain controllers and detects differences.
NTDSUtil.exe	Command	Biased to managing the directory database, although it has other functions too. One function related to this chapter is to remove the Active Directory objects of a selected domain controller or partition. You could use the former function if your demotion process would be interrupted for some reason, leaving some unnecessary objects still in Active Directory.

* These tools are included in Windows 2000 Support Tools, which you need to install separately from the Windows 2000 CD.

Replication Permissions

To be able to use the Replicate Now feature, an administrator must have the Replication Synchronization extended right for the root object of each partition (i.e., schema, configuration, and domain for normal domain controllers, and also the remaining domains for global catalog servers). You can use the ACL Editor to assign this permission to appropriate administrators, as explained in Chapter 4. The easiest way to locate all necessary objects is to use ADSI Edit and launch the ACL Editor from there.

To be able to get replication status, an administrator must have the Manage Replication Topology extended right. All the information in the previous paragraph applies also to this permission.

ADVANCED TOPICS

We have postponed the discussion of the advanced topics until this section. One obvious reason is that this way you could learn the easier skills and concepts before delving into the finer aspects of replication. The other reason is that an administrator could install and use Active Directory quite well without this information, at least if his network doesn't span multiple sites. The subjects covered here are as follows:

- Intrasite and intersite replication topologies
- Configuring SMTP replication
- The replication process
- Time synchronization
- Managing operations masters

Even though you may not need this in-depth knowledge when you first use Active Directory, eventually you will probably encounter situations that require it. An administrator who has a deep understanding of the network's physical structure is equipped for troubleshooting and solving the problems that arise.

Intrasite Replication Topologies

As mentioned earlier, Knowledge Consistency Checkers (KCCs) automatically create topologies for both intrasite and intersite replication. When determining the optimal topology, KCCs base their decisions on replication objects such as sites, site links, and domain controllers (or to be exact, the NTDS Settings objects). If there are changes in these objects, the KCCs automatically make the necessary alterations. They also monitor replication for problems that would necessitate temporary or permanent changes in the topology.

REPLICATION RING

An automatically created intrasite replication topology forms a bidirectional ring, as Figure 5.22 shows.

Each domain controller establishes an inbound *replication partnership* with two other domain controllers. For example, in Figure 5.22 DC1 will pull replication data from DC2 and DC5.

The order of the domain controllers in the ring is determined by the object-GUID property of the NTDS Settings object under their corresponding domain controller objects. The domain controllers are sorted in ascending order and the ones with the smallest and largest GUIDs close the ring.

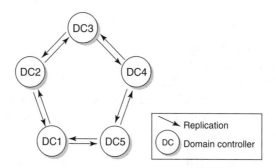

FIGURE 5.22 An intrasite replication topology forms a bidirectional ring.

DRAWING THE REPLICATION RING

It is beneficial to know the order of domain controllers in your replication ring when you diagnose replication problems or use the Replicate Now function to get some changes faster to other domain controllers. Therefore, you may want to document the ring order on each site of your network. If you install five domain controllers and call them DC1, DC2, DC3, DC4, and DC5, they probably won't be in consecutive order in the ring. Figure 5.22 assumes that the GUIDs happen to be in the same order as the server names.

Chapter 11 presents a short script that lists the GUIDs. The list helps you to document your topology.

Another way to get the GUID list is to use the DNS management snap-in, with some manual work. Select Forward Lookup Zones, "your forest name", _msdcs and you will see a list of GUIDs, each corresponding to one of your domain controllers. Export the list to a text file by right-clicking _msdcs with your mouse. Next, edit the file to extract the lines that belong to the site you are interested in. Before you can sort the GUIDs to help you in drawing the ring, you must edit each GUID. When you see a GUID represented with dashes, the byte order is different from the actual binary format. Therefore, you need to swap bytes of the first three parts of the GUID, but not the last two. You change bytes 1, 2, 3, 4 to 4, 3, 2, 1, so if you start with "752d5592-07de-11d3-a61f-4000f006f0d0," you will get "92552d75-de07-d311-a61f-4000f006f0d0." Now you can sort the GUIDs "alphabetically" and draw your ring.

CONNECTION OBJECTS

As you learned earlier, each domain controller object (i.e., NTDS Settings) hosts a connection object for each inbound replication partner—that is, the partners it pulls data from—as Figure 5.23 illustrates.

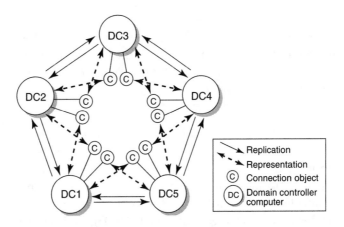

FIGURE 5.23 Each domain controller object (i.e., NTDS Settings) has a connection object for each inbound partner. Thus, in a bidirectional ring there are two connection objects in each domain controller object.

The KCCs add, delete, and possibly modify the connection objects automatically. However, they don't delete or modify any connection objects that you created. If you delete an automatically created connection object, a KCC may soon recreate it, if it determines that it is needed anyway. If you manually modify an automatically created connection object, you have the option to change it to be administered manually.

NOTE   Each connection object has an options property, which determines the "owner" of the object. If the least significant bit of options is 1, the object is maintained automatically by the KCC; if it is 0, you will maintain the object manually.

Intrasite replication should work just fine with the automatic topology, so we explain the process of creating connection objects with the discussion of intersite replication.

AS THE RING GROWS

When you add a domain controller, its place in the ring is determined by its GUID. It kind of "squeezes" in between its two new neighbors.

The KCCs take care that there are almost never more than three hops between any two domain controllers in the intrasite replication topology. Because the replication delay with one hop is 5 minutes, a three-hop maximum means that a change to an Active Directory object will reach all domain controllers in the site in 15 minutes.

NOTE   Remember that the 5-minute delay may actually be slightly longer. When the domain controller with changes notifies its replication partners, it adds 30 seconds for each partner after the first one. Consequently, 15 minutes is not always an accurate time frame.

The largest ring that has three hops at most between any two domain controllers has seven domain controllers. When a ring has eight or more domain controllers, the KCCs add shortcut connections to the basic ring. Otherwise, the greatest "distance" would be four hops or more. In an eight-DC ring, each domain controller has a third (shortcut) inbound connection, and the starting point is chosen randomly regardless of GUIDs. Figure 5.24 shows a ring topology of eight domain controllers.

The exact logic for a KCC to add shortcut connections goes as follows:

1. The KCC knows the number of domain controllers in the ring.

2. Based on this number, the KCC calculates the minimum number of connections that each domain controller must have to get a topology, where the path between any two domain controllers is three hops at the most.

3. If the local domain controller has fewer than this number of connections, the KCC chooses random source domain controllers from the ring and creates connections from them to achieve this minimum number of connections.

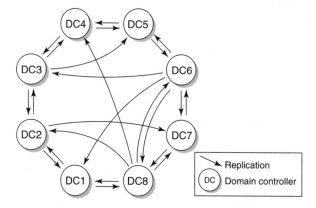

FIGURE 5.24 When the replica ring grows to at least eight domain controllers, it must have shortcut connections to maintain the three-hop maximum.

NOTE   The exact logic of creating shortcut connections means that the KCCs only approximate the three-hop maximum. The minimum number of connections that is calculated in step 2 assumes that those connections will exist between domain controllers in the optimal way. However, in step 3 the connections are created randomly. Therefore, in rare cases of a large ring, the maximum number of hops could be four, resulting in a 20-minute replication latency.

The KCCs run independently in each domain controller and they don't negotiate with each other when building the topology. But because they base their decisions on the same information (the replication objects) and use the same algorithms, they cooperate to build a common topology.

NOTE   The number of connection objects per domain controller can be larger than described here, which might happen if there are some DNS problems or other connectivity problems in the network. If a domain controller cannot contact some of its replication partners, it will create temporary connection objects to bypass the failed connection.

IN TRANSITION

The independence of the KCCs means that each one will change its part of the topology at a slightly different time than the next one. By default, a KCC wakes up 5 minutes after a domain controller boots up and every 15 minutes thereafter.

A new domain controller will add its connection objects right away. The existing domain controllers accommodate the change, as the KCC in each one happens to wake up on its own schedule. Consequently, it may take 15 minutes or longer before the topology shown in Figures 5.22 through 5.24 is actually completed.

When a replication object such as a domain controller object is created or changed in a domain controller, it needs to be replicated to other domain controllers, just like any ordinary Active Directory object does. Also, it may also take 15 minutes for this change to reach all domain controllers in the site. Therefore, if some KCCs check the replication topology during this period, they will find outdated information on which to base their decisions.

The new topology should be applied throughout the site in a half hour—that is, after 15 minutes (for replication latency) plus 15 minutes (for any KCC to wake up). Of course, it will take yet another 15 minutes until the changes any KCC made are replicated back to other domain controllers. Finally, after 45 minutes the replication objects of the site should be consistent again.

NOTE   Remember that a KCC picks a random starting point for a shortcut connection. Therefore, if you delete a shortcut connection object and then initiate Check Replication Topology, the new connection object you get will probably be for a different source domain controller. There is no harm done if you try this out.

SEVERAL PARTITIONS

All that we have said so far about intrasite replication rings assumes that the domain controllers are part of the same domain. The situation is a little different when there are several domains, because each replication partition has its own independent replication topology. When you think about it, it is actually quite obvious, because the whole idea of a partition is to be the unit of replication.

The domain controllers of domain A create a replication topology for that domain, the domain controllers of domain B create another replication topology, and so on. Schema and configuration partitions use a common topology, because every domain controller of an enterprise forest has a replica of each of these partitions.

In addition, the global catalog must be replicated across domains, obviously using the computers that are assigned to be global catalog servers.

Figure 5.25 shows how replication topologies for multiple partitions build up. By *domain replication* we mean the replication of a domain partition between domain controllers of that domain. *Enterprise replication* means the replication of schema and configuration partitions. This figure does not show global catalog replication.

NOTE   To make the figure less crowded, we use bidirectional arrows instead of the unidirectional arrows in previous figures.

In phase 1 we have three domain controllers, all of which belong to domain A. Both the domain partition and the two enterprise partitions replicate with a simple replication ring.

Next, in phase 2 we add the first domain controller for domain B. This, of course, doesn't incur any changes to domain A's topology, but the enterprise replication ring accommodates this new domain controller. Note that the enterprise connection between A2 and A3 is not removed. Because that connection is

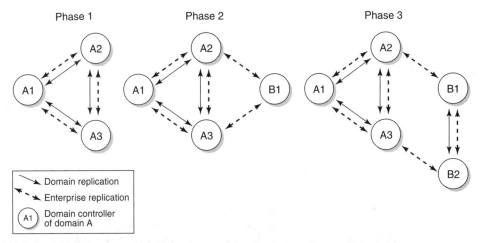

FIGURE 5.25 Domains A and B have their own replication topologies. Schema and configuration partitions use a common topology, shown with the "enterprise replication" arrows. In phase 1 we have only domain A. In phase 2 we add the first domain controller for domain B, and in phase 3 we add a second domain controller for domain B.

needed for the domain A ring, the same connection can be used for the enterprise replication as well.

NOTE Even though each partition has an independent topology, the enterprise topology mostly follows a domain topology while "traveling" in that domain. That is, a domain replication connection is never alone; it always has an enterprise replication connection running parallel to it.

Finally, in phase 3 we add a second domain controller for domain B. Again, this doesn't affect domain A's ring, but the enterprise ring gets one additional member. Domain B also gets a small "ring" as B1 and B2 replicate from each other. This time the old connection between A3 and B1 is removed. It would have been used only for enterprise replication, which didn't need that connection anymore.

Figure 5.26 shows the several partitions of Sanao Corporation's Boston site.

NOTE Starting with Figure 5.26 we simplified the diagrams. Because a domain connection always has an enterprise connection by its side, we show the latter connections only when they exist alone.

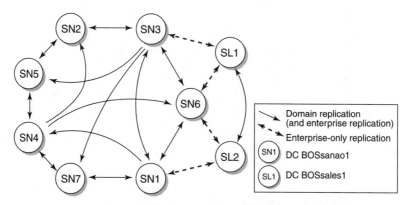

FIGURE 5.26 The seven domain controllers in `sanao.com` comprise one ring, and the two in `sales.sanao.com` another. Together they build a nine-DC enterprise ring. In that ring BOSsanao6 is between BOSsales1 and BOSsales2 because of the GUID order of their NTDS Settings objects.

GLOBAL CATALOG REPLICATION

Each domain controller that is a global catalog server must host all the objects of all the domains in the enterprise. That domain controller has by nature the objects of its own domain. Although global catalog servers host all objects of the forest, they host only part of the properties (those that are part of the global catalog) of the objects in the other domains. A global catalog server must get the objects of other domains by global catalog replication. The corresponding replicas are called *partial replicas* and, obviously, only some of the properties need to be replicated to them. Figure 5.27 shows the replicas and replication of the global catalog in Sanao Corporation's forest. Figure 5.28 shows how global catalog replication fits in the replication topology.

Global catalog replication from a full-domain replica is one-way, such as from B1 to A1 in Figure 5.28. Just as with domain replication, a global catalog replication partnership doesn't exist alone. It always has an enterprise replication partnership by its side.

Figure 5.29 shows the global catalog replication of Sanao Corporation's Boston site.

Intersite Replication Topologies

Now that we have described the intrasite topologies, we are ready to examine the intersite case. Intersite topologies are like intrasite topologies in that KCCs automatically create intersite topologies based on replication objects. The resulting topology, however, is a spanning tree instead of a ring. While in the intrasite case

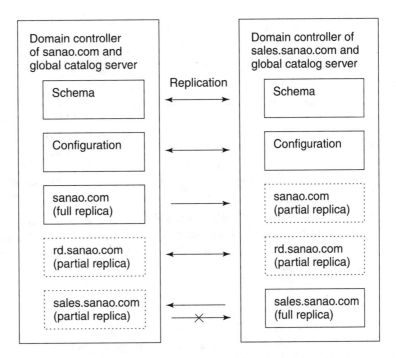

FIGURE 5.27 A normal (full) domain replica can be a source for the global catalog (partial replica), but not vice versa. Also, partial replicas (the ones in the global catalog) can be sources for each other.

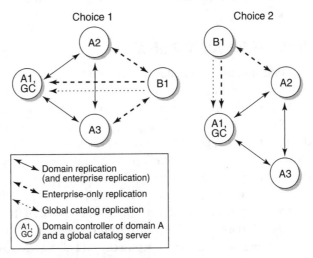

FIGURE 5.28 Global catalog replication takes place from B1 to A1, and in this case it is unidirectional. It must be this way because B1 is the sole domain controller in domain B and A1 is the only global catalog server in the enterprise forest. Whether the forest uses choice 1 or 2 depends on B1's location in the enterprise replication ring.

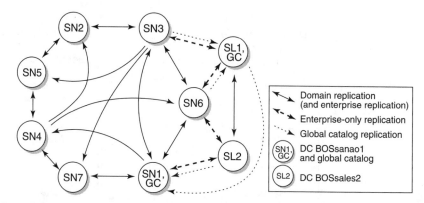

FIGURE 5.29 Sanao Corporation has two global catalog servers in Boston, which happen to be domain controllers in different domains. The two servers get their cross-domain data mainly via existing connections. Only the connection from BOSsales1 to BOSsanao1 is new compared to the topology in Figure 5.26.

the replication objects are created automatically, in the intersite case administrators must plan what objects (excluding the connection objects) to have as well as create them manually. Also, it is more likely in the intersite case that administrators would create all or part of the topology (i.e., the connection objects) manually.

We start by explaining the "operator" that is responsible for creating the topology.

INTER-SITE TOPOLOGY GENERATOR

The first domain controller on each site becomes the *inter-site topology generator (ISTG)* for that site. It means that the KCC in that machine is responsible for managing the incoming intersite connections for all domain controllers on its site.

When building an intrasite topology, it is possible that a number of independent KCCs are operating and still producing a single, agreed-upon topology (based on the GUID ordering). In an intersite topology, however, a single KCC must be responsible for the whole site; therefore, the ISTG is designated.

There is one ISTG on each site. If the original ISTG becomes unavailable, another domain controller automatically assumes that role. The change is easy because no data has to be transferred from the old ISTG to the new one.

The Sites and Services snap-in doesn't allow you to control which domain controller has the role, but you can see the current owner in the property page of the NTDS Site Settings object under each site object. You can change the ISTG role to another domain controller by modifying the `interSiteTopologyGenerator` property of the NTDS Site Settings object, using ADSI Edit, for example. However, there should be no need to change the role manually, unless you have such a large network that you want to change the role to a domain controller, which must have ample CPU power to perform the calculations needed to determine the optimal topology.

SITE LINKS AND THE TOPOLOGY

The automatic intersite topology generation has the following two phases:

1. You create appropriate site link objects and possibly specify some other settings (e.g., in the IP container object) to give Active Directory hints for the kind of topology it should create.

2. Based on the information from the previous phase, the ISTG on each site creates the incoming connection objects for the domain controllers on its site. These connection objects comprise the intersite topology of the forest.

The two phases may overlap. After all, each KCC wakes up every 15 minutes to check if any changes to the topology are necessary.

Next we examine which routes Active Directory uses between sites in an intersite topology. Our samples require only one domain controller on each site and only one domain in the forest. Compare the two cases in Figure 5.30. In case A there is one site link among three sites, and in case B there are two site links.

NOTE   Remember that site link objects represent connections between sites, and the resulting connection objects represent connections between domain controllers.

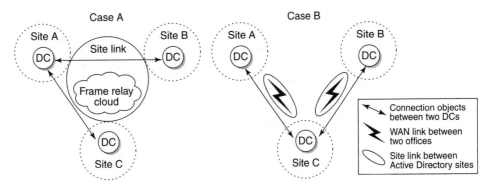

FIGURE 5.30 When Active Directory site links are created according to the physical network, they ensure that connections between domain controllers use the physical network efficiently.

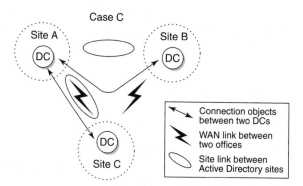

FIGURE 5.31 Poorly selected site links result in inefficient intersite replication.

Case A's network has a cloudlike WAN. It doesn't matter whether domain controllers on sites A and B or on sites B and C communicate. Consequently, we create only one site link object to connect all three Active Directory sites and thus let the ISTGs freely decide which connections to create. Case B has a physical WAN link between offices A and C and another physical WAN link between offices B and C. To ensure that the connections between domain controllers match the physical WAN links, we must create the site links to match the WAN links.

NOTE   Active Directory cannot sense the physical WAN topology. You must describe it using correct site links.

Figure 5.31 presents case C where the site links are not optimal. Site links between sites A and B and between sites A and C cause corresponding connections between the domain controllers. In this case, if we create Jack Brown in the domain controller on site B, that object will be replicated first to the domain controller on site A. However, the network packets will travel through the router in office C. Finally, Jack Brown is replicated from site A to site C, meaning that the object travels again in the wire between offices A and C, although now in the opposite direction. Obviously, this setup is not efficient.

Figure 5.32 illustrates case D. Now there are two consecutive site links from site A to C to B. The difference between case C (in Figure 5.31) and case D (in Figure 5.32) is that in case D the domain doesn't have a domain controller on site C. Consequently, the domain controllers on sites A and B must communicate directly. This is possible because two things are true:

• The two consecutive site links are bridged. This is not shown in this figure but as you saw earlier in this chapter, the IP container by default contains the setting "Bridge all site links." This is sometimes expressed with the words "by

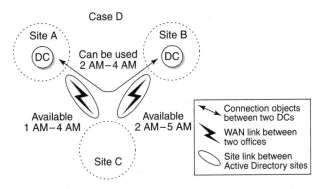

FIGURE 5.32 By default, all site links are bridged together, which allows two domain controllers to create a connection over several consecutive site links.

default site links are transitive." If you remove the default setting, you may need to create site link bridge objects, as discussed later in this chapter.

- The schedules of the two site links overlap so that there is a common time window between 2:00 AM and 4:00 AM every day.

If the two site links have different replication intervals, the longer one is used.

NOTE The cost of site links doesn't matter in cases A, B, C, and D. The cost is meaningful only if there are several alternative routes from which Active Directory can choose.

SITE LINK COSTS

If there are multiple routes between sites, the site link cost is used to determine which route to use. Lower cost is favored over higher cost as Figure 5.33 illustrates.

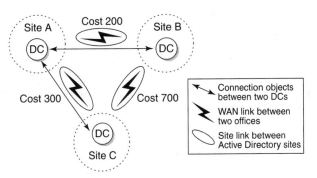

FIGURE 5.33 When multiple routes are available, the ISTGs choose the route with the lowest cost.

In this sample there are three site links, which means that there are two possible routes between any two sites in the sample network. The site link between sites B and C has the highest cost (700), so the other two links will be used.

Site link costs are cumulative. The ISTGs on each site build a minimum-cost spanning tree topology among sites. In a large network with many site links the possible accumulation plays a role when the ISTGs calculate the minimum cost tree.

Site link cost is between 1 and 32,767. The number doesn't represent actual money; it is just a number that Active Directory compares with costs in other site links. Because it is relative to the costs of other site links, you can think of it as representing the priority of a site link. If a network has more than a couple of Active Directory site links, it is a good idea to establish a standard that specifies the cost to use for each kind of WAN link. You should consider at least the following criteria:

- *Link speed*. A link that transmits at 56Kbps or at 64Kbps (i.e., 64,000bps) could correspond to a cost of 32,000; a link that transmits at 128Kbps could correspond to a cost of 16,000; and so on. In this proportional model you would divide 2 billion by the link speed. Consequently, a link that transmits at 2Mbps would mean a cost of 1,000 and a T-3 speed (45Mbps) would mean a cost about 50.

- *Type of link or network*. Instead of a mathematical approach to link speed, you could use simple categories, such as a cost of 100 for company backbone links, a cost of 500 for fast domestic leased lines, a cost of 1,000 for international leased lines, and a cost of 5,000 for dial-up lines.

- *Monetary cost*. If you have a link that transmits at 64Kbps on a leased line or at 64Kbps on an ISDN dial-up line, the latter should have a higher cost. You need to pay the phone company for each minute the ISDN line is open, so it would be wise to specify a lower cost (and consequently, a higher priority) for the leased line.

In addition to these items, link availability, reliability, and latency may affect the costs you choose.

NOTE The cost doesn't affect directly which route the replication packets take. The cost affects only which domain controllers will communicate. It is then up to the routers and other physical routing topology of the network to determine the actual route of the packets.

Cost is not meaningful if there are no domain controllers (of the same partition) between the two endpoint domain controllers. Consider Figure 5.34. When

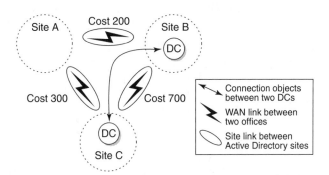

FIGURE 5.34 With Active Directory site links, you cannot specify which routes the network packets will take when there are no domain controllers between the endpoint domain controllers.

the two domain controllers on sites B and C replicate, they might use the WAN link B–C or the two WAN links B–A and A–C. You cannot specify the route with Active Directory, nor will you know which one was chosen.

INTERSITE TOPOLOGY OF ONE DOMAIN

Now that you know how the routes between sites are chosen, we are ready to add several domain controllers per site to give the full picture of the replication topology of one domain. We naturally want to replicate any change in Active Directory data only once from site to site. That is why only one domain controller at each end of the link is doing the intersite replication. These domain controllers are called *bridgehead servers*. As ISTGs create the intersite topology, they choose which domain controllers will be the bridgehead servers and create the appropriate connection objects for them. Figure 5.35 shows how one domain (`sanao.com`) replicates among three sites. To simplify the figure, we have fewer domain controllers on each site than in the examples of intrasite replication.

A KCC creates connection objects only for inbound replication and this applies also when an ISTG is selecting the source domain controllers from other sites to be used in the connection objects of the bridgehead server on the local site. However, the ISTGs on all sites come up with the same result about bridgehead servers on other sites. For example, if BOSsanao3 is pulling from LONsanao1, then LONsanao1 will pull from BOSsanao3 and not from BOSsanao2.

PREFERRED BRIDGEHEAD SERVERS

Instead of letting the ISTG choose bridgehead servers, you can designate the domain controller you want to be the *preferred bridgehead server*. The ISTG will use this domain controller as the bridgehead as long as it is up and running.

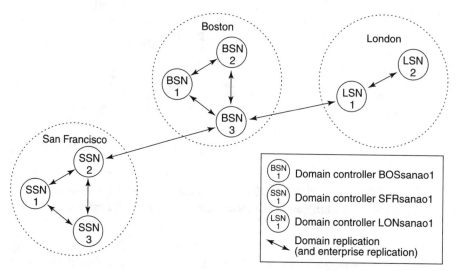

FIGURE 5.35 SFRsanao2 (SSN2), BOSsanao3 (BSN3), and LONsanao1 (LSN1) are the bridgehead servers for the domain `sanao.com`. They replicate the changes in each site to the other sites. As with intrasite replication, enterprise replication topology follows the topology of the only domain in the forest.

You can also designate more than one domain controller per site to be preferred bridgehead servers, in which case the ISTG picks only one of them. If all the (or the only) preferred bridgehead servers fail, intersite replication is no longer possible.

You should designate one or multiple preferred bridgehead servers if you know that they are better suited for intersite replication than just any domain controller that the ISTG happens to choose. Two typical scenarios are the following.

- If you have a large environment with many changes to replicate, the domain controllers you designated as preferred could have the processing power to do the compression used in intersite replication.

- If your site has a firewall and only one domain controller can pass the firewall to the outside world, you obviously need to designate this domain controller to be the preferred bridgehead server.

You do the designation per protocol, as Figure 5.36 shows.

MANAGING BRIDGEHEAD SERVER FAILURES

If an automatically selected bridgehead server fails, the ISTG will choose a new one automatically. It will do this after the second failed replication attempt and

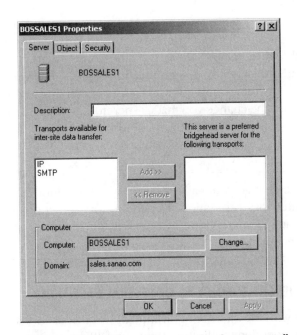

FIGURE 5.36 Server object properties enable you to assign that domain controller as a preferred bridgehead server on either RPC over IP (shown as "IP") or SMTP protocols, or both.

after 2 hours have elapsed from the last successful replication. If the ISTG cannot find a new appropriate domain controller for the role (one that is in the correct domain and site) it will log an event, which you can see using the Event Viewer. Obviously, in this case the intersite replication of the partition or partitions that the failed bridgehead server handled is not possible until the problem has been resolved.

The ISTG responds the same way when you have more than one preferred bridgehead server and one of them fails. If the last preferred bridgehead server fails, the ISTG doesn't select a new one. It is up to you to fix the problem by taking one of the following steps.

- For the site in question, add a new preferred bridgehead server that is capable of replicating the partition(s) that lost their bridgehead. If that includes a domain partition, you must select a domain controller of that domain.

- Remove all preferred bridgehead designations from the site in question. This way the ISTG can pick a bridgehead server. Of course, if only the failed domain controller would be able to pass the firewall, this option wouldn't fix replication.

Once you have performed one of the operations on some domain controller on the site that had lost one of its bridgehead servers, the change will replicate to all domain controllers on that site. Consequently, the ISTG will know about the fix and it will create a new connection object. However, that connection object is only for incoming replication, which means that the other affected sites won't learn about the change you made. Therefore, you need to perform the same fix (add or remove preferred bridgehead servers) on some domain controller on other sites as well (all or some or no other sites, as the Note describes).

NOTE   The change you made is part of the configuration partition, which is part of the enterprise replication. Depending on your domain and site configuration, the change may replicate to other sites using other bridgehead servers that are still functional.

INTERSITE TOPOLOGIES OF SEVERAL PARTITIONS

As with the intrasite replication of several partitions, each intersite partition has an independent replication topology. Different domains have totally separate replication topologies, and the enterprise replication topology follows the domain topologies whenever possible. When there is no domain connection to use (i.e., no intradomain or no global catalog connection), the enterprise replication topology will have a connection created just for it. This means that bridgehead servers must be established per partition also. That is, each domain in a given site that needs to replicate from (and to) other sites will have its own bridgehead server. Thus, there may actually be several bridgehead servers per site. Figure 5.37 shows

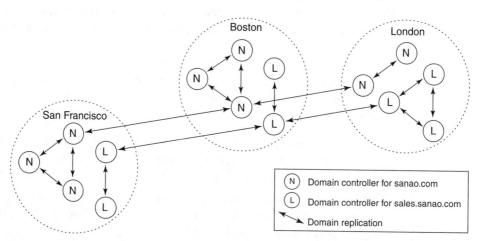

FIGURE 5.37 Different domains have totally different replication topologies. They also have their own bridgehead servers.

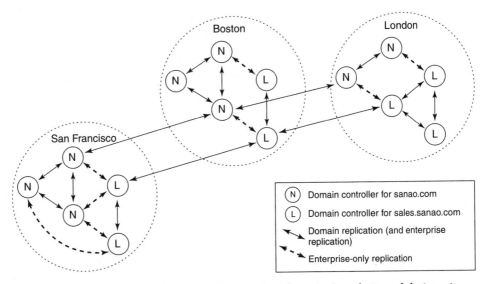

FIGURE 5.38 The enterprise replication topology consists of one ring in each site and the intersite connections. There are no enterprise-only connections between sites, however, because there already are enough domain connections, including enterprise replication.

the intersite replication topologies for two domains. To make room in the figure, we do not include the domain controller names. Figure 5.38 shows the intersite topologies with enterprise replication.

NOTE   Even though both Boston and San Francisco have three domain controllers for sanao.com and two for sales.sanao.com, the two sites have different enterprise replication rings. This is because the GUID order happens to result in two different rings.

In the previous example, both domains had controllers in all three sites. If we transform the three sanao.com domain controllers in San Francisco to a new domain rd.sanao.com, it will naturally have some implication on the topologies. The effect is shown in Figure 5.39.

INTERSITE GLOBAL CATALOG REPLICATION

The last aspect of intersite replication to describe is the global catalog replication. Figure 5.40 and Figure 5.41 show our sample topology with the global catalog replication.

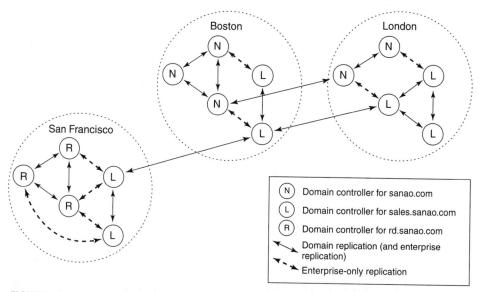

FIGURE 5.39 Because `rd.sanao.com` has domain controllers only in San Francisco, it doesn't replicate to other sites. The only domain link to San Francisco is of `sales.sanao.com`, so that connection will be used for enterprise replication to and from that site.

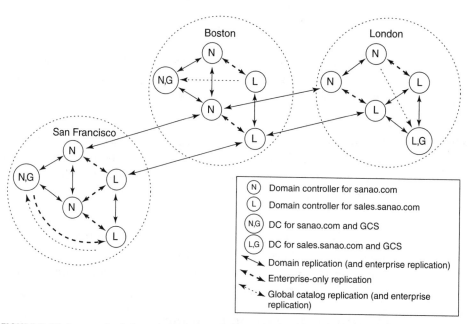

FIGURE 5.40 Because both domains (`sanao.com` and `sales.sanao.com`) have controllers in all three domains, global catalog replication doesn't increase traffic in any WAN links. In this scenario, that replication is always local to a site.

In our first case (Figure 5.37 and Figure 5.38) there were two domains, and both had domain controllers in all three sites. This means that all domain information was present in all sites. Consequently, it is easy to have a global catalog server on each site, because all global catalog replication can take place locally. Figure 5.40 illustrates this case with global catalog replication added.

NOTE   One enterprise replication arrow in San Francisco is one-way. The other direction is included in the global catalog replication arrow. Remember that all arrows are actually one-way. We are just using one two-way arrow instead of two one-way arrows to simplify the figure.

Our other enterprise case in Figure 5.39 introduced the domain rd.sanao.com in San Francisco. In that scenario the domains were not present on all sites, and therefore, part of global catalog replication takes place intersite. This is illustrated in Figure 5.41.

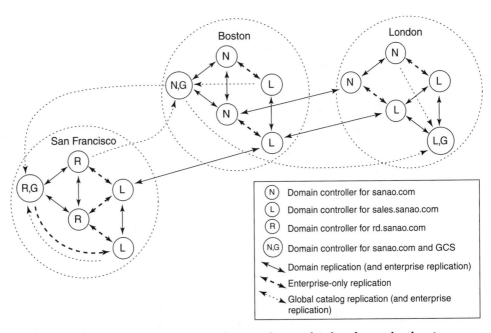

FIGURE 5.41 Each global catalog server needs to get the partial replica of two other domains. This often comes from another site, thus increasing WAN traffic. Because the partial replica of rd.sanao.com is in the Boston global catalog server, it can be the source of this information for the London global catalog server. This connection is one-way, because the Boston global catalog server can read sales.sanao.com intrasite.

NOTE   It is purely coincidental that there is one global catalog server in each domain in Figure 5.41.

The basic rule for global catalog servers is to have at least one in each site. In a very large environment (hundreds of sites), however, you might decide not to comply with this convention because hundreds of global catalog servers might generate more traffic on the WAN links than they can take.

CREATING AND MANAGING SITE LINK BRIDGES

Remember that a site link is an object that symbolizes a physical link between two or more sites. A *site link bridge* object symbolizes two or more site links together that use the same protocol (RPC over IP or SMTP).

NOTE   We explained earlier that there are bridgehead servers at the ends (or edges) of site links. However, don't confuse them with site link bridges.

Site links (including their cost) and site link bridges both give the ISTGs hints about how to create connection objects when building an intersite replication topology. You have three ways to create your intersite topology:

- *Create site links* and let the ISTGs manage the connection objects based on them (as discussed so far).
- *Create site link bridges* (in addition to creating site links) to give additional hints to the ISTGs about which connection objects to create.
- *Create connection objects* manually.

The first choice in the list is by far the most common. Site link bridges are necessary only in some complex scenarios. Also, you don't usually need to create connection objects manually.

We mentioned earlier that there is a "Bridge all site links" check box in the properties of the IP and SMTP container objects. By default, that setting is on for both protocols, so all the site links in your forest are bridged together (i.e., they are transitive) for a given protocol. You don't see a site link bridge object to symbolize this; there is just the check box setting.

Instead of one large automatic site link bridge, you could create several smaller ones. This happens as follows:

1. Turn off site link transitiveness by clearing the aforementioned check box.
2. Create the appropriate site link bridge objects manually in the IP or SMTP containers.

NOTE   Even if you turn off automatic bridging, you might need only a few, if any, site link bridge objects.

NOTE   If you turn off automatic bridging and don't create the necessary site link bridges, an ISTG could no longer include some domain controllers in the replication topology. Consequently, it would log event 1311, which you would see using the Event Viewer.

Any network described by site links and site link bridges can also be described by site links alone, as Figure 5.42 illustrates. The figure assumes that automatic bridging of all site links is off. The goal is to get the domain controllers on sites A and B to communicate.

Solution 1 is to create a site link bridge. It joins the two site links into one, using as the cost the cumulative cost of the two site links. Each site link in a bridge must have a common site with another site link in that bridge.

Solution 2 is to simply create a third site link. This makes sites A and B adjacent, so no bridging (i.e., transitiveness) is necessary. Microsoft has more than 100 site links in their corporate Active Directory network and they don't need any site link bridges (at least during the first year of deployment).

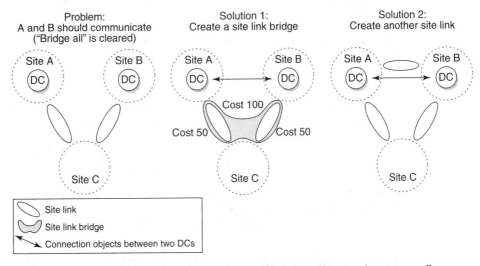

FIGURE 5.42 A site link bridge "chains" two or more site links so that two domain controllers can communicate over this chain. However, the same result can be achieved by creating a new site link. The cost of a site link bridge is the sum of the site link costs.

NOTE   As the number of site links increases, solution 2 may become more complicated. Depending on the topology and placement of domain controllers, you might need to create many site links to replace one site link bridge and consequently you would have to manage the cost and schedule of each site link separately.

We haven't still answered the ultimate question: Automatic bridging of all site links is the easiest choice, so why turn it off? The answer is that in a large network there would be so many permutations in possible routes (including the cumulative costs) that it would take too much CPU power on the ISTG to calculate the optimal topology.

"Too much" is a highly relative expression. Microsoft says in Knowledge Base article Q244368 that you can "Bridge all site links" as long as the following is true:

```
(1 + number of domains) * number of sites^2 <= 100,000
```

According to this formula, if you have just one domain, the limit would be about 220 sites; with two domains, it would be about 180 sites. Because of the aforementioned relativity, this formula is more like a rule of thumb. Server speed and network topology will affect the exact results. Also, if the ISTG calculates the topology every 15 minutes, there is no exact number of seconds or minutes it would be allowed to spend.

If you have a large network, performing the following steps will show you how much time the calculation takes:

1. Find out the current ISTG of a site by looking it up in the NTDS Site Settings object.

2. Select Check Replication Topology on the NTDS Settings object of the ISTG and time the result.

If the ISTG would take too much CPU even after automatic bridging was disabled, the Knowledge Base article Q244368 presents a script that triggers the topology generation process. You can schedule the script to run during off-peak hours to avoid overloading the ISTG domain controller during business hours.

A typical scenario for a large network is a hub-spoke topology with headquarters and 500 branch offices. All replication takes place between headquarters and some branch office, so there is no need to calculate routes and costs from one branch office to another. Disabling automatic bridging would greatly save the CPU on ISTGs. Also, you would probably not need manual site link bridges either.

CREATING AND MANAGING CONNECTION OBJECTS

As you know, the KCCs create and manage connection objects automatically, and this normally produces the best results. If you aren't happy with the resulting topology, the solution is not to create connection objects manually, but to modify the background information, such as site links or site link properties. You can also check that there are no errors in network connectivity, including DNS services. Nevertheless, the following are reasons to create connection objects manually.

- You would have so many (thousands) sites and site links that even without automatic site link bridging it would take the ISTGs too long to calculate the topology. In this case, you would probably create the connection objects programmatically using an ADSI script. You can get such scripts, as well as detailed planning and deployment information, from the Branch Office Guide at `http://www.microsoft.com/` (use the Search feature to locate the correct pages).
- Later in this chapter we explain that each operations master should have a standby domain controller ready to take over the role in case of a failure. There should be a direct replication connection from the operations master to the standby, which you can ensure by creating the connection object manually.
- Sometimes you might want fewer than three hops between two servers on a site with many domain controllers.
- You might want to replicate temporarily from a certain server to another. You could create a connection object, initiate replication, and then delete the connection object.

NOTE   Site links and site link settings (such as cost and schedule) don't affect manually created connection objects. You assign all the properties (most important, the schedule) yourself.

You start creating a connection object by locating the NTDS Settings object of the receiving end's domain controller. When you right-click the latter object, you can select New Active Directory Connection from the context menu. Next you choose the source domain controller in a dialog box, as shown in Figure 5.43.

When you click OK, the next screen appears, and you can type a name for the object, which is probably the same as the source domain controller name (in this example, SFRsales1). We don't show that screen because it contains only the text field for the name.

The properties and schedule dialog boxes for a connection object are shown in Figure 5.44 and Figure 5.45, respectively. The other property you can set besides the schedule is the transport to be used. Table 5.14 lists the transport choices.

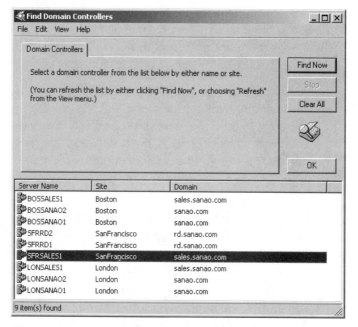

FIGURE 5.43 When you create a connection object manually, you choose the source domain controller from a list.

NOTE   If you choose the SMTP transport, there are some special considerations, which are discussed a little later in the "Configuring SMTP Replication" section.

If the need arises, you can change the source for a connection object in its properties dialog box. You should also rename the object to match the new source domain controller.

TABLE 5.14 Transport Protocols for Replication

Display Name	Protocol	Can Be Used
RPC	RPC over IP (same as next)	Intrasite, for any data
IP	RPC over IP (same as previous)	Intersite, for any data
SMTP	SMTP over IP	Intersite, for schema and configuration partitions, as well as the global catalog; not for domain data

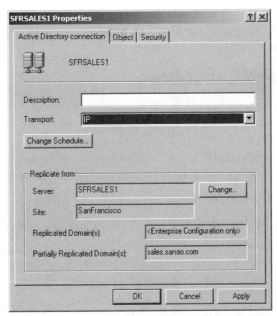

FIGURE 5.44 When you create an intersite connection object, the RPC protocol is called IP. The other protocol option is SMTP. The two lowermost fields tell you that the source and destination domain controllers are in different domains (because only enterprise configuration is replicated) and the latter is a global catalog server (because the source domain is partially replicated).

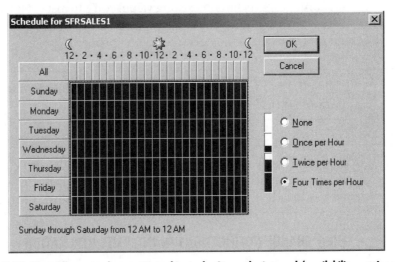

FIGURE 5.45 Manually created connection objects don't use the interval/availability settings pair. Instead, you define the schedule directly with the weekly grid.

If you delete a manually created connection object, you can either create something else for a replacement or you can let the KCCs determine whether some new connections are needed.

RECIPROCAL REPLICATION

If your replication takes place over a dial-up link, you can make use of *reciprocal replication.* When the link is open, you can replicate changes in both directions during one call, which will help you save money on your phone bills. Also, it is possible that the branch office can call the headquarters, but not vice versa. In this case, you must use reciprocal replication. The order of events is the following:

1. The branch office dials up to the headquarters.
2. The branch office bridgehead server requests and receives any changes in the headquarters bridgehead server.
3. The branch office bridgehead server sends a change notification to the headquarters bridgehead server.
4. The headquarters bridgehead server requests and receives any changes in the branch office bridgehead server.

You would define reciprocal replication by modifying the `options` property of the corresponding site link object. The easiest tool for this is ADSI Edit. First, locate the correct site link object in the configuration partition. Then open the properties of that site link and select to view the `options` property.

Reciprocal replication is defined in the second bit from the right. If the `options` property has no existing value, you can just set it to a decimal value 2. If there is already a value (most likely to be 1), you must add 2 to that existing value and set the result as the new value of the property.

NOTE   Adding the two values together is, in this case, equivalent to doing a "bitwise or" operation on them.

NOTE   You must modify the property on a headquarters domain controller. If you modified it on a branch office domain controller, the change would never replicate to the headquarters, if the headquarters cannot dial up to the branch office.

USING CHANGE NOTIFICATIONS IN INTERSITE REPLICATION

As mentioned earlier, change notification is used by default in intrasite replication, but you can enable it also for intersite replication. You might do this in the following cases.

- You want urgent replication to take place also intersite.
- You have a high-speed WAN and you want to achieve the same low-latency replication as what you have intrasite.

To define change notifications on a site link, modify the same `options` property that we just described with reciprocal replication. The difference is that you set the first bit from the right instead of the second. Value 1 means "use change notifications," value 2 means "use reciprocal," and value 3 means "use both."

The two settings end up in the options property of the automatically generated connection objects. In those objects the second bit from right means "use reciprocal" and the third bit from right means "use change notifications." You could also use these bits manually, if you create connection objects manually.

NOTE   If there are several bridged site links in a chain between two domain controllers, all of their `options` properties are "anded" together. In other words, if even one of the site links in the chain doesn't have either bit set, the corresponding setting is not used.

Table 5.15 lists the two bits of site links and Table 5.16 the three bits of connection objects.

TABLE 5.15 Options Property Bits of Site Links

Bit from Right	Hex Value	Description
1	1	Setting this bit causes change notifications to be used.
2	2	Setting this bit causes reciprocal replication to be used.

TABLE 5.16 Options Property Bits of Connection Objects

Bit from Right	Hex Value	Description
1	1	A value of 1 means that the connection object is maintained automatically by the KCC. A value of 0 means that an administrator manually maintains the object.
2	2	Setting this bit causes reciprocal replication to be used.
3	4	Setting this bit causes change notifications to be used.

SITE OPTIONS

In addition to site link objects and connection objects, a third replication object, NTDS Site Settings, may contain the options property. Table 5.17 describes the five bits that you can use to control connection object creation on the corresponding site.

Configuring SMTP Replication

As mentioned previously, you can use Simple Mail Transfer Protocol (SMTP) to replicate the schema and configuration partitions, as well as to replicate global catalog information among domain controllers in different domains. But you cannot use it to replicate normal domain partitions among domain controllers in one domain. SMTP can only be used for intersite replication.

The reason for the limitation with SMTP replication is that intradomain replication must be somewhat synchronized with the File Replication Service (FRS), because the latter is used to replicate Group Policies. While SMTP replication is asynchronous, FRS doesn't yet support asynchronous replication.

SMTP replication encrypts the replicated data. Therefore, for it to work you need to set up Certificate Services (included in Windows 2000) as well as install and configure an enterprise *certificate authority (CA)*.

TABLE 5.17 Options Property Bits of NTDS Site Settings

Bit from Right	Hex Value	Description
1	1	Setting this bit disables the automatic intrasite topology generation by the KCCs.
2	2	Setting this bit disables the cleanup of outdated replication connections.
3	4	Setting this bit disables the automatic generation of shortcut connections in the site's replication ring. Consequently, the three-hop maximum is not maintained.
4	8	Setting this bit disables the detection of failed replication links and the generation of temporary bypass connections.
5	10	Setting this bit disables the automatic intersite topology generation by the ISTG.

Just like with RPC over IP replication, you can create SMTP site links (and perhaps site link bridges) and let the ISTGs create the appropriate connection objects. Or you can create the SMTP connection objects manually.

To route replication requests and responses between domain controllers, the SMTP replication uses two services that are included in Windows 2000: the Intersite Messaging (ISM) service and the SMTP service. The latter service is shown as an IIS component. SMTP replication ignores the availability schedules of site links and uses only the interval settings (i.e., the "Replicate every" fields).

Reasons to use SMTP replication are as follows.

- You have sites where there is no direct connection from any other site.

- Your replication traffic goes over the public Internet, so you can make use of encryption by using the SMTP choice. However, you can also get encryption by using IPsec with normal RPC over IP replication.

- You have unreliable WAN links. If the network is reliable, you can use RPC even though the network would be slow.

If you need to replicate domain partitions to some site, you must always use RPC. Once you use RPC for this, you should use RPC also for enterprise and global catalog replication.

Microsoft's Web site (`http://www.microsoft.com/`) contains a document called "Step-by-Step Guide to Setting up ISM-SMTP Replication." If you point your Web browser to the Microsoft site and perform a search using the document's title, you'll be able to access procedural information on setting up SMTP replication (and Certificate Services).

The Replication Process

Now that you have learned how replication topologies are built, it's time to examine how the data flows along the paths in the topology.

To be efficient, the Active Directory replication process must have the functions listed in Table 5.18.

NOTE   For this replication process section, it doesn't make any difference if the replication is intrasite or intersite.

BACKGROUND

Before we address the five mechanisms in Table 5.18, we need to lay some foundation. We can divide the replication process into the following four steps:

1. A user or an application makes a change to an object or property in a domain controller (domain controller A). This is called an *originating update* and it is stored in the directory database of domain controller A.

2. Domain controller A sends a notification about the change to its outbound replication partner(s) (including domain controller B). This step is skipped in the schedule-based intersite replication.

3. Domain controller B sends a request for updates to domain controller A.

4. Domain controller B receives the change, which is called a *replicated update* (in contrast to an *originating update*), and stores it in its directory database. A replicated update can also correspond to a number of originating updates that originate even from different domain controllers.

TABLE 5.18 Functions of the Active Directory Replication Process

Function	Mechanisms
Because Active Directory replicates individual changed properties and those changes may initiate in any domain controller, there must be a way to identify new and changed objects and properties in each domain controller.	Update sequence numbers
Each domain controller replicates the changes from one or more replication partners. They need to know what new changes the partner has in order to be able to retrieve them.	High-watermark vectors
There may be multiple paths in the replication topology from one domain controller to another. *Propagation dampening* prevents a change from replicating endlessly or replicating several times to the same domain controller.	Up-to-date vectors
When replicating changed properties, the receiving domain controller must determine for each property whether it should keep the property value just received or the property value already in the local database. Also, in a multimaster replication system it is possible that someone changes a property in some domain controller, and before the change has replicated to some other domain controller, someone changes the same property there. This leads to a *collision* (or, conflict), which must be resolved.	Version numbers and timestamps
When an object is deleted, the deletion must be replicated to other domain controllers.	Tombstones

Because Active Directory replication is transitive, after domain controller B has stored the change, it may replicate it to domain controller C, which may replicate it to domain controller D, and so on.

There can be four types of originating updates:

- Creating an object
- Deleting an object
- Moving or renaming an object
- Adding some properties to an object, changing or deleting the properties of an object

Domain controllers and their databases are identified in the replication operations with two GUIDs:

- *Server GUID.* This GUID identifies a domain controller and it is the `object-GUID` property of the NTDS Settings object under the corresponding server object. This is the same GUID that is used to set the order of domain controllers in a replication ring.
- *Database GUID.* This GUID identifies the directory database of a domain controller. It is the `invocationId` property of the NTDS Settings object. The database GUID is originally the same as the server GUID, but when you do a directory database restore, the database GUID changes. This way, you can differentiate an after-restore database from the original database.

Active Directory treats updates to the database as transactions. The entire update operation is either committed as a whole to the database, or it is rejected. This prevents corruption of the database.

UPDATE SEQUENCE NUMBERS

Each domain controller has an independent 64-bit counter called the *update sequence number (USN)*. Whenever a transaction for either an originating update or a replicated update is committed (not aborted) to the database of a domain controller, the domain controller increments its USN by one and stores the new value with the committed change.

Storing the current USN with each change yields an order of the changes—an implied relative "timestamp" that lets other domain controllers request changes that were made after a certain "time." Having USNs in the domain controllers relieves them and you from maintaining an exact time for all your domain controllers. You don't lose or duplicate changes even if the times of two domain controllers disagree by a significant amount.

If the replication was interrupted or a domain controller was down for a while, with the help of USNs it will know where it stopped, and replication can continue from that point.

If the USNs run out, you need to reinstall your forest. However, with 64 bits you can do 100 changes per second, and still your USNs would last for more than 5 billion years. Microsoft has promised an upgrade that solves this forest-reinstallation problem before then.

Each Active Directory object has six USN properties, two of which are used in this context.

- uSNCreated contains the current USN from the time of the object creation. Applications can use uSNCreated to request any new objects, but this property is not used by replication.

- uSNChanged contains the current USN from the time of the latest change to the object (excluding changes to nonreplicating properties). This value is the same as the largest local USN of the object's properties (discussed shortly). We can use uSNChanged to request new changes to any object.

Both these attributes are indexed in the database for fast access and comparison. They are also in the global catalog.

In addition to the two per-object USNs, Active Directory stores two USNs for each property, as well as three other pieces of identifying information:

- *Originating USN.* This is the USN that was stored with the property at the time of the originating update on the originating domain controller.

- *Local USN.* This number is based on the current USN of the local domain controller. Local and originating USNs are the same in the database of the originating domain controller.

- *Version number.* This is a 32-bit number that starts at 1 and is incremented by 1 with each originating update to the property, but not with a replicated update. Unlike a USN, the version number is not domain controller–specific; it follows its property wherever it will be replicated. The version number indicates the number of times a property is changed during its lifetime. However, if you change the property simultaneously on two domain controllers, one of those changes is eventually left out of the count (and also, because of a collision, the corresponding change is lost).

- *Timestamp.* This is a 64-bit time value in GMT/UTC (Greenwich Mean Time/Coordinated Universal Time) for each property change.

- *Originating domain controller.* This is the database GUID of the domain controller where the update was originated.

The local USN never leaves the local domain controller. The other four values together form a *stamp* that follows the property value when it is replicated to other domain controllers. These values can be used when resolving conflicts, as explained a little later.

REPLICATION METADATA

The originating USN, local USN, version number, timestamp, and originating domain controller values are called *replication metadata* and they are stored in binary format in the `replPropertyMetaData` property of each object. If you add their sizes plus 4 bytes to identify the property they relate to, you will notice that they create a 48-byte overhead on disk for each property.

To see the values for a given object, you can use a command such as

```
repadmin /showmeta "cn=jill green,ou=london,dc=sanao,dc=com"
```

Another choice is to start the graphical ReplMon, add a domain controller to the list, and select Show Attribute Meta-Data for Active Directory Object.

`ReplPropertyMetaData`, `uSNCreated`, and `uSNChanged` are not replicated to other domain controllers. However, the four values in `replProperty-MetaData` are transferred with the property value, so that data means a 40-byte overhead for each property on the wire.

NOTE   The transfer overhead is 8 bytes smaller than the storage overhead because the local USN is not transferred.

NOTE   Active Directory doesn't keep track of the newness or changes of nonreplicating properties. Consequently, the "repl" properties, or a property such as `last-Logon`, won't get USNs or timestamps, nor will they advance the `uSNChanged` property of the corresponding object.

Tables 5.19 through 5.22 show how USNs and version numbers work when creating objects and modifying properties. Table 5.19 shows the data when you create a new user on DC1. If the USN on DC1 were 22,113, it would be advanced to 22,114.

TABLE 5.19 A Newly Created Object on DC1

Property	Value	Local USN	Originating DC	Originating USN	Version	Timestamp
uSNCreated	**22114***					
uSNChanged	**22114**					
name	**Sam Brown**	**22114**	DB GUID of DC1	**22114**	**1**	**UT**
givenName	**Sam**	**22114**	DB GUID of DC1	**22114**	**1**	**UT**
homeDirectory	**\\Srv1\Users\Sam**	**22114**	DB GUID of DC1	**22114**	**1**	**UT**

* Bold indicates changed data.

NOTE The example in Table 5.19 is simplified. In reality, when you create a new user, she gets at least 30 properties and the USN counter advances two to five steps. This is because whether you use the snap-in or an ADSI script, behind the scenes there are multiple transactions. These transactions also update properties that you didn't specifically set.

The user that was created on DC1 is next replicated to DC2. The current USN of DC2 is 31,331, so it advances to 31,332. Table 5.20 shows the outcome.

Table 5.21 shows the next step: the change of Sam's home directory on DC2. Because some time has elapsed from the operation in Table 5.20, the USN of DC2 has advanced to 32,522. With the change of the home directory, it advances to 32,523.

TABLE 5.20 A Replicated Object on DC2

Property	Value	Local USN	Originating DC	Originating USN	Version	Timestamp
uSNCreated	**31332***					
uSNChanged	**31332**					
name	*Sam Brown***	**31332**	*DB GUID of DC1*	*22114*	*1*	*UT*
givenName	*Sam*	**31332**	*DB GUID of DC1*	*22114*	*1*	*UT*
homeDirectory	*\\Srv1\Users\Sam*	**31332**	*DB GUID of DC1*	*22114*	*1*	*UT*

*Bold indicates changed data.
** Italics indicate that the data is new to this domain controller, but it is identical to the data in its replication source.

TABLE 5.21 A Change to a Property on DC2

Property	Value	Local USN	Originating DC	Originating USN	Version	Timestamp
uSNCreated	31332					
uSNChanged	**32523***					
name	Sam Brown	31332	DB GUID of DC1	22114	1	UT
givenName	Sam	31332	DB GUID of DC1	22114	1	UT
homeDirectory	**\\Srv2\Users\Sam**	**32523**	**DB GUID of DC2**	**32523**	**2**	**UT**

* Bold indicates changed data.

The last step, shown in Table 5.22, is to replicate the changed property back to DC1. The current USN of DC1 is 23,776, so now it advances to 23,777.

NOTE   The properties cn, ou, dc, l, o, and c are treated differently in replication. Depending on the object class, one of these properties is the "naming attribute" of the object. Because the value is the same as the name property (i.e., RDN), it is sufficient to replicate only the name property. If you look at the metadata of a naming attribute, such as cn, you will notice that the originating DC and originating USN are always the same as the local ones, indicating that the value was generated locally instead of by replication.

TABLE 5.22 A Changed Property Replicated Back to DC1

Property	Value	Local USN	Originating DC	Originating USN	Version	Timestamp
uSNCreated	22114					
uSNChanged	**23777***					
name	Sam Brown	22114	DB GUID of DC1	22114	1	UT
givenName	Sam	22114	DB GUID of DC1	22114	1	UT
homeDirectory	*\\Srv2\Users\Sam***	**23777**	*DB GUID of DC2*	*32523*	*2*	*UT*

* Bold indicates changed data.
** Italics indicate that the data is new to this domain controller, but it is identical to the data in its replication source.

Now that you are familiar with the basic mechanics of USNs, we move on to examine how a domain controller knows what changes to replicate.

HIGH-WATERMARK VECTORS

Each domain controller maintains one high-watermark vector for each partition for which it contains a replica. Consequently, a domain controller that is not a global catalog server has three high-watermark vectors: one for its domain partition, one for the schema partition, and one for the configuration partition.

A high-watermark vector is a table that stores the highest replicated USN of each incoming replication partner of the corresponding partition. In other words, the table has rows at most for the same domain controllers that the owner has connection objects for. If a connection object is used to replicate only some partitions, the corresponding domain controller appears in the high-watermark vectors of only those partitions. Table 5.23 is a high-watermark vector of DC1.

Each high-watermark vector is stored in the nonreplicating `repsFrom` property of the corresponding partition's root object. That property stores other information also.

With the help of the high-watermark vector, a domain controller can detect and request recent changes from its replication partner. When a domain controller requests changes from its partner, it sends the following information in the request:

- The naming context (partition) for which the changes are requested.
- The maximum number of objects requested.
- The maximum number of values requested.
- An indication of whether or not to send parents.
- The highest replicated USN of the partner (taken from the vector). This tells the partner which changes the receiving end already has, so the partner will send only the new changes (i.e., the ones with the USN greater than requested, provided that propagation dampening doesn't kick in).

TABLE 5.23 The High-Watermark Vector of DC1

Incoming Replication Partner	Highest Replicated USN from the Partner
Database GUID of DC2	25882
Database GUID of DC5	6577
Database GUID of DC9	18183

- An up-to-date vector, which takes care of propagation dampening.

The partner (or source domain controller) returns the following information:

- The source DC's server GUID
- The source DC's database GUID
- A number of object-update entries, which all contain the GUID for the object and a list of one or more property-update entries
- The largest uSNChanged so the destination can update its high-watermark vector
- An indication of whether or not there was more data, if the maximum number of objects or values didn't prevent sending it
- If there is no more data, an up-to-date vector from the source DC

UP-TO-DATE VECTORS

Like a high-watermark vector, an up-to-date vector is a table that a domain controller has for each of its partitions (see Table 5.24). Instead of replication partners, these vectors contain entries (i.e., highest USNs) for each domain controller from which the owner has ever received originating updates.

NOTE   Actually, the table has entries for all domain controllers of the forest (current and removed), but only the ones just mentioned have any practical meaning.

The highest USNs in the table are originating USNs, not replicated USNs. Each highest originating USN in the table states that all changes from the corresponding domain controller with a USN less than or equal to the one in the table have been received by the domain controller that owns the table.

TABLE 5.24 The Up-to-Date Vector of DC1

Domain Controller	**Highest Originating USN from the DC**
Database GUID of DC2	25882
Database GUID of DC3	19234
Database GUID of DC5	6577
Database GUID of DC7	32904
Database GUID of DC9	18180

Each up-to-date vector is stored in the nonreplicating `replUpToDateVector` property of the corresponding partition's root object.

With the help of up-to-date vectors, domain controllers can filter out changes that the other party has already received from another domain controller. That is, the vectors provide propagation dampening, which prevents a change from replicating endlessly or from replicating several times to one domain controller.

The next example (Tables 5.25 through 5.29) describes propagation dampening step by step. We have a minimal network with three domain controllers: DC1, DC2, and DC3. They are all replication partners of each other. We will demonstrate how a change made to DC2 propagates to DC1. With each step, we show the contents of the high-watermark vector and up-to-date vector of DC1, as well as the USNs of all three domain controllers.

Table 5.25 shows the initial state.

Now an administrator changes some user's home directory on DC2. This causes the USN of DC2 to advance by one to 8,023, as shown in Table 5.26.

DC1 will get a notification about the change from DC2, so it will request any changes greater than 8,022 (its high-watermark vector for DC2) from there. DC1 also sends its complete up-to-date vector to DC2. It contains USN 8,022 for DC2, so DC2 doesn't filter out the change. Consequently, DC2 will return the new

TABLE 5.25 USN of Each DC and Vectors of DC1: Initial State

DC	Current USN	DC	High-Watermark Vector	Up-to-Date Vector
DC1	9915			
DC2	8022	DC2	8022	8022
DC3	12331	DC3	12331	12320

TABLE 5.26 USN of Each DC and Vectors of DC1: Step 1

DC	Current USN	DC	High-Watermark Vector	Up-to-Date Vector
DC1	9915			
DC2	**8023***	DC2	8022	8022
DC3	12331	DC3	12331	12320

* Bold indicates a changed value.

home directory to DC1. Getting and storing this change advances the USN of DC1 to 9,916.

DC2 also returns its last changed USN (8,023), which DC1 uses to update the DC2 entry of its high-watermark vector, and an up-to-date vector, which DC1 uses to update the DC2 entry of its up-to-date vector. Table 5.27 shows the resulting vectors.

Next, the same change is replicated from DC2 to DC3. Obviously, this doesn't change the vectors of DC1, but the USN of DC3 advances, as Table 5.28 shows.

Now DC3 has a new change, which it presents (or notifies) to DC1. The latter sends a request to DC3 asking for any changes newer than 12,331. This would return the changed home directory (12,332) again to DC1 if there weren't the up-to-date vector.

In the request DC1 sent its complete up-to-date vector, which states that changes originated in DC2 already reside in DC1 up to 8,023. As you remember, there is an originating USN stored with each property (in this case, 8,023 with the new home directory). Therefore, DC3 realizes that DC1 already knows about the new home directory and filters it out. The result is that DC3 returns no objects or properties to DC1, but it does return its last changed USN. DC1 uses this information to update its high-watermark vector, as shown in Table 5.29.

TABLE 5.27 USN of Each DC and Vectors of DC1: Step 2

DC	Current USN	DC	High-Watermark Vector	Up-to-Date Vector
DC1	**9916***			
DC2	8023	DC2	**8023**	**8023**
DC3	12331	DC3	12331	12320

* Bold indicates a changed value.

TABLE 5.28 USN of Each DC and Vectors of DC1: Step 3

DC	Current USN	DC	High-Watermark Vector	Up-to-Date Vector
DC1	9916			
DC2	8023	DC2	8023	8023
DC3	**12332***	DC3	12331	12320

* Bold indicates a changed value.

TABLE 5.29 USN of Each DC and Vectors of DC1: Step 4

DC	Current USN	DC	High-Watermark Vector	Up-to-Date Vector
DC1	9916			
DC2	8023	DC2	8023	8023
DC3	12332	DC3	**12332***	12320

* Bold indicates a changed value.

TIP   You can see the up-to-date vector of a given domain controller and partition using the RepAdmin command (included in Support Tools) with the `/showvector` option.

COLLISIONS

In a multimaster replication system, it is possible that people or applications make changes on different domain controllers that, once they are replicated, are clearly in conflict. There are two steps to minimizing the number of these collisions.

- Active Directory narrows the possibility of collisions, because it keeps track of changes on a per-property basis. Therefore, changing two properties of one object in two domain controllers doesn't create a collision.

- You, the administrator, should organize and delegate administration in such a way that several people are not likely to change the same properties to different values (almost) simultaneously.

When a changed property is replicated to another domain controller, Active Directory must choose whether to keep the replicated property or the one already on the destination. As seems natural, the property being replicated wins almost always. However, the exact logic is as follows:

- If the version numbers are different, let the larger one win, otherwise . . .
- If the timestamps are different, let the later one win, otherwise . . .
- Let the one win that was originated on the domain controller with a higher database GUID

We can call the three values combined a *stamp* and express the three-step logic in only three words: larger stamp wins.

It is highly unlikely that Active Directory would need to use the third value on the list, but it must have some unambiguous way to determine the winner in every possible situation. If you're playing with the first two options, you will have three scenarios:

- A *normal change* (incoming version number is larger). The property was changed only once in only one domain controller. Consequently, the property being replicated has a larger version number (+1) and it will propagate to every domain controller.
- A *collision* (equal version numbers). The same property was changed on two domain controllers. Consequently, both changes have the same version number. Active Directory will use the timestamp to determine the winner.
- A *peculiarity* (incoming version number is smaller). For example, an administrator could change a user's phone number twice on DC1: first accidentally to a wrong value and then to the correct one. This would advance the version number by two, so if 2 minutes later the phone number were changed on DC2, that latter change would lose, because its version number was incremented only by one.

NOTE   The last scenario means that a later change may lose even if clocks are synchronized. However, this shouldn't be a problem in practice.

NOTE   Active Directory doesn't do merges on multivalued properties. When resolving a conflict, it picks one of the alternatives as a whole.

WARNING   Because group memberships are stored as multivalued lists, changing the member list of one group on two domain controllers within the replication cycle would result in one of the changes being destroyed. If the domain controllers are on the same site, the replication cycle is between 5 and 15 minutes.

In addition to the property value conflict just discussed, there are two other types of collisions. Table 5.30 describes how Active Directory handles the three kinds of collisions that could occur. They are possible in domain and configuration partitions, but not in the schema partition—the schema partition is updated in a single-master fashion (as discussed later in the "Managing Operations Masters" section).

TABLE 5.30 How Active Directory Handles Collisions

Collision Type	Example	Resolution
Property value conflict	Someone changes a property in DC1 and before the change has replicated to DC2, someone changes the same property there. This collision is detected when the local version number is the same as the replicated one, and the two values are different.	If timestamps are different, use the later timestamp; otherwise, use the one with a higher database GUID.
Creation or move under a deleted container	Someone creates a user in OU1 on DC1 and someone deletes OU1 on DC2.	OU1 will be deleted and the user will be moved to the LostAndFound container of the domain or to LostAndFoundConfig if the change was made to the configuration partition.
Sibling object name conflict	Two users with identical common names are created on two domain controllers at the same time. Two users could also be moved or renamed to be the same.	The user that has a larger stamp (i.e., usually was created a little later) will get the printable representation of its GUID appended to its common name (and consequently its DN and canonical name).

NOTE   In the name conflict case in Table 5.30, the given name, surname, display name, user principal name, or pre–Windows 2000 name (SAM name) won't change. This means that two users will end up having the same UPN and SAM name. It is up to the administrator to rename them as well for one of the users.

NOTE   Even though schema updates are made in a single-master fashion, they could still conflict with other changes. If you add a class or property and then create an object based on them, the new object might reach some domain controller before the knowledge of the schema modification does. If this happens, the destination domain controller aborts processing the current replication data and writes a "schema mismatch" message to the event log. Then it resyncs the schema from the source domain controller and requests again the normal replication data. This time everything should go fine.

If the conflicting name of the last case in Table 5.30 was originally "Jack Brown," after the append operation it will be something like "Jack Brown*CNF: 507c75a0-28f9-48cb-7c33-cb946d109184." The asterisk (*) represents a reserved character (000A hex) normally seen as a white box. Because of the reserved character, this automatic name can never conflict with anything that you have created.

Remember that the most important feature of conflict resolution is consistency. After things cool down, each domain controller has reached the same state and the same change has won everywhere. It really doesn't matter whether another change that lost was made 2 seconds earlier or later, perhaps in another town.

TOMBSTONES

When an object is deleted, there must be something left to replicate to other domain controllers so that they will learn about the deleted object. This is why Active Directory doesn't immediately delete an object, but instead turns it into a tombstone. The following changes are made to an object when it is "deleted."

- The `isDeleted` property is set to true.
- An internal property, When-Deleted (this property has no LDAP name), is set to the time of the `isDeleted` property's timestamp.
- The `nTSecurityDescriptor` is set to a special value.
- The common name is changed to something like "Jack Brown*DEL: 507c75a0-28f9-48cb-7c33-cb946d109184." As with conflicts, the asterisk (*) represents a reserved character, so this name can never conflict with anything that you have created.
- Most of the properties are stripped, leaving just a few that Active Directory needs.

The following 24 attributes may exist in a tombstone:

attributeID	objectClass
attributeSyntax	objectGUID
dNReferenceUpdate	objectSid
governsID	oMSyntax
groupType	name
instanceType	replPropertyMetaData
lDAPDisplayName	sAMAccountName
legacyExchangeDN	subClassOf
mSMQOwnerID	systemFlags
nCName	userAccountControl
nTSecurityDescriptor	uSNChanged
distinguishedName	uSNCreated

This tombstone is replicated to other domain controllers and consequently the original object is "deleted" from them also. After this, it takes quite a while before the tombstone object is actually deleted from the database of each domain controller. This time is called *tombstone lifetime,* and the default value is 60 days. Microsoft recommends that you never change the value; in normal networks it shouldn't be a problem that deleted objects (i.e., tombstones) reserve space in directory databases for a couple of extra months.

NOTE   If you ignore Microsoft's recommendation and change this value, you do so by modifying the `tombstoneLifetime` property of `CN=Directory Service, CN=Windows NT, CN=Services, CN=Configuration, DC=sanao, DC=com`.

If the tombstone's lifetime were shorter than the worst-case replication latency, the tombstone might be deleted before it has replicated to every appropriate domain controller. As a result, those domain controllers would never know about the deletion of the original object, leaving the directory in an inconsistent state; some domain controllers would contain the object and some wouldn't.

Once a tombstone is deleted, its space can be reused for other objects. However, the database size doesn't shrink unless you do an offline defragmentation. You would do that in Directory Services Restore Mode, as explained in the Resource Kit documentation. The operation is normally unnecessary, but if you have removed a large number of objects and want to recover the disk space, you can perform it.

If you restored a backup that was older than the tombstone lifetime, that domain controller could have missed a number of object deletions. For this reason, the Windows 2000 backup utility doesn't allow restoring directory databases that are older than the tombstone lifetime.

There is a *garbage collector* task that runs on each domain controller. It wakes up by default every 12 hours to check if there are tombstones to delete from the database. The deletion criterion is that the internal When-Deleted property of the tombstone must be at least 60 days older than the current time.

In Chapter 6 we describe the LDAP search that you can use to list the tombstones.

Time Synchronization

As explained with the replication process, Active Directory replication uses timestamps only when resolving collisions. Therefore, time synchronization between domain controllers is nice to have but not essential.

Synchronized time between various computers in a forest is more crucial for the Kerberos authentication protocol. The clocks of two computers must not vary by default more than 5 minutes for Kerberos to work.

A service included in Windows 2000 takes care of time synchronization. The internal name for the service is *W32Time* and the display name is *Windows Time*. This service lives in the process services.exe and it is implemented in a file w32time.dll.

W32Time service can get the time from an external time source using Simple Network Time Protocol (SNTP), which is defined in RFC 1769. SNTP uses UDP port 123, so you must open this port in your routers if you want SNTP packets to pass them. However, between computers of a forest, W32Time communicates with the RPC protocol. It is using the same secure channel mechanism as other domain-related communications.

TIME CONVERGENCE HIERARCHY

W32Time uses the treelike hierarchy that is already in place in a forest.

- Each workstation and member server gets the time from the same domain controller that the client is using anyway for authentication and other domain functions.
- Each domain controller gets the time from the domain controller that owns the PDC emulator operations master role in that domain.
- Each PDC emulator gets the time from the PDC emulator in its parent domain.

When we get up to the root domain of the forest, the PDC emulator there is authoritative for the whole forest. For this domain controller you have three options.

- Maintain time manually.
- Install some hardware that tracks the correct time, such as a card that gets the time from the atomic clock of a Global Positioning System (GPS) satellite.
- Set the domain controller to get the time using the SNTP protocol from some host on the Internet. For more information, visit the U.S. Naval Observatory Web site (http://www.usno.navy.mil/).

CONTROLLING THE TIME SERVICE

You can control the time service, for example, to set the external time source. You have two commands for time service operations: NET TIME and W32TM. To get help for these, you can type either of the following commands:

```
NET TIME /HELP
W32TM /?
```

To set the PDC emulator of the root domain to use two external hosts as time sources, you can use a command like the following:

```
NET TIME /SETSNTP:"tick.usno.navy.mil tock.usno.navy.mil"
```

To set the computer time based on another computer time, you can use the following command:

```
NET TIME \\someotherserver /SET /YES
```

TIME SYNCHRONIZATION PROCESS

When a time client boots up, it contacts its time server up in the hierarchy and the following steps take place:

1. The client and server computers exchange packets to find out the latency of communications between them.

2. When the client receives a timestamp from the server, the W32Time service of the former can add the latency to the received time. This way, it will know the time it should start using. This time is called the *target time.*

3. If the local time of the client is behind the target time, the client will immediately set the local time to the target time. If the local time of the client is ahead of the target time, it will slow down the local clock over the next 20 minutes to "catch down" with the target time. However, if the local time was more than 2 minutes ahead, it will be set to the target time immediately.

After the initial steps, the time client checks the time regularly with its time server. The initial checking period is 8 hours, but it may change between 45 minutes and 8 hours according to the following logic.

- If the difference between the local and target times is more than 2 seconds, the checking period is divided in half.
- If the difference is less than 2 seconds, the checking period is doubled.

Managing Operations Masters

Active Directory uses single-master replication or operation in five special cases where a multimaster approach would be prone to conflicts or extremely difficult to implement. In this section we explain the functions of each of these operations masters, also called flexible single-master operation (FSMO) roles.

Two of the roles are forestwide and three are domainwide. This leads to a simple formula for the number of operation master roles in your forest:

```
number of roles = 2 + (3 X number of domains)
```

Note that any role can be independently placed, so a given domain controller may hold from zero to five roles at a time.

The two forestwide roles are as follows:

- Schema master
- Domain naming master

The three domainwide roles are as follows:

- RID master
- PDC master (or PDC emulator)
- Infrastructure master (or infrastructure daemon)

In the next five subsections we describe the functions of each of the operations masters. After that we discuss the placement considerations and how to transfer or seize any of the roles to another domain controller, perhaps as a response to an operations master failure.

SCHEMA MASTER

If you ever change the base schema of your forest, you make all changes to the domain controller that is holding the forestwide schema master role. These changes to the schema partition are then replicated to every other domain controller in the forest.

DOMAIN NAMING MASTER

The following changes are made to the forestwide domain naming master:

- Adding a domain to the forest or removing a domain from a forest
- Adding or removing a cross-reference to a domain in an external directory

In a future version of Active Directory, the domain naming master may also support moving and renaming domains in a forest.

RID MASTER

As you know, every time a new security principal (i.e., user, computer, security group, trusting domain) is created in some domain, that security principal gets a security ID (SID). You also know that this SID consists of a domain part and a unique relative ID (RID).

Each domain controller has a pool of RIDs to issue to security principals that are created in that domain controller. When the amount of free RIDs falls below 100, the domain controller retrieves 500 new RIDs from the per-domain RID master. This means that every domain controller should always have between 100 and 600 RIDs available.

A RID master is also used when you move an object from one domain to another. It removes the object from the first domain and puts it in the second domain. If you move an Active Directory object between domains with MoveTree, you must initiate the move on the RID master of the source domain. With this requirement, Active Directory makes sure that two administrators cannot move the same object to two domains simultaneously. Such a conflict would lead to two identical objects being in the forest, both using the same GUID. This would be an illegal situation.

PDC EMULATOR

The per-domain PDC emulator has functions for both pre–Windows 2000 computers and for a pure Windows 2000 network. The former case includes the following functions.

- Pre–Windows 2000 computers, such as Windows NT backup domain controllers (BDC), member servers, and workstations, expect to find a primary domain controller (PDC) in their domain. The PDC emulator fills this need. For example, when any change is made from a downlevel computer to a user object, such as a user changing her password, this is written first to the PDC (emulator). After that, each Windows NT BDC will replicate the change from the PDC.

- The old browser service (for building up the Network Neighborhood for users) needs a *domain master browser* to exchange computer lists between IP subnets. The PDC emulator also emulates this function, which is natural, because in old networks the PDC was always the same computer as the domain master browser.

The PDC emulator is used in the following ways for Windows 2000 computers.

- When a user changes his password on any domain controller, the change is pushed by the Netlogon service to the PDC emulator on a best-effort basis (not part of replication). This is beneficial if the user immediately tries to access some other server and his new password hasn't yet been replicated to every domain controller. If the authenticating domain controller notices that the user's password doesn't match, it can check with the PDC emulator to see if there is a new password for the user. The changed password is also normally replicated to other domain controllers.

- All user and computer account lockouts are processed on the PDC emulator. This way, both the setting of lockouts and the releasing of lockouts happens instantly without a replication delay.

- The PDC emulator of each domain gets the network time from the PDC emulator in its parent domain. Each PDC emulator also passes the time on to other domain controllers.

As you can see, Windows 2000 clients use the PDC master only indirectly via a domain controller.

The push of passwords to the PDC emulator can be disabled between sites with the following registry setting (where value 1 means true):

```
HKEY_LOCAL_MACHINE\SYSTEM\CurrentControlSet\Services\Netlogon\Parameters
   AvoidPdcOnWan : REG_DWORD : 1
```

INFRASTRUCTURE MASTER

When an object references another object, such as when a group references its member, and the referenced object is not in the directory database of the domain controller (because the two objects are in different domains), a special record called *phantom* is needed in the directory database to represent the referenced object. A phantom contains two or three identifiers of the referenced object: the GUID, the distinguished name (DN), and if the referenced object is a security principal, a SID.

The GUID never changes, but the DN will change if the object is moved or renamed. The SID will change if the object is moved from one domain to another. Consequently, the DN and SID in the phantom must be updated in these cases. The per-domain infrastructure master of the referencing object's domain is responsible for updating the phantom after a move or renaming operation. It must also replicate changed phantoms to other domain controllers in the domain. The infrastructure master performs its duty by periodically scanning its directory database for references to objects that are not in its database (because they are in other domains of the forest) and by contacting a global catalog server to check if these references are still valid.

For example, the group CN=gsSales, OU=Salesmen, DC=sales, DC=sanao, DC=com has a member from a different domain: CN=Jack Brown, OU=Boston, DC=sanao, DC=com. If Jack were moved from the Boston OU to the London OU, his new DN would be CN=Jack Brown, OU=London, DC=sanao, DC=com. The infrastructure master in the Sales domain would update the reference (i.e., the phantom) accordingly.

Global catalog servers don't need phantoms, and consequently they don't create or update them. A global catalog server contains all objects of the forest, so it will never find references where the target wouldn't be in its database.

NOTE   Don't confuse phantoms with tombstones (i.e., objects marked as deleted) or foreign security principals (references to objects outside the forest).

OPERATIONS MASTER PLACEMENT

As you know, the two forestwide roles go by default to the first domain controller of the forest and the three domainwide roles go to the first domain controller of each domain.

In a small forest you may settle for the default configuration, but in a large forest you probably need to make some changes. Table 5.31 describes the different scenarios as incremental steps. Table 5.32 describes the role placement in a multi-domain forest.

NOTE   In most of the cases in Table 5.31, all five operations master roles are in the same domain controller. You are not forced to use this configuration, but it is simpler to manage, especially when responding to operations master failures (covered in a later section).

TABLE 5.31 Placement Rules for Operations Masters

Number of Domains, DCs	Other Conditions	Placement
1 domain, 1 DC	Any	All five roles are in the only DC.
1 domain, several DCs	Small to medium domain	All five roles are in the first DC (the default). You can call it an *operations master domain controller (OMDC).*
	A large domain with more load	You could select a more powerful computer as the OMDC than the original OMDC might be (i.e., transfer all five roles there). The load on the schema, domain-naming, and infrastructure masters is zero or next to zero. The RID master may experience some load and the PDC emulator is subject to a heavy load (depending on the number of users and workstations).
	Multiple sites	You should select an OMDC that can be accessed from any site reliably and with a decently fast connection.

(continued)

TABLE 5.31 (*continued*)

Number of Domains, DCs	Other Conditions	Placement
1 domain, several DCs	Even more load	If you feel that all five roles are too much for one DC, you can transfer the PDC emulator role to another DC. That new DC should also be accessible from any site, because the downlevel clients communicate directly with it.
Several domains	Any	See Table 5.32.

TABLE 5.32 Placement Rules for Operations Masters in a Multidomain Forest

Roles	Placement
Schema and domain naming masters	You should keep these two roles in the same domain controller—this way, you will have one less special DC to look after. You have the most control over the roles when they are in the root domain. The domain naming master must be on a domain controller that is a global catalog server.
RID and PDC masters (in each domain)	You can apply the instructions from Table 5.31; that is, keep these two roles in the same domain controller, unless a heavy load would make you separate them.
Infrastructure master (in each domain)	This role must not be on a global catalog server. If it is, the domain controller doesn't need (or contain) any phantoms, so it won't notice when the cross-domain references are out of date and need updating. This would hurt the other domain controllers in the domain (the ones that are not global catalog servers), because no one would send them updated phantoms. You would see a warning about this in the event log (see Figure 5.46). The infrastructure master should have a good network connection to a global catalog server, preferably in the same site. As an exception, if all the domain controllers of the domain are global catalog servers, the infrastructure master can be on any of them, because the infrastructure master is actually not needed for anything anymore.

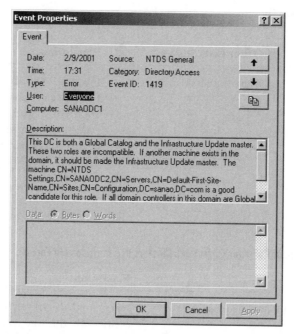

FIGURE 5.46 If the infrastructure master role is in a domain controller that is also a global catalog server, an error message is logged. You can see this error using the Event Viewer.

NOTE   Remember to review your operations master placement if you make changes in your forest that might affect this placement.

In addition to selecting the placement of the operations masters, you should designate standby OMDCs. You can prepare for a possible failure of the original OMDC by using the following guidelines.

- Designate a standby for each OMDC in your forest. A standby is another domain controller on the same site (and naturally in the same domain, for the domainwide roles).

- If you want to prepare for a sitewide disaster, designate a second standby off-site. It should have a reasonably fast and reliable communication link to the primary site.

- Each standby for the roles schema master, domain naming master, and RID master should have a connection object for its primary OMDC to directly replicate from there. If there is an automatically created connection object, you cannot rely on it being there tomorrow; the KCC may have changed the replication topology. Therefore, you should create the needed connection objects manually. This way, the standby OMDC's Active Directory data is as current as possible at the time of the primary OMDC's failure. The requirement in this bullet doesn't apply to the roles PDC emulator and infrastructure master, because they don't carry any vital configuration information that should be transferred to the new role owner.

- If some child domain has only one domain controller, you don't need to install a second domain controller just to get a standby for that domain (although otherwise it is a good idea to have at least two domain controllers in each domain).

- If you have a mixed-mode domain with Windows NT BDCs, it is better to have the standby PDC emulator in the same site as the PDC emulator. This way the Windows NT BDCs don't have to perform a full sync (i.e., replicating the whole domain partition) if the standby PDC emulator ever needs to replace the original one.

- The standby should be capable for the role. For example, because the domain naming master must be on a global catalog server, the standby should already be a global catalog server so that you don't have to promote it in a hurry when the original role owner has failed.

We will discuss in the subsequent "Managing Operations Master Failures" subsection what to do in a case of a failure of an OMDC.

TRANSFERRING OPERATIONS MASTER ROLES

You could change a role to another domain controller to respond to a failure or just to put it in a better place. The former case requires a drastic operation, called *seizing a role*. In this situation, before seizing an operations master role to another domain controller, you must understand failures (see the next section). The latter case, called *transferring a role,* is not a drastic or difficult operation, because it happens in cooperation with the old role owner.

Under the hood, the current owner of each role is identified by an fSMORoleOwner property in a certain object of Active Directory. This property points to the NTDS Settings object of the domain controller that owns the role.

You can see and transfer each role with some graphical MMC snap-in, so you need the fSMORoleOwner property only if you are writing ADSI scripts. We give an example of this in Chapter 11.

Table 5.33 lists the graphical snap-in, as well as the object that contains the fSMORoleOwner property for each role.

TABLE 5.33 How to See or Transfer the Role Owner

Role	Graphical Snap-In	Object That Contains *fSMORoleOwner*
Schema master	Schema Manager, right-click the snap-in root in the left pane and select Operations Master.	CN=Schema, CN=Configuration, *<my forest>*
Domain naming master	Domains and Trusts, right-click the snap-in root in the left pane and select Operations Master.	CN=Partitions, CN=Configuration, *<my forest>*
RID master	Users and Computers, right-click the domain and select Operations Masters.	CN=RID Manager$, CN=System, *<my domain>*
PDC master (or PDC emulator)	Same as for RID master	*<my domain>*
Infrastructure master	Same as for RID master	CN=Infrastructure, *<my domain>*

WARNING   If you transfer one of the first three roles in Table 5.33, you must not restore the domain controller that used to have the role from a backup, where it still holds the role. If you do so, you could corrupt your enterprise forest or one domain.

Another way to see the current role owners is to use the NTDSUtil command-line utility. You can use the following command (all as one line):

```
Ntdsutil roles Connections "Connect to server myserver" Quit
     "select Operation Target" "List roles for connected server"
     Quit Quit Quit
```

NOTE   You must type a real server name instead of "myserver."

Alternatively, you can use just the following command:

```
Ntdsutil
```

Once you see the utility prompt (ntdsutil:), you type one word or part at a time of the command just listed (roles, connections, and so on) and press Enter after each command.

MANAGING OPERATIONS MASTER FAILURES

If a failure does occur, an operations master role is not seized automatically. Instead, you need to do this manually after you consider the following.

- Most of the failures won't affect users (see Table 5.34)—at least not any time soon. Therefore, it is often best to fix the original OMDC to get it back online.

- It is, of course, possible that the failure is not in the OMDC itself, but in the network connection to it. Consequently, you don't want to seize the role to another domain controller, but rather you want to fix the network connection.

- If after a failure you seize the role of the schema master, domain naming master, or RID master to the standby, you must make absolutely sure that the original OMDC never gets back online. Otherwise, you might end up with two competing masters, which could corrupt your forest or corresponding domain. In other words, if the original OMDC just seems not to answer, don't automatically seize any of the three roles. First, consider if you really want to seize the role, and then if you do, turn off the original OMDC, disconnect it from the network, and format or destroy its hard disk. Also make sure that you don't later restore the original role to the original domain controller from a backup.

- The other two roles, PDC master and infrastructure master, you can seize to a standby without fear of drastic consequences. Also, if you later get the original OMDC back online, you can restore the roles to it.

NOTE Because seizing the schema master, domain naming master, or RID master role is quite drastic, the graphical snap-ins listed in Table 5.33 refuse to do it. Instead, you must use NTDSUtil.

Table 5.34 lists what happens if an OMDC fails.

Figure 5.47 shows the error message that appears when the RIDs run out. The outcome is that of the five roles you could consider the PDC master to be some

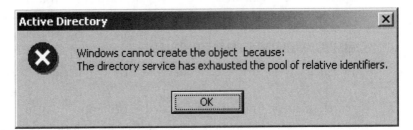

FIGURE 5.47 If a domain controller runs out of RIDs, perhaps because of a RID master failure, it doesn't allow you to create security principal objects anymore.

TABLE 5.34 Impact of Different Operations Master Failures

Role	Failure Affects Users	Impact of a Failure
Schema master	No	Schema administrators cannot make changes to the schema.
Domain naming master	No	Administrators cannot add or remove domains, or manage cross-references to external directories.
RID master	No	Because every DC has 100–600 RIDs in its pool at any time, an administrator starts to notice the failure of the RID master after he has created that number of security principal objects (such as users) on the same domain controller.
PDC master	Yes	Pre–Windows 2000 BDCs don't have a master to replicate from; pre–Windows 2000 clients cannot change their passwords or see Network Neighborhood changes in other sites. If Windows 2000 clients change their passwords, they cannot immediately access other servers with the new password. Until replication completes, they must use the old password. The network time doesn't get synchronized among domain controllers.
Infrastructure master	No	If an administrator in some other domain moves or renames objects that are referenced by objects in this domain (such as users in other domains as members of groups in this domain), those references won't get updated to reflect the move or rename operation.

kind of a single point of failure. However, in a case of a failure, you can rather easily assign a new domain controller to take care of the role.

You can run DCDiag to verify that each operations master is operational.

SEIZING OPERATIONS MASTER ROLES

You can seize the PDC master and infrastructure master roles using the Users and Computers snap-in, as described in Table 5.33. These two roles do not include any vital domain or forest configuration information, so you don't need to worry about the new role owners being up-to-date before the seize operation. If you anticipate that the current role owner is unavailable for an unacceptably long time, you can go ahead and seize the role(s). If the original role owner later becomes available again, you can transfer the role(s) back.

The remaining three roles (i.e., schema master, domain naming master, and RID master) do carry vital configuration information, so you should make sure that the new role owner is as up-to-date as possible before you seize the role using the command-line tool NTDSUtil. Remember also that these three roles are not constantly needed, so you shouldn't seize the role at all if there is a chance that the original role owner will later become available.

Obviously, if the current role owner has failed, there is nothing you can do anymore to make its configuration information up-to-date in other domain controllers. Of course, because most of this configuration information changes infrequently, it is quite possible that the information is already up-to-date in other domain controllers. What you can do is locate the domain controller with the information being closest to up-to-date (even if not quite up-to-date). If your standby OMDC has a connection object to replicate directly from the original OMDC (as instructed earlier in this section), the information in the standby is probably closest of any candidate domain controllers to being up-to-date.

NOTE   It doesn't matter if the new schema master or domain naming master role owner is not up-to-date before the seize operation, as long as it is closest of all candidates to being up-to-date. If the failed role owner had information that even the best candidate doesn't have, that missing information cannot corrupt the domain or forest. After all, there is no one alive that would know about that information.

NOTE   The preceding note does not apply to RID masters. A RID master may have issued RIDs to other domain controllers, even though the state of the RID master has not yet been replicated to them. Fortunately, RID master state changes are replicated using urgent replication, which should minimize the risk of domain corruption in case of a RID master failure. By default, however, urgent replication takes place only intrasite, so it helps only if there is another domain controller of the same domain on the same site as the failed RID master.

To locate the best candidate for the new role owner, you can use the RepAdmin command with the `/showvector` option. It displays the up-to-date vector of a given domain controller for a given partition. For example, the domain naming master of the sanao.com forest was DC2 until it failed an hour ago. Because the hard drive failed completely, and you don't have a backup of it on tape, you decide to seize the role to another DC. The forest had four DCs, so you are left with DC1, DC3, and DC4.

You type the following three commands:

```
repadmin /showvector cn=configuration,dc=sanao,dc=com dc1.sanao.com
repadmin /showvector cn=configuration,dc=sanao,dc=com dc3.sanao.com
repadmin /showvector cn=configuration,dc=sanao,dc=com dc4.sanao.com
```

Each command displays output such as the following:

```
Default-First-Site-Name\DC1        @ USN 15108
Default-First-Site-Name\DC2        @ USN 6792
Default-First-Site-Name\DC3        @ USN 12193
Default-First-Site-Name\DC4        @ USN 9733
```

To find out which DC has the latest information originated in DC2 (the failed role owner), compare the DC2 line of each of the three outputs. If your designated standby has the largest USN (as it should), seize the role to that DC. If another DC has the largest USN, seize the role to that DC instead, or wait until normal replication brings your designated standby up-to-date and make it the role owner after all. You can also use the Replicate Now function so that you don't have to wait so long.

If the new role owner should be DC3, seize the role with the following command (all as one line):

```
Ntdsutil roles Connections "Connect to server dc3.sanao.com" Quit
    "seize domain naming master" Quit Quit
```

Alternatively, you can use this command:

```
Ntdsutil
```

Once you see the utility prompt (ntdsutil:), you type one word or part at a time of the command just listed (roles, connections, and so on) and press Enter after each command.

CONCLUSION

After finishing this long chapter, you should have a good understanding of and be well equipped to manage the physical structure of your Active Directory network. You know what the automatically generated replication topology is for intrasite and intersite replication and what configuration information to enter for this automatic topology to be optimal. You also know when and how to adjust the topology manually. You are familiar with the replication process, so you can diagnose a failure efficiently. Finally, you know how to set up and manage the special domain controllers in your network, the global catalog servers, the bridgehead servers, and the operations masters. Once you read Chapter 6, which covers the logical structure, you are ready to roll.

Domains and Forests

The previous chapter covered replication and the physical structure of Active Directory. We continue the same theme in the beginning of this chapter; when we talk about domains and forests, we also have to talk about domain controller and global catalog placement. This in turn requires that we first examine how much network traffic Active Directory causes.

After we have established the placement of various servers, we examine whether these servers should belong to one or several domains and to one or several forests. We continue this topic by discussing forest structures, such as the forest root domain (FRD), and trust relationships among domains.

After addressing the aforementioned design issues, we move on to managing forests. This includes managing various trusts, moving objects in a forest, managing groups and permissions, examining referrals and cross-references, and delegating domain installation.

In the last section we explain how to use different tools to perform searches in a forest. Within this discussion, we explain many LDAP concepts and techniques.

DOMAIN CONTROLLER PLACEMENT

A major design issue in Active Directory is the placement of domain controllers and, consequently, the directory information. To help us determine these locations, we will first examine the amount of Active Directory's network traffic.

Active Directory Network Traffic

Microsoft has measured how much data traffic Active Directory generates for the following traffic types:

- Windows 2000 client logon traffic
- Active Directory replication traffic
- LDAP client traffic

In this section we present the summary numbers of the first and third traffic types as well as some derived numbers of the second type. If you want to read the full 140-page description of all the numbers, you can refer to the book *Building Enterprise Active Directory Services—Notes from the Field*, by Microsoft Press. You can get numbers also with a tool that Microsoft has written called Active Directory Sizer (ADSizer), which you can download from `http://www.microsoft.com/windows2000`. The tool asks you to enter information about users and other objects you have, how often people log on, how often administrators make changes, and so on.

Once you have entered the requested information, ADSizer estimates the number of domain controllers along with their hardware requirements, the domain database size, the global catalog size, network traffic, and some other information. Unfortunately, we cannot show screen shots of ADSizer because its license strictly forbids publishing any results the tool has given.

NOTE   Even though ADSizer can give you the numbers, you are better off if you have some background in Active Directory replication traffic. Therefore, this section deserves its space in this book.

WINDOWS 2000 CLIENT LOGON TRAFFIC

The logon process has two phases:

1. When a typical Windows 2000 workstation boots up, it generates about 70KB of network traffic. About 12KB of this goes toward obtaining Kerberos tickets and 28KB goes toward an LDAP query for domain controller LDAP functionality and Group Policy query and download.

2. Next, a workstation user logs on to her workstation interactively, which typically generates about 85KB of network traffic. About 28KB of this goes toward exchanging Kerberos tickets and 38KB goes toward querying and downloading Group Policies.

These numbers add up to a total of about 155KB of network traffic, whereas with Windows 95/98 the number was about 50KB. Most of the traffic is exchanged with a domain controller, but a small amount is exchanged with DNS and other servers.

The following factors affect the exact amount of the traffic.

- Each group that the user belongs to adds roughly 600 bytes to the interactive logon traffic. This is due to the Kerberos ticket growth as they include more group SIDs. If you have put the user in 100 universal groups, this means about 60KB of extra traffic. However, if you are using domain local groups instead, only the groups of the home domain are included in the tickets.

- Each Group Policy object (GPO) that affects the computer or user adds perhaps 3KB. Note that even if the same GPO affects the computer and the user, both add their own 3KB. The exact number depends on the GPO size, so 3KB is just a rough estimate. After start-up and logon, group policies are refreshed by default every 90 minutes. This causes more traffic, especially if there are changes in the Group Policies.

- Using a roaming profile adds easily several hundred kilobytes of traffic. When a user logs on, the workstation needs to check if there are changes in the server-based copy of the profile and, obviously, download any changes. During logoff there is likely to be even more traffic, when all changes to the local profile are uploaded back to the server.

- If folder redirection is used so that some user files are on the server, this naturally causes traffic every time the user accesses those files (except that client-side caching probably saves from transferring some bytes between the client and server). If offline folders are used also, the user can read files locally from the workstation, but any changes need to be written to the server. These traffic types are not tied to logon time.

- If a start-up and/or logon script is executed, it adds some traffic, especially if it launches some programs from the domain controller disk to be run in the workstation.

Most communication of the last three items on the list is not necessarily with a domain controller, but it may be with any designated file server.

Because the numbers presented in this subsection are per workstation and user, you can easily scale them up to the number of workstations and users that are (concurrently) booting up and logging on.

ACTIVE DIRECTORY REPLICATION TRAFFIC

Microsoft has measured the actual replication traffic for different numbers of objects in different cases. From these "raw data" tables we have derived the number of bytes each new object adds to the number of bytes that need replication and how many bytes you need to add as a base number.

In other words, we show you the two parameters (A and B) of the following linear function:

```
Y = A × X + B
```

You may have seen this formula in school. The following formula shows the same thing, this time expressed with our replication terms:

```
Amount = Number-of-bytes-per-object × Number-of-objects + Base-
  number-of-bytes
```

The fancy mathematical term for what we just did is *(linear) regression analysis.* There is a mathematical algorithm to find out the most representative line for the data set we had. However, we were more interested in finding out the practically representative parameters than the mathematically representative parameters, so we sought them manually.

NOTE   Setting aside the mathematical approach, there is no single right answer for what the parameters should be. Determining which line best represents some nonlinear data set is to some degree a matter of taste. Therefore, our numbers are a good estimation, but you should not take them as the absolute and only truth.

Table 6.1 shows the results for five replication types and four object types. The rightmost column of the table gives the margin of error when you use this linear formula instead of Microsoft's detailed tables. The numbers without parentheses indicate the replication bytes caused by creating each new object with just

TABLE 6.1 Replication Traffic Amounts When Creating New Objects

Replication Type	User	Security Group	Volume	Printer	Margin of Error (%)
Intrasite domain	3,985 (2,097)	2,087 (2,137)	1,747 (2,134)	3,519 (1,958)	0 to +2
Intrasite GC	3,017 (2,177)	2,087 (2,259)	1,808 (2,196)	2,637 (2,095)	−1 to +1
Intersite domain	256 (8,260)	180 (8,112)	180 (7,476)	192 (8,058)	−1 to +14
Intersite GC	210 (8,114)	180 (8,132)	153 (8,048)	192 (8,090)	0 to +5
Intersite GC with SMTP	408 (29,350)	357 (25,168)	314 (24,780)	372 (25,418)	0 to +24

mandatory attributes (i.e., parameter A). The numbers in parentheses indicate the base number (i.e., parameter B).

NOTE   Even though Table 6.1 shows the same numbers for all group scopes, the numbers for universal groups are a couple of percentage points higher in the case of global catalog replication.

As you can see in Table 6.1, the margin of error in the two intrasite cases is really small. This means that the intrasite replication of Active Directory is quite linear and you can easily calculate the total numbers (except for the effect of additional attributes).

NOTE   Now that the numbers contain only the mandatory attributes, the difference between domain replication (full) and global catalog replication (partial) is small or even nonexistent. In real life when you are using additional attributes, the domain numbers are likely to increase more than the global catalog numbers, thereby increasing the difference.

NOTE   Even though we say that the numbers in Table 6.1 include only the mandatory attributes, this is not quite true. When you create a user with ADSI and specify only the mandatory attributes, some other attributes also get a value (`account-Expires`, `codePage`, `countryCode`, and `pwdLastSet`). This explains why the domain numbers are larger than the global catalog numbers, even though all seven mandatory attributes are part of the global catalog.

The three intersite cases in Table 6.1 are using compression, so the per-object numbers are mostly less than a tenth of the intrasite numbers. However, the base numbers in parentheses are larger because initiating intersite replication takes more bytes. There is no notification of changes, which would specify the changed partition, so the receiving domain controller has to check all three partitions (or more in the case of a global catalog server).

Using SMTP instead of direct RPC doubles the numbers. SMTP packs bytes less efficiently for transportation, and SMTP headers need to be added and they cannot be compressed.

Compression in the three intersite cases introduces nonlinearity, which increases our margins of error. The first error comes from the fact that compression takes place only if there is more than 32KB of data to be replicated.

We have picked up the formula parameters from the data that is above the compression threshold so any results we calculate will represent the compressed traffic quite well. With small object counts without compression, however, the correct numbers could be two to four times larger than the ones that our formula produces. Fortunately, this involves only a few tens of kilobytes in this case.

The compression threshold is between 10 and 20 objects for all other cases, except for users and intersite domain replication, where the threshold is right after five users.

The intersite margins of error shown in Table 6.1 (+14, +5, and +24) are from above the compression threshold. Above this threshold, the formula produces the largest errors around 100 objects. The reason for this is that the proportional savings from compression are the biggest when adding the first tens of objects after the compression has started.

NOTE   The compression threshold also means that replicating 100 objects may take fewer bytes than replicating 10 objects.

In addition to the numbers in Table 6.1, we present some other results.

When adding ten-character Unicode string attributes to existing user objects and replicating them intrasite, we can derive the following formula from the Microsoft numbers:

```
Amount = 2250 B + Number-of-users × (290 B + Number-of-attributes × 92 B)
```

The margin of error is ±3 percent, so the results are quite accurate. You can see that each ten-character string (2 bytes per Unicode character) takes about 90 bytes when replicated. If you add the ten-character attributes when you create user objects, you can use the same 90 bytes as an estimated value per attribute.

The group numbers in Table 6.1 don't include members. We derived the following formula to take the members into account (noncompressed intrasite replication):

```
Amount = 2137 B + Number-of-groups × (2087 B + Number-of-members × 165 B)
```

The margin of error is again quite small, between –1 and +4 percent. The formula means that replication of each group member takes 165 bytes.

NOTE   As you know, all members of a group are stored in one multivalued attribute. Therefore, if you add one member to the existing 3,000 members, all 3,001 get replicated.

In domain replication, members are replicated for both global and universal groups, but in global catalog replication, members are replicated only for universal groups.

Replicating password changes intersite is less efficient than replicating normal string attributes. Active Directory encrypts a password before storing it to the directory database, and this encrypted data doesn't compress as well as normal average data. Each password takes almost a kilobyte to replicate intersite.

When using Active Directory–integrated zones in DNS servers, the DNS record changes are part of Active Directory replication. Each host record (i.e., A record) takes about 120 bytes to replicate intersite in addition to approximately 10KB as a base number.

Replication of the schema and configuration partitions shouldn't add many bytes because you probably do not add schema objects, domains, or sites often. When you do make some of these changes, each new object takes roughly a few hundred bytes to be replicated intersite to all domain controllers of the forest.

LDAP CLIENT TRAFFIC

As you know, clients access Active Directory information using the LDAP protocol. The reasons for access may be queries and other reads or administration and other modifications. The users who cause this traffic may be administrators, end users, directory-enabled applications, or network devices that use Active Directory.

Microsoft tested LDAP traffic using the native LDAP C API, ADSI, user tools such as Windows Address Book, and administrative MMC snap-ins. Here is a brief summary of Microsoft's findings:

- Connecting and authenticating (using the SSPI interface) with LDAP takes about 7KB, with ADSI about 10KB, and with a snap-in about 29KB. An anonymous bind with LDAP takes only 124 bytes.

- Obviously, the traffic increases when retrieving more properties of an object. Retrieving all properties (using the property list "*") of a large number of objects can cause excessive amounts of traffic, so you should avoid it.

- Searching many OUs doesn't increase the traffic because the search is executed inside a single server anyway.

- Modifying objects with native LDAP causes the least amount of traffic. However, using ADSI causes roughly only one and one-half times more traffic, and using a snap-in causes only three times more traffic.

- Reading from the global catalog causes about the same amount of traffic as reading the same information from a normal LDAP port.

- LDAP traffic can be tuned, for example, to set a certain page size. This and similar settings are explained in Chapter 11.

Determining the Placement of Directory Information

Part of Active Directory planning is to determine what directory information to store in each location of your enterprise network.

You may recall from the previous chapter that the replicas of the configuration and schema partitions reside on every domain controller of a forest, whereas the replicas of any given domain reside only on the domain controllers of that domain. You also know that some domain controllers are designated as global catalog servers, in which case they contain a partial replica of every other domain of their forest.

Now we examine the choices you have in placing the domain controllers, which is the same thing as placing Active Directory information. We will discuss three topics:

- Looking at all sites and domains together
- Looking at a single site and domain
- Looking at global catalog server placement

The first section introduces the playing field on a somewhat abstract level. In the second section, we discuss how to make the actual selections about domain controller placement. The third section continues the placement discussion, now concentrating on global catalog servers.

LOOKING AT ALL SITES AND DOMAINS TOGETHER

In this section we present and compare three general scenarios, each of which uses three sites: Boston, San Francisco, and London. The scenarios are as follows:

- One domain that has domain controllers on each site
- Three domains that all have domain controllers on only one site
- Three domains that all have domain controllers on each site

When there is only one domain, as Figure 6.1 shows, all Active Directory information is stored in each domain controller and must be replicated to every site. This involves the maximum possible amount of replication among sites. However, for users it also means that all directory information is local to them (the best possible proximity of information).

Figure 6.2 shows the second scenario. The only replication necessary to be replicated among sites is replication of the enterprise information, meaning the configuration and schema partitions. Because we have placed a global catalog server on each site, we also need to replicate those attributes of the domain partition objects that are part of the global catalog.

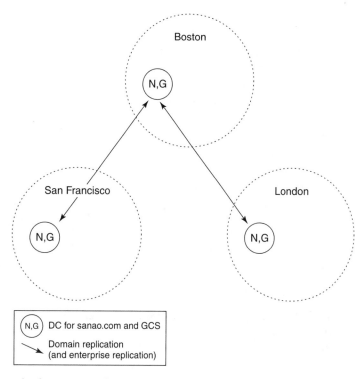

FIGURE 6.1 In this first scenario there is only one domain and this domain has domain controllers on each site.

Setting aside the effect of the global catalog, the scenario in Figure 6.2 requires the minimum amount of replication and offers the worst possible proximity of information. The users would always need to access information in other domains over a WAN link. If we dropped two global catalog servers, the amount of replication would be even less and the proximity of information would be even worse.

NOTE   Whether not having proximity of information is a drawback depends on if the users ever need to access information from other domains.

Figure 6.3 shows a scenario where the domain controllers of each domain are distributed on all sites. This third scenario is actually equivalent to the first scenario with regard to the amount of replication and proximity of information. Therefore, having three domains instead of one brings no savings in replication. Three perhaps independent divisions can now have their own domains, but they also need to buy their own domain controllers on each site.

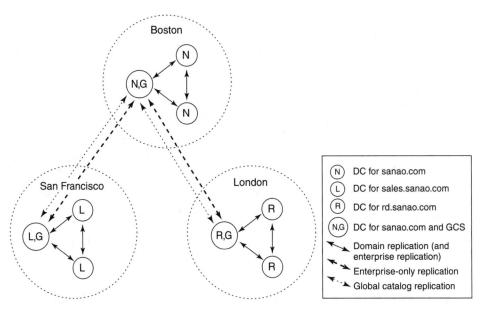

FIGURE 6.2 In this second scenario there are three domains and each of them has domain controllers on only one site.

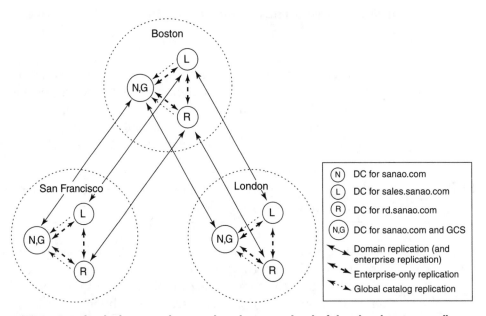

FIGURE 6.3 In this third scenario there are three domains and each of them has domain controllers on each site.

NOTE   The second and third scenarios (see Figure 6.2 and Figure 6.3) represent the two extreme cases of a multidomain forest. In practice, your solution is likely to fall between the two; that is, some of your domains would have all domain controllers on one site, and others would have domain controllers on several but probably not all sites.

Next we examine the placement of a domain controller from the viewpoint of a single site and a single domain.

LOOKING AT A SINGLE SITE AND DOMAIN

When placing directory information, you naturally would like to give your users local access to the information they need. On the other hand, you don't want excessive replication over WAN links.

Having learned the elementary numbers earlier in this chapter, now you should decide if it is better to put a domain controller (and perhaps also a global catalog server) on a remote site causing replication over the WAN link, or not to put one on a remote site causing logon and other traffic over the WAN link.

NOTE   When evaluating whether or not to put a domain controller on a remote site, you cannot simply calculate which one causes less traffic and choose it. Client traffic usually occurs when a user is sitting at a workstation waiting for a transaction to complete, whereas replication takes place "backstage" and can be scheduled to off-peak hours.

Let's consider the London site from the previous section as an example. As we suggested earlier, the least replication occurs in the first of the following cases and the most replication occurs in the last of them:

- We don't place domain controllers of any American domains in London and we don't have a global catalog server there.
- We designate a global catalog server to reside in London (which is normally wise).
- We put a domain controller for some American domain in London.

The exact amount of replication traffic depends also on how you plan sites and domains, and on the size of the domain and the frequency of changes.

The amount of client traffic (logon and other LDAP traffic) depends only on the number of clients and how and how often they use Active Directory and features such as Group Policies and roaming profiles.

This leads to a (quite obvious) conclusion: With a small number of clients, it is better not to place a domain controller on a remote site, but with a large number of clients it probably pays off to place a domain controller on a remote site.

We are not going to give more precise numbers or exact rules because so many variables affect the final traffic numbers. Besides, you can use the ADSizer tool to calculate numbers for various scenarios. You must also remember that your decisions will be only partly based on numbers because intuition plays an important role too.

However, we give the following (also quite obvious) additional considerations:

- The need for an on-site domain controller is probably greater when there are users of that domain on that site, because the users need the logon services. If users are just making LDAP queries to get Active Directory information about foreign domains, they can live better without an on-site domain controller for that domain.

- If you place a domain controller on a remote site, that computer contains all the directory information of that domain, including users' passwords. Consequently, you should see to the physical security of that domain controller in the new site.

- If you place a domain controller on a remote site, you also need to plan who will manage it and how, either locally or remotely.

- If you choose not to place a domain controller on-site, you need to make sure that the users of that site don't suffer too much. You should give them a WAN link that is decent enough (in both speed and reliability) to use for logons and other access. You could have a hub site that contains domain controllers for the branch sites to use.

- A global catalog server is always a domain controller, so if a global catalog server is needed on some site, that site must have at least one domain controller.

If you decide to place a domain controller on a remote site to serve users there, you have one more decision to make, with the following two options:

- Do not create a new domain, which means that you have to replicate an existing domain over the WAN (this is what we have been mainly discussing in this section).

- Create a new domain for the site, so that only the schema, the configuration, and possibly the global catalog need to be replicated. (We will return to this option later in this chapter.)

We have mentioned the global catalog a couple of times. Now we will seriously consider global catalog placement.

LOOKING AT GLOBAL CATALOG SERVER PLACEMENT

A global catalog server must be contacted in the following cases.

- A user (or application) queries something from the global catalog, for example, by using the Start menu (click the Start button and select Search, For People).

- A user or computer logs on and the computer is a member of a native-mode domain. The authenticating domain controller needs to contact a global catalog server to find memberships of any universal security groups to be included in the access token.

- A user uses his user principal name (UPN) to logon or to perform some other operation, such as change a password. If the domain part of the UPN is not the user's domain, the mapping to a correct user account must be resolved from the global catalog information.

- An organization starts to use Exchange 2000, which uses the Active Directory global catalog for its global address list.

If you don't want the traffic to take place over a WAN link in some of these cases, because of either speed or reliability, you must place a global catalog server on a remote site.

The following are considerations for placing global catalog servers.

- Normally you should place a global catalog server on every site. However, this increases replication to the site and one of the domain controllers on that site needs to be powerful enough to host the global catalog.

- The directory database of a global catalog server is larger than the database in a normal domain controller. For this reason you must be sure there is adequate hardware in any domain controller that you assign to be a global catalog server.

- Universal group members are stored in the global catalog. To avoid excessive replication, put users and computers as members in universal groups only via global groups. Be careful with the amount of global catalog replication—for example, refrain from adding many new attributes to the global catalog.

- If the increase in replication or database size is more than you are willing to accept given your WAN links and server hardware, you should leave some sites without a global catalog server. However, make sure that there is adequate service (speed and reliability) for that site also.

- As of this writing, Microsoft has 166 Active Directory sites in its corporate network and 165 of them have a global catalog server.

- If there is only one domain in your forest, make all domain controllers global catalog servers. In the one-domain case, this doesn't add replication, nor will it increase the size of the database, but it will maximize the availability of global catalog servers.

- If you already have a global catalog server on some site, having several global catalog servers on the same site doesn't add intersite replication. Once the data gets to the first global catalog server on the site, it will replicate intrasite to other global catalog servers.

NOTE Combining the first and last listed considerations for placement of global catalog servers can lead to an interesting claim. If there should normally be a global catalog server on each site, and once there is one, there could easily be several, we could claim that you could easily make all the domain controllers of your forest global catalog servers. However, if this were the case, all your domain controllers might need more hardware, so we don't make that claim. Also, if there were many domain controllers (say, over 20) on a site, it would be impractical (because of extra replication) to promote them all to global catalog servers.

NOTE It is possible that you don't need the features of the global catalog, especially if you disable the requirement for a global catalog server during logon (as explained next). In this case, of course, you don't need to worry about their placement.

If it becomes a problem that a site doesn't contain a global catalog server, and one cannot be contacted across a WAN link, you can add the following registry key on the domain controllers on that site:

`HKEY_LOCAL_MACHINE\System\CurrentControlSet\Control\Lsa\IgnoreGCFailures`

With this setting, users logging on may not be recognized as members of correct universal groups. If one of these groups were denied access to some resource, the members of that group could still access the resource.

When you have decided on the placement of domain controllers and global catalog servers, you must then consider the logical structure of your Active Directory. There are three hierarchy options: a single domain, multiple domains in a forest, or multiple forests.

DESIGNING DOMAINS AND FORESTS

When you design the structure of your Active Directory, you must choose whether to use one or multiple domains, and one or multiple forests. If you select a multi-domain forest, you must plan the structure of the forest, choose a root domain, and possibly create shortcut trust relationships to optimize authentication.

Single or Multiple Domains and Forests

Recall the four Active Directory hierarchies that we introduced in Chapter 1:

- One domain with no structure
- OU tree in one domain
- Domain tree
- Forest of domain trees

In this chapter we adjust the list a bit. Because we discussed OUs in Chapter 3, we don't need to differentiate the first two hierarchies for the purposes of this chapter. In both cases we just have a domain, which may or may not have an OU tree. Also, apart from DNS names and some search capabilities, the last two items in the list are the same, so we consolidate them as well. When we add one new item, we get the following list of possibilities:

- A single domain (with or without an OU tree)
- Multiple domains in a single forest (with one or several domain trees)
- Multiple forests

These three options lead to two questions: Will you have a single or multiple domains, and in the latter case, will you have a single or multiple forests? You must select one of the three options as the structure for your Active Directory. In making your choice, you must weigh conflicting benefits and costs, so you must know your priorities. Table 6.2 contains a summary of the differences among the three options.

Note that the three last items in Table 6.2 (policies, administration, and replication) make a difference when choosing one or multiple domains. Similarly, the four first items (number of schemas, configurations, global catalogs, and complete trust areas) make a difference when choosing one or multiple forests.

SINGLE OR MULTIPLE DOMAINS

Microsoft recommends that you use only one domain, unless you can specifically justify each additional domain. In this section we explain what it means to have multiple domains in your organization. We also list the costs related to additional domains. Remember that we already have discussed domains in several chapters. You may wish to review the following subjects in the cited chapters:

- Active Directory building blocks and hierarchies in Chapter 1
- The logical aspects of a domain (the OU tree and other objects of a domain) in Chapter 3
- The physical aspects of a domain (managing domain controllers and operations master roles) in Chapter 5
- Placement of domain controllers earlier in this chapter

TABLE 6.2 Per-Domain and Per-Forest Features

Feature	Single Domain	Multiple Domains in a Single Forest	Multiple Forests
Number of schemas	1	1	1 per forest
Number of forest configurations	1	1	1 per forest
Number of global catalogs	1	1	1 per forest
Number of complete trust areas	1	1	1 per forest
Global catalog placement	Can be in every DC without extra cost	Evaluate which DCs should host the GC	Evaluate which DCs should host the GC
Universal groups	No benefit but no cost	Benefits in certain cases, extra cost in all cases	Depends on whether there is one or several domains in each forest
Number of password, account lockout, and Kerberos policies	1	1 per domain	1 per domain
Units of administration	1	1 per domain	1 per domain
Units of replication	1	1 per domain	1 per domain

You already know that a domain is a unit of administration, unit of policy, and unit of replication. If you need more than one of any of these units, you obviously need multiple domains.

Multiple Domains Because of Units of Administration

A domain is an administrative unit in two senses.

- Administrative groups (most notably Domain Admins, Administrators, and Account Operators) have, by default, wide permissions to Active Directory objects in their own domain. It is possible but cumbersome to change the defaults. Consequently, if some part of your organization must have autonomous control over part of the objects (without Domain Admins being able to get there), you should create a separate domain for them.

- Outside Active Directory, there are a number of fixed rights that Administrators and/or Server Operators have for all domain controllers of a domain.

These rights include formatting hard drives, sharing folders, creating and sharing printers, as well as starting and configuring services. If you want someone to have these rights on London domain controllers, but not on Boston domain controllers, those domain controllers must be in different domains.

Also, geopolitical boundaries or legislation in some countries may prohibit administration in a foreign country.

Multiple Domains Because of Units of Policy

Group Policy includes some policies that apply only per-domain. They are visible also in per-OU GPOs, but they come into play only when set in a per-domain GPO. These policies include all settings in Computer Configuration, Windows Settings, Security Settings, Account Policies, which contains the following policy branches:

- *Password Policy.* For example, if you require a longer password for some users than others, those two kinds of users must be in different domains.

- *Account Lockout Policy.* These settings enable you to specify that too many wrong passwords entered for a user in a given time will lock that account for a specified amount of time. This way, for example, a potential intruder can guess someone's password only three times, and then wait 15 minutes.

- *Kerberos Policy.* These settings enable you to specify how long Kerberos tickets are valid. By default, a ticket-granting ticket (TGT) is valid for 10 hours.

In addition, the following settings in Computer Configuration, Windows Settings, Security Settings, Local Policies, Security Options apply per domain:

- Automatically log off users when logon time expires
- Rename administrator account
- Rename guest account

Multiple Domains Because of Units of Replication

Because a domain is a directory partition, it is a unit of replication: Each object that is created in a domain is replicated to all domain controllers in that domain. When you have more changes in directory information than it is feasible to replicate to every domain controller, you must create additional domains. This includes the following cases:

- *Too many changes (or WAN links that are too slow).* You have more changes than you want to replicate everywhere or to a certain location. Either you feel that you don't want to spend WAN bandwidth to replicate objects to places where they are not needed, or you simply don't have enough (free) bandwidth.

The reasons for this are that the link is too slow, it is unavailable part of the day, or more important traffic needs to use that link.

- *Too many objects.* Even though a single domain can host at least 100 million objects, you don't want all domain controllers to be powerful enough to store all the objects in your forest.

- *Cost by usage.* You have to pay for certain WAN links by usage. As you know, replicated data is compressed and you can optimize replication. For example, you can schedule it to occur only once a day and use reciprocal replication (i.e., once a link is open, replicate to both directions). However, by creating a separate domain, you may reduce traffic even more, and thereby lower monetary cost.

- *SMTP.* You don't have a direct connection to a site, but it can be reached with SMTP mail. Because SMTP replication is possible only between domains (i.e., schema, configuration, and global catalog replication), you must create a separate domain for that site.

Multiple Domains Because of Existing Windows NT Domains

Another reason to have multiple domains is that your existing Windows NT network has multiple domains, and you upgrade those domains to Active Directory *in place.* This leads to having exactly the same domains in Active Directory that you had in Windows NT.

This selection of domains might not be ideal for your organization in the long run, but it is a mandatory intermediate stage when performing this kind of upgrade. If your ideal forest includes fewer domains—perhaps just one—you can later consolidate domains on your path toward this ideal structure. In a large network, however, it could take a year or two to reach the ultimate goal.

Although we don't address migration strategies in this book, we want to mention an alternative to in-place upgrade. You can create an empty new forest with ideal domains and then migrate existing users, groups, and so on to this new forest.

Nonreasons to Create Multiple Domains

With Windows NT you needed to create several domains if there were too many user and computer accounts for one domain. The limit was about 40,000 users, or 26,000 users with computer accounts. This is not a concern with Active Directory because even one domain can host at least 100 million objects, given that the server hardware is capable.

With Windows NT the only way to delegate administration of some users and groups to another administrator was to create another domain. With Active Directory, per-OU permissions allow delegation in a single domain.

Branch Office Environment

As a special case, if you have a large number of branch offices, you can get detailed planning and deployment information from the Branch Office Guide at `http://www.microsoft.com/` (use the Search feature to locate the correct pages). The guide also includes scripts to automate the deployment process.

The basic approach in a branch office environment is to have a domain for the headquarters and another domain common to all branch offices. Or, in a large environment, there might be several domains for the headquarters and a new child domain for every 100 branch offices.

Costs of Additional Domains

Each additional domain introduces the following costs:

- *Additional domain controllers.* Because a domain controller can host only one domain, you need new domain controller computers (including Windows 2000 Server licenses) for the new domain. Fault tolerance requires at least two domain controllers per domain. If the domain is present on several sites (most likely because of user needs), you must have more domain controllers accordingly.

- *More interdomain communications.* The more domains there are, the more likely it is that a user accessing a resource and the resource are in different domains. In this case, the user's workstation must communicate with domain controllers in both domains. In addition, if the two domains don't have a direct trust relationship, the user's workstation must communicate with a domain controller in each domain along the trust path between the two end domains. This is how the Kerberos authentication protocol implements transitive trusts. Figure 6.4 illustrates the process. This item can be costly because the more often interdomain authentication is needed, the more likely it is that some domain on the trust path is sometimes unavailable to some user.

- *Increased risk of having to move users and groups among domains.* As users and groups are scattered in more domains, the possibility increases that in case of reorganization or a job change you must move some of those objects, or users' computer objects, to other domains. This is somewhat more laborious to administrators and somewhat less transparent to the users than moving objects inside a domain. In case of groups, the group scope is also significant in cross-domain moves—universal groups are easier to move than global or domain local groups. (We return to this subject later in this chapter.)

- *Duplicate administration.* Each domain must be administered independently, which may mean unnecessary extra work. For example, group policies must be established, OU trees must be created, and bridgehead servers must be managed separately for each domain.

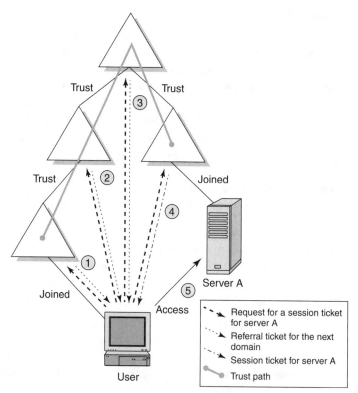

FIGURE 6.4 When a user accesses a server in a different domain, authentication is carried out with the Kerberos protocol and transitive trusts. The user's home domain returns a referral ticket for the next domain along the trust path. A domain controller in that domain returns another referral ticket until the target server's domain is reached. A domain controller in this final domain returns a session ticket for the target server, and this allows the user to access the server. Fortunately, each machine on the path caches Kerberos tickets, so the next time the process will be quicker.

SINGLE OR MULTIPLE FORESTS

If you choose to have multiple domains, you must decide whether to have a single or multiple forests. Again, multiple forests incur additional costs, so you should create only one forest unless you can specifically justify multiple forests.

The following four forest features must be considered when choosing either a single or multiple forests. These four features are possible reasons to create multiple forests and they also represent costs if you do have multiple forests.

- A forest has a common schema.
- A forest has a common enterprise configuration.
- A forest has a common global catalog.
- A forest is an area of complete trust.

Even though we can treat these four features separately, they have one thing in common: The likelihood that an organization will implement multiple forests is greater if that organization has autonomous administration groups that don't trust each other. Consequently, each administration group wants to have its own forest. By "don't trust" we are not suggesting that the IT personnel are an especially suspicious kind of people. It is merely a question of the organization having quite independent divisions, and the upper management of each division not allowing administration from foreign divisions. Alternatively, there are multiple organizations that form a partnership.

NOTE   All four costs affect administrators, but only multiple global catalogs affect end users.

WARNING   Administrators of child domains and domain controllers must be highly trusted also in the traditional sense of "trust." There are several ways (which we don't describe in this book) for a child domain administrator to gain system privileges and modify the forest configuration, which modifications subsequently replicate to all other domain controllers of the forest. Such privileges can also be gained by anyone who has a suitable boot diskette and physical access to one of the domain controllers. If part of the organization feels that another part (either their premises or administrators) is not worth this trust, those parts should deploy separate forests.

Number of Schemas

Someone should "own" the schema; there should be a single person or group to decide which schema changes are allowed as well as to coordinate and implement the changes. If the schema owner cannot be agreed on, there must be multiple schemas, and consequently, multiple forests. Also, if part of the organization wants to have control over the schema, it must create its own forest.

Another schema-related reason for multiple forests is a need to have multiple different schemas. This requirement should be quite rare in a production network. Classes and attributes that are added to the schema have several names and numeric identifiers that ensure their uniqueness. Therefore, a single schema (and forest) can host all schema extensions that applications from various vendors might need. However, you must have a separate forest to test any applications that require schema changes.

Multiple schemas can be slightly costly because they may require duplicate administrative work. If a change is necessary to multiple forests, it must be applied to each forest separately. If there is a setup program to care of this, the amount of administrative work is probably tolerable.

Number of Forest Configurations

Similar to the schema management, there should be a person or group that is responsible for the forest configuration. This configuration includes definitions of the sites and site links in the forest and domains, as well as some other enterprisewide configuration information. Again, if part of the organization wants to maintain autonomous control over this information, it must create its own forest.

Sites and site links must be created and managed separately for each forest, which results in duplicate administrative work. You must consider all the circumstances to decide if the costs are worth the benefits.

Number of Global Catalogs

The global catalog is used mainly for three purposes:

- Searches
- User principal names (UPNs)
- Universal groups

When end users use Windows 2000 to search something from the "Entire Network," they actually search from the global catalog. It would be confusing for users if the Entire Network included only part of the Active Directory objects in the enterprise's network. Thus, there should normally be only one forest. On the other hand, if a service provider maintained Active Directory networks for separate companies, separate global catalogs would probably be acceptable.

In addition to searches, the global catalog is used in two ways for user logons and authentications to servers: locating the user object via a UPN and checking memberships of universal groups. (UPN is called "user logon name" in the Users and Computers snap-in.)

A UPN, such as `jack.brown@sanao.com`, has a *UPN suffix*, such as `sanao.com`. This UPN suffix may be different from the user's domain name. For example, Jack's user object could be in domain `domestic.sales.sanao.com` and still he could have the aforementioned UPN. This has two advantages: The name is easier to remember, and if the user's domain changes his UPN doesn't have to change.

The UPN is a property of a user object, and the property is stored in the global catalog. Whenever someone enters "jack.brown@sanao.com" as a logon name, Active Directory can query the global catalog to locate the actual domain of the user object as well as the user object. Now, if there were two forests and two global catalogs and the user were sitting at a computer in a different forest from the user object, a UPN wouldn't work.

NOTE   Smart card logons rely on UPNs, so whenever a smart card is used to log on from a different forest, a default UPN must be used.

During a user logon or authentication to a server, memberships in universal groups are checked from the global catalog. If the user's account is in a different forest than the workstation he is sitting at, these memberships cannot be checked.

Complete Trust Area

A forest is a complete trust area and, therefore, a forest is the following:

- A scope of security principals (users, computers, and groups)
- A scope of Authenticated Users
- A scope of Enterprise Admins

The domains of each forest form a complete trust area. Any user or computer in the forest can be a member of any group (in accordance with the group scope), and any of the three can be assigned permissions to any object or resource in the forest. If this complete trust setup is not acceptable, multiple forests must be used.

Trusts between forests, or *external trusts,* are unidirectional and nontransitive (i.e., Windows NT–like). Consequently, you must manually create a trust relationship between each pair of domains (in the correct direction) where cross-domain resource access is needed. For example, if users in domain A need access to resources in domain B, domain B must trust domain A (of course, proper permissions must be assigned also). Figure 6.5 illustrates external trusts.

NOTE   Between forests, authentication takes place with NTLM instead of Kerberos.

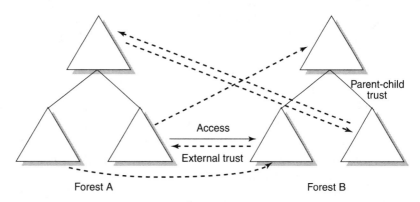

FIGURE 6.5 Interforest access from one domain to another requires an external trust in the opposite direction of the required access. With two three-domain forests there could be 18 trusts between different domain pairs, but this figure contains "only" 5.

NOTE   Another way to provide some access for the resources in a forest to users external to the forest is to use PKI. You can give those users PKI certificates and then map the certificates to user accounts in your forest.

Because a forest is a complete trust area, Authenticated Users includes all users of the forest and, by default, Authenticated Users has permission to read most objects in all domains of the forest. Therefore, all users of a forest can see practically all objects in the forest and read all properties of most of the objects. If you want to hide the objects in one domain from the users of other domains, consider putting that domain in a separate forest.

An alternative approach to creating a separate forest is to modify the default permissions so that the objects in a domain become hidden from the users in other domains in the same forest. However, this approach is somewhat laborious and more prone to errors than putting the domains in separate forests. Authenticated Users has a "Read + List Object" permission entry for the domain object. Phase 1 is not laborious or error-prone: You can use the Change button in ACL Editor to replace Authenticated Users for Domain Users in this entry, which causes only the local domain users to be able to browse the domain's objects and to see their properties (see Figure 6.6).

In phase 2 the process becomes laborious and error-prone. The permission change from Authenticated Users to Domain Users (see Figure 6.6) prevents users from other domains from navigating into the domain. However, savvy outside users can still see the objects in the domain by specifying names such as CN=Users, DC=sales, DC=sanao, DC=com or using tools such as LDP (Ldp.exe), which is included in Windows 2000 Support Tools. Therefore, to really hide all the objects in the domain, you should replace Authenticated Users for Domain Users in all the objects of the domain (and remember to do this also for each new object). If medium security is enough, you can modify the permissions of only the top-level containers in the domain and hope that outsiders don't figure out any object names at lower levels.

Creating an outgoing external trust from a domain to a domain in an external forest makes the users of the target domain part of the Authenticated Users of the source domain. Consequently, those external users can see practically all objects in the source domain. However, note that because external trusts are not transitive, the external users cannot see the objects in the other domains of the forest. Figure 6.7 illustrates this concept.

The root domain of a forest includes the group Enterprise Admins, and that group is a member of Administrators in each domain. Also, Enterprise Admins has Full Control for the domain object, which also applies to all child objects (that allow

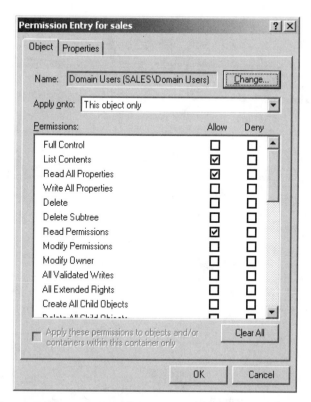

FIGURE 6.6 Authenticated Users has a "Read + List Object" permission entry for each domain object. You can use the Change button in ACL Editor to assign this entry to Domain Users instead of Authenticated Users. This limits access to the objects of the domain to only the local domain users.

inheritance). Therefore, Enterprise Admins has almost the widest possible permissions and rights to all objects in the domain as well as to its domain controllers.

If you want to block Enterprise Admins out of a domain, you can just remove the group from Administrators, and remove that one aforementioned permission entry. It is not necessary to put the domain in a separate forest to achieve this kind of independence.

Other Reasons for Multiple Forests

Because Windows 2000 version of Active Directory doesn't allow merging forests, an organization may have to use multiple forests for "historical" reasons. If independent divisions built Active Directory networks before any central coordination, those divisions have to be separate forests (until there is a version of Active Directory that allows merging forests). Also, company acquisitions, mergers, and partnerships may result in a multiforest network.

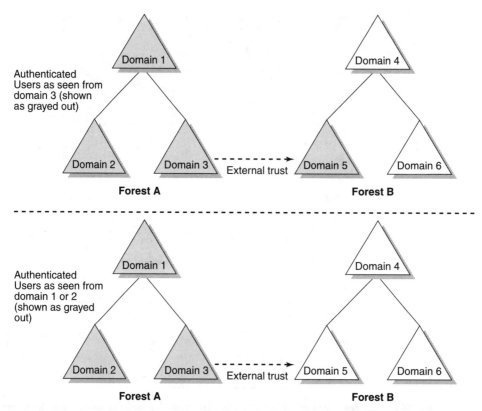

FIGURE 6.7 Each outgoing external trust enlarges the scope of Authenticated Users. Because external trusts are not transitive, however, the enlarged scope applies only to the trusting domain (domain 3 in the figure).

Other Costs of Additional Forests

In addition to the four main reasons for a single or multiple forests, there are the following miscellaneous costs.

- Administrators cannot move user accounts and other objects between forests (as they can between domains in a forest). However, they can clone objects between forests. The latter option doesn't preserve user passwords or maintain object GUIDs.

- Between Active Directory domains in two different forests, only NTLM, not Kerberos, authentication is used.

- Exchange 2000 uses Active Directory's global catalog as its global address list. If there are multiple forests and consequently multiple global catalogs, users of one forest cannot browse potential recipients from other forests. One Exchange organization can operate only in a single forest and only one Exchange organization can operate in a single forest.

Forest Planning Considerations

When you plan a forest for your organization, you must know three topics:

- The three faces of a forest
- How to add shortcut trusts to optimize authentication
- How to choose the root domain

THE THREE FACES OF A FOREST

You can look at the structure of the domains in a forest from three viewpoints (see Figure 6.8).

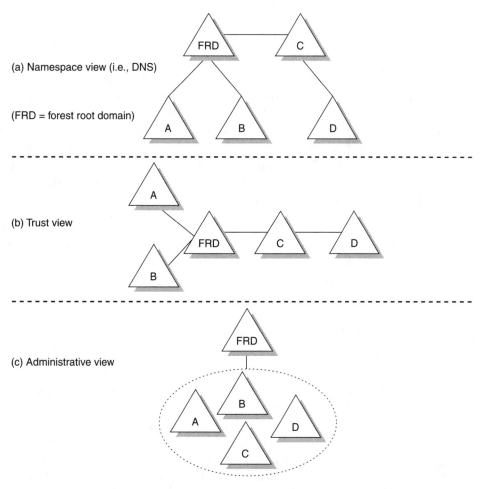

FIGURE 6.8 Three views of a forest: (a) Namespace view, (b) Trust view, and (c) Administrative view.

As Figure 6.8 illustrates, the three faces of a forest are as follows:

- *Namespace view.* This is the traditional view from which forests are presented. Each domain tree (two in Figure 6.8) in the forest has a root domain, and the first of them is also the forest root domain. The domains in this view are arranged according to the DNS namespace. This view also dictates how the search scopes are determined (as explained later in this chapter).

- *Trust view.* If we think only of the trust relationships among the domains, we can forget the traditional levels, where a child domain is on a lower level than its parent. All that matters are the trust paths between various domain pairs. As you saw in Figure 6.4, the user's workstation must contact each domain on the trust path to the target domain where the accessed resource resides. The longer this trust path is, the longer it takes to authenticate. In addition, the authentication speed depends on the speed of the workstation's connection to each domain controller on the path. The forest root domain is the central station of this authentication traffic.

- *Administrative view.* The structure of the domains in a forest has no administrative meaning. In this view you can think of the domains (except the forest root domain) as just a bunch of domains. Group policies or permissions don't inherit from one domain to another. Administrators from parent domains don't get permissions or rights to child domains, and administrators from child domains can be managerial superiors to administrators from parent domains. The forest root domain is special because it contains Enterprise Admins and Schema Admins, and anyone who controls the forest root domain can control these two groups.

NOTE   If domain C in Figure 6.8 were not a separate domain tree, but merely a child domain in the first tree, the namespace view would be different. The trust view and administrative view would still look exactly the same.

SHORTCUT TRUSTS

Administrators can add shortcut trusts to speed up users' authentication from one domain to another. Like external trusts, shortcut trusts are one-way. Unlike external trusts, shortcut trusts are transitive and they are always between domains in the same forest.

Shortcut trusts not only make interdomain authentications faster, but they can also improve fault tolerance. Without shortcut trusts, if the user's workstation cannot contact a domain (i.e., a domain controller of that domain) along the trust part to the target domain, the authentication fails. However, if there is a shortcut trust between the user's domain and the resource domain, the missing domain is bypassed and the authentication succeeds. If the communication failure also prevents part or all of the DNS name resolution, this bypassing mechanism probably will not work.

Shortcut trusts don't cost anything other than the few minutes' work that it takes administrators to create one. Therefore, consider creating a shortcut trust between each pair of domains in which users from one domain relatively frequently access resources in the other domain, and where a normal parent-child trust does not already exist as part of the forest structure. If there are only a few domains in the forest, you can even create all possible shortcut trusts without using energy to consider whether they are needed or not. There are no drawbacks to this approach.

Figure 6.9 illustrates a five-domain forest (using two views), where users of domain D quite frequently access resources in domain B. Therefore, administrators have created a shortcut trust in the opposite direction—in other words, from domain B to domain D. Figure 6.10 illustrates a four-domain forest where all possible shortcut trusts are created.

NOTE   Because shortcut trusts are transitive, creating one trust helps users only in the subsequent domains. All users of the forest can use this new shortcut when it makes the trust path shorter to a target domain.

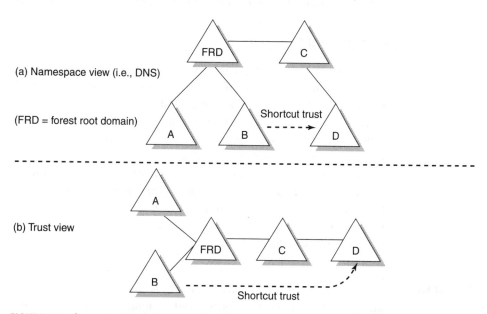

FIGURE 6.9 **If users in domain D quite frequently access resources in domain B, it pays to create a shortcut trust in the opposite direction. Without the shortcut trust, each authentication would need to go via domain C and the forest root domain.**

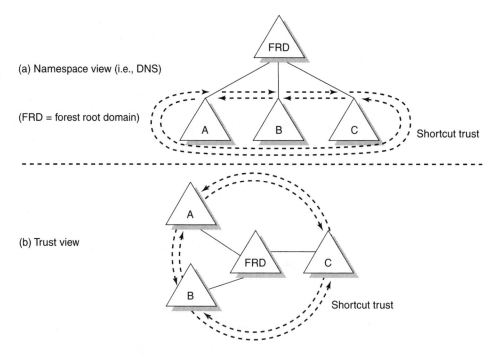

(a) Namespace view (i.e., DNS)

(FRD = forest root domain)

Shortcut trust

(b) Trust view

Shortcut trust

FIGURE 6.10 Because it takes only 15 minutes to create the six (i.e., all possible) shortcut trusts in this figure, it is probably not worth trying to find out which ones are actually needed.

THE FOREST ROOT DOMAIN

If you decide to have multiple domains in a forest, one of those domains is the forest root domain. In addition, if there are multiple domain trees in the forest, each consequent domain tree has a root domain.

Only the forest root domain contains the groups Enterprise Admins and Schema Admins, so members of Domain Admins and Administrators in that domain can control the members of the two former forestwide groups.

Selecting a forest root domain is a permanent choice. It is the first domain you create in a forest, and after you create it you cannot transfer the root "role" to any other domain. You cannot create a new domain above the forest root domain; you can create only child domains. Also, you cannot delete the forest root domain (unless it is the last domain in the forest being removed).

WARNING   You cannot reinstall a forest root domain to an existing forest. Consequently, if all domain controllers of the forest root domain fail, and there is no backup to restore them, you have to install all domains in the forest from scratch. Obviously, you want to avoid this.

The following are two criteria for selecting the forest root domain.

- *The forest root domain should be well monitored and maintained.* The organization cannot afford to lose the forest root domain. That domain contains Enterprise Admins and Schema Admins, and probably the schema master and domain naming master as well.

- *The forest root domain should be easily accessible.* The forest root domain is the central station for interdomain authentications, even though not all interdomain authentications must travel through the forest root domain (it depends on the trust paths and shortcut trusts). Consequently, all parts of the network should be connected to the forest root domain by a reliable and relatively fast link.

The forest root domain can be either "empty" or nonempty. In the latter case, it can contain 30,000 users, for example. We must use quotation marks with the word "empty" because even though we wouldn't create hundreds of users, computers, or other objects in the forest root domain, it would still contain all the predefined objects of any domain. Figure 6.11 illustrates the two choices.

An "Empty" Forest Root Domain

On the left side of Figure 6.11, one of the three child domains would have had to be chosen to be the forest root unless the organization had created an "empty" domain for this purpose. In an organization with relatively independent divisions and decentralized IT administration, it is difficult to raise any division domain above others, so the model with an "empty" forest root domain suits such an organization well (given that the organization didn't opt for multiple forests).

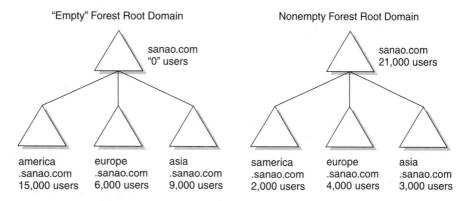

FIGURE 6.11 The forest root domain can be either "empty," in which case all users and other objects are created in child domains (or in other trees), or the forest root domain can contain most of the users in the organization.

Using this approach, the three divisions of Figure 6.11 would have to create and manage a fourth domain and buy domain controllers for it. They would have to establish a committee or team to be responsible for the forest root domain, the schema, and the configuration of the forest. This approach would offer the following benefits for the organization.

- An "empty" FRD never becomes obsolete. If `europe.sanao.com` on the left side of Figure 6.11 were chosen to be the FRD, and two years later the organization decided to sell all European functions, the organization would still have to use europe as the FRD.

- An "empty" FRD is light and easy to replicate to various locations of the network (given that appropriate domain controllers are bought and installed).

- With an "empty" FRD and separate division domains, the administrators of any division domain cannot control the membership of Enterprise Admins or Schema Admins. In other words, the organization can isolate the forest administration (with required permissions and rights) from domain administration.

The forest root domain could contain some objects in addition to the predefined objects that exist in any domain. If Windows 2000 DNS services were used with an Active Directory–integrated zone, all the DNS records of the zone that corresponds to the forest root domain would reside in that domain. The user accounts for enterprise administrators or schema administrators would most likely reside in the forest root domain.

NOTE   You can set a strict password policy for the forest root domain so that passwords of enterprise administrators are required to be longer than in other domains and fewer wrong passwords are tolerated before an account locks up.

A Nonempty Forest Root Domain

On the right side of Figure 6.11, one organization has most of its employees in the headquarters office (assumed to be in North America) and it has centralized IT administration. It is convenient for this organization to have a forest root domain that contains all the headquarters users. The other three domains contain fewer users in South America, Europe, and Asia.

In this scenario, the domain administrators of the main domain also control the forest by controlling the membership of Enterprise Admins and Schema Admins. Therefore, the number of domain administrators in that domain should be limited, and user administration, as well as other normal domain administration, should be structured so that various OUs are delegated to various OU administrators.

WARNING   Only members of Administrators can share folders, format hard disks, and perform some other such tasks on domain controllers. As you assign people to this group so that they can perform these tasks on the domain controllers of the main domain, those same people get permission to modify membership of Enterprise Admins and Schema Admins as well. Unless this is what you want, you should remove Administrators from the permission lists of Enterprise Admins and Schema Admins.

If the users in Europe, Asia, or South America access a foreign domain, it is most likely the main domain in headquarters. However, if a user in Europe sometimes accesses the Asia domain, the authentication needs to travel via the headquarters domain in North America. Placing a domain controller of the headquarters domain in Europe shortens the transmission path, but it results in replicating all the changes in the 21,000 North American users to Europe.

Another way to make authentication from Europe to Asia faster is to create a shortcut trust from Asia to Europe. This solution doesn't require extra hardware or replication traffic. As long as there are only a few domains, it is probably the best choice. If there are 17 domains in the Asia branch of the domain tree and another 17 in the Europe branch, the administrators can (but they shouldn't) create 578 ($2 \times 17 \times 17$) shortcut trusts to directly cover all cases when a user in some of the European or Asian domains accesses a resource in the other continent. However, because shortcut trusts are transitive, creating just two shortcut trusts on the top level (from the top domain of the Europe branch to the top domain of the Asia branch and vice versa) bypasses the need to communicate with North America.

Various Roots

There are actually quite a few different roots related to Active Directory:

- *Forest root domain.* This was explained in the preceding paragraphs.
- *Tree root domain.* This is the root domain of each domain tree in a forest.
- *RootDSE.* This concept is part of the LDAPv3 specification. RootDSE is the root of the directory information tree and it is referred to with an empty distinguished name. Despite its name, rootDSE doesn't operate as a root in the sense that you could browse any tree beneath it. RootDSE is a virtual object that contains 19 properties. The purpose of these properties (and, consequently, of rootDSE) is to provide basic information of an LDAP server to an LDAP client. When the client connects to a server, the former can ask the latter such things as the name of the forest and domain the server is part of, which LDAP controls and authentication mechanisms the server supports, and whether or not the server contains the global catalog.

- *DNS root.* In our sample name `sanao.com`, "sanao" is a *second-level domain (SLD),* and "com" is a *top-level domain (TLD).* Above com and other top-level domains, such as `org`, `gov`, and `edu`, is the root of the DNS namespace. This DNS root is denoted with a single dot (.).
- *Root of an OU tree.* Each domain can have an OU tree, and the root for this tree is the domain object of the domain.

MANAGING DOMAINS AND FORESTS

Now that you are familiar with forest structures, we are ready to examine how to manage various tasks in a forest. We discussed single-domain management in earlier chapters, so here we focus on a multidomain forest.

Managing Trusts

Table 6.3 lists the trust types, some of which we have discussed earlier in this chapter. One of the first two trust types (parent-child or tree root) is created automatically each time a new domain is installed in a forest. The trust relationships of the remaining types (shortcut, external, and non-Windows) must be created manually, typically using the Domains and Trusts snap-in. If a trust does not seem to work, an administrator can verify and reset it.

TRUSTED DOMAIN OBJECTS

Trusts are represented by `trustedDomain` objects, which reside in the System container of each domain. The properties of these objects describe the type and features of the trust, as conveyed in Table 6.3. However, the actual `trustType` property of the object specifies a type for each trust that differs a bit from those in Table 6.3:

- *Value 1: Downlevel Trust.* This trust is with a Windows NT domain (being external).
- *Value 2: Windows 2000 Trust.* This trust is with an Active Directory domain (being parent-child, root domain, shortcut, or external).
- *Value 3: MIT.* This trust is with a (non-Windows) MIT Kerberos version 5 realm.
- *Value 4: DCE.* This trust is with a DCE realm. DCE refers to Open Group's Distributed Computing Environment specification. This trust type is mainly theoretical.

A Windows 2000 trust (value 2) can be of any type listed in Table 6.3, except the last one (non-Windows). Downlevel trusts (value 1) can be only external, and MIT trusts (value 3) can be only non-Windows trusts.

TABLE 6.3 Trust Types

Trust Type	Explicit	Direction	Transitiveness	Purpose*
Parent-child	No	Two-way	Transitive	To create the forest structure and make it a complete trust area; this trust is between a parent and child domain
Tree root	No	Two-way	Transitive	To create the forest structure and make it a complete trust area; this trust is between a tree root domain and the forest root domain
Shortcut	Yes	One-way**	Transitive	To make a trust path shorter between two domains in the same forest
External	Yes	One-way	Nontransitive	To be able to assign group memberships and/or permissions between two domains in different forests or between an Active Directory domain and a Windows NT domain
Non-Windows Kerberos Realm	Yes	One-way or two-way	Transitive or nontransitive	To be able to give access to Windows users for resources in non-Windows Kerberos realms and vice versa; you can think of a Kerberos realm as a kind of Windows domain***

*The general purpose of any trust relationship is to enable administrators and resource owners to give a user or group of one domain permissions to access a resource in another without creating a duplicate user account in the other domain. This column describes the specific purposes of each trust type that are based on this general purpose.
**Shortcut trusts are usually one-way, but if you create a trust with the NetDom tool, you can actually create a bidirectional shortcut trust. The appropriate command is shown later in this section.
***There is more information on creating trusts with a non-Windows Kerberos realm at `http://www.microsoft.com/`.

The other meaningful properties of `trustedDomain` objects are the following:

- `trustPartner`: For Active Directory domains, this is the DNS name of the domain. For Windows NT trusted domains, this is the NetBIOS name of the domain. For non-Windows trusted domains, this is the name of the domain.

- `flatName`: For Windows trusted domains, this is the NetBIOS name of the domain. For non-Windows trusted domains, this is the name of the domain or it is NULL.

- `trustDirection`: 0 = disabled, 1 = incoming (i.e., trusting domain), 2 = outgoing (i.e., trusted domain), 3 = both directions.

- trustAttributes: (hexadecimal values) 1 = The trust is nontransitive; 2 = The trust is valid only for Windows 2000 (and newer) computers; 40 0000 = The trust is to the parent domain; 80 0000 = The trust is to another tree root domain in the forest. Other undocumented values are possible.

VIEWING TRUSTS

There are several ways to view the trusts of a domain. The primary way is to use the Domains and Trusts snap-in. You can also use the NLTest or NetDom command-line tool from Support Tools or view the actual `trustedDomain` objects using the Users and Computers snap-in, LDP, or ADSI Edit (the last two being from Support Tools).

Figure 6.12 shows a sample of the hierarchy of domains that you see when you launch the Domains and Trusts snap-in. Figure 6.13 shows the list of trusts that you see when you right-click a domain, select Properties, and select the Trusts tab. When you select a trust and click Edit, you see the trust properties, as shown in Figure 6.14.

You can see the same trust properties of Figure 6.14 with the Users and Computers snap-in. Turn on Advanced Features and locate the Trusted Domain objects in the System container. Then right-click any of those objects and select Properties.

NLTest lists the trusts of the domain of a certain domain controller when you type the following command:

```
nltest /trusted_domains /server:sanaodc1.sanao.com
```

With the trusts shown in Figure 6.13 the output would be this:

```
List of domain trusts:
    0: SALES sales.sanao.com (NT 5) (Forest: 6) (Direct Outbound)
        (Direct Inbound)
```

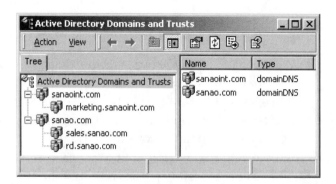

FIGURE 6.12 The Domains and Trusts snap-in displays the domains of a forest and enables you to manage them.

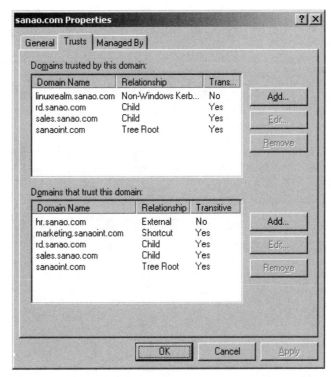

FIGURE 6.13 The Trusts tab of the domain properties lists both trusted and trusting domains of that domain. Domains with bidirectional trust appear in both lists.

```
1: RD rd.sanao.com (NT 5) (Forest: 6) (Direct Outbound)
     (Direct Inbound)
2: SANAOINT sanaoint.com (NT 5) (Forest Tree Root) (Direct Outbound)
     (Direct Inbound) ( Attr: 0x800000 )
3: HR hr.sanao.com (NT 5) (Direct Inbound)
4: LINUXREALM (MIT) (Direct Outbound)
5: MARKETING marketing.sanaoint.com (NT 5) (Forest: 2)
     (Direct Inbound)
6: SANAO sanao.com (NT 5) (Forest Tree Root) (Primary Domain)
     (Native)
The command completed successfully
```

For each trust the output shows a trust index (domain controller–specific), the NetBIOS and DNS names of the trusted domain, and the contents of the `trustType` property ("NT 5" means "Windows 2000 Trust"). The other flags of SALES indicate that its parent domain is index number 6 (i.e., SANAO), and the trust is both incoming and outgoing (i.e., bidirectional). The flags of SANAO indicate that it is a tree root domain, it is the domain of the target server (`sanaodc1.sanao.com`), and it is running in native mode.

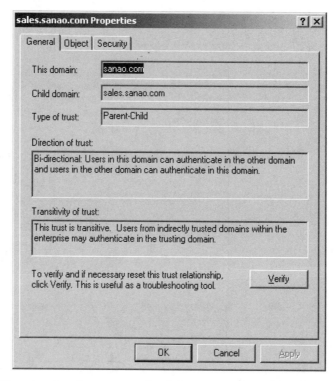

FIGURE 6.14 The properties of a trust viewed in the Domains and Trusts or Users and Computers snap-in.

NOTE   The information about native mode is shown only for the domain of the target domain controller. In other words, SALES could also be a native mode domain, but NLTest doesn't show it.

To list the direct trusts of `sanao.com` using NetDom, you would type the following:

```
netdom query trust /d:sanao.com /direct
```

With the trusts shown in Figure 6.13, the output would be this:

```
Direction Trusted\Trusting domain          Trust type
========= =======================          ==========
<->       sales.sanao.com                  Uplevel
<->       rd.sanao.com                     Uplevel
<->       sanaoint.com                     Uplevel
<-        hr.sanao.com                     Uplevel
```

```
<-          marketing.sanaoint.com              Uplevel
 ->         linuxrealm.sanao.com                Mit
The command completed successfully.
```

Trust type "uplevel" means "Windows 2000 Trust."

VERIFYING TRUSTS

You can verify a trust by clicking the Verify button shown in Figure 6.14. If everything is OK, you see the dialog box shown in Figure 6.15. If there is a problem with the trust, you get a warning like the one in Figure 6.16. When you click OK, the snap-in tries to reset the trust, and if this is successful, you get the OK message of Figure 6.15.

A trust is between two domains, and you could claim that a domain is just an abstract thing in the network. Consequently, it is possible to check only if a trust works between a domain controller in the trusting domain and a domain controller in the trusted domain. These connections between domain controllers that make up the trusts between domains are called *secure channels*. In other words, a trust is between two domains, but a secure channel is between two domain controllers. To be exact, "resetting a trust" means resetting one or more secure channels between domain controllers.

FIGURE 6.15 Normally everything is OK with a trust, so you receive an OK message as a result of the verification of the trust.

FIGURE 6.16 If there is an error in the secure channel making up the trust, the snap-in tries to reset the secure channel to fix the trust.

NOTE There is also a secure channel from each Windows NT/2000 workstation and server that has joined a domain to a domain controller in the domain that the computer has joined. In addition, there are secure channels between the domain controllers of the same domain. However, in this discussion of trusts, we are only talking about the interdomain secure channels.

WARNING When using verification of the graphical Domains and Trusts tool, you cannot control the per-domain controller secure channels, and the results may be confusing. The snap-in verifies the secure channel of only one domain controller: the one that you are connected to. In our scenario, SalesDC2 has a secure channel to SanaoDC1, and SalesDC1 has a secure channel to SanaoDC2, but SanaoDC2 is temporarily offline. If you click the Verify button (see Figure 6.14) on SalesDC2, you get the OK message shown in Figure 6.15, even though the secure channel of SalesDC1 to SanaoDC2 is broken. If you next click Verify on SalesDC1, you may get a series of errors, the last being that "the secure channel cannot be reset because there are no logon servers available." In other words, clicking the Verify button on SalesDC2 didn't reveal the problem with SalesDC1, and clicking it on SalesDC1 didn't fix the secure channel of SalesDC1, even though SanaoDC1 would have been available.

There are three command-line tools that you can use to verify trusts: NLTest, NetDom, and DCDiag. All three are part of Support Tools. We show a sample of each, but you can see more command-line options and examples in the Support Tools help.

To verify the trust from sales to sanao using NetDom, you would type the following:

```
netdom trust sales.sanao.com /domain:sanao.com /verify
    /ud:administrator /pd:*
```

NOTE The command shows on two lines because of wrapping, but it is one command.

The ud option specifies the username for the domain specified with the domain option and pd defines its password. Because of the asterisk (*), the user is prompted to enter a password. If there is a problem with the trust, you can reset it by replacing the verify option of the preceding command with the reset option.

WARNING It is possible that the `reset` option doesn't work. If the target of the secure channel of the local domain controller is offline, the preceding `NetDom /verify` command displays: "The network path was not found. The command failed to complete successfully." If you next try `NetDom /reset`, you may get the same error message, and your secure channel didn't reset to a working target. In this case, try using NLTest instead.

To verify and reset a trust from a domain controller in `sales.sanao.com` to the domain `sanao.com` using NLTest, you would type the following:

```
nltest /server:dc2.sales.sanao.com /sc_query:sanao.com
nltest /server:dc2.sales.sanao.com /sc_reset:sanao.com
```

In addition to verifying or resetting the trust (or secure channel, to be exact), both commands would show to which domain controller in `sanao.com` dc2's secure channel is connected.

WARNING The preceding `sc_query` command may show "success" for a secure channel, even though the target domain controller is offline. Therefore, if you think there is something wrong, you can always run the `sc_reset` command as well. Resetting a secure channel doesn't cause any harm, such as a disruption to the network services of users.

The last sample command uses DCDiag:

```
dcdiag /v /s:dc2.sales.sanao.com /test:outboundsecurechannels
      /testdomain:sanao /nositerestriction
```

NOTE The command shows on two lines because of wrapping, but it is one command.

The `v` option stands for "verbose"—it causes DCDiag to display more output. DCDiag tests all domain controllers of the source domain and `nosite-restriction` specifies that domain controllers from all sites should be checked. If the current target of the secure channel is offline, this DCDiag command should reset the secure channel so that it is established to a working domain controller. If this doesn't happen, you can use NLTest to reset the secure channel manually.

CREATING EXPLICIT TRUSTS

A shortcut trust between two domains in a forest must be established at both ends. By doing this, you get a one-way trust; if you want a trust also in the other direction, that trust must be established at both ends as well.

Our sample scenario has a sanao.com forest that has two child domains: asia and europe (see Figure 6.17). You want to speed up the authentications of users in europe to the resources in asia, so you create a shortcut trust in the opposite direction, from asia to europe. As you remember from Figure 6.13, the properties of each domain show two trust lists: The upper list contains the trusted domains and the lower list contains the trusting domains. To speed the authentication, you must add europe to the upper list of asia and asia to the lower list of europe.

To add the other domain to the list, you must enter its name and a password that matches the one entered for the other end. This process is illustrated in Figure 6.18. The result for europe is shown in Figure 6.19.

If you feel that it is hard to remember which way this goes—that is, which domain is trusting and which is "trusted by," or which one should be in the upper list and which one in the lower to speed up the authentication to a certain direction—don't worry, you are not alone. To help you remember, you can take "ed" from "trusted" and "ing" from "trusting." "Ed" is like a username, so the trusted domain contains the user who will access, and "ing" is like "thing," so the trusting domain contains the thing (i.e., the resource) the user will access.

Creating an external trust is very similar to creating a shortcut trust. If the other end is a Windows NT domain, the user interface is slightly different, because you would use the User Manager tool of Windows NT. Also, if a Windows NT domain should trust an Active Directory domain, it is better to establish the trust first at the Active Directory end. This way the Windows NT domain can verify the trust right away, and you will see a pop-up message stating this.

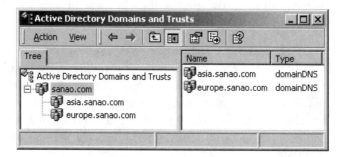

FIGURE 6.17 Our sample forest contains a forest root domain and two child domains.

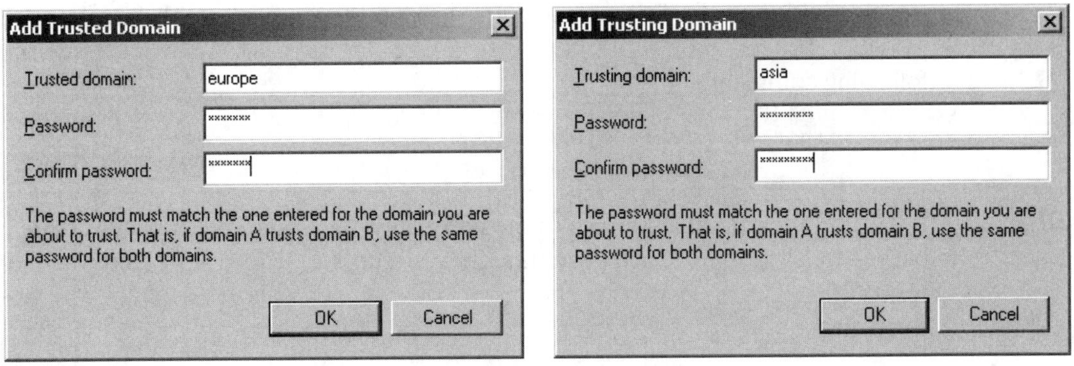

Add Trusted Domain

Trusted domain: europe

Password: xxxxxxx

Confirm password: xxxxxxx

The password must match the one entered for the domain you are about to trust. That is, if domain A trusts domain B, use the same password for both domains.

OK   Cancel

Add Trusting Domain

Trusting domain: asia

Password: xxxxxxxxx

Confirm password: xxxxxxxxx

The password must match the one entered for the domain you are about to trust. That is, if domain A trusts domain B, use the same password for both domains.

OK   Cancel

FIGURE 6.18 A one-way trust from `asia` to `europe` must be established at both ends. `Europe` is a trusted domain for `asia`, and `asia` is a trusting domain for `europe`. The passwords entered at both ends must be identical.

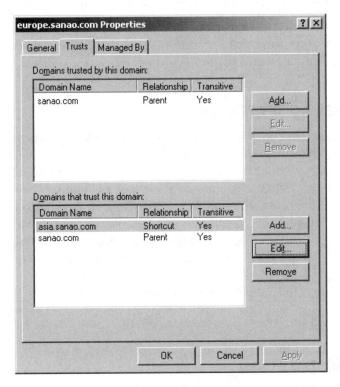

FIGURE 6.19 Once a trust from `asia` to `europe` is created, `asia.sanao.com` shows as a trusting domain in the trust list of `europe.sanao.com`.

In addition to the Domains and Trusts snap-in, you can establish trusts with NetDom. To create the shortcut trust from `asia` to `europe`, you would issue the following command:

```
netdom trust asia.sanao.com /d:europe.sanao.com /ADD
```

NOTE   If you add the option /twoway to the preceding command, you actually create a bidirectional shortcut trust, even though shortcut trusts are supposed to be one-way only.

We don't delve into non-Windows Kerberos trusts in this book, but we do show the NetDom command to create one (at the Active Directory end):

```
netdom trust /d:linuxrealm.sanao.com sanao.com /ADD
    /PT:abc /REALM /TwoWay
```

NOTE   The command shows on two lines because of wrapping, but it is one command.

This command would create (to the Active Directory end) a two-way trust between the Kerberos realm `linuxrealm.sanao.com` and the Active Directory domain `sanao.com`. The trust password is "abc."

FOREIGN SECURITY PRINCIPALS

There is a container called ForeignSecurityPrincipals in each domain. It contains placeholders that represent group members from domains external to the forest. There are placeholders also for well-known security principals such as Authenticated Users, if they are members of some group in the domain.

When you add a member to a group from an external forest, the corresponding placeholder is automatically added to ForeignSecurityPrincipals. The name of this `foreignSecurityPrincipal` object is the security ID (SID) of the object it refers to. If you remove the external member from the group, the corresponding `foreignSecurityPrincipal` object is not deleted.

Objects in ForeignSecurityPrincipals are visible only when Advanced Features of the Users and Computers snap-in are turned on. However, the container is always visible.

Moving Objects in a Forest

The Users and Computers snap-in allows moving objects inside a domain. If you need to move objects to another domain in a forest, you must use the command-line tool MoveTree, which is part of Support Tools. To move objects from one forest to another, you would use the ClonePrincipal tool, which is also part of Support Tools. In this section we explain MoveTree. If you need to use ClonePrincipal—when migrating users from a Windows NT domain, for example—you can read ClonePr.Doc, which is included in Support Tools.

You can also use migration tools to move and/or copy users and other objects between domains. You can download Microsoft Active Directory Migration Tool (ADMT) from `http://www.microsoft.com/`, or you can buy a commercial tool such as NetIQ Domain Migration Administrator (`http://www.netiq.com/`), FastLane Migrator (`http://www.quest.com/solutions/ms.asp`), or BindView bv-Admin (`http://www.bindview.com/`).

MOVETREE FEATURES

The MoveTree tool has the following features:

- MoveTree moves objects from one domain to another in a single forest.
- MoveTree moves a container (along with its contents) or an individual object.
- Each object that is a security principal has a SID. Because SIDs are domain specific, the SID must change when the object is moved to another domain. During the move, MoveTree adds the object's SID in the old domain to the `sIDHistory` property of the object in the new domain. This way, the moved user (or other security principal) maintains all group memberships and permissions in the forest.
- MoveTree maintains users' passwords.
- MoveTree maintains objects' GUIDs.
- MoveTree maintains the Group Policy links of the moved objects. However, this means that after the move, users and computers access their group policies from another domain, which is slower. To restore the earlier performance, you can (and should) recreate similar group policies for the new domain and remove the links from the old ones.
- If a move operation is interrupted, the not-yet-moved objects are left in a special container in the LostAndFound container of the source domain. This *orphan* container has the same name as the GUID of the container that was being moved.
- The source domain controller of the move operation must be the RID master of the source domain.

MOVETREE LIMITATIONS

MoveTree has some limitations, although only the first three in the following list are actual drawbacks. The remaining limitations in the following list are more or less obvious.

- MoveTree can move only empty (i.e., containing no members) global and domain local groups. However, it can move nonempty universal groups without problems. We discuss these options in the next section.

- MoveTree can move only users that are not members of any global or domain local groups. However, it can move members of universal groups.

- MoveTree cannot move computer objects. You should use NetDom instead. To be specific, MoveTree will move computer objects, but the corresponding workstations or member servers won't know about the move, so they cannot build a secure channel to the domain. Consequently, they can no longer use any domain user accounts. In effect, they are cut out of the domain.

- MoveTree requires the target domain to be in native mode. Otherwise, the SID history feature wouldn't work.

- MoveTree moves only Active Directory objects. Profiles, policies, logon scripts, and other file-based information outside Active Directory are not moved.

- MoveTree cannot move the computer objects of domain controllers or any of their child objects.

- MoveTree doesn't move system objects—that is, objects whose class schema object's `systemOnly` property value is True.

- MoveTree cannot move objects in the containers Builtin, ForeignSecurity-Principals, System, and LostAndFound.

- MoveTree cannot move objects that would have a name conflict or other conflict in the target domain. This includes duplicate names and accounts that do not conform to the password restrictions of the target domain.

MOVING GROUPS

As stated in the previous list, MoveTree can move global and domain local groups only if they don't have members. Therefore, you must take special steps to be able to move these groups. You have two options to move global groups.

- Convert any global groups to be moved to universal groups, and then convert them back to global groups after the move. This approach is relatively easy, although because universal group members are stored in the global catalog, converting the groups will cause a peak in your global catalog replication.

- Document the members of each global group, remove the members, move the groups, and then add the same members back. The easiest way to document the members of a group is to issue the command NET GROUP MyGGroup >Members.txt. This command lists all the members and writes them to the Members.txt file. To get the members back to the group in the latter option, you can use two batch files. The first file you get by renaming Members.txt to

Members.bat and modifying it a little. The resulting file is shown in Figure 6.20. The other file AddMember.bat is called from Members.bat and it is shown in Figure 6.21.

Because domain local groups are by nature used for resources in one domain, you shouldn't need to move them to other domains. However, if necessary, you can move them by using one of the options presented here for global groups.

USING MOVETREE

MoveTree has four main options:

- /check causes MoveTree to perform a trial run to check if the requested move operation is possible. After the trial run, you can check the text file movetree.chk to see if there is anything to prevent the actual move.

- /start causes MoveTree to perform a trial run to check if the requested move operation is possible, and if so, to perform the actual move.

- /startnocheck causes MoveTree to perform the actual move without a trial run.

- /continue causes MoveTree to continue a move that was interrupted due to a network fault or the target domain controller becoming unavailable.

In addition to one of the aforementioned main options, you must specify the source and destination domain controllers, as well as source and destination object

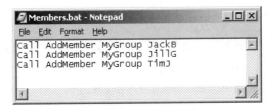

FIGURE 6.20 You can add a number of members back to a group with a batch file that calls another batch file for each member to be added.

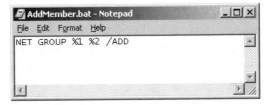

FIGURE 6.21 This command adds the given user (%2 command-line parameter) to the given group (%1 command-line parameter).

distinguished names. However, with the `continue` option, the source DN is optional. The following command moves the OU Salesmen from `sanao.com` to `sales.sanao.com` and renames the OU to SalesRep:

```
movetree /start /s sanaodc1.sanao.com /d salesdc2.sales.sanao.com /sdn
ou=salesmen,dc=sanao,dc=com /ddn ou=SalesRep,dc=sales,dc=sanao,dc=com
```

NOTE   The command shows on two lines because of wrapping, but it is one command.

SanaoDC1 must be the RID master of `sanao.com` for the move operation to succeed. If there are no errors, you see the following output:

```
MOVETREE PRE-CHECK FINISHED.
MOVETREE IS READY TO START THE MOVE OPERATION.

MOVETREE FINISHED SUCCESSFULLY.
```

If the move operation is not possible, you are prompted to read the move-tree.chk file and correct any problems.

Managing Groups and Permissions in a Forest

In a multidomain forest, users of one domain often need permissions in another domain. These permissions can be assigned either directly or via group memberships.

PREDEFINED ADMINISTRATIVE GROUPS IN A FOREST

We explained the predefined administrative groups (Enterprise Admins, Domain Admins, and Administrators) in Chapter 3 and their default permissions in Chapter 4. Here we revisit the topic by showing the default memberships of these groups in a multidomain forest.

Figure 6.22 illustrates the roles of different administrators in a forest and their default memberships. Enterprise Admins from the forest root domain is a member of Administrators in each domain of the forest. Consequently, Enterprise Admins gets quite a few permissions and rights in all domains. However, Enterprise Admins is not a member of Domain Admins in any domain. Consequently, Enterprise Admins doesn't get permissions or rights that are assigned directly to Domain Admins.

In addition to its memberships, Enterprise Admins has direct permissions for Active Directory objects. For example, Enterprise Admins has Full Control for each

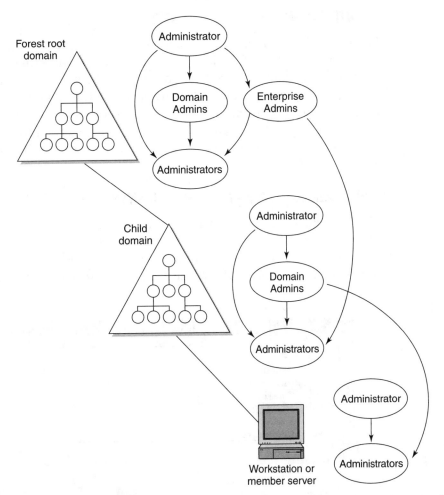

FIGURE 6.22 Enterprise Admins from the forest root domain is a member of Administrators in each domain of the forest.

domain object, and that permission is for "this object and all child objects." Consequently, Enterprise Admins has effective full-control permissions to all objects in each domain, except the few exceptions that don't allow inheritance.

If Enterprise Admins should be blocked out from some child domain, the child domain administrators should do two things:

- Remove Enterprise Admins from the Administrators group.
- Remove the Enterprise Admins' permission entry from the domain object.

PREDEFINED USER GROUPS IN A FOREST

Recall that Table 3.5 in Chapter 3 shows that if you give permissions to Domain Users, only the users of the local domain can use those permissions. If you give permissions to Authenticated Users, all users of the forest can use them.

Figure 3.3 and Figure 3.4 illustrate the default memberships of the various predefined groups, such as Domain Users and Users. Those figures describe the memberships in a single-domain forest, but the figures also apply to a multidomain forest. There are no predefined interdomain end-user memberships that would add anything to these figures.

GROUP MEMBER AND PERMISSION ASSIGNMENTS IN A FOREST

When assigning members to a group or assigning permissions, you can select the domain from which the potential members or permission holders can be selected. You can also choose Entire Directory, in which case the list is retrieved from the global catalog. This is illustrated in Figure 6.23. In each case the list

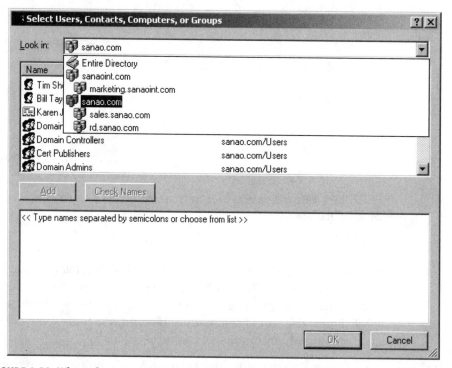

FIGURE 6.23 When selecting members or permission holders, you can choose the domain from which to select them. If you choose Entire Directory, you will get a list of all candidate objects from the whole forest.

shows only those objects that are possible for that case. For example, when you are assigning permissions, the list doesn't contain contacts or distribution groups, and the list never contains domain local groups from other domains.

Referrals and Cross-References

Because a directory is normally divided into partitions (or naming contexts), a single directory server doesn't necessarily contain all directory information. In the case of Active Directory, this is true when there are multiple domains in a forest. Even in a single-domain Active Directory forest, there are three partitions: schema, configuration, and the domain.

When an LDAP client requests an object or objects from an LDAP server (in the case of Active Directory, a domain controller), the client includes the distinguished name of a *base object* in the request (see the "LDAP Searches" section later in this chapter). If the server doesn't contain the partition where the base object should be, the server returns an LDAP *referral* to the client. For example, the client is connected to a domain controller of the Sales domain but requests a user object from the Sanao domain.

A referral points the client to another server (or multiple equal servers), which should contain the base object that the client requested. If this is not the case, the referred server sends another referral to the client, pointing it to yet another server(s). It is up to the client to *chase* these referrals—that is, to request the base object from the referred server. If referral chasing is turned on in a Windows 2000 computer, the operation takes place in the WLDAP32.DLL component of the operating system. Otherwise the referral "error" is returned to the calling application, which can decide whether or not to chase the referral.

NOTE   LDAP search operations may span partition boundaries. This concept is close to referrals, but we discuss it in the "Continuation References" section later in this chapter.

CROSS-REFERENCE OBJECTS

Referrals are based on cross-references, which are forestwide configuration information residing in every domain controller. Cross-references are *internal,* when the referred partition is in the same forest, or *external,* when the reference points outside the forest. An external cross-reference could point to another Active Directory forest or a non–Active Directory LDAP directory.

Cross-references are stored in `crossRef` objects, which reside in the `CN=Partitions` container of the configuration partition. There is a `crossRef`

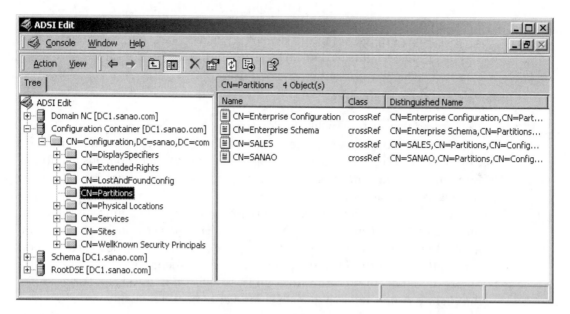

FIGURE 6.24 The `CN=Partitions` container includes a `crossRef` object for each partition of the forest.

object for each partition of the forest (i.e., schema, configuration, and all domains). These internal cross-references are created automatically when the forest or each subsequent domain is installed. In addition, administrators can create external cross-references to partitions outside the forest. Because all domain controllers of a forest host the configuration partition, they all have the knowledge of all partitions of the forest as well as any external cross-references that are defined. Figure 6.24 shows the automatically created (i.e., internal) `crossRef` objects of the `sanao.com` forest. That forest has one child domain: Sales.

   A `crossRef` object has six properties that are worth mentioning. Table 6.4 describes the first five and Table 6.5 describes the last one, the `systemFlags` property.

NOTE   If the `systemFlags` property is not defined for an object, it is equal to both bits having value "0."

CREATING EXTERNAL CROSS-REFERENCES

Members of Enterprise Admins and Domain Admins of the forest root domain can create external cross-references by creating appropriate `crossRef` objects. This

TABLE 6.4 Properties of Cross-Reference Objects

Property	Sample Value (Sales)	Description
dnsRoot	sales.sanao.com	This property specifies where the referred partition resides. It is the DNS name of either the corresponding domain or a specific server. When the client receives this DNS name in the referral, the client can query a DNS server to find out the IP address to connect to.
nCName	DC=sales, DC=sanao, DC=com	This property specifies the distinguished name of the referenced partition (or naming context). The nCName properties of all internal cross-reference objects together define the directory structure of the forest.
trustParent	CN=SANAO, CN=Partitions, CN=Configuration, DC=sanao, DC=com	If the corresponding partition is an Active Directory domain other than a forest or tree root domain, this property specifies the crossRef object corresponding to the parent domain.
rootTrust	<not defined>	If the corresponding partition is an Active Directory tree root domain other than the forest root domain, this property specifies the crossRef object corresponding to the forest root domain (comparable to a parent domain).
superiorDNSRoot	<not defined>	If you want to define a *superior reference* for a forest, add it as a distinguished name to this property of the crossRef object that corresponds to the forest root domain. A superior reference is used (if defined in this property) when the base object of the request doesn't match a partition known to the server. The purpose is to serve as a "last resort" access point to requests that otherwise cannot be resolved. Normally an Active Directory forest doesn't have a superior reference defined. It is always external to the forest.
systemFlags	3	See Table 6.5.

TABLE 6.5 `SystemFlags` **Property Bits of Cross-Reference Objects**

Bit from Right	Hex Value	Description
1	1	Value "1" indicates an internal cross-reference; the corresponding partition is in this forest. Value "0" indicates an external cross-reference; the corresponding partition is outside this forest.
2	2	Value "1" indicates that the partition represents a domain. Consequently, the cross-reference objects for the schema and configuration partitions have value "0" in this bit.

allows end users to access the corresponding external directories without needing to specify the correct external server name or IP address.

NOTE   A trust to an external Active Directory forest doesn't need a `crossRef` object. Any necessary referrals can be generated based on the information registered in DNS.

Although we describe six `crossRef` properties in Table 6.4 and Table 6.5, only two must be defined with external cross-references: nCName and dnsRoot. The administrator enters the distinguished name of the external partition in the former property and the DNS name of the server that hosts it in the latter property. In addition, a descriptive cn must be defined as for any new object.

The partition name referenced by an external cross-reference may or may not be contiguous to the forest namespace. An example of a cross-reference with a noncontiguous partition name results when an administrator of the sanao.com forest adds a `crossRef` object for microsoft.com. In this case, the administrator could define nCName to be DC=microsoft, DC=com and dnsRoot to be ldap.microsoft.com. If a user subsequently queries that external noncontiguous name (i.e., DC=microsoft, DC=com) or one of its child objects, her workstation would be referred to contact ldap.microsoft.com.

While cross-references with noncontiguous names typically refer to directories outside the organization, cross-references with contiguous names probably refer to partitions and servers that are internal to the organization. For example, Sanao Corporation could have calendar information in a Linux-based LDAP server and they want that data to appear under sanao.com/Sales. Therefore, an administrator creates a `crossRef` object and defines nCName to be CN=calendar, OU=sales, DC=sanao, DC=com and dnsRoot to be calendarserver.boston.sanao.com.

As long as the Sales OU exists in the forest and the Linux server is configured to serve the correct distinguished name (CN=calendar, OU=sales, DC=sanao, DC=com), clients should be able to contact and use the calendar server.

Delegating Domain Installation

Only members of Enterprise Admins (and members of Domain Admins of the forest root domain) can install domains to a forest. This is easy if the first domain controller of each domain resides in the headquarters. If this is not the case, the aforementioned administrators, or root administrators, have four options to get the child domains created.

- They can travel to the locations of each new domain to run DCPromo on the first domain controller of each domain.
- They can ask the administrators of the incoming child domains to install Terminal Services on the incoming first domain controllers. This enables the root administrators to perform the domain creation (i.e., to run DCPromo) without leaving the headquarters.
- They can install the first domain controller (or others as well) in the headquarters, and then ship them to appropriate locations.
- They can delegate the child domain installation.

Because in the first three options the root administrators personally perform the actual domain installation, those options are more suitable for an organization with centralized administration. The fourth delegation option is appropriate for organizations with decentralized administration. We first list the summary steps of the fourth option and then describe the process in more detail:

1. A root administrator modifies permissions of certain objects in the schema and configuration partitions.
2. A parent domain administrator modifies the permissions of each (incoming) parent domain.
3. A root administrator precreates a cross-reference object for each child domain using the NTDSUtil command-line tool.
4. A root administrator modifies the permissions of each cross-reference object.
5. A root administrator ensures that the DNS name of the incoming domain controller can be resolved to an IP address.
6. An incoming administrator of each incoming child domain runs DCPromo to install his child domain.

NOTE   Before step 6, the creator should wait until all changes of steps 1 through 4 have replicated to the domain controller with which his new domain controller will communicate with (i.e., "the source domain controller") during the promotion. This domain controller can be found by capturing the network packets of the early promotion process using Network Monitor (included in Windows 2000).

Step 1 is performed only once, and steps 3 through 6 are performed once for each new child domain. Step 2 is performed once for each parent domain that will get child domains installed by delegation.

We list the required permission modifications in Table 6.6 (i.e., steps 1, 2, and 4). As always in permission management, you shouldn't assign permissions directly to any user, but to a group instead. Our sample group is "Domain Creators." It is most natural to create this group in the forest root domain. It could be a global group; if you want to assign members from other domains, however, you must make it a universal group. In addition, we assign Full Control for some objects to the well-known security principal Creator Owner. As explained in Chapter 4, the result is that the one who created the object (and became the owner) gets Full Control for it.

When a root administrator creates the cross-reference object for the incoming child domain, he must specify the child domain's name and the name of its first domain controller. He would use the NTDSUtil command, as demonstrated on the following lines, entering the text in bold.

```
C:\>ntdsutil
ntdsutil: domain management
domain management: connections
server connections: connect to server dc1.sanao.com
Binding to dc1.sanao.com ...
Connected to dc1.sanao.com using credentials of locally logged on user
server connections: quit
domain management: list
Found 4 Naming Context(s)
0 - CN=Configuration,DC=sanao,DC=com
1 - DC=sanao,DC=com
2 - CN=Schema,CN=Configuration,DC=sanao,DC=com
3 - DC=sales,DC=sanao,DC=com
domain management: precreate dc=RD,dc=sanao,dc=com dc6.rd.sanao.com
adding object CN=rd,cn=Partitions,CN=Configuration,DC=sanao,DC=com
domain management: quit
ntdsutil: quit
Disconnecting from dc1.sanao.com ...
```

NOTE   The domain name in the preceding `precreate` command (i.e., "RD") must be in uppercase letters.

TABLE 6.6 Permission Modifications for Delegating Child Domain Installation

Object	Trustee	Permission	Apply To*	Purpose
Schema and Configuration container objects	Domain Creators	Read	This+Ch	To be able to replicate the schema and configuration partitions to the incoming domain controller
	Domain Creators	Replicating Directory Changes	This	
	Domain Creators	Replication Synchronization	This	
	Domain Creators	Manage Replication Topology	This	
The Servers container under the site object for the site where the server object will appear (based on IP address)	Domain Creators	Read	This+Ch	To be able to create a server object and NTDS settings object for the incoming domain controller
	Domain Creators	Create All Child Objects	This+Ch	
	Creator Owner	Full Control	Ch	
CN=System container in the parent domain	Domain Creators	Read	This	To be able to create a trustedDomain object for the incoming child domain
	Domain Creators	Create All Child Objects	This	
	Creator Owner	Full Control	Ch	
Cross-reference object for the child domain**	Domain Creators	Full Control	N/A	To be able to access the cross-reference object

*"This" means "This object only," "Ch" means "Child objects only," and "This+Ch" means "This object and child objects."
**A root administrator creates this object with NTDSUtil, as explained in the text. Consequently, the permissions described in this table can be assigned only after the creation of the object.

NOTE   All domain creations (i.e., cross-reference object creations) take place on the domain naming master. If you connect with NTDSUtil to a domain controller other than the domain naming master, that domain controller refers your `precreate` command to the domain naming master.

A cross-reference object created this way contains an extra property that is not listed in Table 6.4. This new property is `Enabled` and it has a value of "FALSE," meaning that the corresponding partition doesn't exist yet.

Enabled is an LDAP name, but unlike other LDAP names, it starts with an upper-case letter.

The incoming domain controller must have a DNS host record so that its name (such as dc6.rd.sanao.com) can be resolved to an IP address (such as 10.10.1.28). The primary DNS suffix (such as rd.sanao.com) must be set in a dialog box that opens when you click the Start button and select Settings, Control Panel, System, Network Identification, Properties, More. Of course, the computer name (such as dc6) must also be set to match the name in the precreate command. The new name and DNS suffix can be registered to the DNS service with the following command:

```
IPCONFIG /REGISTERDNS
```

At this point you should be able to "ping" dc6.rd.sanao.com from other computers in the forest. If this is not the case, the DCPromo process fails.

If the DNS service allows only secure updates, the DNS name registration is not possible unless the incoming domain controller first joins some domain in the forest, most logically the parent domain. In this case, the computer dc6.rd.sanao.com must be a member of the Active Directory domain sanao.com. This is not possible unless you clear the setting "Change primary DNS suffix when domain membership changes" in the same dialog box where you set the primary DNS suffix.

Once a root administrator has assigned Full Control for the new cross-reference object to Domain Creators (see Table 6.6), a member of this group can start the promotion process by running DCPromo. When asked for credentials, the domain creator enters a name such as JackB and an appropriate password and domain name. Root administrators can assign various members to this group as necessary, and they can remove members from the group when they are no longer necessary.

DELEGATING DOMAIN CONTROLLER INSTALLATION

By default, members of Domain Admins can install new domain controllers to their domain. If they need domain controllers in remote locations, they have the same options as root administrators have in delegating domain installation—to travel, to use Terminal Services, to ship computers, or to use delegation. We explain the last option here.

This time we use a sample group, DC Installers, to be the target of the delegation. Because that group will get some permissions for the schema and configuration partitions, it is logical to create this group in the forest root domain. The person who will perform the domain controller installation needs a user account in the forest, most logically in the domain where the domain controller will appear. We use Jack as our sample installer. This scenario requires DC Installers to be a universal group.

The delegation process consists of the following steps:

1. A root administrator modifies permissions of certain objects in the schema and configuration partitions.

2. A domain administrator modifies permissions of the domain object.

3. A domain administrator assigns Jack the user right to log on locally on domain controllers.

4. Jack installs Windows 2000 on the incoming domain controller computer and joins the computer as a member server in the domain. This way he can be authenticated with a domain account (which is required) when he later performs the DCPromo process.

5. Jack makes his domain account a member of the local Administrators group of the member server.

6. A domain administrator modifies permissions of the computer object of the incoming domain controller.

7. A domain administrator defines the computer object to have a setting "Trust computer for delegation."

8. A domain administrator moves the computer object from CN=Computers to OU=Domain Controllers.

9. Jack (using his domain account) runs DCPromo to promote the member server to a domain controller.

NOTE   Before step 9, Jack should wait until all changes of steps 1 through 8 have replicated to the domain controller with which his new domain controller will communicate ("source domain controller") during the promotion.

Step 1 is performed only once per forest; steps 2 and 3 are performed one time for the domain. The remaining steps are performed once for each new domain controller. Table 6.7 lists the required permission modifications (i.e., steps 1, 2, and 6).

TABLE 6.7 Permission Modifications for Delegating Domain Controller Installation

Object	Trustee	Permission	Apply To*	Purpose
Schema and Configuration container objects and the domain object	DC Installers	Read	This+Ch	To be able to replicate the schema, configuration, and domain partitions to the incoming domain controller
	DC Installers	Add/Remove Replica In Domain**	This	
	DC Installers	Replicating Directory Changes	This	
	DC Installers	Replication Synchronization	This	
	DC Installers	Manage Replication Topology	This	
The Servers container under the site object for the site where the server object will appear (based on IP address)	DC Installers	Read	This+Ch	To be able to create a server object and NTDS settings object for the incoming domain controller
	DC Installers	Create All Child Objects	This+Ch	
	Creator Owner	Full Control	Ch	
Computer object for the incoming domain controller***	DC Installers	Read and Write	This+Ch	

*"This" means "This object only," "Ch" means "Child objects only," and "This+Ch" means "This object and child objects."
**This permission can and should be assigned only to the domain object.
***You should assign these permissions to the computer object of the member server. During the promotion process, the object will be converted to the domain controller object.

LDAP AND SEARCHES

Active Directory access takes place using LDAP, so obviously any Active Directory searches must be LDAP searches. We first explain the mechanics of LDAP searches and then show how to implement them using different tools.

LDAP Searches

One of the LDAP operations listed in Table 1.6 (in Chapter 1) is Search. This operation retrieves the selected properties of one or more objects that meet the given criteria.

When an LDAP client sends a search request to an LDAP server, the client includes eight parameters in the search that specify what is to be searched and what is to be returned. Table 6.8 describes the four main parameters (`baseObject`, `scope`, `filter`, and `attributes`). The remaining four parameters—

TABLE 6.8 The Main Parameters of an LDAP Search

Parameter	Example	Description
Base object	`DC=sanao, DC=com`	This parameter is the distinguished name of the *base object* of the query. The base object is also called the *root object*, because the scope of the query is from this object downward.
Scope	`SubTree`	This parameter defines which objects are evaluated to see if they pass the filter. `Base` means that the query targets only the base object itself. If the base object doesn't pass the filter, no objects are returned. `OneLevel` means that the query targets only the immediate children of the base object (which itself is excluded). `SubTree` means that the whole tree beneath the base object is evaluated. By default, even with the `SubTree` option, the scope of the query doesn't cross partition (naming context) boundaries, such as from a parent domain to a child domain.
Filter	`(&(objectCategory=person)` `(sn=a*))`	This parameter specifies the criteria that each object must meet to be included in the search result set. This example filter includes users and contacts whose last name starts with A. We elaborate on LDAP filters later in this chapter.
Property List	`distinguishedName, givenName, sn`	This parameter lists the property LDAP names* that are to be returned for each matching object in the result set of the search.

The properties in the Filter and Property List parameters are usually identified by their LDAP names. Another way to identify properties is to use their object identifiers (OIDs), which are explained in Chapter 8. The OID of sn is 2.5.4.4, so (sn=a) would change to (2.5.4.4=a*).

`derefAliases`, `sizeLimit`, `timeLimit`, and `typesOnly`—are described in Table 11.8 in Chapter 11. You might need that information when you use scripts to perform searches. (Note that Table 11.8 also includes some other options. They are implemented using extended LDAP controls, which are discussed later in this chapter.)

NOTE   LDAP searches are also called LDAP queries.

Figure 6.25 illustrates the Scope parameter described in Table 6.8.

PROPERTY LISTS

You can specify the property list of an LDAP search in the following ways.

- The property list contains a comma-separated list of LDAP names (or OIDs) of the properties that are to be included in the search results.

- The property list is empty or *, in which case all nonconstructed properties are returned. Constructed properties are explained in Chapter 8.

- The property list explicitly contains a constructed property—for example, `canonicalName`. In this case, it must be the only property in the list.

- The property list contains *, `canonicalName`, for example. This list retrieves all nonconstructed properties and `canonicalName`. However, this form does not seem to work in Active Directory.

- The property list is `1.1`, in which case no properties are returned. `1.1` is an imaginary OID. It doesn't correspond to any property; therefore, no properties are returned.

- The property list is `"otherHomePhone;range=0-2"`, for example. This form returns the first three values of the multivalued property `otherHomePhone`.

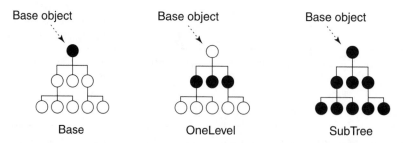

FIGURE 6.25   The Scope parameter of an LDAP search operation specifies which objects are evaluated to see if they pass the LDAP search filter.

To request the next three values, you would use the list `"otherHomePhone;`
`range=3-5"`. Note that when using ranges, you must include the quotes.

LDAP SEARCH FILTERS

An LDAP search filter is a text string that sets the criteria that an object must meet
to be included in the search results. All conditions in the filter inspect whether
certain properties in an object have certain values. Here's an example of a simple
filter:

`(sn=a*)`

Properties are usually identified by their LDAP names. For an object to
pass this filter, the first character of the object's last name (surname) must be
"A" or "a." Almost all properties of the base schema that use string syntax are
case-insensitive, so uppercase and lowercase *a* are equal in the filter. The only
exceptions are 13 properties that use syntax "Printable string." The wildcard character (*) specifies that the remaining characters (zero, one, or several) can be any
characters.

If we want to include only certain types of objects, we use `objectClass`
and/or `objectCategory` properties. For example:

`(objectCategory=person)`

It is usually better to use `objectCategory` because it is an indexed attribute,
while `objectClass` is not. If you are searching among thousands of objects,
using indexed attributes is more efficient. Using either property may actually
include several types of objects.

- Several object classes may use a common object category. For example, both
  users and contacts belong to the category `person`. Consequently, `(object-`
  `Category=person)` includes both users and contacts.

- Using an object class in the filter includes the child classes of that class. For
  example, computer is a child class of `user`, so `(objectClass=user)`
  includes both users and computers. If we wanted only users, we could use the
  two conditions together. The resulting filter would be this:

`(&(objectCategory=person)(objectClass=user))`

NOTE   An LDAP search requires that a filter be present. If you want to include all objects,
you can use the filter `(objectClass=*)`.

NOTE	Object classes, child classes, categories, and property syntaxes are explained in more detail in Chapter 8.

Filters can be combined to create more complex filters. The sample filter presented in Table 6.8 is as follows:

```
(&(objectCategory=person)(sn=a*))
```

This filter includes two conditions. The ampersand character (&) at the beginning stands for "AND," so both conditions must be true.

Table 6.9 describes the various filter elements that you can use.

TABLE 6.9 LDAP Search Filters

Type	Format	Examples	True If
Presence	(prop=*)	(sn=*)	The sn property (i.e., last name) exists.
Equality	(prop=value)	(sn=brown)	The last name is Brown, brown, BROWN, or some other permutation of the same letters in uppercase/lowercase.
Substrings	(prop=[initial]*[any]*[final])	(sn=a*)	The last name starts with "A" or "a."
		(sn=*son)	The last name ends with "son" (or some uppercase/lowercase permutation).
		(sn=*z*)	The last name contains "z" or "Z."
		(sn=a*z*son)	The last name starts with "a," contains "z," and ends with "son" (or some uppercase/lowercase permutation).
Greater than or equal to	(prop>=value)	(sn>=x)	The last name starts with "x" or a later letter.
		(salary>=30000)	The salary is at least $30,000. This property is not part of the base schema, so this filter is meaningful only if such property is added to the schema.
Less than or equal to	(prop<=value)	(sn<=d)	The last name starts with "a," "b," "c," or "d."

(continued)

TABLE 6.9 (*continued*)

Type	Format	Examples	True If
Approximate	(prop~=value)	(sn~=bruwn)	The last name is approximately "bruwn." Note that the exact logic of this filter type is implementation specific, and Active Directory doesn't support this filter type at all.
And	(&(filter A) (filter B))	(&(object-Category=person) (sn=a*))	The object is a user or contact and the last name starts with "A" or "a."
Or	(|(filter A) (filter B))	(|(sn=a*) (sn=k*))	The last name starts with "A," "a," "K," or "k."
Not	(!(filter))	(!(sn=k*))	The last name does not start with "K" or "k."
		(&(!(sn=*)) (objectcategory= person))	The object is a user or contact and the last name is missing.
Extensible	(prop: ruleOID:=value)		Active Directory supports two extensible matching rules, which are explained in the "Specifying Values" section.

Because parentheses and asterisks have special meanings in the search filter, you must use an *escape sequence* instead of them if any value should contain one of these characters. An escape sequence consists of a backslash (\) and the ASCII value of the character in hexadecimal form. Table 6.10 lists these escape sequences. In addition to the values in the table, any bytes can be expressed with the corresponding hexadecimal escape sequence. For example, to include the byte E2 (hex), you can use the escape sequence "\E2."

As you can see, Table 6.9 includes "greater/less than or equal to," but not just "greater/less than." You can achieve the same result by using the fact that "greater than or equal to" is the opposite of "less than." For example, if you needed to specify "salary less than 30,000," the following filter would be illegal:

```
(salary<30000)
```

Therefore, you must use the following filter instead:

```
(&(!(salary>=30000))(salary=*))
```

TABLE 6.10 The Escape Sequences in LDAP Search Filters

Character	Escape Sequence
(	\28
)	\29
*	\2A
\	\5C

The first part of this filter reads "salary not greater than or equal to 30,000." The second part specifies that the salary property must exist. Otherwise, in addition to the correct objects, objects would be included that don't have a salary defined at all.

SPECIFYING VALUES

Table 6.9 shows how you could use normal strings and integers in the search filter comparison values. Next we expand the topic by explaining how to specify values using various syntaxes:

- *Boolean.* Possible values are TRUE and FALSE. A sample filter is (`showInAdvancedViewOnly=TRUE`).

- *Integer.* Possible values are integers in a decimal form. Hexadecimal values are not accepted. A sample filter is (`salary=30000`).

- *Unicode string (or directory string).* This is the most common string syntax, and you specify the values, as you have seen in the examples so far. A sample filter is (`sn=Brown*`).

- `Octet string`. An `octet string` is binary data, so the value must be defined using escape sequences. For example, a three-byte (24-bit) value "E277BD" would be expressed as \E2w\BD. Note that "77" is the ASCII code of "w," so we use "w" instead of \77. For example, to list all properties that belong to the General Information property set (see Table 4.15 and Figure 4.27 in Chapter 4), you would use the filter (`attributeSecurityGuid=\42\2f\ba\59\a2\79\d0\11\90\20\00\c0\4f\c2\d3\cf`). Some of the escape sequences in this filter could be changed to letters, such as the first \42 to uppercase "B." However, doing so would make the filter look even more ugly. The 16 bytes in the filter are the `rightsGuid` of the corresponding property set converted to a binary GUID representation. (The section "List Binary GUIDs.vbs" in Chapter 11 sheds more light on this messy topic.)

- *DN (or distinguished name or DN String).* The entire DN value must be supplied and the wildcard (*) is not allowed. For example, to list all objects (in practice, group objects) where Jack is a member you would use the filter (member=cn=jack brown, ou=boston, dc=sanao, dc=com). Note that technically objectCategory uses the DN syntax. However, it enables you to use LDAP display names such as (objectCategory=person).

- *OID string.* The entire OID value must be supplied and the wildcard (*) is not allowed. As with the DN syntax, you can use the LDAP display name instead of the OID value.

- *Generalized time string.* The form of the value in a filter is either "YYYYMMDDHHMMSS.0Z" or "YYYYMMDDHHMMSS.0[+/-]HHMM." The "Z" in the former form means "no time differential"; that is, the time is in GMT/UTC time. The latter form includes a time zone differential to GMT/UTC. For example, Finland is 2 hours ahead of GMT/UTC. If you wanted to list objects that were created on or after February 26, 2001, 3:20 PM (local time), you would use the filter (whenCreated>=20010226152000.0+0200). The same filter using the GMT/UTC time would be (whenCreated>= 20010226132000.0Z).

- *UTC time string.* The principles described for the Generalized time string apply also to this syntax. However, the forms of the values are either "YYM-MDDHHMMSSZ" or "YYMMDDHHMMSS[+/-]HHMM." As you see, the year is expressed with two digits and there are no tenths of a second. Also, the seconds value (SS) is optional.

NOTE   The description for the Integer syntax applies also to the syntaxes Enumeration and Large integer (or INTEGER8). The description for the Octet string syntax applies also to the syntaxes NT security descriptor, SID string, Access point DN, Presentation address, Replica link, DN with Unicode string, DN with binary (or DN with octet string), and OR name.

Active Directory supports two extensible matching rules: a bitwise AND and a bitwise OR. The general format of an extensible matching rule is as follows:

```
(property:ruleOID:=value)
```

The rule OID for bitwise AND is 1.2.840.113556.1.4.803, and the rule OID for bitwise OR is 1.2.840.113556.1.4.804. Therefore, to do a bitwise AND, you would use a filter:

```
(property:1.2.840.113556.1.4.803:=value)
```

In a sample scenario you would need to list all global security groups. The group scope and type are both stored in a single `groupType` property that is using the `Integer` syntax. Figure 11.8 in Chapter 11 shows that a global group is denoted by value "2," and a security group is denoted by value "8000 0000" (hex). In bitwise arithmetic, we add these two values to get "8000 0002" (hex). Then we must convert this to a decimal to be able to use it in an LDAP filter. Using Windows Calculator, for example, we get "2,147,483,650." The resulting filter is as follows:

```
(groupType=2147483650)
```

We didn't need the rule OID yet in the preceding example. Next, we want to list all global groups, whether they are security or distribution groups. This means that we need to study only one bit in `groupType`, which requires use of the AND operators. The resulting filter is as follows:

```
(groupType:1.2.840.113556.1.4.803:=2)
```

MULTIDOMAIN SEARCHES

Normal LDAP searches are limited to one partition (naming context), which means that you get objects of only one domain at a time. You have two options to direct a search to multiple partitions: either turn on *referral chasing* or use the global catalog.

- *Referral chasing.* This is a special LDAP feature that allows a search to travel to other partitions to find more objects. Normally this means extending the search to child domains. In a large network, the LDAP client might need to communicate with servers all over the world to be able to fulfill the query. Consequently, the global catalog option is usually much more effective.

- *The global catalog.* Normal LDAP searches use the standard LDAP port 389, but if you direct the search to the port 3268, you perform a global catalog search. Because every global catalog server stores the whole global catalog (and these global catalog servers are usually located on each site), you can usually perform a global catalog search without communicating with domain controllers on remote sites. When searching the global catalog, you can also use a nonexistent object as the base object. For example, if you specify an empty distinguished name, or `dc=com`, your search covers both `sanao.com` and `sanaoint.com` if they are part of your forest. If you're using the referral chasing approach, you cannot reach both these domain trees in one query. Figures 6.26, 6.29, 6.34, and 6.35 are examples of searching the global catalog.

CONTINUATION REFERENCES

We explained in the "Referrals and Cross-References" section that if an LDAP server doesn't contain the partition where the base object specified in an LDAP request should be, the server will return a referral that points the client to another server. A slightly different case is when the client performs an LDAP search and the base object *is* found on the server, but the server is unable to search all the objects in the scope. In this case, the server returns the matching objects residing in its partition, as well as *continuation references* to subordinate partitions.

For example, a client that is connected to dc1.sanao.com wants to find all users with the last name of Brown. The client specifies the starting point of the search (i.e., the base object) to be DC=sanao, DC=com and the scope to be Sub-Tree. The steps of the process are as follows:

1. The client sends a query to dc1.sanao.com for the base object DC=sanao, DC=com and the scope SubTree.

2. Dc1.sanao.com returns the two Browns that exist in sanao.com. The server also returns continuation references to all immediate child partitions of sanao.com. There is one child domain, sales.sanao.com, and the configuration partition, so the server returns two LDAP URLs: ldap://sales.sanao.com/DC=sales, DC=sanao, DC=com and ldap://sanao.com/CN=Configuration, DC=sanao, DC=com.

3. The client queries DNS and learns that dc1.sales.sanao.com serves sales.sanao.com. The client connects and authenticates to this server.

4. The client sends a query to dc1.sales.sanao.com for the base object DC=sales, DC=sanao, DC=com and the scope SubTree.

5. Dc1.sales.sanao.com returns the only Brown that exists in sales.sanao.com. There are no more child domains, so the server doesn't return continuation references.

6. The client sends a query to dc1.sanao.com for the base object CN=Configuration, DC=sanao, DC=com and the scope SubTree.

7. There are no Browns in the configuration partition, so dc1.sanao.com returns only the continuation reference for the schema partition—that is, an LDAP URL ldap://sanao.com/CN=Schema, CN=Configuration, DC=sanao, DC=com.

8. The client sends a query to dc1.sanao.com for the base object CN=Schema, CN=Configuration, DC=sanao, DC=com and the scope SubTree.

9. There are no Browns in the schema partition either (nor are there any child partitions), so dc1.sanao.com returns an empty LDAP search result.

The term "continuation reference" is used in the LDAP RFC 2251. Microsoft documentation uses the term "subordinate reference" instead.

Search Tools

Windows 2000 includes a number of tools that enable you to perform searches in various ways:

- *The Find dialog box.* End users can access this tool by opening My Network Places and selecting Entire Network, Directory, and then selecting Find in the context menu of any visible domain tree. Administrators can access the same tool in the Users and Computers snap-in by selecting Find in the context menu of any container. The Find dialog box provides a graphical interface for performing searches, as shown in Figure 6.26. If you select Entire Directory as the target for the query, you will actually use the global catalog. If you select Custom Search, Advanced, you can enter LDAP filters (called LDAP queries here).

- *ADSI Edit.* This tool enables you to enter an LDAP filter, which specifies the objects that you see in the right-hand pane of the tool. To target the query to a

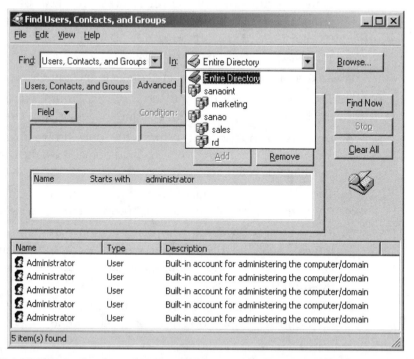

FIGURE 6.26 This search is directed to Entire Directory, meaning the global catalog. Therefore, the Administrator accounts of all five domains in the forest are found. If you click Browse in the upper-right corner, you can target the search to an individual OU instead of a domain.

domain partition, right-click the Domain NC and select New, Query. This opens a dialog box (shown in Figure 6.27) that enables you to define the query. When you click OK, you get the list shown in Figure 6.28.

- *The Users and Computers snap-in.* The View menu of the snap-in includes an item called Filter Options that enables you to specify which objects to show when you browse various container objects. If you select the custom filter type and the Advanced tab, you can enter an LDAP filter.

- *LDIFDE.* This tool allows importing and exporting objects between Active Directory and a text file using LDIF format. LDIFDE stands for "LDIF Directory Exchange," and LDIF stands for "LDAP Data Interchange Format." LDIF is defined in RFC 2849. When exporting data, you can specify as command-line arguments the base object, scope, LDAP filter, and list of properties to be exported. However, you cannot turn on referral chasing. See the example later in this section of how to export (i.e., search) objects with LDIFDE.

- *LDP.* This tool deserves a longer description, so we dedicate the next section to it.

- *Scripts.* Using scripts to perform searches is explained in Chapter 11.

Figure 6.29 illustrates an example of how to export (i.e., search) objects with LDIFDE. We have issued an LDIFDE command three times, with slight modifications each time. In each command we use the verbose mode (/v) to see the names

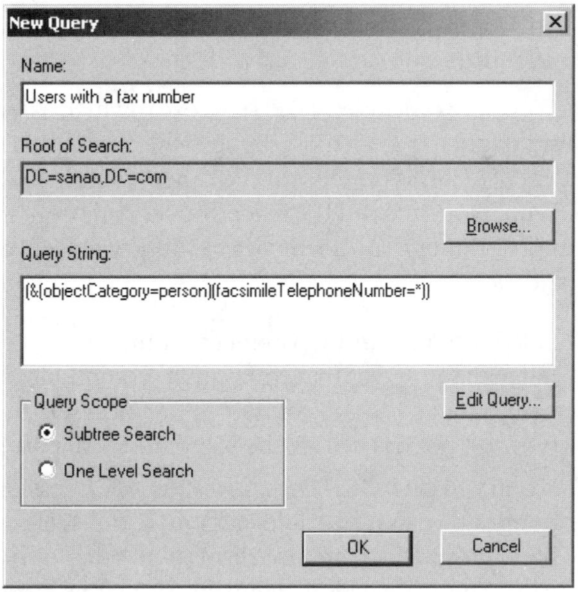

FIGURE 6.27 ADSI Edit enables you to enter an LDAP filter that specifies the objects to include in the right-hand pane.

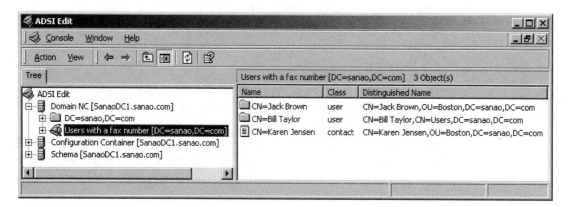

FIGURE 6.28 By using an LDAP filter, you can select objects that meet certain criteria to be listed in the right-hand pane. These objects can reside in different containers, so you effectively remove the tree structure in this view.

of the exported objects ("entries" in LDAP terminology) and direct the output to the file Output.txt. In each command we want to list all objects that have the common name Administrator. The first command is a normal LDAP query, so we get the only Administrator in our domain. The second query is directed to the global catalog (-t 3268), so we get these users from all three domains that exist in sanao.com or its child domains. The third query is also directed to the global catalog, but now we use dc=com as the base object. Consequently, we get all five Administrator users, not only from sanao.com, but also from sanaoint.com.

THE LDP TOOL

Support Tools includes LDP (Ldp.exe), which is a versatile although not very polished tool to access most of the LDAP features. LDP uses the native LDAP C API instead of ADSI, as do most of the other administrative tools of Windows 2000.

When you launch LDP (click the Start button and select Run, type LDP, and then press Enter), you see only an empty window. Performing the following steps gets you started:

1. Select Connect in the Connection menu. This enables you to type the DNS name of the server that you want to communicate with. If you leave the server name empty, you will connect to the local server. You can also specify the port number, but it is usually the standard LDAP port 389.

2. When you click OK, LDP establishes a TCP session with the given LDAP server, queries the rootDSE information, and displays this information in the right-hand pane. That pane also displays all other output as you continue to use the tool. The Connection menu includes the Save and Print functions, which enable you to transfer the generated output to a text file or to paper. You can also use Copy/Paste with Ctrl-C/Ctrl-V.

3. So far you have connected anonymously. When you select Bind in the Connection menu, you can type the username, password, and domain to authenticate with.

4. When you click OK, LDP binds to the previously specified server using the given credentials. You should see the text "Authenticated as dn:'administrator'" (or whatever your username is) in the right pane.

At this point you are connected and have proved your identity, which allows you to perform any LDAP operations that you have permissions for. You have two paths to choose from: You can either open a tree that you can navigate or perform various LDAP operations listed in the Browse menu (Add, Delete, Modify, Modify DN, Search, Compare, and so on). We'll briefly explain the tree navigation option and the Search operation.

FIGURE 6.29 Depending on the options used with LDIFDE, the tool returns a different number of objects. In this figure, the command was issued three times, with slight modifications each time.

To open a navigation tree, select Tree in the View menu, and then enter the distinguished name of the base object to navigate from. If you entered "dc=sanao,dc=com," you would get a tree like the one in Figure 6.30. The right-hand pane displays all the (nonconstructed) properties of the base object. The number in front of the property indicates the number of values the property has. For example, "3> subRefs" means that that multivalued property has three values.

As you double-click any child object, the properties of that object are displayed and the children of that child are listed in the tree.

You initiate a search operation by selecting Search in the Browse menu. The dialog box that opens is shown in Figure 6.31. If you click Options, the dialog box shown in Figure 6.32 appears. These two dialog boxes enable you to specify the search parameters, as described earlier in this section when we discussed LDAP searches in general.

When you perform the search specified in Figure 6.31 and Figure 6.32, you get the result shown in Figure 6.33. In other words, the only object matching the query is the Administrator of sanao.com. If you select "Chase referrals" and

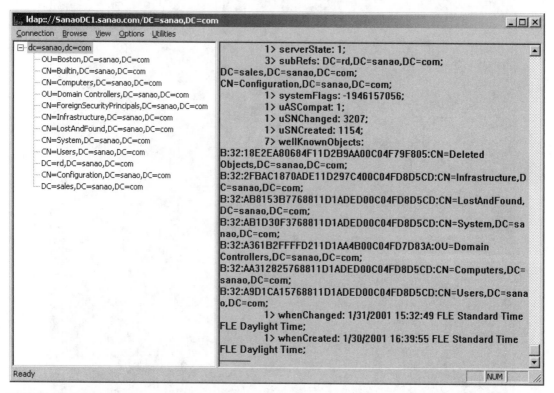

FIGURE 6.30 LDP enables you to specify a starting point (dc=sanao, dc=com here) from which to navigate the tree and to see all the properties of each object.

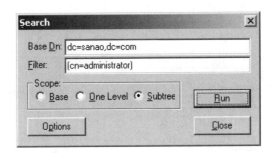

FIGURE 6.31 When performing an LDAP search, you must specify the base object, search filter, and the scope of the search.

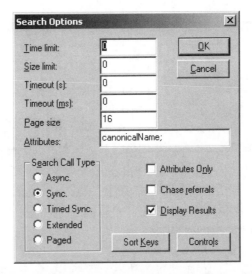

FIGURE 6.32 In addition to the basic parameters of the preceding figure, you may need to modify other search options, most often the list of properties (i.e., attributes) to be returned.

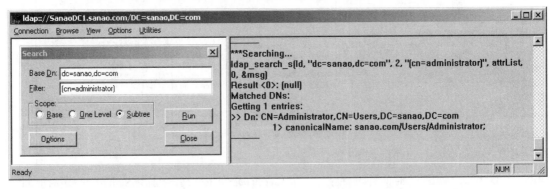

FIGURE 6.33 A normal LDAP query covers only one domain, so you get only one Administrator.

rerun the query, it covers the child domains also, so you get three Administrator users instead of just one. This is illustrated in Figure 6.34.

If you want to reach all domain trees of the forest, you must switch to use the global catalog. First disconnect the current connection, and then establish a new connection, this time using the port 3268. Bind again using the same credentials as you used in the first connection. When you perform the query specified in Figure 6.31 and Figure 6.32, you get three Administrator users as in Figure 6.34, even though you didn't turn on referral chasing. If you next change the base DN to be just dc=com or an empty string, you get all Administrator users from all domain trees, as shown in Figure 6.35.

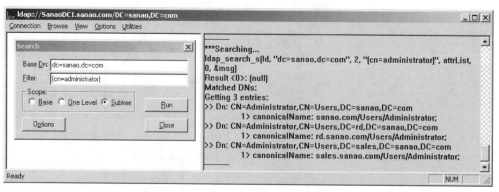

FIGURE 6.34 When referral chasing is turned on, or when the global catalog is queried, all child domains are also covered, so you get three Administrator users.

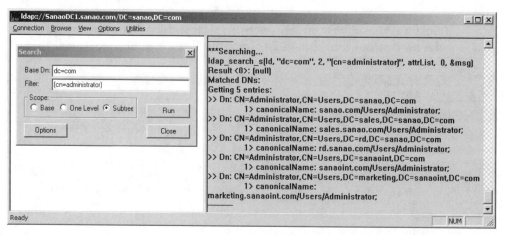

FIGURE 6.35 When searching the global catalog, you can specify nonexistent base objects, such as dc=com or an empty string. This means that you can search sanao.com and sanaoint.com at the same time.

Extended LDAP Controls

The LDAP specification allows vendors to extend existing operations and add operations. `RootDSE` includes two properties, `supportedControl` and `supportedCapabilities`, that list the extended controls that Active Directory supports. We list these controls in Table 6.11, along with a short description. Developers may need to use these controls frequently, but administrators need them only occasionally, if at all.

LISTING DELETED OBJECTS

As an example of extended controls, we explain how to list the deleted objects (i.e., tombstones) of a domain. This requires the use of the corresponding control 1.2.840.113556.1.4.417.

After you have connected and bound to a server LDP, you perform a search with the following parameters:

- The base object is the domain (such as `dc=sanao, dc=com`).
- The search filter is (`isDeleted=*`).
- The scope is `SubTree`.
- The list of attributes should be `1.1` if you want to list just the names of the objects.
- The search call type is Extended.

TABLE 6.11 Extended LDAP Controls of Active Directory

Control	Description
1.2.840.113556.1.4.319	Paging search results. This control allows the client to request the results in chunks, instead of all objects at once.
1.2.840.113556.1.4.417	Show deleted object. This control allows listing the tombstones.
1.2.840.113556.1.4.473	Sorting search results. This control allows the client to request that the results be sorted.
1.2.840.113556.1.4.474	Server response sort. A server can respond to the client that initiated a sort request using the previous control.
1.2.840.113556.1.4.521	Cross-domain move. This control allows an object to be moved from one domain to another in a forest.

(continued)

TABLE 6.11 Extended LDAP Controls of Active Directory (*continued*)

Control	Description
1.2.840.113556.1.4.528	Server notification. The client can register to be notified when changes are made to objects in Active Directory.
1.2.840.113556.1.4.529	Return extended distinguished names. This control makes the server return a special form of the distinguished name that includes the GUID of the object. This name never changes even though the object was moved or renamed.
1.2.840.113556.1.4.619	Server lazy commit. The server commits a modify operation to the client before the modify is actually written to disk, so the client doesn't have to wait as long.
1.2.840.113556.1.4.800	Windows 2000–supported capabilities. This control indicates that the responding server is a Windows 2000 server and it has all the capabilities of Active Directory. This control is a kind of version number for the directory service.
1.2.840.113556.1.4.801	Server security descriptor operations. This control allows the client to pass flags to the server to control security descriptor behaviors.
1.2.840.113556.1.4.805	Tree delete. This control allows a client to request deletion of a container including the whole tree beneath it (inside a single partition).
1.2.840.113556.1.4.841	Directory synchronization. This control allows the client to search and retrieve the latest changes from the directory.
1.2.840.113556.1.4.970	Not documented.
1.2.840.113556.1.4.1338	Verify distinguished name server. If an object was recently added, and you want another object to refer to it by its DN, the DC that you are using might not yet be aware of the new object. This control allows you to specify the global catalog server that should know the new object.
1.2.840.113556.1.4.1339	Do not generate referrals. This control tells the server not to return referrals, so the search is limited to one partition only.
1.2.840.113556.1.4.1340	Server search operations. This control allows the client to pass flags to the server to control search behaviors. A flag with value 1 is the same as the previous control (Do not generate referrals). A flag with value 2 allows nonexistent search base objects, such as dc=com.
1.2.840.113556.1.4.1413	Server permissive modify. This control modifies the behavior of an extended LDAP modify request so that no error is returned if a nonexistent property is trying to be deleted, or if a property is added that already exists, as long as the old and new values are the same.

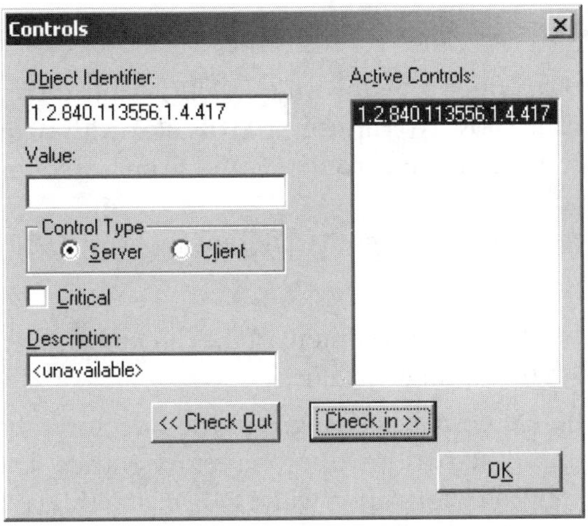

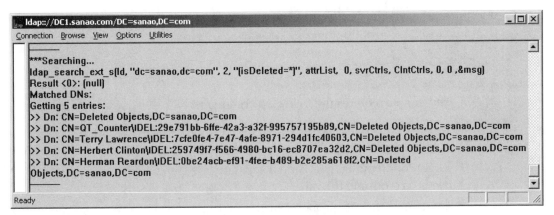

FIGURE 6.36 You can add extended controls to perform operations that are not part of the basic LDAPv3 functionality. This control enables you to list the deleted objects of a domain.

In addition, you must click the Controls button in the Search Options dialog box. This opens the Controls dialog box that enables you to add the control 1.2.840.113556.1.4.417 as an active control. Type this long number in the Object Identifier field, make sure that the control type is Server, and then click "Check in". You don't need to specify a value. The resulting screen is shown in Figure 6.36. Click OK a couple of times to get back to the Search dialog box and then click Run. Figure 6.37 contains the resulting output.

FIGURE 6.37 Deleted objects (i.e., tombstones) have special names and they are stored in a hidden container Deleted Objects.

LDAP Data Interchange Format

LDAP Data Interchange Format (LDIF) is a text file format that is defined in RFC 2849. The most typical use of LDIF files with Active Directory is to export and import directory information to and from a text file using the LDIFDE command-line tool.

There are two slightly different types of LDIF files, which are used for the following purposes:

- The file describes content of the directory; that is, one or several objects along with their property values.

- The file describes changes to the directory; that is, one or several modifications to be performed on directory entries. This type of file is created when exporting information with LDIFDE and this is also the file type that you could import back to the directory.

LDIF FILES TO DESCRIBE CONTENT

The following lines illustrate a sample of the first case (i.e., a content-describing file):

```
dn: CN=Jack Brown, OU=Boston, DC=sanao, DC=com
objectClass: user
givenName: Jack
sn: Brown
# This is a comment line
otherHomePhone: 123 123
otherHomePhone: 321 321
description: Here is a description
 for Jack
thumbnailPhoto:: xyzxyz==

dn: CN=Jill Green, OU=Boston, DC=sanao, DC=com
objectClass: user
givenName: Jill
etc.
```

The sample requires the following comments:

- The contents of an object are on consecutive lines, starting with the DN property. There is an empty line between objects.

- Each property/value pair is on a separate line (to contain the property LDAP name, a colon, and the value).

- Apart from the DN property in the first line of each object, the remaining properties of an object can be in any order.

- Multiple values of a property are on separate lines (see the `otherHomePhone` property).

- A line may be folded to continue on the next line by adding one space in the beginning of the subsequent line(s) (see the `description` property).

- An empty value can be denoted by including only the property LDAP name and a colon (e.g., `sn:`).

- A line that starts with a pound sign (#) is a comment line.

- Binary values are encoded using base64, in which case there are two colons after the property LDAP name (see the `thumbnailPhoto` property). Also, other values that contain "unsafe" characters, such as the European characters é, ö and ä, are encoded with base64. Safe characters are the ones with an ASCII code between 1 and 127, except carriage return (code 0D) and linefeed (code 0A). In addition, the first character must not be a space, a colon (:), or a less-than sign (<) to be safe. The given name of Björn Borg, the famous tennis player from the 1970s, is "QmrDtnJu" (without quotes) when expressed in base64.

NOTE   When importing information with LDIFDE, you can have the line `givenName:` `Björn`, but when exporting, LDIFDE will generate the line `givenName: QmrDtnJu`.

Base64 Encoding
Base64 encoding works as follows.

1. The value to be encoded is divided into three-byte sections (i.e., 24 bits each).

2. Each 24-bit section is divided into four 6-bit values (i.e., from 0 to 63).

3. Each 6-bit value is mapped to one of the following 64 characters: uppercase alphabets A through Z, lowercase alphabets a through z, numbers 0 through 9, plus sign (+), or slash (/).

This results in a string of basic alphabets, numbers, and possibly some plus signs and slashes. If the number of bytes in the original value is not a multiple of three, the encoded value will have one or two equal signs (=) at the end so the number of character is always a multiple of four.

LDIF FILES TO DESCRIBE CHANGES

The previous discussion of content-describing LDIF files applies also to LDIF files that describe changes to the directory. As a new element, the latter files contain extra lines that specify the operations to perform.

An LDAP client can manipulate objects in an LDAP server using four operations: Add, Delete, Modify DN, and Modify (see Table 1.6 in Chapter 1). These four operations are referred to in an LDIF file when defining the changes to be applied to a directory. Table 6.12 lists the choices, along with a sample file of the first three. Compared to content-describing LDIF files, there is one extra line in each sample: "changetype: something."

The fourth choice, Modify, has three further choices. Table 6.13 lists them, showing a sample file of each. Compared to content-describing LDIF files, there are now the following three extra lines:

- `changetype: modify`
- `add:`, `delete:`, or `replace:`, along with the property LDAP name
- A hyphen (-) to end the block of lines that add/delete/replace started

TABLE 6.12 LDIF Operations

Operation	Sample File

Add object	`dn: CN=Jack Brown, OU=Boston, DC=sanao, DC=com`
	`changetype: add`
	`objectClass: user`
	`givenName: Jack*`

Delete object	`dn: CN=Jack Brown, OU=Boston, DC=sanao, DC=com` `changetype: delete`

Modify object DN
(i.e., rename and/or move)
	`dn: CN=Jack Brown, OU=Boston, DC=sanao, DC=com`
	`changetype: moddn`
	`newrdn: CN=John Brown**`
	`deleteoldrdn: 1***`
	`newsuperior: OU=London, DC=sanao, DC=com****`

Modify object	See Table 6.13.

*In addition, mandatory properties, which Active Directory does not automatically fill, must be specified and other optional properties may be defined (each on a separate line). For a user object, at least `sAMAccountName` must be specified, and `userAccountControl` and `userPrincipalName` should be specified.

**This line must be present even if the RDN stays the same (e.g., from `CN=Jack Brown` to `CN=Jack Brown`).

***Active Directory requires that this value always be 1 (i.e., True); you are not allowed to leave the old name present in the directory. This line must be right after the newrdn line.

****If this line is omitted, the object is not moved, but only renamed. If present, this line must be right after the deleteoldrdn line.

TABLE 6.13   LDIF Modify Operations

Operation	Sample File
Add a property or additional value(s)	dn: CN=Jack Brown, OU=Boston, DC=sanao, DC=com changetype: modify add: otherHomePhone otherHomePhone: 123 456 -
Delete a property or individual value(s)	dn: CN=Jack Brown, OU=Boston, DC=sanao, DC=com changetype: modify delete: otherHomePhone otherHomePhone: 123 456* -
Replace all existing value(s) with new value(s)	dn: CN=Jack Brown, OU=Boston, DC=sanao, DC=com changetype: modify replace: otherHomePhone otherHomePhone: 123 457 -

*This line specifies the value of a multivalued property that must be deleted. If this line is omitted, all the values are deleted and the property becomes "<not set>." Multiple values can be specified, each on a separate line.

You can perform several Modify operations on one object. In this case the DN and changetype appear only once. The following example adds a phone number for Jack and deletes his office property:

```
dn: CN=Jack Brown, OU=Boston, DC=sanao, DC=com
changetype: modify
add: otherHomePhone
otherHomePhone: 123 456
-
delete: physicalDeliveryOfficeName
-
```

This section is not an exhaustive description of LDIF files. For example, you can include extended LDAP controls in LDIF files, which we don't cover here. For more information, refer to RFC 2849.

Setting user passwords with LDIF files requires special handling. See Microsoft Knowledge Base article Q263991 for more information.

CONCLUSION

In this chapter you have learned the logical structure of Active Directory and you've also learned which aspects to consider when you plan the optimal Active Directory structure for your organization. This chapter, along with the three previous chapters, covered the management of Active Directory content and structure. These topics are what we consider the core skills of Active Directory: planning, deploying, and administering. There is one more to come, however, as we explain Group Policy in the next chapter.

Chapter 7

Group Policy

GROUP POLICY CONCEPTS

Microsoft's *IntelliMirror* initiative groups various technologies for the purpose of helping administrators manage user environments efficiently and consequently reduce the *total cost of ownership (TCO)*. In order to achieve the lower TCO, these technologies, of which Group Policy is one, enable centrally administering users' data, applications, and settings. *Change and Configuration Management (CCM)* includes IntelliMirror coupled with workstations installed with Windows 2000 Remote Installation Services (RIS). With CCM, a user's Windows 2000 Professional computer can literally break apart, and an administrator can install a new computer within minutes. When the user starts the computer and logs on for the first time, he will receive the centrally stored previous settings together with administrator-assigned settings and applications. When data is stored centrally, it will also be still available to the user.

Group Policy doesn't only make users' lives easier. It also gives administrators an efficient and pervasive tool to manage logon scripts, security settings such as password policies, and user interface restrictions.

The term "Group Policy" is a bit misleading. Although it implies a direct relationship with user groups, there is actually no such relationship. Rather, the term "Group Policy" refers to a group of policy settings. And to complicate matters more, you can control the effect of these Group Policy settings by filtering them with permissions defined for security groups. Thus, Group Policy is loosely related to security groups.

Group Policy facilitates both centralized and decentralized management of machine and user settings. In the former method, the policy settings are stored in *Group Policy objects (GPOs)* within Active Directory. If Active Directory is not available, or if you want to apply a specific setting on a particular computer, you might want to configure the computer's *Local GPO (LGPO)*. Used in this decentralized manner without Active Directory, the policies contain fewer settings and are more difficult to manage. In addition to Group Policy, System Policies introduced in Windows NT 4 can still be used to control individual Windows 2000 workstations or servers. The same applies if Windows 2000 computers are members of a Windows NT 4 domain.

Used with Active Directory, GPOs are identified with 128-bit globally unique identifiers (GUIDs). GPOs can be associated with a site, a domain, or an OU and are stored at domain partition(s). Settings defined in these GPOs are processed by so-called *client-side extensions (CSE)* based on the location of user and computer objects in the Active Directory structure. Thus, in order to deploy Group Policy effectively, Group Policy must be taken into consideration in the planning stage of Active Directory deployment.

NOTE   Sometimes the terms "local" and "nonlocal" are used to refer to the local GPOs available in every Windows 2000 computer and to Group Policy objects stored in Active Directory.

Group Policy settings are divided into computer and user categories. These settings are processed in various stages, the most obvious being when the computer starts up or when a user logs on. They are also processed periodically, and they can be refreshed manually.

In order to process the settings, Group Policy has client-side and server-side components. The client-side extensions interpret and process the settings that are read either from the local machine or from Active Directory. The server-side components take care of storing and replicating the GPOs.

The management of Group Policies can be divided into three main tasks: creating Group Policy objects, managing Group Policy links, and configuring Group Policy settings. You can accomplish all tasks with an MMC snap-in. The Group Policy snap-in has ten extensions, which all open by default whether all of them can be used or not.

When you install Active Directory, two GPOs are created in the new domain. The Default Domain Policy is linked to the domain and the Default Domain Controllers Policy is linked to the Domain Controllers OU.

MMC Group Policy Snap-In

There are two alternative means to manage Group Policies. The first is to use either the Active Directory Users and Computers snap-in (for GPOs linked to a

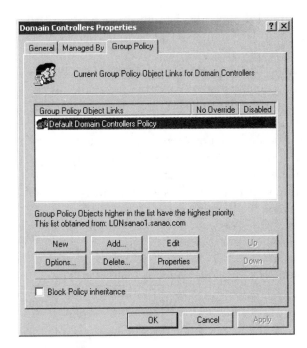

FIGURE 7.1 Group Policy tab for the Domain Controllers OU

domain or to OUs) or the Active Directory Sites and Services snap-in (for GPOs linked to a site). By default, these snap-ins open with the Group Policy extension, which enables you to manage Group Policies. To access Group Policies, you right-click any container that a Group Policy is linked to or into which you intend to link a GPO. Select Properties and open the Group Policy tab. Figure 7.1 shows the Group Policy tab for the Domain Controllers OU.

The second way to manage Group Policies is to access them directly by creating a new MMC console and adding the Group Policy snap-in into it. Then you can browse for the desired GPO.

The Group Policy dialog box is used to perform almost all Group Policy management tasks.

NT 4 System Policy Compared to Windows 2000 Group Policy

Windows NT 4 had a feature called System Policy. Group Policy retains the functionality of the NT 4 System Policy, but with vast improvements. Group Policy also contains new functionalities that were previously found via various management tools or that were not at all there in NT 4.

In NT 4 networks, System Policy was primarily used to restrict users' actions on their workstations. The System Policies were by default stored on one file, ntconfig.pol, that was most often stored on the Netlogon share on domain controllers. The settings were read when users logged on. There was no other means to process the System Policy but to ask the user to log off and to log on again. The changes could be made during the night, but in a larger network it was difficult to ensure that every user had been subjected to the new policy set.

Another major problem with NT System Policy was *registry tattooing*. This means that a System Policy–initiated change in a registry setting could be removed only by making another change in the same setting. Thus, it could be difficult to ensure a consistent state of one specific setting through a number of workstations or servers.

Table 7.1 lists the major differences between NT 4 System Policy and Windows 2000 Group Policy.

TABLE 7.1 NT 4 System Policy Compared to Windows 2000 Group Policy

Feature	System Policy	Group Policy
Purpose	Restricting users' desktop	Efficient management and control of users' desktops and settings; part of IntelliMirror
Number of registry settings	72	More than 450
Number of security settings	N/A	More than 100
Scope	Domain	Site, domain, OU
Focus	Computer, user, global group	Filtering with permissions given for groups
Security	Share and NTFS permissions on shared folder Netlogon, users have write permission for registry keys	Active Directory and NTFS permissions, users have only read permission for default registry keys
Registry tattooing	Yes	No (for registry settings defined in administrative templates)
Settings are processed	At logon	When computer starts or user logs on, when the computer is shut down or user logs off, automatically at adjustable periodic intervals, manually with command secedit

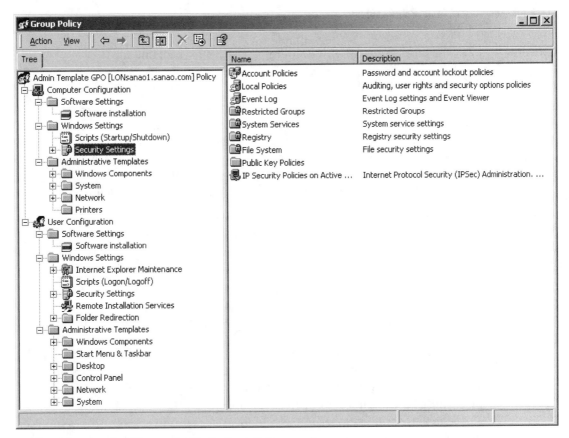

FIGURE 7.2 A sample GPO opened with the Group Policy snap-in

GROUP POLICY CONTENTS

By default, there are at least 116 security-related settings, 111 registry-based computer settings, and 354 registry-based user settings that you can configure through Group Policy. Figure 7.2 shows a GPO opened for editing so that all major categories are visible. We discuss each category in this section.

Table 7.2 describes the three main categories. All three exist for both computers and users.

Computer versus User

You can define policy settings separately for computers and users. Some settings make sense when applied to computers, and others make sense when applied to

TABLE 7.2 Summary of Group Policy Contents

Category	Purpose	Available for Computer	Available for User
Software settings	Installing, upgrading, and removing applications	Yes	Yes
Windows settings	Defining scripts and security settings; for users, some other settings (see next columns)	Start-up and shutdown scripts, numerous security settings	Logon and logoff scripts, few security settings, Internet Explorer settings, RIS settings, folder redirection
Administrative templates	Defining registry settings centrally	Yes	Yes

users. For example, you'll usually want to specify security settings appropriate to individual computers.

A computer's settings are processed when the computer starts and at periodic intervals afterward. When a user logs on, the user policy settings are processed. There is one exception to this rule, and you may want to use it if certain user settings must be the same, no matter who logs onto the computer. For example, although a user who belongs to the Administrators group is assigned a certain set of applications, we do not want those applications to be installed when the user logs on to domain controllers. We describe this exception, called *loopback processing,* in greater detail later in this chapter.

Software Settings

Previous operating system versions of Windows (NT, 9x, and Me) offer no centralized way to manage software applications. Finally, Active Directory together with Group Policy provides a method to centrally define which applications are available or installed to which users or computers. You can manage the whole software application life cycle from installation through upgrades and patches to removal with Group Policy application management. You can define the following policies with software settings:

- *Application deployment.* Application shortcuts appear either in Add/Remove Programs in the Control Panel or in users' Start menus when their computers start or they log on to their workstations. A new service called Windows

Installer installs the applications unless they are legacy (i.e., installed with setup routines).

- *Patches and upgrades for existing packages.* An application that was deployed with Group Policy can be *redeployed.* Redeployment could take place if, for example, few files required by the application were updated. Larger modifications such as new versions of the application can also be deployed with Group Policy. Upgrades can be optional or mandated. You may want to use the mandated upgrade if, for example, you want to ensure the version compatibility of saved application files when the storage format has changed.

- *Application removal.* Applications that were deployed with Group Policy can also be removed automatically.

Group Policy–managed application deployment settings are not processed periodically, but rather take place only when users log on or log off, or a computer starts. This makes sense when you think about the possibility of an administrator removing a word-processing application in the middle of a user's typing a letter with that application.

Group Policy might not be the optimal deployment solution in larger environments or if alternative software deployment methods have been developed in-house. This is a result of shortcomings of the management such as the limited reporting/logging it provides and the lack of scheduling. Thus, a system/enterprise management software such as CA Unicenter or Microsoft's Systems Management Server might be more applicable in these scenarios.

The use of Group Policy for software management is discussed later in this chapter in the "Software Management with Group Policy" section.

Scripts

When you administer a large number of Windows 2000 computers, especially servers, scripting is very convenient. This is also true of workstation administration and logon scripts. You can still use legacy batch files, but de facto scripting in Windows 2000 uses VBScript or JScript scripts, which are interpreted with Windows Script Host (WSH). Scripts are run hidden by default.

Scripts for stand-alone workstations and servers can be defined in the LGPO. You can access the LGPO with a built-in MMC console called gpedit.msc. Alternatively, you can define scripts with an MMC console with the Group Policy snap-in added and targeted to Local Computer.

IF YOU KNOW NT User logoff scripts as well as computer start-up and shutdown scripts are new to Windows 2000.

You can still define logon scripts in the user settings in Windows 2000 Active Directory and store them in the Netlogon share of the domain controllers. However, defining a logon script with Group Policy is recommended because this offers more options. It is also better to use only one method rather than both.

Security Settings

Security settings can easily be controlled centrally with Group Policy. In addition to configuring various security settings manually for different GPOs, you may want to use the Security Configuration Toolset. It consists of the secedit command and two MMC snap-ins: Security Configuration and Analysis, and Security Templates. Microsoft has created 11 sample configurations for different configurations and environments. These configurations are stored into security templates, which are stored as text-based files with extension .inf in %systemroot%\ security\templates. However, modifying them with a text editor such as Notepad can quickly become too complicated. The Security Templates snap-in is the tool for modifying them. It is not available by default and, as a result, you would have to create your own MMC console and add this snap-in into it. If you want to start with an empty configuration with all settings undefined, you can create a new template. Later, you could import the settings into one or more GPOs. Alternatively, you can analyze your computer with the Security Configuration and Analysis snap-in and compare its security settings to those defined in one of the templates. And if you want, you can configure the security settings based on a template. You can also perform analysis and configuration from the command line with the secedit command.

The Security Configuration Toolset was ported to Windows NT 4 in Service Pack 4. You can find the tools in the Security Configuration Manager (SCM) subfolder on the Service Pack 4 (or later) CD or at `ftp://ftp.microsoft.com/bussys/ winnt/winnt-public/tools/scm/`.

TIP The Windows 2000 Server Resource Kit contains two security templates (SECUREINTERNETWEBSERVER.INF and SECUREINTRANETWEBSERVER.INF) useful for securing Internet and intranet Web servers. They are incorrectly copied into the \Program Files\Resource Kit folder during the Resource Kit installation. You can copy them into %systemroot%\security\templates to have them visible straight away in the Security Templates snap-in. This was corrected in the Windows 2000 Server Resource Kit, Supplement 1.

ACCOUNT POLICIES

Account policies include password, account lockout, and Kerberos policies. When defined in Active Directory–stored GPOs, these policies are effective only at the domain level (i.e., they must be defined in GPOs linked to the domain), although they appear on GPOs linked to other container types (site and OU) as well. These settings can also be defined in the local GPO for stand-alone and domain member workstations and servers. If the workstation or server is a member of a domain and the same setting in an Active Directory–stored GPO has no other value configured, the policy defined in the local GPO can remain in effect. Local GPO does not have Kerberos policies.

TIP   In addition to password, account lockout, and Kerberos policies, three other security options also apply only when defined in GPOs linked to the domain. These are renaming administrator and guest accounts and automatically logging off users when their logon times expire. See Knowledge Base article Q259576 for more information.

IF YOU KNOW NT   In Windows NT 4 you had to either install passfilt.dll from Service Pack 2 or newer and make registry changes manually or install Passprop.exe from the Resource Kit to force complex passwords. In Windows 2000, this is just one policy option in the password policies.

LOCAL POLICIES

Local policies include Audit Policy, User Rights Assignment, and Security Options. There are nine types of events to be audited and you can define whether successful or failed events are logged into the security log. There are 34 user rights, including change system time and log on locally. (We discuss user rights in detail in Chapter 4.)

TIP   By default, auditing is defined not to collect any events for successes or failures in Default Domain Controllers Policy. Thus, turning auditing on only on the domain level would leave no trails for logon attempts with incorrect passwords on domain controller security logs unless you change the Default Domain Controllers Policy too.

NOTE   To collect security events for file and folder access, you must specify "Audit object access." In addition, you must also define which user or group and what type of action you want to audit in the system access control list (SACL) of the file or folder. You can access the SACL from the Audit tab in the file or folder properties, Security—Advanced. The same applies for "Audit directory service access." You should first enable auditing in the GPO, and then the user or group and type of actions to be audited in the SACL of the Active Directory object.

The importance of security in Windows 2000 can be seen in the number of security options, of which there are 40. Some of them were available in Windows NT 4 System Policies or directly with changing registry settings, but most are new. For example, you can set the LAN Manager authentication level so that the more secure NTLMv2 authentication is required. You must remember that defining this level carries implications for clients connecting to the computers that are controlled by this policy (i.e., Windows 9*x* and NT 4 with SP3 and lower cannot connect if NTLMv2 is required). For more information on this setting, see the Group Policy Reference in the Windows 2000 Server Resource Kit.

NOTE   One option to enable NTLMv2 in Windows 9*x* and NT 4 computers is to install the Active Directory client extension. For Windows 9*x*, it is available on the Windows 2000 distribution CD. For Windows NT, you can find the client on the Microsoft site at `http://www.microsoft.com/windows2000/server/evaluation/news/bulletins/adextension.asp`.

Other very interesting security options are the ability to prevent users from installing unsigned drivers, the ability to rename administrator and guest accounts, and the ability to define the action that takes place when a smart card that was used for logon is removed (either locking the computer or logging off the current user).

NOTE   When the security log fills, Microsoft recommends using the audit log setting "Shut down system immediately if unable to log security audits" in Security Options rather than "Shut down the computer when the security audit log is full in AuditLog." The former causes the system to halt with the blue screen message "STOP: C0000244 {Audit Failed} An attempt to generate a security audit failed."

IF YOU KNOW NT NT has seven event categories for auditing. The new categories in Windows 2000 are "Audit account logon events" and "Audit directory service access." The former can be used to log on events where the computer was used to validate/authenticate a user (e.g. on domain controller). The latter is similar to "Audit object access" in which the access of registry keys or NTFS files or folders was audited. With "Audit directory service access," you can audit the access to Active Directory objects as defined in their SACL. In NT 4, there were 10 basic and 17 advanced user rights. Most security options are new in Windows 2000.

EVENT LOG

You can define various settings for application, security, and system logs. For example, you can restrict guest access to these logs, define their maximum sizes, and define how full logs are handled. By default, this policy is not defined in Default Domain and Default Domain Controller policies. Local GPO does not have Event Log Policy.

RESTRICTED GROUPS

You may want to control the membership of some groups, which the Restricted Groups policies enable you to do. You can either add members to a certain group or define the set of group(s) to which a certain group belongs. If you leave the "Members of this group" list empty, it means that the group should have no members. If you leave the "This group is a member of" list empty, of course, you do not indicate which groups the group belongs to. By default, this policy is not defined in Default Domain and Default Domain Controller policies. Local GPO does not have Restricted Groups Policy.

SYSTEM SERVICES

You can set the default state (Automatic, Manual, or Disabled) of services upon start-up. You can also define permissions, such as start, stop, and pause, for all system services. By default, this policy is not defined in the Default Domain and Default Domain Controller policies. Local GPO does not have System Services Policy.

NOTE If you define the start-up status of a certain service as Automatic and stop the service, it will not be started automatically during the periodic refresh of Group Policy, but rather upon the next start-up of the system.

REGISTRY

You can define the permissions and audit settings for registry keys. By default, this policy is not defined in Default Domain and Default Domain Controller policies. Local GPO does not have Registry Policy.

FILE SYSTEM

The File System Policy enables you to define the permissions and audit settings for file system objects such as files and folders. By default, this policy is not defined in the Default Domain and Default Domain Controller policies. Local GPO does not have File System Policy.

PUBLIC KEY POLICIES

The Encrypted Data Recovery Agents setting enables you to add certificates for users who should be able to decrypt files or folders encrypted by other users in case these files are needed while users are away (for example, on vacation). By default, the domain administrator account has the necessary certificate added to this policy to be able to recover files encrypted on any Windows 2000 computer on the domain. If you delete this policy, no files can be encrypted with Encrypting File System (EFS). For stand-alone computers, the local administrator has the ability to recover the files encrypted on that computer. If a certification authority (CA) does not exist in the network, the key pairs and certificates required for EFS are generated automatically by the operating system. This is the only public key policy available on local GPO.

With Automatic Certificate Request Settings, you can define types of certificates that computers can automatically request. With this setting, an administrator could, for example, define computers in a certain OU to request an IPSec certificate in order to use IPSec encryption later for securing data communication between computers.

Trusted Root Certification Authorities are authorities that are automatically trusted when, for example, a user opens a Web page that requires a secured communication link. With this policy, you can specify that a group of computer and user resources trust certain CAs.

The Enterprise Trust policy, an extension of the Trusted Root Certification Authorities, enables you to add certificate trust lists (CTLs), which are signed lists of Trusted Root CAs.

With the exception of the Encrypted Data Recovery Agents policy, these policies are not defined in the Default Domain and Default Domain Controller policies.

IP SECURITY POLICIES

IP Security (IPSec) enables authenticated and/or encrypted data communication between computers. By default, there are three IPSec policies defined with a lot of settings for each. However, none of the IPSec policies is assigned and as a result none of them is in effect.

Administrative Templates

The Administrative Templates section contains registry-based settings. If you are familiar with Windows NT, you already know the principle. The configurable settings are defined in template files. These templates, which have extension .adm, define which options are available for you to change in the graphical UI (Group Policy snap-in or System Policy Editor) and how the selected settings modify the registry. You can leave a setting undefined, or you can select Enabled or Disabled. In some policies, you might also have to define the value (i.e., not only Enabled or Disabled), as illustrated in the Figure 7.3. If you select Enabled or Disabled, the setting in the registry is configured according to the value defined in the template when Group Policy is processed.

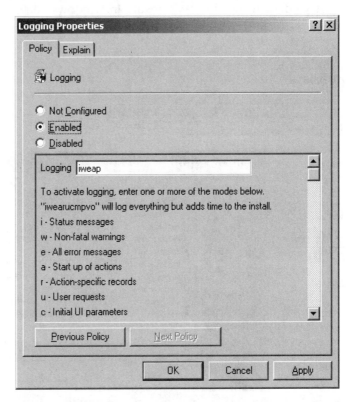

FIGURE 7.3 Defining the settings for administrative templates can be more complex than simply selecting Enabled or Disabled. You can use the Explain tab to see more information about the setting and its effect.

The existing templates are Unicode-based text files that are stored in %SystemRoot%\Inf. By default, three templates (conf.adm, inetres.adm, and system.adm) are loaded. If you want to add more templates, right-click Administrative Templates in either the Computer or User configuration and click Add/Remove Templates. Figure 7.4 illustrates the templates that are loaded by default as well as the templates that come with Windows 2000 and are located in %SystemRoot%\inf. Table 7.3 lists these templates and their purpose as well as whether they can be used with Group Policy.

NOTE The same templates are used for both Computer and User configurations.

In Windows NT 4, the settings specified in the System Policy templates were modifying registry values under many locations in the registry. Removing a changed setting was problematic because you had to use another policy or registry editor to do this. As a result, in Windows 2000, all registry-based settings

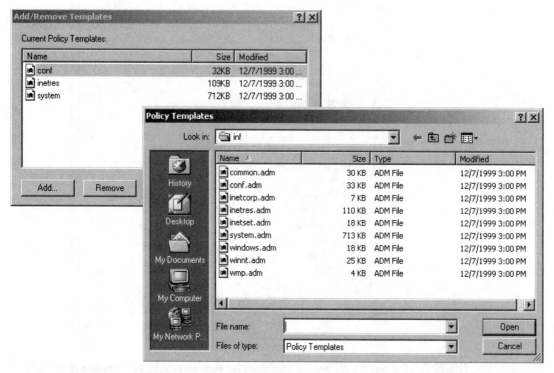

FIGURE 7.4 By default, three templates are loaded. You can add more by right-clicking Administrative Templates and selecting Add/Remove Templates.

TABLE 7.3 Default Template Files in %SystemRoot%\Inf

File	Contents	Note
common.adm	Settings for Windows NT	Cannot be used with Group Policy
conf.adm	Settings for NetMeeting	—
inetcorp.adm	IEAK settings for previous versions of Internet Explorer	Cannot be used with Group Policy
inetres.adm	Settings for Internet Explorer	—
inetset.adm	IEAK settings for previous versions of Internet Explorer	Cannot be used with Group Policy
system.adm	All other settings apart from NetMeeting, IE, and Windows Media Player	By far the largest template file with most settings
windows.adm	Settings for Windows 9x	Cannot be used with Group Policy
winnt.adm	Settings for Windows NT	Cannot be used with Group Policy
wmp.adm	Settings for Windows Media Player	—

that are modified with Group Policy are grouped under four keys. The preferred locations are HKEY_CURRENT_USER\Software\Policies and HKEY_LOCAL_MACHINE\Software\Policies. In addition, HKEY_CURRENT_USER\Software\Microsoft\Windows\CurrentVersion\Policies and HKEY_LOCAL_MACHINE\Software\Microsoft\Windows\CurrentVersion\Policies can be used.

If the existing 450 registry-based settings do not include the settings that you want to control, you can always create your own .adm files. Try to stick to those settings that are stored under the previously mentioned keys. To use a value that is defined somewhere else in the registry, you have to create a new .adm file or modify an existing one. We recommend creating a completely new one so that it is easy to distinguish between the original and your own templates.

In Windows 2000, a value that is stored outside the previously mentioned four registry keys is called a *preference*. By default, preferences are not displayed in the Group Policy snap-in. This is to discourage administrators from using Group Policy to configure settings outside the keys defined for the purpose.

In order to see the preferences, you must right-click Administrative Templates, click View, and deselect Show Policies Only. To distinguish preferences from "true" policies, preference icons have a red dot instead of the blue dot that appears on policy settings.

TIP   You can also deselect Show Policies Only from the View menu of the MMC snap-in.

As an example, Figure 7.5 illustrates the contents of a template file with which you can configure a setting to prevent a computer from taking part in browser elections. This could be desirable if you have Windows 2000 Server and Professional computers that you do not want to become so-called master browsers, thus causing them unnecessary load. This could happen if your domain controllers are still NT 4. A Windows 2000 computer wins the master browser election based on an operating system version criterion. The NetBIOS Browser service maintains a list of computers with shared resources so that users can browse them through My Network Places (or Network Neighborhood in NT).

When you add this template to Administrative Templates, a new node called Browser is created under Computer Configuration, Administrative Templates, Network, as you can see in Figure 7.6.

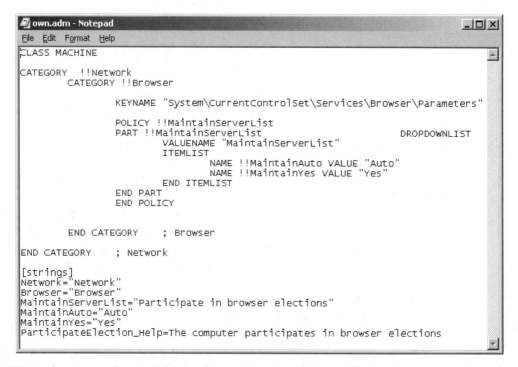

```
own.adm - Notepad                                                    _|□|x|
File  Edit  Format  Help
CLASS MACHINE

CATEGORY   !!Network
        CATEGORY !!Browser

                KEYNAME  "System\CurrentControlSet\Services\Browser\Parameters"

                POLICY !!MaintainServerList
                PART !!MaintainServerList                        DROPDOWNLIST
                        VALUENAME "MaintainServerList"
                        ITEMLIST
                                NAME !!MaintainAuto VALUE "Auto"
                                NAME !!MaintainYes VALUE "Yes"
                        END ITEMLIST
                END PART
                END POLICY


        END CATEGORY    ; Browser

END CATEGORY     ; Network

[strings]
Network="Network"
Browser="Browser"
MaintainServerList="Participate in browser elections"
MaintainAuto="Auto"
MaintainYes="Yes"
ParticipateElection_Help=The computer participates in browser elections
```

FIGURE 7.5 The contents of a user-defined template with which a Windows 2000–based computer can be prevented from taking part in browser elections

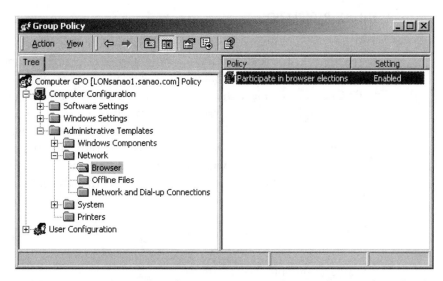

FIGURE 7.6 You can see the sample preference "Participate in browser elections" created with own.adm with the Group Policy snap-in after clicking View and deselecting Show Policies Only.

TIP   You can use the Resource Kit tools browmon or browstat to see the current browser status.

TIP   You can centrally prevent administrators from seeing and using preferences by enabling the "Enforce Show Policies Only" setting, which you can locate under User Configuration, Administrative Templates, System, Group Policy.

You can use Unicode characters in Windows 2000 Group Policy templates. To edit Unicode files, you have to use an editor, such as Notepad, that supports them.

Other Policies

There are three other categories of policies that you can define for users: folder redirection, remote installation services, and Internet Explorer maintenance.

FOLDER REDIRECTION

The user profile contains certain subfolders that would be better stored on the server rather than in the local profile (%SystemDrive%\Documents and Settings\User). When the data in these folders is physically on the server, it can be backed up centrally. One way to achieve this is to use roaming profiles. Roaming profiles introduce their own problems, such as replicating temporary Internet Explorer files, which can be a large number of files. This would cause delays for users logging on or off their computers because these files have to be copied from or to a file server.

Folder redirection in Windows 2000 enables you to redirect certain folders from the user profile to a file server. The folders that you can redirect include the following:

- Application Data
- Desktop
- My Documents
- My Pictures
- Start Menu

You can define each of these folders to be stored on different UNC paths. And with advanced settings, users in different security groups can have their folders stored in different network locations, according to the security group(s) to which they belong (see Figure 7.7). If a user belongs to at least two groups for which the redirection has been defined, the first redirection with a matching group remains in effect. There are no Up/Down buttons for rearranging the redirections, so you have to create them in the correct order.

The steps that the operating system performs during folder redirection are as follows.

1. Determine which folders to redirect based on the policy at logon time.
2. Desired redirected location is determined and access is verified.
3. If the folder does not exist, it is created and NTFS permissions are set. If the folder exists, NTFS permissions and ownership are checked.
4. If desired, the contents are moved.

REMOTE INSTALLATION SERVICES

Remote Installation Services (RIS) is one way to deploy the Windows 2000 Professional operating system. In addition to adding and configuring RIS, the operation of RIS requires Active Directory, DHCP, and DNS services. RIS can be used to deploy the operating system only or the operating system with applications already installed.

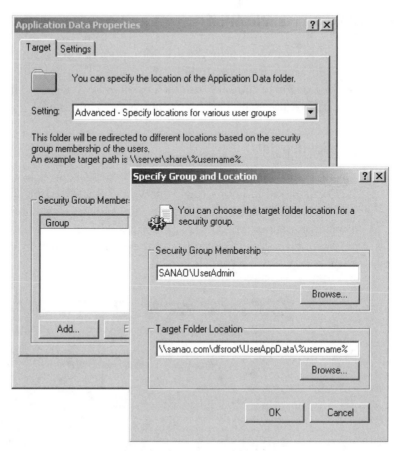

FIGURE 7.7 With advanced folder redirection, you can redirect certain users' profile subfolders into different network locations based on those users' security group membership.

With four "Choice Screen" settings, the user can be allowed or denied permission to make certain choices during the installation. One example is to restrict the user from seeing Custom Setup choice when he starts installing Windows 2000 with RIS into a new computer.

INTERNET EXPLORER MAINTENANCE

Internet Explorer maintenance enables administrators to centralize the configuration of users' Internet Explorer browsers, such as the contents of Favorites or proxy or security zone settings. In earlier Windows networks, the Internet Explorer Administration Kit (IEAK) was used to accomplish the same task. Even in Windows 2000 networks, the IEAK still has its role in creating Internet Explorer installation packages.

GROUP POLICY OBJECTS AND LINKS

In this section we explain the common pool of Group Policy objects (GPOs) in a domain. You may choose to link one or several of these GPOs to each OU (as well as the domain or the site), so that a number of GPOs may affect a given computer or user. We also examine how to control GPO inheritance and priorities.

Group Policy Objects

Group Policies are stored and edited in virtual Group Policy objects. Two kinds of GPO exist: local and nonlocal. Every Windows 2000–based computer has one local GPO. Nonlocal Group Policies are Active Directory–based and stored in the domain container. The GPOs are identified by GUIDs, which are also used in the replication process. You can locate the GUID of a GPO by clicking Properties on the Group Policy tab (see Figure 7.8).

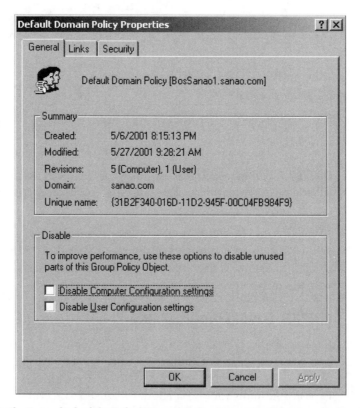

FIGURE 7.8 The General tab of the Default Domain Policy Properties dialog box displays the GUID for a GPO. The GUID for the Default Domain Policy GPO is the same in all Active Directory networks.

Because the Group Policy extension in the Active Directory Users and Computers and Active Directory Sites and Services snap-ins does not contain all information for GPOs, you can use either ADSI Edit or LDP to see additional information. Figure 7.9 displays all defined properties of the Default Domain GPO with the LDP tool. You can find the instructions for opening this view in Chapter 6.

The components of the GPOs reside in Active Directory and the file system and are illustrated in Figure 7.10. The component that resides in Active Directory is called the Group Policy container (GPC). The actual class in schema is called Group-Policy-Container with LDAP display name `groupPolicyContainer`. Table 7.4 lists the most important properties of a GPC.

TIP   The node that contains Group Policies in the Active Directory Users and Computers snap-in is not visible by default. To make it visible, select View, Advanced Features, and then locate System, Policies under your domain.

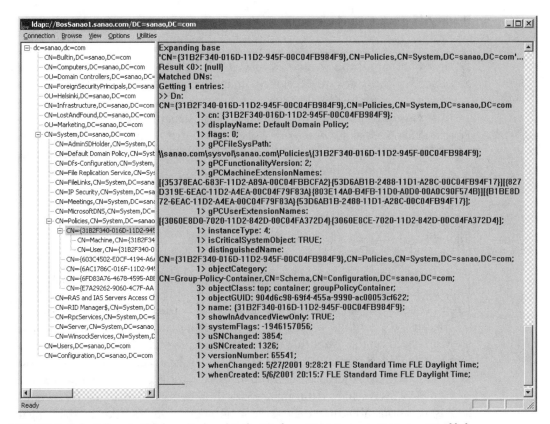

FIGURE 7.9 Default Domain Policy as displayed in the Windows 2000 Resource Kit Support Tool lpd.exe

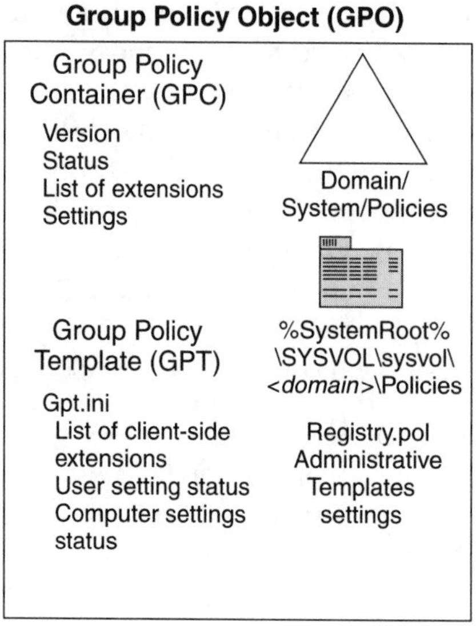

Group Policy Object (GPO)

Group Policy
Container (GPC)

Version
Status
List of extensions
Settings

Domain/
System/Policies

Group Policy
Template (GPT)

Gpt.ini
List of client-side
extensions
User setting status
Computer settings
status

%SystemRoot%
\SYSVOL\sysvol\
<domain>\Policies

Registry.pol
Administrative
Templates
settings

FIGURE 7.10 Components of a Group Policy object

In addition to these properties, all GPCs contain two subcontainers, Machine and User, which a software developer can extend in order to use Active Directory to store policies for her applications.

The Group Policy template (GPT) is a folder structure stored in the %System-Root%\SYSVOL \sysvol\<*domain*>\Policies folder of domain controllers. It contains information about applications managed with Group Policy, security settings, scripts, and Administrative Template–based policy settings. Figure 7.11 displays a GPT folder structure for a sample GPO under \\sanao.com\sysvol\sanao.com\Policies\{2CF3B5F6-2058-4857-B50E-A6BB30B9EEAD}.

The GPT contains a file called GPT.INI in the root of an individual policy folder. For the Active Directory–based GPOs, GPT.INI contains only the version number. The version numbers for GPT and GPC are used by the client components to determine whether the settings in a GPO have changed and also to check that the GPT and GPC are in sync. This is to ensure reliable processing of the Group Policy. If the version numbers do not match, the GPO is not processed.

Because the settings in either Computer Configuration or User Configuration are read based on the event that takes place (e.g., the computer starts or the user logs on), their versions must be kept separate. This is in order for the client extensions to determine if there has been a change in the settings of the applicable section of the GPO. This is achieved through revision numbers kept separately for computer and user sections. You can see the revision numbers of each section by checking the properties of the GPO. See Figure 7.8 earlier in this chapter for an example.

TABLE 7.4 Important Properties of a Group Policy Container

Property	Description
DisplayName	The name that is displayed in the Group Policy tab.
gPCFileSysPath	The location of the file system–based component of GPO.
gPCFunctionalityVersion	The version of the MMC Group Policy extension that created this GPC. For Windows 2000, this value is 2.
gPCMachineExtensionNames	GUIDs for machine extensions defined in this GPO. If Disable Computer Configuration Settings is checked in the policy's properties, this property has no value.
gPCUserExtensionNames	GUID(s) for user extensions defined in this GPO. If Disable User Configuration Settings is checked in the policy's properties, this property has no value.
flags	Indicates whether computer or user sections are disabled. If both are enabled, the value for this property is 0. If Disable User Configuration Settings is checked in the policy's Properties, this property has value 1 and if Disable Computer Configuration Settings is checked in the policy's properties, this property has value 2.
versionNumber	The version of the GPC. It is compared with the version number in a GPT component, the gpt.ini file by client extensions in order to determine whether the components of a GPO are in sync.

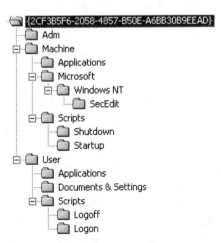

FIGURE 7.11 A sample Group Policy template folder structure

The version number is 0 for a new GPO. For the default GPOs (Default Domain Policy and Default Domain Controllers Policy), the version number is 1 because one change has occurred in the computer section (the change in security settings that were all stored at the same time). When you make a change in any setting of the computer section, the version number is increased by 1. A change in the user section increases the version number by 65536. Thus, we can derive the following formula for the version number:

```
Version = 1 C + 65536 U, where C is the number of changes in the
computer section and U is the number of changes in the user section.
```

For example, if you have changed five settings in the computer section and seven settings in the user section, the revision numbers are 5 for the computer section and 7 for the user section. Consecutively, the version number stored in GPT.INI and the versionNumber property of the GPC is 458757.

Windows 2000 can determine the values for the revisions with the following formulas (shown here in Microsoft Excel format):

```
User Revision = INT(Version/65536) and
Computer Revision = MOD(Version, 65536)
```

Empty subfolders Machine and User are created when you create a new GPO. When you open a new GPO for editing, three default .adm files (conf.adm, inetres. adm, and system.adm) are copied from %Systemroot%\inf into the Adm folder.

TIP   You can use setting User Configuration, Administrative Templates, System, Group Policy, "Disable automatic update of ADM files" to prevent the system from loading the most recently revised copies of the adm template files from %Systemroot%\inf folder.

Files Machine\Registry.pol and Computer\Registry.pol store all registry-based settings that you define in the Administrative Templates. The file Machine\ Registry.pol is created when you make the first change to any setting in the Administrative Templates under Computer Configuration. The file User\Registry.pol is created similarly after the first change. The subfolders Machine\Scripts\Shutdown and Machine \Scripts\Startup are created when you click the Windows Settings node under Computer Configuration. As the name implies, these folders are used to store the computer start-up and shutdown scripts. Folders User\Scripts\Logoff, User\Scripts\Logon, and User\Documents and Settings are created when you click the Windows Settings node under User Configuration. The script folders again store user-specific scripts, whereas Folder Redirection settings are stored in Documents and Settings. These settings are stored in a text file called fpdeploy.ini.

Machine\Microsoft\Windows NT\SecEdit contains the file GptTmpl.inf, which stores security settings. This subfolder tree and file is created when you click Security Settings in the Group Policy snap-in. User\Microsoft\IEAK is created when you open the Internet Explorer Maintenance node in the MMC console, and it stores Internet Explorer settings in various files and subfolders in a similar manner to IEAK. User\Microsoft\RemoteInstall stores RIS settings in a text file called oscfilter.ini.

Finally, the Applications subfolder under both the user and computer folders contains the files required for application deployment with Group Policy. These include the application assignment scripts using the filename format {GUID}.aas.

If a third-party software developer wants to use Group Policy to store the application settings as policies, they can use the registry.pol for registry settings. They may also create subfolders for Machine and User folders in a manner similar to the way Microsoft stores RIS and IE settings.

By default, an Active Directory domain contains two GPOs—namely, the Default Domain Policy and the Default Domain Controllers Policy. By default, there is no GPO associated with the first site of a new Active Directory forest: Default-First-Site-Name.

LOCAL GROUP POLICY OBJECT

You can use the local Group Policy object (LGPO) to define settings for a Windows 2000 Professional or Server computer that is not a member of a domain. It is stored in the %SystemRoot%\SYSTEM32\GroupPolicy folder. The file Gpt.ini in this folder contains information about

- Whether the computer or user portion is disabled
- Which client-side extensions of the Group Policy snap-in contain computer or user data in the GPO
- The version number of the Group Policy snap-in extension that created the GPO

The subfolders for the local GPO are the same as for the Active Directory–based GPOs apart from the folders for application deployment, folder redirection, and RIS, which are not available without Active Directory.

TIP   If you do not have Active Directory yet and you want to use the same LGPO policies for several Windows 2000 computers, you can define the settings for one of the computers and then copy the contents of %SystemRoot%\SYSTEM32\Group-Policy to other computers.

NOTE   You can use the LGPO to define settings also for computers that are members of an Active Directory domain. You just have to remember that if the same setting with a different value in Active Directory–stored GPOs applies to a computer or a user, it will override the setting stored in the LGPO.

Group Policy Links

A Group Policy is associated to an Active Directory container by a link. You can link GPOs to three types of Active Directory container objects: sites, domains, and OUs. You cannot link a GPO to the default containers (Builtin, Computers, and Users) because they are not OUs.

As Figure 7.12 shows, a GPO can be linked to several containers. Alternatively, a container can be associated with several GPOs. In the latter case, you can define the priority of the GPOs by clicking the Up and Down buttons in the Group Policy dialog box. The links in the list are read from bottom to top (i.e., the first link is read last),

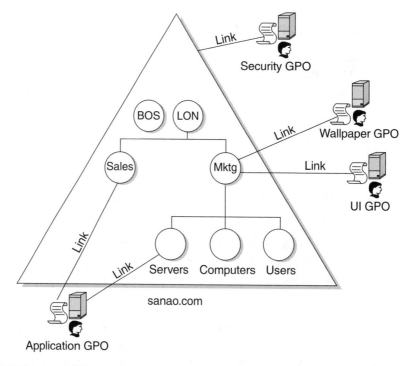

FIGURE 7.12 You can link a GPO (Application GPO) to several containers or several GPOs to one container (Mktg).

and as a result settings in the GPO that this link associates remain in effect should the same setting with a different value be defined in another GPO lower in the list.

Scope of Group Policies

Group Policies can be defined on site, domain, and OU levels. As also mentioned earlier, they cannot be set on container objects such as computers and users. However, the policies that affect the parent container (in this case, domain) also affect the objects in the child containers. Figure 7.13 illustrates GPOs linked to different containers.

Inheritance

By default, Group Policy settings are inherited from the parent container down the tree to the objects in the child containers. The path through the tree is based on the user or computer object's location. If there are conflicting settings, the nearest setting usually remains in effect. Consider the example illustrated in Figure 7.14.

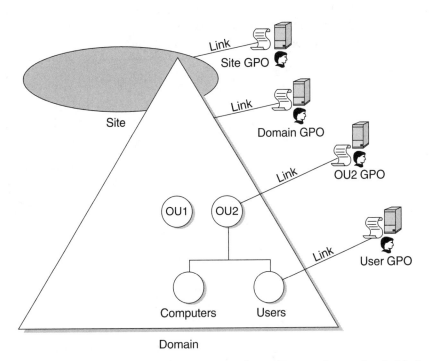

FIGURE 7.13 GPOs that contain policies for computer and user objects can be associated with sites, domains, and OUs.

In the case illustrated in Figure 7.14, three GPOs are linked to three containers.

- A GPO that contains security settings is linked to a domain. Such settings could include the maximum password age and the minimum number of characters in the password.

- An administrative template GPO that contains a setting for common wallpaper is linked to the LON (London) OU. Thus, all users in London would have similar wallpaper on their desktops.

- An administrative template that contains some user interface modifications is linked to the Production OU. For example, the Documents menu could be removed from the Start menu.

All users and computers in the sanao.com domain receive the same security settings. All users in the LON OU and the OUs below it receive the same wallpaper. In addition, users in the Production OU receive the same user interface restrictions.

NOTE   GPOs do not span over domain boundaries. The only way to have a GPO apply to several domains is to use a GPO linked to a site. Theoretically, it is possible to link a GPO from one domain to containers in another. However, you should not do so because it can slow the logon process dramatically.

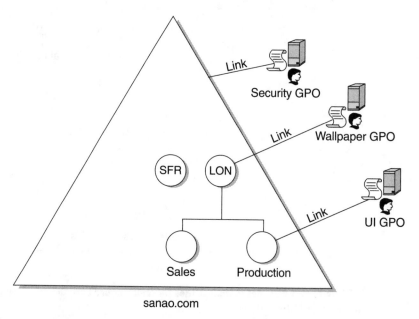

FIGURE 7.14 A sample domain sanao.com with three linked GPOs

SOLVING CONFLICTING POLICY SETTINGS

Some policy settings can have conflicting settings on different GPOs. As we mentioned earlier, in these cases the setting in effect closest to the object wins. Another sample situation is where the same setting exists for both user and computer categories. If, for example, there was a setting defined for connection sharing for both computer and user, the computer configuration would take precedence, as displayed in Figure 7.15. The same figure illustrates well how the Explain tab for each Administrative Template setting has a wealth of information, including information on processing conflict situations.

BLOCKING INHERITANCE

You may want to block inheritance from Group Policies linked to parent containers. In this case, the policies set in GPOs linked to the parent containers do not affect objects on this container or its children. By blocking, you cannot define specific policies to be blocked. In other words, it is all or nothing. The mouse pointer in Figure 7.16 indicates the "Block Policy inheritance" setting.

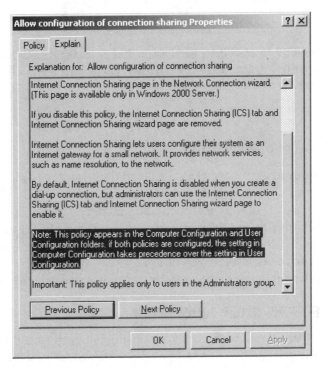

FIGURE 7.15 This sample setting can be defined for both user and computer. Usually the setting defined for computer wins in this kind of situation.

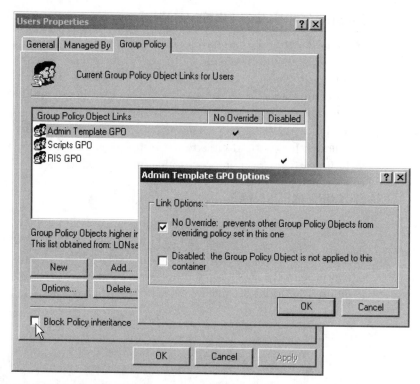

FIGURE 7.16 Block Policy inheritance is done on the Group Policy tab per Active Directory container. If you click Options and check No Override, you force settings in a linked GPO to affect all user and computer objects in child containers.

FORCING GROUP POLICY

To override blocking, a domain administrator may want to force the settings in a given GPO linked to the domain to apply to every object within the domain, regardless of whether inheritance has been blocked by another lower-level administrator. This is achieved by checking No Override for the GPO link. You can either double-click the No Override column or click Options and select No Override from the Options dialog box, as displayed in Figure 7.16. The third way to define this setting is to right-click the GPO link and select No Override.

FILTERING GROUP POLICIES WITH GROUPS

Finally, we get to create a relationship between Group Policy and security groups. The relationship comes through the fact that certain permissions are required for the policies to have an effect on objects in a container. You can display the permissions in the Security tab for a GPO by clicking Properties in the Group Policy dialog box.

In order to be affected by settings in a GPO, a User or Computer account needs to have Read and Apply Group Policy permissions for the given GPO. By default, the Authenticated Users security group has these permissions for all new GPOs. This is illustrated in Figure 7.17.

Domain Admins, Enterprise Admins, and System have Read, Write, and Create/Delete All Child Objects permissions for all GPOs. Because the Domain Admins and Enterprise Admins groups are also members of Authenticated Users, the settings defined in GPOs also affect them. If you do not want Group Policies to affect users in these groups, you have two options.

- You can remove the Apply Group Policy permission from these groups by checking the Deny column.
- You can remove the Apply Group Policy permission from Authenticated Users, create another group to which you give Read and Apply Group Policy permissions for this GPO, and assign appropriate users as members in that new group.

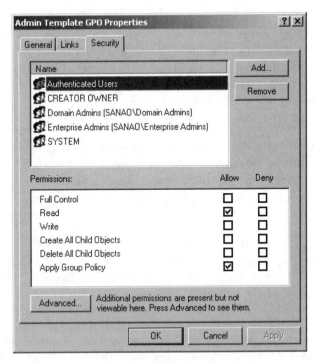

FIGURE 7.17 Default permissions for a GPO include the Read and Apply Group Policy permissions to Authenticated Users.

In addition to the permissions just mentioned, the well-known security principal Creator Owner has Full Control except All Extended Rights, applying to child objects only. This permission (along with permissions to the GPO itself) allows anyone who creates a GPO to administer it.

PROCESSING GROUP POLICY

Workstations and servers apply Group Policies by processing them at start-up/logon time and periodically thereafter. You can also trigger this processing manually if you want to test a certain setting or if you want to get policies to apply immediately.

Processing Basics

Group Policies are processed when certain events occur, the most obvious being when the computer starts and when the user logs on. The local Group Policy is processed first, and then the Active Directory tree is processed starting from site, going to domain, and then moving to the OUs to which the computer or user object belongs. Table 7.5 lists different events, along with their actions, that cause Group Policy processing to start.

TIP   An acronym to remember the sequence of GPO processing is LSDOU: L for LGPO, S for GPO(s) linked to the site, D for GPO(s) linked to the domain, and finally OU for GPO(s) linked to the OU(s).

NOTE   Changes that you make to the local Group Policy are implemented immediately unless they conflict with an Active Directory–based setting that overrides the change. The immediate processing is a result of the fact that changing a setting in the local Group Policy triggers the Group Policy processing to start.

By default, Group Policies are processed synchronously, which means that computer policy is completed before the Ctrl-Alt-Delete dialog box is presented, and user policy is completed before the shell (i.e., Windows Explorer) becomes active so the user can start using it.

TIP   You can change the synchronous processing behavior with the "Apply Group Policy for computers asynchronously during startup" and "Apply Group Policy for users asynchronously during logon" settings under Computer Configuration, Administrative Templates, System, Group Policy.

TABLE 7.5 Processing Group Policies

Event	What Gets Applied	Based On
Computer starts	Computer settings	Location of computer object
User logs on	User settings	Location of user object
User logs off	Logoff scripts	Location of user object
Computer shuts down	Shutdown scripts	Location of computer object
Periodic refresh	User and computer settings	Locations of user and computer objects
SECEDIT/REFRESHPOLICY command	MACHINE_POLICY; Computer settings	Location of computer object
	USER_POLICY; User settings	Location of user object

PROCESSING GROUP POLICY PERIODICALLY

Most Group Policies are processed periodically in the background. Two exceptions are folder redirection and software deployment. These two policies only take place when the computer starts or the user logs on.

The periodic processing helps to distribute the centrally defined policies for users and computers without the need for users to restart their computers or to log off and log back on again. Usually, the settings in GPOs are reapplied only if the GPOs have changed. You can use the "Process even if the Group Policy objects have not changed" option to reapply a certain GPO even if there is no change in the GPO. This could be the case if you doubt that a user somehow managed to change the setting.

TIP   You can disable background processing while someone is logged on by enabling the policy Computer Configuration, Administrative Templates, System, Group Policy, "Disable background refresh of Group Policy."

The default processing interval for domain controllers is 5 minutes. It can be modified in Computer Configuration, Administrative Templates, System, Group Policy, "Group Policy refresh interval for domain controllers." For computers and users, the default interval is 90 minutes with a 0–30 minute offset (i.e., between 90 and 120 minutes). The random offset prevents all clients from refreshing their policies simultaneously.

NOTE   You cannot specify a time for Group Policy background processing.

MANUAL REFRESH OF GROUP POLICY

You can refresh Group Policy manually with the following command:

```
SECEDIT /REFRESHPOLICY MACHINE_POLICY for machine settings and
SECEDIT /REFRESHPOLICY USER_POLICY for user settings.
```

Starting Group Policy processing manually would be useful if, for example, you wanted to implement a certain policy immediately without waiting through the refresh policy interval. You can ensure that the policies defined in the GPOs are reapplied even if there are no changes in the GPOs by using the /ENFORCE parameter at the end of the command.

Slow Link Processing

There is no point in processing certain policies over a slow connection. Consider, for example, a user dialing in with his cellular phone to check e-mail. If you have set up a software installation policy to upgrade users' e-mail applications, it would take a long time for the upgraded package to be loaded over the slow connection. Thus, certain Group Policy extensions are not processed if a slow link is detected.

On the other hand, it is a security problem if the security settings are not processed over the slow connection. Table 7.6 lists the default status of slow link processing, as well as whether or not the behavior can be changed.

Loopback Processing

By default, a user obtains settings that are the result of Group Policy processing based on the location of the user object. Sometimes you may want to configure users' settings based on the location of the computer object—for example, for software installation. A user could be assigned certain applications by specifying them in a Group Policy object linked to an OU in which the user object is located. However, when the user logs onto a server computer, you may not want all applications to be installed onto that server. The feature you use to modify the default behavior is called *loopback processing*. It is defined in Computer Configuration, Administrative Templates, System, Group Policy, "User Group Policy loopback processing." Two modes of operation are available:

- Replace mode
- Merge mode

TABLE 7.6 Slow Link Processing Options

Extension	Processed When Slow Link Is Detected	Behavior Can Be Modified to Allow Processing When Slow Link Is Detected
Security settings	Yes	No
Administrative templates (Group Policy option is called "Registry processing")	Yes	No
Software installation	No	Yes
Remote installation	Not applicable because it only takes place when a new computer is installed. It would not make much sense to even try to install Windows 2000 over a slow speed connection because of the amount of data to be transferred.	
Scripts	No	Yes
EFS recovery	Yes	Yes
IPSec	Yes	Yes
Disk quota	No	Yes
Folder redirection	No	Yes
Internet Explorer Maintenance	No	Yes

In replace mode, the user settings defined in the GPOs that affect the computer object replace the settings that the user would have normally received. In merge mode, the user settings defined in GPOs that affect the user object are processed first, and then the user settings defined in GPOs that affect the computer object are processed. Thus, the settings defined in the GPOs that affect the computer object have higher priority if settings come into conflict.

GROUP POLICY PROCESSING IN DETAIL

Let's walk through the Group Policy processing in detail when a computer is started and a user logs on to that computer.

1. The user starts his computer. If his computer's IP information is configured to be assigned dynamically, a DHCP server is contacted to obtain this information. Otherwise, the information is retrieved from the registry.

2. The computer locates a domain controller with a DNS name query. It then creates a secure channel with one of the domain controllers in its site.

3. The computer determines its location from the Active Directory configuration container based on its IP address. If it has already done so, the information is cached in the registry from where it is retrieved. The registry key is `HKLM\System\CurrectControlSet\Services\Netlogon\Parameters\DynamicSiteName`.

4. The computer Group Policy processing starts. First the network connection speed to the domain controller is determined in order to decide whether the link is considered slow.

5. The computer executes the GetGPOList application programming interface (API) call to the domain controller. This call is used to determine which GPOs apply to the computer object. The applicable GPOs are determined based on the computer object's location in the Active Directory hierarchy.

6. Once the list is obtained, the version information and GPO options are studied in order to determine which GPOs must be processed. The GPOs are sorted by priority. The value of the `gPCFileSysPath` of the applicable GPOs is obtained in order to determine the location of the GPTs.

7. The client-side extensions (CSEs) process the policies defined in the local Group Policy and the GPTs. The user sees at least two dialog boxes with "Applying computer settings" and "Applying security policy" messages. In addition, software may be installed. A number of registry settings affect the processing. For example, if loopback processing mode is defined for a GPO, it sets `HKEY_LOCAL_MACHINE\Software\Policies\Microsoft\Windows\System\UserPolicyMode` to 1 for merge mode and 2 for replace mode. This forces the processing to be altered when the user logs on.

8. The time for next Group Policy refresh is determined—for example, 92 minutes.

9. The user sees the logon screen. He types his username and password.

10. The user is authenticated by a domain controller with Kerberos authentication.

11. If the authentication is successful, the user profile type and location are determined.

12. The user Group Policy processing starts. First, the network connection speed to the domain controller is determined in order to decide whether the link is considered slow.

13. The GetGPOList call is executed again. This time the applicable GPOs are determined based on the user object's location in the Active Directory hierarchy unless the loopback processing mode is enabled.

14. Once the list is obtained, the version information and GPO options are studied in order to determine which GPOs must be processed. The GPOs are sorted by priority.

15. The value of the `gPCFileSysPath` of the applicable GPOs is obtained in order to determine the location of the GPT.

16. The CSEs process the policies defined in the local Group Policy and the GPTs. The user sees at least two dialog boxes with "Loading your personal settings" and "Applying your personal settings" messages. In addition, software may be installed at this stage.

17. The user's profile is loaded. The default user shell (usually Windows Explorer) is started and user may start using the computer.

Determining Effective Group Policies

Because there is no specific tool to determine effective policies for a given user in Windows 2000 yet, it may be a rather difficult task to accomplish. The Windows 2000 Professional and Server Resource Kits contain one tool, Group Policy Results, that we discuss later in this chapter. Some third-party tools are also available to assist in this task.

NOTE   Windows XP Professional and Windows .NET Server will have a Resultant Set of Policies (RsoP) feature for determining effective policies.

Modifying and also determining effective policies for the security settings has been made easy. On domain controller computers, there are shortcuts for accessing security policies for all default levels (i.e., Domain, Domain Controller, and Local). To see the effective security settings, click the Start button, and then select Programs, Administrative Tools, Local Security Policy. For example, to determine maximum tolerance for computer clock synchronization for Kerberos authentication, go to Account Policies, Kerberos Policy, as shown in Figure 7.18. As you can see, this setting has not been defined for the local GPO. However, because the account policies are effective only when defined at the domain level, the setting 5 minutes must come from the Default Domain Policy or some other policy linked to the domain.

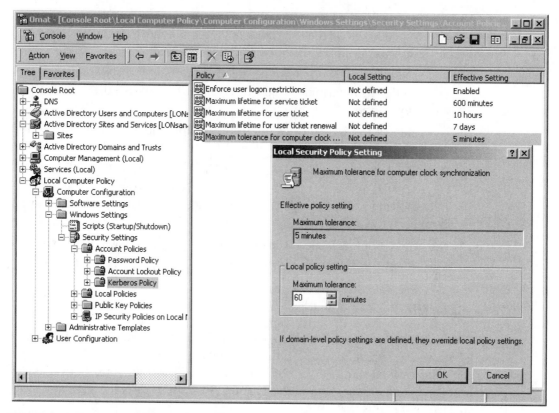

FIGURE 7.18 Clicking the Start button and selecting Programs, Administrative Tools, Local Security Policy enables you to see the effective security settings.

Because user rights can be given to several users and groups, the Local Policy Setting and the Effective Policy Setting are displayed slightly differently in the dialog box shown in Figure 7.19.

In this case, the right to change the system time has been given to the Administrators and Power Users groups in the local GPO. We took the screen shot in Figure 7.19 from a domain controller, which by default does not have a Power Users group although it had one prior to becoming a domain controller. In addition, the setting has been overridden by the Group Policies inherited from higher in the tree. The Server Operators group currently has the right to change the system time, and if you go and see the default GPOs, you will find that Administrators and Server Operators have been given this right in the Default Domain Controllers Policy GPO.

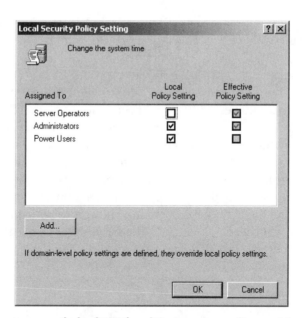

FIGURE 7.19 When you open the local GPO for editing, you can see the user rights settings defined in the local GPO as well as the effective setting. The Effective Policy Setting may be different from the Local Policy Setting due to the settings defined in Active Directory–based GPOs.

TIP When you want to see whether certain security settings are in effect after you have changed something and refreshed the policy with the secedit command, you can refresh the displayed effective settings in the Local Security Policy console by right-clicking Security Settings and clicking Reload.

TIP If you want to display only those Administrative Templates policies that have been configured, right-click Administrative Templates and select View, Show Configured Policies Only. You may have to click Administrative Templates first in order to see the View option in the context menu.

TIP You can create views similar to the restricted ones in built-in Security consoles, such as Default Domain Security, in any stand-alone MMC snap-ins by right-clicking any node and selecting New Window from Here.

To help you further grasp Group Policy processing, we have created a scenario with a few simple registry-based settings. Figure 7.20 shows this scenario, in which the Sanao Corporation has organized its resources into one Active Directory domain called `sanao.com` with two sites: Boston (BOS) and London (LON). Each site has one or more domain controllers. There are four OUs: MFG, Users, Computers, and Servers. Two user accounts, Jack and Jill, are located in the Users OU. In addition, one security group called Assistants is also located in this OU. Jill is a member of this group. A Windows 2000 Professional computer named BosSanao100 is located logically in the Computers OU and physically in the Boston site. A server computer named LonSanao10 is located logically in the Servers OU and physically in the London site. Altogether, nine GPOs (GPO1 through GPO9) have been linked to these containers. These GPOs contain five settings called A through E. The GPOs differ from each other by specifying a value for certain settings—the value being the sequence number of the GPO.

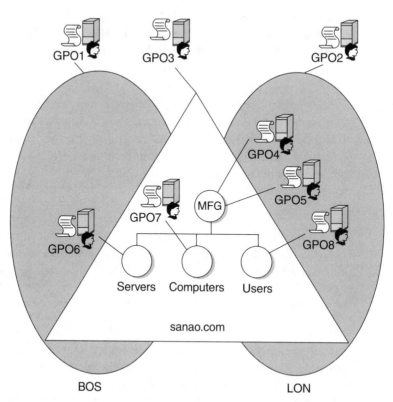

FIGURE 7.20 Sanao GPO infrastructure for the sample scenario

In addition to creating the specified GPOs and specifying the settings shown in Table 7.7, the following was performed:

- GPO2 was marked "No override" in order to ensure that every user logging on a computer on that site would receive certain site-specific settings (such as wallpaper).

- GPO5 was moved up on the GPO link list of the MFG OU properties so that it has higher priority over GPO4.

- The user administrator responsible for administering the Users OU blocked policy inheritance on the Group Policy tab of the Users OU properties.

- The Assistants security group was defined Deny ACE for Apply Group Policy permission for GPO5.

- The Group Policy loopback processing mode was enabled and defined as Replace for GPO6.

When users log on to these computers, they receive certain settings in their registry under HKEY_CURRENT_USER\Software\Policies\Sanao. Table 7.7 illustrates these effective settings. Let's walk through the GPO process in order to determine the final value for the settings when Jill starts the server computer LonSanao10 and logs on to it.

1. Jill starts her computer.

2. Jill's computer determines which GPOs apply to the computer object. The applicable GPOs are GPO2, GPO3, Default Domain Policy, GPO4, GPO5, and GPO6. GPO6 contains the setting for loopback processing, and as a result user settings based on the computer object are the ones that define the final results. The value for loopback processing is set in the registry. Settings are defined only in the user sections of the GPOs and, thus, no other value is entered into the registry.

3. Jill logs on to the computer.

4. Jill's computer determines which GPOs apply to the user object. Because the registry setting for loopback processing is set, the evaluation is done based on Jill's computer object. As a result, the applicable GPOs are GPO2, GPO3, Default Domain Policy, GPO4, GPO5, and GPO6. GPO5 is not applied because the Assistants group, of which Jill is a member, has a Deny ACE for the Apply Group Policy permission.

5. Based on this information, the GPO2 linked to site LON is processed and consequently, SettingB is set value 2.

6. Next, GPO3 linked to domain sanao.com is processed. It defines value 3 for SettingA, SettingC, and SettingE. These values are entered into the registry.

7. Default Domain Policy is processed. It doesn't contain any setting of interest for our scenario.

8. GPO4 linked to the MFG OU is processed. It defines value 4 for SettingA, SettingC, and SettingD. These values are entered into the registry.

9. As the last applicable GPO, GPO6, is processed. It defines value 6 for SettingA, SettingC, and SettingE. These values are entered into the registry. The final values stored in the registry are as displayed in Table 7.7.

10. Jill's profile is loaded. Windows Explorer starts and Jill is able to start using the computer.

You can use the following instructions to create a simple ADM file to determine the effective settings in your environment. You would need at least three

TABLE 7.7 Settings Used in Sample Scenario for Determining Effective Group Policy Settings

Setting	Values for Group Policy Settings on Boston (BOS) Site					Values for Group Policy Settings on London (LON) Site				
	A	B	C	D	E	A	B	C	D	E
Group Policy										
GPO1	—	1	—	—	—	—	1	—	—	—
GPO2	—	2	—	—	—	—	2	—	—	—
GPO3	3	—	3	—	3	3	—	3	—	3
No override										
GPO4	4	—	4	4	—	4	—	4	4	—
GPO5	5	—	5	—	—	5	—	5	—	—
GPO6	6	—	—	6	6	6	—	—	6	6
GP loopback processing mode: Replace										
GPO7	7	—	—	—	7	7	—	—	—	7
GPO8	—	—	8	—	—	—	—	8	—	—
	Jack logs on workstation BosSanao100					Jill logs on server LonSanao10				
Effective policy	—	—	8	—	—	6	2	4	6	6

computers in order to run this scenario: two domain controllers and one member server. In addition, you would need to configure one Windows 2000 computer as a router or use a "real" router to create two subnets. You also want to create two sites, BOS and LON, and assign subnets for them.

TIP   You may want to refer to Chapter 5 for further instructions on sites and replication before trying this scenario.

To create and configure the GPOs, perform the following steps:

1. Start Notepad and type the following lines. Add the missing lines for Settings C through E.

```
CLASS USER
CATEGORY !!_TestSettings
   KEYNAME " Software\Policies\Sanao"
   POLICY !!SettingA
      PART !!A                   NUMERIC REQUIRED SPIN 1
         DEFAULT 1
         MAX    10
         MIN     1
         VALUENAME "SettingA"
      END PART
   END POLICY

   POLICY !!SettingB
      PART !!B                   NUMERIC REQUIRED SPIN 1
         DEFAULT 1
         MAX    10
         MIN     1
         VALUENAME "SettingB"
      END PART
   END POLICY
*Repeat the same for Policies C through E
END CATEGORY    ; _TestSettings

[strings]
TestSettings=" TestSettings "
A="A"
SettingA="SettingA"
B="B"
SettingB="SettingB"
*Repeat the same for Policies C through E
```

2. Save the file as testsettings.adm in %SystemRoot%\inf on the domain controller.

3. Open the Active Directory Users and Computers snap-in.

4. Right-click the Active Directory container into which you want to link the new GPO. Select Properties, and then select the Group Policy tab.

5. Click New and type the name for the new GPO.

6. Open the GPO for editing by clicking Edit, selecting the Administrative Templates node for User Configuration and right-clicking it, and selecting Add/ Remove Templates.

7. Click Add and select testsettings.adm. Click Open, Close.

8. Open User Configuration, Administrative Templates, TestSettings.

9. Change the settings according to Table 7.7.

10. Repeat steps 3 through 9 for each GPO.

11. Replicate changes to the other domain controller with Active Directory Sites and Services.

12. Try to log on as Jack or Jill and use the Registry Editor or Resource Kit tool gpresult.exe to see the effective settings.

MANAGING GROUP POLICIES

Management of Group Policies involves two specific tasks:

- Managing GPOs
- Managing GPO links

Managing GPOs can also be divided into two tasks:

- Creating GPOs
- Editing GPOs

In addition to these tasks, it is usually useful to be able to delegate the management. Also, Group Policies should be backed up. In this section we describe how to perform each of these management tasks.

Group Policy Dialog Box

You can accomplish all Group Policy management tasks through the Group Policy dialog box. The buttons Add and Options are for managing links, whereas Edit and Properties are purely for managing GPOs. With New you can create a new GPO and link it to the current container. With Delete, you either remove the link between the current container and the GPO, or delete a GPO and its associated links.

Notice that there is no Save button for Group Policy—all changes are stored immediately when you click the OK or Apply button. However, they will be replicated to other domain controllers only through normal Active Directory replication.

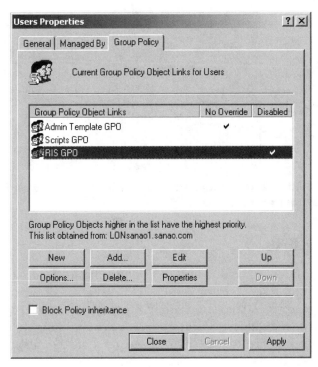

FIGURE 7.21 All management tasks related to Group Policy are accomplished in the Group Policy dialog box.

TARGET DOMAIN CONTROLLER FOR GROUP POLICY OPERATIONS

By default, the MMC Group Policy extension is targeted at the operations master server that holds the PDC emulator role. This setup prevents two administrators from modifying settings on two domain controllers, and then one change overriding another later through replication. You can change this behavior by selecting View, DC Options while editing any Group Policy object.

As Figure 7.22 shows, the options for domain controller selection are in the most preferred order. If possible, you should always target the PDC emulator to prevent data loss. However, if the PDC emulator server is behind a slow WAN link, you might want to change the setting to use the same domain controller as your Active Directory snap-in, for example, Active Directory Users and Computers.

TIP   You can force your administrators to target the PDC role holder by setting User Configuration, Administrative Templates, System, Group Policy, "Group Policy domain controller selection."

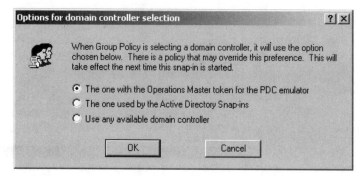

FIGURE 7.22 You can select the target domain controller for Group Policy operations by selecting DC Options from the View menu.

Creating GPOs

In order to create a new GPO, a user has to be a member of Administrators or Group Policy Creator Owners, either directly or indirectly. The Domain Admins, Enterprise Admins, and Group Policy Creator Owners group have the permission to create child objects in the `cn=Policies, cn=System, dc=<domain>` container, as Figure 7.23 shows. However, only the Administrators and Group Policy

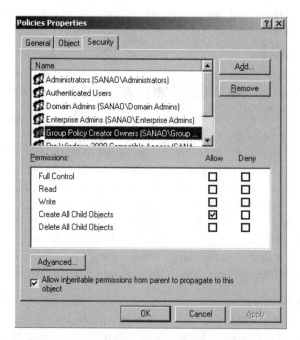

FIGURE 7.23 Group Policy Creator Owners has the Create All Child Objects ACE on the `cn=Policies, cn=System, dc=<domain>` container.

Creator Owners groups (and local system account) have the necessary NTFS permissions for SysVol.

You can create a linked or an unlinked GPO. To create a linked GPO, right-click the appropriate container (Site, Domain, or OU), and after selecting Properties, open the Group Policy tab. Click New and give a name to the new GPO.

There are two ways to create an unlinked GPO:

- Select any container that can host a GPO (i.e., Site, Domain, OU) in the Active Directory Users and Computers snap-in or in the Active Directory Sites and Services snap-in. Open properties for the container and navigate to the Group Policy tab. Click Add and select the All tab. Select the domain that you want to create the GPO in by selecting it in "Look in" field. Right-click anywhere in the list and then click New or click Create Group Policy on the toolbar. Type a name for the GPO. Click Cancel twice unless you want to edit the new GPO, in which case you have to link it to some container first or use a stand-alone MMC console.

- Open MMC. Add a new Group Policy snap-in and click Browse. On the All tab in the Browse for a Group Policy Object dialog box, select the domain that you want to create the GPO in by selecting it in the "Look in" field. Right-click anywhere in the list and then click New (as shown in Figure 7.24) or click Create Group Policy on the toolbar. Type a name for the GPO. Click Cancel twice unless you want to edit the new GPO, in which case you can simply select the new GPO, click OK, click Finish, and then click OK again.

The members of the Group Policy Creator Owners group cannot change the permissions for the Group Policy folders on the System Volume folder. Neither do

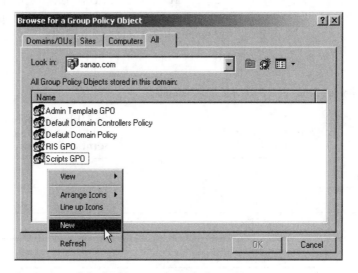

FIGURE 7.24 Creating an unlinked GPO is a rather complex operation.

the members of this group have permission to take the ownership of a GPO. However, all GPOs created by the members of this group have the group as the owner of the GPOs.

Editing GPOs

You can edit existing GPOs either with a stand-alone MMC console or with the default Active Directory administration consoles. To edit a GPO, the user must have both Read and Write ACEs for that GPO.

By default, Windows 2000 has one MMC console for editing a local GPO called gpedit.msc. There is no shortcut in the Start menu for it, but you could create one for it or you can start it by clicking the Start button, selecting Run, and typing gpedit.msc. In addition, Windows 2000 has one shortcut under Administrative Tools in the Start menu for editing security settings in the local GPO. The shortcut is called Local Security Policy and it opens the security node of the local GPO. If the computer is a domain controller, it also has shortcuts for editing domain and domain controller security policies. Table 7.8 lists these MMC consoles.

As displayed in Figure 7.25, you can create a your own MMC console for editing Group Policy so that the focus of the saved console can be changed by starting the console from the command line or by clicking the Start button and selecting Run. You can start the Group Policy console with the following two command-line switches:

- /gpcomputer:"machinename", where machinename can be a NetBIOS or DNS name, which opens the local GPO of the given computer

- /gpobject:"ADSI path", where ADSI path could be LDAP://CN={GUID of the target GPO},CN=Policies,CN=System,DC=Sanao,DC=com, which opens the specified GPO for editing

TABLE 7.8 Default Group Policy–Related MMC Consoles

Filename	Name Displayed in Start Menu	Available on Professional and Stand-alone or Member Servers	Available on Domain Controllers
gpedit.msc	N/A	X	X
secpol.msc	Local Security Policy	X	X
dompol.msc	Domain Security Policy		X
dcpol.msc	Domain Controller Security Policy		X

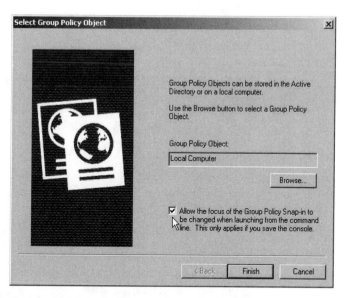

FIGURE 7.25 When you add the Group Policy snap-in to an MMC console, you can check the option to allow changing the focus of the saved console.

TIP   In order to document the GPO settings, you can use the Excel spreadsheet included in the Group Policy scenarios package or FAZAM 2000. These tools are introduced briefly later in this chapter.

Managing GPO Links

If you are using the Add button of the default Group Policy snap-in extension in the Active Directory Users and Computers or Active Directory Sites and Services snap-ins to create a new GPO, you always automatically associate this GPO to the current Active Directory container with a link. Either this link or parts of the newly created GPO can be disabled.

DISABLING PARTS OF GPO OR GPO LINKS

To speed up the start-up or logon process, it might be beneficial to disable unused parts of a GPO, as shown in Figure 7.26.

Especially when testing the effect of Group Policy settings, you may want to disable a GPO link temporarily. You do this by either double-clicking the Disabled column or clicking Options and selecting Disabled in the Group Policy dialog box.

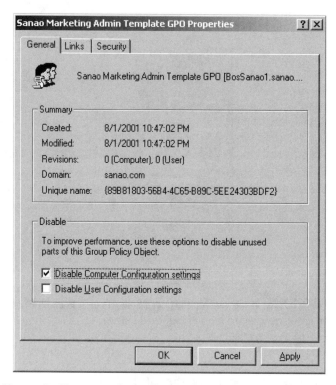

FIGURE 7.26 You can disable an unused part of a GPO from GPO Properties.

TIP   To ensure that policies in a new GPO do not apply before you enable the link, you
             can force links to new GPOs to be disabled. The policy is located at User Configu-
             ration, Administrative Templates, System, Group Policy, "Create new Group Policy
             Object links disabled by default."

Deleting GPOs

Deleting a linked GPO is easy: Just locate the Active Directory container that a
GPO is linked to, open the Group Policy dialog box, and click Delete. You are
presented with two choices for deletion: You can delete only the link that associates the GPO to the container or the link and the GPO. The former option
removes the link but leaves the GPO unlinked or with its other existing links in
Active Directory. The latter option removes the GPO and all links associated with
it (see Figure 7.27).

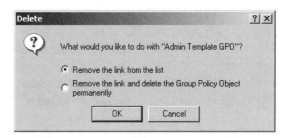

FIGURE 7.27 Deleting a GPO link enables you to delete the GPO as well.

If you want to delete an unlinked GPO, you have to think in "Windows ways"; that is, in order to delete, you access the Add GPO dialog box from any container (Site, Domain, or OU). (This add/delete is like shutting down Windows 2000 by clicking the Start button and selecting Shutdown on the desktop.) Open the property dialog box for any container, click Add on the Group Policy tab, select the unlinked GPO on the All tab, right-click the unlinked GPO, and then click Delete (see Figure 7.28).

Backing Up Group Policy

The only supported way to back up Group Policy is to back up the entire Active Directory as part of the System State with the Windows 2000 Backup tool. The shortcoming of the System State is that it cannot be used partially. In other words,

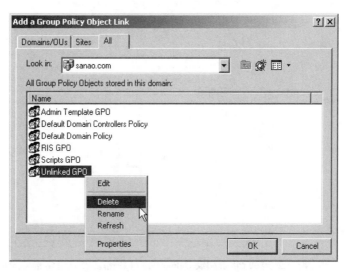

FIGURE 7.28 You delete an unlinked GPO from the Add a Group Policy Object Link dialog box.

one individual GPO cannot be backed up or restored. For larger environments, a third-party backup application that supports backing up individual GPOs (e.g., Full Armor's FAZAM 2000) might be a wise purchase. The so-called reduced functionality version of this FAZAM tool is included in the Windows 2000 Server Resource Kit, Supplement 1 in the apps folder. To back up Group Policy in an unsupported way, see the Group Policy scenarios later in this chapter.

Delegating Management of GPOs

Although you can delegate the administration of a specific OU with the Delegation of Control Wizard, it does not imply that the members of the group to whom you delegated control could fully administer GPOs. The only common task that can be delegated with the wizard is the ability to manage Group Policy links associated with a given container, as displayed in Figure 7.29.

When you delegate to a user or group the ability to manage Group Policy links, the user or group gets Read and Write ACEs to the `gpLink` and `gpOptions` attributes. Table 7.9 lists the groups that have permission to link GPOs to different container objects.

If you want to enable the members of a certain group to edit a GPO, that group must have Read and Write permissions for the GPO. In order to modify the

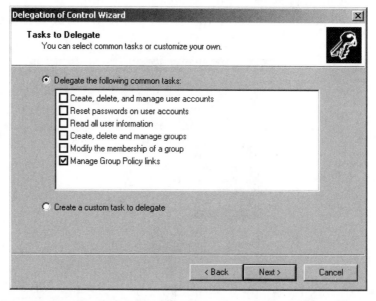

FIGURE 7.29 You can use the Delegation of Control Wizard to delegate administration of GPO links associated with a container.

TABLE 7.9 Groups with Permissions to Link GPOs

Container	ACE Assigned Directly to the Container	Inherited ACE
Site	System	Enterprise Admins
		FRD (forest root domain) Domain Admins
Domain	Domain Admins	
	Administrators	
	System	
	Enterprise Admins	
OU	System	Administrators
	Domain Admins	Enterprise Admins

permissions, click Properties on the Group Policy tab and then select the Security tab. Add the necessary group and give it Read and Write allow ACEs. By default, Domain Admins and Enterprise Admins groups along with System have Write permission for new GPOs.

CREATING AN MMC CONSOLE FOR A DELEGATED GPO

You can create an MMC console for editing the GPO that you just delegated. First start MMC, add the Group Policy snap-in, browse for the delegated GPO, and click Finish, Close, OK. If you want to restrict the user to a specific node, you can right-click Node and click New Window from Here. Close the original window (you might have to use the Window menu to make it visible). Then select Options from Console menu. Finally, select User mode, limited access, single window, and save the console to an appropriate folder (e.g., C:\Documents and Settings\ YourAdminUser\Desktop). Changing the mode restricts the user from seeing menus and modifying snap-ins or views.

TIP You can open the default administrative tools, the Active Directory Users and Computer snap-in, and the Active Directory Sites and Services snap-in in author mode by running dsa.msc and dssite.msc with the /a parameter. The author mode, for example, enables adding other snap-ins.

TIP   You can prevent other users from opening consoles in author mode with the policy User Configuration, Administrative Templates, Windows Components, Microsoft Management Console, "Restrict users from entering author mode."

Another way to restrict the user is to modify the snap-in extensions that open when the user starts the console. There are ten extensions, some of which are shown in Figure 7.30.

TIP   To ensure that the user will or won't be able to use specific MMC snap-ins, use the following policies: the policy User Configuration, Administrative Templates, Windows Components, Microsoft Management Console, "Restrict users to the explicitly permitted list of snap-ins," and the 12 policies under User Configuration, Administrative Templates, Windows Components, Microsoft Management Console, Restricted/Permitted snap-ins, Group Policy. Should you exclude yourself, seek help from Microsoft Knowledge Base article Q263166.

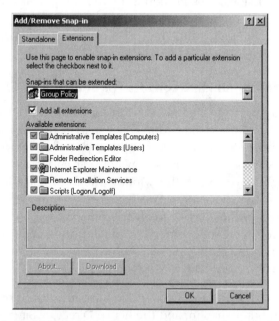

FIGURE 7.30 By default, all MMC snap-in extensions are added to the Group Policy snap-in. When delegating control of GPOs, you can select only some of the extensions.

DELEGATING LOCAL GROUP POLICY

The only way to delegate control of a local Group Policy object is to define NTFS permissions for the %SystemRoot%\System32\GroupPolicy folder. Because there is no Apply Group Policy ACE among the file system ACEs, every user who has Read permission for the folder will be affected by local Group Policy. If there is a conflicting setting in Active Directory, however, the setting in Active Directory wins. If you want to prevent the settings in the local GPO from applying to the members of a certain group, you can deny Read permission to the NTUser.pol file.

Additional Tools

At the moment, apart from the Group Policy snap-in, there are not many additional tools you can use with Group Policies. For troubleshooting, you may want to consult the "Troubleshooting Group Policies" section later in this chapter.

SOFTWARE MANAGEMENT WITH GROUP POLICY

Group Policy can help you simplify the administration of software applications in your network.

Windows Installer

In the past, software applications were deployed and installed with various setup engines in Windows environments. Developers did not always follow the standards, especially the Windows logo requirements for applications (http://msdn.microsoft.com/certification/description.asp). These requirements have to be fulfilled in order to get the application approved by a certifying company and, as a sign they have been fulfilled, a "Certified for Windows" sticker attached to the product box. Consequently, we have applications that store files in the wrong folders and settings in the wrong registry paths, unsuccessful uninstallation programs, DLL conflicts, and so on. Windows 2000 includes a new setup method that is enabled by the Windows Installer service. By including this service, the setup procedure has been standardized. Figure 7.31 illustrates the setup process.

The Microsoft Software Installer (MSI) database includes information stored on tables, based on which Windows Installer creates the actual setup script.

Using Windows Installer offers the following benefits to the Windows environment:

- *Rollback for the installation in case of interrupted or failed process.* The computer (and especially the registry) is returned to the state it was in before the setup process was started.

- *Actual setup only on first use.* Only the shortcut appears on the Start menu prior to first use.

- *Division of the setup into various components.* It is not necessary to install the whole application at once.

- *Option to store all files used during the setup in one .msi file.*

- *Merge modules.* These modules contain components used often in several packages.

- *Customizable installation packages.* You can customize a package to meet specific requirements.

- *Self-repairing applications.* If you start an application and Windows Installer finds a problem with, for example, one corrupted file, the file is replaced automatically by the Windows Installer service.

- *Setup with privileged rights.* The setup is performed in the security context of the system account and, consequently, there is no need for an administrator to attend to the computer during setup if the user's privileges are insufficient for installing the application.

NOTE   The policy Administrative Templates, Windows Components, Windows Installer, "Always install with elevated privileges" exists in both in the Computer Configuration and User Configuration folders. The policy is effective only if you enable it in both locations.

- *Additional information in the Add/Remove applet in the Control Panel.* For example, you can find the URL for the software vendor's support pages.

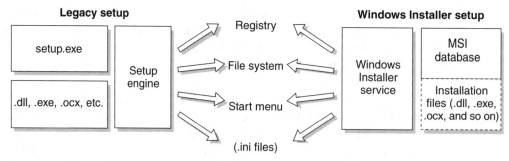

FIGURE 7.31 The applications are installed with a legacy setup or Windows Installer.

NOTE	Windows Installer service must be used to install a third-party application in order to display "Certified for Windows 2000" in the product documentation.

IF YOU KNOW NT	If you try to install an MSI package into NT 4, the Windows Installer service is installed first, after which you must restart the computer and restart the setup. An example of this type of application is Office 2000.

The stages of software installation process are as follows:

1. Copy files.
2. Create shortcuts.
3. Associate file types.
4. Register COM, COM+, and DCOM files.
5. Register application for removal.

The Windows Installer service performs all these tasks as defined in the MSI databases in Windows Installer packages.

Creating Windows Installer Packages

The first stage of deploying software with Group Policy is to create a Windows Installer package. Various tools are available for this task. The Windows 2000 CD-ROM contains Veritas WinInstall LE in the Valueadd\3rdparty\Mgmt\Winstle folder. Other tools include the following:

- Microsoft Visual Studio Installer (http://msdn.microsoft.com/vstudio/)
- Wise for Windows Installer (http://www.wisesolutions.com/)
- InstallShield (http://www.installshield.com/)
- Veritas WinInstall2000 (http://www.veritas.com/)

Deploying Software with Group Policy

The next step is to store the installation package in a shared folder on a file server. You could use a distributed file system (DFS) service to create a fault-tolerant file distribution infrastructure. Then you have to choose whether to publish or assign the application. You also must decide whether to deploy the software for the computer or user.

PUBLISHED VERSUS ASSIGNED APPLICATION

The two ways to deploy applications are as follows:

- The application is published so that it appears in the Add/Remove Programs applet in the Control Panel.

- An application is assigned to a user or computer and appears in the Start menu after the user logs on or the computer is started. The actual installation takes place when the user clicks the shortcut for the application.

A published application can also be installed if the user opens a file with an extension that has been associated with a certain application. You can study the differences between published and assigned applications in Table 7.10.

DEPLOYING NON-MSI PACKAGES

To deploy an older application, you have two options: create an MSI file for the installation with one of the tools mentioned earlier or create a .zap file that contains

TABLE 7.10 Comparison of Published and Assigned Applications

	Published	**Assigned to User**	**Assigned to Computer**
When is software available for installation?	The next user logs on	When the next user to whom the GPO applies logs on	The next time the computer is started
Who starts installation?	User	User	Automatic when the computer starts
Where is the installation started?	Add/Remove Programs in the Control Panel	Start menu	N/A
Is installation by opening an associated file?	Yes, if Auto-Install is selected	Yes	N/A
Removal from Add/Remove software?	Yes	Yes	No—only local administrator can remove the application, but user can repair it
What are the supported installation file types?	Windows Installer packages and .zap files	Windows Installer packages	Windows Installer packages

instructions so that Windows Installer can install the application. The contents for a sample .zap file for installing Excel 97 are as follows:

```
[Application]
FriendlyName = "Microsoft Excel 97"
SetupCommand = setup.exe
DisplayVersion = 8.0
Publisher = Microsoft
URL = http://www.microsoft.com/office
Architecture = Intel
```

Upgrading Applications

The applications that you deploy with Group Policy can be easily upgraded. For example, you can use Group Policy to deploy the current service pack to the Windows 2000 computers in your infrastructure and when a new service pack is released, you can upgrade the computers with the new one. The example GPO in Figure 7.32 is used to install Windows 2000 Service Pack 1 and then upgrade it to Service Pack 2.

Patching Applications

Software developers issue patches to their applications every now and then. As a result, maintaining an application includes the task of deploying these minor upgrades. You can redeploy an application that was deployed originally with Group Policy so that users who have it installed will receive the patched version automatically from the server.

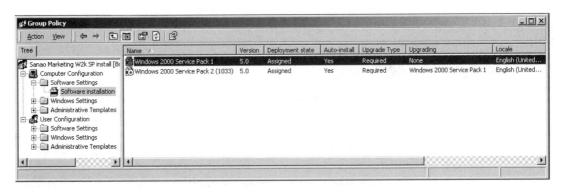

FIGURE 7.32 A GPO used to install and upgrade Windows 2000 service packs

Removing Applications

The applications that were deployed with Group Policy can also be removed with Group Policy. The removal can be optional, in which case users can continue using the application that they installed earlier. However, new users can no longer install the application. The other option is to use mandated removal, in which case the application is removed from the computer when it is restarted or when the user next logs on.

NOTE   Applications deployed with .zap files cannot be removed with Group Policy.

TROUBLESHOOTING GROUP POLICY

The only graphical tools that Windows 2000 provides for expediting the effect of Group Policy settings are the Local Security Policy console and the Security Analysis and Configuration snap-in. With the former, you can see which security settings are in effect, although it does not give a clue as to where the settings came from (if not from local GPO). The Security Analysis and Configuration snap-in enables you to analyze your computer's security settings against settings stored in some of the security templates. The categories that this tool analyzes are as follows:

- Account policies
- Local policies
- Event log
- Restricted groups
- System services
- Registry
- File system

Logging Group Policy Events

In order to gather Group Policy events in logs, you must edit the registry. We recommend using registry editor RegEdt32 for the task rather than RegEdit because it has better support for different value types such as REG_MULTI_SZ and REG_EXPAND_SZ, and for permissions. RegEdit is still useful when you want to search for something in the registry.

You can turn on the Verbose flag in the registry to generate more detailed information on Group Policy processing. Enabling this flag starts verbose logging in the

application event log. The value is located under HKEY_LOCAL_MACHINE\
Software\Microsoft\WindowsNT\CurrentVersion\Diagnostics, and to
turn on the logging, you create a value RunDiagnosticLoggingGroupPolicy
of type REG_DWORD, and set its value to 1. Figure 7.33 illustrates a sample event generated by turning this value on.

TIP   The Diagnostics key does not exist by default. Thus, you must create it prior to
creating the value RunDiagnosticLoggingGroupPolicy.

TIP   Remember to remove the setting from the registry when it is no longer appropriate. If you leave it on, the application log will become full within a few hours as the
default application log size is 512KB.

Another useful log, especially for in-depth understanding of Group Policy
processing, is the Group Policy Processing Log. You can enable it by creating
a REG_DWORD value called UserEnvDebugLevel under HKLM\Software\
Microsoft\Windows NT\CurrentVersion\Winlogon and setting its value

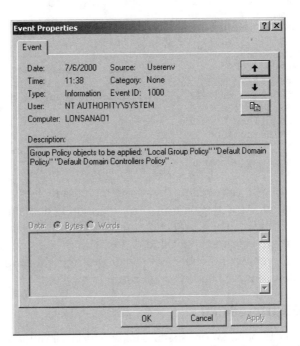

FIGURE 7.33 A sample event from an application log after turning on the Verbose flag

to 0x10002. After setting the value, a log file %Systemroot%\Debug\userenv.log is created.

TIP

Other possible values for UserEnvDebugLevel are 0x10001, which logs only errors and warnings, and 0x10000, which logs nothing.

IF YOU KNOW NT

In order to create a detailed NT 4 System Policy processing log for analysis or troubleshooting purposes, you'd have to use the Checked Build version of Windows NT 4 Workstation or Server.

The following is sample output for a Group Policy Processing Log:

```
USERENV(cc.300) 13:27:12:646 PingComputer:  First time:  10
USERENV(cc.300) 13:27:12:646 PingComputer:  Second time:  0
USERENV(cc.300) 13:27:12:646 PingComputer:  Fast link.  Exiting.
USERENV(cc.300) 13:27:12:656 ProcessGPOs:  User name is:  CN=LON-
SANAO1,OU=Domain Controllers,DC=sanao,DC=com, Domain name is:  SANAO
USERENV(cc.300) 13:27:12:666 ProcessGPOs: Domain controller is:
\\LONsanao1.sanao.com  Domain DN is sanao.com
USERENV(cc.300) 13:27:12:676 ProcessGPOs: Calling GetGPOInfo for
normal policy mode
USERENV(cc.300) 13:27:12:676 GetGPOInfo:
*******************************
USERENV(cc.300) 13:27:12:676 GetGPOInfo:  Entering...
USERENV(cc.300) 13:27:12:736 GetGPOInfo:  Server connection
established.
USERENV(cc.300) 13:27:12:756 GetGPOInfo:  Bound successfully.
USERENV(cc.300) 13:27:12:766 SearchDSObject:  Searching <OU=Domain
Controllers,DC=sanao,DC=com>
USERENV(cc.300) 13:27:12:766 SearchDSObject:  Found GPO(s):
<[LDAP://CN={6AC1786C-016F-11D2-945F-00C04fB984F9},CN=Policies,
CN=System,DC=sanao,DC=com;0]>
```

As you can see, the first thing the engine does is check the speed of the connection. Next the name of the computer, domain controller, and domain are determined. Then, an LDAP query can be done against the domain controller in order to find the applicable GPOs. The processing continues by checking if the GPO version numbers have changed and then determining which client-side extensions are needed to interpret the policies.

DETAILED LOGGING

You can obtain more specific information for different Group Policy categories by enabling the logging in the registry. Table 7.11 lists the most common settings.

TABLE 7.11 Registry Values for Starting Detailed Logging

Key	Value*	Type	Data	Log File	Purpose
HKLM\Software\ Microsoft\ Windows NT\ CurrentVersion\ Winlogon	GPEdit-DebugLevel	REG_DWORD	0x10002	%windir%\ debug\ usermode\ gpedit.log	Troubleshooting GPO editing
HKLM\Software\ Microsoft\ Windows NT\ CurrentVersion\ Winlogon	GPText-DebugLevel	REG_DWORD	0x1002	%windir%\ debug\ usermode\ gptext.log	Troubleshooting GPO Administrative Template behavior
HKLM\Software\ Microsoft\ Windows NT\ CurrentVersion\ Diagnostics	Fdeploy-DebugLevel	REG_DWORD	0x0f	%windir%\ debug\ usermode\ fdeploy.log	Troubleshooting folder redirection
HKLM\Software\ Microsoft\ WindowsNT\ CurrentVersion\ Winlogon\ GpExtensions\ {827d319e-6eac-11d2-a4ea-00c04f79f83a}\	Extension-DebugLevel	REG_DWORD	0x2	%windir%\ security\ logs\ winlogon.log	Troubleshooting security CSE
HKEY_LOCAL_ MACHINE\ logging SOFTWARE\ Microsoft\ Windows NT\ CurrentVersion\ Diagnostics	Appmgmt-debuglevel	REG_DWORD	0000009b	%windir%\ %\debug\ usermode\ appmgmt.log	Detailed software installation
HKEY_LOCAL_ MACHINE\ SOFTWARE\ Policies\ Microsoft\ Windows\ Installer	Debug Logging	REG_DWORD REG_STRING	00000003 "voice-warmup"	%windir%\ temp\ MSI*.log %temp%\ MSI*.log	Windows Installer troubleshooting

*All Values are one word; hyphens are added to indicate this.

Resource Kit Tools for Group Policy

Both the Windows 2000 Server and Professional Resource Kits include two tools for analyzing and troubleshooting Group Policy–related issues: Group Policy Results and Group Policy Verification Tool. You can find them in the Network Management Tool category. A third tool, Group Policy Migration, helps you to migrate NT 4 System Policy settings into Group Policy. It is located in the Deployment Tools category.

TIP	You can also find some of these tools at `http://www.microsoft.com/ windows2000/techinfo/reskit/tools/default.asp`

GROUP POLICY RESULTS

Group Policy Results (gpresult.exe) is a client-side analysis and troubleshooting tool that you can use to find, for example, the source of a client's Group Policy settings. Here is sample output of this tool:

```
Microsoft (R) Windows (R) 2000 Operating System Group Policy Result
tool
Copyright (C) Microsoft Corp. 1981-1999
Created on 9/7/2001 at 1:31:01 PM
Operating System Information:
Operating System Type:          Server
Operating System Version:  5.0.2195.Service Pack 2
Terminal Server Mode:           None
###########################################################
   User Group Policy results for:
   CN=Jill,OU=Users,OU=MFG,DC=sanao,DC=com
   Domain Name:          SANAO
   Domain Type:          Windows 2000
   Site Name:          LON
   Roaming profile:    (None)
   Local profile:      C:\Documents and Settings\Jill
   The user is a member of the following security groups:
        SANAO\Domain Users
        SANAO\Assistants
        \Everyone
        BUILTIN\Users
        \LOCAL
        NT AUTHORITY\INTERACTIVE
        NT AUTHORITY\Authenticated Users
###########################################################
Last time Group Policy was applied: 9/7/2001 at 1:30:34 PM
Group Policy was applied from: LonSanao1.sanao.com
===========================================================
The user received "Registry" settings from these GPOs:
        GPO4
        GPO5
```

```
        GPO7
        GPO3
##############################################################
   Computer Group Policy results for:
   CN=LONSANAO10,OU=Servers,OU=MFG,DC=sanao,DC=com
   Domain Name:           SANAO
   Domain Type:           Windows 2000
   Site Name:         LON
   The computer is a member of the following security groups:
        BUILTIN\Administrators
        \Everyone
        BUILTIN\Users
        SANAO\LONSANAO10$
        SANAO\Domain Computers
        NT AUTHORITY\NETWORK
        NT AUTHORITY\Authenticated Users
##############################################################
Last time Group Policy was applied: 9/7/ 2001 at 11:57:04 AM
Group Policy was applied from: lonsanao1.sanao.com
==============================================================
The computer received "Registry" settings from these GPOs:
        Local Group Policy
        GPO6
==============================================================
The computer received "EFS recovery" settings from these GPOs:

        Local Group Policy
```

The previous sample was run with no parameters. You can use /v for more detailed information and /s to see even the hex registry values. You can find further explanation of the output in the Resource Kit Help under "Interpreting GPResult Output."

NOTE   Group Policy results do not process the local GPO. You must take this into consideration when you try to determine the effective policy settings.

GROUP POLICY VERIFICATION TOOL

Group Policy Verification Tool (gpotool.exe) is a server-side troubleshooting tool. You can use it to determine if the Group Policy components GPC and GPT are synchronized in a specific domain controller and among the domain controllers in the domain. The most valuable information the tool provides is an indication of whether all GPOs are synchronized. When everything has gone smoothly, the last line of the output is "Policies OK," as in the following sample:

```
C:\>gpotool
Validating DCs...
Available DCs:
```

```
BosSanao1.sanao.com
BosSanao2.sanao.com
Searching for policies...
Found 2 policies
===============================================================
Policy {31B2F340-016D-11D2-945F-00C04FB984F9}
Policy OK
===============================================================
Policy {6AC1786C-016F-11D2-945F-00C04FB984F9}
Policy OK

Policies OK

C:\>
```

In the preceding example, there were two domain controllers and only the default policies (Default Domain Policy and Default Domain Controllers Policy) existed. In the next example, we add one GPO called Sanao General GPO with one computer setting. The output of the gpotool command is as follows:

```
C:\>gpotool
Validating DCs...
Available DCs:
BosSanao1.sanao.com
BosSanao2.sanao.com
Searching for policies...
Found 3 policies
===============================================================
Policy {31B2F340-016D-11D2-945F-00C04FB984F9}
Policy OK
===============================================================
Policy {6AC1786C-016F-11D2-945F-00C04FB984F9}
Policy OK
===============================================================
Policy {6FD83A76-4678-4595-ABE6-90B3B96CCF2F}
ADsGetObject(LDAP://BosSanao2.sanao.com/CN={6FD83A76-4678-4595-
ABE6-90B3B96CCF2F},CN=policies,CN=system,DC=sanao,DC=com) returned
0x80072030, retry...
Error: ADsGetObject(LDAP://BosSanao2.sanao.com/CN={6FD83A76-4678-4595-
ABE6-90B3B96CCF2F},CN=policies,CN=system,DC=sanao,DC=com) failed with
0x80072030
Details:
-------------------------------------------------------------
DC: BosSanao1.sanao.com
Friendly name: Sanao General GPO
Created: 5/27/2001 6:09:42 AM
Changed: 5/27/2001 6:10:43 AM
DS version:     0(user) 1(machine)
Sysvol version: 0(user) 1(machine)
Flags: 0
User extensions: not found
```

```
Machine extensions: [{35378EAC-683F-11D2-A89A-00C04FBBCFA2}
{0F6B957D-509E-11D1-A 7CC-0000F87571E3}]
Functionality version: 2
------------------------------------------------------------
------------------------------------------------------------
DC: BosSanao2.sanao.com
Friendly name: (null)
Created: (null)
Changed: (null)
DS version: (null)
Sysvol version: (null)
Flags: (null)
User extensions: (null)
Machine extensions: (null)
Functionality version: (null)
------------------------------------------------------------

Errors found

C:\>
```

In the preceding example, the GPO had not yet replicated to domain controller BosSanao2. Thus, there was an error because the GPO did yet not exist on that domain controller. This can be interpreted from all fields having a NULL value.

As you may have noticed, gpotool only expands those GPOs that have errors. If you want to also analyze the processing and the contents of the GPOs with no errors, you can use the /verbose switch.

REPLICATION MONITOR

Replication Monitor is part of the Windows 2000 Support Tools. It has many capabilities for advanced analysis of replication issues. If you want to analyze GPOs on a domain controller within your Active Directory forest with this tool, you right-click the domain controller and select Show Group Policy Object Status from the context menu. Figure 7.34 displays sample output for this option. The column Version shows the GPC version and the column SysVol version shows the version of GPT. If they are not in sync for any GPO, a check mark is displayed in the Sync Status column.

GROUP POLICY MIGRATION

Because the location of the System Policy settings in the registry differs between Windows NT 4 and Windows 2000, a tool, gpolmig.exe, was created to enable the migration of the settings from NT 4 System Policy files (ntconfig.pol) into the Windows 2000 GPO structure.

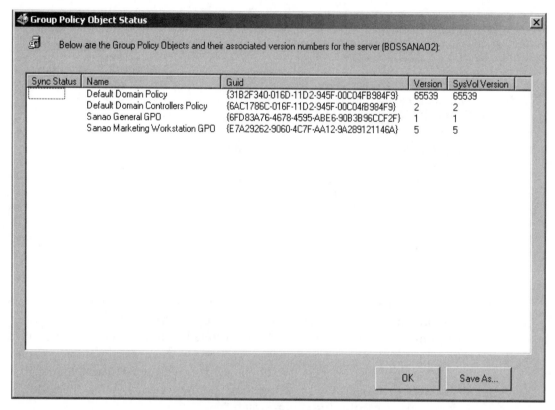

FIGURE 7.34 You can use Replication Monitor to display Group Policy object status.

GROUP POLICY REFERENCE

The Windows 2000 Resource Kit Group Policy Reference (gp.chm) is an online Help file that contains all the same information as the Explain tabs for the Administrative Templates. In addition, the Reference contains hyperlinks and explanations for the security settings that are not available through the Group Policy dialog boxes.

FAZAM 2000 RFV

The Windows 2000 Server Resource Kit Supplement 1 contains a third-party product called FAZAM 2000 RFV (Reduced Functionality Version). You can use this tool to analyze and report on Group Policies. In addition, it provides the capability to back up GPOs. However, most of the valuable functionality has been removed from this free version, and the full version is only available at http://www. fullarmor.com/.

Group Policy Scenarios

Group Policy Scenarios is a tool that you can download from Microsoft Web site (`http://www.microsoft.com/windows2000/techinfo/howitworks/ management/grouppolicy.asp`). It includes six usage scenarios, each with supporting GPOs. It also includes various files, of which two command batch files, loadpol.bat and savepol.bat, are the most interesting. Although they are not supported for transferring GPOs from one domain to another, based on our experiments they work just fine. At the same time, these two tools can be used to back up GPOs.

In addition to over 70 pages of documentation, settings for each scenario have been defined in a Microsoft Excel spreadsheet file. Although there are small errors in the settings, you could use one of these spreadsheets as a template for documenting your own GPOs.

ADVANCED TOPICS

In this last section, we discuss some topics that might be good for you to know, especially when you're troubleshooting or if you want to know Group Policy in more detail. First we present Group Policy–related registry settings that you can define centrally with Group Policy Administrative Templates. We also list the client-side extensions for Group Policy as well as registry values that they use, Group Policy History and Default permissions for GPOs. Last, we present the slow link detection algorithm.

Registry-Based Settings for Group Policy Processing

In order to centrally manage Group Policy processing, there are 16 Group Policy–related registry settings for computer objects and 6 for user objects. You can locate the settings for both Computer and User Configurations in any GPO under Administrative Templates, System, Group Policy. Table 7.12 and Table 7.13 list each setting along with its purpose.

Client-Side Extensions

Client-side extensions (CSEs) are the components that actually process the Group Policy settings defined in the local GPO or in GPOs stored in the Active Directory. These CSEs are registered in the registry in `HKEY_LOCAL_MACHINE \SOFTWARE\ Microsoft\Windows NT\CurrentVersion\Winlogon\GPExtensions`. Table 7.14 lists the GUIDs for different client-side extensions along with the names of

TABLE 7.12 Registry-Based Settings for Group Policy Processing for Computer Objects

Setting	Is Used to Define	Note
Disable background refresh of Group Policy	Whether Group Policies can refresh periodically while someone is logged on	
Apply Group Policy for computers asynchronously during start-up	Whether the logon dialog box is displayed before computer policies are completely processed	
Apply Group Policy for users asynchronously during start-up	Whether the user sees and can use the shell (Windows Explorer by default) before user policies are completely processed	
Group Policy refresh interval for computers	How often the computer policies are refreshed in the background for Windows 2000 workstations and servers that are not domain controllers	Default 90 minutes plus offset of 0 to 30 minutes. Default also applies if this policy is disabled. Available range for the interval is 0 to 64,800 minutes (45 days). If set to 0, the Group Policies are refreshed every 7 seconds. Available range for the offset is 0 to 1,440 minutes (24 hours).
Group Policy refresh interval for domain controllers	How often the computer policies are refreshed on the background for Windows 2000 domain controllers	Default 5 minutes. Default also applies if this policy is disabled. Available range for the interval is 0 to 64,800 minutes (45 days). If set to 0, the Group Policies are refreshed every 7 seconds. Available range for the offset is 0 to 1,440 minutes (24 hours).
User Group Policy loopback processing mode	Whether user policies based on the location of the computer object are in effect	Options: Replace and Merge.
Group Policy slow link detection	Threshold for determining if the connection to the authenticating domain controller is slow	Default 500Kbps; enabled with value 0 disables slow link detection (i.e., all connections are considered fast). Available range is 0 to 4,294,967,196Kbps.

(continued)

TABLE 7.12 (*continued*)

Setting	Is Used to Define	Note
Registry policy processing	When the policies changing registry settings are processed	Options for background and unchanged GPO.
Internet Explorer Maintenance policy processing	When the Internet Explorer Maintenance policies are processed	Options for slow link, background, and unchanged GPO.
Software Installation policy processing	When software is deployed	Options for slow link and unchanged GPO.
Folder Redirection policy processing	When folder redirection policies are processed	Options for slow link and unchanged GPO.
Scripts policy processing	When any Group Policy scripts are processed	Options for slow link, background, and unchanged GPO.
Security policy processing	When security policies are processed	Options for background and unchanged GPO.
IP Security policy processing	When any Group Policy IPSec policies are processed	Options for slow link, background, and unchanged GPO.
EFS recovery policy processing	When EFS policies are processed	Options for slow link, background, and unchanged GPO.
Disk Quota policy processing	When disk quota policies are processed	Options for slow link, background, and unchanged GPO.

the dynamic link library (DLL) files. The only Group Policy component that does not have a client-side extension is the Remote Installation Services (RIS). This is because the purpose of the RIS is to install the operating system, which obviously cannot have any DLLs before the installation is complete.

In Figure 7.35, notice that some of the registry settings that we introduced in the previous section are also defined per CSE.

Registry Settings for Group Policy History

As a result of Group Policy processing, certain settings for GPOs are written to the client's registry, forming what is called *Group Policy History.* These settings are

TABLE 7.13 Registry-Based Settings for Group Policy Processing for User Objects

Setting	Is Used to Define	Note
Group Policy refresh interval for users	How often the user policies are refreshed on the background	Default 90 minutes plus offset of 0 to 30 minutes. Default also applies if this policy is disabled. Available range for the interval is 0 to 64,800 minutes (45 days). If set to 0, the Group Policies are refreshed every 7 seconds. Available range for the offset is 0 to 1,440 minutes (24 hours).
Group Policy slow link detection	Threshold for determining if the connection to the authenticating domain controller is slow	Default 500Kbps; enabled with value 0 disables slow link detection (i.e., all connections are considered fast). Available range is 0 to 4,294,967,196Kbps.
Group Policy domain controller selection	Which domain controller the Group Policy snap-in focuses (i.e., on which DC the changes are actually made)	Options for PDC, same as Active Directory snap-ins and any domain controller.
Create new Group Policy object links disabled by default	Whether links are created disabled	You can enable them later after you have configured GPOs and tested them.
Enforce Show Policies Only	Whether the user can deselect Show Policies only in the Group Policy snap-in	Determines if preferences can be displayed and configured.
Disable automatic update of ADM files	Whether the system loads the most current .adm files from %SystemRoot%\inf	If enabled, you must manually update the .adm files if they are changed. You can achieve this through right-clicking Add/Remove Templates for Administrative Templates.

organized by the client-side extension that processed them. You can find them under `HKEY_LOCAL_MACHINE\Software\Microsoft\Windows\Current-Version\Group Policy\History` for GPOs applied to the computer, and `HKEY_CURRENT_USER\Software\Microsoft\Windows\CurrentVersion\Group Policy\History` for GPOs applied to the user. Under each of the

TABLE 7.14 Client-Side Extension GUIDs and DLLs

Client-Side Extension	GUID	DLL
Folder Redirection	25537BA6-77A8-11D2-9B6C-0000F8080861	Fdeploy.dll
Microsoft Disk Quota	3610EDA5-77EF-11D2-8DC5-00C04FA31A66	Dskquota.dll
Scripts	42B5FAAE-6536-11D2-AE5A-0000F87571E3	Gptext.dll
Security	827D319E-6EAC-11D2-A4EA-00C04F79F83A	Scecli.dll
EFS Recovery	B1BE8D72-6EAC-11D2-A4EA-00C04F79F83A	Scecli.dll
Application Management	c6dc5466-785a-11d2-84d0-00c04fb169f7	Appmgmts.dll
Internet Explorer Settings	A2E30F80-D7DE-11d2-BBDE-00C04F86AE3B	Iedkcs32.dll
Registry Settings	35378EAC-683F-11D2-A89A-00C04FBBCFA2	Userenv.dll
IP Security	e437bc1c-aa7d-11d2-a382-00c04f991e27	Gptext.dll

GUIDs for installed CSEs there is a key for each GPO applied. These are given numbers starting from zero and incremented by one. The larger the number, the later in the processing cycle this GPO was processed (i.e., its priority would be higher). Table 7.15 lists these values and their purposes.

Default Permissions for GPOs

By default, four security principals have all Group Policy–specific permissions for new Group Policy objects. They are Domain Admins, System, Creator Owner, and Enterprise Admins. In addition, the Authenticated Users group has Read permission to certain properties and can apply Group Policy permission to Group

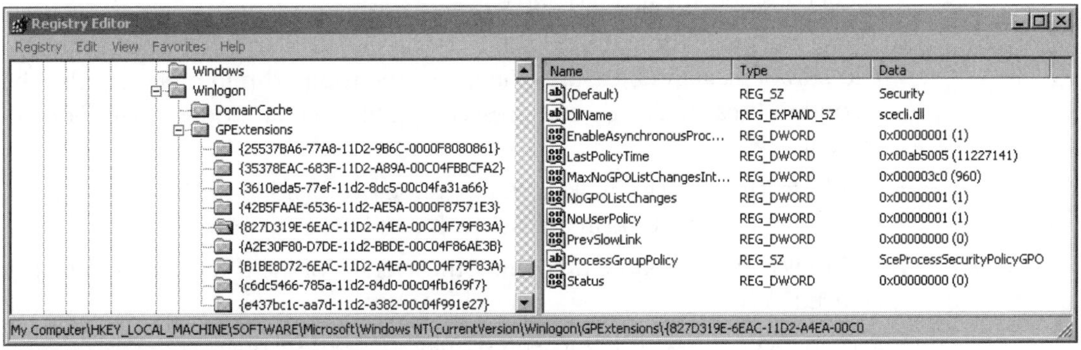

FIGURE 7.35 Client-side extensions are registered in the registry.

TABLE 7.15 Group Policy History Registry Values

Value	Purpose
DisplayName	Name displayed in the Active Directory administration tools.
DSPath	Distinguished Name path to the GPC. Not available for LGPO.
Extensions	List of CSEs required to process this GPO.
FileSysPath	Path of the GPT for Active Directory–based GPO; %SystemRoot%\system32\GroupPolicy for LGPO.
GPOLink	Indicates what type of container this GPO is linked to: 0=unlinked, 1=local, 2=site, 3=domain, 4=OU.
GPOName	GUID of the GPO stored in Active Directory; Local Group Policy for LGPO.
Link	Domain where this GPO resides; Local for LGPO.
Iparam	Used to perform various functions.
Options	Options for the GPO link, such as whether or not either section is disabled.
Version	Version number of the GPO that was last applied.

Policy object itself. Table 7.16 lists these permissions and Figure 7.36 illustrates the properties and permissions that Authenticated Users group has.

Slow Link Detection Algorithm

Active Directory uses the following algorithm to determine if a link is slow:

1. The client pings the authenticating domain controller with a 0-byte file and calculates Time1 for the round trip. If the time is less than 10 milliseconds, the client considers the link fast and exits.

2. The client pings the authenticating domain controller with an uncompressible 2KB of data and measures Time2 for the round trip in milliseconds. The algorithm uses an already compressed .jpg file so that modems cannot compress it.

3. DELTA = Time2 – Time1. This removes the overhead of headers and session setup. DELTA is the time in milliseconds that it takes to move 2KB.

4. DELTA is measured three times, and the average of the three values of DELTA is called AVG.

5. The connection speed Z, measured in kilobits per second (Kbps), is Z = 2 × (2KB) × (8 bits/byte) × (1,000 milliseconds/second) /AVG milliseconds.

TABLE 7.16 Default Permissions for GPOs

ACE	Object	Property	Group That Has the Permission (in Addition to Domain Admins, System, Creator Owner, and Enterprise Admins)
Apply Group Policy	X		Authenticated Users
Create groupPolicyContainer objects	X		
Delete groupPolicyContainer objects	X		
Create IntelliMirror Group Objects	X		
Create IntelliMirror Group Objects	X		
Create IntelliMirror Service Objects	X		
Delete IntelliMirror Service Objects	X		
Read All Properties		X	Authenticated Users
Write All Properties		X	
Read gPCFileSysPath		X	Authenticated Users
Write gPCFileSysPath		X	
Read gPCFunctionalityVersion		X	Authenticated Users
Write gPCFunctionalityVersion		X	
Read gPCMachineExtensionNames		X	Authenticated Users
Write gPCMachineExtensionNames		X	
Read gPCUserExtensionNames		X	Authenticated Users
Write gPCUserExtensionNames		X	

Because the 2KB of .jpg file has moved through each modem, Ethernet card, or other device in the loop once in each direction, we multiply the speed by a factor of 2 in order to determine the one-way bandwidth.

The system compares Z with either the default value (500Kbps) or the values defined in the policy (Administrative Templates, System, Group Policy, "Group Policy slow link detection"). If Z is lower, the speed is considered slow.

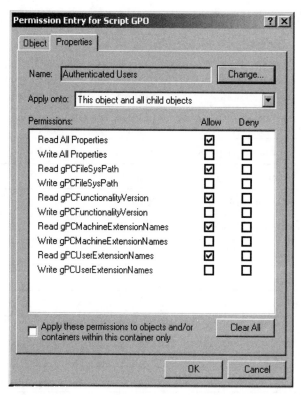

FIGURE 7.36 The Authenticated Users group has Read permission for all GPO properties.

CONCLUSION

Group Policy is the main management infrastructure for administering resources in Active Directory. It is complex, but after you have mastered it and deployed Group Policy in your Windows 2000 network, you'll surely reap the benefits.

However, as you can see from the rather cumbersome and sometimes complicated ways of performing tasks, there is still room for improvement. Also, in order to be a significant software deployment tool, diagnostics, timing, and reporting will surely improve over time. At the time of this writing, the launch of Windows XP is just around the corner. The Windows XP Professional includes Resultant Set of Policy functionality along with an improved Group Policy Results tool that is included with the operating system.

PART

III

ADVANCED SKILLS

Active Directory Schema

This chapter describes the Active Directory data model and the way in which the rules of the schema enforce it. You can approach this chapter with the following three purposes:

- To understand better how Active Directory works behind the scenes
- To enhance administration by learning, for example, which attributes are indexed to make searches faster
- To learn the technical background to extend the schema of your forest and to prepare you for the next chapter about schema extensions

  This chapter has the following sections:

- Overview of the Active Directory data model
- Schema in general
- Classes
- Attributes and syntaxes

OVERVIEW OF THE ACTIVE DIRECTORY DATA MODEL

Active Directory uses the LDAP data model, which is derived from the X.500 data model and, consequently, Active Directory implements many of X.500 features. However, Active Directory is not a full X.500 directory service.

In this first section we introduce the Active Directory data model, including most notably classes and attributes, as well as their relationship to the normal user and other objects that you see in your domains.

Classes, Objects, and Attributes

As you know, information in Active Directory is represented as objects, and there is an object for each user, computer, printer, and so on. Objects of the same type belong to the same *class,* so all user objects belong to the class user, all computer objects to the class computer, and all printer objects to the class printQueue.

You also know that information in an object is stored as values of various *properties,* which the corresponding class supports. For example, a user may have a phone number and home folder, whereas a printer might have knowledge about supported forms or print speed. Because this chapter is about the inner architecture of Active Directory, we want to use the slightly fancier term *attribute* instead of *property.* You can use these two words interchangeably.

The *schema* dictates which object classes and attributes a given forest supports. The *base schema* that ships with Windows 2000 supports 142 object classes and 863 attributes for those classes. The user class uses 207 attributes of the pool of 863. Active Directory implements most of the X.500 standard classes, but not quite all. The classes that it does not implement are alias, strongAuthenticationUser, and groupOfUniqueNames.

NOTE   The attribute pool is common to all classes. The description attribute, for example, may be used by several classes (actually, all classes use it).

Bringing in another fancy term, you could say that each object is an *instantiation* of the corresponding class. For example, the Jack Brown object is an instantiation of the user class. Just as the class contains a number of attributes, the instantiated object contains the values for those attributes. However, only some of the attributes for a class are *mandatory,* which means that they must contain a value (a *single-valued* attribute such as homePhone) or values (a *multivalued* attribute such as otherHomePhone). Most of the attributes for a given class are *optional;* that is, they may contain a value, but more often they don't. Figure 8.1 shows these relationships.

NOTE   You can see only a small subset of object types in the Users and Computers snap-in and only a subset of attributes for each object.

NOTE   To create user objects with the Users and Computers snap-in, you must enter the user principal name (i.e., user logon name), even though it is just an optional attribute behind the scenes.

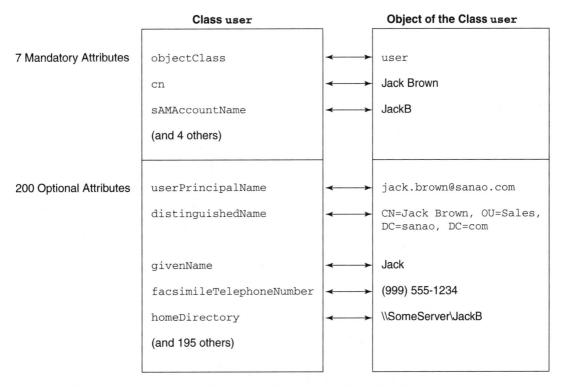

FIGURE 8.1 The class `user` defines 7 mandatory and 200 optional attributes for which any user object must *or* may contain values.

Each attribute has one of 23 *syntaxes,* such as `Integer` 14, `Unicode string` "abc", or `Generalized time` 04/26/2000 2:59:01 PM. We discuss syntaxes later in this chapter.

As you see in Figure 8.2, some of the classes (actually, most of them) are something other than the familiar users, groups, and computers.

Container and Leaf Objects

Active Directory objects of some classes are *container objects,* and the objects of the remaining classes are *leaf objects.* If you compare this to a file system, container objects correspond to folders and leaf objects correspond to files. We call these two types of classes *container classes* and *leaf classes.*

One obvious example of a container class is `organizationalUnit`. There are also many others, however, because a total of 56 classes of the base schema are container classes and 86 are leaf classes. Interestingly, `user` is also a container class; `user` objects may contain `nTFRSSubscriptions` and `classStore` objects.

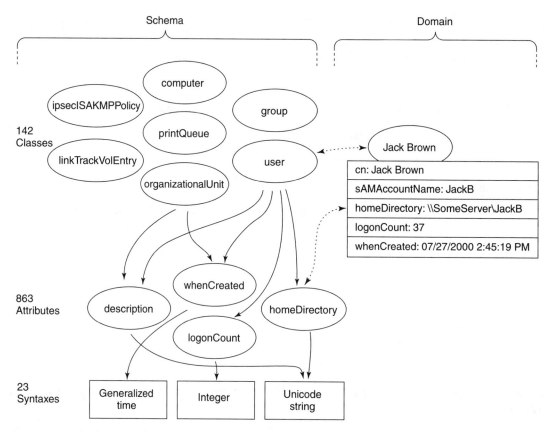

FIGURE 8.2 Each of the 142 classes uses a number of attributes, which in turn use a certain syntax.

NOTE "Container" can also mean a specific class—one of the 56 container classes is called `container`. Two examples of this class are `CN=Users` and `CN=Computers`, which you see with the Users and Computers snap-in under any domain.

Even though the base schema contains 86 leaf classes, those classes are not doomed to "eternal leafhood." You can modify the schema to make a leaf class a possible superior (i.e., a parent) to some other class. When you do so, a former leaf class (except for schema objects) becomes a container class.

One difference in our file system analogy is that in Active Directory both containers and leafs contain data, whereas in a file system files contain data, but folders don't.

NOTE Just as there is a class called `container`, one of the 86 leaf classes is called `leaf`. You can make also that class a container, so one of your container classes could be called `leaf`.

Indexing and the Global Catalog

An Active Directory database can contain thousands or even millions of objects. Therefore, we obviously need *indexing* to locate the right object or objects fast. Of the base schema, 64 attributes are indexed, examples being `givenName`, `sn` (Surname) and `birthLocation`. Searching and retrieving objects via indexed attributes is naturally much faster and efficient than using nonindexed attributes.

The *global catalog* helps in making local searches in a multidomain forest. One hundred thirty-eight attributes of the base schema are part of the global catalog, including `cn`, `userPrincipalName`, `givenName`, `sn` (Surname), and `printStaplingSupported`.

SCHEMA

In this section we explain the role of the schema, its location, and its inspection. We also explain briefly the topics of subschema subentry and schema cache.

Role of the Schema

The schema contains rules for object instantiation—that is, it dictates which objects a directory can contain, their relationships, and their possible content. (This is true for other directory services as well as Active Directory.) In other words, the schema governs the structure and content of Active Directory with structure and content rules. Table 8.1 explains these uses of the schema.

Table 8.1 describes why the schema is necessary to maintain a directory. In addition, the schema contains information that helps to maintain the schema itself. This is described in Table 8.2. We explore the topics introduced in Table 8.1 and Table 8.2 in the later sections "Classes" and "Attributes and Syntaxes."

Location of the Schema

Because everything in Active Directory is stored in objects, the schema is implemented as a number of objects. There is one object for each class in the schema (`classSchema` objects) and one for each attribute (`attributeSchema` objects).

TABLE 8.1 Uses of the Schema

Category	Description
Structure rules	• Possible parent classes for each class (i.e., under what classes of objects each object can exist). For example, a user object may exist under the container types `organizationalUnit`, `domainDNS`, `builtinDomain`, `container`, and `lostAndFound`.
Content rules	• The mandatory and optional attributes for each object class.
	• For each attribute there is a certain syntax and value range, as well as the choice between single-value and multivalue.
Miscellaneous	• Which attributes are indexed and which are stored in the global catalog.
	• The default security descriptor, category, and hiding value for each new object.
	• The name type (i.e., the naming attribute) of a class: CN, OU, or DC.

TABLE 8.2 Inside Uses of the Schema

Category	Description
Naming and identification	• Various names and ID numbers for schema classes, attributes, and syntaxes
Schema class hierarchy	• Whether a class is *structural, abstract,* or *auxiliary*
	• The parent of a class in the inheritance chain
	• The auxiliary classes that give a class additional attributes
Protection	• Whether a class or attribute is *system only*
	• The security descriptor for a class or attribute

However, there are no objects for the syntaxes; they are hard-coded into Active Directory. This means that classes and attributes can be created and modified, but syntaxes cannot.

NOTE   A directory service vendor could implement the schema as a long text file. Microsoft chose to implement the Active Directory schema as Active Directory objects. This enables administrators and applications to query the schema contents and add or modify classes and attributes using the same object manipulation techniques as would be used with any Active Directory objects.

Consequently, the location of the schema is the location of the schema objects.

THE PHYSICAL LOCATION OF THE SCHEMA

As you learned in Chapter 5, every domain controller stores a full replica (or copy) of three partitions (or replication units): the schema, configuration, and domain partitions. Obviously, the schema (i.e., the schema objects) is physically located in the schema partition.

You also learned that the schema partition is replicated to every domain controller in a forest, so that all domain controllers contain identical information. Any changes to the schema would have to be initiated on the domain controller that holds the schema master role (as explained in Chapter 5).

Even though there are three separate partitions, their replicas in a given domain controller are stored in the same database table. That table resides in the Active Directory database file, which is called ntds.dit. The default location for the file is the folder C:\Winnt\NTDS.

There is another ntds.dit file located in C:\Winnt\System32. That file serves as the initial database file and it is copied to C:\Winnt\NTDS (or whatever location you choose) during the DCPromo process.

NOTE   You may also come up with a file schema.ini (in C:\Winnt\System32). Despite its name, it doesn't initialize the schema in any way. Instead, it contains the information for the initial objects in your tree—mostly for the domain and configuration partitions.

THE LOGICAL LOCATION OF THE SCHEMA

All the 1,005 schema objects (142 classes and 863 attributes) are located in the *Schema container.* That container is of class dMD (the letters stand for "directory management domain") and its distinguished name is CN=Schema, CN=Configuration, DC=*forest_root_domain*. Figure 8.3 shows the location of the schema container in the directory tree.

NOTE   Although there seems to be a CN=Configuration object under your root domain, you won't see it in the Users and Computers snap-in, even with Advanced Features turned on. That snap-in is meant to show contents of only domain partitions.

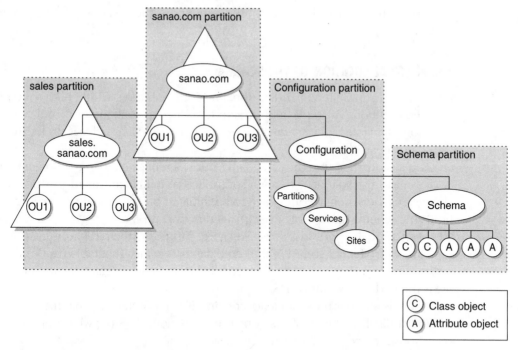

FIGURE 8.3 The schema container is logically under the configuration container, which in turn is under the forest root domain. Physically, however, the three are different partitions.

Inspecting the Schema with ADSI Edit

Now that you know that the schema is implemented as a number of objects and you know where to find them, we can start studying them in the user interface. The two main tools for the job are as follows:

- ADSI Edit, a general tool for viewing all the objects in Active Directory
- The Schema Manager snap-in, a specialized tool for viewing and managing the schema

We begin our discussion of these two tools with ADSI Edit. Because it is a general tool, it nicely shows you the general picture and the location of the schema objects, not just the schema contents.

NOTE   There are other tools that you can use to view the schema. For example, Support Tools contains LDP, which enables you to do various LDAP operations—among others, to view the schema.

We mentioned previously that with the Users and Computers snap-in you see only part of the objects and only part of the attributes of each object. With ADSI Edit you see all the objects and all of their attributes.

ADSI Edit is part of Support Tools, which you have to install separately. Locate the folder Support\Tools on your Windows 2000 CD and run Setup.Exe. After the installation, you will find the tool by clicking the Start button and then selecting Programs, Windows 2000 Support Tools, Tools.

Figure 8.4 shows the screen that opens when you launch ADSI Edit. ADSI Edit shows container objects with yellow folder icons and leaf objects with white icons similar to the icons used for text documents in Windows Explorer. The left pane shows only container objects, and the right pane shows both container and leaf objects.

To familiarize yourself with ADSI Edit, it's a good idea to first check the properties (or attributes) of one of your users before you start to explore the schema objects.

INSPECTING ATTRIBUTES OF CLASSES AND ATTRIBUTES

When you are ready to move to the schema objects, you can start inspecting their attributes. For example, you can check the attributes of the user class schema object (see Figure 8.5).

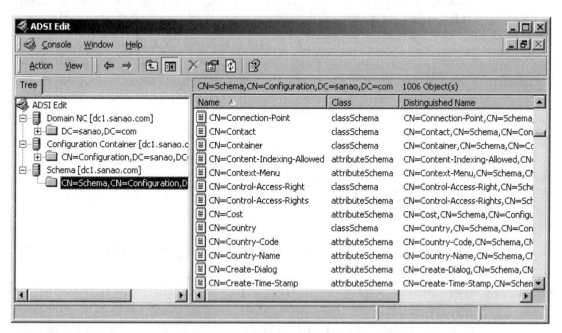

FIGURE 8.4 When you first start ADSI Edit, it shows three partitions (aka naming contexts). Under the Schema container you can see all the class and attribute objects.

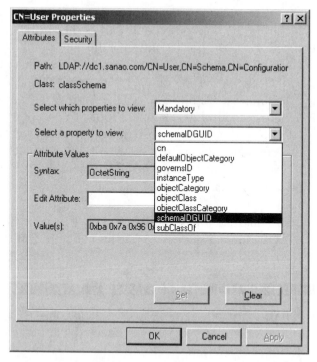

FIGURE 8.5 When you select Properties in the context menu of any object, ADSI Edit opens a dialog box that enables you to browse all the attributes of that object. From the first drop-down list, you can choose Mandatory, or Optional, or Both.

WARNING   ADSI Edit enables you to change the attribute values. When you study schema objects, be sure to click Cancel at the end. Do not click OK or Apply.

Note that because all objects contain attributes, `classSchema` and `attributeSchema` objects also contain attributes. For example, the object `CN=Jack Brown` has an attribute `givenName`, with the value "Jack." The schema contains the object `CN=Given-Name`, which in turn contains such attributes as `schemaIDGUID` and `attributeSyntax`.

We discuss the contents of `classSchema` objects a little later in the section "Classes" and `attributeSchema` objects in the section "Attributes and Syntaxes."

NOTE   ADSI Edit displays all the attributes of a class or attribute object, but only some of them are meaningful to the schema. Most of the attributes are the same ones that all objects in Active Directory have, such as `uSNChanged`, which helps to track replication.

TIP SchemaIDGUID and some other attributes use OctetString syntax, which is about the same as binary. If you want to see just the bytes without "0x"s, you can copy and paste the string to Notepad and then replace all "0x"s with nothing.

VARIOUS ATTRIBUTE NAMES

You may have noticed that each attribute has two slightly different names. Table 8.3 summarizes the two naming conventions together with the administrative tool name.

NOTE Unlike the example in Table 8.3, the three attribute names may be quite different, such as "Surname"—"sn"—"Last name" or "WWW-Page-Other"—"url"—"Web Page Address (Others)." This is the case especially with attributes that have long-established X.500 names.

Just as attributes do, classes have both common names and LDAP names.

Sometimes the common name and LDAP name are the same, but they refer to different attributes. Table 8.4 gives two examples of this (using four attributes).

The attribute names that you see in administrative snap-ins, such as Users and Computers, are not usually stored in the schema. Instead, you find them under the DisplaySpecifiers container, which in turn is under the Configuration container. In this container, first locate the object with your locale identifier (e.g., 409

TABLE 8.3 Various Attribute Names

Name	Example	Naming Convention	Where to Find
Common name	Facsimile-Telephone-Number	Each word starts with an uppercase letter; a dash occurs between words	The common name of the attributeSchema object.
LDAP name	facsimileTelephoneNumber	Name starts with a lowercase letter; each subsequent word starts with an uppercase letter; no dash between words	The lDAPDisplayName attribute of the attributeSchema object.
Name in admin tools	Fax Number	Any name that is descriptive and consistent	See the explanation in the text.

TABLE 8.4 Some Confusing Name Pairs

LDAP Name	Common Name
info	Comment
comment	User-Comment
street	Street-Address
streetAddress	Address

for "English (United States)"). Then open the properties for `CN=user-Display` and select the attribute `attributeDisplayNames`. It is a multivalued attribute that contains pairs of LDAP names and display names.

NOTE   The list of name pairs is not likely to contain display names for all attributes. For names that are not on the list, each attribute schema object has an attribute `adminDisplayName`, which the administrative tools can use instead.

NOTE   In reality, the Users and Computers snap-in doesn't use all the display specifier attributes (even though it is suggested here and in Microsoft's documentation). For example, most of the field names in user properties (such as Description or Office) are hard-coded in the tool instead of readable from the `attribute-DisplayNames` attribute.

We use mainly LDAP names in this book for three reasons:

- If you use ADSI scripts, you need LDAP names.
- If you use LDAP filters, you need LDAP names.
- The Schema Manager snap-in, Replication Monitor, and many other administration tools use LDAP names.

Inspecting the Schema with the Schema Manager Snap-In

The Schema Manager snap-in is made specifically for viewing and managing the schema. Because Microsoft doesn't make it available to casual users, you have to take some extra steps to access it.

WARNING   Just as with ADSI Edit, do not select OK or Apply in the Schema Manager snap-in dialog boxes. Always exit by clicking Cancel.

TIP   If you want to run the Schema Manager snap-in in a workstation, you must first install the Admin Pak. Locate the file AdminPak.MSI in the I386 folder of a Windows 2000 Server CD. When you double-click that file, it will install the Admin Pak.

1. In the Run window (click the Start button and select Run) or at the command prompt, enter the command regsvr32 schmmgmt.dll and press Enter. You should get a message indicating that the registration was successful.

2. Start MMC (Microsoft Management Console) by typing mmc and press Enter (again, either in the Run window or at the command prompt).

3. In the Console menu, select Add/Remove Snap-in. In the dialog box that opens, click Add.

4. From the list of snap-ins, select Active Directory Schema, click Add, and click Close. Click OK to close the original dialog box.

5. To save what you just did, in Console menu select Save As, select the name and location of the .msc file that you want, and click Save. Next time you want to start the snap-in, double-click the .msc file you just saved.

Now you are ready to take a look at your schema from a slightly different view than what you saw with ADSI Edit. Figure 8.6 and Figure 8.7 illustrate this view.

Using the Schema Manager snap-in, you can also see the mandatory and optional attributes for any class, which would be quite cumbersome with ADSI Edit. Note that this time we don't mean the attributes of a classSchema object, such as schemaIDGUID, but the attributes that the instances of the class may use, such as homeDirectory or givenName.

In addition to the lists in the screen shots in Figure 8.6 and Figure 8.7, you can open a properties dialog box for any class or attribute. We show those dialog boxes and discuss them in the later sections "Classes" and "Attributes and Syntaxes."

NOTE   You must select an attribute in the Attributes container to be able to open the properties dialog box for it. If you select the attribute from the list shown in Figure 8.7, you will see just one item, Help, when you right-click the attribute.

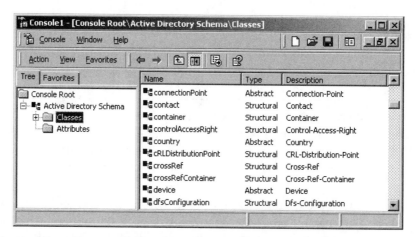

FIGURE 8.6 When you start the Schema Manager snap-in, it shows two containers: one for all the classes and one for attributes. Unlike with ADSI Edit, the objects are listed by their LDAP names.

Dumping the Schema to a Spreadsheet

Although the two graphical tools we just described are nice to use to explore the schema, they both have one problem: You can see the attributes for only one `classSchema` or `attributeSchema` object at a time.

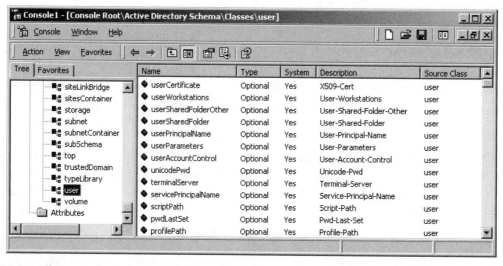

FIGURE 8.7 When you select a class in the left pane, the right pane shows the attributes for that class. Again, they are listed by their LDAP names. The text in the description column is usually the same as the common name you can see with ADSI Edit.

In this section we explain how you can dump all the information in your schema to a spreadsheet. It allows a broader view to the schema contents. Also, you can sort and filter the data, which gives you a better idea of how the various attributes are used. As you read on in this chapter, you can use the tables created here as a reference.

We use Excel in our explanation of how to dump the schema into a spreadsheet, but you can use other spreadsheet and database applications. First, you dump all your `classSchema` and `attributeSchema` objects into two text files, and then import those text files to Excel.

At a domain controller, you must type the following two commands at the command prompt (click the Start button and select Programs, Accessories, Command Prompt) and press Enter after each command:

```
C:\>csvde -f classes.txt -d cn=schema,cn=configuration,dc=sanao,dc=com
-r (objectCategory=classSchema)
C:\>csvde -f attributes.txt -d cn=schema,cn=configuration,dc=sanao,
dc=com -r (objectCategory=attributeSchema)
```

You should see output like the following for each command:

```
Connecting to "(null)"
Logging in as current user using SSPI
Exporting directory to file classes.txt
Searching for entries...
Writing out entries...........................
.............................................
Export Completed. Post-processing in progress...
142 entries exported
The command has completed successfully
```

Each of the two commands specifies an output file, a base distinguished name from which to dump, and an LDAP filter.

NOTE   You can also use the CSVDE tool on a workstation. See its online help for more information.

Next you must launch Excel and perform the following steps for both of your text files:

1. Select File, Open.

2. Select one of your newly created text files and click Open. A text import wizard should start up.

3. Specify that your data is delimited (instead of fixed width).

4. Specify that the delimiter is a comma.

5. Click Finish to complete the wizard. You should now have about 30 columns of data, one column for each attribute.

6. Click cell A2 to activate it. Choose Freeze Panes in the Window menu. Now your first row with the column labels (i.e., attribute names) stays visible, even if you scroll down the sheet.

7. Adjust the width of each column as you like. You can also double-click the right border of each column header (F, G, H, and so on) to autosize the columns. Note that some of the data values may be longer than the width of your screen. If you cannot resize a wide column by dragging its right border with a mouse, you can use the Format menu option Column, Width.

8. If they are present, remove the columns uSNChanged, uSNCreated, whenChanged, whenCreated, dITContentRules, extendedClassInfo, modifyTimeStamp, and extendedAttributeInfo. You are not interested in them because they don't define schema characteristics.

9. Open the Data menu and select Filter, AutoFilter. This turns each column header into a drop-down list filter. When you open a list, you see all the distinct values for that column (i.e., attributes). If you select a value, your sheet will be filtered to show only the lines with that value.

10. Save the sheet in XLS format.

Figure 8.8 shows an Excel sheet that results from the preceding steps. We haven't sorted the lines—you might want to sort them by the lDAPDisplayName column (using the Sort feature in the Data menu of Excel).

Subschema Subentry

Active Directory supports LDAPv3, which requires a directory service to expose its schema in a single subSchema object. Active Directory stores this object in the Schema container with the name CN=Aggregate.

The Aggregate object contains some multivalued attributes, which list the classes and attributes available in the schema. If you want to take a look, those attributes are as follows:

- objectClasses
- attributeTypes
- extendedClassInfo
- extendedAttributeInfo
- dITContentRules

In Chapter 10 and Chapter 11, we use the ADSI interface for directory access. When you specify a path such as LDAP://sanao.com/schema for ADSI, or just

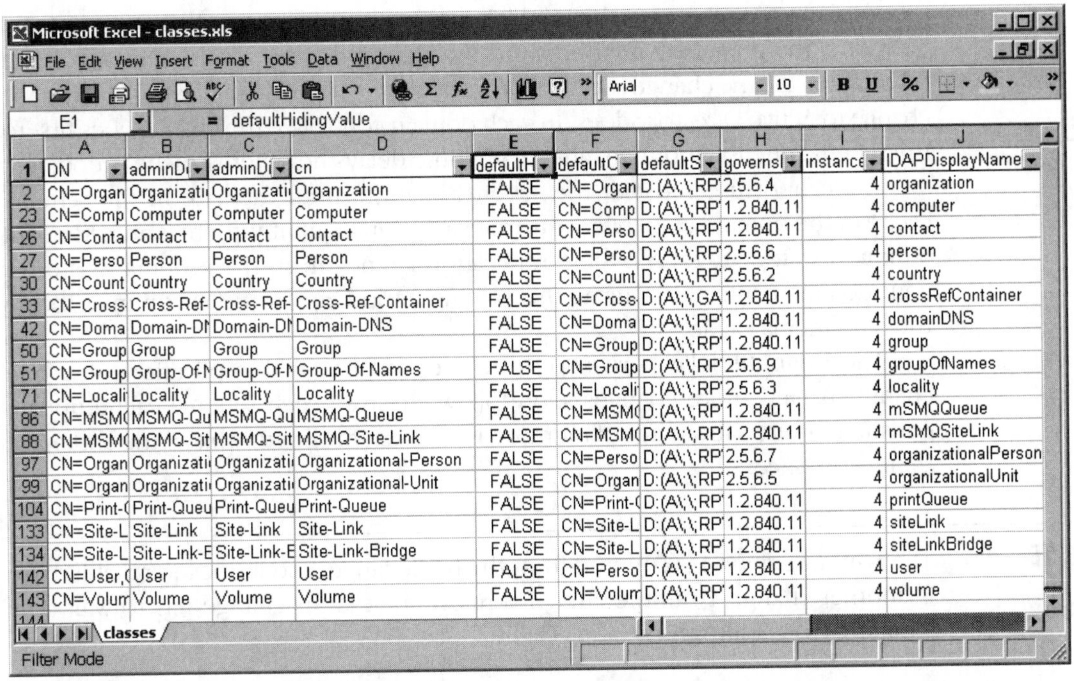
Microsoft Excel - classes.xls

E1 = defaultHidingValue

	DN	adminD	adminDi	cn	defaultH	defaultC	defaultS	governsI	instance	lDAPDisplayName
2	CN=Organ	Organizati	Organizati	Organization	FALSE	CN=Organ	D:(A\;\;RP	2.5.6.4	4	organization
23	CN=Comp	Computer	Computer	Computer	FALSE	CN=Comp	D:(A\;\;RP	1.2.840.11	4	computer
26	CN=Conta	Contact	Contact	Contact	FALSE	CN=Perso	D:(A\;\;RP	1.2.840.11	4	contact
27	CN=Perso	Person	Person	Person	FALSE	CN=Perso	D:(A\;\;RP	2.5.6.6	4	person
30	CN=Count	Country	Country	Country	FALSE	CN=Count	D:(A\;\;RP	2.5.6.2	4	country
33	CN=Cross	Cross-Ref-	Cross-Ref-	Cross-Ref-Container	FALSE	CN=Cross	D:(A\;\;GA	1.2.840.11	4	crossRefContainer
42	CN=Doma	Domain-DI	Domain-DI	Domain-DNS	FALSE	CN=Doma	D:(A\;\;RP	1.2.840.11	4	domainDNS
50	CN=Group	Group	Group	Group	FALSE	CN=Group	D:(A\;\;RP	1.2.840.11	4	group
51	CN=Group	Group-Of-N	Group-Of-N	Group-Of-Names	FALSE	CN=Group	D:(A\;\;RP	2.5.6.9	4	groupOfNames
71	CN=Locali	Locality	Locality	Locality	FALSE	CN=Locali	D:(A\;\;RP	2.5.6.3	4	locality
86	CN=MSM(	MSMQ-Qu	MSMQ-Qu	MSMQ-Queue	FALSE	CN=MSM(	D:(A\;\;RP	1.2.840.11	4	mSMQQueue
88	CN=MSM(	MSMQ-Sit	MSMQ-Sit	MSMQ-Site-Link	FALSE	CN=MSM(	D:(A\;\;RP	1.2.840.11	4	mSMQSiteLink
97	CN=Organ	Organizati	Organizati	Organizational-Person	FALSE	CN=Perso	D:(A\;\;RP	2.5.6.7	4	organizationalPerson
99	CN=Organ	Organizati	Organizati	Organizational-Unit	FALSE	CN=Organ	D:(A\;\;RP	2.5.6.5	4	organizationalUnit
104	CN=Print-(	Print-Queu	Print-Queu	Print-Queue	FALSE	CN=Print-(	D:(A\;\;RP	1.2.840.11	4	printQueue
133	CN=Site-L	Site-Link	Site-Link	Site-Link	FALSE	CN=Site-L	D:(A\;\;RP	1.2.840.11	4	siteLink
134	CN=Site-L	Site-Link-E	Site-Link-E	Site-Link-Bridge	FALSE	CN=Site-L	D:(A\;\;RP	1.2.840.11	4	siteLinkBridge
142	CN=User,(	User	User	User	FALSE	CN=Perso	D:(A\;\;RP	1.2.840.11	4	user
143	CN=Volum	Volume	Volume	Volume	FALSE	CN=Volum	D:(A\;\;RP	1.2.840.11	4	volume

classes

Filter Mode

FIGURE 8.8 After you have all the class definitions in Excel, you can filter in just the classes you specify—for example, classes that have `defaultHidingValue = False`.

`LDAP://schema`, ADSI will expose the `subSchema` object as one container with 142 classes, 863 attributes, and 33 syntaxes under it. The properties for these "virtual objects" are more limited than those with the real Schema container, but they have some advantages for scripting.

NOTE Active Directory supports 23 syntaxes, as discussed later in this chapter. The ADSI interface is using 33 syntaxes because it must support other environments also—most notably, NetWare. The ADSI syntaxes are listed in Chapter 10.

Schema Cache

Because the schema guards the structure and content of Active Directory objects, it is needed every time any object (such as the user Jack Brown) is added or modified. Accessing the schema from the ntds.dit file would be too slow; therefore, every domain controller holds a copy of the schema in RAM. This copy is called the *schema cache*.

Internally the schema cache is not an identical copy of the bytes on disk; it is structured a little differently for easy and fast access.

Naturally the schema cache is built based on the information in the disk version each time the domain controller starts. If a change is made to the schema on the schema master, the change starts to replicate to other domain controllers, just as any change to Active Directory does. In each domain controller, the change goes first to the schema on disk and then, after a 5-minute delay, the schema cache is updated.

You cannot use most of the schema changes until they are in the schema cache of the domain controller you are using. Consequently, there is an additional 5-minute wait after the possible replication latency from the schema master to your domain controller. During this waiting period, applications continue to use the old schema cache.

The 5-minute delay here is for the same reason as with replication. After one change, usually more changes soon follow. Because each schema cache update consumes quite a few bytes of memory, it is more efficient to wait a little and make them all at once.

NOTE   The 5-minute period is counted from the first change, and it doesn't reset if there is another change 1 minute later. Therefore, that latter change has to wait only 4 minutes to get into the schema cache.

The extra memory consumption in schema reload is due to the fact that when a new schema version is reloaded in cache, the old schema cache stays in memory for all the threads that were already running. Once all the old threads have exited, the older schema cache copy is released from memory. This also means that if you test schema changes, you probably need to restart your admin tools, so that they start to use the new schema cache and therefore can see the changes.

TRIGGERING THE SCHEMA CACHE UPDATE

If 5 minutes is too long for you to wait, you can trigger the cache update immediately with the Schema Manager snap-in. In the left pane, right-click the node Active Directory Schema and select Reload the Schema. There is also a programmatic way to trigger the schema cache update. You must write the value 1 to an attribute schemaUpdateNow residing in a special rootDSE virtual object. We cover this in later chapters:

- Chapter 9 contains an example of adding a new attribute and class to the schema and triggering the update using the LDIFDE tool.
- Chapter 10 describes the rootDSE object in more detail.
- Chapter 11 contains an example of adding a new attribute and class to the schema and triggering the update using the ADSI interface in a script.

Before we conclude our discussion about the schema in general, we'll mention the constructed attributes.

Constructed Attributes

Not all attributes for an object are stored in the schema on disk. Instead, they are built from other attributes. Twenty-two of the 863 attributes in the base schema are constructed.

The 22 constructed attributes are as follows:

```
primaryGroupToken                extendedClassInfo
allowedAttributes                fromEntry
allowedAttributesEffective       modifyTimeStamp
allowedChildClasses              objectClasses
allowedChildClassesEffective     parentGUID
aNR                              possibleInferiors
attributeTypes                   sDRightsEffective
canonicalName                    subSchemaSubEntry
createTimeStamp                  tokenGroups
dITContentRules                  tokenGroupsGlobalAndUniversal
extendedAttributeInfo            tokenGroupsNoGCAcceptable
```

CLASSES

In the overview section of this chapter we introduced classes, and in the "Schema" section we mentioned that there is a class schema object for each class. In this section we examine classes and their schema objects in more detail.

Each class is defined by the attributes of its schema object. This means that examining classes actually means examining those attributes. Each `classSchema` object may contain at most 95 attributes. However, remember that many of these attributes are not related to defining the schema, but instead are "normal" attributes for any object. Examples of these normal attributes are `wWWHomePage` and `uSNChanged`. Here we discuss 36 attributes and omit 59 normal "uninteresting" attributes.

NOTE   You could claim that some of the 36 attributes we address are also uninteresting. For example, they include 5 attributes that are not used at all. We include them so that you don't need to wonder what they are if you run into them with ADSI Edit or some other tool.

NOTE   We list a few numbers of attributes in the text and in Table 8.5. The exact numbers are not important; we mention them to give you an idea of how many different kinds of attributes there are.

Classes can inherit from other classes attributes their instances must and may contain. Of the 95 `classSchema` attributes, 22 are the class' own attributes and 73 are inherited from the `top` class. In the list of 36 attributes in Table 8.5, 22 are the class' own attributes and 14 are inherited attributes.

We have divided the 36 attributes into four categories. These categories resemble those listed in the "Role of the Schema" section earlier in this chapter (see Table 8.1 and Table 8.2).

- *Names and identifiers.* There are 14 of these attributes (plus 1 naming-type attribute). Fortunately, not all of them are used.
- *Structure and containment rules.* These 7 attributes define where in the tree each object may be created (or instantiated) and which attribute values it must and may contain.
- *Class inheritance.* A class may inherit containment from another class. The 4 attributes in this category define how this happens.
- *Miscellaneous.* The remaining 10 attributes provide some defaults, for example, to the objects that will be created to the corresponding class.

Table 8.5 lists the 36 attributes by their LDAP names. If the common name has no resemblance to the LDAP name, the common name appears in parentheses

TABLE 8.5 Attributes of a `classSchema` Object

Name	Type	Source Class	Base Schema Classes (142)	user Class Example
Names and Identifiers				
`lDAPDisplayName`	O	`classS.`	All values are unique	`user`
`cn` (Common-Name)	M	`classS.`	All values are unique	User
`adminDisplayName`	O	`top`	Same as cn	User
`name` (RDN)	O	`top`	Same as cn	User
`distinguishedName` (Obj-Dist-Name)	O	`top`	All values are unique	`CN=User, CN=Schema, CN=Configuration, DC=sanao, DC=com`

(continued)

TABLE 8.5 (*continued*)

Name	Type	Source Class	Base Schema Classes (142)	user Class Example
canonicalName	O	top	All values are unique	sanao.com/ Configuration/ Schema/User
displayName	O	top	Not used	—
displayNamePrintable	O	top	Not used	—
classDisplayName	O	classS.	Not used	—
adminDescription	O	top	Same as cn	User
description	O	top	Not used	—
governsID	M	classS.	125 are Microsoft IDs (1.2.840.113556), 17 are X.500 IDs (2.5)	1.2.840.113556.1.5.9
schemaIDGUID	M	classS.	All values are unique	ba7a96bf e60dd011 a28500aa 003049e2
objectGUID	O	top	All values are unique	4856468b 62963047 8c32fcfe 70f6ca9b
rDNAttID	O	classS.	134 x cn, 4 x dc, 1 x c, 1 x l, 1 x o, 1 x ou	cn

Structure and Containment Rules

Name	Type	Source Class	Base Schema Classes (142)	user Class Example
mustContain	O	classS.	All are <not set>	—
systemMustContain	O	classS.	51 are set; 91 are <not set>	—
mayContain	O	classS.	All are <not set>	—
systemMayContain	O	classS.	116 are set; 26 are <not set>	A long list of attributes
possSuperiors	O	classS.	All are <not set>	—
systemPossSuperiors	O	classS.	134 are set; 8 are <not set>	builtinDomain + organizationalUnit + domainDNS
possibleInferiors	O	top	56 are set (=container); 86 are not (=leaf)	nTFRSSubscriptions + classStore

(*continued*)

TABLE 8.5 Attributes of a `classSchema` Object (*continued*)

Name	Type	Source Class	Base Schema Classes (142)	user Class Example
Class Inheritance				
objectClassCategory	M	classS.	124 are structural; 14 are abstract; 4 are auxiliary; none are 88-classes	1 (=structural)
subClassOf	M	classS.	89 are top; 53 are others	organizationalPerson
auxiliaryClass	O	classS.	All are <not set>	—
systemAuxiliaryClass	O	classS.	7 are set, 135 are <not set>	securityPrincipal + mailRecipient
Miscellaneous				
nTSecurityDescriptor	M	top	All are set	A DACL, SACL, and so on
isDefunct	O	classS.	All are <not set>	—
defaultObject-Category	M	classS.	Almost all are same as the class distinguished name	CN=Person, CN=Schema, CN=Configuration, DC=sanao, DC=com
defaultHidingValue	O	classS.	123 are True; 19 are False	False
defaultSecurity-Descriptor	O	classS.	138 are set; 4 are <not set>	Almost a 1,000-character-long string, starting with D:(A;;RPWPCRCCDC
systemOnly	O	classS.	8 are True; 134 are False	False
systemFlags	O	top	140 are set; 2 are <not set>	16
objectClass	M	top	All are top+ classSchema	top + classSchema
objectCategory	M	top	All are CN=Class-Schema, CN=Schema, CN=Configuration, DC=sanao, DC=com	CN=Class-Schema, CN=Schema, CN=Configuration, DC=sanao, DC=com
schemaFlagsEx	O	classS.	Not used	—

(such as "`distinguishedName (Obj-Dist-Name)`"). The Type column indicates whether the attribute is mandatory or optional. The Source Class column indicates either `classSchema` or `top`, the latter meaning the attribute was inherited from the `top` class. The Base Schema Classes column gives a summary of the kind of values the 142 classes have for the attributes in the table. Finally, the `user` Class Example column lists the values for the `user` class.

In the remaining subsections, we examine each of the four categories.

Names and Identifiers

The various names and identifiers identify the classes by both people and Active Directory. This category of 15 attributes includes nine different names, two descriptions, and three identifiers. The fifteenth attribute (`rDNAttID`) is none of these, but we include it in this category because it is name-related.

Table 8.6 describes the 15 attributes. Fortunately, Active Directory doesn't use quite all of them, as indicated in the table. Consequently, we are left with "only" six different names and one description. Furthermore, `canonicalName`, `distinguishedName`, and RDN are redundant with `cn`, because you can derive them directly from `cn`. This leaves us with three "nonredundant" names (the first three in Table 8.6) and one description.

Object Identifiers

As you see in Table 8.6, one of the many identifiers for each class schema object is an *object identifier (OID)*. An OID consists of numbers that have dots in between them, such as 1.3.6.1.4.1.123123. The number is hierarchical, so the first number in an OID is the highest level of the tree.

Anyone who "owns" a certain OID can allocate new child OIDs to it. For example, if you have the *base OID* 1.2.3, you could allocate to it OIDs, such as 1.2.3.1, 1.2.3.77, and 1.2.3.77.4.3.2.1.

Just like IP addresses, OIDs are administered globally so that no two organizations in the world can have the same base OID. OIDs allow unique identification of all kinds of things—they are used to identify classes, attributes, and syntaxes in X.500 directories and variables in Simple Network Management Protocol (SNMP), among other things.

Microsoft uses the base OID 1.2.840.113556.1 in many Active Directory classes (and attributes). Table 8.7 describes the history of that OID.

NOTE   Not all class schema objects and attribute schema objects of the Active Directory base schema use the OIDs in Table 8.7. Some use OIDs defined in X.500 or some other source.

TABLE 8.6 Name and Identifier Attributes of a `classSchema` Object

Name	Syntax*	Multi-valued	Description	`user` Class Example
`lDAPDisplayName`	Unicode string	No	Name to identify the class in ADSI scripts, LDAP filters, many low-level admin tools, and internally with all LDAP access.	`user`
cn (Common-Name)	Unicode string	No	Actual name of the class schema object.	User
`adminDisplayName`	Unicode string	No	Name that admin tools can use as their display name if there isn't a name in the `Display-Specifiers` container. If `adminDisplayName` is also not specified, the system will use cn instead.	User
name (RDN)	Unicode string	No	Same as cn.	User
`distinguishedName` (Obj-Dist-Name)	Distinguished name	No	"cn with a path," identifies the location of the object (which is always the Schema container).	`CN=User, CN=...`
`canonicalName`	Unicode string	Yes	"cn with a path," but using a different format from `distinguishedName`.	`sanao.com/ Configuration/ Schema/User`
`displayName`	Unicode string	No	Not used.	—
`displayName-Printable`	Printable string	No	Not used.	—
`classDisplayName`	Unicode string	Yes	Not used.	—
`adminDescription`	Unicode string	No	Descriptive text for the class for admin tools.	User

(continued)

TABLE 8.6 (*continued*)

Name	Syntax*	Multi-valued	Description	user Class Example
description	Unicode string	Yes	Not used.	—
governsID	OID string	No	Object ID (OID) of the class (see the section, "Object Identifiers").	1.2.840.113556.1.5.9
schemaIDGUID	Octet string	No	128-bit unique GUID to identify the class.	ba7a96bf e60dd011 a28500aa 003049e2
objectGUID	Octet string	No	128-bit unique GUID to identify this class schema object (as well as any object in Active Directory).	4856468b 62963047 8c32fcfe 70f6ca9b
rDNAttID**	OID string	No	Whether the class prefix is cn=, ou=, dc=, c=, l=, or o=. This attribute also specifies whether the naming attribute (i.e., RDN) of the instances of this class is cn, ou, or some of the other choices just listed.	cn

*We discuss the syntaxes in the "Attributes and Syntaxes" section.

**The rDNAttID attribute choices c, l, and o are used by the country, locality, and organization classes, respectively. These classes exist in Active Directory, but are not used in any way. Consequently, you won't see them unless you install Exchange 2000 or some other software that would use them.

Another base OID that Microsoft owns is 1.3.6.1.4.1.311. Each numeric part has a name, so we can express this same base OID as iso.org.dod.internet. private.enterprise.microsoft. "Org" in the name indicates an "identified organization" that ISO acknowledges and "dod" indicates the U.S. Department of Defense. These "private enterprise numbers" are currently assigned by the Internet Corporation for Assigned Names and Numbers (ICANN, http://www. icann.org/). In addition to assigning enterprise OID numbers, ICANN coordinates the assignment of Internet domain names and IP address numbers. You can see the current list of assigned private enterprise numbers at ftp://ftp. isi.edu/in-notes/iana/assignments/enterprise-numbers.

TABLE 8.7 **Microsoft Active Directory OIDs**

Value	Owner
1	ISO, which issued 1.2 to ANSI
1.2	ANSI, which issued 1.2.840 to USA
1.2.840	USA, which issued 1.2.840.113556 to Microsoft
1.2.840.113556	Microsoft, which issued 1.2.840.113556.1 to Active Directory
1.2.840.113556.1	Active Directory, where class schema objects use either 1.2.840.113556.1.3 or 1.2.840.113556.1.5, and attribute schema objects use either 1.2.840.113556.1.2 or 1.2.840.113556.1.4.

Recall that we discussed the X.500 standards in Chapter 1. OIDs have similar roots, as they were first defined in ITU-T X.208, which corresponds to ISO/IEC 8824. However, X.208 has been superseded by the ITU-T recommendation X.680 (12/97): "Abstract Syntax Notation One (ASN.1): Specification of basic notation."

In addition to the OID notation, X.680 specifies the following base OIDs:

- 0: ITU-T assigned.

- 1: ISO assigned.

- 2: Joint ISO/ITU-T assigned. Active Directory contains some classes and attributes from X.500, and they use the base OIDs 2.5.6 and 2.5.4, respectively. There is also one "2.5.20" class ("X.500 schema object class") and six "2.5" attributes other than 2.5.4.

You can inspect various assigned OIDs at `http://www.alvestrand.no/domen/objectid/top.html`.

OBTAINING A BASE OID

If your organization needs to add classes or attributes to the schema, it must obtain a base OID. This need could rise from two situations.

- You need to modify the Active Directory schema of your organization.

- You sell applications to other organizations, and those applications need to modify the schema of the customer Active Directory.

There are three ways to get a base OID.

- Run the OIDGEN utility included in the Windows 2000 Resource Kit. It generates one base OID for classes and another for attributes. A resulting OID could be 1.2.840.113556.1.4.7000.233.28688.28684.8.96821.760998.1196228.1142349. You can use these OIDs in your tests, but for a production network you should register a base OID, as explained in the next two choices.

- Apply for a free private enterprise number from ICANN using the form at `http://www.isi.edu/cgi-bin/iana/enterprise.pl`. You should receive a number (1.3.6.1.4.1.something) in a few days by e-mail.

- Apply for a base OID from another issuing authority, perhaps for a fee. Many countries have a country-specific organization to issue OIDs. For organizations in United States, you can try ANSI and the Web page `http://web.ansi.org/public/services/reg_org.html`. (However, ANSI seems not to be very responsive. We sent e-mail to three people whose e-mail addresses appeared on the ANSI Web page regarding OIDs, but we have not received an answer from them in 6 months.)

Once you get the base OID, you should establish the policy regarding administration of the numbers in your organization, just like you probably have had to do with IP addresses. For example, you can dedicate the branch ".1" to new classes and ".2" to new attributes. Because OIDs are a general standard, you may also need the base OID for uses other than Active Directory.

Structure and Containment Rules

The main job of the schema is to establish the structure and content rules for Active Directory. This is done with the first six attributes described in Table 8.8. They consist of three pairs of a normal attribute and a system attribute (`must-Contain` + `systemMustContain`, `mayContain` + `systemMayContain`, and `possSuperiors` + `systemPossSuperiors`).

When creating classes, administrators can set all six attributes. For existing classes, they can change only the three normal attributes, not their system counterparts. The base schema uses only the three system attributes; it does not use their normal counterparts. This way, Active Directory can protect the base schema definitions. You cannot remove base schema attributes from any base schema class, nor can you remove possible parent classes.

NOTE   Even if an attribute is not a system attribute, it doesn't mean that you can change it freely. There are other restrictions to modifying the schema, which we discuss in the next chapter.

Because all seven attributes here are multivalued and use the `OID string` syntax, Table 8.8 does not include this information. Table 8.8 indicates if each

TABLE 8.8 Structure and Containment Attributes of a `classSchema` Object

Name	Constructed	System Only	Description	user Class Example
`mustContain`	No	No	Admin-changeable list of mandatory attributes for the instances of this class	—
`systemMust-Contain`	No	Yes	Same as previous, but only the Directory System Agent (DSA) can change the list after the class has been created	—
`mayContain`	No	No	Admin-changeable list of optional attributes for the instances of this class	—
`systemMay-Contain`	No	Yes	Same as previous, but only the DSA can change the list after the class has been created	A long list of attributes
`possSuperiors`	No	No	Admin-changeable list of possible parent containers for the instances of this class	—
`systemPoss-Superiors`	No	Yes	Same as previous, but only the DSA can change the list after the class has been created	`builtinDomain + organizational-Unit + domainDNS`
`possible-Inferiors`	Yes*	Yes	List of the classes that an instance of this class can contain instances of (i.e., possible child object types)	`nTFRS-Subscriptions + classStore`

*`PossibleInferiors` is a constructed attribute. It is calculated from the attributes `possSuperiors` and `systemPoss-Superiors` to kind of sum up the effect, but the value is not stored in the schema on disk.

attribute is constructed and if only the system, but not an administrator, can alter the value.

NOTE   If you compare the constructed `possibleInferiors` attribute to the attributes on which it is based, they seem not to match. The reason is that `possible-Inferiors` accounts for the effect of inheritance, as discussed in the next subsection.

Figure 8.9 illustrates the role of the structure and containment attributes. The `systemMayContain` attribute of a `classSchema` object lists some of the attributes (inheritance may list more) that the instances of that class may contain (i.e., optional attributes). `SystemPossSuperiors` specifies some of the possible parents that the instances may have, and `possibleInferiors` displays the list of possible children.

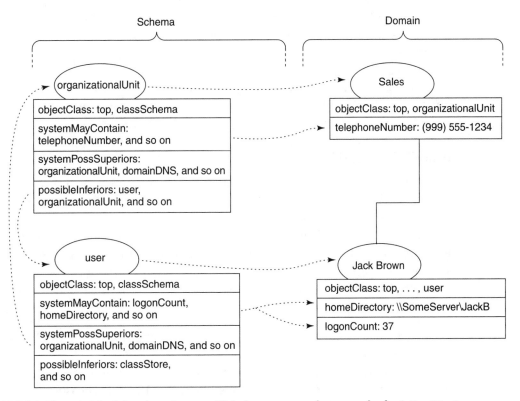

FIGURE 8.9 The main job of the schema is to establish the structure and content rules for Active Directory.

Four constructed attributes that are based on the attributes in Table 8.8 reside in the normal objects, such as users. Therefore, these attributes are not part of the schema, but still, you can study the schema by studying them.

- `AllowedChildClasses` and `allowedChildClassesEffective` both contain the same information as `possibleInferiors` (mentioned in Table 8.8), but they reside in normal objects, such as the user Jack Brown.

- `AllowedAttributes` and `allowedAttributesEffective` both contain a list of all mandatory and optional attributes of an object. For example, with Jack Brown, these two attributes both contain a list of 207 attributes, the number of mandatory and optional attributes of any `user` class object.

These four constructed attributes also take into account class inheritance.

Class Inheritance

A class gets most of its characteristics from the corresponding class schema object. However, a class inherits some features from several class schema objects, using *class inheritance*. We can also say that a class is *derived* from another class.

In this section we explain how, by means of inheritance, the list of possible superiors, mandatory attributes, and optional attributes are built from the information in several objects.

Class inheritance makes defining new classes easier, because they can build on existing classes. There is no need to list all possible superiors and attributes from the ground up. Table 8.9 lists the four attributes relevant to class inheritance.

USER CLASS EXAMPLE

Figure 8.10 illustrates the way the three lists (possible superiors, mandatory attributes, and optional attributes) are built up for the user class. We picked the user class as an example because it is by far the most intuitive.

The inheritance chain in Figure 8.10 (`top—person—organizational-Person—user`) has nothing to do with the hierarchy of the schema objects. They all exist as siblings in `CN=Schema, CN=Configuration, DC=sanao, DC=com`. Nor is there any connection with the normal directory hierarchy (domain—OU—user).

Figure 8.10 requires several explanatory comments.

- To save space, we abbreviated attribute names—`sMayContain` instead of `systemMayContain`, and so on.

- In addition to the system attributes shown in Figure 8.10, `mustContain`, `mayContain`, and `possSuperiors` also will inherit. This base schema example just doesn't happen to use them.

TABLE 8.9 Class Inheritance Attributes of a `classSchema` Object

Name	Syntax	Multi-valued	Description	user Class Example
objectClass-Category	Enumeration	No	1 = Structural 2 = Abstract 3 = Auxiliary 0 = 88-class	1 (=structural)
subClassOf	OID string	No	The class from which this class inherits containment and structure attributes. The parent is called a *superclass* and the child a *subclass*.	organizational-Person
auxiliaryClass	OID string	Yes	Admin-changeable list of auxiliary classes from which this class inherits containment attributes.	—
system-AuxiliaryClass	OID string	Yes	Same as previous, but only the Directory System Agent (DSA) can change the list.	securityPrincipal + mailRecipient

- `Top` has 69 optional attributes and `person` has 4 of its own. Still, the sum is 72 instead of 73 because there is 1 common attribute. For the same reason, the other sums may be a little less than you might expect.

- The two auxiliary classes `securityPrincipal` and `mailRecipient` are also subclasses of `top`. To keep the figure simple, and because this relationship has no effect, Figure 8.10 does not show this relationship.

- In Figure 8.10, only the `user` class happens to use auxiliary classes. Any superclass could also use auxiliary classes, in which case those attribute lists would also affect the subclasses.

- We show LDAP names (such as `mailRecipient`) as object names, even though to be precise the object names should be common names (such as Mail-Recipient). LDAP names appear because in this book we systematically call classes and attributes by their LDAP names.

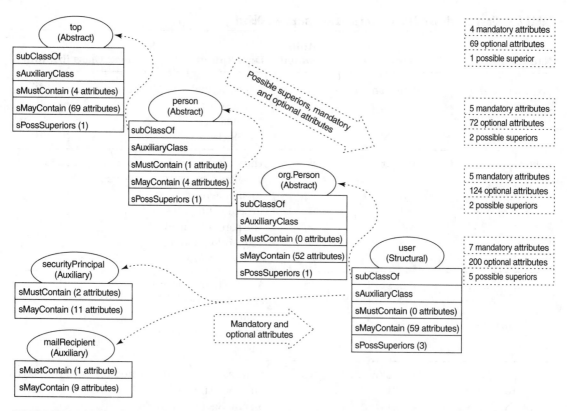

FIGURE 8.10 The list of possible superiors, mandatory attributes, and optional attributes for each class is the sum of its own list and the lists of all its superclasses. Also, auxiliary classes may add attributes to the list of mandatory and optional attributes.

CLASS CATEGORIES

Each class in Figure 8.10 was marked to be in one of three categories: *structural, abstract,* or *auxiliary.* Active Directory classes belong to four categories, as Table 8.10 describes. Figure 8.11 shows three categories of classes and their relationships as superclasses and subclasses.

Miscellaneous Characteristics of Classes

As the last set of class characteristics, we discuss ten miscellaneous attributes. Three of them provide defaults for objects to be created and four are quite general attributes that any Active Directory object will have. See Table 8.11 for details.

TABLE 8.10 Class Categories

Category	Number of Classes in the Base Schema	Can Be Instantiated*	Purpose and Comments
Structural	124	Yes	• Structural classes are the normal ones, because you can actually create objects for these classes. • Structural classes are derived from abstract or other structural classes and they can include auxiliary classes.
Abstract	14	No	• Abstract classes act as templates from which you can derive the actual structural classes or auxiliary and other abstract classes, if necessary.
Auxiliary	4	No	• Auxiliary classes just store lists of mandatory and optional attributes, which you can include in other classes. • Auxiliary class can be derived from another auxiliary class.
88-class	0	Yes	• The 1993 version of X.500 introduced the three previous categories. Any class created before that time belongs to a generic 88-class, which refers to the year 1988 when the previous version of the standard was approved. You shouldn't create any 88-class classes.

*Remember that *instantiation* means creating an object of some class. For example, when you create user Jack Brown, you just made an instance (or object) of the class user.

Table 8.11 introduces the following four concepts:

- showInAdvancedViewOnly
- Category 1 and 2 schema objects
- objectCategory
- Security Descriptor Definition Language (SDDL)

SHOWINADVANCEDVIEWONLY

All Active Directory objects have a showInAdvancedViewOnly attribute, which is derived from the top class. If the value of this attribute is set to True, an administrative snap-in can choose not to show the object in the user interface. If the attribute value is False or missing, an administrative snap-in should show the object.

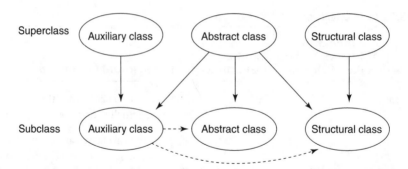

FIGURE 8.11 A class of any category can be inherited, or derived, from an abstract class. Only an auxiliary class can be inherited from another auxiliary class and only a structural class can be inherited from another structural class. In addition, the attribute lists in auxiliary classes can be used in abstract and structural classes (indicated by the dashed arrows).

Many objects are not interesting even to administrators, so setting this attribute helps to hide those objects. When you turn on Advanced Features in the Users and Computers snap-in, you make visible those objects that have the showInAdvanced-ViewOnly attribute set to True.

TABLE 8.11 Miscellaneous Attributes of a `classSchema` Object

Name	Syntax	Multi-valued	Description	user Class Example
nTSecurity-Descriptor	NT security descriptor	No	Security descriptor of the class schema object; allows Schema Admins to modify and other users to read schema objects.	A DACL, SACL, and so on
isDefunct	Boolean	No	If set to True, the class is disabled.	—
defaultObject-Category	Distinguished name	No	Default value for objectCategory attribute for each new instance of this class.	CN=Person, CN=...
defaultHiding-Value	Boolean	No	Default value for showInAdvanced-ViewOnly attribute for each new instance of this class.	False

(continued)

TABLE 8.11 (*continued*)

Name	Syntax	Multi-valued	Description	user Class Example
defaultSecurity-Descriptor	Unicode string	No	Default value for the security descriptor for each new instance of this class, using Security Descriptor Definition Language (SDDL). The program that will create the instance can also specify a security descriptor to replace this default.	Long string, starting with D:(A;;RPWPCR
systemOnly	Boolean	No	If set to True, only the Directory System Agent (DSA) can create and modify instances of this class.	False
systemFlags	Integer	No	Fifth bit from right (0x10) tells whether this class belongs to *category 1* (part of the base schema) or *category 2* (an extension).	16 (=0x10)
objectClass	OID string	Yes	Class of this class schema object itself, the value is obviously classSchema for all class schema objects (plus the superclass top—see discussion about object categories later in this chapter).	top + classSchema
objectCategory	Distinguished name	No	Object category of this class schema object itself, the value is the distinguished name of the object CN=Class-Schema for all class schema objects.	CN=Class-Schema, CN=Schema, CN=...
schemaFlagsEx	Integer	No	Not used	—

NOTE `CN=Dfs-Configuration` has the value False for this attribute. However, it doesn't show in the normal view of the Users and Computers snap-in because the parent container, `CN=System`, has a value True. Once you turn on Advanced Features, they will both show.

CATEGORY 1 AND 2 SCHEMA OBJECTS

One bit in the `systemFlags` attribute tells whether the class belongs to category 1 or 2. *Category 1* classes and attributes are part of the base schema, and *category 2* schema objects are something that you or your application have added. In other words, category 2 schema objects are part of the schema extensions.

The reason for the two categories is that there can be (and there are) stricter rules for modifications of category 1 schema objects.

OBJECT CATEGORY

You have seen the word "category" used in more than one context in this chapter. Here is one more: As you know, each object belongs to some class—to be exact, it also belongs to all superclasses of the main class. For example, the object Jack Brown belongs to the classes `user`, `person`, `organizationalPerson`, and `top`. To be able to contain this list, the `objectClass` attribute is multivalued.

Each object belongs also to some *object category,* as expressed with a single-valued attribute `objectCategory`. The object category is usually the same as the class, but it may be different, most likely one of the superclasses. For example, the `objectCategory` of most `user` class objects is `person`, which is two steps up in the class hierarchy.

As you can see in Table 8.11, the schema defines only the `defaultObject-Category` of each class, but the actual `objectCategory` attribute is per object. Consequently, two objects of the same class could belong in theory to two categories. However, this would only make things more confusing when you used the category as a search criterion. Also, Active Directory doesn't allow changing the `defaultObjectCategory` of any base schema object or the `objectCategory` of any existing object, which fortunately makes this confusing situation difficult to achieve.

Using object categories in LDAP filters and queries has the following advantages over using object classes.

- `ObjectCategory` is an indexed attribute, whereas `objectClass` is not. Therefore, LDAP filters and queries that use `objectCategory` are much faster than those that use just `objectClass`.

- Objects of several classes can use the same category. If you use a filter or query `objectCategory=person`, you will get a list of all people, regardless of whether they are users or contacts. Apart from this "`person = user + contact`," however, the base schema doesn't contain practical examples of several classes using the same object category.

SECURITY DESCRIPTOR DEFINITION LANGUAGE

Microsoft uses Security Descriptor Definition Language (SDDL) whenever a security descriptor should be described in a string format. Two examples of this are as follows:

- The `defaultSecurityDescriptor` attribute, mentioned in Table 8.11
- Security templates, which are INF files in C:\Winnt\Security\Templates

We explain SDDL briefly here by interpreting the `defaultSecurityDescriptor` for the `group` class (i.e., for each new group that you create). We don't use the `user` class as an example because the string would be ten times longer. For a detailed description of SDDL, refer to the Microsoft Platform SDK (software development kit) at `http://msdn.microsoft.com/library`.

The SDDL string for the `group` class is

```
D:
(A;;RPWPCRCCDCLCLORCWOWDSDDTSW;;;DA)
(A;;RPWPCRCCDCLCLORCWOWDSDDTSW;;;SY)
(A;;RPLCLORC;;;AU)
(A;;RPWPCRCCDCLCLORCWOWDSDDTSW;;;AO)
(A;;RPLCLORC;;;PS)
(OA;;CR;ab721a55-1e2f-11d0-9819-00aa0040529b;;AU)
```

NOTE   The string is divided here on seven lines to make it easier to read. In reality, it is one long string.

To interpret the string, you must be familiar with the contents of a security descriptor, as discussed in Chapter 4.

The `D:` in this string means that the subsequent data is a discretionary ACL. The owner, group, and system ACL are not included in this case.

The rest of the string consists of six pairs of parentheses, each of which is one ACE. The ACE in turn consists mostly of two-letter acronyms specifying who has what permissions.

The semicolons divide each ACE into six fields:

- ACE type
- ACE flags

- Permissions
- Object GUID
- Inherit object GUID
- Account SID

Table 8.12 shows the interpretation of the six ACEs. You can compare its elements to the SDDL string. Table 8.13 lists the SDDL acronyms, their spelled-out names, and their corresponding permission names in the user interface (i.e., in ACL Editor).

ClassSchema Object Property Pages

We conclude our discussion on classes by showing the Schema Manager snap-in property pages for a classSchema object. We picked (once again) the user class as an example.

TABLE 8.12 Default ACEs for a Group Object

ACE Type	Permissions*	Object GUID	Account SID
Access allowed	Read Prop, Write Prop, Control Access, Create Child, Delete Child, List Children, List Object, Read Control, Write Owner, Write DAC, Standard Delete, Delete Tree, Self Write		Domain Admins
Access allowed	Read Prop, Write Prop, Control Access, Create Child, Delete Child, List Children, List Object, Read Control, Write Owner, Write DAC, Standard Delete, Delete Tree, Self Write		System
Access allowed	Read Prop, List Children, List Object, Read Control		Authenticated Users
Access allowed	Read Prop, Write Prop, Control Access, Create Child, Delete Child, List Children, List Object, Read Control, Write Owner, Write DAC, Standard Delete, Delete Tree, Self Write		Account Operators
Access allowed	Read Prop, List Children, List Object, Read Control		(Personal) Self
Object access allowed	Control Access (i.e., extended rights)	Send to	Authenticated Users

*Domain Admins, System, and Account Operators have a list of 13 permissions. That list is the same as Full Control in the user interface. Authenticated Users and Self have a list of four permissions. The list is equal to the standard permission Read + special permission List Object.

TABLE 8.13 SDDL Permissions

AccessMask Bit Name	SDDL Acronym	SDDL Spelled-Out Name	Name in the User Interface
ADS_RIGHT_DS_CREATE_CHILD	CC	Create Child	Create All Child Objects
ADS_RIGHT_DS_DELETE_CHILD	DC	Delete Child	Delete All Child Objects
ADS_RIGHT_ACTRL_DS_LIST	LC	List Children	List Contents
ADS_RIGHT_DS_SELF	SW	Self Write	All Validated Writes
ADS_RIGHT_DS_READ_PROP	RP	Read Prop	Read All Properties
ADS_RIGHT_DS_WRITE_PROP	WP	Write Prop	Write All Properties
ADS_RIGHT_DS_DELETE_TREE	DT	Delete Tree	Delete Subtree
ADS_RIGHT_DS_LIST_OBJECT	LO	List Object	List Object
ADS_RIGHT_DS_CONTROL_ACCESS	CR	Control Access	All Extended Rights
ADS_RIGHT_DELETE	SD	Standard Delete	Delete
ADS_RIGHT_READ_CONTROL	RC	Read Control	Read Permissions
ADS_RIGHT_WRITE_DAC	WD	Write DAC	Modify Permissions
ADS_RIGHT_WRITE_OWNER	WO	Write Owner	Modify Owner

We show three screen shots (Figures 8.12 through 8.14)—one for each property page. We exclude the Security tab because it is a normal access control screen. For each screen, we list the attributes that correspond to the fields in the screen.

In the course of this section we have discussed 38 attributes of a class. The screens in Figures 8.12 through 8.14 show the values for only 12 of them (13 if you count the Security tab) corresponding to the nTSecurityDescriptor attribute. To see the remaining attributes, you need to use ADSI Edit.

Figure 8.12 shows the General tab. The corresponding attributes from top to bottom are as follows (the values are shown in parentheses):

- lDAPDisplayName ("user")
- adminDescription ("User")
- cn ("User")
- governsID ("1.2.840.113556.1.5.9")
- objectClassCategory ("Structural")

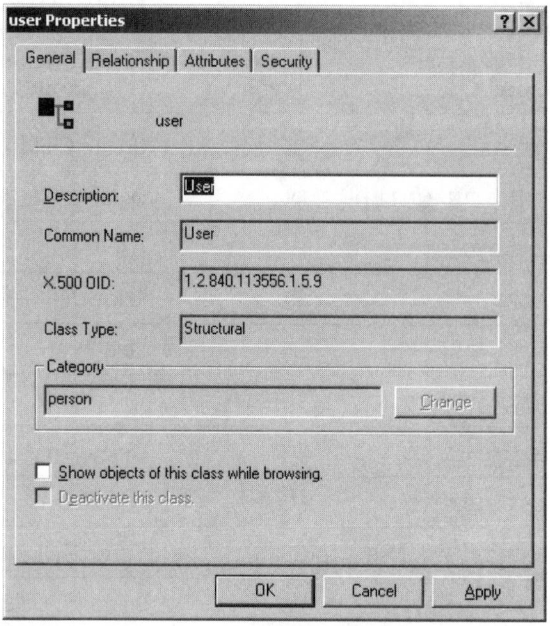

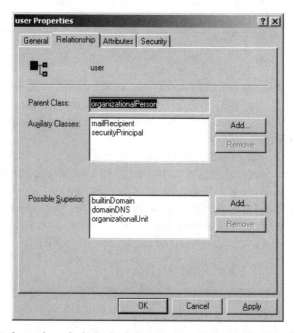

FIGURE 8.12 With the Schema Manager snap-in you can see the attributes of various classes, such as the `user` class.

FIGURE 8.13 The Relationship tab shows both the inheritance hierarchy in the schema and the possible superiors in the normal directory tree.

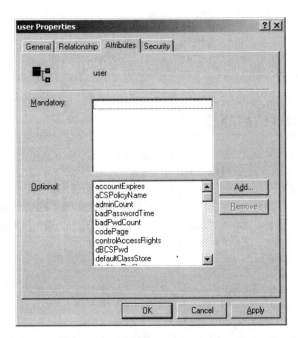

FIGURE 8.14 The Attributes tab lists the mandatory and optional attributes for the class, excluding inherited attributes.

- `defaultObjectCategory` ("person")
- `showInAdvancedViewOnly` (Note that the snap-in shipping with the original Windows 2000 has a bug so that setting this check box doesn't have the desired effect. The check box should control `defaultHidingValue`, which in turn controls the `showInAdvancedViewOnly` attribute of the objects to be created.)
- `isDefunct` ("not set")

Figure 8.13 shows the Relationship tab. The corresponding attributes from top to bottom are as follows (the values are shown in parentheses):

- `subClassOf` ("organizationalPerson")
- `auxiliaryClass`, `systemAuxiliaryClass` ("mailRecipient, security-Principal")
- `possSuperiors`, `systemPossSuperiors` ("builtinDomain, domainDNS, organizationalUnit")

Figure 8.14 shows the Attributes tab. The corresponding attributes from top to bottom are as follows (the values are shown in parentheses):

- `mustContain, systemMustContain` (empty list)
- `mayContain, systemMayContain` (a number of attributes)

Now that we have covered the different aspects of schema classes, we are ready to move on to the attributes and syntaxes. Attribute characteristics have something in common with class characteristics, but obviously there are also quite a few differences.

ATTRIBUTES AND SYNTAXES

In this section we discuss the attributes that define the attributes in the schema.

As with classes, there is a schema object for each attribute, which means a total of 863 `attributeSchema` objects in the base schema. Each of these 863 attributes is characterized by the attributes of its schema object and those `attribute-Schema` objects themselves use 94 attributes out of the 863. Figure 8.15 shows the relationship between the attribute schema objects and their attributes.

NOTE   The other figures that we have included in this chapter show LDAP names as schema object names (although this is imprecise). In Figure 8.15 we show the common names (which is more correct), because we want to show the actual object name and the LDAP name attribute separately.

Of the 94 attributes that the `attributeSchema` class uses, it inherits 73 attributes from `top` and defines 21 on its own level. As with classes, most of the inherited attributes are quite general (after all, they apply to any Active Directory object). We cover only 13 of the inherited attributes and all 21 "own" attributes for a total of 34 attributes.

NOTE   When discussing classes, we listed 14 inherited attributes and now 13. The list is the same except that `possibleInferiors` doesn't apply here. For example, the `homePhone` of a user cannot have child objects.

We divide the 34 attributes into four categories.

- *Names and identifiers.* You probably remember that `classSchema` objects have 14 various names, descriptions, and identifiers. `attributeSchema` objects have even more: 17 names, descriptions, and identifiers.
- *Syntax and content rules.* These 7 attributes define the kind of data the attribute accepts and the values that are possible for it.
- *Searches.* The 2 attributes in this category control things such as indexing of the attribute and whether it is part of the global catalog.
- *Miscellaneous.* There are 8 miscellaneous attributes.

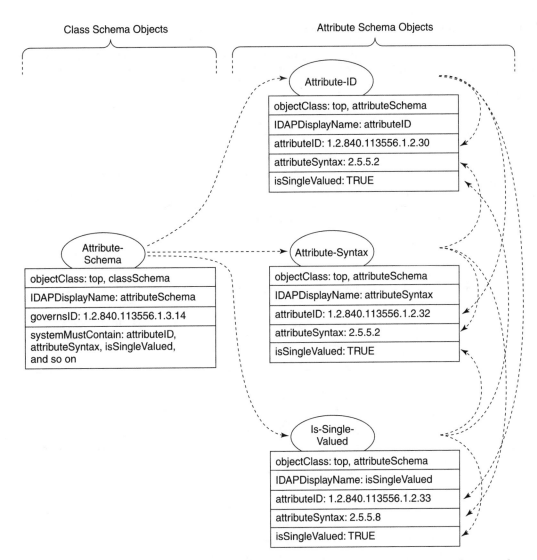

FIGURE 8.15 The `attributeSchema` class has 863 instances (i.e., `attributeSchema` objects) in the base schema. Each of these 863 objects defines the syntax and other aspects of one attribute. The definitions reside in the attributes of the objects, which means that the `attributeSchema` objects define attributes also for themselves. This figure shows three `attributeSchema` objects, which result in 3 × 3 arrows on the right side.

Table 8.14 shows all 34 attributes listed by their LDAP names. If the common name is quite different from the LDAP name, it appears in parentheses. The four sections following Table 8.14 describe the attributes in more detail. The Type column indicates whether the attribute is mandatory or optional. The Source Class column contains either `attributeSchema` or `top`—the latter meaning the

TABLE 8.14 Attributes of an `attributeSchema` Object

Name	Type	Source Class	Base Schema Attributes (863)	LDAP Display Name Attribute Example
Names and Identifiers				
lDAPDisplayName	M	attr.S.	All values are unique	lDAPDisplayName
cn (Common-Name)	M	attr.S.	All values are unique	LDAP-Display-Name
adminDisplayName	O	top	Same as cn	LDAP-Display-Name
name (RDN)	O	top	Same as cn	LDAP-Display-Name
distinguishedName (Obj-Dist-Name)	O	top	All values are unique	CN=LDAP-Display-Name, CN=Schema, CN=Configuration, DC=sanao, DC=com
canonicalName	O	top	All values are unique	sanao.com/ Configuration/ Schema/LDAP-Display-Name
displayName	O	top	Not used	—
displayName-Printable	O	top	Not used	—
classDisplayName	O	attr.S.	Not used	—
adminDescription	O	top	Same as cn	LDAP-Display-Name
description	O	top	Not used	—
attributeID	M	attr.S.	801 are Microsoft IDs (1.2.840.113556), 51 are X.500 IDs (2.5), 4 are Netscape IDs (2.16.840.1.113730), and 7 are "ITU-T data - PSS" IDs (0.9.2342)	1.2.840.113556.1.2.460
schemaIDGUID	M	attr.S.	All values are unique	9a7996bf e60dd011 a28500aa 003049e2
objectGUID	O	top	All values are unique	22a9624f 4b998f46 a658e3c2 7a357859
attribute-SecurityGUID	O	attr.S.	128 are set; 735 are <not set>	—

(continued)

TABLE 8.14 (*continued*)

Name	Type	Source Class	Base Schema Attributes (863)	LDAP Display Name Attribute Example
mAPIID	O	attr.S.	70 are unique values; 793 are <not set>	33137
linkID	O	attr.S.	32 are unique values; 831 are <not set>	—

Syntax and Content Rules

Name	Type	Source Class	Base Schema Attributes (863)	LDAP Display Name Attribute Example
attributeSyntax	M	attr.S.	All are set to 1 of 15 values	2.5.5.12
oMSyntax	M	attr.S.	99 are set to "127"; 764 are set to 1 of 14 values	64
oMObjectClass	O	attr.S.	99 are set; 764 are <not set>	—
isSingleValued	M	attr.S.	620 are True; 243 are False	True
rangeLower	O	attr.S.	163 are set; 700 are <not set>	1
rangeUpper	O	attr.S.	162 are set; 701 are <not set>	256
extendedChars-Allowed	O	attr.S.	All are <not set>	—

Searches

Name	Type	Source Class	Base Schema Attributes (863)	LDAP Display Name Attribute Example
searchFlags	O	attr.S.	106 are nonzero; the rest 757 are zero	9
isMemberOf-Partial-AttributeSet	O	attr.S.	138 are True; 725 are <not set>	True

Miscellaneous

Name	Type	Source Class	Base Schema Attributes (863)	LDAP Display Name Attribute Example
nTSecurity-Descriptor	M	top	All are set	A DACL, SACL, and so on
isDefunct	O	attr.S.	All are <not set>	—
systemOnly	O	attr.S.	93 are True; 770 are False	False

(*continued*)

TABLE 8.14 Attributes of an `attributeSchema` Object (*continued*)

Name	Type	Source Class	Base Schema Attributes (863)	LDAP Display Name Attribute Example
Miscellaneous (continued)				
systemFlags	O	top	849 are set; 14 are \<not set>	16
objectClass	M	top	All are top + attributeSchema	top + attributeSchema
objectCategory	M	top	All are CN=Attribute-Schema, CN=Schema, CN=Configuration, DC=sanao, DC=com	CN=Attribute-Schema, CN=Schema, CN=Configuration, DC=sanao, DC=com
schemaFlagsEx	O	attr.S.	Not used	—
isEphemeral	O	attr.S.	Not used	—

attribute was inherited from the `top` class. The Base Schema Attributes column indicates the kinds of values the 863 attribute objects have for the attributes in the table. Finally, the LDAP Display Name Attribute Example column lists the values for the `lDAPDisplayName` attribute.

NOTE As a detail, `lDAPDisplayName` is a mandatory attribute of an `attribute-Schema` object, but it is only an optional attribute of a `classSchema` object.

Names and Identifiers

Most of the names, descriptions, and identifiers for attribute schema objects are exactly the same as names, descriptions, and identifiers for class schema objects. Consequently, there is no need to repeat the descriptions of the following nine attributes:

- `lDAPDisplayName`
- `cn` (Common-Name)
- `adminDisplayName`
- `name` (RDN)
- `distinguishedName` (Obj-Dist-Name)
- `canonicalName`

TABLE 8.15 Some Name and Identifier Attributes of an `attributeSchema` Object

Name	Syntax	Multi-valued	Description	LDAP Display Name Attribute Example
attributeID	OID string	No	Object ID (OID) of the attribute.	1.2.840.113556.1.2.460
attribute-SecurityGUID	Octet string	No	ID that links the attribute to belong to some property set; permissions may then be given for this property set (see Chapter 6).	—
mAPIID	Integer	No	Messaging API (MAPI) applications identify attributes with this ID. Note that only 70 attributes have the `mAPIID` attribute set.	33137
linkID	Integer	No	Some attributes form forward-back link pairs, as discussed in the "Linked Attributes" section.	—

- `adminDescription`
- `schemaIDGUID`
- `objectGUID`

Also, the following four attributes are not used, as they were not used with class schema objects:

- `displayName`
- `displayNamePrintable`
- `classDisplayName`
- `description`

This leaves us with four not-yet-familiar attributes. They are described in Table 8.15.

LINKED ATTRIBUTES

When an attribute refers to another object in the directory, it is often beneficial that the target object has a reference to the first object. An example is a user's membership in a group. The group has a member attribute, which includes the user (a forward link) and the user has a `memberOf` attribute, which includes the group (a back link). Figure 8.16 shows an example.

An even value in the `linkID` attribute denotes a forward link and a larger-by-1 odd value denotes a back link.

The base schema contains the following 13 linked attribute pairs:

- `member–memberOf` (Is-Member-Of-DL)
- `manager–directReports`
- `siteObject–siteObjectBL`
- `nonSecurityMember–nonSecurityMemberBL`
- `queryPolicyObject–queryPolicyBL`
- `privilegeHolder–isPrivilegeHolder`
- `managedBy–managedObjects`
- `hasMasterNCs–masteredBy`
- `serverReference–serverReferenceBL`
- `bridgeheadTransportList–bridgeheadServerListBL`
- `netbootServer–netbootSCPBL`
- `frsComputerReference–frsComputerReferenceBL`
- `fRSMemberReference–fRSMemberReferenceBL`

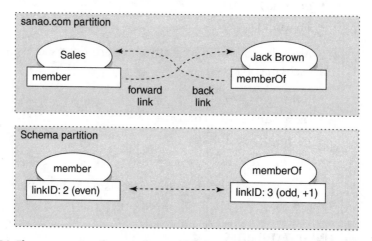

FIGURE 8.16 The `member` attribute is a forward link from a group object to a user object. The `memberOf` attribute is a back link from the user to the group. The relationship is defined in the corresponding `attributeSchema` objects.

NOTE   If you count the attributes that have `linkID` defined, the number is not $2 \times 13 = 26$, but 32 instead. The reason is that the base schema includes 6 attributes that have `linkID` defined, but which are missing the corresponding back-link pair.

All back-link attributes, such as `memberOf`, are "system only"—that is, users or administrators cannot modify them. Active Directory is responsible for updating these attributes, maintaining *referential integrity* in the process. If either of the referenced objects is moved, Active Directory modifies the reference accordingly.

A forward-link attribute must use one of the following syntaxes: `DN`, `DN with Unicode string`, `DN with binary`, `access point DN`, and `OR name`. A back-link attribute must be of syntax `DN`.

Syntax and Content Rules

Seven `attributeSchema` attributes control the type of data and the values each attribute accepts. Table 8.16 describes these syntax and content attributes.

The data type is called syntax in this context and it is defined by three attributes: `attributeSyntax`, `oMSyntax`, and `oMObjectClass`. Naturally, the three attributes must be consistent, as you see in Tables 8.17 through 8.20 where we describe all the syntax choices.

Several attributes are necessary to express the syntax because more than one standard is involved. The first attribute (`attributeSyntax`) defines an X.500 syntax, and the two others a XOM syntax. "XOM" stands for "XAPIA X/Open Object Management," an interface for ASN.1 messaging defined by X.400 API Association (XAPIA) and X/Open (a former vendor standards organization). Currently, "X/Open" is a trademark that belongs to Open Group (`http://www.opengroup.org/`).

NOTE   In "XAPIA," the *X* refers to X.400 and X.500 ITU-T standards, whereas in "X/Open," the *X* refers to UNIX.

NOTE   The letters *XOM* can also stand for "X/Open OSI-Abstract-Data Manipulation."

SYNTAX CHOICES

Active Directory supports 23 syntaxes, but it uses only 19 of them in the base schema. Because the syntax choices are hard-coded and don't appear as objects in Active Directory, you cannot add syntaxes.

TABLE 8.16 Syntax and Content Attributes of an `attributeSchema` Object

Name	Syntax	Multi-valued	Description	LDAP Display Name Attribute Example
attribute-Syntax	OID string	No	Identifies with an X.500 OID whether the value of this attribute is integer, string, or some other data format.	2.5.5.12
oMSyntax	Integer	No	About the same as `attributeSyntax` but expressed with a XOM code.	64
oMObject-Class	Octet string	No	If the XOM code is 127 (=object distinguished name), this attribute defines the "subsyntax."	—
isSingle-Valued	Boolean	No	Specifies whether the attribute is single- or multivalued.	True
rangeLower	Integer	No	The lowest possible value for an integer attribute or the shortest possible value for a string attribute.	1
rangeUpper	Integer	No	The largest possible value for an integer attribute or the longest possible value for a string attribute.	256
extended-CharsAllowed	Boolean	No	Specifies whether the attribute can contain extended characters; used only with the syntax `Teletex string`.	—

We can divide the syntaxes into the following categories:

- Simple data types (4 syntaxes)
- String data types (10 syntaxes)
- Time data types (2 syntaxes), which are actually also strings
- Reference data types (7 syntaxes), which are various object references

Tables 8.17 through 8.20 describe the syntaxes of each category. Some syntaxes have two names, in which case we mention the second name in parentheses.

TABLE 8.17 Syntaxes for Simple Data Types

Syntax	attribute-Syntax	oMSyntax	Description	Count in Base Schema
Boolean	2.5.5.8	1	Values can be either TRUE or FALSE.	54
Integer	2.5.5.9	2	32-bit number.	149
Enumeration	2.5.5.9	10	32-bit number. Active Directory treats this as an integer.	6
Large integer (INTEGER8)	2.5.5.16	65	64-bit number.	66

TABLE 8.18 Syntaxes for String Data Types

Syntax	attribute-Syntax	oMSyntax	Description	Count in Base Schema
OID string	2.5.5.2	6	An object ID string (e.g., 2.5.5.2) consisting of digits (0–9) and dots	20
Case-sensitive string (case-exact string)	2.5.5.3	27	Case-sensitive* string, each character of which belongs to the General-String character set**	0
Case-ignore string (teletex)	2.5.5.4	20	Case-insensitive string, each character of which belongs to the teletex character set**	8
Printable string	2.5.5.5	19	Case-sensitive string, each character of which belongs to the Printable character set**	13
IA5 string	2.5.5.5	22	Case-sensitive string, each character of which belongs to the *International Alphabet 5* (IA5) character set**	7
Numeric string	2.5.5.6	18	String, each character of which is a digit**	2
Octet string	2.5.5.10	4	Array of bytes (i.e., binary data)	120

(continued)

TABLE 8.18 Syntaxes for String Data Types (*continued*)

Syntax	attribute-Syntax	oMSyntax	Description	Count in Base Schema
Unicode string (directory string)	2.5.5.12	64	Normal case-insensitive string using any Unicode characters	298
NT security descriptor	2.5.5.15	66	An octet string that contains a Windows NT/2000 security descriptor (SD)	3
SID string	2.5.5.17	4	An octet string that contains a Windows NT/2000 security identifier (SID)	8

*Whether a string is case-sensitive or case-insensitive matters when you start to use LDAP filters to specify which values match certain criteria.
**Active Directory doesn't currently enforce General-String, teletex, Printable, or IA5 character sets, or the digit restriction. However, this may change, so you should use only valid characters.

TABLE 8.19 Syntaxes for Time Data Types

Syntax	attribute-Syntax	oMSyntax	Description	Count in Base Schema
UTC time string	2.5.5.11	23	Time-string format defined by ASN.1 standards. See standards ISO 8601 and X.680 for more information.* UTC, or Coordinated Universal Time, is roughly the same as GMT, or Greenwich Mean Time. This syntax uses only two characters to represent the year.	4
Generalized time string	2.5.5.11	24	Time-string format defined by ASN.1 standards. See standards ISO 8601 and X.680 for more information.* This syntax uses four characters to represent the year.	6

*These two time formats are further described in Chapter 6 in the "Specifying Values" section.

TABLE 8.20 Syntaxes for Reference Data Types

Syntax	attribute-Syntax	oMSyntax	Description	Count in Base Schema
DN (dis-tinguished name or DN String)	2.5.5.1	127	Distinguished name of an object in the directory. If the target object is moved or renamed, Active Directory updates the DN attribute accordingly.	92
DN with binary (DN with octet string)	2.5.5.7	127	This syntax stores a distinguished name along with some binary data. Active Directory keeps the DN up-to-date. The format is B:*hex digit count*:*bytes as hex*:*DN* (e.g., B:6:F12A4B:*someDN*).	4
OR name	2.5.5.7	127	An X.400 syntax (related to e-mail addresses).	0
Replica link	2.5.5.10	127	Syntax that repsFrom and repsTo attributes use to control replication. The corresponding attributes contain things such as the up-to-date vector of a replication partition.	2
Presentation address	2.5.5.13	127	OSI application entities use presentation addresses to address other application entities. See RFCs 1278 and 2252 and ISO DIS 7498-3 for more information.	1
DN with Unicode string	2.5.5.14	127	This syntax stores a distinguished name along with a string. Active Directory keeps the DN up-to-date. The format is S:*character count*:*string*:*DN* (e.g., S:5:hello:*someDN*).	0
Access point DN	2.5.5.14	127	An X.400 distinguished name.	0

All seven syntaxes in Table 8.20 have oMSyntax = 127, which means that they must have oMObjectClass also defined. The latter attribute distinguishes them, because some of them have identical attributeSyntax and oMSyntax. We list the oMObjectClass values in Table 8.21.

TABLE 8.21 `oMObjectClass` Values for "127" Syntaxes

Syntax	`attributeSyntax`	`oMSyntax`	`oMObjectClass` (hexadecimal)
DN	2.5.5.1	127	2B0C0287731C00854A
DN with binary (DN with octet string)	2.5.5.7	127	2A864886F7140101010B
OR name	2.5.5.7	127	56060102050B1D
Replica link	2.5.5.10	127	2A864886F71401010106
Presentation address	2.5.5.13	127	2B0C0287731C00855C
Access point DN	2.5.5.14	127	2B0C0287731C00853E
DN with Unicode string	2.5.5.14	127	2A864886F7140101010C

MULTIVALUED ATTRIBUTES

Each multivalued attribute can have up to 850 values, except for linked multivalued attributes, such as group members, which can have 5,000 values (i.e., group members).

When one value is added, deleted, or modified, the whole attribute is replicated to other domain controllers. Therefore, it is not a good idea to make multivalued attributes too large. Another reason to favor relatively small multivalued attributes is that when you read the attribute, all values are normally returned together.

The values are returned in random order; if you write a program or script to read the values, you cannot depend on the order.

Even though returning all values of a multivalued attribute is the normal behavior, LDAP allows specifying the range of values. This is explained in Chapter 6.

Searches

Some attributes are indexed, which allows fast searches based on those attributes, and some attributes are part of the global catalog. The indexed and global catalog attributes are defined with two `attributeSchema` attributes, which are described in Table 8.22.

NOTE   Indexing and global catalog membership are per-attribute settings, not per-class settings. In other words, if the `givenName` attribute is indexed, this will apply to any class that happens to use `givenName`.

TABLE 8.22 Search Attributes of an attributeSchema Object

Name	Syntax	Multi-valued	Description	LDAP Display Name Attribute Example
SearchFlags	Enumeration	No	The bits in this number define whether the corresponding attribute is indexed and how it is treated in searches. (Table 8.23 describes the bits.)	9
isMemberOf-Partial-AttributeSet	Boolean	No	If True, the corresponding attribute is part of the global catalog and consequently is replicated to all global catalog servers.	True

NOTE   You might wonder how it is possible that the member attribute is part of the global catalog (isMemberOfPartialAttributeSet is True), but only universal group members appear in the global catalog, whereas global and domain local group members don't. The answer is that Microsoft hard-coded this difference to Active Directory; that is, group membership doesn't care about isMemberOfPartial-AttributeSet attribute.

SearchFlags is a *bit-field* attribute. It contains 32 bits, 5 of which have a meaning. Those 5 bits are the least significant ones, which means that they are the rightmost bits if you use Windows Calculator to convert a decimal number to binary. The bits are described in Table 8.23. The bit value "1" means True—that is, the setting is on.

AMBIGUOUS NAME RESOLUTION

Ambiguous Name Resolution (ANR), which is mentioned in Table 8.23, needs a few words of explanation. ANR is an LDAP feature that allows using a simple LDAP filter instead of a complex filter in certain LDAP searches. You can use ANR manually with LDAP filters (discussed in Chapter 6). Also, when you perform a search with Windows 2000 Address Book, it will use ANR for you.

The following eight attributes are part of the ANR set in the base schema:

- displayName
- givenName

TABLE 8.23 `SearchFlags` **Bits**

Bit from Right	Hex Value	Description	Count in Base Schema
1	1	If set, the attribute is indexed.	64
2	2	If set, the attribute is indexed over container and attribute.	0
3	4	The attribute is part of the Ambiguous Name Resolution (ANR) set, which is explained in the "Ambiguous Name Resolution" section. This bit should be used in conjunction with the first bit.	8
4	8	The attribute is preserved when an object is changed to a tombstone (i.e., "deleted"). All attributes without this bit are deleted.	24
5	10	If set, the attribute is copied when duplicating a user with the Users and Computers snap-in.	33

- `legacyExchangeDN`
- `name` (RDN)
- `physicalDeliveryOfficeName` (user properties, General tab, Office)
- `proxyAddresses`
- `sAMAccountName` (user properties, Account tab, Pre-Windows 2000 name)
- `sn` (Surname)

ANR gives flexibility in two ways:

- Only a partial match is required from the beginning of the text. If you search for "Brown," you will get both "Brown" and "Brownfield."
- The search is performed on several attributes (those eight just listed). If you search for "Brown," it can be the starting part of not only the surname (last name), but also `displayName`, `sAMAccountName`, or any of the other five attributes.

If you search for two words, ANR works as just described, with one addition. It will also try if the words are "first name—last name" or "last name—first name." If you want to find Jack Brown, you can type either "jac bro" or "brow jack." The corresponding LDAP filters would be

```
(anr=jac bro)
(anr=brow jack)
```

It is possible to suppress the first name/last name functionality and/or the last name/first name functionality. You do this by modifying the same dSHeuristics attribute that is used to enable the List Object permission. We explained the procedure in Chapter 4 in the "Enabling and Using the List Object Permission" section.

Miscellaneous Characteristics for Attributes

Most of the miscellaneous attributeSchema attributes are also classSchema attributes. Because we described the classSchema attributes when discussing classes, there is no need to repeat the discussion of the following attributes:

- nTSecurityDescriptor
- isDefunct
- objectClass
- objectCategory
- schemaFlagsEx

One new attribute, isEphemeral, is not used, so we are left with only two attributes to address here: systemOnly and systemFlags. Although those two attributes also appeared in the discussion of classes, they have some new aspects. Table 8.24 describes the attributes systemOnly and systemFlags, and Table 8.25 continues the description of the systemFlags.

NOTE   For some peculiar reason, 14 of the base schema attributes and two of the classes are not marked to belong to category 1. Therefore, you could deactivate them, for example, even though you are not supposed to be able to do that for category 1 attributes or classes.

AttributeSchema Object Property Pages

There is only one property page for attributeSchema objects in the Schema Manager snap-in, and there is no Security tab. Figure 8.17 shows the property page for the object LDAPDisplayName.

TABLE 8.24 Miscellaneous Attributes of an `attributeSchema` Object

Name	Syntax	Multi-valued	Description	LDAP Display Name Attribute Example
systemOnly	Boolean	No	If True, you can set the value for the attribute only when creating an object. Afterward, only the DSA can change the value.	False
systemFlags	Integer	No	The bits in this number define things such as whether the corresponding attribute is replicated or constructed. (Table 8.25 describes the bits.)	16

TABLE 8.25 `SystemFlags` Bits

Bit from Right	Hex Value	Description	Count in Base Schema
1	1	If set, the attribute is not replicated from one domain controller to another.	39
2	2	This is an undocumented bit used by the system.	43
3	4	If set, the attribute is constructed. It is built from other attributes and not stored in the schema on disk.	22
5	10	If set, the attribute belongs to category 1 (part of the base schema); otherwise, it belongs to category 2 (an extension).	849
28	800 0000	This is an undocumented bit used by the system.	21

Of the 34 `attributeSchema` attributes that we have discussed in this section, Figure 8.17 shows the following 11, with the values in parentheses (we didn't count `showInAdvancedViewOnly`). To see all of the attributes, you need ADSI Edit.

- `lDAPDisplayName` ("lDAPDisplayName")
- `adminDescription` ("LDAP-Display-Name")

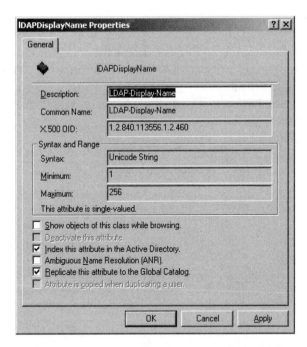

FIGURE 8.17 With the Schema Manager snap-in you can see the attributes of various attributes, such as lDAPDisplayName.

- cn ("LDAP-Display-Name")
- attributeID ("1.2.840.113556.1.2.460")
- attributeSyntax, oMSyntax, oMObjectClass ("Unicode String")
- rangeLower ("1")
- rangeUpper ("256")
- isSingleValued ("This attribute is single-valued")
- showInAdvancedViewOnly (Note that even though checking the "Show objects of this class while browsing" box sets this attribute to False, it doesn't have any practical meaning.)
- isDefunct ("Deactivate this attribute" not checked)
- searchFlags ("Index this attribute in the Active Directory" checked, "ANR" not checked, "Attribute is copied when duplicating a user" not checked)
- isMemberOfPartialAttributeSet ("Replicate this attribute to the Global Catalog" not checked)

CONCLUSION

In this chapter we discussed how the schema is built up from classes, attributes, and syntaxes. We also described the attributes of `classSchema` and `attribute-Schema` objects.

We have examined the schema in detail thus far, but we have not made changes to it. In the next chapter we evaluate if we need to extend the schema, and if so, how to extend it.

Chapter 9

Extending the Schema

One of the advantages Windows 2000 has over its predecessor Windows NT is that Active Directory has an extensible schema. Even though the Active Directory base schema has quite a few classes and attributes, they cannot accommodate all data and anticipate every need that an organization may have. In this chapter we explain how to extend the schema by addressing the following topics:

- When and why to extend or modify the schema
- How to plan for various modifications
- How to perform modifications
- How to show the extensions in the user interface

These topics build on the knowledge that you gained in the preceding chapter.

In this chapter we talk about modifying the schema, and most of those modifications are extensions. The phrase "extending the schema" is well established to cover both extensions and other modifications. Therefore, we use the terms "extend" and "modify" somewhat interchangeably.

NOTE Even if you are not going to extend the schema, you should check the example in the "Bringing the Extensions to the User Interface" section later in this chapter. In that section, we demonstrate how to view logon counts and other information about users without extending the schema.

At the end of the chapter we show how to extend the user class. The example works as a summary of this chapter; however, it might be helpful to check the example first, and then read the chapter from the beginning with the example in mind as a point of reference.

WHEN AND WHY TO MODIFY

One reason to modify the schema is that the current schema doesn't contain the classes and attributes that would accommodate data that you as an administrator want to put in Active Directory. Another reason is that a directory-enabled application (DEA) wants to modify the schema to store its data in the directory.

Even though an extensible schema is a selling point for Active Directory, Microsoft discourages modification of the base schema unless absolutely necessary. You should first evaluate if the current schema would fill the need without modification. Unfortunately, the only way to do the evaluation is to examine the base schema and try to find out if a certain class or attribute would suit that need.

If you must modify the schema, you can modify some category 1 (base schema) classes and/or attributes, or you can create new (category 2) classes and/or attributes. There are two approaches to modifying or extending attributes.

- *Use an existing attribute unmodified.* Add an existing category 1 attribute to an existing or new class or classes.

- *Create a new attribute.* Create a new category 2 attribute and add it to an existing or new class or classes.

Note that neither approach includes modifying an existing attribute. We didn't include such approach, because about all you can (or should) do to an existing attribute is to modify its indexing, ANR, and global catalog settings. None of the three options enables you to store any new kind of data in Active Directory—they are only for administrative tuning of Active Directory.

There are also two approaches to modifying or extending classes.

- *Modify (extend) an existing class.* Add category 1 and/or 2 attributes to the `mayContain` list of some category 1 class or classes and/or add new possible superiors for the class.

- *Create (and derive) a new subclass.* Create a new category 2 class using as a superclass a class that already has most of the attributes and possible superiors that you need. If none is suitable, you can derive from the `top` class (keeping in mind that from the `top` class alone you inherit 73 attributes to your new class). When you create the class, add any appropriate category 1 and/or 2 attributes (to the `mayContain` list and/or the `mustContain` list) and possible superiors.

NOTE   You cannot add `mustContain` attributes to an existing class. This would lead to an illegal situation, because you might already have a number of instances of that class, and those instances wouldn't have this new mandatory attribute set to any value.

Creating new attributes or classes requires more planning than just modifying existing ones. Once you create a new schema object, you cannot delete it, at least in the first version of Active Directory included in Windows 2000 (the version included in Windows .NET Server should support schema deletion). Consequently, the enterprise organization may be stuck with the extensions for some time. Further, if different departments all add something in addition to purchased applications, the number of attributes and classes in your directory would be much higher after a few years. When a directory accumulates a large number of category 2 classes and attributes, using and managing the directory and its schema is easier if they all are well documented and systematically named.

When adding new classes or attributes, you need to get all of their characteristics right, whereas if you modify an existing class or attribute, you need to focus on only some characteristics. Creating new attributes or classes seems less desirable than modifying existing ones, but it has one big advantage: The new attributes and classes are guaranteed to be for the exclusive use of your organization. Even though there are already 863 attributes in the base schema and you could imagine that there is an attribute for every need, how can you ever know which ones are safe to use? Microsoft doesn't offer a list to indicate "these 450 are OK to use," or anything similar. If you add some nice-sounding category 1 attribute to the `mayContain` list of a category 1 class, Microsoft might do the same in a future version of Windows 2000, but for a different purpose. However, if you create a new category 2 attribute, it should be safe to use that attribute with a category 1 class and vice versa—using category 1 attributes in your new category 2 classes should also be fine. Not to mention that both the attribute and class are category 2.

Guidelines

Based on the preceding discussion, we offer the following guidelines for schema modifications.

- Evaluate the need to change the schema.
- If you need to modify the schema, go ahead, but plan the modification thoroughly and put the plan on paper (or in an electronic file at least). You

must plan the attribute values of each new and modified `classSchema` and `attributeSchema` object. You should also plan how to use class inheritance.

- Document the modifications. This document is likely to be about the same as the documented plan we mentioned in the previous point.

- If you are a software vendor and the modification will be applied in customer directories, give your customers the document. If you are the customer, require your vendor to provide you with the documentation.

- Consider not modifying category 1 classes, except for adding new attributes and possible superiors to some classes.

- Consider the impact that your modifications might have on other departments in the organization and on future modifications, whether they originate from manual modifications within the organization or from purchased applications.

- If you are a vendor of directory-enabled applications (that need to modify the schema of the customer directories), write a separate installation program for the schema modification. Include instructions that only the Schema Admins are able to run it as well as other information that a customer needs to perform a successful schema extension. This information is presented throughout the course of this chapter, especially in the "Order of Tasks" section.

- Put only one or two users in the Schema Admins group, which has a permission to modify the schema. Store the users' passwords in a safe and perhaps require them to use a smart card for logon. You could also remove all users from Schema Admins and add them only when actually changing the schema.

- Establish a committee (or nominate a responsible person) to analyze and approve the applications to modify the schema (and probably also carry the modifications out).

- When the people on the committee in the previous point get a request for a modification, they should consider if the modification will fill one isolated need or if it could be used throughout the organization. Also, the committee should determine if they will consolidate multiple requests from different departments.

- When you have a set of attributes that you may need to add to several classes, consider using an auxiliary class instead of adding attributes directly to a class.

- Don't create a subclass of the `user` class and start putting your users in that new class. User management is much simpler if they are all in the plain old `user` class.

- Consider if you can use existing attributes and perhaps add them to some additional classes (either new or existing), or if you need to create new attributes. For example, the `birthLocation` attribute is in the base schema, which you could add to the user class. However, that attribute accepts only binary data, so you might end up creating a new attribute that accepts text data.

Now we turn to consideration of the kind of data to put in Active Directory.

What Data to Put in Active Directory

Active Directory as an information store has the following characteristics.

- Because of intrasite and intersite replication, the data is highly available. There is fault tolerance and a geographically spanned network has proximity of information.

- As a result of replication, the data in some domain controllers may be out-of-date at any given time (i.e., loose consistency).

- Active Directory hierarchies and permissions allow distributed management of the data. Permissions also allow control of which users see which objects and attributes.

- Active Directory is optimized for a high number of reads.

- Active Directory allows standards-based read and write access using the LDAP protocol.

Keep these characteristics in mind when you plan what data to put in Active Directory. In addition, there are the following three basic requirements for the data that will go in Active Directory.

- *"Globally" useful.* The data should be "globally" useful, because Active Directory provides an easy way to replicate data to different sites, as well as an efficient means to search, read, and modify the data. To be precise, your data doesn't have to be globally useful, but if it is not, it doesn't use this benefit of Active Directory, and it is replicated to several sites in vain (depending on the domain controller placement).

- *Not volatile (i.e., relatively static).* The data should not be volatile. Examples of volatile data are a single print job or e-mail message. If it would take 1 hour to replicate a change to all necessary domain controllers in a multisite network, there would be no sense in putting in data that would change every hour. Such data would be out-of-date most of the time.

- *Relatively small.* The data items should be relatively small. Large, multivalued attributes would be costly to replicate among domain controllers and retrieve to clients. However, some clients are able to use the LDAP control that allows incremental reading of multivalued attributes. We cannot give you numbers because they depend on physical network connections, among other things.

Especially the last two requirements are important because Active Directory data is replicated to several domain controllers, often on different sites. When you consider which attributes to put in the global catalog, the requirements are even more important. The level of importance increases further if you plan to store some data in the configuration partition instead of the domain partitions.

If you are a programmer, you should know some additional things about Active Directory. Active Directory is different from a relational database, such as SQL Server. A relational database allows joins with tables and views, but Active Directory does not. There is no distributed lock management in Active Directory, just the aforementioned loose consistency. Each object is a flat list of attributes, which has no substructure or nesting. Even though attributes can be multi-valued, the multiple values are sets instead of vectors—you can never retrieve them in a particular order. You can perform complex queries, but there are only two bitwise operations available (implemented as LDAP extensions). Also, you cannot evaluate expressions in queries, which is quite different from SQL queries.

In addition, if your application must store several data elements in Active Directory, it is better to add one binary attribute that contains all of them than to add many individual attributes for the various needs of the application. In other words, Active Directory doesn't need to see the data structure of your application data. On the other hand, creating several smaller attributes may be better in terms of replication.

In summary:

- If your data is not globally useful, is volatile, or is too large, you should probably store it somewhere other than in Active Directory. Some alternate locations are the file system, a database application such as SQL Server, and the registry.

- Or, if the data fills the criteria, you can store the data in Active Directory. First examine the existing classes and attributes to determine if some of them will fill the need.

- Or, if the existing classes and attributes are not enough, plan, implement, and document the necessary extensions to the schema.

PLANNING THE MODIFICATIONS

In planning modifications, you must consider the changes you could make, as well as gather and determine the necessary information relevant to each possible modification. Here we address the following operations:

- Creating a class
- Modifying a class

- Creating a attribute
- Modifying an attribute
- Deactivating a class
- Deactivating an attribute

Remember that creating or modifying a class or an attribute means creating or modifying the corresponding `classSchema` or `attributeSchema` object.

Creating a Class

When we discussed `classSchema` objects in the previous chapter, we described 36 attributes for them. If you create a new `classSchema` object, you must define only 5 attributes and you may define 16 more. Table 9.1 lists these 21 attributes,

TABLE 9.1 Attributes of a New `classSchema` Object

Name	Must/ May	System Only	Guidelines
Names and Identifiers			
cn (Common-Name)/ name (RDN)	Must	cn: No/ name: Yes	Microsoft strongly advises you to use the following convention: "Registered DNS name of the company + year of DNS name registration with four digits + product name which is unique in the company and descriptive enough, first letter being uppercase and the rest according to the product + attribute or class name, again descriptive." Between each part and word there should be a hyphen (e.g., `Sanao-Com-2000-MyProduct-Config-Info`).
lDAPDisplayName	Must	No	Derive this name from cn by changing the first letter to lowercase and removing all hyphens except those right before and after the product name (e.g., `sanaoCom2000-MyProduct-ConfigInfo`).
adminDisplayName	May	No	Use any name you want, but usually it is best to define this to be the same as cn. Also, if you don't specify a name, the system will use cn.
adminDescription	May	No	Use any description you want.

(continued)

TABLE 9.1 Attributes of a New `classSchema` Object (*continued*)

Name	Must/ May	System Only	Guidelines
Names and Identifiers (continued)			
governsID	Must	Yes	Allocate an OID that is unique within all classes and attributes in the world from the "range" that was issued to your organization by an issuing authority.
schemaIDGUID	May	Yes	Active Directory generates this value if not specified. However, especially if you are an application vendor, you should provide a value so that your class will have the same value in all installations (this helps in tasks such as defining property sets and managing permissions programmatically). The value should be a 128-bit octet string that is unique within all classes and attributes in all directories that this class will be used. To get a GUID, use UUIDGen or GUIDGen, which are part of the Platform SDK (see `http://msdn.microsoft.com/library`).
rDNAttID	May	Yes	Microsoft encourages you to use only "cn," which is also the default if you don't specify a value. You shouldn't use values other than "cn," "dc," "l," "o," "c," and "ou" because all LDAPv3 clients recognize them.
Structure and Containment Rules*			
mustContain	May	No	Include whichever mandatory attributes you want. Even though this attribute is not "system only," you cannot change the list.
systemMustContain	May	Yes	Include whichever mandatory attributes you want. You cannot change the list.
mayContain	May	No	Include whichever optional attributes you want.
systemMayContain	May	Yes	Include whichever optional attributes you want. You cannot change the list.
possSuperiors	May	No	Include whichever possible superiors (parents) you want. (See the end of this chapter for considerations of where in the directory to place the instances of new classes.)
systemPossSuperiors	May	Yes	Include whichever possible superiors (parents) you want. You cannot change the list.

(*continued*)

TABLE 9.1 *(continued)*

Name	Must/ May	System Only	Guidelines
Class Inheritance			
objectClass-Category	Must	Yes	Specify structural, abstract, or auxiliary as you need, but don't create 88-classes.
subClassOf	Must	Yes	Specify top or some other existing class appropriate to your need (and inheritance plan).
auxiliaryClass	May	No	Include whichever auxiliary classes are appropriate according to your inheritance plan.
systemAuxiliary-Class	May	Yes	Include whichever auxiliary classes are appropriate according to your inheritance plan. You cannot change the list.
Miscellaneous			
defaultObject-Category	May	No	If you don't specify a value, this attribute defaults to the DN of the classSchema object itself (which is often fine). You can also specify a superclass if that is used in searches more frequently. If you inherit this new class from a category 1 class (other than top), specify the DN of that class for this attribute. This way, the instances of the new class are easier to find.
defaultHiding-Value	May	No	Set this value to True if the instances of your new class should not be visible in the user interface (normal view of the Users and Computers snap-in [without Advanced Features turned on] and the Windows shell).
defaultSecurity-Descriptor	May	No	Set a default if you want, using Security Descriptor Definition Language (SDDL).
systemOnly	May	Yes	Don't set this value. None of your classes should be "system only," because you couldn't use them.

*We indicate in the table that you don't need to define the mayContain, systemMayContain, mustContain, and systemMustContain attributes. However, you cannot use the new class for anything unless you define at least one of them.

with some guidelines. The remaining 15 attributes you cannot define, because they are one of the following:

- Not used
- Filled by the system
- Constructed attributes

The second column of Table 9.1 indicates whether you must or may specify a value for each attribute. Note that this is not the same as the attribute's being mandatory or optional. Some mandatory attributes are filled by the system and some attributes you need to assign a value, even though technically they are optional.

NOTE   If you want to set an attribute that is marked as "system only" in Table 9.1, you must do this when you create the `classSchema` object. Afterward, you cannot change a system-only attribute.

TIP   When generating the value for `defaultSecurityDescriptor`, you can probably do fine by taking a `defaultSecurityDescriptor` of one of the existing classes and modifying it to your needs. C programmers also have the option of generating the string with the `ConvertSecurityDescriptorToStringSecurity-Descriptor` Win32 API function.

Table 9.1 recommends class names such as `sanaoCom2000-MyProduct-ConfigInfo`. That recommendation is targeted primarily to application vendors—such a long name doesn't matter when an application is using it internally. However, if you create some classes, and especially attributes, for your own administrative use, the recommended names may be impractically long. At the (tiny) risk of future name conflicts, you could use a shorter name, such as `sanaoITExtensions`.

When a class is created, it must pass a series of *consistency checks*. Otherwise, Active Directory refuses to create the class schema object. Basically, the checks ensure that classes conform to certain requirements—for example, if the `governsID` should be unique, the checks verify that it really is unique. They also check that any attribute or class that is referred in `mayContain`, `auxiliaryClass`, or any other attribute that refers to another attribute or class exists and is the right type (e.g., an auxiliary really is an auxiliary).

Modifying a Class

When creating a new class, you could use 21 `classSchema` attributes. If you later modify the class, the number of possible attributes narrows to 9. The rest are either "system only" or the schema *safety checks* prevent the change. Table 9.2 lists the attributes that you can change.

NOTE   In addition to guidelines here, keep in mind also the guidelines for creating classes.

The safety checks ensure that changes made by one application or user won't harm other applications and users.

As a safety check, Active Directory doesn't allow you to add or delete mandatory attributes of a class, either directly with `mustContain` or indirectly with inheritance/auxiliary. The reason is that there could already be a number of instances of that class that would suddenly become illegal because they didn't contain that mandatory attribute.

For category 1 classes (i.e., the base schema), Active Directory has the following additional restrictions as safety checks.

- You cannot change the `lDAPDisplayName`.
- You cannot change the `defaultObjectCategory`.
- You cannot change the `objectCategory` of any instance of a category 1 class.

TABLE 9.2 `ClassSchema` **Object Attributes That Can Be Changed**

Name	Guidelines
`lDAPDisplayName`	You shouldn't change this. However, if you accidentally create a class that is not quite what you want, you can rename the first class to something obsolete and create a new one.
`adminDisplayName`	No guidelines.
`adminDescription`	No guidelines.
`mayContain`	If you want additional optional attributes, add them here directly or use an auxiliary class as a set of attributes.
`possSuperiors`	No guidelines.
`auxiliaryClass`	If you want additional optional attributes, add them directly to `mayContain` or add an auxiliary class as a set of attributes.
`defaultObjectCategory`	No guidelines.
`defaultHidingValue`	No guidelines.
`defaultSecurityDescriptor`	No guidelines.

NOTE   Because two of the base schema classes don't have their `systemFlags` attribute set, they are not recognized as in category 1. Consequently, you can do modifications such as change their `lDAPDisplayName`.

TIP   If you want to see which classes and attributes are without protection (not that you need that information for anything), you can use ADSI Edit to apply an LDAP filter `(!(systemFlags:1.2.840.113556.1.4.803:=16))` to the Schema container. Or, because the attribute is not set at all, you can also use a shorter form `(!(systemFlags=*))`.

Creating an Attribute

When creating new `attributeSchema` objects, 13 of the 34 attributes that we discussed earlier are filled by the system, constructed, or not used. One attribute is discussed later when we cover deactivating attributes. Table 9.3 contains the remaining 20 attributes. You must use 5 of them and you may use 15 others. (Although to be exact, the list of 20 includes also a few that you can but should not use.)

TABLE 9.3 Attributes of a New `attributeSchema` Object

Name	Must/ May*	System Only	Guidelines
Names and Identifiers			
cn (Common-Name)/ name (RDN)	Must	No/Yes	Specify a name using the conventions we described when we covered creating classes (e.g., `Sanao-Com-2000-MyProduct-User-Data`).
lDAPDisplayName	Must	No	Specify a name derived from the cn (e.g., `sanaoCom2000-MyProduct-UserData`).
adminDisplayName	May	No	Use any name you want, but usually it is best to define this to be the same as cn. Also, if you don't specify a name, the system uses cn.
adminDescription	May	No	Use any description you want.
attributeID	Must	Yes	Allocate an OID that is unique within all classes and attributes in the world, from the "range" that was issued to your organization by an issuing authority.

(continued)

TABLE 9.3 *(continued)*

Name	Must/ May*	System Only	Guidelines
schemaIDGUID	May	Yes	Active Directory generates this value if not specified. However, especially if you are an application vendor, you should provide a value so that your class will have the same value in all installations (this helps in tasks such as managing permissions programmatically). The value should be a 128-bit octet string that is unique within all classes and attributes in all directories that this class will be used. To get a GUID, use UUIDGen or GUIDGen, which are part of the Platform SDK (see http://msdn.microsoft.com/library).
attribute-SecurityGUID	May	No	If you want your new attribute to be part of some property set, store the rightsGuid of that property set to the attributeSecurityGUID of your new attribute. (See Chapter 4 for more information on property sets.)
mAPIID	May	Yes	Don't set this value. You won't have MAPI applications that would identify your new attributes with this ID.
linkID	May	Yes	Set this value if you are creating a linked attribute.

Syntax and Content Rules

Name	Must/ May*	System Only	Guidelines
attributeSyntax	Must	Yes	Set this according to the syntax you have chosen.
oMSyntax	Must	Yes	Set this according to the syntax you have chosen.
oMObjectClass	May	Yes	Set this according to the syntax you have chosen, when oMSyntax is 127. If you don't specify a value, Active Directory provides a default value that matches your chosen attributeSyntax. Remember, however, that one attributeSyntax may correspond to more than one oMObjectClass value, and if using the default, you cannot choose which one.
isSingleValued	May	Yes	Set this according to your needs. If you don't specify anything, the default is False (i.e., multivalued).
rangeLower	May	No	Specify this if you want a lower limit. There is no default.

(continued)

TABLE 9.3 Attributes of a New `attributeSchema` Object (*continued*)

Name	Must/ May*	System Only	Guidelines
Syntax and Content Rules			
rangeUpper	May	No	Specify this if you want an upper limit. There is no default.
extendedChars Allowed	May	Yes	If you happen to use the syntax Case-ignore string (teletex), you can set this value.
Searches			
searchFlags	May	No	Set this value if you want the new attribute to be indexed or part of the ANR set. You should index only attributes that have relatively unique values (such as last name). A Boolean attribute with True/False values is a bad choice for indexing. Also, multivalued attributes are bad choices because they are all but light to index. Note that indexing doesn't generate more data to be replicated, because indexes are created locally in each domain controller.
isMemberOf- Partial- AttributeSet	May	No	Set this to True if you want your new attribute to be part of the global catalog. Unlike indexing an attribute, adding an attribute to the global catalog increases the amount of replication traffic in your enterprise WAN, because subsequent value changes to this attribute in any object must be replicated to all global catalog servers of the forest. Consequently, you should use this setting only for attributes, which are relatively small, change quite seldom, and are probably of interest to most of the enterprise. See also the Warning in the text.
Miscellaneous			
systemOnly	May	Yes	Don't set this value. None of your attributes should be "system only," because in that case you couldn't use them.
systemFlags	May	Yes	Don't set this value. The bits in systemFlags are only for system use.

*As with classes, the division of whether you must or may define an attribute is not the same as the attribute's being mandatory or optional. Some mandatory attributes are filled by the system and some attributes you need to fill, even though technically they are optional.

NOTE   As with classes, if you want to set an attribute that is marked as "system only" in Table 9.3, you must do this when you create the `attributeSchema` object. You cannot change a system-only attribute later.

WARNING   Adding a new attribute as part of the global catalog causes a full replication (or "full sync") of all partial replicas of all global catalog servers in the forest. For example, if you have a forest where the directory database on a global catalog server is 1GB larger than in a normal domain controller, the size of the partial replicas combined is 1GB (although the number varies in different domains). If your forest contains 25 global catalog servers, adding a new attribute to the global catalog will generate about 25GB of replication in your LANs and WAN. This slight disadvantage will be removed in the next version of Active Directory included in Windows .NET Server. Already in the Windows 2000 version of Active Directory, removing attributes from the global catalog doesn't cause any replication. The global catalog servers remove the attributes locally from their databases.

When we discussed creating classes, we mentioned that a new class must pass some consistency checks. This is also true for new attributes. Two of these checks are not as evident as the rest.

- If `rangeLower` and `rangeUpper` are specified, `rangeUpper` must be larger than `rangeLower`.
- When you define link IDs, keep in mind that a back link must have a corresponding forward link.

Modifying an Attribute

Recall that when creating a new `attributeSchema` object, you can set 20 attributes. You can modify 8 of them, which we list in Table 9.4.

In addition, the following safety checks apply to category 1 (the base schema) attributes:

- You cannot change the `lDAPDisplayName`.
- You cannot change the `rangeLower` or `rangeUpper`.
- You cannot change the `attributeSecurityGUID`.

Actually, the only sensible changes to any category 1 attribute would be the settings for indexing, global catalog membership, and perhaps ANR.

TABLE 9.4 `AttributeSchema` **Object Attributes That Can Be Changed**

Name	Guidelines
`lDAPDisplayName`	Specify a name derived from the cn (e.g., sanaoCom2000-MyProduct-UserData).
`adminDisplayName`	No guidelines.
`adminDescription`	No guidelines.
`attributeSecurityGUID`	If you change an attribute to a new property set, it affects the permission of your Active Directory, so be very careful.
`rangeLower`	If you make a tighter range, you should first change the values of all instances to match the new limit.
`rangeUpper`	If you make a tighter range, you should first change the values of all instances to match the new limit.
`searchFlags`	If you index an attribute, the index will be built dynamically. If you choose not to index the attribute anymore, the index will be dropped from the database.
`isMemberOfPartialAttributeSet`	Be sparing in what you store in the global catalog. See also the previous Warning.

NOTE   Because 14 of the base schema attributes don't have their `systemFlags` attribute set, they are not recognized as being in category 1. Consequently, you can perform modifications on them, such as changing their `lDAPDisplayName`.

Deactivating Classes and Attributes

When you decide that a class or attribute is no longer necessary in your enterprise forest, you can deactivate it. This is also known as making it *defunct*. However, you cannot delete a class or attribute schema object.

Deactivating, rather than deleting, classes and attributes has two advantages.

- If the class or attribute were deleted, all the instances using it would have to be cleaned up from the forest in the deletion process. This would be a slow and difficult task, especially if your network spanned the globe.

- If you deactivate a class or attribute by mistake and you need it later, you can resurrect it, and nothing is lost or corrupted in the process. Active Directory doesn't do any cleanup of the instances when a class or attribute is deactivated.

RESTRICTIONS ON DEACTIVATION

The following are the restrictions on deactivating classes or attributes.

- You cannot deactivate any category 1 class or attribute, except those few in which Microsoft did not include the `systemFlags` protection.
- You cannot deactivate a class if it is in use by any nondefunct class. In other words, the class to be deactivated cannot be a "source" of any inheritance/ auxiliary relationships or possible superiors.
- You cannot deactivate an attribute if it is a member of any nondefunct class, either as a mandatory or optional attribute, and either directly or through inheritance/auxiliary. This means that if you start "tearing down" some of your classes and attributes, you must deactivate the classes first and only then can you deactivate the attributes.

HOW TO DEACTIVATE

Before you deactivate an attribute that is indexed or part of the global catalog, you may want to remove indexing or the global catalog membership to save space in the Active Directory database. Of course, if you expect to delete all instances of the deactivated class soon, the storage would be of little concern. In this case you would also benefit from the attribute being indexed and/or part of the global catalog; searching for instances to delete would be more efficient. An attribute cannot change after deactivation, so there will be no replication even if you don't remove the global catalog membership.

To deactivate a class or attribute, set the `isDefunct` attribute of the corresponding schema object to True. There is a check box for this that appears when you open the property page of a class or attribute in the Schema Manager snap-in.

The order of events could be the following:

1. Deactivate the classes.

2. Deactivate the attributes.

3. Search for any instances you want to delete and delete them.

If you have any instances that you want to keep in the directory, but you don't need their deactivated attributes in the indexes or the global catalog, you can perform the following additional steps:

1. Reactivate each deactivated attribute that is indexed or part of the global catalog.

2. Remove the indexing and/or global catalog settings.

3. Deactivate the attributes once more.

HOW DEACTIVATED CLASSES AND ATTRIBUTES BEHAVE

After deactivation, the class or attribute behaves as if it still exists, or doesn't exist, depending on what you are trying to do. The class or attribute *seems not to exist* in the following cases. You will receive an error if you try to

- Create a new instance of the deactivated class
- Change an existing instance of the deactivated class
- Change the deactivated class (i.e., the `classSchema` object), except to activate it again
- Extend the schema by relying on the deactivated class or attribute (use the class in inheritance/auxiliary or possible superiors, or add the attribute as a new mandatory or optional attribute)

However, the class or attribute still *exists quite normally* for the following operations:

- Searching or viewing instances of the deactivated class or attribute
- Deleting an instance of the deactivated class
- Extending the schema and reusing in new classes or attributes some name or identifier of the deactivated class or attribute (such as `lDAPDisplayName`, `governsID`, `attributeID`, `mAPIID`, or `schemaIDGUID`)

NOTE   Because a deactivated attribute can be a member of only a deactivated class, and you cannot create or modify the instances of that class, you obviously cannot create, modify, or even delete a value of a single deactivated attribute.

Because you can still see and delete all the instances of the deactivated classes and attributes, you can clean up the instances from your forest and be sure that no one can add new ones at the same time.

NOTE   Because of the fact stated in the previous Note, if you have any instances that you want to keep in the directory, but you don't need their (soon-to-be) deactivated attributes at all, you must delete those attributes prior to deactivating the class.

NOTE   Removing an auxiliary class from a structural class is somewhat similar to deactivating attributes. However, in this case the corresponding attributes become invisible, so you should first delete their values to save space in the directory database. For example, the user class of your forest is using the sanaoHumanResources auxiliary class, which contains the salary attribute. If you don't need the attributes (such as salary) of that auxiliary class anymore, you should first delete all their values, and after that remove sanaoHumanResources from the auxiliary class list of user. Using this order of tasks, any salary data is removed from your directory database.

REACTIVATING CLASSES AND ATTRIBUTES

As we mentioned previously, the only change that you can make to a deactivated class or attribute is to activate it again—that is, make it nondefunct. To do this, either set the isDefunct attribute to False or remove that attribute. Another way is to clear the appropriate check box in the Schema Manager snap-in.

NOTE   When you reactivate a class or attribute, Active Directory performs the same checks as if you were creating the class or attribute. For example, the attributes in the mayContain list must exist and be nondefunct.

THE MODIFICATION PROCESS

Now that we have explained in theory how to modify the schema, it is time to put this into practice. In this section we discuss

- The order in which you should perform the various tasks
- The means and tools you have for the job
- Some additional issues related to schema modifications

Order of Tasks

You may want to add your own custom extensions to the schema, either for administrative purposes or for some in-house application, or you may have bought a commercial directory-enabled application (DEA) that you are about to install. In any case, when you want to add some classes and attributes to your schema, there is a preferred order in which to proceed.

NOTE   A commercial DEA should have a separate installation program for any possible schema changes that it needs.

NOTE   The text in this section is written from an administrator's point of view. If you are an application vendor, part of the discussion doesn't apply to you, except in the manner in which your customers will use your application.

We have divided the procedure into the following 15 steps.

1. *Assign responsibilities.* Decide who is responsible for the schema and its modifications, keeping in mind that the schema is an enterprisewide "asset." Do you have a schema team and do the same people who decide on the changes implement them? You also need someone to allocate OIDs in the organization, which is a similar process to allocating IP addresses in that OIDs must be unique and administered in an organized way. Because OIDs have uses outside Active Directory (e.g., SNMP management), the OID administrators might or might not be the same as the schema administrators.

2. *Obtain an OID.* If you haven't already done so, obtain a base OID from an issuing authority. From this base OID, you can create OIDs for all future classes and attributes. In the case of a commercial DEA, the OIDs of the application vendor are used so the customer organization does not need its own.

3. *Plan the new classes and attributes.* We have described many attributes for the classSchema and attributeSchema objects. Either decide the value for each or decide not to assign a value. You should also have a strategy for the use of class inheritance and auxiliary classes. One of the guidelines at the beginning of this chapter recommends documenting all changes thoroughly. If you have a commercial DEA, evaluate the vendor's documentation to determine if you can employ those schema changes in your enterprise forest.

4. *Try the modifications in a test forest.* By following the remaining steps here, you should make any modifications first to a test forest (one domain controller in that forest is enough) that is separate from your production enterprise forest. You might make the changes to the test forest with the Schema Manager snap-in (and maybe with a little help from ADSI Edit). Then, using the LDIFDE tool, you could export the changes from the test forest and import them to your production forest. This way, the possibility of errors is minimized.

5. *Choose your schema master.* As you may recall from Chapter 5, one domain controller of your forest is holding the schema (operations) master role. All

schema changes should be made on that domain controller. Unless you have already done so, choose your schema master according to the instructions in Chapter 5.

6. *"Unlock" Schema Admins.* If you normally don't have members in Schema Admins, add one now, or if the smart card for the Schema Admin logon is stored in a safe, get it now and log on.

7. *Enable schema modifications.* By default, schema modifications are not possible in any domain controller, even in the schema master. You should enable the modifications on the domain controller that is holding the schema master role. With a commercial DEA, the schema installation program may do this for you; otherwise, you have to do it manually (as described in the section that follows this list).

8. *Create the attributes.* Create the attributes you need. Naturally, you will use the values from the plan that you made earlier. With a commercial DEA, the schema installation program will do this.

9. *Create the classes.* Create the classes according to your plan. Now that your new attributes exist, you can also add them to your new classes. If you create classes that depend on each other (inheritance/auxiliary, possible superiors), you must first create the classes that others depend on. If you refer to the earlier attributes and classes with an OID, the 5-minute wait before the schema cache update is not necessary. An OID refers to the disk version of the schema and, therefore, it doesn't matter if the schema cache is updated. If you use LDAP names instead of OIDs, you must either wait 5 minutes or update the schema cache manually. Note that if you use the Schema Manager snap-in, it shows LDAP names, but internally it uses OIDs. Again, with a commercial DEA, the schema installation program will do this.

10. *Check the changes.* If you made any errors, if there were other errors, or if the schema *concurrency control* kicks in, it is possible that some of your intended changes didn't complete. You should check that all the changes are OK by querying the modified schema objects and verifying that they exist and that their attribute values are what you specified. (We return to the topic of concurrency control in the "Some Gotchas in Changing the Schema" section later in this chapter.) A commercial DEA's schema installation program should perform the check (and fix anything that didn't pass in the first round).

11. *Disable schema modifications.* To prevent accidental changes, restore the protection that you removed four steps ago. A commercial DEA's schema installation program may do this. However, it is a good idea to double-check it manually.

12. *Re-establish Schema Admin locks.* If you have a policy of doing so, remove again any members from Schema Admins and return the smart card for the Schema Admin logon to a safe.

13. *Don't boot the schema master.* There is no need to boot any servers after the schema changes.

14. *Perhaps force a schema update.* If you need to use the schema modifications to create new instances, for example, before the 5-minute wait, you may update the schema cache. A commercial DEA's schema installation program may or may not do this, depending on how the vendor chose it to work.

15. *Perhaps trigger replication.* Schema changes are like any other Active Directory changes: They are normally replicated to other domain controllers of the forest. If you need to create instances on a domain controller other than the schema master and you don't want to wait for normal replication, you could trigger it to happen sooner.

ENABLING SCHEMA MODIFICATIONS

We mentioned in the previous list that you need to enable schema modifications on the schema master and also disable them after you have made the changes. There are two ways to do this.

- If you know how to use RegEdt32, start it and select the `HKEY_LOCAL_MACHINE` window. Next, locate the key `SYSTEM—CurrentControlSet—Services—NTDS—Parameters`. Under that key, add a value (if it doesn't exist already) named `Schema Update Allowed`, with a data type `REG_DWORD` and data "1" (without quotes). If the value already exists, change the data to "1". When you later disable schema changes, either change the data to "0" or remove the whole value (i.e., the parameter line).

- Start the Schema Manager snap-in and right-click the Active Directory Schema tree node in the left pane. Select Operations Masters from the context menu. The dialog box that opens includes a "The Schema may be modified on this Domain Controller" check box. By checking it, you actually turn on the aforementioned registry setting.

You could automate the registry change with the Resource Kit tool RegIni or use REG files with RegEdit. However, it is probably not a good idea to automate removal of such a protective setting.

The Means to Make Changes

There are several interactive and programmatic ways to change the schema:

- The Schema Manager snap-in
- ADSI Edit
- The LDIFDE utility and a text file in LDIF format
- The CSVDE utility and a text file in CSV (comma-separated values) format

- A script (e.g., in VBScript language) using the ADSI interface
- A schema installation program for some directory-enabled application (an EXE file)

Table 9.5 describes the pros and cons of each means.

TABLE 9.5 Means to Modify the Schema

Means	Description	Pros	Cons
The Schema Manager snap-in	The basic tool for managing the schema.	Specially made for manual simple schema changes.	Cannot set all the attributes you might want.
ADSI Edit	The tool to manage any attribute of any object in the directory.	Can set any attribute.	You must be careful to do things right.
LDIFDE	A command-line tool that exports objects to an LDIF format text file. LDIFDE can also add, modify, and delete objects based on an LDIF text file.	Can export changes from a test forest and import them in a production forest. The learning curve is not as steep as with scripts.	Not graphical or interactive.
CSVDE	A command-line tool that exports objects to a CSV format text file. CSVDE can also add objects based on a CSV text file.	Many spreadsheet, database, and other applications support CSV, so you can import and export Active Directory data to and from other applications.	Not graphical or interactive; can create objects but not change them; CSV format is not well suited for schema extensions.
Script*	A short text file containing script language (e.g., VBScript) that, by using ADSI operations, can modify the schema.	You can do just about anything you want. You can test the script in a lab network before deploying it to your production forest.	A learning curve in the beginning; possibility of bugs.
An installation EXE file	Typically a software vendor might write a schema installation EXE file for its directory-enabled application.	Cannot be tampered with; can handle errors and provide feedback; also the pros of scripts.	The administrator of a customer cannot see in advance how the program will change his schema. The learning curve is steeper than with scripts and the possibility of bugs is greater.

*See Chapter 11 for a sample script that creates an attribute and a class.

If you create a class with ADSI Edit, LDIFDE, or scripting, you cannot see the permissions for the new object using the Schema Manager snap-in. When you select the Security tab, you see just the text "Unable to display security information." However, using ADSI Edit you can see the permissions. We haven't been able to determine if the Schema Manager snap-in has a bug here, or if the reason is the funny `defaultSecurityDescriptor` value (just `D:S:`) in the object `CN=classSchema`. Whatever the reason is, it seems to cause no harm when you create new classes with any of the three ways mentioned.

The Schema Manager Snap-In

You can use the Schema Manager snap-in to create and modify both attributes and classes.

CREATING AND MODIFYING ATTRIBUTES

We listed earlier 20 `attributeSchema` attributes that you might want to set when you create new `attributeSchema` objects. With the Schema Manager snap-in you can set most of these attributes, but not quite all. Table 9.6 lists these attributes and specifies if you can set them when creating an object or later.

NOTE If you sometimes want to change the `lDAPDisplayName`, you cannot do it with the Schema Manager snap-in.

NOTE You cannot set the attributes `schemaIDGUID`, `linkID`, or `extendedChars-Allowed` at creation time. Because they are system only (i.e., they cannot change afterward), if you need a value for any of them, you must use a means other than the Schema Manager snap-in to create the `attributeSchema` object.

To create a new attribute, right-click the Attributes container and select Create Attribute. A general warning will appear, as shown in Figure 9.1. When you click Continue, the dialog box shown in Figure 9.2 appears, where you can enter the attributes for the `attributeSchema` object.

Once you have created the attribute, you can open its property dialog box, as shown in Figure 9.3.

TABLE 9.6 The Schema Manager Snap-in and the Attributes of an `attributeSchema` Object

Attribute	Schema Manager Creation Time	Schema Manager Later	System Only	Name in the User Interface (Creation Time/Later)
cn (Common-Name)/ name (RDN)	Yes	No	No/Yes	Common Name
lDAPDisplayName	Yes	**No***	No	LDAP Display Name/—
adminDisplayName	No	No	No	—
adminDescription	No	Yes	No	—/Description
attributeID	Yes	No	Yes	Unique X500 Object ID/X.500 OID
schemaIDGUID	**No**	No	Yes	—
attribute- SecurityGUID	No	No	No	—
mAPIID	No	No	Yes	—
linkID	**No**	No	Yes	—
attributeSyntax	Yes	No	Yes	Syntax
oMSyntax	Yes	No	Yes	Syntax
oMObjectClass	Yes	No	Yes	Syntax
isSingleValued	Yes	No	Yes	Multivalued/This attribute is …
rangeLower	Yes	Yes	No	Minimum
rangeUpper	Yes	Yes	No	Maximum
extended- CharsAllowed	**No**	No	Yes	—
searchFlags	No	Yes	No	—/Index…, Ambiguous…, Attribute is copied…
isMemberOf- Partial- AttributeSet	No	Yes	No	—/Replicate this attribute …
systemOnly	No	No	Yes	—
systemFlags	No	No	Yes	—

*Bold "No" indicates what we consider a (perhaps slight) shortcoming of the tool.

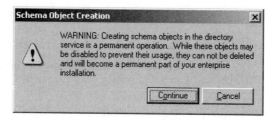

FIGURE 9.1 When you start creating schema objects, the snap-in warns that the operation is permanent.

FIGURE 9.2 To create a new `attributeSchema` object in your test forest, you can use the seven sample values shown here. Because `rangeLower` and `rangeUpper` are both 200, the octet string values that are later stored in this attribute must be exactly 200 bytes. The syntax choice corresponds to the `attributeSyntax`, `oMSyntax`, and `oMObjectClass` attributes.

CREATING AND MODIFYING CLASSES

With new `classSchema` objects, there are 21 attributes that you might want to set. Table 9.7 lists these attributes and indicates if you can manage them with the Schema Manager snap-in at creation time or later.

When you create a `classSchema` object in the Classes container, you see the same warning as with attributes. After you dismiss the warning, you enter the `classSchema` attributes in a two-page wizard, as shown in Figure 9.4 and Figure 9.5.

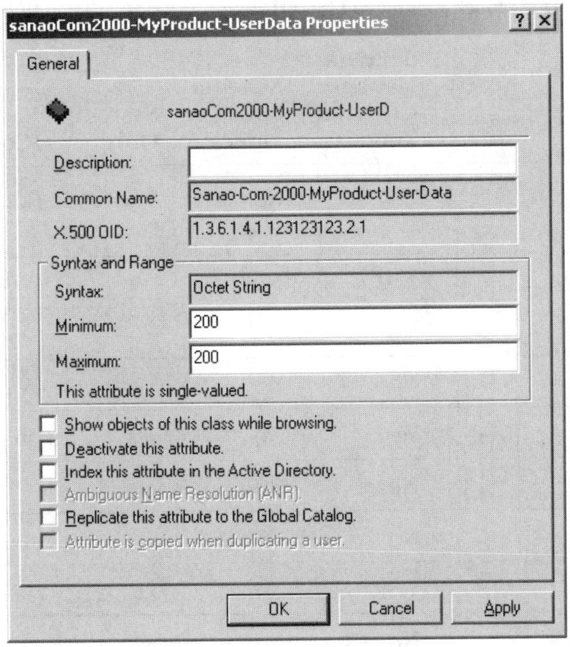

FIGURE 9.3 In the Property dialog box, you can check what you just created and make some changes.

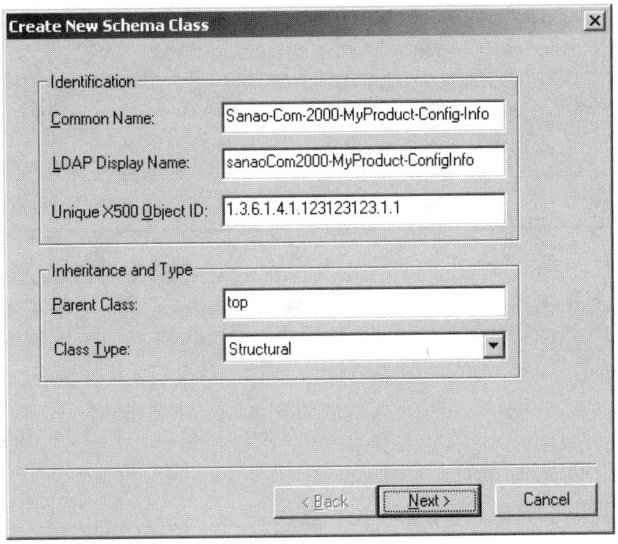

FIGURE 9.4 In the first page of the two-page wizard to create a new schema class, you enter the name and inheritance information.

TABLE 9.7 The Schema Manager Snap-in and the Attributes of a classSchema Object

Attribute	Schema Manager Creation Time	Schema Manager Later	System Only	Name in the User Interface (Creation Time/Later)
cn (Common-Name)/ name (RDN)	Yes	No	No/Yes	Common Name
lDAPDisplayName	Yes	**No***	No	LDAP Display Name/—
adminDisplayName	No	No	No	—
adminDescription	No	Yes	No	—/Description
governsID	Yes	No	Yes	Unique X500 Object ID/X.500 OID
schemaIDGUID	**No**	No	Yes	—
rDNAttID	No	No	Yes	—
mustContain	Yes	No	No	Mandatory
systemMustContain	**No**	No	Yes	—
mayContain	Yes	Yes	No	Optional
systemMayContain	**No**	No	Yes	—
possSuperiors	No	Yes	No	—/Possible Superior
systemPossSuperiors	**No**	No	Yes	—
objectClassCategory	Yes	No	Yes	Class Type
subClassOf	Yes	No	Yes	Parent Class
auxiliaryClass	No	Yes	No	—/Auxiliary Classes
systemAuxiliaryClass	**No**	No	Yes	—
defaultObjectCategory	No	Yes	No	—/Category
defaultHidingValue	**No**	No	No	—
defaultSecurity-Descriptor	No	No	No	—
systemOnly	No	No	Yes	—

*Bold "No" indicates a shortcoming, which may or may not affect you.

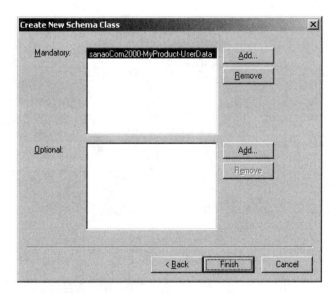

FIGURE 9.5 In the second page of the two-page wizard to create a new schema class, you can list mandatory and optional properties for the new class.

Having created the object, you can see its attributes in three property pages. We show the first two in Figure 9.6 and Figure 9.7. The third property page has the same lists of mandatory and optional properties that you see in Figure 9.5 when creating the object. The only obvious difference is that you can no longer change the list for mandatory attributes. Remember that Active Directory doesn't allow this.

ADSI Edit

To create a new attribute with ADSI Edit, you progress through a short wizard that prompts you for the values of the cn, oMSyntax, lDAPDisplayName, isSingleValued, attributeSyntax, and attributeID attributes for the new attribute. If you need to enter other system-only attributes (which you cannot change later), you must click More Attributes.

Creating a new class is a similar procedure to creating an attribute. This time the wizard asks you to enter values for cn, subClassOf, and governsID. You must click More Attributes to enter values of at least lDAPDisplayName and objectClassCategory.

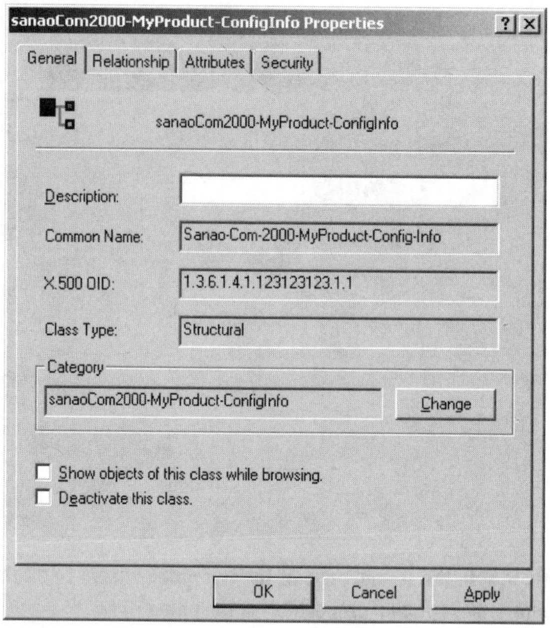

FIGURE 9.6 You can enter a description for the class, but unfortunately you cannot edit the `lDAPDisplayName` with the Schema Manager snap-in.

WARNING   Be sure to set `objectClassCategory` through More Attributes. Otherwise, you will get an 88-class, and you won't be able to ever fix the situation. You may also want to set `schemaIDGUID`, `mustContain`, or any of the system-only attributes before you click Finish to create the class.

If you would like to try to create some new schema objects with ADSI Edit, you can use the sample values in the LDIFDE example in the next section.

LDIFDE

With LDIFDE you can create and modify any objects, so you can use it to create `classSchema` and `attributeSchema` objects. Recall that earlier in this chapter we introduced the following process as a preferred way to modify your schema (we'll now add more detail):

1. Use the Schema Manager snap-in and perhaps also ADSI Edit to create your objects to a test forest.

2. Verify that all creations and changes are OK.

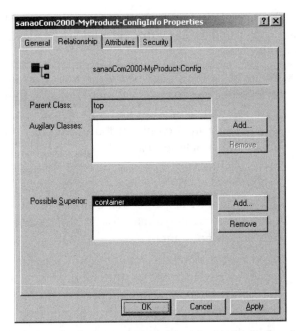

FIGURE 9.7 You must add at least one possible superior for a new class. Otherwise, you cannot use the class for anything (provided, of course, that it is a structural class).

3. Use LDIFDE to export the creations and changes to a text file.

4. Edit the text file (or rather, a copy of it).

5. Use LDIFDE to test the edited text file in a second test forest.

6. Use LDIFDE to import the creations and changes from the text file into your production forest.

Now we explain how to export, edit, and import the text file.

If you type just "ldifde" and press Enter, you will get the online Help for the tool. To export the changes to a text file, use the following command:

```
C:\>ldifde -f myext.txt -d cn=schema,cn=configuration,dc=testsanao,
dc=com -r (cn=sanao*)
```

This command writes all the schema objects that start with "sanao"—that is, those that you have created—to a text file called myext.txt.

NOTE   There is an m parameter in LDIFDE to be used when you export and import objects from one Active Directory forest to another. However, even if you use it, you still need to edit the file, so it doesn't actually save any work.

Next you have to edit the text file with an ASCII text editor such as Notepad. First copy the file to myextmod.txt and then make the following changes to the latter file.

- Remove the lines that specify the following attributes: cn, instanceType, distinguishedName, name, objectCategory, objectGUID, uSNChanged, uSNCreated, whenChanged, whenCreated, and systemOnly. (Object-GUID is actually the only attribute you must remove. Removal of the others makes the file a little cleaner.)

- Remove also the lines for defaultObjectCategory, schemaIDGUID, rDNAttID, defaultSecurityDescriptor, and adminDisplayName, unless you have a specific value stored in them. Note that the Schema Manager snap-in created a value for defaultSecurityDescriptor, which you may or may not want to use.

- If you were using the testsanao.com forest, change the distinguished names to sanao.com. Another method is to use the c parameter to replace the names when you later import the text file. (We show an example of this command line a little later in this chapter.)

- Order the lines so that the lines that create attribute objects appear before the lines that create class objects. Order also the lines for dependent class objects to follow the lines for the classes on which they depend.

- Because you now refer to the new attribute with an LDAP name instead of an OID, you must update the schema cache before you try to create the dependent class object. The update takes place when you insert the following lines in the correct position in your LDF file:

```
dn:
changetype: modify
add: schemaUpdateNow
schemaUpdateNow: 1
-
```

The empty distinguished name refers to the rootDSE virtual object. The hyphen in the last line designates the end of the attribute block.

The resulting file should look something like the following:

```
dn: CN=Sanao-Com-2000-MyProduct-User-Data, CN=Schema, CN=Configuration,
  DC=sanao, DC=com
changetype: add
attributeID: 1.3.6.1.4.1.123123123.2.1
attributeSyntax: 2.5.5.10
isSingleValued: TRUE
lDAPDisplayName: sanaoCom2000-MyProduct-UserData
objectClass: attributeSchema
oMSyntax: 4
```

```
rangeLower: 200
rangeUpper: 200
showInAdvancedViewOnly: TRUE

dn:
changetype: modify
add: schemaUpdateNow
schemaUpdateNow: 1
-

dn: CN=Sanao-Com-2000-MyProduct-Config-Info, CN=Schema, CN=Configuration,
  DC=sanao, DC=com
changetype: add
governsID: 1.3.6.1.4.1.123123123.1.1
lDAPDisplayName: sanaoCom2000-MyProduct-ConfigInfo
mustContain: sanaoCom2000-MyProduct-UserData
objectClass: classSchema
objectClassCategory: 1
possSuperiors: container
defaultHidingValue: TRUE
showInAdvancedViewOnly: TRUE
subClassOf: top
```

Binary values and some other attributes have a second colon, such as

```
schemaIDGUID:: 8b9KkY41PES0YAF8iAA+4A==
```

In this case, the value is coded using the same *base64* representation that MIME attachments use in SMTP messaging.

Because you had to make a number of modifications, you should test your LDF file on another empty test forest. You cannot use the first test forest because it already contains the new classes and attributes.

TIP If you want to clean up a one-server test forest, you can run DCPromo to demote the domain controller and then run DCPromo again to build up a new forest.

Use the following command to import the text file to both the second test forest and your production forest:

```
C:\>ldifde -i -f myextmod.txt
```

If you didn't edit the forest name in your LDIF file (i.e., the test forest name is still there), you can use the following command instead when you import the file to your production forest:

```
C:\>ldifde -i -f myextmod.txt -c "DC=testsanao,DC=com" "DC=sanao,
DC=com"
```

WARNING   The first forest distinguished name after the c parameter is the one that you have in the LDIF file. For LDIFDE to work, the name on the command line must exactly match the name in the file. You must have identical lowercase/uppercase letters and spacing (i.e., if one name has a space after the comma, the other one must also have a space after the comma).

The output for either command should look like the following:

```
Connecting to "dc1.sanao.com"
Logging in as current user using SSPI
Importing directory from file "myextmod.txt"
Loading entries....
3 entries modified successfully.
The command has completed successfully
```

CSVDE

An LDIF file has a pair of an attribute name and value on each line. A CSV file has a list of all attribute names on the first line and a list of values on another line, one line per object. This latter format is not practical for schema extensions, so we do not describe this option.

CSVDE is best suited for dumping an existing schema to a text file to be imported to a spreadsheet, as explained in Chapter 8.

An Installation EXE File

A commercial application vendor would probably choose to write an installation EXE file and ship it with its directory-enabled application. Although an EXE file doesn't show the customer administrator the changes that are going to happen to the schema, the EXE has the following advantages.

- Because it is a binary file, it is difficult to alter intentionally and impossible to alter unintentionally. If the file is corrupted by transmission, it is more likely to fail completely.

- The vendor can put more intelligence and interactivity into the program to adapt to various customers and error situations.

- LDIF uses base64 encoding for binary data, which is a somewhat awkward format for human beings. The programmer can handle various hexadecimal and

Unicode data more easily when using the C language, for example, to write an EXE file.

- An EXE file can be digitally signed to prove its origin and to ensure that it hasn't been corrupted or infected by a virus.

Some Gotchas in Changing the Schema

We want to mention two minor issues before we conclude our discussion about the schema modification process. They are the replication of schema changes and the concurrency control.

SCHEMA REPLICATION

When you add a new class to the schema and then an instance (object) of that class, it is possible that the new instance reaches some other domain controller before the new class does.

We explained the situation in Chapter 5. We also described the following solution: If a domain controller receives an instance of an unknown class, it will abort processing the current replication data and write a "schema mismatch" message to the event log. Then it automatically resyncs the schema from the source domain controller and requests again the normal replication data. This time everything should go fine.

CONCURRENCY CONTROL

The schema has *concurrency control*—that is, only one schema object change can take place at a time. This prevents a situation in which two conflicting changes occur at the same time. Therefore, if two people or applications try to modify the schema simultaneously, some of the changes may not complete.

Because concurrency control controls each object change separately, it is possible that when two people try to make ten changes, eight of one person's changes and six of the other person's changes will complete. Consequently, to have all the changes in place, the former person should repeat two changes and the latter person should repeat four changes.

Any schema installation program, especially a commercial program, should accommodate concurrency control. If the installation program is run a second time, it should notice that some of the extensions are already in and gracefully add only the missing extensions.

BRINGING THE EXTENSIONS TO THE USER INTERFACE

Now that you have extended your Active Directory under the hood (i.e., added some attributes and classes to the schema), you are probably anxious to see the extensions in the user interface.

In this section we discuss three things about the instances of your new classes:

- Where to place them
- How to manage permissions for them
- How to create and display them, including their attributes

For brevity, we call the instances of your new classes "new objects."

Where to Place the New Objects

Depending on the intended purposes of the new objects, you can choose to place them in various places of a domain partition or sometimes in the configuration partition. You have the following five options:

- *Under the corresponding user objects.* If each new object directly relates to one user object, you should store the new objects under the corresponding user objects. This way, when you delegate administration of the user objects, the delegation applies also to these child objects. In addition, when you delete or move a user object, the child objects are deleted or moved with their parent.

- *Under corresponding other objects.* If each new object directly relates to some other object type, such as computer, you should store the new objects under these corresponding objects.

- *In any convenient OU.* If the new objects are not related to any specific objects in the domain, you can place them in any convenient OU. You would control their visibility to users, as well as delegate administration, using Active Directory permissions.

- *In the System container.* If you don't want the new objects to be part of the normal OU tree, you can store them in the System container, which exists in every domain. You should first create (using ADSI Edit, for example) a container that includes your organization's name and then store the new objects in this new container. This ensures that if you later buy a directory-enabled application, the objects it will create won't collide with the objects you are now creating. An example container would be CN=Sanao Corp, CN=System, DC=sales, DC=sanao, DC=com.

- *In the configuration partition*. You might want the new objects to be replicated to all domain controllers of your forest instead of just one domain. You can achieve this by placing the new objects in the configuration partition. Recall that the data in Active Directory should be globally useful, relatively static, and small. Obviously, when you place the objects in the configuration partition, these requirements are even more important than in the single-domain case. Microsoft recommends storing the objects in either the Services container or in a site object. Again, the container you create for new objects should include your organization's name.

NOTE   In the list of where to place new objects, we recommend in two situations that you create a container for the new objects and that it includes your organization's name. You might consider this for other situations as well (e.g., when creating child objects under a user object).

Managing Permissions

One important part of managing the new objects is to manage permissions for them. You can assign permissions either to individual attributes or to several attributes at once using property sets. We discuss both possibilities in the following two sections.

We use the `sanaoClass` class as an example. One of its mandatory attributes is `sanaoAttribute1` and one of its optional attributes is `sanaoAttribute2`. The recommended names, such as `sanaoCom2000-MyProduct-ConfigInfo`, are so long that they are somewhat clumsy to use in these examples.

MANAGING PERMISSIONS FOR INDIVIDUAL ATTRIBUTES

When you add attributes to either new or existing classes, those attributes automatically become visible on the property permission page of the ACL Editor, as Figure 9.8 illustrates. (You can hide some of the attributes from the list using DSSec.Dat, as described in Chapter 4.) Consequently, you can manage their per-attribute permissions as with any other attribute.

USING PROPERTY SETS

Now that you have new attributes, you can put them in a property set. This enables you to assign permissions for them as one entity. We show here an example of how to create a property set and put two attributes, `sanaoAttribute1` and `sanao-Attribute2`, in it. The set will apply to the instances of the `sanaoClass class`.

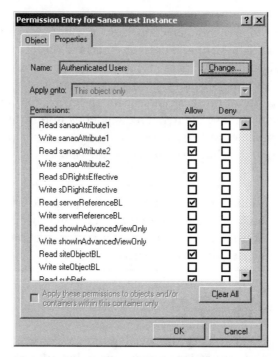

FIGURE 9.8 When you have two new attributes, `sanaoAttribute1` and `sanaoAttribute2`, in the `sanaoClass` class, the attributes automatically appear in the permission list.

First, use ADSI Edit to locate `CN=Extended Rights, CN=Configuration`, which resides in the configuration partition. Next, create a new `controlAccess-Right` object in that container. Give the object a name (i.e., the cn attribute) such as Sanao Property Set. It is not necessary to set any other values yet. Figure 9.9 shows the ADSI Edit windows and the Create Object dialog box.

Now that you have the Sanao Property Set object, you need to set four attributes for it, as explained in the following list.

- *AppliesTo*. This attribute specifies the class or classes to which the property set applies. The value(s) must be the `schemaIDGUID` attribute of the corresponding `classSchema` object, although unfortunately in a different format. If `sanaoClass` has the `schemaIDGUID` of "0x73 0xa7 0x49 0xad 0x86 0x05 0xe8 0x44 0xaa 0x46 0xa9 0xd3 0xbb 0xe7 0xf9 0xbf," you must first remove the "0x"s to get "73a749ad8605e844aa46a9d3bbe7f9bf." Next, you add three dashes to get "73a749ad-8605-e844-aa46-a9d3bbe7f9bf." As the last step, you swap some bytes (remember that a byte corresponds to two hex characters). The first "word" up to a dash must be swapped—for example, you would replace 12345678 with 78563412. The two bytes in the second and third

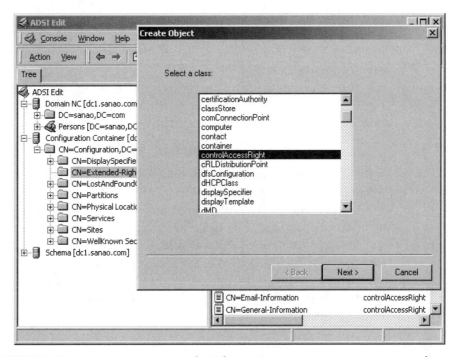

FIGURE 9.9 To create a new property set, begin by creating a `controlAccessRight` object. It will represent the property set.

"words" must be swapped, such as 1234 to 3412. The result is "ad49a773-0586-44e8-aa46-a9d3bbe7f9bf," so now you (finally) have a GUID to store in the `appliesTo` attribute.

- *DisplayName*. This attribute specifies the text to show in the ACL Editor. You can enter "Sanao Properties" as the value.

- *RightsGuid*. This attribute serves as an identifier to which the attributes in the set will refer. You need a fresh GUID for this one, so you would run UUID-Gen from the Platform SDK and get something like "55f648e1-f367-4ebb-9589-7e74fc2f8d84." If you haven't downloaded the Platform SDK, you can type any random hexadecimal characters to get a GUID. However, for production purposes, you must use UUIDGen or GUIDGen from the Platform SDK.

- *ValidAccesses*. This attribute specifies the possible permissions for the property set. The value 16 means that only Read is visible in the list, whereas the value 32 shows only Write. Normally you would define the value 48, which results in both Read and Write being visible. (The values correspond to `ADS_RIGHT_DS_READ_PROP` and `ADS_RIGHT_DS_WRITE_PROP`.)

After setting the four attribute values for the property set object, you must specify the attributes it should contain. You do this by setting the `attribute-SecurityGUID` of each appropriate attribute to be the same as the `rightsGuid` of the property set object.

The value of our `rightsGuid` was "55f648e1-f367-4ebb-9589-7e74fc2f8d84." Unfortunately, `attributeSecurityGUID` uses the same format of GUIDs as `schemaIDGUID` did, which means that you must perform a reversed conversion process of what we described with the `appliesTo` attribute. The result is "0xe1 0x48 0xf6 0x55 0x67 0xf3 0xbb 0x4e 0x95 0x89 0x7e 0x74 0xfc 0x2f 0x8d 0x84." This is the value that you need to store in `attributeSecurityGUID` of each appropriate `attributeSchema` object.

At this point, you can try the new property set. Obviously, you need to create an instance of `sanaoClass` to be able to apply any permissions. You must create the test object with ADSI Edit, but after that you can use either ADSI Edit or the Users and Computers snap-in to see and modify the permissions.

Figure 9.10 shows the new property set. You will see the same two lines for Sanao Properties (Read and Write) if you click Advanced, click View/Edit, and click the Properties tab.

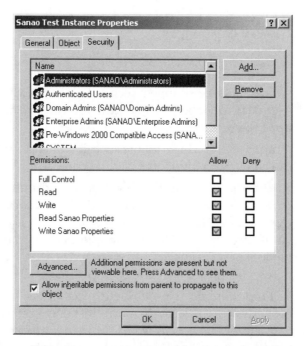

FIGURE 9.10 If you add a property set as a `controlAccessRight` object to the configuration partition, you can use the property set (such as Sanao Properties) to give permissions for applicable objects.

Creating and Displaying the Objects

Active Directory's architecture facilitates showing the new classes and attributes in various administrative tools as well as in the end-user interface. This architecture covers the following display elements:

- Property pages, which are different in admin tools (e.g., the Users and Computers snap-in) and end-user applications, including the Windows shell (My Network Places and Start menu, Search)
- Context menus, again different for administrators and end users
- Icons
- Creation wizards
- Class and attribute display names

You can, of course, always use ADSI Edit to browse and manage any old and new classes and attributes. Using the listed display elements, however, facilitates building an easier user interface.

The good news is that the display elements are defined in Active Directory itself, which means that they are available to any user of the forest. The bad news is that the definitions in Active Directory refer to DLL and other files, which must be on any local computer where the new display elements are to be used. This brings up the question of distributing the files.

Another piece of bad news is that adding display elements usually requires programming. Especially the property pages and creation wizards require that you create them as Component Object Model (COM) objects. Each COM object also needs to implement the appropriate COM interfaces, such as `IShellProp-SheetExt` or `IContextMenut`.

NOTE   Administration scripts are as far as we go toward programming in this book. Because you can write COM objects for property pages and creation wizards only with real programming languages, such as Visual Basic or C/C++, you need to turn elsewhere for that information.

Although you may not be a programmer, we briefly explain the display architecture here for two reasons.

- You wouldn't write COM objects, but you could buy an application that extends your displays, or your company might have an in-house developer to write those applications.
- Even without writing COM objects, you can still create some display elements. For example, at the end of this section we show how you can view logon

counts and other information about your network users by adding an item to the context menu of users.

Display Specifiers

Each class that needs some of the display elements previously listed has a *display specifier* object to define the elements. You can use ADSI Edit to find these objects in the configuration container. First locate the DisplaySpecifiers container and then your locale identifier, such as 409 for English (United States). The common name for the container is similar to the following:

```
CN=409,CN=DisplaySpecifiers,CN=Configuration,DC=sanao,DC=com
```

Figure 9.11 shows some of the contents of the 409 container. As you can see, the display object names are the same as the class LDAP names, but "-Display" is appended.

NOTE   As mentioned, the actual property or wizard pages must be implemented as COM objects. These objects are often stored in DLL files. Applications don't refer to various COM objects with their filenames, but use instead *class identifiers* (CLSID). Class identifiers are about the same as globally unique identifiers (GUIDs) or

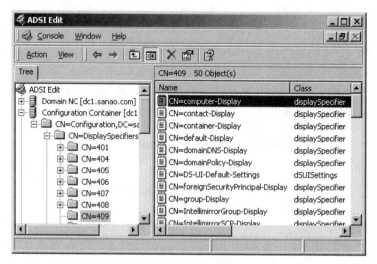

FIGURE 9.11 Each class that needs user interface elements has a corresponding object in the DisplaySpecifiers container. There can be separate display objects for each locale.

universally unique identifiers (UUIDs), and an example of all three is {6dfe648b-a212-11d0-bcd5-00c04fd8d5b6}. You can find in the registry all the class identifiers registered in your computer. You must use either RegEdt32 or RegEdit and locate the path `HKEY_CLASSES_ROOT—CLSID`. The class identifier keys in that location specify, among other things, the file that the COM object lives in.

Table 9.8 describes the attributes that define the various display elements.

NOTE   In reality, the Users and Computers snap-in doesn't use all the display specifier attributes (even though it is suggested here and in Microsoft's documentation). For example, most of the field names in user properties (such as Description or Office) are hard-coded in the snap-in, so the snap-in does not read them from the `attributeDisplayNames` attribute.

TABLE 9.8 Display Specifier Attributes

Attribute	Description
`adminPropertyPages`, `shellPropertyPages`	These two multivalued attributes define the COM objects that contain property pages for admin tools and the end-user Windows shell, respectively. Each element defines one COM object as follows: `<order-number>`, `<CLSID>`, `[optional data]`. The order numbers determine the position of each page, and they are not required to be consecutive. Each COM object may implement more than one property page.
`adminContextMenu`, `shellContextMenu`, `contextMenu`	These three multivalued attributes define the context menus for admin tools and the end-user Windows shell, or both, respectively. Each element defines either one COM object (as with property pages: `<order-number>`, `<CLSID>`, `[optional data]`) or an application.
	The syntax for the latter choice is `<order-number>`, `<context menu name>`, `<program name>`. The context menu name appears as the text in the context menu and the program name defines which program is launched. If the full path hasn't been defined, the application must be in the search path of the computer where the new menu item is used. The LDAP path to the selected object and its class are passed as the first and second arguments for the program, respectively.
	The latter choice (an application instead of a COM object) allows using scripts also (see the next section for an example).

(continued)

TABLE 9.8 Display Specifier Attributes (*continued*)

Attribute	Description
iconPath	This multivalued attribute defines the icons for the class. Each element uses either the syntax `<state>, <ICO-file-name>` or `<state>, <DLL-file-name>, <resource-ID>`. The state is a value between 0 and 15, where 0 means "default" or "closed," 1 means "open," and 2 means "disabled." The ICO or DLL file must be in the search path of the local computer. Resource-ID is an index to the icon in the file.
creationWizard	This single-valued attribute defines the COM object that contains the pages for the creation wizard of an object class. The syntax is `<CLSID>`. Using this attribute completely replaces an existing wizard.
createWizardExt	This multivalued attribute defines the COM objects that contain additional pages for a creation wizard. The syntax is `<order-number>, <CLSID>`. Again, the order number determines the extension's position in the wizard.
createDialog	This single-valued attribute allows modifying the formation of a user's or contact's full name. If you type "Jack" for the first name and "Brown" for the last name, the full name is normally "Jack Brown." If you set `createDialog` to be `%<sn>, %<givenName>`, the full name will be "Brown, Jack."
classDisplayName	This multivalued attribute defines the display name for the class to be used in admin tools and the end-user shell.
attributeDisplayNames	This multivalued attribute defines the display name for each attribute of the class. Each element contains a pair of `LDAP name, display name`, such as `samAccountName,Computer name (pre-Windows 2000)`.
treatAsLeaf	If true, this single-valued Boolean attribute defines that the corresponding class should be displayed as a leaf object in the user interface, even though it technically would be a container object. An example of this is the user class.

As an example of a display specifier object, we used LDIFDE to dump the attributes of `computer-Display`. The appropriate lines of the dump are as follows:

```
dn: CN=computer-Display, CN=409, CN=DisplaySpecifiers, CN=Configuration,
  DC=sanao, DC=com
adminPropertyPages: 1,{6dfe6492-a212-11d0-bcd5-00c04fd8d5b6}
adminPropertyPages: 3,{77597368-7b15-11d0-a0c2-080036af3f03}
adminPropertyPages: 4,{6dfe648b-a212-11d0-bcd5-00c04fd8d5b6}
```

```
adminPropertyPages: 5,{6dfe6488-a212-11d0-bcd5-00c04fd8d5b6}
adminPropertyPages: 6,{4E40F770-369C-11d0-8922-00A024AB2DBB}
adminPropertyPages: 10,{0F65B1BF-740F-11d1-BBE6-0060081692B3}
shellPropertyPages: 1,{f5d121f4-c8ac-11d0-bcdb-00c04fd8d5b6}
shellPropertyPages: 2,{dde2c5e9-c8ae-11d0-bcdb-00c04fd8d5b6}
adminContextMenu: 1,{08eb4fa6-6ffd-11d1-b0e0-00c04fd8dca6}
contextMenu: 0,{62AE1F9A-126A-11D0-A14B-0800361B1103}
createWizardExt: 1,{D6D8C25A-4E83-11d2-8424-00C04FA372D4}
classDisplayName: Computer
attributeDisplayNames: samAccountName,Computer name (pre-Windows 2000)
attributeDisplayNames: operatingSystemVersion,Operating System Version
attributeDisplayNames: operatingSystem,Operating System
attributeDisplayNames: managedBy,Managed By
attributeDisplayNames: description,Description
attributeDisplayNames: cn,Name
treatAsLeaf: TRUE
```

Now that you know the attributes, you are ready to test-change a couple of them.

Testing to Change the Displays

If you have a test forest, you can test the following two things:

- Change the class display name
- Add an item to a context menu

If you locate the `computer-Display` object with ADSI Edit, you can see that the value for the `classDisplayName` attribute is "Computer." As an experiment, change this to "Television." If you now open up the Users and Computers snap-in, you will notice that the type of any computer object is shown as "Television."

NOTE The information in the display specifiers is cached per process and per class. This means that if you already had the Users and Computers snap-in running, you might need to restart it to see the change.

Next we test adding a context menu item for user objects. To achieve this, we need to perform the following steps.

1. Add the two menu definitions to the `contextMenu` attribute of the `user-Display` object.
2. Create and test the first corresponding program (a batch file).
3. Create and test the second corresponding program (a VBScript file).

ADDING THE MENU DEFINITIONS

Locate the `user-Display` object with ADSI Edit and select the `contextMenu` attribute. Add to the attribute the following two values, but don't remove existing values:

```
11, Test Item &1, c:\test\testitem.bat
12, Test Item &2, c:\test\testitem.vbs
```

We use numbers 11 and 12 to leave room in case a future version of Active Directory uses 1 and 2. (A proper way for a C programmer would be to list the existing values to find out which values are available.) The ampersand character (&) defines that the next character will be underlined, which allows you to use it as a hot key.

Your resulting property page should look like the one in Figure 9.12, although the order of the values may vary.

You would already see the new items in the context menu of any user, as shown in Figure 9.13. Selecting a new item would do nothing, however, because the corresponding program does not exist yet.

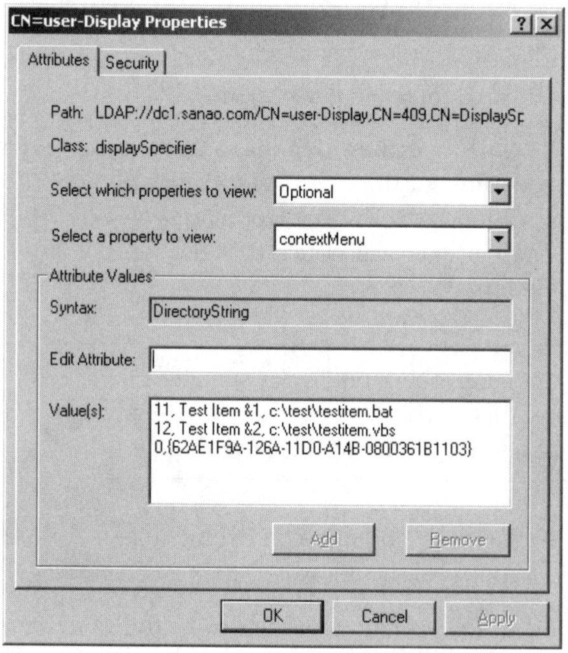

FIGURE 9.12 You can add context menu items to existing or new classes by adding the corresponding definitions as values in a display specifier object.

FIGURE 9.13 **The new items appear in the context menu.**

CREATING AND TESTING A BATCH FILE

Create the folder C:\Test. Using an ASCII text editor (i.e., Notepad), create the file C:\Test\TestItem.Bat and add the following lines:

```
@echo off
echo Name is: %1
echo Class is: %2
pause
```

Next, launch the Users and Computers snap-in and open any user's context menu. You should see the two new items you just added. When you select the first new item, a screen like the one shown in Figure 9.14 should appear.

We used a batch file as the first example to keep it simple but give you an idea of the process. In practice, however, if you are using batch files, your possibilities are limited.

```
C:\WINNT\system32\cmd.exe                          _ □ ×
Name is: "LDAP://dc1.sanao.com/CN=Jack Brown,OU=Sales,DC=sanao,DC=com"
Class is: user
Press any key to continue . . .
```

FIGURE 9.14 **The LDAP path to the selected object and its class are passed to the launched program. This example doesn't use the two values, except for showing them to you.**

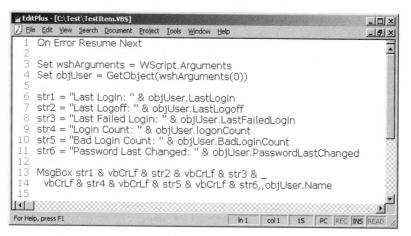

FIGURE 9.15 TestItem.VBS. This script displays logon information about a user.

CREATING AND TESTING A VBSCRIPT SCRIPT

The Users and Computers snap-in doesn't show when a user has last logged on or if someone has tried wrong passwords for that user account. You can create a script to fill this need. Our example uses EditPlus (a shareware program from http://www.editplus.com/), but Notepad is also fine.

First create the file C:\Test\TestItem.VBS and add the lines shown in Figure 9.15. (You can also download the file from the book's Web site at http://www.kouti.com/.) Line 1 specifies that if a later line contains an error, continue with the next line instead of quitting the script right away. The most likely error source is that some attribute value is not set, in which case we just list all the others. Line 2 collects all arguments and line 3 creates a user COM object from the first (denoted by "0") argument. As you remember, the first argument is the LDAP path to the selected user.

Next the script retrieves each attribute and stores the values to six string variables, along with the description text. The last line (split across lines 13 and 14 with the underscore) pops up the result, putting a carriage return/linefeed (CrLf) between each attribute. It also puts the name property of the object in the caption text of the message box.

NOTE

On line 9 of TestItem.VBS, "logonCount" starts with a lowercase letter, whereas "BadLoginCount" and others start with uppercase letters. The reason is that "logonCount" is an attribute LDAP name, but the others are ADSI property method names.

NOTE	Actually, both "logonCount" and "LogonCount" would work. VBScript is not a case-sensitive language.

After saving the file, select your second menu item in the context menu of any of your users. A screen like the one in Figure 9.16 should appear. In this example, Jack has logged on 37 times. He has never tried to log on with a wrong password, nor has someone else tried to use his account. Consequently, the last failed logon time is A.D. 1601, when Henry IV (le bon Henri) still ruled France! The corresponding large integer attribute `badPasswordTime` has a value of zero, which indicates that ancient date. The time shows 3:00 AM instead of midnight, because the local time when running the script was 3 hours ahead GMT/UTC (2 hours for the time zone and another hour for daylight saving time).

A bad login count of zero indicates that there were no unsuccessful logon attempts after the last successful logon. Upon each successful logon, the bad login count is reset to zero.

WARNING	In the example in Figure 9.16, all settings except `PasswordLastChanged` correspond to nonreplicating attributes. Therefore, each domain controller knows the values only for itself; you will get different results if you read the settings from different domain controllers.

NOTE	`LastLogoff` doesn't work, at least in the first version of Active Directory included in Windows 2000. Therefore, the second line of the output is empty.

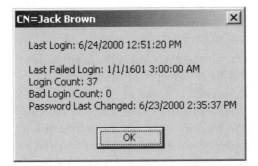

FIGURE 9.16 By adding a context menu item for user objects, you can display sometimes useful attributes that the Users and Computers snap-in doesn't show you.

NOTE   Microsoft uses "logons," but Novell uses "logins." Because ADSI is designed to work also with NetWare networks, Microsoft chose to use the name `LastLogin` instead of `LastLogon`.

NOTE   If the default in your computer is CScript instead of WScript, you will see an extra character-based window when you select the menu item. We discuss this, as well as other aspects of scripting, in Chapter 10.

EXTENDING THE USER CLASS

To summarize the discussion of extension and modification to the schema, we present an example of how to extend the `user` class.

You could use the `user` class extensions (i.e., new attributes) at least for two purposes:

- Human resources management for data such as the date each user started to work for your organization or the name of his or her previous employer
- IT management for data such as the primary workstation of each user

We use the first situation in this example. We will plan the extensions, implement them, and also show how to manage the values and permissions for the new attributes.

Planning the Extensions

We expect to have quite a few new human resources attributes for user objects. Therefore, it is convenient to put the attributes first into an auxiliary class and then add this auxiliary class to the `user` class. Figure 9.17 shows the new auxiliary class as well as the two sample attributes it will contain.

We cannot add new mandatory attributes to an existing class, so both our new attributes are optional (i.e., `mayContain`).

The recommended format for class and attribute names that we presented earlier in this chapter could lead to very long names. We use somewhat shorter names here because we will use the attributes in our scripts and LDAP queries. Having shorter names will save us a lot of typing in the future.

Our company has a base OID "1.3.6.1.4.1.123123123." Below that base we have allocated "11" to human resources classes and "12" to human resources attributes.

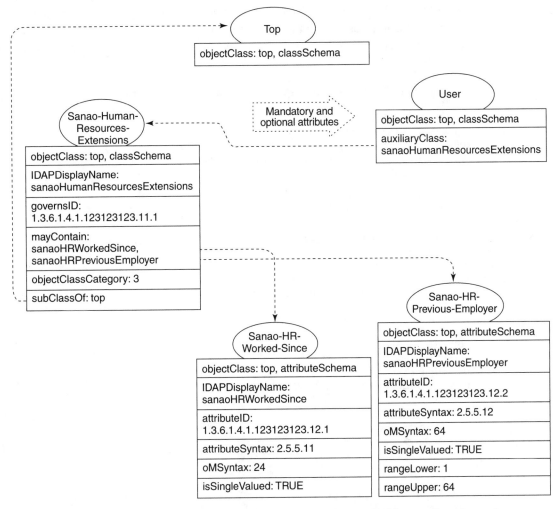

FIGURE 9.17 `ObjectClassCategory` 3 means that the new class on the left is auxiliary. It contains two optional attributes, which will be used in the `user` class through this auxiliary class.

The `sanaoHRWorkedSince` attribute uses the `Generalized time` syntax, whereas `sanaoHRPreviousEmployer` uses a normal `Unicode string` syntax. The latter attribute has a maximum length of 64 characters.

Implementing the Extensions

We use LDIFDE to create the three new schema objects and to extend the `user` class. It is a straightforward tool once we know the values for all needed attributes.

Besides, an LDIF file allows us to list the extensions in an exact and compact way (both for the in-house document and this book). We don't want to repeat the numerous screen shots that you saw earlier in this chapter. The following 54 lines will do the trick:

```
dn: CN=Sanao-HR-Worked-Since, CN=Schema, CN=Configuration,
   DC=sanao, DC=com
changetype: add
objectClass: attributeSchema
lDAPDisplayName: sanaoHRWorkedSince
attributeID: 1.3.6.1.4.1.123123123.12.1
attributeSyntax: 2.5.5.11
oMSyntax: 24
isSingleValued: TRUE
showInAdvancedViewOnly: TRUE

dn: CN=Sanao-HR-Previous-Employer, CN=Schema, CN=Configuration,
   DC=sanao, DC=com
changetype: add
objectClass: attributeSchema
lDAPDisplayName: sanaoHRPreviousEmployer
attributeID: 1.3.6.1.4.1.123123123.12.2
attributeSyntax: 2.5.5.12
oMSyntax: 64
isSingleValued: TRUE
rangeLower: 1
rangeUpper: 64
showInAdvancedViewOnly: TRUE

dn:
changetype: modify
add: schemaUpdateNow
schemaUpdateNow: 1
-

dn: CN=Sanao-Human-Resources-Extensions, CN=Schema, CN=Configuration,
   DC=sanao, DC=com
changetype: add
objectClass: classSchema
lDAPDisplayName: sanaoHumanResourcesExtensions
governsID: 1.3.6.1.4.1.123123123.11.1
mayContain: sanaoHRWorkedSince
mayContain: sanaoHRPreviousEmployer
objectClassCategory: 3
subClassOf: top
defaultHidingValue: TRUE
showInAdvancedViewOnly: TRUE

dn:
changetype: modify
add: schemaUpdateNow
schemaUpdateNow: 1
-
```

```
dn: CN=User, CN=Schema, CN=Configuration, DC=sanao, DC=com
changetype: modify
add: auxiliaryClass
auxiliaryClass: sanaoHumanResourcesExtensions
-
```

We added `showInAdvancedViewOnly = True` to each object to keep them hidden from normal administrative tools and end-user interface. We did this because all the base schema objects have the setting also. This is not part of the actual schema characteristics.

Managing the Attribute Values

Unfortunately the Users and Computers snap-in doesn't notice our new attributes and start magically showing them on one of the property pages. We would have to start writing a COM component (using the C language, for example) to implement a new property page.

We have two other choices to read and modify the values, although neither of them is particularly handy:

- Use ADSI Edit
- Use scripts

For the scripting option, you could create a new menu item for the `user` class and when selecting that item on some user, you would see the current value and perhaps enter a new value. Another choice is to apply a script to a number of users, again either just displaying current values or modifying them. You could have the values in a large Excel spreadsheet and write them to the new Active Directory attributes.

We demonstrate here the scripting option for a single user. Chapter 11 has examples of listing attribute values for a number of users and using an Excel spreadsheet as a means of input.

ADDING A SCRIPT TO THE CONTEXT MENU

We explained earlier in this chapter how to add new menu items and use them. Here we briefly list the steps that apply to our user extension example.

1. Using ADSI Edit, locate the `user-Display` object (in `CN=409, CN=DisplaySpecifiers, CN=Configuration`).

2. Select the `adminContextMenu` attribute. Add to the attribute the value 2, `S&anao Human Resources, c:\test\sanaohr.vbs`. Do not remove existing values and if number 2 is already in use, select a free number.

3. Create the file c:\test\sanaohr.vbs and add the lines shown in Figure 9.18.

```
EditPlus - [C:\Test\SanaoHR.VBS]
File  Edit  View  Search  Document  Project  Tools  Window  Help
1   On Error Resume Next
2
3   Set wshArguments = WScript.Arguments
4   Set objUser = GetObject(wshArguments(0))
5
6   str1 = "The current information"
7   str2 = "Worked for Sanao since: " & objUser.sanaoHRWorkedSince
8   str3 = "Previous employer: " & objUser.sanaoHRPreviousEmployer
9   str4 = "Would you like to modify the previous employer?"
10
11  intAnswer = MsgBox(str1 & vbCrLf & vbCrLf & str2 & vbCrLf & str3 & _
12     vbCrLf & vbCrLf & str4, _
13     vbYesNo, _
14     "Human Resources Information for " & objUser.Name)
15
16  If intAnswer = vbNo Then WScript.Quit
17
18  strEmployer = InputBox("Enter the previous employer", _
19     "Sanao Human Resources", objUser.sanaoHRPreviousEmployer)
20
21  If strEmployer = "" Then WScript.Quit   'User clicked Cancel
22
23  objUser.sanaoHRPreviousEmployer = strEmployer
24  objUser.SetInfo
25
For Help, press F1                                    ln 1   col 1   25   PC  REC INS READ
```

FIGURE 9.18 SanaoHR.VBS

On lines 7 and 8 of Figure 9.18 we read the current values for the two human resources attributes. On line 11 we use the MsgBox function to display the results. Line 13 specifies that there are Yes and No buttons instead of the default OK button.

If the user clicks No, the script will terminate on line 16. If she clicks Yes, we use the InputBox function to ask for a new value for one of the attributes. Finally, on lines 23 and 24 we store the new value back to Active Directory.

After saving the file, you can select the menu item Sanao Human Resources in the context menu of any of your users. A screen like the one in Figure 9.19 should appear. If the user clicks Yes, he will face the dialog box shown in Figure 9.20.

Searching on the New Attributes

The new attributes will show in the Find dialog box of My Network Places if you only add a display name for each of the attributes.

As with adding menu items, you need to modify the attributes of the user-Display object. Add the following two new values to the attributeDisplay-Names attribute:

```
sanaoHRWorkedSince,Sanao HR Worked Since
sanaoHRPreviousEmployer,Sanao HR Prev. Employer
```

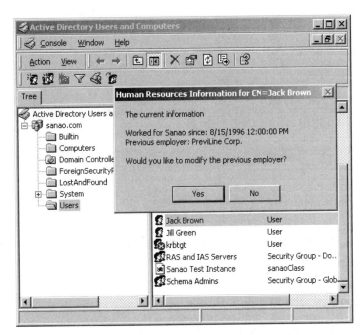

FIGURE 9.19 When you select Sanao Human Resources in the context menu of Jack Brown, you see the contents of our two new attributes.

Once you log off and log on again, you can start using the new attributes. Open My Network Places, Entire Network, Directory, and then open the Find dialog box from the context menu of sanao. The new attributes are available in the Advanced tab, as shown in Figure 9.21.

It is not practical to use the Find dialog box with date attributes. With the fields shown in Figure 9.21 you cannot choose to find "all users that have joined our company since 1996." However, you can find those users with an LDAP query, which you can enter if you select Custom Search, Advanced. (LDAP queries are discussed in Chapter 6.)

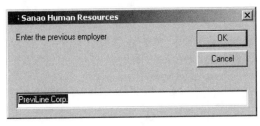

FIGURE 9.20 You can enter a new value for one of the attributes. We show the existing value as a default.

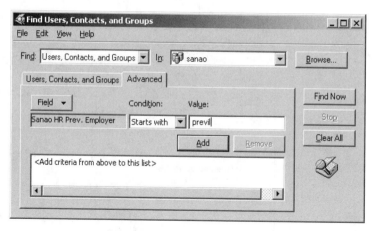

FIGURE 9.21   You can use the Find dialog box to list all users who have a certain previous employer.

Managing the Attribute Permissions

The new attributes will automatically show in the ACL Editor, as explained earlier in this chapter. You can also create a property set to assign permissions to several attributes at once. Creating a property set requires quite a few steps, as described earlier in this chapter. We won't repeat the steps here.

CONCLUSION

Schema modifications should not be taken lightly, but they are also not forbidden. If you feel that the base schema doesn't serve all your needs, you must evaluate which changes are necessary, plan them carefully, and implement them efficiently. In this chapter, you learned guidelines and saw examples of how to do so.

Chapter 10

Administration Scripts: Concepts

We discuss administration scripts in two chapters. This chapter covers the concepts; the next is full of examples and explanations of how they work. We also include more concepts in the next chapter so as not to pack too much background theory in this chapter.

If you want to learn to speak a new language, you first need some basic vocabulary, grammar, and so forth. After a while you will learn more effectively—and more entertainingly—if you read some good novels in that language or travel to a country where the people speak that language. This chapter gives you the basic "vocabulary and grammar" of scripts, and the next will increase your skills. These two chapters will be useful if you are in one of the following three situations.

- You want to learn to write scripts to enhance administration and save work.

- You want to learn to read scripts. If you download scripts from the Internet or get them from other sources, you'll want to check what they do before you use them in your organization.

- You want to learn more about Active Directory architecture. Outputs of many of the examples in the next chapter provide architectural information about Active Directory and you can run those scripts without knowing what they do on each line. You should, of course, read the description first to check that that script isn't going to modify your Active Directory in any way. For instance, one example extends your schema (although we do include safety mechanisms in that script).

This first chapter covers the following topics:

- Getting started (i.e., how to download everything you need and how to use the Windows Script Host environment)

- The basics of the VBScript language
- ADSI concepts
- Additional scripting techniques, such as how to input and output information and how to debug scripts

You can download the scripts presented in the two chapters from `http://www.kouti.com/`.

GETTING STARTED

You have probably written and/or used batch files, which contain DOS/Windows NT/Windows 2000 commands. As you know, they are a convenient way to automate administrative tasks.

Scripts are like "super batch files." They are usually more powerful and versatile than batch files; however, because they are a step toward real programming, there is a steeper learning curve than with batch files. Fortunately, you don't have to be a rocket scientist to use scripts. If you read this chapter and practice a little, you should be able to create quite useful administration scripts.

This chapter has another goal that is perhaps even more important than the goal of teaching you how to write scripts: This chapter aims to teach you how to *read* scripts. Quite a few scripts are available from Microsoft and on the Internet. Depending on the source, you might want to read through a downloaded script to learn what it does before you apply it in your enterprise.

You can use scripts for at least the following administrative tasks:

- To manage Active Directory objects
- To manage servers and services, such as Internet Information Server (IIS)
- To manage user workstations
- To create logon scripts for users and/or workstations

In this book we cover the first item in the list and give brief examples of the second one.

The Script Execution Environment

The following list contains three things that make up the environment to run Active Directory scripts, and the fourth item in the list could be beneficial.

- *Windows Script Host (WSH)* is a generic environment included in Windows 2000 for running scripts written in various languages.
- *VBScript* is the language interpreter for the VBScript language. It is included in WSH.

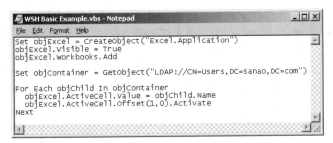

FIGURE 10.1 You can use Notepad to write a script that contains lines in the VBScript language. The WSH environment enables you to run this sample script, so it can open Excel, use ADSI to bind to the `CN=Users` container in a given domain, and write the names of all child objects in an Excel spreadsheet.

- *Active Directory Service Interfaces (ADSI)* is the programmatic interface to Active Directory.
- *ActiveX Data Objects (ADO)* is a programmatic interface to any database or data source that has implemented an OLE DB provider, such as SQL Server, Oracle database server, or Active Directory.

Figure 10.1 shows a WSH script that uses the VBScript language and uses ADSI to access Active Directory.

All four items in the previous list are purely Microsoft technologies. We discuss WSH in this section, focus on VBScript and ADSI in later sections of this chapter, and present ADO in the next chapter. The four technologies make a good team, but there are alternatives (except for ADO). We list some choices along with their pros and cons in the following three sections.

THE WSH ENVIRONMENT

Windows Script Host, or WSH, is a generic environment for running scripts written in various languages. It includes VBScript and JScript (Microsoft's implementation of JavaScript), but the architecture enables vendors to create and install other languages as well. Windows 2000 includes WSH 2.0 and Windows 98 includes WSH 1.0. You can download WSH 1.0 for Windows 95/NT from `http://msdn. microsoft.com/scripting`.

The WSH environment has the following advantages.

- In general, scripts are easier to learn to write than real programs, and they are more powerful than batch files.
- You can call and use any services based on Component Object Model (COM). This opens up a world in which you can interact with Active Directory via ADSI, with databases via ADO, with Office applications via their COM support, and with local file system and registry via WSH COM components. You can

also do messaging via Collaborative Data Objects (CDOs), or do anything for which some vendor has written a COM component. For example, you could write a WSH script that displays the correct numbers for the next week's lottery if you can find a vendor that is selling a COM component for that.

- WSH is included in the operating system. It is present in all the Windows 2000 computers of your company, meaning that they are ready to execute any WSH script (including malicious scripts, such as LOVE-LETTER-FOR-YOU.TXT.vbs).

- WSH is widely accepted and used and it has broad support from Microsoft and other vendors.

- WSH takes only a few megabytes of a computer's RAM.

- You can run scripts both on the command line and in the graphical user interface.

- If you prefer, in WSH you can use the JScript language instead of VBScript. You can also download, buy, and install other languages that vendors have made for WSH.

The disadvantages of the WSH environment are as follows.

- In general, scripts are less powerful than real programs, and they are harder to learn and write than batch files.

- You cannot create full-fledged interactive programs that use the graphical user interface. You can display and input text in graphical pop-up messages, but you cannot go any further.

- WSH is not an *integrated development environment (IDE),* which would contain features such as an intelligent editor, debugging support, and integrated Help files.

- WSH does not include an integrated method for running a script in a computer other than your local computer. However, there have always been ways in Windows NT/2000 to start programs in remote computers and you can still use those ways with scripts. Those methods include logon scripts, the Startup folder, and the Task Scheduler service. In addition, a script running in your workstation could manage a server or another workstation if the COM component that you are calling from the script supports remote access. For example, ADSI supports remote access.

- There are some features in ADSI that you can access only with compiled programming languages and not with a scripting environment. An example of this is the `IDirectorySearch` interface; fortunately, you can pretty much achieve its functionality by using ADO.

- You cannot manage Group Policy in WSH. However, this is more of an ADSI restriction than a WSH restriction.

In addition to, or instead of, WSH you can use the following solutions for administrative tasks:

- *Visual Basic.* You can buy this development environment separately from Microsoft. Visual Basic enables you to write real programs that are compiled to binary EXE files (or DLL and OCX files, if needed). The programming language is a superset of VBScript. Compared to WSH scripts, Visual Basic applications may include an interactive graphical user interface, but learning to write those applications takes more time than learning to write scripts. Typical users of Visual Basic are in-house programmers who develop solutions for their own company. Commercial vendors may also use it, and sometimes administrators use it.

- *C/C++ compiler (and others).* C and C++ are (much) harder to learn than Visual Basic, but many professional developers prefer these languages because of their greater versatility and power.

- *Visual Basic for Applications (VBA).* Excel and other Microsoft Office applications, as well as some third-party applications, use VBA. The language is almost the same as VBScript. You need to learn the object model of the hosting application, such as Excel, but once you do, you can integrate your scripting solutions to that application. If you write something with VBA, it is called a "macro" instead of a "script." However, in this book we tend to call these macros "scripts."

- *Active Server Pages (ASP) scripts in IIS.* You can write and run ASP scripts for your IIS Web server. Those scripts can be integrated with Active Directory via ADSI and they can be used by administrators and end users.

- *Commercial scripting and management environments.* These include WinBatch (http://www.windowware.com/), XLNT (http://www.advsyscon.com/), and FastLane Developer (http://www.quest.com/solutions/ms.asp).

- *Batch files.* You can do amazing things with plain old batch files that use standard Windows 2000 commands or other suitable EXE file commands acquired separately (including the ones in Windows 2000 Support Tools and Resource Kit).

Note that apart from VBA, commercial scripting environments, and batch files, the other items in the list are probably off limits for an administrator. He could learn any of the others, but it would probably be an inappropriate way to spend his working hours. In a large company, in-house developers may be able to spend more time on learning the more difficult but powerful alternatives.

In conclusion, because WSH is the most natural choice to cover, we focus on it in this book.

NOTE   Batch files and scripts are executed "sequentially." When we launch one, the processing begins from line 1. After that, the processing continues to line 2, line 3, and so on, unless there are some *conditional* or *loop statements* to control the flow. In contrast, normal Windows programs written in Visual Basic or C/C++ are written to react to various events, such as user actions.

THE VBSCRIPT LANGUAGE

WSH includes two scripting languages, VBScript and JScript, either of which you could use in your administrative scripts.

Windows 2000 includes version 5.1 of both languages. As of this writing, version 5.5 is available for at `http://msdn.microsoft.com/scripting`. Microsoft's policy is to add to VBScript what has already been in JScript, and vice versa, and ultimately have identical features in both. The newer version of both languages is a step toward this goal. (The examples in this book don't require the new features of version 5.5.) JScript 5.5 also conforms to ECMAScript, a standard scripting language for the Web.

VBScript is considered the easier of the two languages, and because administrators cannot dedicate their lives to learning a programming language, VBScript should be a better choice for them. JScript is more C-like, and while it has some fancier features, it is also more difficult to learn. Consequently, we use VBScript in this book for administrators.

THE ADSI INTERFACE

Active Directory Service Interfaces, or ADSI, is the programmatic interface to Active Directory, as well as to Windows NT and NetWare 3, 4, and later versions. Windows 2000 includes ADSI 2.5, and you can download it for Windows 95/98/NT from `http://www.microsoft.com/adsi`. Also, if you install the Directory Service Client (DSClient) on Windows 95/NT, you will get ADSI. ADSI offers almost the full range of access to Active Directory from your scripts. The following alternatives provide some of the functionality of ADSI.

- You can call NET commands from your WSH scripts, such as `NET USER Jack /add`. They are somewhat easier than pure ADSI, but you will have access only to some of the user properties (those that existed already in Windows NT).

- There is an LDAP C API that gives you access to Active Directory. However, as the name implies, you must use the C language, so WSH wouldn't be an option. Even for C programmers, Microsoft recommends ADSI.

- Windows Management Instrumentation (WMI) is a COM interface that enables you to access (among many other targets) Active Directory. WMI is more difficult than ADSI, but a person who already knows WMI for other purposes can leverage this knowledge for Active Directory scripts.

- ADO is a way to read (but not write) Active Directory information.

   Clearly, ADSI is the best choice.

Launching WSH Scripts

There are various ways to launch WSH scripts on the command line or through the graphical user interface. Before we get into that, however, we'll say a few words about the different script file types.

SCRIPT FILE TYPES

As a default, WSH interprets the following file types as executables:

- *VBS:* The file contains VBScript.
- *JS:* The file contains JScript.
- *WSF:* The file contains either VBScript or JScript along with some Extensible Markup Language (XML) tags.
- *WSH:* The file contains settings for a script, along with the actual script file-name (VBS, JS, or WSF).

To launch a script via one of these four file types, use any of the traditional ways to launch a file.

- Double-click the file with your mouse.
- While the file is selected in the graphical user interface, press Enter.
- Type the filename on the command line (specify the path if the file is not in the current folder or search path).
- Click the Start button, select Run, type the filename (and maybe the path), and press Enter.
- Drag and drop with a mouse another file over the script file. In this case, the dropped file (or files) will be an argument for the script.

WSCRIPT VERSUS CSCRIPT

You run a WSH script either in the graphical environment ("WScript") or the command window ("CScript"). The differences are explained in Table 10.1.

TABLE 10.1 WScript and CScript Comparison

Feature	WScript	CScript
The process that is executing the script and that you will also see in the Task Manager process list	wscript.exe	cscript.exe
An extra (black) command window appears if you start the script from the graphical environment	No	Yes
Errors show as	Graphical dialog box (pop-up)	Line or lines in the command window
Script output that is using the `WScript.Echo` method appears as	Graphical dialog box (pop-up)	Line or lines in the command window

You choose WScript or CScript by typing the corresponding word in front of the script filename. If you don't specify the choice in the launch command, there is a per-computer default, as explained in the next section.

The following lines are some examples of possible commands:

```
hello
c:\test\hello
cscript hello.vbs
cscript c:\test\hello.vbs
wscript hello.vbs
wscript c:\test\hello.vbs
```

NOTE   When typing just the script filename (and maybe the path), you can drop the file extension, but you cannot drop the file extension when you also type `wscript` or `cscript`.

NOTE   If you type just `hello`, and you have both Hello.VBS and Hello.WSH, the former takes precedence.

TESTING WITH A SMALL SCRIPT

To test a small script on your own, you can launch Notepad and type the following line:

```
WScript.Echo "Hello, world"
```

Save this line to a file called Hello.VBS (case is not important) and try to start your script in various ways. Figure 10.2 and Figure 10.3 show examples of the WScript and CScript output, respectively.

NOTE   If you launch the CScript example in Figure 10.3 from the graphical environment (for example, by clicking the Start button, selecting Run, and typing the script file-name), you will see the command window with the output for less than half a second. The same applies to any error messages. Consequently, you probably want to use the actual command window (i.e., cmd.exe).

The choice between the two environments depends on your needs. WScript is perhaps better suited to "end user–like" scripts, and CScript is better suited to serious administrative tasks. If you print a list of 100 users, for example, you don't want that many pop-up messages, but rather a 100-line list in a command window.

You can also redirect the CScript output to a file with the following command:

```
cscript hello.vbs >results.txt
```

For many scripts, it doesn't matter which environment you use.

TIP   As you write more scripts, you also tend to make their names longer in order to make them easy to find. If you don't want to type a script's long name when starting it at the command line, you can use the `CompletionChar` feature. Start RegEdt32 and select either the `HKEY_LOCAL_MACHINE` or `HKEY_CURRENT_USER` window

FIGURE 10.2 Hello.VBS launched with WScript

```
C:\Test>Hello
Hello, world

C:\Test>
```

FIGURE 10.3 Hello.VBS launched with CScript

(depending on whether you want the feature for the computer or for the user). Next, locate the `CompletionChar` parameter in the key `Software`, `Microsoft`, `Command Processor`, and change the value to 9. The value 9 is the ASCII value for the Tab character, which means that now you need to type only a few characters from the beginning of the script name and then press Tab. This will autocomplete the name, or if there are several matches, it will cycle through several names.

Next we look at how you can change the default for WScript/CScript and control the other aspects of script execution.

Controlling WSH Scripts

You can store some per-computer, per-user, and per-script settings. Before we discuss them, however, we'll explain the command-line options.

COMMAND-LINE OPTIONS

If you have used commands on the command line, you have noticed that command options are often preceded by a slash—for example, `dir /p`. With WSH we must have a way to separate the options for the script host from the options for the script. You separate them by using two slashes for the script host options. The command would be something like this:

```
cscript //hostopt1 //hostopt2 scriptname scriptopt1 scriptopt2
```

Actually, you can also use just one slash for the host options, as long as these options appear before the script name on the command line. Because Microsoft always uses two slashes in its documentation and help files, we use that convention as well.

There are 13 host options for `cscript` and `wscript`, and we describe them in Table 10.2.

NOTE   The script options could be whatever your script happens to use.

WARNING   You can use the `//S` option with any other option and you will always get the message "Command line options are saved." However, only the timeout and logo settings are actually saved. For the other options, the message is erroneous.

TABLE 10.2 Host Options for CScript and WScript

Option	Description
`//T:n`	Timeout. The option specifies how many seconds (n) the script is allowed to run. If n is zero or the option is omitted, there is no time limit.
`//Nologo`	By default there is a two-line Microsoft copyright notice at the beginning of the `cscript` output. This option omits those two lines.
`//Logo`	This option is the opposite of the `//Nologo` option. Once you change the default setting to "no logo," you can use this option (but you probably don't want to).
`//S`	Save. When used with `//T`, `//Nologo`, or `//Logo`, this option saves the timeout or logo visibility as a per-user setting.
`//B`	Batch mode. This option suppresses any script error messages or other output from showing on the screen, either on the command line or in pop-up windows.
`//I`	Interactive. This option is the opposite of `//B`. Note that in the previous version of WSH you could make the batch mode the default. Now the interactive mode is always the default, so this `//I` option is obsolete.
`//H:cscript`	Host. This option changes the default environment to CScript.
`//H:wscript`	Host. This option changes the default environment to WScript (which is also the initial default).
`//U*`	Unicode. If you redirect the script input or output when using CScript, this option assumes that that I/O is using Unicode, instead of the traditional PC-ASCII character set.
`//X`	"Execute script in debugger." This option opens your script in the Script Debugger, placing the debugging cursor over the first script line.
`//D`	"Enable Active Debugging." This option starts running your script, but if there is an error, your script will open in the Script Debugger and the debugging cursor will be on the line that contains the error. Unfortunately, you receive no indication of what the error was.
`//E:engine`	With this option, you can specify a certain engine to process your script. Two examples are VBScript and JScript. Normally the file type (VBS or JS) specifies the engine, so there is no need to specify it using this option.
`//Job:name`	If you include several script jobs in one WSF file, you can use this option to specify which job to run. The online Help for WSH 2.0 explains how to do this.

*The last five options (`//U`, `//X`, `//D`, `//E`, and `//Job`) were introduced in WSH 2.0 and don't exist in WSH 1.0.

Even though you can use the host options with `wscript`, you would normally use them with `cscript`. Also, three of the options (`//Nologo`, `//Logo`, and `//U`) are meaningful only with `cscript`.

NOTE   As mentioned, you can launch a script by just typing its name. If you want to specify host options, however, you must first type `cscript` (or sometimes `wscript`).

SCRIPT SETTINGS

Some of the command-line options described in the previous section are used to make a default setting. Apart from that, any command-line options are in effect only for one invocation of a script.

Unless you change them, some settings remain in effect permanently. Table 10.3 lists these settings and also indicates where they are stored and how to change them. You are already familiar with the actual settings, because they are the same ones you saw with command-line options.

You don't need the following information to run scripts, but if you are interested, you can examine the `HKEY_CLASSES_ROOT` contents by performing the following steps:

TABLE 10.3 WSH Script Settings

Type	Settings	Stored In	How to Change
Per-computer	WScript or CScript as the default	Registry `HKEY_CLASSES_ROOT`	`cscript //H:cscript` or `cscript //H:wscript.`
Per-user	Logo or no logo, Timeout	Registry `HKEY_CURRENT_USER`, `Software`, `Microsoft`, `Windows Script Host`, `Settings*`	Start wscript.exe to open a settings page or use the command-line host options with `//S`.
Per-script**	Logo or no logo, Timeout	Text file <script name>.WSH	Right-click a script file, select Properties, and select the Script tab.

*The registry path `HKEY_LOCAL_MACHINE`, `Software`, `Microsoft` also contains the keys `Windows Script Host` and `Windows Scripting Host`. They may look similar to the path in this table, but they don't contain your settings.

**The per-script and per-user settings are the same. If you use both, the per-script settings take precedence.

1. Locate the key .VBS (note the dot as the first character). It has a reference to the key VBSFile.

2. Locate the key VBSFile, ScriptEngine. It has a reference to the key VBScript.

3. Locate the key VBScript. It has a reference to the key {B54F3741-5B07-11cf-A4B0-00AA004A55E8.}.

4. Locate the long key name from the previous step under the CLSID key (they are sorted alphabetically).

5. Once you find the key, you will see the InprocServer32 key, which has a reference to vbscript.dll.

This way, you have found the file (vbscript.dll) that actually interprets your VBScript file and carries out the operations defined in that script.

Table 10.3 briefly mentions how to change the various settings. Now we will elaborate on these procedures with a few examples.

You can use the following commands to change the default environment to either CScript or WScript:

```
cscript //H:cscript
cscript //H:wscript
```

Or, if you like, you can use the following two commands:

```
wscript //H:cscript
wscript //H:wscript
```

NOTE   There is a slight bug in Windows 2000: If you launch a script using a WSH file, it will use WScript, even though your default environment is CScript.

To open the per-user settings page (see Figure 10.4), use this command:

```
wscript
```

Another way to set the two per-user settings is to use commands such as the following:

```
cscript //nologo //s
cscript //t:15 //s
```

As mentioned in Table 10.3, to see the per-script settings, right-click a script file, select Properties, and select the Script tab. That property page is similar to the per-user page shown in Figure 10.4.

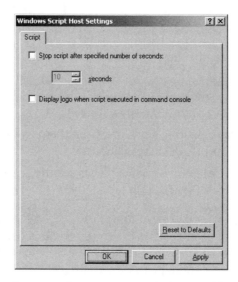

FIGURE 10.4 If you type the command `wscript`, a settings page with two general per-user settings will appear.

When you click OK to save the per-script settings, a file with a WSH extension is created with the same name and in the same folder as the script. See Figure 10.5 for an example.

NOTE   If you are using WSH 1.0 (e.g., with Windows NT), you can also add a third setting in the `Options` section: `BatchMode=1`. This setting corresponds to the `//B` command-line option.

KILLING A SCRIPT

Sometimes a script goes into an *infinite loop,* which means that it will never stop (unless you have specified a timeout, of course). The script could also spend more time on some operation than you are willing to wait. It is possible to kill a script without harming your system in any way.

WARNING   There is a theoretical possibility that the script that seems to be in an infinite loop is just in the middle of some Active Directory batch update, in which case killing the script would cause part of the update not to take place. It shouldn't cause any other damage, though, if you happen to kill a script in such a moment.

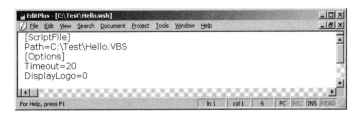

FIGURE 10.5 The per-script settings are stored in a WSH file.

The following factors affect how a running script is visible in the user interface:

- Whether the script is running in WScript or CScript
- Whether the script was started from the command line or from the graphical environment
- Whether the script is doing any input or output

Depending on these three factors, you may see your script in the Windows taskbar or in the Applications tab of the Task Manager (press Shift-Ctrl-Esc to launch the Task Manager). If so, you can just select Close or End Task and that may kill your script. The taskbar Close operation probably closes just one pop-up message of your script, but the End Task operation of the Task Manager should kill the whole script, at least if you wait a few seconds. If the script is running in a command window (i.e., CScript), pressing Ctrl-C should kill the script.

To check if those operations helped, and possibly to finish the job, you can perform the following steps:

1. Select the Processes tab of the Task Manager.
2. Click the Image Name column twice to sort the processes alphabetically (the first click sorts them in the reverse order).
3. Locate any cscript.exe and wscript.exe processes, select one, and click End Process. Then select the next process, click End Process, and so on.

TIP You can use the Task Manager to see the amount of I/O that each process is doing. While in the Processes tab, select View, Select Columns and check I/O Reads and I/O Writes. The numbers in these new columns may help you deduce whether a script is actually doing something or has just "hung."

Being able to kill a script requires appropriate privileges. If you start a script with the Task Scheduler service that is running with the credentials of LocalSystem, you cannot kill that script later, even though you are an administrator.

WARNING   Be careful not to kill the wrong process.

Setting Up the Development Environment

Although the minimum requirements for writing scripts are Notepad and quick fingers, your work will be easier with the following extra tools:

- An effective and convenient editor
- The Help file for VBScript
- The Help file for WSH
- The Help file for ADSI

GETTING A SCRIPT EDITOR

An editor that is made especially for writing scripts or programs has the following advantages over Notepad.

- It shows you line and column numbers. If you try to run a script, but WSH tells you that there is an error on line 137, you can easily locate the problem line.
- It has *syntax highlighting,* which means that you will see the reserved keywords, comments, strings, and function names all in different colors. This is a tremendous improvement over a black and white view. Colors help you quickly notice typing errors and they make any script much more readable.

Of course, if a company is trying to sell an editor to replace Notepad, it has probably included various other enhancements in its product. One such editor is EditPlus (http://www.editplus.com/), a shareware program from ES-Computing. Figure 10.6 shows a basic view of the program.

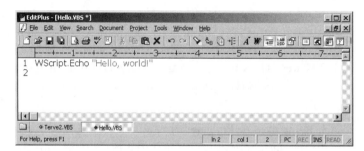

FIGURE 10.6 EditPlus is made for scripting, programming, and HTML editing.

We use EditPlus for our examples in this and the next chapter—not because of color highlighting, but because of the line numbers. As we explain each code example, you can easily locate the corresponding line of the script. EditPlus also provides us with nice frames around the examples. Note that after Figure 10.6 we have stripped away the toolbars, status bars, and rulers to save some space in the examples.

Other script editors include Primal*script* (http://www.sapien.com/), UltraEdit (http://www.ultraedit.com/), VBScript Editor (http://www.koala.it/Eng/script.htm), and WinEdit (http://www.winedit.com/).

TIP   You can make EditPlus or any other editor the default editor instead of Notepad, at least for VBS files. To do this, open any folder in Windows Explorer, select the Tools menu, select Folder Options, select the File Types tab, locate and select the extension VBS, click Advanced, select the action Edit on the list, and click the Edit button. Now you should see the text that defines the editor application. Using the Browse button, change the path to your favorite editor to replace Notepad. Finally, click OK a few times to save your changes. Now you can right-click any VBS file with your mouse and when you select Edit from the context menu, your script opens in your favorite editor.

GETTING THE HELP FILES

Even though WSH (including VBScript) and ADSI are part of Windows 2000, you need to download the Help files separately. As of this writing, the starting point for the download is the Microsoft Scripting Technologies site (http://msdn.microsoft.com/scripting).

There you can download a 280KB wshdoc.exe and a 620KB vbsdoc.exe. When you download and run each one, it will install the Help files for WSH and VBScript into your Start menu (click the Start button and select Programs, Microsoft Windows Script). Figure 10.7 shows the opening page of the VBScript Help.

The Help file for ADSI is available from Microsoft's ADSI Web pages at http://www.microsoft.com/adsi. There you can download a 1.5MB ADSI25.CHM file and place it in any convenient folder on your hard disk.

The ADSI25.CHM file fulfills its purpose, but there is also a more complete and current Help file with the name NetDir.CHM. The latter file includes other Active Directory and LDAP documentation and it is part of the Platform SDK (therefore, it is continuously updated). You can access the Platform SDK online at the MSDN Library address http://msdn.microsoft.com/library. There you can also download the Platform SDK Core SDK. This 230MB package includes the 3MB NetDir.CHM file. You may also be able to find an individual NetDir.CHM

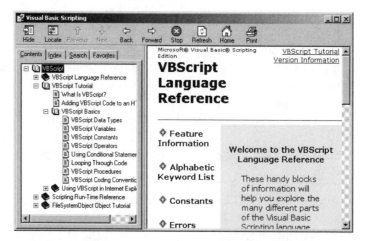

FIGURE 10.7 The VBScript Help file is created in the compiled HTML (CHM) format. The navigation tree contains both a tutorial and a reference for the VBScript language.

file on the Internet using a search engine. Another option is to buy the Platform SDK CD for the cost of shipping and handling at `http://developerstore.com/`.

SOURCES OF ADDITIONAL INFORMATION

This chapter and the next chapter give you a good basis for reading, using, and writing scripts to administer Active Directory. The information in these two chapters alone may even suffice for your purposes. However, if you want to keep up with new developments, learn additional aspects of scripting, and see more sample scripts than fit on these pages, you can use the Web and Internet news areas to update your knowledge. The following list contains some Web sites for you to visit:

- `http://www.kouti.com/` (this book's Web pages)
- `http://msdn.microsoft.com/scripting` (Microsoft Scripting Technologies)
- `http://www.microsoft.com/adsi` (Microsoft's Active Directory Service Interfaces Overview)
- `http://msdn.microsoft.com/library` (Microsoft's MSDN Library documentation including the Platform SDK)
- `http://www.15seconds.com/` (15 Seconds)
- `http://communities.msn.com/windowsscript` (Windows-Script community site)

- `http://cwashington.netreach.net/` (Win32 Scripting)
- `http://www.win2000mag.com/` (*Windows 2000 Magazine,* formerly *Windows NT Magazine*)
- `http://www.win32scripting.com/` (*Windows Scripting Solutions,* from the publisher of *Windows 2000 Magazine*)

Microsoft has a news server at `nntp://news.microsoft.com`. It contains, among others, the following scripting newsgroups:

- `microsoft.public.scripting.wsh`
- `microsoft.public.scripting.vbscript`
- `microsoft.public.adsi.general`

With a browser, you can also access any developer-related Microsoft public newsgroups at address `http://msdn.microsoft.com/newsgroups`.

Obviously, we can list only a few Internet resources out of the many available. You can use a search engine to find more sites if you feel the need.

VBSCRIPT LANGUAGE

Batch files are often just a series of commands that you have typed in a text file (of type BAT or CMD) so that you don't have to type the same series again and again.

With scripts, you use a programming language and that enables you to use the following programming constructs:

- Constants and variables of different data types
- Arrays
- Objects
- Operators
- Conditional statements to control program flow
- Looping statements to control program flow
- VBScript functions
- Procedures and functions

NOTE   A batch file isn't necessarily just a series of commands; some of the items on the list are available also in the batch language.

In this section we explain the basic features and use of the VBScript language. At the same time we give some general guidelines for programming. If you are anxious to learn about ADSI, you may skip this section. Learning and understanding ADSI doesn't require you to know the information presented this section. To make good use of ADSI in scripts, however, you must be conversant with some aspects of VBScript.

By no means can we cover VBScript fully here. We try to offer enough information for you to gain an elementary understanding of it, while keeping the section to a reasonable length. The Help file that you downloaded includes the language reference with a complete list of all keywords, functions, and so on. The Help file also lists how VBScript is different from VBA, both of which are subsets of Visual Basic.

Dissecting a Sample Script

We start exploring VBScript by introducing and explaining a short sample script. It contains the most basic features of the language. After the first sample, we show two other scripts that do about the same things as the first one but in fewer lines.

The script first asks for your height in feet and in inches. Then it calculates your height in centimeters and displays it. Figure 10.8 shows the input box for the first question (feet). The input box for the second question (inches) looks nearly the same, so we don't show it separately. Figure 10.9 shows the script output.

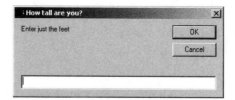

FIGURE 10.8 Using VBScript, you can ask the user for script input.

FIGURE 10.9 In VBScript, a script can display a message box to show some text, warnings, or results.

The First Sample (Normal)

Now that you have seen how the script works, we show the contents of the script source (see Figure 10.10). This first version represents the typical style of scripting. To write a VBScript:

- You should write *comment lines* at the beginning of the script to explain what the script does. Each comment line starts with an apostrophe ('). Our example in Figure 10.10 has only three comment lines (lines 1 through 3), but you are encouraged to write several lines, particularly for more complex scripts.

- You can add *comments at the end of any line* in the script (e.g., lines 7 and 8 in the sample). Again, the apostrophe indicates the beginning of comment

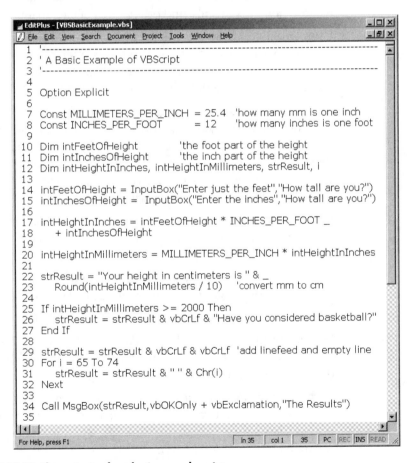

```
1 '---------------------------------------------------------------
2 ' A Basic Example of VBScript
3 '---------------------------------------------------------------
4
5 Option Explicit
6
7 Const MILLIMETERS_PER_INCH  = 25.4   'how many mm is one inch
8 Const INCHES_PER_FOOT       = 12     'how many inches is one foot
9
10 Dim intFeetOfHeight          'the foot part of the height
11 Dim intInchesOfHeight        'the inch part of the height
12 Dim intHeightInInches, intHeightInMillimeters, strResult, i
13
14 intFeetOfHeight = InputBox("Enter just the feet","How tall are you?")
15 intInchesOfHeight =  InputBox("Enter the inches","How tall are you?")
16
17 intHeightInInches = intFeetOfHeight * INCHES_PER_FOOT _
18     + intInchesOfHeight
19
20 intHeightInMillimeters = MILLIMETERS_PER_INCH * intHeightInInches
21
22 strResult = "Your height in centimeters is " & _
23     Round(intHeightInMillimeters / 10)   'convert mm to cm
24
25 If intHeightInMillimeters >= 2000 Then
26     strResult = strResult & vbCrLf & "Have you considered basketball?"
27 End If
28
29 strResult = strResult & vbCrLf & vbCrLf 'add linefeed and empty line
30 For i = 65 To 74
31     strResult = strResult & " " & Chr(i)
32 Next
33
34 Call MsgBox(strResult,vbOKOnly + vbExclamation,"The Results")
35
```

FIGURE 10.10 The contents of our basic example script

text. Comments help other people understand quickly what the script does, as well as how and why it does it. Comments will help you also, when after a couple of years you try to remember what the script does. It is not necessary to comment on every line, however—some lines are self-explanatory.

- You can use *empty lines* to make the script easier to read (e.g., lines 6, 9, 13 in our example).

- *Constants* are known values that do not change as the script runs. When you define them with the `Const` keyword, their values cannot change. The formulas that calculate inches and millimeters (lines 17 and 20) are descriptive when you use names (such as `INCHES_PER_FOOT`) instead of just 12. By convention, names of constants are all uppercase letters.

- *Variables* can change their values, so the script can calculate the height in millimeters and store the answer in the corresponding variable. You use variables to store numbers, strings, and other kinds of data that the script needs.

- Using good and descriptive *constant and variable names* helps in understanding what the script does. The three-letter prefix of the name indicates the data type to be used with the variable. "int" stands for integer and "str" stands for string. The Help file has a list of recommended prefixes.

- Using `Option Explicit` in the beginning forces you to *declare* each variable with the `Dim` keyword (short for "dimension"). Although this may seem to be unnecessary extra work, it is actually a good thing. Without `Option Explicit` you could mistype a variable name and not notice it. Everything would seem to work, so such bugs could be hard to locate and fix. You can list several variable names in one `Dim` line.

- VBScript language is *not case-sensitive,* which means that instead of `Dim` you can also use `dim`, `DIM`, or `DiM`. Likewise, `intMyVar` and `Intmyvar` are the same variable.

- You must use a *decimal point* in decimal numbers (line 7), even though your regional options might define another decimal symbol.

- You must put any *string values in quotation marks* (e.g., line 22).

- Your script may use VBScript *functions,* such as `InputBox` to ask for user input, Round to get rid of too many decimals in the number, and `MsgBox` to display some output to the user.

- Each function may require some number of *arguments.* In our example, `InputBox` is using two arguments separated with a comma (e.g., line 14). Round takes just one argument (line 23), and `MsgBox` takes three arguments separated by commas (line 34).

- Each *function returns one value,* which you typically store in a variable (e.g., in the `InputBox` lines 14 and 15 of our example). `MsgBox` would also return a value to tell you whether the user clicked OK, Cancel, or some other button. Because we don't need the return value, we just use the `Call` statement to call the function.

- Many arguments are *optional,* which means that they have a default value and you can just omit them. For example, `InputBox` could take seven arguments, but we need only the first two, leaving the remaining five to their default values. If you omit an argument from the middle, you must insert a comma to indicate this.

- You can use various *control statements* to control the program flow. The `If` statement in the sample script has two parts—the conditional and consequence clauses. The conditional clause on line 25 (`If intHeightInMillimeters >= 2000 Then`) is evaluated first, and if true, the consequence clause on line 26 is executed. The lines in the For statement (line 30) are carried out a certain number of times.

- You should *indent the lines* inside `If` and `For` statements to enhance readability.

- You can use *operators,* such as an asterisk (`*`) to multiply, a plus sign (`+`) to add, a slash (`/`) to divide, and an ampersand (`&`) to concatenate two strings into one.

- Note that when forming the `strResult` string (line 22), you actually concatenate a string with a number. They are two *different data types.* Some other programming language would generate a "type mismatch" error, but VBScript changes the number 200 to a string 200, so the concatenation succeeds.

- Sometimes the automatic conversion doesn't work, so you have to use a *conversion function* (such as `CStr`) to convert a number to a string, for example.

- You can *cut long lines* by typing an underscore (`_`) and continuing the line on the next physical line (lines 17 and 18). This way the lines are nicely visible in the editor window.

- You can also put *two short script lines together* with a colon between them. We don't use this in the sample script, however.

- In addition to two of your own constants, the script also contains some *intrinsic constants.* `VbCrLf` (standing for carriage return/linefeed) equals the characters that cause the output to scroll to the beginning of the next line. `VbOKOnly` (line 34) corresponds to value 0, which causes `MsgBox` to show just the OK button and no other buttons, such as Cancel. `VbExclamation` equals 48, which causes `MsgBox` to show an exclamation mark. Again, a script is more readable when it says "vbExclamation" instead of just "48."

NOTE The term "carriage return/linefeed" was born back in the 1970s when computer terminals printed all output on paper. The terminals had a carriage with a device (ball, cylinder, or row of rods) that contained all necessary characters (just like the old IBM typewriters). Once the carriage neared the right edge of the paper, it needed to return to the left edge. Linefeed rolled the paper up one line.

The Second Sample (Short)

Next, we write the same sample in 10 lines (see Figure 10.11) instead of 34. To be able to shorten the script

- We drop out all comments.
- We drop out the `For` loop, which adds letters A–J to the output.
- We drop out `Option Explicit` as well as all `Const` and `Dim` statements.
- We do not store the user input to a variable first, but instead place the `Input-Box` functions directly in the formula.
- We do not calculate intermediate results, such as `intHeightInInches`.

Although 10 lines may seem better than 34 lines, shorter is not always better. A shorter script is usually less readable. We show it here so you can see some possibilities. We consider the longer sample better in many regards.

The Third Sample (Very Short)

If we don't need the comment "Have you considered basketball?" (lines 7 and 8 of Figure 10.11), we do not need intermediate results. In this case, we can squeeze

```
 1  HeightCM = Round(25.4 * _
 2    (InputBox("Enter just the feet","How tall are you?") * 12 + _
 3    InputBox("Enter the inches","How tall are you?")) / 10)
 4
 5  strResult = "Your height in centimeters is " & HeightCM
 6
 7  If HeightCM >= 200 Then strResult = strResult & vbCrLf & _
 8    "Have you considered basketball?"
 9
10  Call MsgBox(strResult)
```

FIGURE 10.11 The contents of a shorter version of the sample script in Figure 10.10

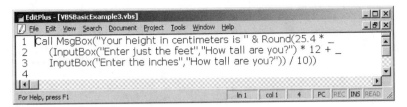

FIGURE 10.12 The contents of the shortest version (just one line) of the VBScript sample in Figure 10.10

everything to one line (which we cut into three to fit it on a book page). Figure 10.12 shows the result.

Notice that the return values of `InputBox` can be used directly as arguments for `MsgBox`.

ADSI CONCEPTS

In this section we explain the general concepts of ADSI. We also show some small code fragments to demonstrate the concepts. However, we leave most of the code details to the next chapter, which is full of ADSI examples and explanations.

ADSI provides access from a number of programming environments to a number of directory services (see Figure 10.13). Because ADSI is implemented as COM objects, any programming environment that understands COM will understand ADSI.

There are two kinds of COM clients:

- Automation clients (that use *late binding*), such as WSH + VBScript and WSH + JScript

- Nonautomation clients (that use *early binding*), such as Visual Basic, VBA, and C/C++

Using ADSI differs depending on which client type is in use. Because this chapter is about scripting, we discuss ADSI from the automation client's point of view. Our examples will use late binding, but we don't discuss what late binding or early binding actually means in the background. We introduced the terms so that when you see one of them in documentation, you'll know if it is related to scripting.

In addition to early-binding fashion, you can use Visual Basic and VBA also in late-binding fashion. Consequently, the information and sample scripts of this chapter and the next chapter apply also to these two environments. Because of language differences, however, you must modify any sample script in the following ways to make it work in Visual Basic.

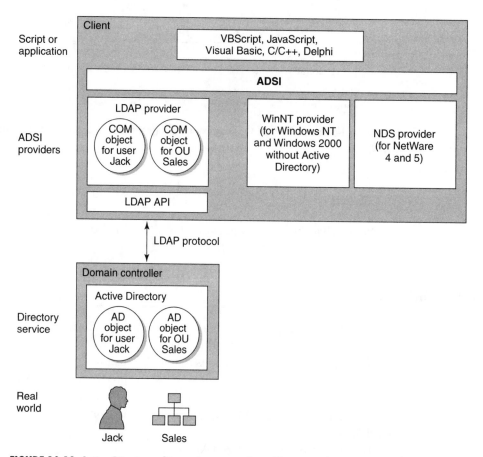

FIGURE 10.13 Active Directory objects abstract real-world users and resources. ADSI COM objects in turn abstract Active Directory objects. When your script manipulates the COM objects, it eventually affects the corresponding Active Directory objects.

- Change any `WScript.Echo` output method to `Debug.Print` (or, if you want to compile an EXE file, use other suitable means for output, such as `MsgBox`).

- When you declare variables in `Dim` statements, add the data type of each variable (e.g., change `Dim i` to `Dim i As Integer`).

To make the sample scripts work in VBA, you must also replace the `WScript.Echo` output method. If you're working in Excel, for example, you can dump the script output into Excel spreadsheet cells.

TIP   If you like VBA's integrated development environment, you can use it instead of WSH for your administrative script. The best platform application in this case is probably Excel.

NOTE   The term "automation" comes from "OLE automation." OLE stands for "Object Linking and Embedding" and it is a Microsoft technology that facilitates cooperation among applications. An automation client can also be called an "OLE automation controller," and ADSI (or any other COM component) would be an "OLE automation server."

Even though ADSI stands for "Active Directory Service Interfaces," it supports different directory services by using the following providers:

- *LDAP.* This provider supports Active Directory and any other LDAP directory service from vendors such as Netscape and Novell. You can also access Exchange 5.5 with the LDAP provider.
- *WinNT.* This provider supports not only Windows NT, but also Windows 2000 workstations and stand-alone/member servers that don't contain Active Directory. In addition, you can manage on Windows 2000 domain controllers some server services, such as file shares and print queues, using the WinNT provider.
- *NDS.* This provider supports Novell NDS, which is included in NetWare 4, 5, and beyond.
- *NWCOMPAT.* This provider supports NetWare 3, which stores users and groups in a place called "the Bindery."

The four providers match four identically named namespaces. Even though ADSI is an interface common to all of them, the features (which object types are supported and in which way) are somewhat different in each namespace. Also, the naming conventions to address an object, such as a certain user account, are somewhat different in different namespaces.

NOTE   Some of the ADSI features support only NDS, and because this book is about Active Directory, we don't discuss those features.

In addition to the four system providers on the list, any vendor can write a provider for its directory service. Microsoft has written a provider for IIS and

Novell has written a provider for NDS to replace the one that Microsoft is shipping with ADSI.

The term *directory service* is used quite loosely with ADSI. To be exact, Windows NT, NetWare 3, and IIS don't include a true directory service.

Basic ADSI

This section lists some typical operations that you would do with ADSI and shows some fragments of scripts to demonstrate some of these operations.

ADSI OPERATIONS

A typical flow of events consists of the following steps:

1. Bind to an Active Directory container object or directly to some target object.

2. If bound to a container, list all or certain child objects in that container.

3. Read or write properties of the target object or listed child objects.

Some other ADSI operations that you can perform on Active Directory objects include the following:

- Create, delete, move, and rename objects.
- Manage the schema.
- List and manage permissions (ACLs) for Active Directory objects.

The sample script in the next section demonstrates the first three operations (bind, list, and read).

A SAMPLE ADSI SCRIPT

The script in Figure 10.14 demonstrates the basic operation of ADSI. It lists all the user objects in the CN=Users container along with the descriptions of the users. If you run the script, you will see the output shown in Figure 10.15. As you see, our test forest sanao.com has only the predefined users in CN=Users.

On line 3 of Figure 10.14 we declare two object variables. Later in the script we will need one for the target container and another for the child objects. On line 5 we bind to a certain object in Active Directory. As a result, we get an instance of an object variable (objContainer) in our script that we can use from that point on. The *binding string* in quotation marks specifies the provider/namespace (LDAP:), two slashes, and the distinguished name of an object. Because we

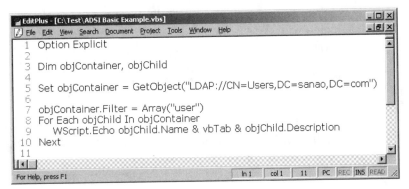

FIGURE 10.14 A basic example of ADSI

bound to a container object, we can list its child objects. On line 7 we define a filter for the container that includes only those children whose LDAP class name is user.

Now we are ready to list the names and descriptions of all child objects. We use a For Each ... Next loop that browses through the contents. Within each cycle we print out one username along with the user's description.

NOTE

This note may sound a little confusing, but if you apply the sample script shown in Figure 10.14 to some container that contains computer objects, those objects are listed as well. The reason is that in the schema the computer class is a subclass of the user class and the filter will also include all subclasses.

LDAP BINDING STRINGS

When you bind to a container or some other object, you need to specify the target with a *binding string*, which is synonymous with *ADSI path* or ADsPath.

```
C:\Test>"ADSI Basic Example.vbs"
CN=Administrator        Built-in account for administering the computer/domain
CN=Guest                Built-in account for guest access to the computer/domain
CN=IUSR_SKOUTI3 Built-in account for anonymous access to Internet Information Se
rvices
CN=IWAM_SKOUTI3 Built-in account for Internet Information Services to start out
of process applications
CN=krbtgt               Key Distribution Center Service Account
CN=TsInternetUser       This user account is used by Terminal Services.

C:\Test>
```

FIGURE 10.15 The output of the example of ADSI in Figure 10.14

As mentioned previously, a binding string is (normally) the text `LDAP://` concatenated with the distinguished name of the target object. An example of this is as follows:

```
LDAP://CN=Guest,CN=Users,DC=sanao,DC=com
```

NOTE   The binding strings for namespaces other than LDAP, such as WinNT, are somewhat different. We discuss here only the LDAP version. In the next chapter we present examples of WinNT binding strings.

You could also include the target server name and, if needed, a TCP/IP *port number*. An example of this longer path is as follows:

```
LDAP://dc1.sanao.com:389/CN=Guest,CN=Users,DC=sanao,DC=com
```

In the binding string, "389" is the standard LDAP port number. You don't usually need to include it. If you omit the port number, the default "389" is used.

In most of the examples in this chapter and the next chapter, we don't specify the server name either. We just let ADSI pick a domain controller (or sometimes another LDAP server) for us. When using this *serverless binding*, ADSI selects a domain controller of the default domain, which is the domain of the user whose credentials are being used (normally the logged-on user).

Instead of 389, we could sometimes use the port 3268, which is the default port for the global catalog. However, instead of changing the port, we can change the first letters to "GC"; that is, we use the following binding string:

```
GC://CN=Guest,CN=Users,DC=sanao,DC=com
```

All the binding examples you have seen use the credentials of the logged-on user. In the next chapter we show how you can bind with some alternative credentials. However, binding with credentials is not usually necessary.

The distinguished name can be replaced with some other provider-specific path. An example of this is to bind using the `objectGUID` attribute of an object. The path would look like the following:

```
LDAP://<GUID=a434e4ee3da56b4a81a282fcb79e1748>
```

When you use `objectGUID` attributes instead of distinguished names, your script will still work even if the object name is changed. However, you'll lose the descriptiveness of the names.

USING ROOTDSE

The examples you have seen so far include a domain name in the binding string. In other words, the domain name is hard-coded in the script. This presents a slight disadvantage, because if you want to execute the scripts in another domain, you need to change all the domain names. By adding one line to each script, you can remove the hard-coded domain name and use rootDSE instead.

The root of the directory information tree in every LDAPv3 directory server (i.e., domain controller in Active Directory) is called rootDSE. It is a virtual object that is not part of any partition (i.e., naming context) and it includes 19 attributes that provide information about the directory server and directory. DSE stands for "DSA-Specific Entry." DSA, in turn, stands for "Directory System Agent." DSA is an X.500 term for a directory server, which in Active Directory is the same as a domain controller.

The attributes that are most interesting for our scripts are the distinguished names for the default domain, the root domain, the Schema container, and the Configuration container. The corresponding attribute names are as follows:

- defaultNamingContext
- rootDomainNamingContext
- schemaNamingContext
- configurationNamingContext

With these four attributes, you can access every object in Active Directory without knowing the domain or forest name at the time you write the script. The following lines show how to bind to the user Guest in the default domain:

```
Set objDSE = GetObject("LDAP://rootDSE")
Set objUser = GetObject("LDAP://CN=Guest,CN=Users," & _
    objDSE.Get("defaultNamingContext"))
```

NOTE   To be exact, the "default domain" means the domain that the domain controller belongs to. However, because you don't specify a domain controller, ADSI will find a domain controller from the domain of the user whose credentials are being used (normally the logged-on user). In other words, defaultNamingContext refers to the user's domain.

The other 15 attributes of rootDSE are as follows:

- currentTime
- subschemaSubentry

- dsServiceName
- namingContexts
- supportedControl
- supportedLDAPVersion
- supportedLDAPPolicies
- highestCommittedUSN
- supportedSASLMechanisms
- dnsHostName
- ldapServiceName
- serverName
- supportedCapabilitie
- isSynchronized
- isGlobalCatalogReady

We do not discuss these attributes here, but we provide the names in case you encounter them or find use for them. Most of the attributes are described in the ADSI documentation.

Basic COM

COM is a standard mechanism that, among other things, enables you to control binary components from text-based scripts. These components are called *COM objects,* and using them gives your scripts tremendous power to do a variety of things.

As you know, you can enhance your batch files by calling appropriate EXE files. They enable you to do tasks that a basic batch file couldn't accomplish. This same principle applies to scripts and binary COM objects—in this case, however, the ways in which a text file can interact with the binary component are more versatile than with the batch files.

A COM object is an entity that often represents something concrete. In the case of ADSI, COM objects mostly represent Active Directory objects, as you saw in Figure 10.13 about ADSI.

A COM object has one or more *interfaces* that enable you to interact with the object. An interface is likely to have *methods;* each time you call a method, it invokes an operation for the interface to perform. An interface also has *properties,* which store some values about the COM object just as Active Directory attributes store values about an Active Directory object. You read and write COM property values using *property methods.* In addition, the normal methods may return values.

Figure 10.13 shows the ADSI COM object for OU Sales. That object could have (or one of its interfaces could have, to be exact) a property `FaxNumber`, a property method `FaxNumber`, and a method `Delete`. If the name of the COM object in a script were `objOU`, you could read and display the `FaxNumber` property using the `FaxNumber` property method with the following script line:

```
WScript.Echo objOU.FaxNumber
```

As you can see, in VBScript you refer to a property method or method with the following syntax:

```
object_name.property_method_or_method_name
```

NOTE   The property names and property method names are the same in VBScript, which usually makes things quite easy. If you used the C language, you would need to read the `FaxNumber` property with the `get_FaxNumber` property method.

NOTE   Echo is a method of the `WScript` COM object.

You write to a property with a command such as

```
objOU.FaxNumber = "555-3159"
```

Finally, you call the `Delete` method with one of the following commands:

```
Call objOU.Delete("user", "CN=Jack")
objOU.Delete "user", "CN=Jack"
```

NOTE   From here on we use mostly the first version of the two commands (the one with `Call` and parentheses), because it is more in line with the next command, where a method returns a value. We like to have parentheses around the arguments in both commands. However, when you read the ADSI documentation and some other sources, you often see the latter version (without `Call` or parentheses). We may also use the latter version when there are no arguments for the method.

If the same method returns a value, you use a command like the following:

```
ret = objOU.Delete("user", "CN=Jack")
```

Because ADSI uses COM technology, it has objects and properties, and as you already know, Active Directory is full of objects and properties. In the next section we examine the relationship between the two.

The Property Cache

The ADSI documentation talks about an attribute when it means a phone number in Active Directory and about a property when it means the same phone number in ADSI. We follow the same convention in this chapter (and the next), even though we may have used the two terms interchangeably in other chapters.

A script does not read and write attributes of Active Directory objects directly, but it goes through the *property cache.* The benefit of the property cache is that if you read five attributes, this doesn't generate five small separate network requests and replies; instead, it generates one larger request. The latter choice is more efficient in terms of speed and network utilization.

There are ADSI methods that you use to read and write attributes between Active Directory and the property cache, as well as methods you use between the property cache and the script variables. Figure 10.16 shows the principle of the property cache along with the ADSI method names.

NOTE   You might wonder why if there are `Get` and `GetInfo`, there aren't also `Put` and `PutInfo`, instead of the current `Put` and `SetInfo`. One answer could be the following: `Get` and `Put` are traditional statements for I/O in the Microsoft Basic language (and others) and they existed back in the 1970s. `GetInfo` and `SetInfo` are traditional function names that appeared in 1988 to enable programmers to read and write user and group properties in OS/2 LAN Manager, which is the ancestor of Windows NT.

Technically, the property cache is common to all objects, but you can think of it as a per-object instance.

As you can see in Figure 10.16, there are reads and writes

- Between the property cache and Active Directory
- Between your script and the property cache

BETWEEN THE PROPERTY CACHE AND ACTIVE DIRECTORY

The property cache for a certain object gets attributes from Active Directory in one of the following three ways.

- The script calls the `Get` or `GetEx` methods and the property cache for that object is empty. This will invoke an *implicit* `GetInfo` method. Therefore,

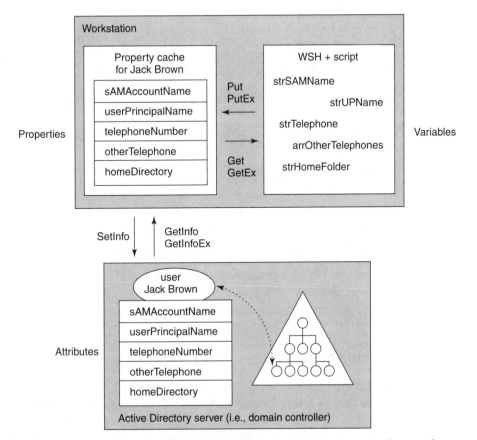

FIGURE 10.16 **When your script reads attributes of an object in Active Directory, those attributes first go to the property cache in your workstation. After that they can be stored in the variables of the script.**

you don't normally need to use GetInfo explicitly in your scripts. However, if you want to *refresh* the nonempty property cache (i.e., retrieve the new and changed attributes from Active Directory), you must call GetInfo explicitly.

- The script calls the GetInfo method *explicitly* in your script. This will retrieve all the attributes of the corresponding object in Active Directory, which have some value set and which are not constructed attributes (for more information and a list of the 22 constructed attributes, see Chapter 8).

- The script calls the GetInfoEx method *explicitly* in your script. This will retrieve only those attributes that you listed as method call arguments. The only way to retrieve any constructed attributes is to use GetInfoEx.

NOTE   Performance is usually not an issue with scripting, but if you are concerned about it, you could retrieve with `GetInfoEx` only those attributes that you need instead of letting the implicit `GetInfo` retrieve all 30 attributes (or whatever the count is).

The properties in the property cache get written back to Active Directory in the following way.

- The script calls the `SetInfo` method *explicitly* in your script. If you don't call `SetInfo`, it is like writing text into Notepad but not saving the text to a file. Similarly, nothing gets written to Active Directory if you forget to call `SetInfo`.

NOTE   Methods (except property methods) bypass the property cache. If you delete an object in an OU with `objOU.Delete` or set a user's password with `objUser.SetPassword`, you don't need to use `SetInfo` after those methods.

BETWEEN YOUR SCRIPT AND THE PROPERTY CACHE

This part is a little tricky because there are several ways to read and write properties and because there are special considerations associated with some attributes.

Figure 10.16 shows that you read properties from the property cache with the `Get` and `GetEx` methods and write them with the `Put` and `PutEx` methods. This is actually a simplification. Table 10.4 offers a fuller picture (we don't cover `GetEx` and `PutEx` yet).

NOTE   A static property method sometimes modifies the value to a different format before returning it, instead of returning the raw value. For example, many dates are expressed as `large integers` in Active Directory. If you retrieve the property with `Get`, you will get that `large integer` value, but if you retrieve the value with a static property method, it will be converted to a date string.

Choices A and B in Table 10.4 are fairly equivalent, but there are two differences.

- When a value is not in the property cache, choice A will return an error ("property not found"), whereas choice B will return a `vbEmpty` "value." Consequently, choice B is easier to use because it avoids the extra hassle of error checking.

TABLE 10.4 Ways to Read and Write the Property Cache

Way	Read and Write Code Examples	Description
A. Explicit `Get/Put` methods with attribute LDAP names	```strLastName = objUser.Get("sn") Call objUser.Put("sn", strLastName)```	This choice enables you to read and write "any" property of any object using the LDAP name of the corresponding attribute as an argument. We put "any" in quotation marks because there are some exceptions and special considerations with some attributes (explained in the text).
B. Dynamic property methods (i.e., attribute LDAP names without `Get/Put`)	```strLastName = objUser.sn objUser.sn = strLastName```	When a new object is fetched in the property cache, ADSI lists all attributes of the corresponding class and dynamically creates a new property method for each of them. Choice B uses attribute LDAP names, as does choice A, but this time you don't see any `Get` or `Put`. (The differences between choices A and B are explained in the text.)
C. Static property methods	```strLastName = objUser.LastName objUser.LastName = strLastName```	You can access some properties of some classes with static property methods. For example, with the user class, you can access 36 out of 207 properties this way. (See the "The IADsUser Interface" section later in this chapter.)
D. Property cache interfaces	```Set objPropEntry = objUser.Item("sn"),``` and so on	ADSI includes *property cache interfaces,* which help in listing, reading, and writing the properties in the property cache. Just like `Get/Put`, you can use these interfaces to any Active Directory object class. (See Chapter 11 for more information and examples.)

- Because the attribute names are not arguments in choice B, you cannot use string variables for them. When we show examples of displaying user properties in the next chapter, you will see how handy it is to use string variables with choice A.

When we later read and write properties, we use mostly choice A. We like to see (and also show you) the explicit `Get/Put` methods along with the attribute

LDAP names. This way you will know each time that we are referring to a certain LDAP name and not just some new mysterious ADSI method name. At the same time, we admit that the script lines using choice B would look a little easier.

However, we use choice B when we specifically want to avoid getting those "property not found" errors.

In the next chapter, we show how to apply choices A, C, and D to list all properties of the user Guest.

- The property cache interfaces example (choice D) finds about 30 properties in the cache and lists those property names along with their values.
- The `Get/Put` example (choice A) lists all 207 property names of the `user` class and values for those that Guest has a value for.
- The static property method example (choice C) lists those of the 36 properties that have a value, which results in a list of about 20 properties.

Table 10.4 mentions that there are exceptions and special considerations with some attributes.

- You are naturally subject to normal Active Directory access control when you try to read or write any property value. Normally your scripts run with the privileges of your logged-on user account.
- As noted earlier, constructed attributes will be missing from the property cache unless you specifically retrieve them using the `GetInfoEx` method. And if they are missing from the property cache, you will get a "property not found" error when you try to read them with the `Get` method or some static property method.
- Multivalued properties require special handling, as explained in the next section.
- Properties that use normal data types (integer, string, date, or Boolean) are easy to read and handle in VBScript. `DN with binary`, `DN with Unicode string`, `NT security descriptor`, and `large integer`, as well as binary data types, are more difficult and require special handling.

HANDLING SPECIAL DATA TYPES

VBScript is not well suited for some special data types. The following list briefly describes how to handle these special data types.

- `DN with binary` and `DN with Unicode` string both consist of two components, as explained in Chapter 8. ADSI has two special interfaces, `IADs-DNWithBinary` and `IADsDNWithString`, that help to get access to the DN component and the binary or string component of the property. Both data types are extremely rare—refer to ADSI Help for more information if you need either data type.

- There is an interface called `IADsSecurityDescriptor` for accessing NT security descriptor properties. We explain how to use it in the next chapter.

- Because VBScript doesn't understand 64-bit `large integers`, you can access the high and low 32 bits of any `large integer` single-valued property using the `IADsLargeInteger` interface. You could use the parts separately and try to figure out what they mean, or you could count the total value with the formula `HighPart * 2^32 + LowPart`. However, if the resulting number were too large for VBScript's 32-bit integers, it would be converted to a floating-point number. The result could be "3.26074403172981E+17," where "E+17" would mean that you should move the decimal point 17 spaces to the right. Because there are "only" 14 decimals in the number, you would need to add three zeros—the resulting number could be wrong by several hundreds. With some extra work you can handle `large integer` properties, perhaps losing some accuracy. (Chapter 11 has examples of handling `large integers` when listing user properties.)

- Properties with binary values will give you some headaches. ADSI returns their values as arrays of bytes, but VBScript is not very good at handling them. We show one tricky but effective way in the next chapter.

NOTE The previous list mentions that you can access single-valued `large integer` properties. The `IADsLargeInteger` interface seems not to work with multivalued properties, but fortunately there are none in the base schema.

SINGLE-VALUED AND MULTIVALUED PROPERTIES

The `Get` method is meant for single-valued properties and `GetEx` is meant for multivalued properties. However, you can use either method for either type of property, as Table 10.5 describes.

Given this flexibility, you can use one of three "strategies" with `Get` and `GetEx`:

- *Always use `Get`.* This choice is possible, but more difficult, because for multivalued attributes you would need to examine each time whether you received an array or not.

- *Use `Get` with single-valued and `GetEx` with multivalued.* This choice is normally the best. It is easy to handle the normal data types for single-valued properties and arrays for multivalued.

TABLE 10.5 `Get` versus `GetEx`

	Single-Valued	**Multivalued***
`Get`	Returns a normal data type value (e.g., string)	If there is only one value, returns a normal data type value (e.g., string); if there are multiple values, returns an array of normal data type values (e.g., strings)
`GetEx`	Returns an array of normal data type values (e.g., strings); however, there is only one element in the array	Returns an array of normal data type values (e.g., strings)

*When you retrieve the values of a multivalued property, they are not in any particular order in the array. You cannot rely on them to be in the same order as you stored them. This is a feature of Active Directory and not ADSI.

- *Always use* `GetEx`. For example, if you list all 207 user attributes, it is probably easier to always use `GetEx` than to figure out when to use `Get` and when to use `GetEx`. We show an example of this when we list user properties in the next chapter.

When writing properties, `Put` is meant for single-valued and `PutEx` for multivalued properties. Again, you could use either method for either type of property.

Before comparing `Put` and `PutEx`, Table 10.6 describes the four modes of the `PutEx` method. The method includes an additional argument that enables you to specify the mode. Consequently, `PutEx` takes three arguments:

- The mode as a value between 1 and 4
- The attribute LDAP name
- An array of values to be added or removed

For example, to delete two home phone numbers, you would use a line like the following (divided into two lines):

```
Call objUser.PutEx(ADS_PROPERTY_DELETE, "otherHomePhone", _
    Array("111-1111","444-4444"))
```

In Table 10.7, we describe how `Put` and `PutEx` work with single-valued and multivalued properties. The result of the table is that you only need to use `PutEx` if you need one of the `append`, `delete`, or `clear` modes.

ADSI Interfaces

As with COM in general, ADSI interfaces enable you to interact with ADSI objects, because each interface has properties and/or methods to use. An ADSI provider,

TABLE 10.6 The Four Modes of PutEx

Mode	Value	Description
ADS_PROPERTY_UPDATE	2	The values you specify are stored in the property and they replace any previous values. If you had a list of five phone numbers and updated them with a list of two, only those two would remain.
ADS_PROPERTY_APPEND	3	The values you specify are stored in the property with existing values. You could append two phone numbers to a list of five, resulting in a total of seven numbers.
ADS_PROPERTY_DELETE	4	The values you specify are removed from the property. You could delete two of five phone numbers, resulting in three numbers.
ADS_PROPERTY_CLEAR	1	All the values are cleared from the property. If you later tried to read the property with Get, you would get the "property not found" error. You can include any array of values as an argument, or rather, use the vbEmpty constant.

such as the LDAP provider, is responsible for implementing most of the ADSI objects and interfaces. Some of them are implemented also by the *router* component, which corresponds to the file activeds.dll.

The ADSI documentation lists 58 interfaces. All of their names start with "IADs" and each is meant to give access to something. For example, IADs-LargeInteger gives access to the high part and low part of a 64-bit number, IADsUser gives access to user objects, and so forth.

TABLE 10.7 Put versus PutEx

	Single-Valued	Multivalued
Put	Writes a normal data type value (e.g., string)	Works almost like PutEx in update mode. If there is only one value, you can use either a normal data type or an array. If there are multiple values, you must use an array.
PutEx	Works like Put, but you must use the update mode and store the value to be written in a one-element array*	Allows you to use any of the four modes (update, append, delete, and clear). You must always use an array, even if there is only one value.

*You can use PutEx for a single-valued property also in the clear mode to put it in a "not set" state.

Some interfaces are meant to give access to only one object class—for example, `IADsUser` is meant just for user objects. Other interfaces are meant to give access to any object class, such as `IADs` and `IADsPropertyList`.

All access capabilities that ADSI offers are implemented as various interfaces. Many of the interfaces give access to Active Directory, but some of them give access to other services, such as file shares and print queues.

Even though there is the class `user` in Active Directory and the corresponding interface `IADsUser` in ADSI, it doesn't follow that there is an interface for each Active Directory class. Fewer than ten ADSI interfaces correspond to Active Directory classes.

One interface, called merely `IADs`, contains the familiar methods `Get`, `GetEx`, `Put`, `PutEx`, `GetInfo`, `GetInfoEx`, and `SetInfo`. You can use this generic interface with any Active Directory objects, so it doesn't matter that only some classes have their own interfaces dedicated. Even when you are managing user objects, you will use `IADs` instead of `IADsUser` when you use any of the methods just listed.

This raises the following question: What do we need `IADsUser` for if `IADs` alone would be enough? The answer is twofold.

- A dedicated interface may add some useful methods, such as `SetPassword` to set a user's password in a secure manner.

- A dedicated interface may add some static property methods, such as those 36 for `IADsUser`. Static property methods exist mainly for the `user` class, so we get back to the topic in the "The IADsUser Interface" section.

In Visual Basic you would define two object variables as follows:

```
Dim objUser As IADsUser
Dim objGroup As IADsGroup
```

Even when specifying that `objUser` is using the `IADsUser` interface, you can use in addition the properties and methods of the `IADs` interface. The reason is that `IADsUser` and the other per-class interfaces inherit the features of `IADs`.

Interestingly, in VBScript you don't need to (and cannot) specify which interfaces you will use. You can just use them. A VBScript equivalent for the previous lines is as follows:

```
Dim objUser
Dim objGroup
```

This is easier, but it doesn't mean that you can forget the existence of interfaces. When you read the ADSI documentation, you still need to locate either the `IADsUser` or `IADsGroup` part to see what methods and properties there are.

NOTE   One consequence of not specifying the interface is that you can use `IADsUser` properties and methods also for classes other than `user`. However, if `IADsUser` contains the `Lastname` static property method, there is not much point in trying to read the last name of an OU.

NOTE   The official convention of expressing a certain method of a certain interface is to use two colons between them. An example is `IADsUser::SetPassword`. We don't use this convention in this book because with VBScript it is not important in which interface each method is implemented.

THE LIST OF ADSI INTERFACES

Of the 58 interfaces, almost all are *dual interfaces,* which means that they can be used from both automation clients (e.g., VBScript) and nonautomation clients (e.g., C/C++).

When you read the documentation for the dual interfaces, you will see lists of `IUnknown` methods and `IDispatch` methods. You cannot call these methods from VBScript scripts. However, `IDispatch` methods are made for automation clients, but they are called automatically behind the scenes.

A couple of interfaces can be used only from nonautomation clients. Some interfaces are obsolete or meant to be used only with Novell NDS. Therefore, we are left with 43 interfaces, which we list in Table 10.8 (divided into categories).

In the following four sections we describe these four interfaces:

- `IADs`
- `IADsContainer`
- `IADsUser`
- `IADsGroup`

The discussions of these interfaces, which are relatively brief, give you an idea of what you can do with them. Because they are the most basic interfaces, they appear frequently in the examples of the next chapter.

THE IADS INTERFACE

As mentioned previously, you can use the methods and properties of `IADs` to manage any Active Directory object, and those features are also inherited to the class-specific interfaces, such as `IADsUser` and `IADsGroup`.

TABLE 10.8 Relevant ADSI Interfaces

Category	`IADs` Interfaces*	Description
Core	`IADs, Container, Namespaces, OpenDSObject`	These interfaces provide the common features to manage any Active Directory object, such as the familiar `GetInfo` and `SetInfo` methods.
Persistent object**	`Collection, Computer, Domain, FileService, FileShare, Group, Members, OU, PrintJob, PrintQueue, Service, User`	These interfaces enable you to browse and modify Active Directory objects and some server services, such as file shares and print queues.
Dynamic object	`ComputerOperations, FileServiceOperations, PrintJobOperations, PrintQueueOperations, Resource, ServiceOperations, Session`	These interfaces enable you to browse and manage current user sessions to a server, current open files, and other dynamic server services.
Schema**	`Class, Property, Syntax`	These interfaces enable you to browse and modify the classes and attributes of your Active Directory and browse the syntaxes.
Property cache**	`PropertyEntry, PropertyList, PropertyValue, PropertyValue2`	These interfaces enable you to browse and modify properties in the property cache.
Data type	`DNWithBinary, DNWithString, LargeInteger`	These interfaces enable you to access some special data types.
Security**	`AccessControlEntry, AccessControlList, SecurityDescriptor`	These interfaces enable you to browse and modify the ACLs of Active Directory objects.
Extension	`Extension`	This interface enables organizations (e.g., independent software vendors [ISVs]) to add new properties and methods to existing ADSI interfaces.
Utility	`ADSystemInfo, DeleteOps, NameTranslate, ObjectOptions, PathName, WinNTSystemInfo`	These interfaces provide additional helper functions.

*We left "IADs" out of every name to save space. An exception is the first interface, because its name is just IADs.

**We present examples of many of the interfaces in the next chapter. Specifically, we cover the following interface categories: persistent objects, schema, property cache, and security.

The IADs interface has the following methods: Get, GetEx, Put, PutEx, GetInfo, GetInfoEx, and SetInfo. ("The Property Cache" section of this chapter provides descriptions of these methods.)

The IADs interface has six properties, which are listed in Table 10.9. Their contents vary slightly depending on the namespace, so we explain them from the LDAP namespace's point of view. All six properties are read-only and return a string.

The script in Figure 10.17 displays the values of all six properties for the user Guest. When you execute the script, you will see the output shown in Figure 10.18.

THE IADSCONTAINER INTERFACE

The IADsContainer interface contains properties and methods that are meaningful with container objects, such as browsing, creating, and deleting child objects. Table 10.10 lists three properties and Table 10.11 lists five methods for the interface.

The following lines demonstrate the use of GetObject (on the second line), which is described in Table 10.11:

```
Set objContainer = GetObject("LDAP://CN=Users,DC=sanao,DC=com")
Set objUser = objContainer.GetObject("user", "CN=Guest")
WScript.Echo objUser.Name & vbTab & objUser.Description
```

Normally you would combine the first two lines and use the traditional Get-Object to create the objUser variable. However, this longer form can be handy if, for example, you need to access several objects in one container.

TABLE 10.9 Properties of the IADs Interface

Property	Description
ADsPath	This property contains the ADsPath, which is the binding string to the target object. With the LDAP provider this is normally in the form LDAP://distinguished name.
Class	This property contains the LDAP name of the schema class of the target object.
GUID	This property contains the objectGUID of the target object. Of the two GUID formats, this property uses the format without curly braces or dashes.
Name	This property contains the RDN (i.e., naming attribute) of the target object.
Parent	This property contains the ADsPath to the parent container of the target object. Note that even though it would seem that you could build up an ADsPath to an object from its Parent and Name properties, you shouldn't do this, because it is not guaranteed to work always.
Schema	This property contains the ADsPath to the schema class object of the target object.

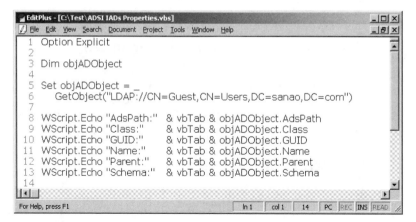

FIGURE 10.17 The properties of the `IADs` interface enable you to display six basic values for any Active Directory object.

FIGURE 10.18 Output from the script in Figure 10.17

TABLE 10.10 Properties of the `IADsContainer` Interface

Property	Description
Count	This read-only property is not implemented in Microsoft's LDAP provider (for performance reasons). Otherwise, it would give the number (perhaps filtered) of child objects in the container.
Filter	This property is an array, where each element is an LDAP class name. When you list the contents of the target container, only the objects that match the filter (including any subclasses) are returned. (For an example of the `Filter` property, see the basic ADSI example in Figure 10.14.)
Hints	This property is an array, where each element is an LDAP attribute name. When you list the contents of the target container, only the specified attributes for each object are retrieved to the property cache, possibly optimizing the network traffic and speed. However, the LDAP provider doesn't implement the `Hints` property.

TABLE 10.11 Methods of the `IADsContainer` Interface

Method	Description
GetObject	This method creates a new object variable for the specified object in the target container. After that, you can access the child object directly.
Create*	This method creates the specified object in the target container.
Delete*	This method deletes the specified object from the target container.
CopyHere	This method copies the specified object to the target container. You cannot use this method with Active Directory.
MoveHere	This method moves the specified object to the target container. You can also use this method to rename an object without moving it.

*Examples of these methods appear in Chapter 11.

If you want to move Jack from Sales to Users, use the `MoveHere` method as follows:

```
Set objContainer = GetObject("LDAP://CN=Users,DC=sanao,DC=com")
Set objUser = _
    objContainer.MoveHere( _
    "LDAP://CN=Jack,OU=Sales,DC=sanao,DC=com", "CN=Jack")
```

If you would also like to rename Jack, change the last argument (`"CN=Jack"`) to the new name—for example, `"CN=Jill"`. If the source and target containers are the same, the object is just renamed, not moved.

If you don't need an object variable for the moved object, you can ignore the returned value and put a `Call` instead. The replaced second line (divided into lines 2, 3, and 4) would be the following:

```
Call objContainer.MoveHere( _
    "LDAP://CN=Jack,OU=Sales,DC=sanao,DC=com", "CN=Jack")
```

THE IADSUSER INTERFACE

The `IADsUser` interface offers three methods and a number of static property methods to help you manage user objects.

In the discussion of reading and writing the property cache, we list the following syntax choices to read the last name of a user:

```
A: strLastName = objUser.Get("sn")
B: strLastName = objUser.sn
C: strLastName = objUser.LastName
D: Set objPropEntry = objUser.Item("sn"), etc.
```

Choices A (explicit Get/Put) and B (dynamic property methods) are about equivalent and they both use the attribute LDAP name to retrieve the value. Choice C (static property method) uses something other than an LDAP name. Choice D uses the property cache interfaces, which we explain in Chapter 11.

Now it's time to compare choice A/B to choice C. We use the user class as an example because of the following reason: Choice C requires a per-class ADSI interface. IADsUser is the most common per-class interface to use, and that interface is the most comprehensive in the number of static property methods.

Table 10.12 lists the 36 IADsUser static property methods that correspond to attributes in Active Directory (excluding the 7 that apply only to NetWare). Note that these 36 property methods are not the same as the most common attributes. You see only 22 of them in the Users and Computers snap-in.

TABLE 10.12 Static Property Methods of the IADsUser Interface

Property Method	Attribute LDAP Name	Syntax	Visible in Users and Computers Snap-In
AccountExpirationDate	accountExpires	Large integer	Yes
BadLoginCount	badPwdCount	Integer	No
Department	department	Unicode string	Yes
Description	description	Unicode string	Yes
Division	division	Unicode string	No
EmailAddress	mail	Unicode string	Yes
EmployeeID	employeeID	Unicode string	No
FaxNumber	facsimileTelephoneNumber	Unicode string	Yes
FirstName	givenName	Unicode string	Yes
FullName	displayName	Unicode string	Yes
HomeDirectory	homeDirectory	Unicode string	Yes
HomePage	wWWHomePage	Unicode string	Yes
LastFailedLogin	badPasswordTime	Large integer	No

(continued)

TABLE 10.12 (*continued*)

Property Method	Attribute LDAP Name	Syntax	Visible in Users and Computers Snap-In
LastLogin	lastLogon	Large integer	No
LastLogoff	lastLogoff*	Large integer	No
LastName	sn	Unicode string	Yes
LoginHours	logonHours	Octet string	Yes
LoginScript	scriptPath	Unicode string	Yes
LoginWorkstations	userWorkstations	Unicode string	Yes
Manager	manager	DN	Yes
MaxStorage	maxStorage	Large integer	No
NamePrefix	personalTitle	Unicode string	No
NameSuffix	generationQualifier	Unicode string	No
OfficeLocations	physicalDeliveryOfficeName	Unicode string	Yes
OtherName	middleName	Unicode string	No
PasswordLastChanged	pwdLastSet	Large integer	No
Picture	thumbnailPhoto	Octet string	No
PostalAddresses	postalAddress	Unicode string	No
PostalCodes	postalCode	Unicode string	Yes
Profile	profilePath	Unicode string	Yes
SeeAlso	seeAlso	DN	No
TelephoneHome	homePhone	Unicode string	Yes
TelephoneMobile	mobile	Unicode string	Yes
TelephoneNumber	telephoneNumber	Unicode string	Yes
TelephonePager	pager	Unicode string	Yes
Title	title	Unicode string	Yes

*LastLogoff isn't maintained in Windows 2000.

In addition to the 36 static property methods in Table 10.12, there are two that correspond to individual bits in the `userAccountControl` attribute:

- `AccountDisabled`
- `PasswordRequired`

NOTE

There is also a third similar property method: `IsAccountLocked`. You can use it with Windows NT, but it doesn't work with Active Directory and ADSI LDAP provider. The reason is that in Active Directory this setting is in the `lockoutTime` attribute, but the property method tries to read it from the `userAccountControl` attribute.

With choices A and B you would get the "raw" value of an attribute, as you would with most choice C static property methods. However, some static property methods may return a "better" value than just the attribute value in Active Directory. For example, `userWorkstations` is a single-valued attribute, which could contain a string "PC25,PC37,PC38." When you retrieve it with the `Login-Workstations` static property method, the string has been modified to a multi-valued property containing three values: "PC25," "PC37," and "PC38."

Using static property methods (i.e., choice C) has the following advantages.

- When you use the two static property methods that correspond to the bits in `userAccountControl`, you don't have to do bitwise arithmetic in your script.

- Some of the static property method names are more descriptive than the LDAP names (such as `LastName` versus `sn`). Therefore, it may be more comfortable for you to use the static property method names.

- `LastLogin`, `LastFailedLogin`, and the other dates in Table 10.12 are stored as `large integers` in Active Directory. If you use choices A or B to read the `badPasswordTime` property, you get a 64-bit number (in two parts) telling you how many 0.1 microsecond intervals (i.e., 1/10,000,000 seconds) have passed since the beginning of the seventeenth century (i.e., January 1, 1601). It would be very difficult to convert this to a meaningful date in your script (although you can use the RepAdmin tool manually as shown in Chapter 11). Using the corresponding `LastFailedLogin` property method would give you a meaningful date and time string right away, including time zone correction.

NOTE

When reading attributes with date syntaxes using choices A or B, you will get UTC times (about the same as GMT). Active Directory stores times in UTC, regardless of whether the syntax is `UTC time string` or a `generalized time string`.

Static property methods have the following disadvantages.

- There are only 36 + 2 of them. For example, there is a static property method for `HomeDirectory` but not one for `HomeDrive`. Also, 14 of those attributes that correspond to static property methods are not found in the Users and Computers snap-in (as listed in Table 10.12); therefore, it is possible that you will never use them.

- You cannot use a variable as the attribute name to browse through all static property methods in a single loop, as you could when using choice A (i.e., `objUser.Get("attrLDAPname")`).

- You may still have to do bitwise arithmetic, because `userAccountControl` contains other settings than just those two.

- The behavior is not always consistent. If you are reading `PostalAddresses`, which is multivalued, you will get an error, a string, or an array, depending on whether there are zero, one, or multiple values defined. With `LoginWorkstations`, you will get an error or an array but not a string. Similarly, a single-valued `EmployeeID` returns an empty string if it is not set, but FaxNumber returns a "property not found" error.

Consequently, you must use choices A or B anyway for some of the properties. As mentioned previously, for consistency we use only choice A in this book, unless there is a specific advantage to using a property method (choice B dynamic or choice C static).

`IADsUser` also has three normal methods, which are listed in Table 10.13.

TABLE 10.13 Methods of the `IADsUser` Interface

Method	Description
Groups	This method returns a collection of groups to which the user belongs. They are managed by the `IADsMembers` interface, which works much like `IADsContainer`. You can set a filter and list all members in a `For Each ... Next` loop. However, all the members in the collection belong to the class `group`, so the filter is obsolete.
SetPassword	This method sets the user's password. In Active Directory this happens with the secure Kerberos protocol as long as the target object is in the same forest and you either use a serverless `ADsPath` (e.g., `LDAP://CN=Guest, CN=Users, DC=sanao, DC=com`) or include a DNS server name in the path (e.g., `LDAP://dc1.sanao.com/CN=Guest, CN=Users, DC=sanao, DC=com`).
ChangePassword	This method changes the user's password as long as you are able to enter the old password as an argument.

The following lines demonstrate the `Groups` method:

```
Set objUser = _
    GetObject("LDAP://CN=Administrator,CN=Users,DC=sanao,DC=com")
For Each objChild In objUser.Groups
    WScript.Echo objChild.Name & vbTab & objChild.Description
Next
```

THE IADSGROUP INTERFACE

The `IADsGroup` interface provides some methods that help in managing group memberships. It has one static property method, `Description`, which corresponds to the `description` attribute in Active Directory. Table 10.14 describes the normal methods.

WARNING   All members of a group are stored as one multivalued attribute. Because Active Directory replication is attribute-based, changing the membership on two domain controllers at the same time results in the loss of one of the changes. Therefore, you should make a habit of modifying group memberships on only one domain controller, which could be the PDC emulator, for example. In this case, the `ADsPath` would be `"LDAP://dc1.sanao.com/CN=SomeGroup, CN=Users, DC=sanao, DC=com"`.

TABLE 10.14 Methods of the `IADsGroup` Interface

Method	Description
Members	This method returns a collection of objects that are the members of this group. They are managed by the IADsMembers interface. You can set a filter* and list all members in a `For Each ... Next` loop. Because the members could be users, contacts, computers, or other groups, you can narrow the list with a filter. You can also use the `Count` property to get the number of members.
IsMember	This method returns True or False depending on whether a given object is a member in the target group.
Add	This method adds a given object to the target group.
Remove	This method removes a given object from the target group.

*You would do this using the `Filter` property, but it seems not to work with IADsMembers in Windows 2000.

NOTE The `Members` method normally returns an empty list for Domain Users, because the method lists only members that are stored in the `members` attribute. This attribute doesn't include users that have the group as their primary group, and Domain Users is by default the *primary group* for every user. The primary group membership is stored in the `primaryGroupID` attribute of each user.

The following lines demonstrate how you can list the members of Domain Admins:

```
Set objGroup = _
    GetObject("LDAP://CN=Domain Admins,CN=Users,DC=sanao,DC=com")
WScript.Echo objGroup.Members.Count
For Each objChild In objGroup.Members
    WScript.Echo objChild.Name '& vbTab & objChild.Description
Next
```

ADSI Syntaxes

Chapter 8 lists 23 syntaxes (or data types) that Active Directory supports. They are mapped to 20 LDAP types, which in turn are mapped to 13 ADSI data types, or `AdsTypes`, in the ADSI LDAP provider. Finally, the 13 `ADsTypes` are mapped to 6 OLE automation data types (see Figure 10.19).

In Figure 10.19, `large integer` is an example to show values for various data type identifiers. As you can see, `large integer` has quite a few identifiers, as do the other 22 syntaxes. (See Chapter 8 for some of the identifiers.)

NOTE There are more than 40 LDAP types (e.g., `LDAPTYPE_AUDIO` and `LDAPTYPE_TELEXNUMBER`), but Active Directory uses only 20. There are also 28 `ADsTypes`, but again, only 13 are used in Active Directory.

You are probably happy to hear that for scripting it is quite sufficient if you just know the list of `ADsTypes` and how they correspond to Active Directory syntaxes. Table 10.15 lists the 23 Active Directory syntaxes and how they map to the 20 LDAP types and 13 ADSI types. Table 10.15 also shows how many attributes of the base schema use each of the syntaxes.

Table 10.16 shows which Active Directory syntaxes map to which OLE automation data type. This information is not essential to write a script, but it may help you to understand how your script handles various types of data.

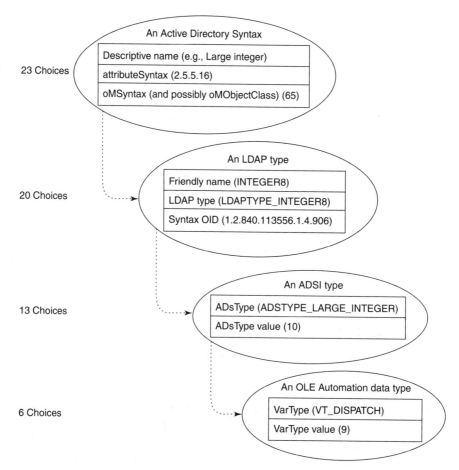

FIGURE 10.19 Twenty-three Active Directory syntaxes map to 20 LDAP types, which map to 13 ADSI types, which map to 6 OLE automation data types. Example values for each identifier appear in parentheses, using the `large integer` syntax as an example.

TABLE 10.15 Syntaxes and Data Types

Descriptive Name	Count in Schema	LDAP Type–Friendly Name	ADsType	ADsType Value
DN (aka distin-guished name)	92	DN	ADSTYPE_DN_STRING	1
Case-sensitive string	0	CaseExactString	ADSTYPE_CASE_EXACT_STRING	2
Unicode string	298	DirectoryString	ADSTYPE_CASE_IGNORE_STRING	3

(continued)

TABLE 10.15 (*continued*)

Descriptive Name	Count in Schema	LDAP Type–Friendly Name	ADsType	ADsType Value
OID string	20	OID	ADSTYPE_CASE_IGNORE_STRING	3
Case-ignore string (teletex)	8	CaseIgnore-String	ADSTYPE_CASE_IGNORE_STRING	3
IA5 string	7	IA5String	ADSTYPE_CASE_IGNORE_STRING	3
Presentation address	1	Presentation-Address	ADSTYPE_CASE_IGNORE_STRING	3
OR name	0	ORName	ADSTYPE_CASE_IGNORE_STRING	3
Access point DN	0	AccessPointDN	ADSTYPE_CASE_IGNORE_STRING	3
Printable string	13	PrintableString	ADSTYPE_PRINTABLE_STRING	4
Numeric string	2	NumericString	ADSTYPE_NUMERIC_STRING	5
Boolean	54	Boolean	ADSTYPE_BOOLEAN	6
Integer	149	INTEGER	ADSTYPE_INTEGER	7
Enumeration	6	INTEGER	ADSTYPE_INTEGER	7
Octet string	120	OctetString	ADSTYPE_OCTET_STRING	8
SID string	8	OctetString	ADSTYPE_OCTET_STRING	8
Replica link	2	OctetString	ADSTYPE_OCTET_STRING	8
Generalized time string	6	GeneralizedTime	ADSTYPE_UTC_TIME	9
UTC time string	4	UTCTime	ADSTYPE_UTC_TIME	9
Large integer	66	INTEGER8	ADSTYPE_LARGE_INTEGER	10
NT security descriptor	3	ObjectSecurity-Descriptor	ADSTYPE_NT_SECURITY_DESCRIPTOR	25
DN with binary (aka DN with octet string)	4	DNWithBinary	ADSTYPE_DN_WITH_BINARY	27
DN with Unicode string	0	DNWithString	ADSTYPE_DN_WITH_STRING	28

TABLE 10.16 OLE Automation Data Types and Corresponding Active Directory Syntaxes

VarType	Value	Comment	Active Directory Syntaxes
`VT_I4`	3	4-byte (32-bit) signed integer	`Integer`, `Enumeration`
`VT_DATE`	7	Date	`Generalized time string`, `UTC time string`
`VT_BSTR`	8	OLE automation string	`DN`, `Case-sensitive string (aka case-exact string)`, `Unicode string (aka directory string)`, `Case-ignore string (teletex)`, `Printable string`, `Numeric string`, `Presentation address`, `Access point DN`, `OID string`, `IA5 string`, `OR name`
`VT_DISPATCH*`	9	`IDispatch`	`Large integer (aka INTEGER8)`, `NT security descriptor`, `DN with binary`, `DN with Unicode string`
`VT_BOOL`	11	Boolean	`Boolean`
`VT_VARIANT`	12	VARIANT	`Octet string`, `SID string`, `Replica link`

*`VT_DISPATCH` is the type that handles the four syntaxes that have dedicated ADSI interfaces to give you access to the corresponding data. For more information, see the "Handling Special Data Types" section.

ADDITIONAL TECHNIQUES

It is good to be aware of the following additional scripting techniques:

- Ways to input and output information
- Using executables (such as the NET commands) from scripts
- Using COM components
- Using the Win32 API
- Debugging scripts
- Including script lines from another file

We describe the techniques in the following sections and present many examples of the first three list items in Chapter 11.

Ways to Input and Output Information

As mentioned, WSH scripts cannot be very interactive. There are still several ways to input information to your scripts and output information from your scripts. The methods to input information are as follows:

- Use the `InputBox` function of VBScript to prompt the user to enter text in a pop-up window.
- Use command-line options (arguments).
- Read a text file or an Excel spreadsheet.
- Read standard input (likely to be redirected from a text file).
- Read another source of information, such as Active Directory or a database.

The ways to output information are as follows:

- Use the `MsgBox` function of VBScript to display a pop-up window.
- Use the `WScript.Echo` method to display a pop-up window or lines of output in the command window, depending on whether WScript or CScript is used.
- Use the `WScript.Popup` method to display a pop-up window.
- Write to a text file or an Excel spreadsheet.
- Write to standard output to display lines of output in the command window (equal to `WScript.Echo` used with CScript).
- Write to another destination, such as Active Directory or a database.

Using Executables from Scripts

You can start applications from your WSH scripts. These applications may be graphical or command-line tools, including any Windows 2000 "DOS" commands (DIR, COPY, and so on) and NET commands (e.g., NET USER). You can probably solve your administrative scripting tasks without these old commands, but you should keep in mind that they are available.

Using COM Components

To write scripts that interact with Active Directory, you will use ADSI and often also ADO. In addition, you could use, among others, the following COM components in your scripts.

- *VBScript* includes `FileSystemObject`, which enables you to browse and manipulate drives, folders, and files. One thing you cannot do, however, is manage file and folder permissions. There is also an `Err` object, which you can use in error handling of the scripts.

- *WSH* includes the objects `WScript`, `WshArguments`, `WshEnvironment`, `WshNetwork`, `WshShell`, `WshShortcut`, `WshSpecialFolders`, and `WshUrlShortcut`. They enable you to perform such operations as use command-line arguments and environment variables, modify the registry, and create network mappings and desktop shortcuts.

- *Microsoft Office* components enable you to control the Office applications. For example, you can write and read information to and from Excel sheets.

- *The ADSI Resource Kit* includes the files ADsEncode.dll, ADsError.dll, ADsFactr.dll, ADsFSMO.dll, ADsLocator.dll, ADsRAS.dll, ADsSecurity.dll, and ADsVersion.dll. These eight files provide additional functions to manage Active Directory and other things. For example, ADsFSMO enables you to list the operations master role owners and ADsSecurity enables you to manage file and folder permissions. The ADSI Resource Kit is not an actual product, and you will get the files if you download the Platform SDK. You could say that the files are included in the SDK as samples. There are also some sample scripts that demonstrate use of the functions, but unfortunately, as of this writing, there is no documentation. Of the eight components, ADsSecurity is relatively popular. Because standard WSH + VBScript + ADSI doesn't enable you to manage file and folder permissions, ADsSecurity fills a specific need in scripting.

- *IADsTools* includes well over 100 functions to access and manage Active Directory. Most of the functions are site- and replication-related—the Replication Monitor utility uses them. IADsTools.dll and the documentation in IADsTools.doc are included in Windows 2000 Support Tools (which you can install from the Windows 2000 CD-ROM).

- *Homemade components* enable your scripts to do "anything." You just need a developer in your organization who can write these components.

- *Purchased components* could be shrink-wrapped products or custom-made products for you. Just like homemade components, purchased components could do "anything."

- *Windows Management Instrumentation (WMI)* is a COM interface that enables you to manage the operating system, services, and devices in Windows 2000 computers (and other Windows computers if you download WMI for them). WMI is quite extensive—it includes providers for Active Directory, Windows Installer, performance counters, registry, SNMP, event log, Win32 API, and Windows Driver Model (WDM). You could use WMI to manage Active Directory; however, WMI is beyond the scope of this book. For more information, see the documentation at `http://msdn.microsoft.com/library` and browse to Setup and System Administration, Windows Management Instrumentation (WMI).

Using the Win32 API

Without learning WMI, you can call at least some Win32 APIs (application program interfaces) from your scripts. You use the same RunDLL32 command that you can use on the command line.

You can try the following command either on the command line or in the Run window (click the Start button and select Run):

```
rundll32.exe user32.dll,LockWorkStation
```

NOTE   The last word (`LockWorkStation`) is case-sensitive.

The command calls the `LockWorkStation` API function, which locks your computer. To do the same in your script, use the following lines:

```
Set WshShell = CreateObject("WScript.Shell")
WshShell.Run "rundll32.exe user32.dll,LockWorkStation"
```

Unfortunately there are two difficulties in using the Win32 API.

- You need to study a huge amount of information (available at `http://msdn.microsoft.com/library`) to find the right function.
- Most of the functions require passing parameters and you can pass only some of the data types on the RunDLL32 command line.

You may occasionally see an example of Win32 API usage (such as the one here); otherwise, using those functions is not a viable option in scripts.

Debugging Scripts

Recall that there is no integrated development environment for WSH scripts. Despite this shortcoming, you have two satisfactory means to debug your scripts: extra output commands or the Microsoft Script Debugger.

DEBUGGING WITH EXTRA OUTPUT COMMANDS

You can add output commands in appropriate places within your script. The output commands could print just "Here we are" or "Next we'll try to create the user."

You could also include some variable values in the output to help you determine what is going on in your script at that moment.

MICROSOFT SCRIPT DEBUGGER

Microsoft has made a debugger to be used when you debug scripts in HTML or ASP files, which execute in Internet Explorer or Internet Information Server, respectively. This Script Debugger also works to some degree with WSH scripts.

Windows 2000 includes a version of the Script Debugger, which is dated May 1997. You can download a newer version from `http://msdn.microsoft.com/scripting`, but that version is not much newer (it is dated October 1997).

NOTE   Because the Script Debugger program was made for a different environment, it has features that are not meaningful with WSH scripts. Also, it is quite possible that the Script Debugger itself halts when you try to start it, or stops responding later, so that you need to kill it with the Task Manager.

TIP   If the Script Debugger starts without your script in it, you can try to fix this by logging off and on again.

You can launch the Script Debugger with either the `//X` or `//D` host options.

- The `//X` option opens your script in the Script Debugger and places the debugging cursor over the first script line.

- The `//D` option starts running your script. If there is an error, however, your script opens in the Script Debugger and the debugging cursor will be on the line that contains the error. Unfortunately, you don't receive information that would identify the error.

The corresponding two example commands are as follows:

```
cscript //x myscript.vbs
cscript //d myscript.vbs
```

Figure 10.20 shows the Script Debugger when it was launched using the `//X` option with our earlier VBS basic example.

Figure 10.20 requires some explanation.

- The arrow symbol on the left indicates the line where the debugging cursor currently is. You have executed the script up to this line (excluding the line where the debugging cursor is).

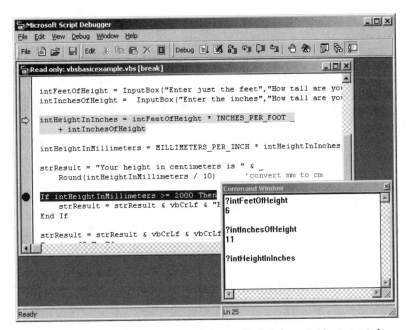

FIGURE 10.20 Our earlier basic example script (in Figure 10.10) shown in the Script Debugger

- You can execute the line (and advance to the next line) by pressing F8.
- You can move the normal "vertical line" text cursor to any line and insert a *breakpoint* on that line by pressing F9. The line will turn dark red and a ball will appear on the left. The If statement in the figure is an example of this.
- When you press F5, the script starts executing from the line where the debugging cursor is. It will continue executing until the script ends, until there is a line with an error, or until there is a line where you have set a breakpoint.
- You can use the Command Window to query the current value (or set a new value) for any variable. In the figure there is no value for intHeightIn-Inches yet, because the line where it would get a value is the next one to be executed.

NOTE   You cannot edit the contents of a WSH script with the Script Debugger.

NOTE   In more complex scripts, a certain part of the script might not be used for a long time and sudden bugs could arise once the functions in that part are used.

Including Script Lines from Another File

You may have script lines that you would like to reuse in other script files. Of course, you could copy and paste the lines from one file to another, but if you later wanted to modify the lines, you would have to do this in (at least) two files. The solution is to have the lines in only one file and use some special XML tags to include them in others.

The lines to include could be a series of *constant definitions.* (They could also be some *functions* or *subprograms,* which we address in the next chapter.)

Figure 10.21 shows a "huge" amount of constant definitions that you would like to include in many of your scripts. As you can see, the file to be included is just like any script. However, the receiving file is a little different. It must use the file extension "WSF" instead of "VBS," and some XML tags must be in the beginning of the file and their closing pairs must be at the end of the file (see Figure 10.22).

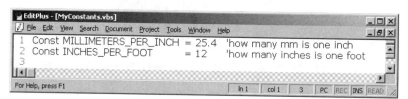

FIGURE 10.21 The same constant definitions are typically needed in many scripts. You can gather all constant definitions in a single file and include that file in your scripts, as shown in Figure 10.22. The figure shows only two definitions—it is not useful to show a 200-line file here.

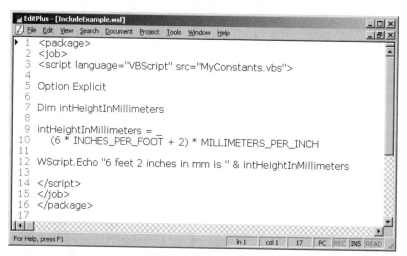

FIGURE 10.22 By using the XML tags shown in the figure, you can include another script file (see line 3). The result is the same as if the lines of the included file were directly in the receiving file.

Lines 1 through 3 in Figure 10.22 contain the required XML tags and lines 14 through 16 contain the corresponding closing tags. The file to be included is specified on line 3 and the reference can be either an absolute or relative path to the file. Lines 4 through 13 are normal VBScript lines.

NOTE   You'll see tens of constant definitions in the various ADSI examples in the next chapter. We have gathered all the definitions in one file that you can download from `http://www.kouti.com/`.

CONCLUSION

This chapter presented the ADSI concepts and explained how to set up a script-writing environment. Now you are ready to explore and test-run the sample scripts.

Administration Scripts: Examples

This chapter is the second of the two scripting chapters. The first scripting chapter presented the concepts, and this chapter focuses on providing practical examples. In addition, this chapter presents a few more concepts so as not to pack too much background theory in the previous chapter. Also, any concepts in this chapter are explained with immediate examples.

You may recall from the introduction to the previous chapter that these two chapters will be useful to people in one of three situations.

- You want to learn to write scripts to enhance administration and save work.

- You want to learn to read scripts. If you download scripts from the Internet or get them from other sources, you'll want to check what they do before you use them in your organization.

- You want to learn more about Active Directory architecture. Outputs of many of the examples in this chapter provide architectural information about Active Directory and you can run those scripts without knowing what they do on each line. You should, of course, read the description first to check that a script isn't going to modify your Active Directory in any way. For example, one script extends your schema (although we do include safety mechanisms in that script).

Let the journey begin.

ADSI EXAMPLES

Now that you know the concepts of scripting and ADSI, the best way to continue learning is to see examples of various tasks. Therefore, in this section we show a number of sample scripts.

We have divided the sample scripts into the following categories:

- User management
- Schema access
- Configuration information
- Access control lists
- OU, group, and computer management
- ADSI without Active Directory
- Additional techniques
- Using ADO

NOTE Several of the samples in the user management category apply to any class. All you need to do is change the binding string to point to some other object.

The scripts also include more programming techniques than the category name suggests. Some scripts may prompt for user input with the `InputBox` function, some may accept command-line arguments, and some may use Excel spreadsheets for input or output. When you build your own administration scripts, you can pick up these various techniques from different samples and combine them to create a solution that serves you best.

TIP To find all scripts that use Excel, for example, you can use the Search feature of Windows 2000. Once you have downloaded the samples from `http://www.kouti.com/` and placed them in a folder on your local hard drive, right-click the folder and select Search. If you type "excel" in the Containing Text field, you will get a list of all scripts that somehow use Excel. Instead of the Search feature, you can use the command-line commands Find, FindStr, and QGrep.

We use the following principles with the sample scripts.

- When a section covers a sample script, the script name (although without a number) is the section heading, including the extension .vbs or .xls.
- Most of the sample script filenames start with "ADSI," "WSH," "ADO," or some other prefix to indicate the main technology in the sample.
- To save space, we don't do error checking in the scripts. We discuss error checking in one special example toward the end of the chapter.

- Also to save space, we use comments sparingly, but after each sample we explain how it works. We encourage you to use plentiful comments in your own scripts.

- We explain the first scripts thoroughly, and as the chapter proceeds, our explanations become shorter. Also, if a later script uses a technique that we have explained with an earlier script, we don't repeat the explanation.

- We may hard-code a script to display information only of the Guest account, for example. Depending on your needs, you can apply various input techniques to apply the script to one object or a number of objects.

- When reading or writing Active Directory attributes (or rather, property cache properties), we mostly use explicit `Get` and `Put` methods. For example, we use `objUser.Get("givenName")` instead of `objUser.givenName`. Although the latter format may be shorter and simpler, we consider the former format clearer—it emphasizes that now we are using an Active Directory attribute's LDAP name instead of an ADSI interface method or some other new mysterious function name.

We show the examples as screen shots in EditPlus if they fit nicely on one page. Longer, multipage examples appear as multiple screen shots or are included in the normal text, but in a different font.

NOTE The sample scripts use quite a few constant definitions to specify various values. We have gathered them all in one file, which you can download from `http://www.kouti.com/`.

TIP The third field in the EditPlus status bar indicates the length of the script in lines. If you see only 14 lines in a figure, but the third field in the EditPlus status bar indicates that the total length is 112 lines, you will know that you are looking at only part of the script.

NOTE The output of several sample scripts is tens or hundreds of lines long. Therefore, we show only some lines, if any. We have manipulated the output so that it seems complete, but lines are still missing.

USER MANAGEMENT

This section includes the following sample scripts:

- CH11-01 ADSI List the Users of One Container.vbs
- CH11-02 ADSI List the Users of One Container to Excel.vbs
- CH11-03 ADSI List the Property Cache Contents.vbs
- CH11-04 ADSI List User Properties with Get.vbs
- CH11-05 ADSI List User Properties with Methods.vbs
- CH11-06 ADSI List the Account Options of a User.vbs
- CH11-07 ADSI Create a User with Minimum Attributes.vbs
- CH11-08 ADSI Create a User with More Attributes.vbs
- CH11-09 BAT Create a User with a Batch File.bat
- CH11-10 WSH Create a Home Folder for a User—ver 1.vbs
- CH11-11 WSH Create a Home Folder for a User—ver 2.vbs
- CH11-12 Read User Information from Excel.xls
- CH11-13 Read User Information from Standard Input.xls

The first two examples list all the users in one container, and the next three list the properties of one user with three different approaches. The rest of the examples do just what their names imply.

In addition to this user management section, two user management scripts appear later in the chapter.

- In the "Additional Techniques" section we show how to list users of several containers.
- In the "Using ADO" section we add a home folder for users that don't yet have one.

The other examples are normal WSH scripts, but number 12 is written in VBA to run as an Excel macro.

List the Users of One Container.vbs

This sample script asks you to enter a container name and then lists all users, along with their descriptions, in that container. The sample is quite similar to the basic ADSI example that you saw in the previous chapter (in Figure 10.14). Now it just has a few more bells and whistles.

Figure 11.1 shows the input box for the distinguished name of the container. Figure 11.2 shows the script's contents.

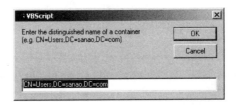

FIGURE 11.1 The input box for "ADSI List the Users of One Container.vbs"

On line 5 in Figure 11.2 we bind to the `rootDSE` object, so that we can read the default domain of the logged-on user. This way, we get a default for the distinguished name.

On line 8 we ask the user to enter a container name and on line 9 we add a second line to the prompt text (see Figure 11.1). We don't specify a title for the input box, so we have two commas before we put the default name as an argument. The entered text you saw in the input box was provided by this default.

On line 11 we will quit the script if the user clicks Cancel. Number 1 as an argument returns an *error level,* which any possible calling application or batch file may use to recognize that there was an error.

On line 13 we finally bind to the chosen container, which is something that we could have done on line 1 if we had hard-coded it (and if there weren't any `Option Explicit` and `Dim` statements).

```
EditPlus - [C:\Test\ADSI List the Users of One Container.vbs]
File  Edit  View  Search  Document  Project  Tools  Window  Help

 1  Option Explicit
 2
 3  Dim objDSE, strDefaultDN, strDN, objContainer, objChild
 4
 5  Set objDSE = GetObject("LDAP://rootDSE")
 6  strDefaultDN = "CN=Users," & objDSE.Get("defaultNamingContext")
 7
 8  strDN = InputBox("Enter the distinguished name of a container" & _
 9      vbCrLf & "(e.g. " & strDefaultDN & ")", , strDefaultDN)
10
11  If strDN = "" Then WScript.Quit(1)     'user clicked Cancel
12
13  Set objContainer = GetObject("LDAP://" & strDN)
14
15  objContainer.Filter = Array("user")
16  For Each objChild In objContainer
17      WScript.Echo objChild.Name & vbTab & objChild.Description
18  Next
19
```

FIGURE 11.2 The contents of "ADSI List the Users of One Container.vbs"

On line 15 we set a filter for the `user` class and then browse through all appropriate child objects of that container and display their names and descriptions.

NOTE   As we mentioned in the basic ADSI example (see Chapter 10, the Note after Figure 10.14) the filter for the `user` class accepts also its subclasses, such as `computer`. It is not a bug in your script if you see some computer objects on your output list.

On line 17 we use `objChild.Description` instead of `objChild.Get-("Description")`. This way, we don't run into the "property not found" error.

List the Users of One Container to Excel.vbs

Like the script in the previous example, this script displays the usernames and descriptions of one container. The only difference is that this time we dump the information into an Excel spreadsheet instead of the command-line window. We also removed the lines to create a default DN.

Figure 11.3 shows the script result when you choose to list the contents of the `CN=Users` container with the default objects. Figure 11.4 shows the script's contents.

On lines 7 through 9 in Figure 11.4 we instantiate a COM object for Excel, which also starts the application (it must be installed in your computer), makes the application visible, and creates a workbook with an empty spreadsheet.

On line 11 we define a name for the spreadsheet. We need to cut the distinguished name, because Excel allows only 31 letters for the spreadsheet name. Note that if the DN is short, we needlessly truncate it and append the ellipses, but we didn't want to add extra lines that would have taken care of this.

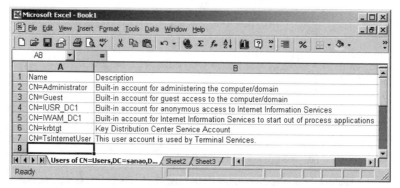

FIGURE 11.3   The output of "ADSI List the Users of One Container to Excel.vbs"

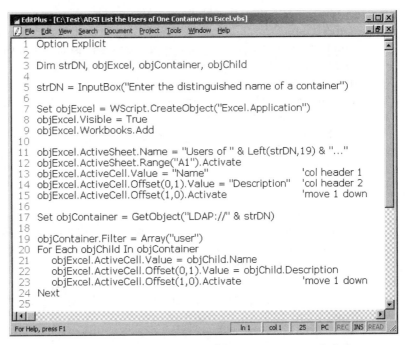

FIGURE 11.4 The contents of "ADSI List the Users of One Container to Excel.vbs"

On line 12 we move to the upper-left corner, on lines 13 and 14 we put the column headers in place, and on line 15 we move to the next line in Excel, where the first username will appear. The first argument in `Offset` means the vertical offset, and the second argument means the horizontal offset.

After binding to the container and setting the filter, we browse all child objects. On lines 21 and 22 we write the name and description to Excel cells and on line 23 we move to the next line in Excel.

List the Property Cache Contents.vbs

In this sample we take one object, user Guest, and list all the properties and their values that he has in his property cache. We do this by using the ADSI property cache interfaces.

TIP   You can use this script for any object class by just changing the target object to bind to.

Figure 11.5 shows some lines of the script's output. As you see, each property name is on its own line in column 1. The number in parentheses is the ADsType (integer, string, and so on) of the property, as discussed in the previous chapter. In column 26 (i.e., character position 26 from left) we have all the values, and in the case of multivalued attributes, each consequent value appears on a new line. You can see that Guest is a member not only of the user class, but also of any of the user superclasses (organizationalPerson, person, and top).

The property cache and, therefore, the script's output don't contain constructed attributes. We would need to use GetInfoEx for them, but we don't (until the next example).

TIP   You can use RepAdmin (part of the Support Tools) to see what date/time a large integer value corresponds to. For example, the output in Figure 11.5 indicates that Guest's password was last changed at the time "1.26078189483997E+17." To convert this value, first divide it by 10,000,000, so you get 12607818948. Then use the command repadmin /showtime 12607818948, which gives you the result 00-07-11 19:55.48 UTC. The tool also shows the local time, but we didn't include it in the book, because it depends on your time zone setting.

WARNING   Some of the attributes that this script displays are nonreplicating (such as lastLogon or badPwdCount). Therefore, each domain controller knows the values only for itself; you will get different results if you read the settings from different domain controllers. To get exact answers, query all domain controllers and pick the latest value or sum the values depending on the attribute.

FIGURE 11.5 Some lines of output of "ADSI List the Property Cache Contents.vbs." Because the original output is tens of lines long, we display only selected lines.

PROPERTY CACHE INTERFACES

Before we show the script, we need to explain how the property cache interfaces work. There are four property cache interfaces, which are illustrated in Figure 11.6.

- `IADsProperyList` has a property method to indicate how many properties there are in the cache. It also enables you to browse through the properties in the cache, perhaps skipping some of them. The `Item` method (and also `Next` or `GetPropertyItem`) retrieves one property from the list to a property entry object. You can select the property either by name (e.g., `.Item("givenName")`) or by index number (e.g., `.Item(2)`).

- `IADsPropertyEntry` enables you to see the name and `ADsType` of the property, as well as browse the values. You can also modify all of these if you are writing some properties to the property cache.

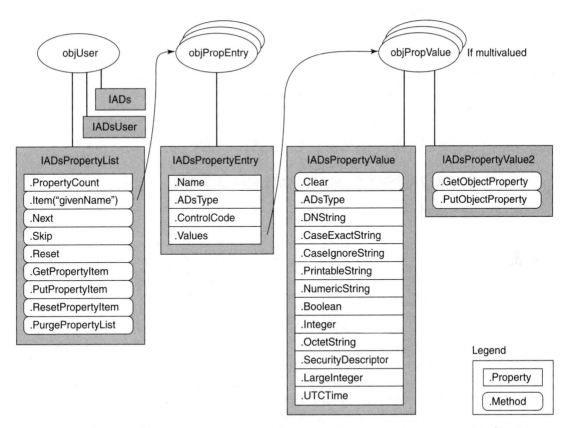

FIGURE 11.6 To list everything in one user's property cache, you use the `IADsPropertyList` interface. It enables you to browse through the properties in the cache and access each entry with `IADsPropertyEntry`. That interface in turn enables browsing through the values of that property.

- `IADsPropertyValue` and `IADsPropertyValue2` enable you to read and write individual values. The former uses the `ADsType` as a property and the latter uses the `ADsType` as an argument to the `GetObjectProperty` method.

The following two lines show an example of `IADsPropertyValue` and `IADsPropertyValue2`, respectively:

```
strAbc = objPropValue.CaseIgnoreString
strAbc = objPropValue.GetObjectProperty(ADSTYPE_CASE_IGNORE_ STRING)
```

The latter example looks more difficult, but it is better for our sample script, as you will soon see.

NOTE   We have drawn several `objPropEntry` and `objPropValue` variables in Figure 11.6. In practice, however, there is usually only one of each and they represent different entries or values one at a time.

NOTE   You don't create a new object for `IADsPropertyList`, but you use that interface with the original object, such as `objUser`.

Now it is finally time to show the sample script.

LIST THE PROPERTY CACHE CONTENTS SAMPLE SCRIPT

We show the script in two parts. Figure 11.7 shows part A and Figure 11.8 shows part B.

Later in the script we need to recognize octet strings, large integers, and security descriptors in order to handle them differently. Consequently, we included the constant definitions for them on lines 3 through 5. We copied and pasted the constant names and values from the ADSI documentation and added the keyword `Const` to each line.

After binding to Guest with the help of `rootDSE` we need to call `GetInfo` on line 13. Otherwise, we wouldn't have anything to list in the property cache.

On lines 15 and 16 we use the `IADsPropertyList` interface to display the number of properties in the cache. Note that the host object (`objADObject`) is not a new object, but rather it is the existing object that represents Guest.

We use a `For ... Next` loop (lines 18 through 41 in Figure 11.8) to browse through the whole property list (i.e., property cache). Because the indexing starts from 0, we must go on only until `count - 1`.

```
1  Option Explicit
2
3  Const ADSTYPE_OCTET_STRING              = 8
4  Const ADSTYPE_LARGE_INTEGER             = 10
5  Const ADSTYPE_NT_SECURITY_DESCRIPTOR    = 25
6
7  Dim objDSE, objADObject, i, strName, intGap
8  Dim objPropEntry, varPropValue, objPropValue, objLargeInt
9
10 Set objDSE = GetObject("LDAP://rootDSE")
11 Set objADObject = GetObject("LDAP://CN=Guest,CN=Users," & _
12     objDSE.Get("defaultNamingContext"))
13 objADObject.GetInfo
14
15 WScript.Echo "Number of properties in the property cache: " & _
16     objADObject.PropertyCount & vbCrLf
17
```

FIGURE 11.7 Part A of "ADSI List the Property Cache Contents.vbs"

On line 19 we use the index number (0, 1, 2, and so on) to retrieve a property entry and create an object for it. On line 20 we read the name and `ADsType` (which we display in parentheses in the script's output) of the property. We store them in a string that we print later on line 38.

On lines 21 through 40 we have a `For Each ... Next` loop that browses through all values of a single property. If the syntax (i.e., `ADsType`) is either a

```
17
18 For i = 0 To objADObject.PropertyCount - 1
19     Set objPropEntry = objADObject.Item(i)
20     strName = objPropEntry.Name & " (" & objPropEntry.ADsType & ")"
21     For Each objPropValue In objPropEntry.Values
22         Select Case objPropEntry.ADsType
23             Case ADSTYPE_NT_SECURITY_DESCRIPTOR
24                 varPropValue = "some security descriptor"
25             Case ADSTYPE_OCTET_STRING
26                 varPropValue = "some octet string"
27             Case ADSTYPE_LARGE_INTEGER
28                 Set objLargeInt = _
29                     objPropValue.GetObjectProperty(objPropEntry.ADsType)
30                 varPropValue = _
31                     objLargeInt.HighPart * 2^32 + objLargeInt.LowPart
32             Case Else
33                 varPropValue = _
34                     objPropValue.GetObjectProperty(objPropEntry.ADsType)
35         End Select
36         intGap = 25 - Len(strName)
37         If intGap < 1 Then intGap = 1
38         WScript.Echo strName & String(intGap, " ") & varPropValue
39         strName = ""
40     Next
41 Next
42
```

FIGURE 11.8 Part B of "ADSI List the Property Cache Contents.vbs"

`security descriptor` or `octet string`, we don't retrieve the actual value because it would be too complicated for this example.

In the case of a `large integer` (lines 27 through 31) we retrieve the value to an object variable (`objLargeInt`). Then we use that variable to access the upper 32 bits and the lower 32 bits of the value. We get the result with the formula on line 31. However, if the high part is not zero, the result is too large for a VBScript integer, in which case the result will be converted to a floating-point number, losing some accuracy.

All other data types are easy, so we can just retrieve the value using the `ADsType` number as an argument (lines 33 and 34).

NOTE   We use the `IADsPropertyValue2` method's `GetObjectProperty` on line 34. This way, we can specify the `ADsType` number as an argument. The clumsier choice would be to use `IADsPropertyValue` and lines such as `varPropValue = objPropValue.CaseIgnoreString`, because in the latter case we would need to use a different line for each `ADsType` (lengthening the `Select Case` statement quite a bit).

Line 36 calculates the space required after the property name to align all the values to column 26 onscreen. The next line makes sure that the result is not negative or zero.

Finally, on line 38 we display the property name (and `ADsType`), a proper number of spaces, and the actual value. On line 39 we clear the property name part so that any additional values of the same property will have just the value on each line.

List User Properties with Get.vbs

As in the previous example, this one lists the properties of Guest and their values. This time we retrieve all 207 mandatory and optional attribute names from the schema and try to access them all with `Get` or `GetEx`.

TIP   You can also use this script for any object class by just changing the target object to bind to.

Figure 11.9 shows some lines of the script's output. On each line we have the attribute number (1 through 207), attribute LDAP name, syntax in parentheses, and the value aligned to column 41. In a case of multiple values, each one is on a

FIGURE 11.9 Some lines of output of "ADSI List User Properties with Get.vbs". The original output is over 600 lines long, so we selected only some lines to show.

new line. Because only some of the optional attributes have a value, quite a few show just <not set>.

Attribute 8, `accountExpires`, specifies the date and time when the account expires. However, 0 is a special value, which indicates that the account never expires. New users that are created to a domain get by default a value 9,223,372,036,854,775,807, which is equal to $2^{63} - 1$. In practice, those accounts never expire either.

If you try running the script yourself, you will get more than 600 lines of output. The attribute `AllowedAttributes` alone produces over 200 lines (which shouldn't surprise you, because it lists all 207 attribute names of the `user` class). You can use one of the following command lines to handle this:

```
ListUsers.vbs >result.txt
ListUsers.vbs | find /i "integer)"
ListUsers.vbs | find /v "not set"
```

The first command redirects the output to a text file, the second command shows only the lines with integer syntax, and the last command shows all lines except those that include the text "not set."

We show the script in six parts (Figures 11.10 through 11.15). Figure 11.10 shows part A.

Later in the script we need to recognize which attributes don't have values in the property cache, so we include the error constant for that on line 3. The characters "&H" mean that the number is in hexadecimal format.

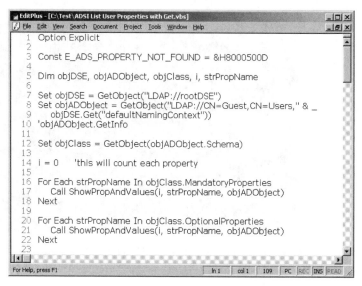

FIGURE 11.10 Part A of "ADSI List User Properties with Get.vbs"

On line 10 we have the `GetInfo` call, but unlike in the previous example, it is now "commented out." In that example we needed to call it explicitly, but now an implicit call (with the first property access) is enough.

On line 12 we bind to the `user` class of the schema, so that we can list the names of all mandatory and optional attributes on lines 16 and 20. We discuss schema access further in the appropriate examples later in the chapter.

As we browse through all mandatory and optional attribute names, we call a subprogram (or procedure) `ShowPropAndValues`. We also pass three variables as arguments to the subprogram.

NOTE   The subprograms (`Sub`) and functions (`Function`) can be at the beginning, middle, or end of the script. In our examples we put them at the end.

Figure 11.11 shows part B of the script, which is the `ShowPropAndValues` subprogram.

On line 25 we declare two variables for the subprogram, which means that they are valid only in this subprogram. In this case, their *scope* is said to be *procedure level*.

FIGURE 11.11 Part B of "ADSI List User Properties with Get.vbs"

NOTE Another choice is to declare all variables to be *script level* by adding the Dim statements to the beginning of the script outside any subprograms. We could also use these script-level variables to pass any information between subprograms, so we wouldn't need any arguments. This may be easier in short scripts, but as your scripts get longer, procedure-level variables and passing values in arguments helps you to avoid nasty bugs.

In order to handle various property values, we need to know the syntax of each attribute and whether it is multivalued. On line 29 we bind to the attribute in the schema to get this information.

On line 30 we store the name and syntax of the attribute to later display them.

We have three more subprograms, ShowBinary, ShowLargeInteger, and ShowOtherTypes, to retrieve and handle the attributes of various syntaxes. Based on the syntax, we call one of these subprograms on line 34, 36, or 39.

Figure 11.12 shows part C of the script, which is the ShowBinary subprogram.

It is quite expected that some attribute values won't be in the property cache, and we don't want the whole script to stop running in this case. We need to take error control into our own hands with the On Error statement on line 46. It defines that if there is an error on some line, the script just continues running from the next line.

```
EditPlus - [C:\Test\ADSI List User Properties with Get.vbs]                    _ □ ×
File  Edit  View  Search  Document  Project  Tools  Window  Help              _ ⓔ ×
42
43  Sub ShowBinary(strName, strPropName, objADObject)
44      Dim varPropValue, arrPropValues
45
46      On Error Resume Next
47
48      Err = 0
49      arrPropValues = objADObject.GetEx(strPropName)
50      If Err = E_ADS_PROPERTY_NOT_FOUND Then
51          varPropValue = "<not in property cache>"
52      Else
53          varPropValue = "???"
54      End If
55      Call ShowValue(strName, varPropValue)
56  End Sub
57
For Help, press F1                              ln 1    col 1    109   PC  REC INS READ
```

FIGURE 11.12 Part C of "ADSI List User Properties with Get.vbs"

NOTE　In theory, you can put the On Error statement just once in the beginning of the script. However, in practice it doesn't always work unless you put it in each subprogram that needs the feature.

WARNING　The On Error statement also hides other errors besides ADSI-related ones. For example, it nullifies the effect of Option Explicit so you don't get any warning when you use undeclared variables.

In the case of an error, the Number property of the Err object contains the error code. Because that property is the default property of Err, we can use just "Err" instead of "Err.Number."

To detect an error we perform the following steps:

1. On line 48 we set Err to 0.

2. On line 49 we try the possibly failing operation.

3. On line 50 we test if Err now contains the error code.

The error we may get just indicates that the property value is not in the property cache. We don't know if there is a value in Active Directory or not. Therefore, on line 51 we don't display <not set>, but only <not in property cache>. Even if there is a value, we are not interested enough in the value to add the extra lines that would retrieve and show it.

On line 55 we call the last subprogram that will show the property name and "value."

Figure 11.13 displays part D of the script, which contains the ShowLarge-Integer subprogram.

The IADsLargeInteger interface doesn't seem to be able to retrieve multivalued properties. Fortunately, there aren't any such properties in the base schema and it is safe to use line 64. In other words, we should never get to line 64.

With single-valued attributes we do the same error handling as in the previous subprogram, only this time we need to access the property with the IADs-LargeInteger interface. We explained the procedure in the previous example involving property cache contents.

Figure 11.14 displays part E of the script. It contains a subprogram that handles all other data types.

This subprogram has a few additions compared to the previous subprograms. On line 84 we use GetEx, which works with both single-valued and multivalued properties.

Lines 85 through 90 contain an extra step. If the property was not in the cache yet on line 84, we try to read it again from Active Directory with GetInfoEx. The result is that we will also get all constructed attributes. For GetInfoEx to work, we need to put the property name in an array (line 86) and add an extra 0 as a second argument. It is not used for anything, but it must be there.

If we still have an error on line 91, this time we know that the attribute really doesn't exist and we can display <not set> instead of the previous <not in property cache> text.

```
57
58   Sub ShowLargeInteger(strName, strPropName, objADObject, _
59       objAttribute)
60       Dim varPropValue, objLargeInt
61
62       On Error Resume Next
63       If objAttribute.MultiValued Then
64           varPropValue = "<cannot retrieve multivalued large integers>"
65       Else
66           Err = 0
67           Set objLargeInt = objADObject.Get(strPropName)
68           If Err = E_ADS_PROPERTY_NOT_FOUND Then
69               varPropValue = "<not in property cache>"
70           Else
71               varPropValue = objLargeInt.HighPart * 2^32 + _
72                               objLargeInt.LowPart
73           End If
74       End If
75       Call ShowValue(strName, varPropValue)
76   End Sub
77
```

FIGURE 11.13 Part D of "ADSI List User Properties with Get.vbs"

FIGURE 11.14 Part E of "ADSI List User Properties with Get.vbs"

Because we used `GetEx`, whether there is a single value or multiple values they will always be in an array. As a result, we need to browse through this array on lines 95 through 97.

Figure 11.15 shows the last part of the script (part F), which is the subprogram that displays any results onscreen.

This part works in the same way as the display part of the previous example. On line 104 we count the number of spaces between the property name and value to align the values. On line 107 we clear the property name so that additional lines of multivalued properties will show just the value.

In this example, we used the explicit `Get` method and put the attribute LDAP name as an argument. This enabled us to get a list of 207 attribute names and feed

FIGURE 11.15 Part F of "ADSI List User Properties with Get.vbs"

them one at a time to be that argument. If we used the other syntax (e.g., `objUser.givenName`), we would have needed to include 207 such lines in our script. Additionally, that version would have worked only with user objects (and any subclasses). The current script will work with any object class.

List User Properties with Methods.vbs

In this example, we list the properties and values of user Guest for the third time. Now we use the static property methods of the `IADsUser` interface. This has the following implications:

- This script works sensibly only for user objects.
- We need to hard-code the static property method names into the script.
- We will get 40 properties at the most.

Figure 11.16 shows the script's output. In this script, we don't align all the values to a certain column. We just put a tab character before each colon, so there is some aligning effect.

Many properties are missing from the output, because the corresponding attributes are not set in Active Directory and those static property methods return an error. However, some static property methods, such as `EmployeeID`, return an empty string in this case; therefore, they show in the output, although without a value.

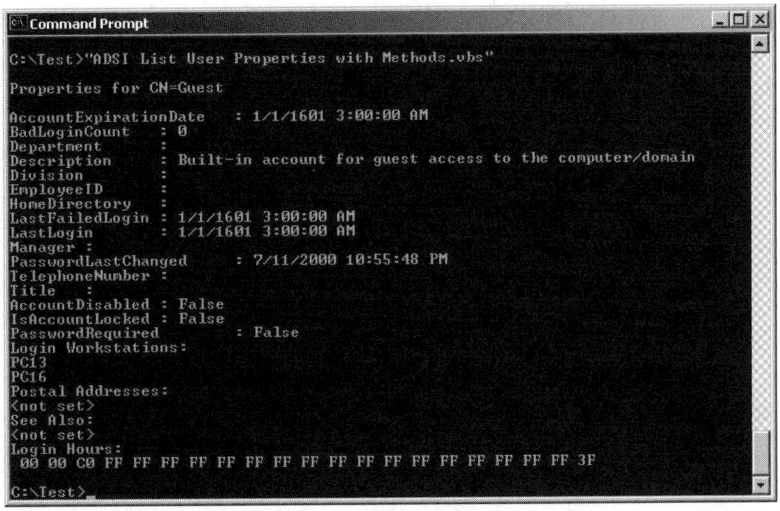

FIGURE 11.16 Output of "ADSI List User Properties with Methods.vbs." In contrast with the two previous examples, this figure shows all the lines of the script's output.

NOTE The first property of the output in Figure 11.16 doesn't mean that the Guest account expired in A.D. 1601. The attribute value in the background is 0, which indicates that the account never expires. 3:00 AM comes from the fact that the computer is in a time zone GMT + 3 hours (Finland is 2 hours east of Greenwich, plus 1 hour because of daylight saving time).

We show the script in five parts (Figures 11.17 through 11.21). Figure 11.17 shows part A.

Part A doesn't introduce anything new. Note that when we print the object name on line 14, that Name property is one of the general properties in the IADs interface.

Figure 11.18 shows part B of the script. It lists all the property methods that we can handle, on one line each.

We have a tab character before each colon in Figure 11.18, but we don't use the vbTab constant. Instead we just pressed the Tab key in the editor. This is a "quick and dirty" solution, but it makes the script look cleaner as long as the editor supports this feature.

NOTE The description attribute is defined in the schema to be multivalued, but the corresponding static property value exposes it as single-valued.

Figure 11.19 shows part C of the script, which handles LoginWorkstations.

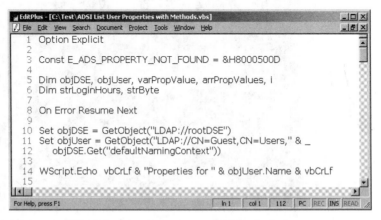

FIGURE 11.17 Part A of "ADSI List User Properties with Methods.vbs"

```
16  WScript.Echo "AccountExpirationDate : " & _
17      objUser.AccountExpirationDate
18  WScript.Echo "BadLoginCount    : " & objUser.BadLoginCount
19  WScript.Echo "Department    : " & objUser.Department
20  WScript.Echo "Description : " & objUser.Description
21  WScript.Echo "Division : " & objUser.Division
22  WScript.Echo "EmailAddress : " & objUser.EmailAddress
23  WScript.Echo "EmployeeID    : " & objUser.EmployeeID
24  WScript.Echo "FaxNumber : " & objUser.FaxNumber
25  WScript.Echo "FirstName   : " & objUser.FirstName
26  WScript.Echo "FullName   : " & objUser.FullName
27  WScript.Echo "HomeDirectory   : " & objUser.HomeDirectory
28  WScript.Echo "HomePage : " & objUser.HomePage
29  WScript.Echo "Languages : " & objUser.Languages
30  WScript.Echo "LastFailedLogin   : " & objUser.LastFailedLogin
31  WScript.Echo "LastLogin   : " & objUser.LastLogin
32  WScript.Echo "LastLogoff : " & objUser.LastLogoff
33  WScript.Echo "LastName   : " & objUser.LastName
34  WScript.Echo "LoginScript : " & objUser.LoginScript
35  WScript.Echo "Manager : " & objUser.Manager
36  WScript.Echo "MaxStorage: " & objUser.MaxStorage
37  WScript.Echo "NamePrefix: " & objUser.NamePrefix
38  WScript.Echo "NameSuffix : " & objUser.NameSuffix
39  WScript.Echo "OfficeLocations   : " & objUser.OfficeLocations
40  WScript.Echo "OtherName : " & objUser.OtherName
41  WScript.Echo "PasswordLastChanged : " & _
42      objUser.PasswordLastChanged
43  WScript.Echo "Picture   : " & objUser.Picture
44  WScript.Echo "PostalCodes   : " & objUser.PostalCodes
45  WScript.Echo "Profile   : " & objUser.Profile
46  WScript.Echo "TelephoneHome   : " & objUser.TelephoneHome
47  WScript.Echo "TelephoneMobile : " & objUser.TelephoneMobile
48  WScript.Echo "TelephoneNumber   : " & objUser.TelephoneNumber
49  WScript.Echo "TelephonePager   : " & objUser.TelephonePager
50  WScript.Echo "Title : " & objUser.Title
51  WScript.Echo "AccountDisabled : " & objUser.AccountDisabled
52  WScript.Echo "IsAccountLocked : " & objUser.IsAccountLocked
53  WScript.Echo "PasswordRequired   : " & objUser.PasswordRequired
```

FIGURE 11.18 Part B of "ADSI List User Properties with Methods.vbs"

```
54
55  WScript.Echo "Login Workstations:"
56  Err = 0
57  arrPropValues = objUser.LoginWorkstations
58  If Err = E_ADS_PROPERTY_NOT_FOUND Then
59      WScript.Echo "All allowed"
60  Else
61      For Each varPropValue In arrPropValues
62          WScript.Echo varPropValue
63      Next
64  End If
65
```

FIGURE 11.19 Part C of "ADSI List User Properties with Methods.vbs"

In contrast with `Description`, `LoginWorkstations` is single-valued in the schema, but the static property method exposes it as multivalued.

If the corresponding property (`userWorkstations`) is not in the cache, it means that there are no workstation restrictions (line 59). Otherwise, there is an array of names, which we display on lines 61 through 63.

Figure 11.20 shows part D of the script, which handles `PostalAddresses` and `SeeAlso`.

Whereas `LoginWorkstations` may return an error or an array, `Postal-Addresses` and `SeeAlso` may return one of three things.

- `PostalAddresses`: 1) An error, 2) a string, or 3) an array
- `SeeAlso`: 1) vbEmpty (different from an empty string), 2) a string, or 3) an array

Consequently, we need to adapt to these various possibilities on the lines shown in Figure 11.20.

```
65
66  WScript.Echo "Postal Addresses:"
67  Err = 0
68  arrPropValues = objUser.PostalAddresses
69  If Err = E_ADS_PROPERTY_NOT_FOUND Then
70      WScript.Echo "<not set>"
71  Else
72      If VarType(arrPropValues) = vbString Then
73          WScript.Echo arrPropValues
74      Else
75          For Each varPropValue In arrPropValues
76              WScript.Echo varPropValue
77          Next
78      End If
79  End If
80
81  WScript.Echo "See Also:"
82  Err = 0
83  arrPropValues = objUser.SeeAlso
84  If VarType(arrPropValues) = vbEmpty Then
85      WScript.Echo "<not set>"
86  Else
87      If VarType(arrPropValues) = vbString Then
88          WScript.Echo arrPropValues
89      Else
90          For Each varPropValue In arrPropValues
91              WScript.Echo varPropValue
92          Next
93      End If
94  End If
95
```

FIGURE 11.20 Part D of "ADSI List User Properties with Methods.vbs"

NOTE   You will probably never use `PostalAddresses` and `SeeAlso`, but we show the lines so that you can learn the different techniques to retrieve various values. Because Microsoft hasn't been very consistent with these static property methods, it offers a nice way to demonstrate all possible variations.

Figure 11.21 shows part E of the script, which is the last part. It displays the allowed logon hours.

Because each day has 24 hours, we need the bits of 3 bytes ($3 \times 8 = 24$) to store the permit/deny settings for one day. For the whole week we need 21 bytes ($3 \times 7 = 21$).

Each permitted hour of the week is represented by bit "1" and each denied hour is represented by bit "0." If all times are permitted, that would mean 21 times hexadecimal "FF" bytes. Also, if the property is not set, all times are permitted.

The first 3 bytes correspond to Sunday, the next 3 to Monday, and so on.

The 21 bytes are returned in a binary array `arrPropValues`. We browse through the array from the start-up to its length (i.e., `LenB`) and convert each byte to a hexadecimal number.

VBScript is not well suited to handle binary data types, but we are still able to read the value properly. We need to use the binary versions (or "B" versions) of the functions `Len`, `Mid`, and `Asc`, and the resulting line 105 looks a little complicated.

```
95
96   WScript.Echo "Login Hours:"
97   Err = 0
98   arrPropValues = objUser.LoginHours
99   If Err = E_ADS_PROPERTY_NOT_FOUND Then
100      WScript.Echo "All times allowed"
101  Else
102      strLoginHours = ""
103      'We need to use the "B" versions of Len, Asc and Mid
104      For i = 1 To LenB(arrPropValues)
105          strByte = Hex(AscB(MidB(arrPropValues, i, 1)))
106          'The following insures two characters for every byte
107          If Len(strByte) = 1 Then strByte = "0" & strByte
108          strLoginHours = strLoginHours & " " & strByte
109      Next
110      WScript.Echo strLoginHours
111  End If
112
```

FIGURE 11.21 Part E of "ADSI List User Properties with Methods.vbs"

TIP   If you need to manage complicated binary data in your scripts, you can find some tips at `http://www.pstruh.cz/tips/detpg_binarytostring.htm`. This Web page also contains a shareware COM component, ScriptUtilities, that among other things includes functions to handle binary data.

The bits of the `logonHours` attribute are stored in UTC/GMT time. When you define the permitted logon hours in the Users and Computers snap-in, the tool will take into account your time zone, but not any daylight saving time setting. For example, if you deny Sunday from a user, and you are in a time zone UTC + 2 and have DST + 1 also on, the tool will make a 2-hour correction instead of the 3-hour correction.

WARNING   When you retrieve the permitted logon hours with `LoginHours`, that static property method doesn't use any time zone correction, so you should do this in your script. Guest in our sample domain is not allowed to log on on Sundays (for a time zone UTC + 2). You can see this restriction when you look at the script output in Figure 11.16. The first three bytes (i.e., Sunday) are "almost zero." However, in the output there are bytes "C0" and "3F." They are in binary "1100 0000" and "0011 1111," meaning a 2-hour difference.

List the Account Options of a User.vbs

There is one user attribute, `userAccountControl`, that is a 32-bit number. It contains a number of account options, one in each bit of the number. In this script we explore those options. There are also account options that are stored in other attributes, as explained in this section.

Figure 11.22 shows the script's output. First we display the two settings that the `IADsUser` static property methods can provide us (and a third one that doesn't work). Then we display the `userAccountControl` attribute value, both in decimal (here "66082") and hexadecimal (here "10222"). If you enter one of these values in Windows Calculator and convert it to binary (in Scientific view), you will get a result of "1 0000 0010 0010 0010." As you probably know, each hex character corresponds to 4 bits.

The next 11 lines mimic the Users and Computers snap-in, using the same text labels and order. The last 6 lines are not visible in the snap-in and of them Active Directory doesn't use the last 4 lines. The requirement for logon script and home folder was used 10 years ago in LAN Manager. `UF_PASSWD_CANT_CHANGE` was

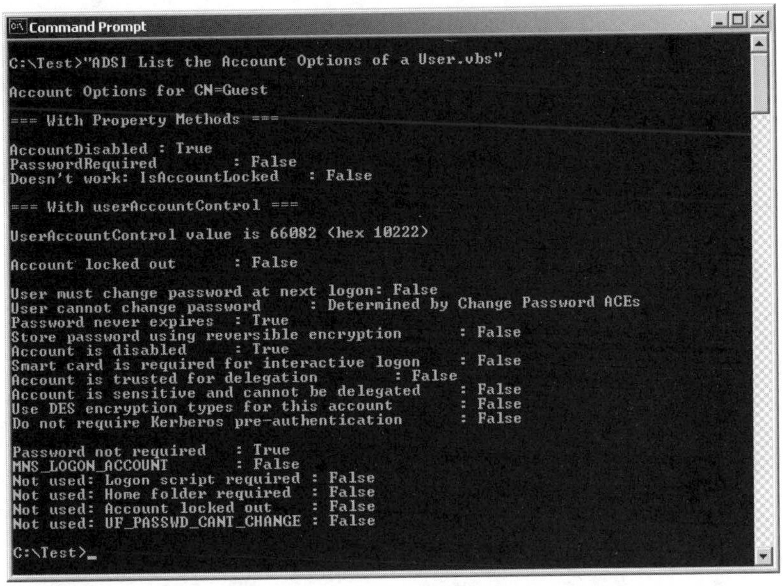

FIGURE 11.22 The output of "ADSI List the Account Options of a User.vbs"

still used in Windows NT, but now in Active Directory the ACL in the user object determines if the user can change her password.

"Account locked out" appears twice in the output. The first occurrence displays the actual value from the `lockoutTime` attribute. The second occurrence is listed as "Not used," because it corresponds to the `UF_LOCKOUT` bit in `userAccountControl`, but that is not used in Active Directory anymore.

NOTE Even though you cannot set "Password not required" with the Users and Computers snap-in, you can do so with the command `NET USER JackB /passwordreq:no`. The name "JackB" here is the pre–Windows 2000 name of the user.

WARNING You can also use the command `NET USER JackB /passwordchg:no` to state "User cannot change password." This command, however, changes JackB's ACEs more than needed by removing other permissions from the list in addition to the one it should remove. This may or may not harm you, but you are better off using just the graphical tool for this setting.

We show the script in three parts (Figures 11.23 through 11.25). Figure 11.23 displays part A.

```
     EditPlus - [C:\Test\ADSI List the Account Options of a User.vbs]
     File  Edit  View  Search  Document  Project  Tools  Window  Help
 1   Option Explicit
 2
 3   Const UF_SCRIPT                            = &H0001
 4   Const UF_ACCOUNTDISABLE                    = &H0002
 5   Const UF_HOMEDIR_REQUIRED                  = &H0008
 6   Const UF_LOCKOUT                           = &H0010
 7   Const UF_PASSWD_NOTREQD                    = &H0020
 8   Const UF_PASSWD_CANT_CHANGE                = &H0040
 9   Const UF_ENCRYPTED_TEXT_PASSWORD_ALLOWED = &H0080
10   Const UF_DONT_EXPIRE_PASSWD                = &H10000
11   Const UF_MNS_LOGON_ACCOUNT                 = &H20000
12   Const UF_SMARTCARD_REQUIRED                = &H40000
13   Const UF_TRUSTED_FOR_DELEGATION            = &H80000
14   Const UF_NOT_DELEGATED                     = &H100000
15   Const UF_USE_DES_KEY_ONLY                  = &H200000
16   Const UF_DONT_REQUIRE_PREAUTH              = &H400000
17
18   Const UF_TEMP_DUPLICATE_ACCOUNT          = &H0100 'local account
19   Const UF_NORMAL_ACCOUNT                  = &H0200 'global account
20   Const UF_INTERDOMAIN_TRUST_ACCOUNT = &H0800 'incoming trust
21   Const UF_WORKSTATION_TRUST_ACCOUNT= &H1000 'ws or ms comp
22   Const UF_SERVER_TRUST_ACCOUNT            = &H2000 'dc computer
23
24   Const E_VBS_OBJECT_REQUIRED              = 424
25
26   Dim objDSE, objUser, intUserFlags, objLargeInt
27   Dim bolLockedOut, bolMustChange
28
29   Set objDSE = GetObject("LDAP://rootDSE")
30   Set objUser = GetObject("LDAP://CN=Guest,CN=Users," & _
31       objDSE.Get("defaultNamingContext"))
32
33   objUser.GetInfo
34
```

FIGURE 11.23 Part A of "ADSI List the Account Options of a User.vbs"

Nineteen of the possible 32 bits in `userAccountControl` are defined and they are listed in Figure 11.23 as constant definitions. The constant names and values are copied from the ADSI documentation. We had to pick two values (lines 15 and 16) from the file lmaccess.h, which is part of the Platform SDK, because they were missing from the documentation. "UF" stands for "user flags." Each hexadecimal value corresponds to 1 bit. If you want to find out which bit, you can again use Windows Calculator.

The 5 bits on lines 18 through 22 are not actual account options, but they indicate the account type. Each account should be one of the five types and consequently have one of the bits set. Line 24 contains a VBScript error code definition, which we need later in the script.

The `GetInfo` call on line 33 is not mandatory, because the first property read later will notice that the cache is empty and call `GetInfo` implicitly.

Figure 11.24 shows part B of the script.

There is no bit in `userAccountControl` that indicates whether or not the account is locked. This is defined in the `lockoutTime` attribute instead. If the attribute value is not set (corresponding to line 39) or equals 0, the account is not

FIGURE 11.24 Part B of "ADSI List the Account Options of a User.vbs"

locked out. If the value is nonzero, the account is locked, as we test on line 42. Because the attribute is a `large integer`, we need line 37 to retrieve it in an object variable. We also need to include the error handling, because if the attribute value is not set, it will cause a VBScript error.

If the value of the `pwdLastSet` attribute is 0, the user must change his or her password at the next logon. This attribute is also a `large integer`, so we need lines 46 through 48 to check if this setting is on and store the result in the Boolean variable `bolMustChange`.

On line 60 we retrieve the value of `userAccountControl`, and on lines 62 and 63 we display it in decimal and hexadecimal. We would display it also in binary if there were a function for it in VBScript.

Figure 11.25 displays the last part of the script (part C). It shows the value of each setting.

Each of the `UF` constants has 1 bit set (i.e., "1") and all other bits not set (i.e., "0"). To find out if the corresponding setting is on in `userAccountControl`, we need to do a bitwise logical `And` operation between the two (see Figure 11.25). If the result is zero, the setting is off, and if the result is nonzero, the setting is on.

For example, if `userAccountControl` (stored in `intUserFlags`) is "1 0000 0010 0010 0000" and `UF_DONT_EXPIRE_PASSWD` is "&H10000" or binary "1 0000

```
EditPlus - [C:\Test\ADSI List the Account Options of a User.vbs]
File  Edit  View  Search  Document  Project  Tools  Window  Help
 64
 65  WScript.Echo "Account locked out   : " & bolLockedOut
 66  WScript.Echo ""
 67  WScript.Echo "User must change password at next logon: " & _
 68      bolMustChange
 69  WScript.Echo "User cannot change password   : " & _
 70      "Determined by Change Password ACEs"
 71  WScript.Echo "Password never expires   : " & _
 72      ((intUserFlags And UF_DONT_EXPIRE_PASSWD) <> 0)
 73  WScript.Echo "Store password using reversible encryption : " & _
 74      ((intUserFlags And UF_ENCRYPTED_TEXT_PASSWORD_ALLOWED) _
 75      <> 0)
 76  WScript.Echo "Account is disabled  : " & _
 77      ((intUserFlags And UF_ACCOUNTDISABLE) <> 0)
 78  WScript.Echo "Smart card is required for interactive logon : " & _
 79      ((intUserFlags And UF_SMARTCARD_REQUIRED) <> 0)
 80  WScript.Echo "Account is trusted for delegation   : " & _
 81      ((intUserFlags And UF_TRUSTED_FOR_DELEGATION) <> 0)
 82  WScript.Echo "Account is sensitive and cannot be delegated : " & _
 83      ((intUserFlags And UF_NOT_DELEGATED) <> 0)
 84  WScript.Echo "Use DES encryption types for this account   : " & _
 85      ((intUserFlags And UF_USE_DES_KEY_ONLY) <> 0)
 86  WScript.Echo "Do not require Kerberos pre-authentication : " & _
 87      ((intUserFlags And UF_DONT_REQUIRE_PREAUTH) <> 0)
 88  WScript.Echo ""
 89  WScript.Echo "Password not required : " & _
 90      ((intUserFlags And UF_PASSWD_NOTREQD) <> 0)
 91  WScript.Echo "MNS_LOGON_ACCOUNT    : " & _
 92      ((intUserFlags And UF_MNS_LOGON_ACCOUNT) <> 0)
 93  WScript.Echo "Not used: Logon script required : " & _
 94      ((intUserFlags And UF_SCRIPT) <> 0)
 95  WScript.Echo "Not used: Home folder required : " & _
 96      ((intUserFlags And UF_HOMEDIR_REQUIRED) <> 0)
 97  WScript.Echo "Not used: Account locked out    : " & _
 98      ((intUserFlags And UF_LOCKOUT) <> 0)
 99  WScript.Echo "Not used: UF_PASSWD_CANT_CHANGE   : " & _
100      ((intUserFlags And UF_PASSWD_CANT_CHANGE) <> 0)
101
For Help, press F1                                    ln 1    col 1    101    PC   REC   INS   READ
```

FIGURE 11.25 Part C of "ADSI List the Account Options of a User.vbs"

0000 0000 0000," the And between those two is "1 0000 0000 0000 0000," meaning that the setting is on.

Line 72 performs this check for the "Password never expires" setting and the consequent lines for all other settings. On lines 65 and 68 we can use the results that we calculated in part B.

Whether a user can change his password or not is determined by the access control ACEs in the user object. We don't start to inspect them here, so on line 70 we just state this.

Create a User with Minimum Attributes.vbs

So far we haven't made any changes in our Active Directory—we have just listed objects and their properties. In this example, we create 1 user or 100 users, but we use only the more or less mandatory attributes (not quite the same as what the schema lists as mandatory attributes).

We could, of course, add some output to indicate that the "command completed successfully," but at present, this script doesn't display anything.

Figure 11.26 shows the script's contents.

We put the actual creation as a subprogram (lines 13 through 27) so that you can call it either one time or several times. Currently, lines 7 through 11 are commented out, but if you uncomment them, they will create users Uu00, Uu01, Uu02, and so on, up to Uu99.

Now the usernames are hard-coded in the script, but you could use a command-line argument or input box to get the names, as shown in earlier examples. A couple of examples later we also show how to read the usernames from Excel (see the "Read User Information from Excel.xls" section).

We need to bind to the container where the user will appear, and we do this on lines 16 and 17. Next, on line 19 we use the `Create` method of `IADs-Container` to create a class `user` object with a common name `CN=whatever`.

Before we write this from the property cache back to Active Directory with the `SetInfo` method (line 24), we need to set some attributes. `SAMAccountName` on line 20 is a mandatory attribute. `UserAccountControl` and `userPrincipal-Name` are not mandatory in the schema, but we want to set them anyway.

The ADSI default for `userAccountControl` is hexadecimal "222" (password not required, account disabled), but the Users and Computers snap-in default for `userAccountControl` is hexadecimal "200" (password required, account

```
EditPlus - [C:\Test\ADSI Create a User with Minimum Attributes.vbs]
File  Edit  View  Search  Document  Project  Tools  Window  Help
 1   Option Explicit
 2
 3   'Dim i, j
 4
 5   Call CreateUser("Jack")
 6
 7   'For i = 0 To 9
 8   '   For j = 0 To 9
 9   '       Call CreateUser("Uu" & CStr(i) & CStr(j))
10   '   Next
11   'Next
12
13   Sub CreateUser(strName)
14       Dim objContainer, objUser
15
16       Set objContainer = _
17           GetObject("LDAP://OU=Sales,DC=sanao,DC=com")
18
19       Set objUser = objContainer.Create("user", "CN=" & strName)
20       Call objUser.Put("sAMAccountName", strName)
21       Call objUser.Put("userAccountControl", &H200)
22       Call objUser.Put("userPrincipalName", strName & "@sanao.com")
23
24       objUser.SetInfo
25       objUser.SetPassword ("secret")
26       Set objUser = Nothing
27   End Sub
28

For Help, press F1                                    ln 1    col 1    28    PC  REC  INS  READ
```

FIGURE 11.26 Contents of "ADSI Create a User with Minimum Attributes.vbs"

enabled). With the setting on line 21 we are using the same value as the latter default.

We want to set the UPN because the graphical tool also requires it and we want to ensure that all users can log on with a UPN.

TIP   If you don't want to hard-code your enterprise name (such as `sanao.com`), you can read the value from the `dnsRoot` attribute of the object `CN=Enterprise Configuration, CN=Partitions, CN=Configuration, DC=<yourforest-name>, DC=com`. If you want to use other UPN suffixes (defined in the Domains and Trusts snap-in), you can use the `uPNSuffixes` attribute of the object `CN=Partitions, CN=Configuration, DC=<yourforestname>, DC=com`.

After you have called `SetInfo` on line 24, you can set the password with the `SetPassword` method on the next line.

On line 26 we release the object that we have used. This also releases any memory it has used. This is actually not needed because when our script completes, all variables are released anyway and so is all memory. We put line 26 there to symbolize that now we are done with the object.

Create a User with More Attributes.vbs

In this example, we expand the user creation process by including many more attributes, as is likely the need in the real world. Of course, we cannot know which of the 207 attributes you are going to use, so we've picked the most representative attributes to demonstrate various techniques and because you are more likely to use them as the remaining attributes.

As with the previous example, the creation process is a subprogram and the username is hard-coded. Again, you can use command-line arguments, input boxes, or Excel to get the usernames.

We show the script in three parts (Figures 11.27 through 11.29). Part A is in Figure 11.27.

The first part is almost similar to the previous "minimum attributes" example. In addition, on line 3 we define one user flag, which we are going to use later. We assign the user a common name "last name first name," but later on line 55 we assign the `displayName` as "first name last name." Whether you will do the same obviously depends on how your e-mail application and other applications use either the common name or the display name.

On line 18 we generate a SAM name like "JackB." After writing the creation and first settings back to Active Directory (line 24), we need to (or at least it is very

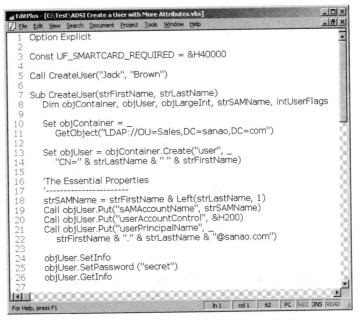

FIGURE 11.27 Part A of "ADSI Create a User with More Attributes.vbs"

preferable to) refresh the property cache on line 26 to also get all predefined or default values.

Figure 11.28 shows part B of the script, which sets the rest of the significant properties (for a description of the differences between significant and informational properties, see Chapter 3).

On lines 30 through 33 we set the usual paths, but we leave the logon script name to be defined in Group Policy. Because the Prof$ share name has a dollar sign as the last character, that share is hidden so that our users don't mess with the files and folders in that share.

In this example, we don't want to require the user to change her password at the next logon, so we need to write the value of –1 to pwdLastSet. In hexadecimal, that value is all F's. On lines 36 through 39 we set the appropriate value to this large integer property.

NOTE   PwdLastSet normally indicates when the user changed her password the last time. If you later write 0 to it to indicate that the user must again change her password at the next logon, or if you set it back to –1 to relieve the user from having to change her password at the next logon, the actual last change time is lost. When you write –1 to this attribute, what actually gets stored is the current date and time.

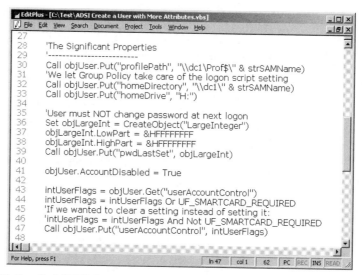

FIGURE 11.28 Part B of "ADSI Create a User with More Attributes.vbs"

On line 41 we disable the account, even though we just enabled it on line 20. We do this just to demonstrate the various settings.

On line 44 we turn on the smart card requirement by using the `Or` operator. Before that, we needed to read the current property into a variable so that the `Or` operator will change just 1 bit. In case we need to clear some `userAccount-Control` bit, we need to use line 46, replacing `Or` with `And` and adding a `Not` in front of the flag constant.

Figure 11.29 shows the third and last part of the script (part C). It sets all the desired informational properties.

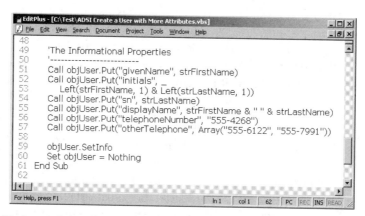

FIGURE 11.29 Part C of "ADSI Create a User with More Attributes.vbs"

We don't need to use `PutEx` even for multivalued attributes, such as the one on line 57, because we don't need to use any special flags (`append` and so on).

Note that we store the first letter of the first name and last name (such as "JB" for "Jack Brown") in the `initials` attribute, whereas the Users and Computers snap-in uses that attribute to store the middle name initial.

In this example, we defined a home folder and roaming profile folder path for the user but didn't create either one. After the next example, we present two short sample scripts that address creating a home folder. We don't need to worry about the roaming profile folder, because the user's workstation creates it automatically when the user logs on for the first time.

Create a User with a Batch File.bat

Our next few examples use some traditional command-line commands instead of pure scripting. As a comparison to WSH + VBScript, we first want to show a batch file that creates a user. The same batch file works also in Windows NT and with minor modifications it worked in LAN Manager as early as 1988.

The motivation behind this comparison is the fact that sometimes you have to use traditional commands in your scripts, and sometimes you don't have to, but if you do so it is somewhat easier to get the job done.

You get the most obvious benefits of using commands in the scripts when managing folders and their permissions. The latter is not even possible with standard WSH + VBScript + ADSI (unless you run a command from the script or use ADsSecurity from the ADSI Resource Kit).

This example of creating a user is much shorter and simpler than a WSH script. However, it doesn't enable you to set features that are new to Active Directory. It is like managing Active Directory users with the Windows NT User Manager. Figure 11.30 shows the batch file.

You would launch the batch file with a command like the following (with a shortened filename):

```
createuser JackB
```

The argument `JackB` will replace `%1` in the batch file when it runs. Line 5 adds the user, line 6 sets some properties, line 9 creates a home folder, line 12 grants the Administrators group Full Control to the new folder, and line 13 grants the user the Change permission. The `/e` option means "edit"—that is, previous permissions are not removed. Finally, on line 16 the new home folder is shared with the same sharename as the user's username.

TIP   You can get help with the commands `NET HELP USER` and `CACLS /?`.

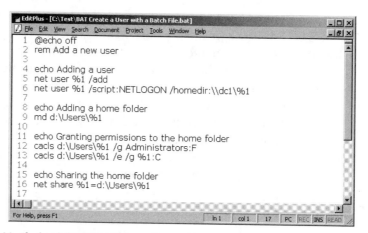

FIGURE 11.30 The batch file "BAT Create a User with a Batch File.bat"

WARNING CACLS has two potential problems. First, CACLS doesn't understand Windows 2000 permission inheritance, so in some cases the tool blocks permission inheritance without asking or warning you. Such cases are if you use CACLS to assign permission without the /e option (i.e., replace all permissions) or replace certain permissions with the /p option. Second, CACLS may order ACEs incorrectly and when you open such permission list in ACL Editor, you'll receive a warning: "The permissions on *folder* are incorrectly ordered, which may cause some entries to be ineffective." The second problem was fixed in Windows 2000 Service Pack 2.

NOTE Other command-line tools for permission management are XCACLS in the Windows 2000 Resource Kit and FILEDACLS.PL in the Windows 2000 Resource Kit Supplement 1.

Create a Home Folder for a User—Ver 1.vbs

This sample script creates a home folder for a user, grants some permissions for it, and shares the folder. We use the same commands as in the previous batch example, and the script launches the commands with the Run method of the WshShell object. That method allows us to start new programs, such as Notepad or some command-line command. Figure 11.31 shows the script.

In order to be able to use the WshShell object, we need to instantiate one on line 11. Then we need four commands for our home folder task, so we store them

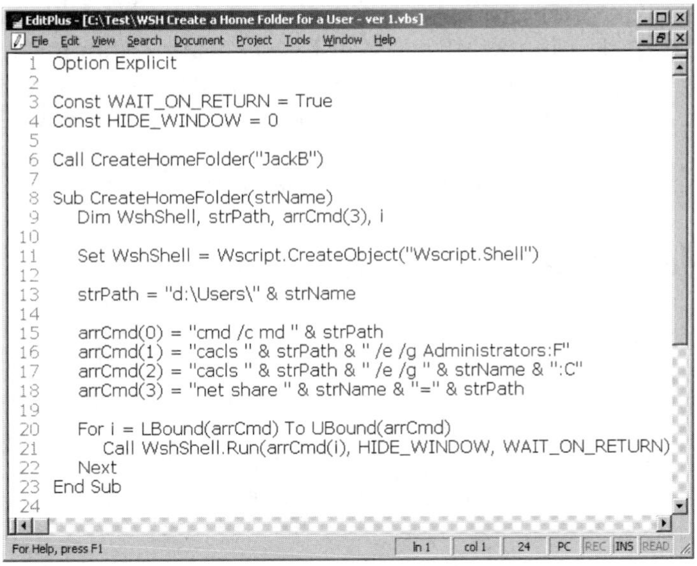

FIGURE 11.31 WSH Create a Home Folder for a User—ver 1.vbs

in a four-element array on lines 15 through 18. Finally, on lines 20 through 22 we run each command as a hidden window and wait for each command to complete before moving to the next one.

The MD command that we use to create the folder is implemented in CMD. EXE and there is no MD.EXE. Therefore we need CMD /C on that command line.

NOTE   Compared to the previous batch example, we now have / e also on the first "cacls" line (line 16). Without this "edit" option the script would want confirmation (i.e., "are you sure, yes/no") and would stop to ask for it. If you don't want to use the "edit" option (i.e., to remove all previous ACEs), you should remove the HIDE_WINDOW setting (but keep the comma) so you can answer "yes" when you are prompted for it.

TIP   If you want to automate pressing the *y* key, you can create a small file with just that letter and Enter in it, and use the file as input. In this case you would need to append "<yourfilename.txt" at the end of the CACLS command.

The script in its current form must be run locally on the server where the home folder is created. If you want to run it from another computer, you can use a

UNC path (such as \\dc1\users\JackB) instead of a local path (such as d:\Users \JackB) in the MD and CACLS commands. Unfortunately, NET SHARE doesn't work this way, but if you have the Windows NT Server Resource Kit, you can use RMTSHARE from the kit. For some reason, the Windows 2000 Server Resource Kit doesn't include it.

See also the CACLS warning in the "Create a User with a Batch File.bat" section.

Create a Home Folder for a User—Ver 2.vbs

This second version does the same things as the first, but this time the folder creation and sharing is done using COM components (WSH and ADSI). We have also enhanced the script so that you can run it from any workstation. Figure 11.32 shows the script's contents.

We still grant permissions with the CACLS command. Later in the "Access Control Lists" section we present a script that modifies folder permissions using the

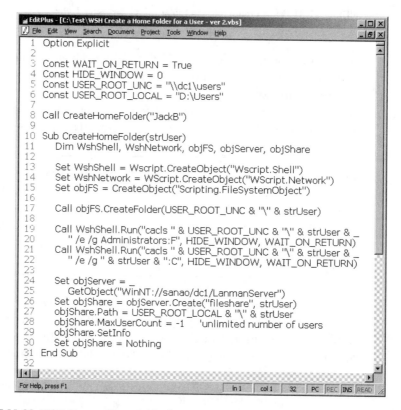

```
1   Option Explicit
2
3   Const WAIT_ON_RETURN = True
4   Const HIDE_WINDOW = 0
5   Const USER_ROOT_UNC = "\\dc1\users"
6   Const USER_ROOT_LOCAL = "D:\Users"
7
8   Call CreateHomeFolder("JackB")
9
10  Sub CreateHomeFolder(strUser)
11      Dim WshShell, WshNetwork, objFS, objServer, objShare
12
13      Set WshShell = Wscript.CreateObject("Wscript.Shell")
14      Set WshNetwork = WScript.CreateObject("WScript.Network")
15      Set objFS = CreateObject("Scripting.FileSystemObject")
16
17      Call objFS.CreateFolder(USER_ROOT_UNC & "\" & strUser)
18
19      Call WshShell.Run("cacls " & USER_ROOT_UNC & "\" & strUser & _
20          " /e /g Administrators:F", HIDE_WINDOW, WAIT_ON_RETURN)
21      Call WshShell.Run("cacls " & USER_ROOT_UNC & "\" & strUser & _
22          " /e /g " & strUser & ":C", HIDE_WINDOW, WAIT_ON_RETURN)
23
24      Set objServer = _
25          GetObject("WinNT://sanao/dc1/LanmanServer")
26      Set objShare = objServer.Create("fileshare", strUser)
27      objShare.Path = USER_ROOT_LOCAL & "\" & strUser
28      objShare.MaxUserCount = -1    'unlimited number of users
29      objShare.SetInfo
30      Set objShare = Nothing
31  End Sub
32
```

FIGURE 11.32 WSH Create a Home Folder for a User—ver 2.vbs

ADsSecurity component, which is part of the ADSI Resource Kit. However, that choice is much more laborious than CACLS and has some problems, which we describe there.

We want to create a constant for the root of all home folders, both as a UNC path and a local path. Note that we need to know the local path for the share, even though we would run the script on another computer.

On lines 13 through 15 we need to create three objects that we can use on the later lines. On line 17 we use the `CreateFolder` method of `FileSystem-Object` to create the home folder. On lines 19 through 22 we use the CACLS command to apply the permissions. The CACLS commands are similar to the ones in the previous example, except that now we use a UNC path for the script to work remotely.

On lines 24 and 25 we use the WinNT provider for the first time in this chapter. We need it because even though we are using ADSI, we are not using Active Directory now. The file shares are owned by the server service (or `Lanman-Server`), and therefore we need to bind to that service on the right server. In the binding string we have the domain NetBIOS name, server name, and `Lanman-Server` as the service name.

By using the Server service object ("Server" here doesn't refer to a server machine), we create a file share with the user's name (line 26) and use the object that was also created to set the path and save the changes. Without the `MaxUser-Count` setting on line 28, only one user at a time could connect to the share. This might not be a problem with a home folder share, but we wanted to show you the setting—you will need it when you create normal shares.

If you combine this last example with the "Create a User with More Attributes" example, you will have a complete script to create user accounts.

See also the CACLS warning in the "Create a User with a Batch File.bat" section.

Read User Information from Excel.xls

In an earlier an example, we dumped usernames into Excel by controlling Excel from outside using the WSH + VBScript environment. Now we use Excel VBA inside Excel to retrieve a number of usernames from an Excel spreadsheet.

Figure 11.33 shows how the first name and last name of each user would be stored in a spreadsheet.

To get to the script part (or macro, in other words) you must select the Tools menu, Macro, Visual Basic Editor, or just press Alt-F11. The Visual Basic environment opens, even though you must remember it is not a real Visual Basic environment (despite the title). If you already have a script file, you'll see something similar to the screen in Figure 11.34. If you don't, you need to select the Insert menu, Module and start typing in the lines.

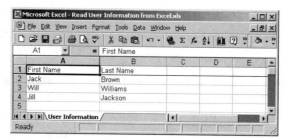

FIGURE 11.33 The input data of "Read User Information from Excel.xls"

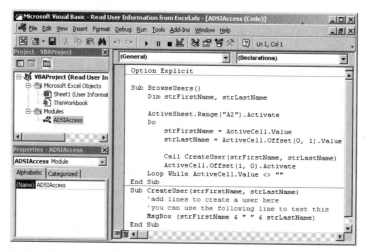

FIGURE 11.34 Read User Information from Excel.xls

This script is different from WSH + VBScript in two ways.

- We don't have any main program—just subprograms. The subprograms that don't have any arguments appear in Excel's Macro dialog box (select the Tools menu, Macro, Macros), so you can run them manually.

- Because we are already inside Excel, we don't need to add lines `WScript.CreateObject("Excel.Application")`, and so on. Also, we don't need to refer to Excel elements via an Excel object, but we can do this directly.

In the script we first activate cell A2 and then read the names from that line. Next we call a subprogram to create a user (a fake one, in this case) and then move to the next line. These lines will be repeated (or looped) as long as we don't run into an empty cell, which indicates the end of the list.

Read User Information from Standard Input.vbs

A program (including a WSH 2.0 script) running in the command window can read from *standard input* and write to *standard output* and/or *standard error output*. Standard input typically means your keystrokes, while the two latter options typically show as lines of output in the command window.

ABOUT STANDARD I/O

Standard I/O features become useful when you start redirecting them to or from text files. You redirect standard input to be read from a text file with the less-than sign (<). An example command is as follows:

```
someprogram <myinput.txt
```

You could redirect standard output when you want to capture program output to a text file. This is useful at least in two cases. In the first case, a program could output some list that you want to capture in a file. In the second case, you want to schedule a program to be run as a background process in the night and by capturing the output in a file you could see the next morning what it did. By saving the output (and probably error output) to a text file, you would have log files of the otherwise mysterious events of the night.

The redirection character for standard output is the greater-than sign (>). When you add 2, you will capture the error output as well. An example command is as follows:

```
listusers >userlist.txt 2>possibleerrors.txt
```

NOTE   Some programs also use standard output for errors and some may use error output for output other than errors. Therefore, you may have to experiment with a program before you learn what is output where. Or you can just capture both, as shown in the previous command example.

Sometimes you would like to append new output to an existing file and not destroy the old lines. This is possible by adding another greater-than sign using a command such as this:

```
listusers >>moreuserlist.txt 2>>morepossibleerrors.txt
```

You can redirect the output of one command to the input of another command by using the pipe sign (|). A sample command is as follows:

```
someprogram | anotherprogram
```

Because you already know how to output from a script (i.e., use `WScript.Echo`) you probably don't need to use standard output inside your scripts. Therefore, our next sample script shows only the input part.

THE READ USER INFORMATION FROM STANDARD INPUT SAMPLE SCRIPT

Our previous sample script read user information from an Excel spreadsheet. Now we do the same with a text file. Figure 11.35 shows the contents of the sample text file.

To use the input data with our script, you would use the following command (we have somewhat shortened the script name):

```
cscript ReadUserInfo.vbs <UserInfo.txt
```

NOTE   You must use "cscript" at the beginning of the command line, even if CScript is your default environment.

The script lines are shown in Figure 11.36.

FIGURE 11.35 The input data from "Read User Information from Standard Input.vbs"

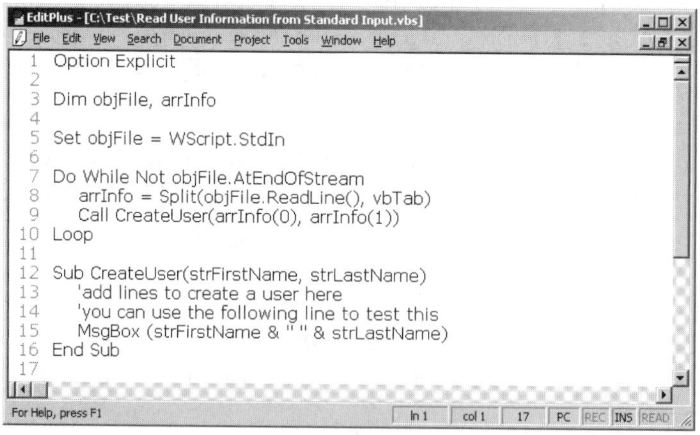

FIGURE 11.36 Read User Information from Standard Input.vbs

We read standard input just like we would read a file—as a result, we name the variable `objFile`. On line 5 we create this `objFile` by associating it with the `StdIn` property of `WScript`.

On lines 7 through 10 we have a loop that goes on as long as we haven't reached the end of the text stream. On line 8 we read a line of input and use the `Split` function to separate the tab-separated elements. Each line element is stored in an element of the `arrInfo` array, so we can pass them on to the sub-program as each user's first name and last name.

We could, of course, read the input from a named file, but the beauty of standard input is the fact that we don't need to include any file or folder names in the script. Of course, we must include the filename on the command line, but that choice is often easier than to include it in the script lines.

If you would rather have the filename inside your script and forget standard input, you can do so by replacing line 5 with the following three lines:

```
Const ForReading = 1
Set objFS = CreateObject("Scripting.FileSystemObject")
Set objFile = objFS.OpenTextFile("C:\Test\UserInfo.txt", ForReading)
```

The lines use the VBScript `FileSystemObject` functionality to open and read the input file. We have included the folder name (C:\Test) on the last line, but you can omit it if the file is in your current folder.

SCHEMA ACCESS

Before we show any schema access script samples we describe some schema access concepts.

Concepts

There are two ways to access the schema with ADSI:

- Using the real schema objects
- Using the abstract schema objects that ADSI creates based on the schema definition in the `subSchema` object (`CN=Aggregate, CN=Schema, CN=Configuration, DC=sanao, DC=com`)

We introduced the latter concept in Chapter 8. We compare the two choices in Table 11.1.

NOTE   We identify the real schema objects with their common names, but we identify the abstract schema objects with the LDAP names of the class or attribute.

TABLE 11.1 The Two Ways to Access the Schema with ADSI

Feature	Real Schema Objects	Abstract Schema Objects

ADsPath to schema root	`LDAP://CN=Schema,`
	`CN=Configuration,`
	`DC=sanao,DC=com`
		`LDAP://schema` (or
		`LDAP://sanao.com/schema`
		or
		`LDAP://dc1.sanao.com/schema`)

ADsPath to user class	`LDAP://CN=User,`
	`CN=Schema,`
	`CN=Configuration,`
	`DC=sanao,DC=com`
		`LDAP://schema/user`

ADsPath to `givenName` attribute	`LDAP://CN=Given-Name,`
	`CN=Schema,`
	`CN=Configuration,`
	`DC=sanao,DC=com`
		`LDAP://schema/givenName`

Class name of class	`classSchema`	Class
Class name of attribute	`attributeSchema`	Property
Class name of syntax	Not available	Syntax
Allows schema extensions and modifications	Yes, create and modify objects just as any Active Directory objects	No
Available schema object properties	All	Only some

While the abstract schema objects contain only a subset of all the schema information, they have the following advantages over the real schema objects.

- The `ADsPaths` (i.e., the binding strings) are easier because they are shorter and use LDAP names, and you don't have to specify a forest name if you don't want to.

- The abstract schema objects combine information from several real schema objects and show it in an easier form. For example, they indicate with a True or False value whether or not each class is a container. If you were using the real schema objects, you would need to browse through all other classes and check if the first class was a possible superior in any of them.

We discussed the attributes of the real `classSchema` and `attribute-Schema` objects in Chapter 8. In the next subsection, we briefly list the properties of the abstract schema objects.

PROPERTIES OF THE ABSTRACT SCHEMA OBJECTS

You access the abstract `class`, `property`, and `syntax` schema objects with the interfaces `IADsClass`, `IADsProperty`, and `IADsSyntax`, respectively. The interfaces have a number of read/write properties, but because the `subSchema` is read-only, you should only read the interface properties.

Table 11.2 lists the properties for abstract schema classes.

WARNING   If there is only one element in the array—for example, with the `Containment` property—the property method returns a string instead of an array. This makes writing scripts a little harder, because you first need to check the data type and then handle it accordingly.

Table 11.3 lists the properties for abstract schema properties.

We don't have a table of abstract syntax objects, because `IADsSyntax` has just one property. `OleAutoDataType` indicates which OLE automation data type the syntax maps to.

TABLE 11.2 Relevant Properties of the Abstract Schema Classes (`IADsClass` Interface)

Property	Description
Container	True if some other class has this class as a possible superior; otherwise, False
Containment	An array of LDAP names for the classes that can be children of this class
PossibleSuperiors	An array of LDAP names for the classes that can be parents of this class
MandatoryProperties	An array of LDAP names for the mandatory attributes of this class
OptionalProperties	An array of LDAP names for the optional attributes of this class
NamingProperties	An array of LDAP names for the naming attributes of this class (i.e., "cn," "ou," and so on)
OID	The object ID of this class
Auxiliary	True if this is an auxiliary class; otherwise, False
Abstract	True if this is an abstract class; otherwise, False
DerivedFrom	The LDAP name of the superclass (subClassOf) of this class
AuxDerivedFrom	An array of LDAP names for the auxiliary classes of this class

TABLE 11.3 Properties of the Abstract Schema Properties (`IADsProperty` Interface)

Property	Description
Syntax	The LDAP type–friendly name of the property (see the "ADSI Syntaxes" section in Chapter 10)
MultiValued	True or False depending on whether or not the property is multivalued
MinRange	Possible minimum for the value(s)
MaxRange	Possible maximum for the value(s)
OID	The object ID of this attribute

RETRIEVING THE PATH TO AN ABSTRACT SCHEMA CLASS OBJECT

In Chapter 10 we introduced the Schema and Class properties of the IADs interface. For example, for user objects they contain the values LDAP://schema/user and user, respectively.

With the help of these two properties (or just one) we can bind to the abstract schema class object that corresponds to any object, such as Jack. We would use the following line to do this:

```
Set objClass = GetObject(objADObject.Schema)
```

Now that you have an understanding of schema access concepts, it is now time to move on to the sample scripts.

Schema Sample Scripts

We present the following sample scripts (and a section on ANR, nonreplicated, and constructed attributes) for schema access:

- CH11-14 ADSI List All Abstract Schema Objects.vbs
- CH11-15 ADSI List the Member Attributes of a Given Class.vbs
- CH11-16 ADSI List the Member Attributes of a Given Class to Excel.vbs
- CH11-17 ADSI Show Property Properties.vbs
- CH11-18 ADSI Container or Leaf.vbs
- CH11-19 ADSI List All Real Schema Objects.vbs
- CH11-20 ADSI List Indexed Attributes.vbs
- List ANR, Nonreplicated, and Constructed Attributes

- CH11-21 ADSI List Global Catalog Attributes.vbs
- CH11-22 ADSI List All classSchemas to Excel.vbs
- CH11-23 ADSI List All attributeSchemas to Excel.vbs
- CH11-24 ADSI Create an Attribute and a Class.vbs

Examples 14 through 18 use the abstract schema and the rest use the real schema objects.

List All Abstract Schema Objects.vbs

Our first schema sample script reads the abstract schema and lists all 142 classes, 863 properties, and 33 syntaxes. As with any command-line output, you can redirect the output to a text file using the greater-than sign (>).

Figure 11.37 shows part of the output of the script. We show only the beginning of each category. Figure 11.38 shows the entire script.

We could have used just one short For loop instead of three, but this way we could order and number the output and also print some extra fields depending on the schema object type.

List the Member Attributes of a Given Class.vbs

This example takes a class LDAP name as a command-line argument and then lists all mandatory and optional property names of that class.

Figure 11.39 shows the beginning of the output of the script when the user class is specified. Again, you can redirect this to a text file using the greater-than sign (>). Figure 11.40 shows the script's contents. As you can see, we use the abstract schema.

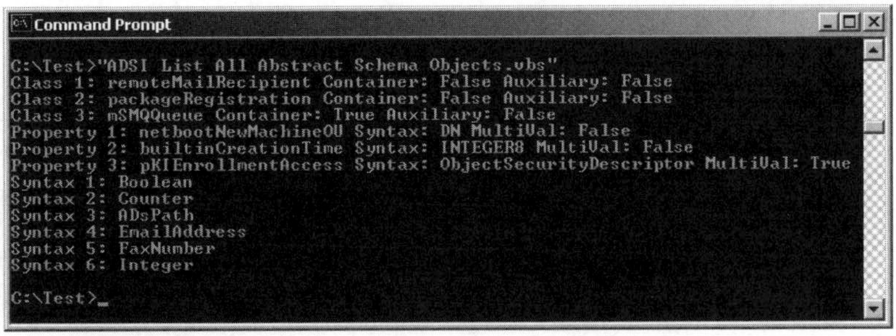

FIGURE 11.37 Some lines of the output of "ADSI List All Abstract Schema Objects.vbs"

```
1  Option Explicit
2
3  Dim objSchema, objChild, i
4
5  Set objSchema = GetObject("LDAP://schema")
6
7  i = 0
8  For Each objChild In objSchema
9      If objChild.Class = "Class" Then
10         i = i + 1
11         WScript.Echo "Class " & i & ": " & objChild.Name & _
12             " Container: " & objChild.Container  & _
13             " Auxiliary: " & objChild.Auxiliary
14     End If
15 Next
16
17 i = 0
18 For Each objChild In objSchema
19     If objChild.Class = "Property" Then
20         i = i + 1
21         WScript.Echo "Property " & i & ": " & objChild.Name & _
22             " Syntax: " & objChild.Syntax  & _
23             " MultiVal: " & objChild.MultiValued
24     End If
25 Next
26
27 i = 0
28 For Each objChild In objSchema
29     If objChild.Class = "Syntax" Then
30         i = i + 1
31         WScript.Echo "Syntax " & i & ": " & objChild.Name
32     End If
33 Next
34
```

FIGURE 11.38 ADSI List All Abstract Schema Objects.vbs

NOTE   You cannot bind to the real classSchema object CN=User and use objClass.
Get("mustContain") or mayContain in a similar way. The reason is that
the mandatory and optional properties of the user class are the sum of the
mustContain, systemMustContain, mayContain, and systemMayContain
attributes from not only the user class, but also from all of its superclasses and
auxiliary classes. The mustContain and mayContain attributes are not even set
for the user class.

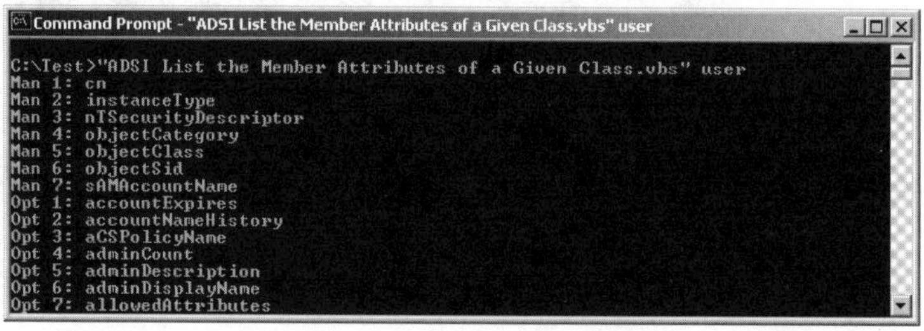

FIGURE 11.39 Some lines of output of "ADSI List the Member Attributes of a Given Class.vbs"

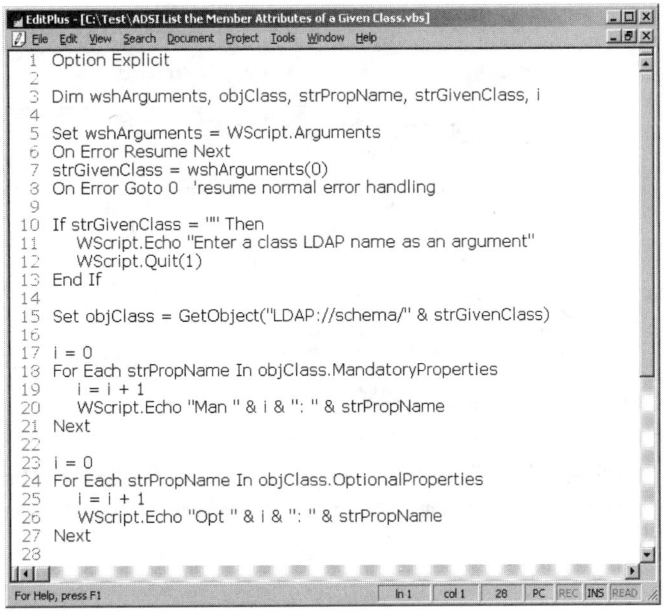

FIGURE 11.40 ADSI List the Member Attributes of a Given Class.vbs

List the Member Attributes of a Given Class to Excel.vbs

This next example extends the previous one. We now ask the class name in an input box and dump the attribute names into Excel. Because Excel is well suited for tables, we can also write other attribute information besides just the name there. Figure 11.41 shows the beginning of the output of the script.

When you start to manage objects of some particular class, you can first dump all its attributes into Excel, so you'll get a nice documentation of the attributes you can start playing with.

Next, we show the script's contents:

```
Option Explicit

Dim objExcel, objClass, strPropName, strGivenClass, strSheetName

strGivenClass = InputBox("Enter a class LDAP name")

Set objExcel = WScript.CreateObject("Excel.Application")
objExcel.Visible = True
objExcel.Workbooks.Add
```

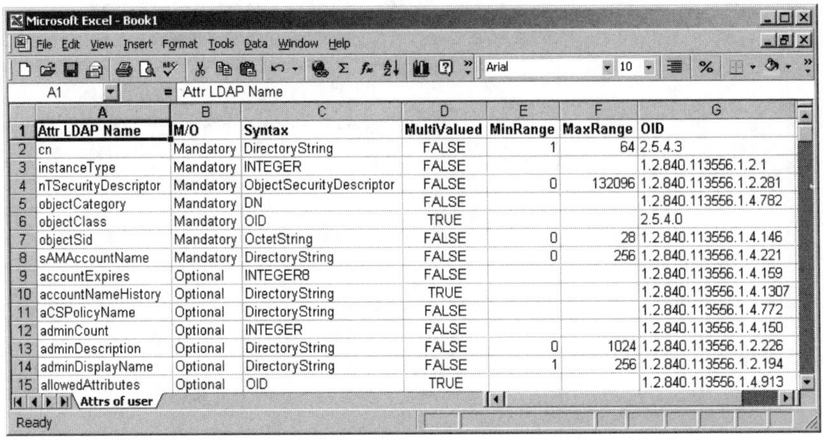

	A	B	C	D	E	F	G
1	Attr LDAP Name	M/O	Syntax	MultiValued	MinRange	MaxRange	OID
2	cn	Mandatory	DirectoryString	FALSE	1	64	2.5.4.3
3	instanceType	Mandatory	INTEGER	FALSE			1.2.840.113556.1.2.1
4	nTSecurityDescriptor	Mandatory	ObjectSecurityDescriptor	FALSE	0	132096	1.2.840.113556.1.2.281
5	objectCategory	Mandatory	DN	FALSE			1.2.840.113556.1.4.782
6	objectClass	Mandatory	OID	TRUE			2.5.4.0
7	objectSid	Mandatory	OctetString	FALSE	0	28	1.2.840.113556.1.4.146
8	sAMAccountName	Mandatory	DirectoryString	FALSE	0	256	1.2.840.113556.1.4.221
9	accountExpires	Optional	INTEGER8	FALSE			1.2.840.113556.1.4.159
10	accountNameHistory	Optional	DirectoryString	TRUE			1.2.840.113556.1.4.1307
11	aCSPolicyName	Optional	DirectoryString	FALSE			1.2.840.113556.1.4.772
12	adminCount	Optional	INTEGER	FALSE			1.2.840.113556.1.4.150
13	adminDescription	Optional	DirectoryString	FALSE	0	1024	1.2.840.113556.1.2.226
14	adminDisplayName	Optional	DirectoryString	FALSE	1	256	1.2.840.113556.1.2.194
15	allowedAttributes	Optional	OID	TRUE			1.2.840.113556.1.4.913

FIGURE 11.41 Some lines of output of "ADSI List the Member Attributes of a Given Class to Excel.vbs." The column widths were adjusted and the headers were bolded manually.

```
strSheetName = "Attrs of " & strGivenClass
If Len(strSheetName) > 31 Then _
   strSheetName = Left(strSheetName,28) & "..."
objExcel.ActiveSheet.Name = strSheetName
objExcel.ActiveSheet.Range("A1").Activate
objExcel.ActiveCell.Value = "Attr LDAP Name"
objExcel.ActiveCell.Offset(0, 1).Value = "M/O"
objExcel.ActiveCell.Offset(0, 2).Value = "Syntax"
objExcel.ActiveCell.Offset(0, 3).Value = "MultiValued"
objExcel.ActiveCell.Offset(0, 4).Value = "MinRange"
objExcel.ActiveCell.Offset(0, 5).Value = "MaxRange"
objExcel.ActiveCell.Offset(0, 6).Value = "OID"
objExcel.ActiveCell.Offset(1, 0).Activate

Set objClass = GetObject("LDAP://schema/" & strGivenClass)

For Each strPropName In objClass.MandatoryProperties
   Call ShowAttrAndFeatures("Mandatory", strPropName)
Next

For Each strPropName In objClass.OptionalProperties
   Call ShowAttrAndFeatures("Optional", strPropName)
Next

Sub ShowAttrAndFeatures(strManOrOpt, strPropName)
   Dim objAttribute

   On Error Resume Next

   Set objAttribute = GetObject("LDAP://schema/" & strPropName)
```

```
      objExcel.ActiveCell.Value = strPropName
      objExcel.ActiveCell.Offset(0, 1).Value = strManOrOpt
      With objAttribute
         objExcel.ActiveCell.Offset(0, 2).Value = .Syntax
         objExcel.ActiveCell.Offset(0, 3).Value = .MultiValued
         objExcel.ActiveCell.Offset(0, 4).Value = .MinRange
         objExcel.ActiveCell.Offset(0, 5).Value = .MaxRange
         objExcel.ActiveCell.Offset(0, 6).Value = .OID
      End With
      objExcel.ActiveCell.Offset(1, 0).Activate
End Sub
```

The `With` statement is something that we now use for the first time. Instead of `objAttribute.Syntax`, we can write just `.Syntax` while we are inside the `With` statement.

TIP
Another way to get data into Excel is to first print it onscreen with `WScript.Echo`, then redirect the output to a text file with the greater-than sign (>), and finally import the text file into Excel. If you print several properties on each line, you can put tabs in between them so that the data will import nicely into Excel.

Show Property Properties.vbs

This example is a subset of the previous one. It takes one attribute LDAP name as a command-line argument and then shows its properties. It doesn't introduce any new techniques, but it is a handy, small script if you quickly want to check some properties. Figure 11.42 shows the output of the script. Figure 11.43 shows the script's contents.

Container or Leaf.vbs

This is our last example that uses the abstract schema. The script binds to a container (CN=Users) and lists the names of all child objects and whether they are

FIGURE 11.42 The output of "ADSI Show Property Properties.vbs"

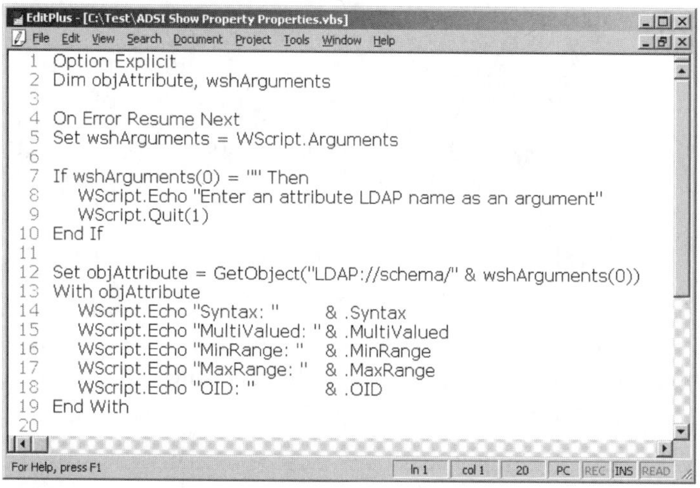

```
EditPlus - [C:\Test\ADSI Show Property Properties.vbs]
File  Edit  View  Search  Document  Project  Tools  Window  Help
 1  Option Explicit
 2  Dim objAttribute, wshArguments
 3
 4  On Error Resume Next
 5  Set wshArguments = WScript.Arguments
 6
 7  If wshArguments(0) = "" Then
 8      WScript.Echo "Enter an attribute LDAP name as an argument"
 9      WScript.Quit(1)
10  End If
11
12  Set objAttribute = GetObject("LDAP://schema/" & wshArguments(0))
13  With objAttribute
14      WScript.Echo "Syntax: "       & .Syntax
15      WScript.Echo "MultiValued: "  & .MultiValued
16      WScript.Echo "MinRange: "     & .MinRange
17      WScript.Echo "MaxRange: "     & .MaxRange
18      WScript.Echo "OID: "          & .OID
19  End With
20
For Help, press F1                                   ln 1   col 1   20   PC   REC  INS  READ
```

FIGURE 11.43 ADSI Show Property Properties.vbs

containers or leafs. Figure 11.44 shows some lines of the output. Figure 11.45 shows the script's contents.

The Schema property contains a string such as LDAP://schema/user, which binds to the abstract schema class object of the hosting object.

NOTE   By default, there are no leaf objects in the CN=Users container, because users and groups are containers. If you want to check that the script really works, you can add one contact object to that container.

NOTE   If we wanted to make the script three times longer, we could have added lines to check the treatAsLeaf attribute of the corresponding display specifier object. It would specify that even though user and group are technically containers, the Users and Computers snap-in should treat them as leaf objects.

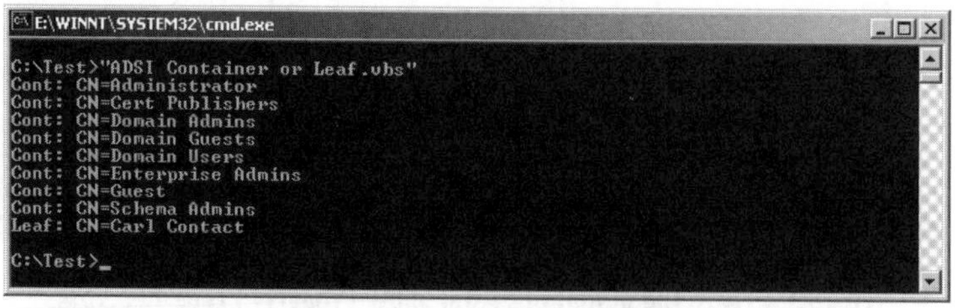

```
E:\WINNT\SYSTEM32\cmd.exe
C:\Test>"ADSI Container or Leaf.vbs"
Cont:  CN=Administrator
Cont:  CN=Cert Publishers
Cont:  CN=Domain Admins
Cont:  CN=Domain Guests
Cont:  CN=Domain Users
Cont:  CN=Enterprise Admins
Cont:  CN=Guest
Cont:  CN=Schema Admins
Leaf:  CN=Carl Contact

C:\Test>_
```

FIGURE 11.44 Some lines of output of "ADSI Container or Leaf.vbs"

```
Option Explicit

Dim objDSE, objContainer, objChild, objClass

Set objDSE = GetObject("LDAP://rootDSE")
Set objContainer = GetObject("LDAP://CN=Users," & _
    objDSE.Get("defaultNamingContext"))

For Each objChild In objContainer
    Set objClass = GetObject(objChild.Schema)
    If objClass.Container Then
        WScript.Echo "Cont: " + objChild.Name
    Else
        WScript.Echo "Leaf: " + objChild.Name
    End If
Next
```

FIGURE 11.45 ADSI Container or Leaf.vbs

List All Real Schema Objects.vbs

With this example, we begin using the real schema objects instead of the abstract schema. The sample script reads the schema container and lists all 142 classes and 863 attributes. This time we don't list syntaxes because they don't exist as objects in the real schema.

Figure 11.46 shows part of the output of the script. We show only the beginning of each category. After classes and attributes we list the `subSchema` object named `Aggregate`. It is the single object that contains the abstract schema definitions.

Figure 11.47 shows the script's contents.

We could also use just one loop instead of three, but this way we were able to sort the objects by their class.

If you want, you can add `objChild.Get("lDAPDisplayName")` to the output line, because the `Name` property method retrieves only the common name this time. We implement this in the next example. However, the `subSchema` object doesn't have an LDAP display name, so you will get an error in that case.

```
C:\Test>"ADSI List All Real Schema Objects.vbs"
1: classSchema: CN=ACS-Policy
2: classSchema: CN=ACS-Resource-Limits
3: classSchema: CN=ACS-Subnet
1: attributeSchema: CN=Account-Expires
2: attributeSchema: CN=Account-Name-History
3: attributeSchema: CN=ACS-Aggregate-Token-Rate-Per-User
1: subSchema: CN=Aggregate

C:\Test>_
```

FIGURE 11.46 Some lines of output of "ADSI List All Real Schema Objects.vbs"

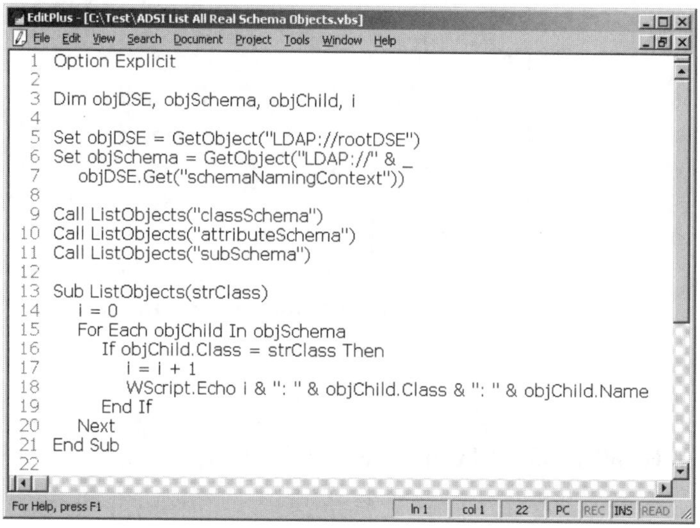

```
EditPlus - [C:\Test\ADSI List All Real Schema Objects.vbs]
File  Edit  View  Search  Document  Project  Tools  Window  Help
 1   Option Explicit
 2
 3   Dim objDSE, objSchema, objChild, i
 4
 5   Set objDSE = GetObject("LDAP://rootDSE")
 6   Set objSchema = GetObject("LDAP://" & _
 7      objDSE.Get("schemaNamingContext"))
 8
 9   Call ListObjects("classSchema")
10   Call ListObjects("attributeSchema")
11   Call ListObjects("subSchema")
12
13   Sub ListObjects(strClass)
14      i = 0
15      For Each objChild In objSchema
16         If objChild.Class = strClass Then
17            i = i + 1
18            WScript.Echo i & ": " & objChild.Class & ": " & objChild.Name
19         End If
20      Next
21   End Sub
22
```

FIGURE 11.47 ADSI List All Real Schema Objects.vbs

List Indexed Attributes.vbs

The abstract schema doesn't know whether an attribute is indexed, so we need to use the real `attributeSchema` objects and their `searchFlags` attribute. This script browses through all those objects and checks if one certain bit of `search-Flags` is set.

Figure 11.48 shows the first few lines of the output of the script. Figure 11.49 shows the script's contents.

You can modify this script for other purposes, as described in the next subsection.

NOTE   The base schema has the `searchFlags` attribute set for all `attributeSchema` objects, but if there are any new attributes in your test forest, they might not. The sample script won't work in this case, unless you either add at least the `On Error Resume Next` statement or modify the script as described in the next example.

FIGURE 11.48 Some lines of output of "ADSI List Indexed Attributes.vbs"

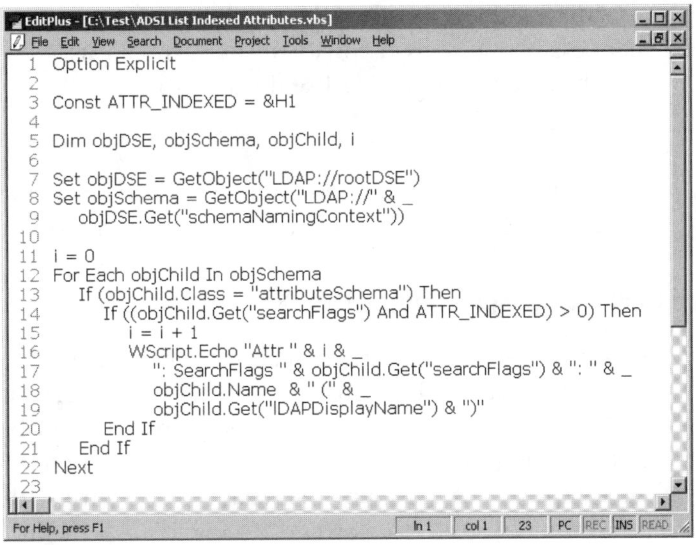

FIGURE 11.49 ADSI List Indexed Attributes.vbs

List ANR, Nonreplicated, and Constructed Attributes

Now that you have a script that scans the `searchFlags` attribute for one certain flag, you can also use it to scan other search flags as well as system flags.

To scan other search flags, just replace `ATTR_INDEXED` with one of the following constants:

```
Const ATTR_PART_OF_ANR_SET = &H4
Const ATTR_SURVIVE_DELETION = &H8
Const ATTR_COPY_WITH_USER = &H10
```

If you replace the `searchFlags` attribute with `systemFlags`, you can use the following constants:

```
Const ATTR_NOT_REPLICATED = &H1
Const ATTR_IS_CONSTRUCTED = &H4
Const ATTR_IS_BASE_SCHEMA = &H10
```

For more information on these flags, see Chapter 8.

The `systemFlags` attribute is not defined for 14 base schema attributes, as discussed in Chapter 8. Therefore, you need to modify the script a little so that you don't get the "property not found" error.

The easiest way to avoid the error is to remove the explicit `Get` method from the `If` statement and use a dynamic property method instead. When you retrieve an attribute value with the `.LDAPname` syntax instead of `.Get("LDAPname")`, you will get `vbEmpty` when the attribute is not set. It is equal to 0 in the `If` statement evaluation, so you don't need any extra lines for error checking.

The resulting line looks like the following:

```
If ((objChild.systemFlags And ATTR_NOT_REPLICATED) > 0) Then
```

Obviously, you can use the same syntax for `searchFlags` if some of the new `attributeSchema` objects don't have that attribute set.

List Global Catalog Attributes.vbs

This script lists all attributes that are part of the global catalog.

The global catalog setting is in the `isMemberOfPartialAttributeSet` attribute, which is usually present only on those attributes that are part of the global catalog. To avoid dealing with the "property not found" error, we use the same approach as in the previous example. We retrieve the value with the `.LDAP-name` syntax instead of `.Get("LDAPname")`.

Figure 11.50 shows the first few lines of the output of the script. Figure 11.51 shows the script's contents.

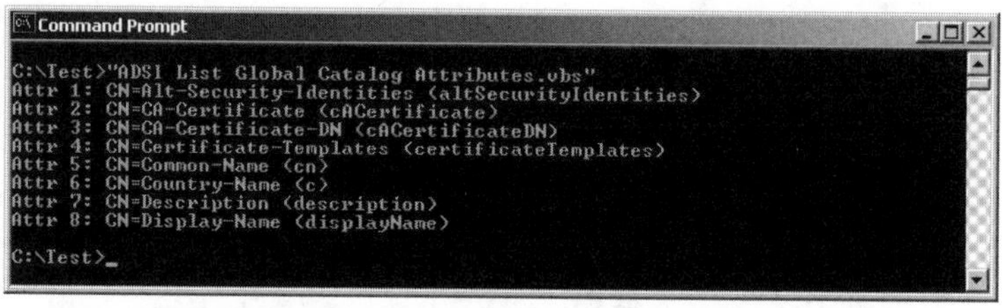

FIGURE 11.50 Some lines of output of "ADSI List Global Catalog Attributes.vbs"

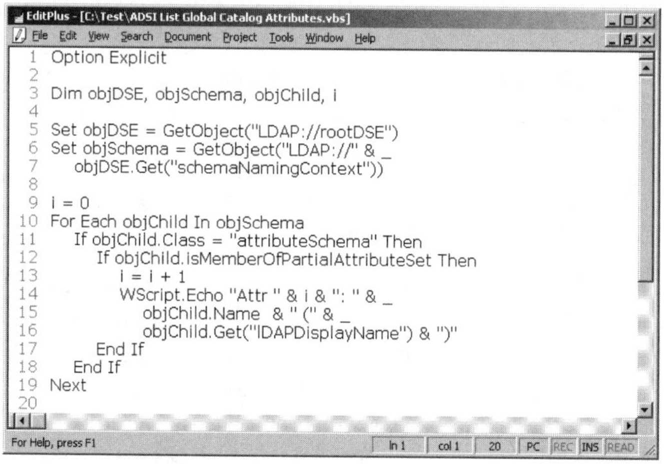

FIGURE 11.51 ADSI List Global Catalog Attributes.vbs

A missing attribute causes a `vbEmpty` situation, which the `If` statement considers to be False. Therefore, we can directly use `objChild.isMemberOf-PartialAttributeSet` in the `If` statement (see line 12).

List All classSchemas to Excel.vbs

This script dumps all `classSchema` objects into Excel and includes all their attributes that are easy to read. In other words, it doesn't include any multivalued, binary, or constructed attributes. We also omitted the attributes that `classSchema` objects don't use, such as `displayName`.

First we list the attribute names in a table using the same order and categories that we introduced in Chapter 8. Then we browse through the Schema container, picking up all `classSchema` objects and reading the listed attributes.

Figure 11.52 shows the resulting Excel spreadsheet. We have manually chosen Freeze Panes and bolded the first line. We haven't adjusted the column widths yet.

If you are interested in the attributes we didn't include, you have two options.

- Enhance this script with the reading techniques that we showed when reading user information earlier in this chapter (see the "List User Properties with Get.vbs" section).

- Use the script "List User Properties with Get.vbs", but replace the target object `CN=Guest` with a `classSchema` object such as `CN=User`. That modified script lists all constructed and multivalued attributes, but not any binary attributes (i.e., the two GUID attributes).

The script is as follows:

```
Option Explicit

Dim objExcel, objDSE, objSchema, objChild, i, varValue
Dim arrParamList(14)
```

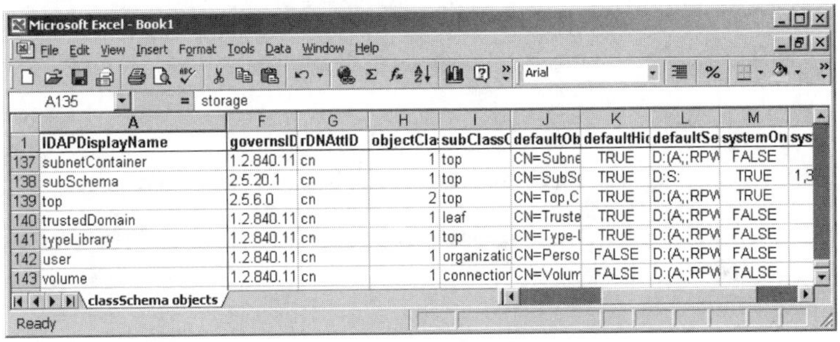

FIGURE 11.52 The output of "ADSI List All classSchemas to Excel.vbs"

```
'Names and Identifiers
arrParamList(0) = "lDAPDisplayName"
arrParamList(1) = "cn"
arrParamList(2) = "adminDisplayName"
arrParamList(3) = "distinguishedName"
arrParamList(4) = "adminDescription"
arrParamList(5) = "governsID"
arrParamList(6) = "rDNAttID"
'Structure and Containment Rules: None
'Class Inheritance
arrParamList(7) = "objectClassCategory"
arrParamList(8) = "subClassOf"
'Miscellaneous
arrParamList(9) = "defaultObjectCategory"
arrParamList(10) = "defaultHidingValue"
arrParamList(11) = "defaultSecurityDescriptor"
arrParamList(12) = "systemOnly"
arrParamList(13) = "systemFlags"
arrParamList(14) = "objectCategory"


Set objExcel = WScript.CreateObject("Excel.Application")
objExcel.Visible = True
objExcel.Workbooks.Add
objExcel.ActiveSheet.Name = "classSchema objects"


objExcel.ActiveSheet.Range("A1").Activate
For i = LBound(arrParamList) To UBound(arrParamList)
   objExcel.ActiveCell.Offset(0,i).Value = arrParamList(i)
Next
objExcel.ActiveCell.Offset(1,0).Activate'Move to next line


Set objDSE = GetObject("LDAP://rootDSE")
Set objSchema = GetObject("LDAP://" & _
   objDSE.Get("schemaNamingContext"))


On Error Resume Next
For Each objChild In objSchema
   If objChild.Class = "classSchema" Then
      For i = LBound(arrParamList) To UBound(arrParamList)
         varValue = objChild.Get(arrParamList(i))
         If Err <> 0 Then      'property not found or some other error
            Err.Clear
            varValue = ""
         End If
         objExcel.ActiveCell.Offset(0,i).Value = varValue
      Next
      objExcel.ActiveCell.Offset(1,0).Activate'Move to next line
   End If
Next
```

In previous examples, we cleared the error code with a line `Err = 0`, but this time we used a cooler way: `Err.Clear`.

List All attributeSchemas to Excel.vbs

This script is identical to the previous one, except that now we pick up `attributeSchema` objects and the list of their attributes is naturally slightly different.

Figure 11.53 shows the resulting Excel spreadsheet. Again, we have manually chosen Freeze Panes and bolded the first line. We haven't adjusted the column widths yet.

The script is as follows:

```
Option Explicit

Dim objExcel, objDSE, objSchema, objChild, i, varValue
Dim arrParamList(18)

'Names and Identifiers
arrParamList(0) = "lDAPDisplayName"
arrParamList(1) = "cn"
arrParamList(2) = "adminDisplayName"
arrParamList(3) = "distinguishedName"
arrParamList(4) = "adminDescription"
arrParamList(5) = "attributeID"
arrParamList(6) = "mAPIID"
arrParamList(7) = "linkID"
'Syntax and Content Rules
arrParamList(8) = "attributeSyntax"
arrParamList(9) = "oMSyntax"
arrParamList(10) = "isSingleValued"
arrParamList(11) = "rangeLower"
arrParamList(12) = "rangeUpper"
arrParamList(13) = "extendedCharsAllowed"
```

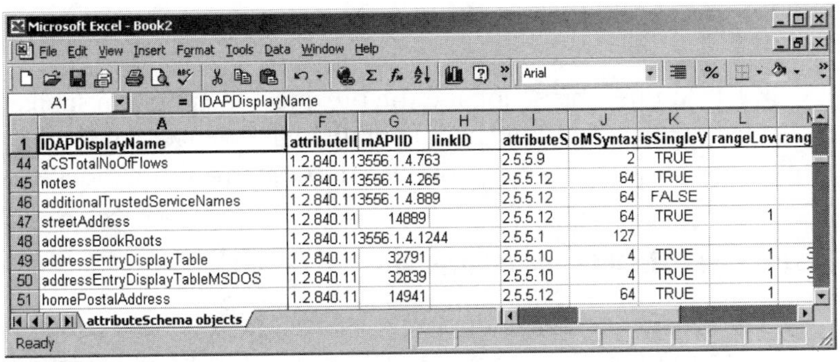

FIGURE 11.53 Output of "ADSI List All attributeSchemas to Excel.vbs"

```
'Searches
arrParamList(14) = "searchFlags"
arrParamList(15) = "isMemberofPartialAttributeSet"
'Miscellaneous
arrParamList(16) = "systemOnly"
arrParamList(17) = "systemFlags"
arrParamList(18) = "objectCategory"

Set objExcel = WScript.CreateObject("Excel.Application")
objExcel.Visible = True
objExcel.Workbooks.Add
objExcel.ActiveSheet.Name = "attributeSchema objects"


objExcel.ActiveSheet.Range("A1").Activate
For i = LBound(arrParamList) To UBound(arrParamList)
    objExcel.ActiveCell.Offset(0,i).Value = arrParamList(i)
Next
objExcel.ActiveCell.Offset(1,0).Activate'Move to next line

Set objDSE = GetObject("LDAP://rootDSE")
Set objSchema = GetObject("LDAP://" & _
    objDSE.Get("schemaNamingContext"))


On Error Resume Next
For Each objChild In objSchema
    If objChild.Class = "attributeSchema" Then
       For i = LBound(arrParamList) To UBound(arrParamList)
          varValue = objChild.Get(arrParamList(i))
          If Err <> 0 Then      'property not found or some other error
             Err.Clear
             varValue = ""
          End If
          objExcel.ActiveCell.Offset(0,i).Value = varValue
       Next
       objExcel.ActiveCell.Offset(1,0).Activate'Move to next line
    End If
Next
```

Because this script and the previous one perform similar actions (but for different data), we could have combined the two and used a subprogram to perform the action. However, we preferred to use two short, independent scripts.

Create an Attribute and a Class.vbs

In our last schema example, we create one attributeSchema and one class-Schema object. We use the same values for the object attributes that we had in Chapter 9.

Because schema extensions are something that we don't want to accidentally create, we have a confirmation box at the beginning of the script (see Figure 11.54). For the same reason, we don't take the forest name from `rootDSE`. You have to edit the forest name manually for each forest that you are going to use this script in. Without these precautions, you might just double-click the script and it would create an attribute and class for you.

There is also one new element in the binding string. We want to specify the server, because any schema changes are possible only on the schema master. With the serverless binding strings we have used so far, you probably bind to a domain controller that is not the schema master and some of your change operations might fail.

If you try to modify the schema on a domain controller that is not the schema master, that wrong domain controller will forward your request to the schema master. Consequently, the modify operation may very well succeed. However, this doesn't apply to the part when the script updates the schema cache using `rootDSE`. As a result, any subsequent modify operations in the same script may fail. The easiest way to ensure that the script works is to specify the schema master in all the binding strings of the script.

The script is as follows:

```
Option Explicit

Dim intYesNo, objSchema, objAttr, objClass, objDSE

intYesNo =  MsgBox("Create a new attribute and class?", _
    vbYesNo + vbQuestion +vbDefaultButton2, _
    "Extending the Schema")
If intYesNo = vbNo Then
    WScript.Quit(0)     'no error so no errorlevel
End If

Set objSchema = GetObject("LDAP://dc1.sanao.com/" & _
    "CN=Schema,CN=Configuration,DC=sanao,DC=com")

On Error Resume Next
```

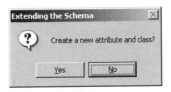

FIGURE 11.54 The confirmation message box of "ADSI Create an Attribute and a Class.vbs." Note that we have set "No" as the default.

```
Set objAttr = objSchema.Create("attributeSchema", _
    "CN=Sanao-Com-2000-MyProduct-User-Data")

Call objAttr.Put("lDAPDisplayName", _
    "sanaoCom2000-MyProduct-UserData")
Call objAttr.Put("attributeID", "1.3.6.1.4.1.123123123.2.1")
Call objAttr.Put("attributeSyntax", "2.5.5.10")
Call objAttr.Put("oMSyntax", 4)
Call objAttr.Put("isSingleValued", True)
Call objAttr.Put("rangeLower", 200)
Call objAttr.Put("rangeUpper", 200)
Call objAttr.Put("showInAdvancedViewOnly", True)
Call objAttr.Put("searchFlags", 0)

Err.Clear
objAttr.SetInfo      'write the new attribute to the server
Call CheckIfError("create the attribute")
WScript.Echo "Created the attribute"

'Err.Clear
'Set objDSE = GetObject("LDAP://dc1.sanao.com/rootDSE")
'Call objDSE.Put("schemaUpdateNow", 1) 'trigger schema cache update
'objDSE.SetInfo
'Call CheckIfError("trigger schema cache update")
'WScript.Echo "Updated the schema cache"

Set objClass = objSchema.Create("classSchema", _
    "CN=Sanao-Com-2000-MyProduct-Config-Info")

Call objClass.Put("lDAPDisplayName", _
    "sanaoCom2000-MyProduct-ConfigInfo")
Call objClass.Put("governsID", "1.3.6.1.4.1.123123123.1.1")
Call objClass.Put("mustContain", _
    Array("1.3.6.1.4.1.123123123.2.1"))
'Call objClass.Put("mustContain", _
'     Array("sanaoCom2000-MyProduct-UserData"))
Call objClass.Put("possSuperiors", Array("container"))
Call objClass.Put("objectClassCategory", 1)       'Structural
Call objClass.Put("subClassOf", "top")
Call objClass.Put("defaultHidingValue", True)
Call objClass.Put("showInAdvancedViewOnly", True)

Err.Clear
objClass.SetInfo 'write the new class to the server
Call CheckIfError("create the class")
WScript.Echo "Created the class"

Err.Clear
Set objDSE = GetObject("LDAP://dc1.sanao.com/rootDSE")
Call objDSE.Put("schemaUpdateNow", 1) 'trigger schema cache update
objDSE.SetInfo
Call CheckIfError("trigger schema cache update")
WScript.Echo "Updated the schema cache"
```

```
Sub CheckIfError(strAttemptedOperation)
   If Err <> 0 Then
      MsgBox "Couldn't " & strAttemptedOperation & vbCrLf & _
         "Error code " & Hex(Err), _
         vbOKOnly + vbCritical, "Error"
      WScript.Quit(1)    'there was an error so we set the errorlevel
   End If
End Sub
```

Note that the `showInAdvancedViewOnly` attribute is not part of the schema definition, nor do we need to add `searchFlags = 0`. However, we included them to be consistent with the base schema objects.

We wouldn't have to use arrays for the two multivalued attributes (because we include only one value), but we wanted to emphasize their nature with the `Array` keyword.

Between adding the attribute and class we have six lines that are commented out. If you uncommented them, they would trigger the schema cache update. The reason we don't need them is that we add the attribute to the `mustContain` list of the class using the `attributeID`. If we wanted to use the attribute LDAP name (the two next commented lines), we would need the schema cache update first.

Anyway, we trigger the schema cache update at the end of the script. It saves us the 5-minute waiting period, so we can start creating instances of this new class right away (e.g., using ADSI Edit). The main reason, however, for triggering the update is that we want to demonstrate how you can do it.

An alternative way to trigger the schema cache update is to use the `IADsADSystemInfo` interface. The following two lines do the trick:

```
Set objSystemInfo = CreateObject("ADSystemInfo")
Call objSystemInfo.RefreshSchemaCache
```

If all goes well when the script runs, you will see the output shown in Figure 11.55. If all doesn't go well, you will see an error box like the one in Figure 11.56 and the script will quit.

Some other errors that are quite possible with this script are as follows:

```
Const ERROR_DS_NO_ATTRIBUTE_OR_VALUE = &H8007200A
Const ERROR_DS_UNWILLING_TO_PERFORM = &H80072035
```

FIGURE 11.55 Output of "ADSI Create an Attribute and a Class.vbs" if all goes well

FIGURE 11.56 Error box of "ADSI Create an Attribute and a Class.vbs." The error code in the figure means `ERROR_OBJECT_ALREADY_EXISTS`. **If you run the script several times without changing the object names and identifiers each time, you will see this error.**

The former error you will get, for example, if you try to use an attribute name in the `mustContain` assignment and you haven't updated the schema cache. The latter error occurs if you haven't allowed schema changes on the schema master (as described in Chapter 9).

CONFIGURATION INFORMATION

The sample scripts in this section mostly access the configuration partition of Active Directory, but some of the examples also do other things. The section presents the following examples:

- CH11-25 ADSI List the Supported Namespaces.vbs
- CH11-26 ADSI List Attribute Display Names.vbs
- CH11-27 ADSI List the DC GUIDs.vbs
- CH11-28 ADSI List the rootDSE Property Cache.vbs
- CH11-29 ADSI List the GPO GUIDs.vbs
- CH11-30 ADSI List the Operations Masters.vbs
- CH11-31 ADSI List the Operations Masters with ADsFSMO.vbs
- CH11-32 ADSI List ADSystemInfo.vbs

All the examples just list information, because you probably don't want to make any changes to the information using scripts. If you do, you already know how to create objects of any class and modify their attributes.

List the Supported Namespaces.vbs

We start the configuration category with a short sample script that lists the ADSI namespaces that are currently installed on your computer. The script uses a

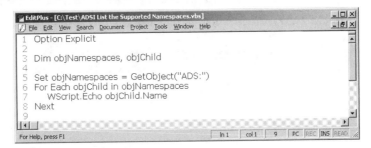

FIGURE 11.57 Output of "ADSI List the Supported Namespaces.vbs"

```
1  Option Explicit
2
3  Dim objNamespaces, objChild
4
5  Set objNamespaces = GetObject("ADS:")
6  For Each objChild in objNamespaces
7      WScript.Echo objChild.Name
8  Next
9
```

FIGURE 11.58 ADSI List the Supported Namespaces.vbs

special binding string, `ADS:`, to do this. The script's output appears in Figure 11.57 and the script's contents are in Figure 11.58.

Because the IIS namespace is also on the output list in Figure 11.57, the script was run on a computer that had the IIS service running.

List Attribute Display Names.vbs

This sample takes a class LDAP name as a command-line argument and lists all attribute display names versus their LDAP names. The information is read from the `attributeDisplayNames` attribute that resides in the display specifier object of the class.

If you want to manage objects of a certain class with ADSI or LDAP filters, you can first use this script to list the attribute names that correspond to the names that you see in the user interface.

Figure 11.59 shows the first lines of output for the user class. Figure 11.60 shows the script's contents.

`AttributeDisplayNames` is a multivalued attribute, where each value consists of a `display name, LDAP name` pair. As we browse through the values in the `For` loop, the `Split` function splits the value using the comma character as a separator.

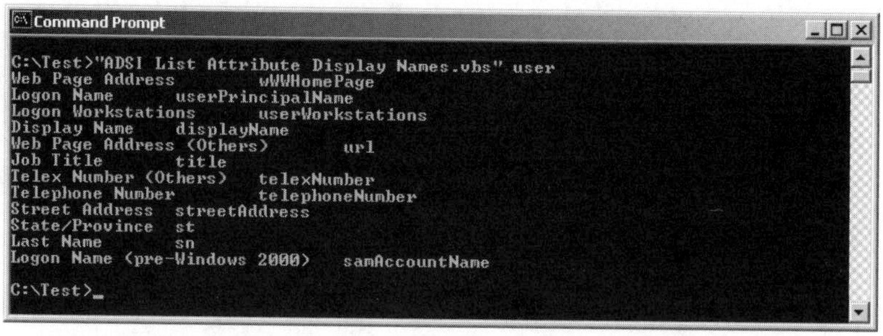

FIGURE 11.59 Some lines of output of "ADSI List Attribute Display Names.vbs"

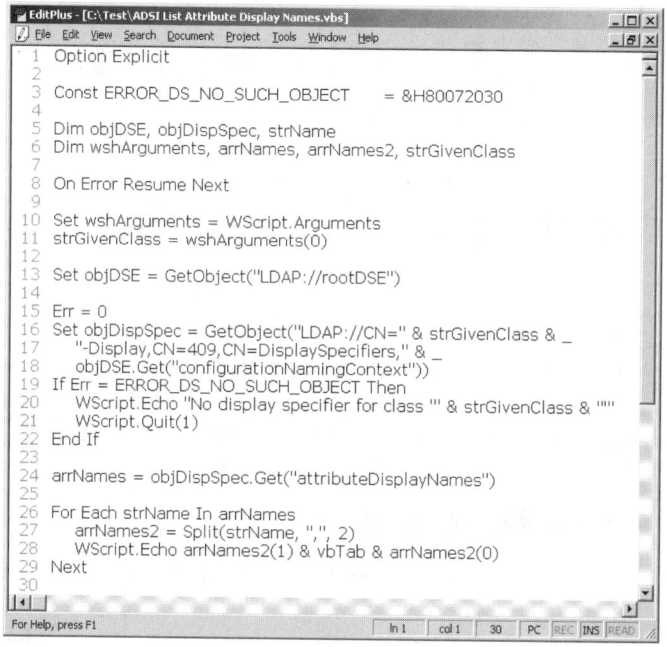


```
Option Explicit

Const ERROR_DS_NO_SUCH_OBJECT     = &H80072030

Dim objDSE, objDispSpec, strName
Dim wshArguments, arrNames, arrNames2, strGivenClass

On Error Resume Next

Set wshArguments = WScript.Arguments
strGivenClass = wshArguments(0)

Set objDSE = GetObject("LDAP://rootDSE")

Err = 0
Set objDispSpec = GetObject("LDAP://CN=" & strGivenClass & _
    "-Display,CN=409,CN=DisplaySpecifiers," & _
    objDSE.Get("configurationNamingContext"))
If Err = ERROR_DS_NO_SUCH_OBJECT Then
    WScript.Echo "No display specifier for class '" & strGivenClass & "'"
    WScript.Quit(1)
End If

arrNames = objDispSpec.Get("attributeDisplayNames")

For Each strName In arrNames
    arrNames2 = Split(strName, ",", 2)
    WScript.Echo arrNames2(1) & vbTab & arrNames2(0)
Next
```

FIGURE 11.60 ADSI List Attribute Display Names.vbs

List the DC GUIDs.vbs

This script reads the Sites container in the configuration partition and lists three things about each domain controller in the forest:

- The domain controller name (i.e., the common name of the server object)
- The DC GUID (i.e., the `objectGUID` attribute of the NTDS Settings object under the server object)
- The site name

Figure 11.61 shows the script's output.

You can use the script if you want to document the replica ring of one of your Active Directory sites. The GUIDs listed determine the order of the domain controllers in the ring. The easiest way to get the correct ring order is to first redirect the output to a text file, such as dcguids1.txt, then delete lines containing other sites, and finally use the following command:

```
sort /+14 <dcguids1.txt >dcguids2.txt
```

This command reads the file, sorts it based on column 14, and outputs the result to dcguids2.txt.

To refresh your memory, Figure 11.62 shows the Sites and Services snap-in. You can refer to it when you read through the script in Figure 11.63.

Because the NTDS Settings objects are quite deep in the hierarchy, we need several nested For loops and If statements to reach them. Even though the objectGUID attribute is binary, it is easy to retrieve. The Guid property method of the IADs interface returns it in a nice text format.

```
Command Prompt                                                            _|□|×|
C:\Test>"ADSI List the DC GUIDs.vbs"
CN=BOSSALES1 6f9092ef369beb4590714dfaee357c21 CN=Default-First-Site-Name
CN=BOSSALES2 b7ef457ff8ab93449f2a3a736e2a98eb CN=Default-First-Site-Name
CN=BOSSANA01 c5ccf9a2cb309c489ef69d0c27b3f675 CN=Default-First-Site-Name
CN=BOSSANA02 636d3c023da3a64b92ec7e2c06965e1d CN=Default-First-Site-Name
CN=BOSSANA03 6f606c1087960d489035295b90681a23 CN=Default-First-Site-Name
CN=BOSSANA04 12c3dd185037034bba8ac1f95dfaf8eb CN=Default-First-Site-Name
CN=BOSSANA05 48b6597ae112bf44883b6d531393594a CN=Default-First-Site-Name
CN=BOSSANA06 a6e61913d72a234c8e5737a5850dcbd1 CN=Default-First-Site-Name
CN=BOSSANA07 fb8b1bd46d640843a266360be9e6e1ea CN=Default-First-Site-Name

C:\Test>_
```

FIGURE 11.61 Output of "ADSI List the DC GUIDs.vbs"

FIGURE 11.62 The Sites and Services snap-in. The sample forest in the figure has just one domain controller: DC1.

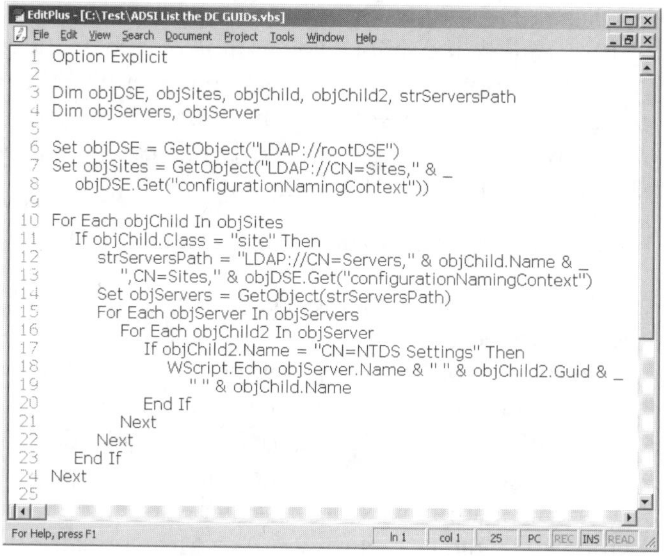

FIGURE 11.63 ADSI List the DC GUIDs.vbs

List the rootDSE Property Cache.vbs

So far we have used some of the rootDSE information to bind to objects without hard-coding the domain name. This script reads and displays everything that is in its property cache. Figure 11.64 shows most properties of the output. Figure 11.65 shows the script's contents.

We explained rootDSE at the end of Chapter 10.

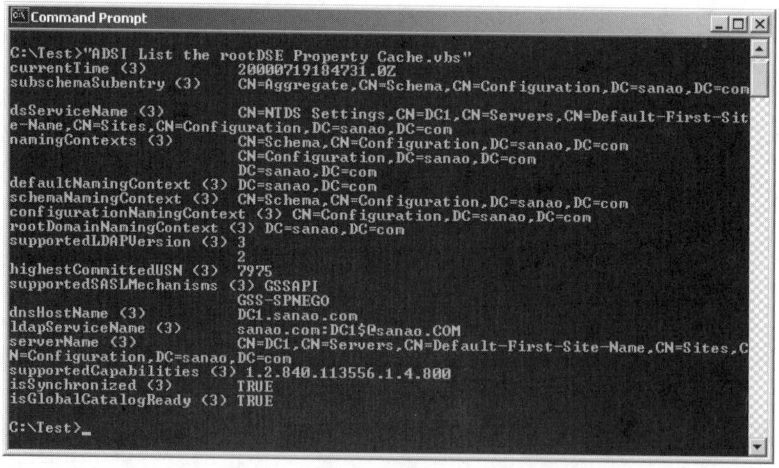

FIGURE 11.64 Most properties of the output of "ADSI List the rootDSE Property Cache.vbs"

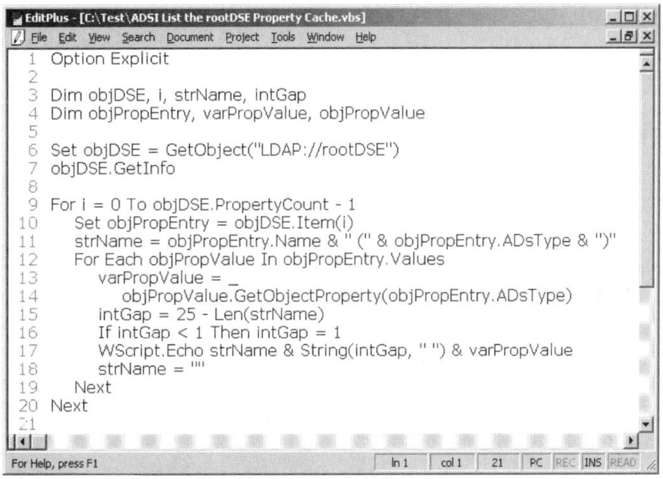


```
Option Explicit

Dim objDSE, i, strName, intGap
Dim objPropEntry, varPropValue, objPropValue

Set objDSE = GetObject("LDAP://rootDSE")
objDSE.GetInfo

For i = 0 To objDSE.PropertyCount - 1
   Set objPropEntry = objDSE.Item(i)
   strName = objPropEntry.Name & " (" & objPropEntry.ADsType & ")"
   For Each objPropValue In objPropEntry.Values
      varPropValue = _
         objPropValue.GetObjectProperty(objPropEntry.ADsType)
      intGap = 25 - Len(strName)
      If intGap < 1 Then intGap = 1
      WScript.Echo strName & String(intGap, " ") & varPropValue
      strName = ""
   Next
Next
```

FIGURE 11.65 ADSI List the rootDSE Property Cache.vbs

List the GPO GUIDs.vbs

You can use this sample script to list all Group Policy objects (GPOs) that exist in your domain. The listed GUIDs are used as folder names when GPOs are stored in Active Directory and the file system. Figure 11.66 shows the script's output for a domain that has only the two default GPOs. Figure 11.67 shows the script's contents.

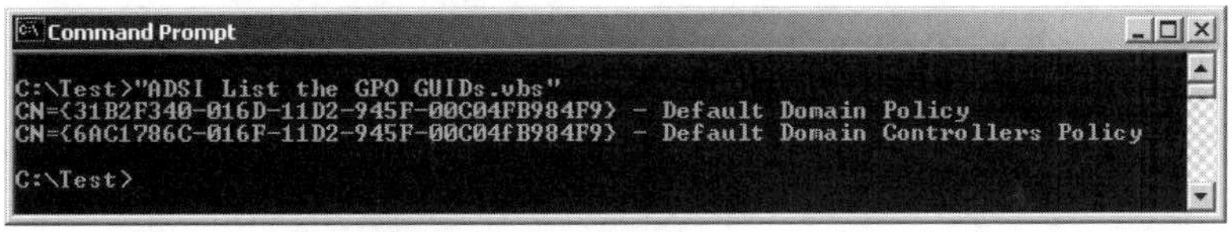


```
C:\Test>"ADSI List the GPO GUIDs.vbs"
CN={31B2F340-016D-11D2-945F-00C04FB984F9} - Default Domain Policy
CN={6AC1786C-016F-11D2-945F-00C04fB984F9} - Default Domain Controllers Policy

C:\Test>
```

FIGURE 11.66 Output of "ADSI List the GPO GUIDs.vbs"

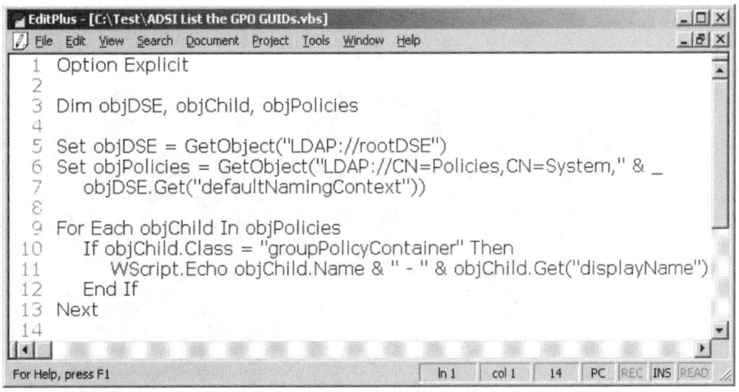


```
Option Explicit

Dim objDSE, objChild, objPolicies

Set objDSE = GetObject("LDAP://rootDSE")
Set objPolicies = GetObject("LDAP://CN=Policies,CN=System," & _
   objDSE.Get("defaultNamingContext"))

For Each objChild In objPolicies
   If objChild.Class = "groupPolicyContainer" Then
      WScript.Echo objChild.Name & " - " & objChild.Get("displayName")
   End If
Next
```

FIGURE 11.67 ADSI List the GPO GUIDs.vbs

The GUID is easy to retrieve because instead of a binary attribute, it is the common name of the object in this case.

List the Operations Masters.vbs

In Chapter 5 we listed the objects that contain an fSMORoleOwner attribute that points to the NTDS Settings object of each role owner. This script reads those attributes and displays the five role owners. You can enter the domain name into an input box that has your default domain as a default.

Figure 11.68 shows the script's output. As you see, all five roles are in the same domain controller in this case.

The script is as follows:

```
Option Explicit

Dim objDSE, strDefaultDom, strDom
Dim objSchema, objPartitions, objRID, objDom, objInfra

Set objDSE = GetObject("LDAP://rootDSE")
strDefaultDom = objDSE.Get("defaultNamingContext")

strDom = InputBox("Enter the distinguished name of a domain" & _
    vbCrLf & "(e.g. " & strDefaultDom & ")", , strDefaultDom)

If strDom = "" Then WScript.Quit(1)   'user clicked Cancel

'Get the objects that have a pointer to each operations master
Set objSchema = GetObject("LDAP://" & _
    objDSE.Get("schemaNamingContext"))
Set objPartitions = GetObject("LDAP://CN=Partitions," & _
    objDSE.Get("configurationNamingContext"))
Set objRID = GetObject("LDAP://CN=RID Manager$,CN=System," & _
    strDom)
Set objDom = GetObject("LDAP://" & strDom)
Set objInfra = GetObject("LDAP://CN=Infrastructure," & strDom)
```

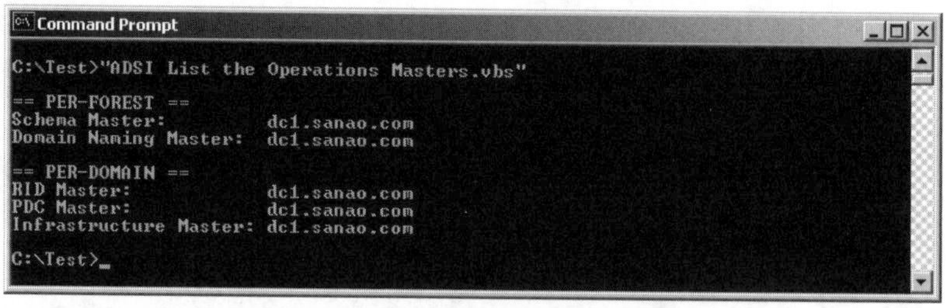

FIGURE 11.68 Output of "ADSI List the Operations Masters.vbs"

```
WScript.Echo vbCrLf & "== PER-FOREST =="
Call ShowFSMO("Schema", objSchema)
Call ShowFSMO("Domain Naming", objPartitions)
WScript.Echo vbCrLf & "== PER-DOMAIN =="
Call ShowFSMO("RID", objRID)
Call ShowFSMO("PDC", objDom)
Call ShowFSMO("Infrastructure", objInfra)

Sub ShowFSMO(strName, objPointerObj)
    Dim objNTDS, objDC, intGap

    Set objNTDS = GetObject("LDAP://" & _
        objPointerObj.Get("fSMORoleOwner")) 'pointer to CN=NTDS Settings
    Set objDC = GetObject(objNTDS.Parent)   'server object

    intGap = 14 - Len(strName)
    WScript.Echo strName & " Master: " & String(intGap, " ") & _
        objDC.dnsHostName
End Sub
```

This is the first example in which we pass an object variable as an argument to a subprogram. In the variable name objPointerObj, the first "obj" means that the variable is a VBScript object. The second "Obj" means that this is an Active Directory pointer object.

CHANGING AN OPERATIONS MASTER

We explained in Chapter 5 how to manually transfer or seize an operations master role to another domain controller. There shouldn't be a great need to script either of these tasks, because they are quite infrequent. However, we introduce the principles briefly.

To initiate a role transfer (i.e., in cooperation with the previous role owner), you must write the value 1 to the appropriate operational attribute of rootDSE. As a result, an atomic transfer of the role occurs, including the synchronization of any vital configuration information. The five attributes that correspond to the transfers of the five roles are as follows: becomeSchemaMaster, becomeDomainMaster, becomeRidMaster, becomePdc, and becomeInfrastructureMaster. For example, executing the following lines transfers the infrastructure master to dc2.sanao.com.

```
Set objDSE = GetObject("LDAP://dc2.sanao.com/rootDSE")
Call objDSE.Put("becomeInfrastructureMaster", 1)
objDSE.SetInfo
```

If you need a role-transferring script in practice, you can use the preceding lines and incorporate error checking from the "Create an Attribute and a

Class.vbs" section. You can also add lines from this section to list the new role owner. However, of the five listed attributes, becomePdc seems not to work—if you use it, you may get the "server is unwilling to perform" error (corresponding to the error code "80072035").

To initiate a role seizure (i.e., when the previous role owner has failed), you must write a pointer to a new domain controller in the fSMORoleOwner attribute of the appropriate object. For information on which objects to use and what to put in fSMORoleOwner, refer to the listing script in this section.

WARNING   Performing a role seizure in a wrong way can corrupt your forest. Before attempting a seizure, be sure to throroughly understand the information on role seizures presented in Chapter 5.

List the Operations Masters with ADsFSMO.vbs

One of the components in the ADSI Resource Kit is ADsFSMO. We can use it to list the same operations master roles that we listed in the previous example.

To use the component, you must perform the following two steps:

1. Locate the file adsfsmo.dll in your Platform SDK folder (perhaps C:\Program Files\Microsoft Platform SDK\Samples\NetDS\ADSI\ResourceKit). You can either leave the file where it is or copy it to some other folder, such as C:\Winnt\System32.

2. Register the component with the command regsvr32 adsfsmo.dll. If the DLL file is not in the current folder, you must include the location in the command. You should see a pop-up message indicating that "DllRegisterServer in adsfsmo.dll succeeded."

Now you are ready to use the component in the script shown in Figure 11.69.

First we create the ADsFSMO object, and then we connect to some domain controller. This determines the domain for which we query the operations master roles.

Because the component knows right away the role owners of each operations master, all we need to do is list them.

NOTE   Even though this operations master script is easier and shorter than the former operations master script, we wanted to include the former one too, because it is much more educational.

```
EditPlus - [C:\Test\ADSI List the Operations Masters with ADsFSMO.vbs]
File  Edit  View  Search  Document  Project  Tools  Window  Help
  1   Option Explicit
  2
  3   Dim objADsFSMO
  4
  5   Set objADsFSMO = CreateObject("ADsFSMO")
  6   objADsFSMO.Connect "dc1.sanao.com"
  7
  8   WScript.Echo vbCrLf & "== PER-FOREST =="
  9   WScript.Echo "Schema Master: " & objADsFSMO.SchemaRoleOwner
 10   WScript.Echo "Domain Naming Master: " & _
 11       objADsFSMO.DomainRoleOwner
 12   WScript.Echo vbCrLf & "== PER-DOMAIN =="
 13   WScript.Echo "RID Master: " & objADsFSMO.RidRoleOwner
 14   WScript.Echo "PDC Master: " & objADsFSMO.PDCRoleOwner
 15   WScript.Echo "Infrastructure Master: " & _
 16       objADsFSMO.InfrastructureRoleOwner
 17
For Help, press F1                                    ln 1    col 1   17   PC  REC  INS  READ
```

FIGURE 11.69 ADSI List the Operations Masters with AdsFSMO.vbs

List ADSystemInfo.vbs

ADSI includes an `ADSystemInfo` interface, which shows you some general configuration information. The output of this information is in Figure 11.70 and the script's contents are in Figure 11.71.

There is nothing to explain about this script, except that we have put line 18 with `GetDCSiteName` as a comment, because that property method seems not to work.

The `ADSystemInfo` interface includes also the method `RefreshSchema-Cache`, which we explained in the "Create an Attribute and a Class.vbs" example.

```
Command Prompt
C:\Test>"ADSI List ADSystemInfo.vbs"
Username: CN=Administrator,CN=Users,DC=sanao,DC=com
Computername: CN=DC1,OU=Domain Controllers,DC=sanao,DC=com
Sitename: Default-First-Site-Name
Domain NetBIOS name: SANAO
Domain DNS name: sanao.com
Forest DNS name: sanao.com
PDC Master: CN=NTDS Settings,CN=DC1,CN=Servers,CN=Default-First-Site-Name,CN=Sit
es,CN=Configuration,DC=sanao,DC=com
Schema Master: CN=NTDS Settings,CN=DC1,CN=Servers,CN=Default-First-Site-Name,CN=
Sites,CN=Configuration,DC=sanao,DC=com
Native Mode: True
DC name: dc1.sanao.com
Tree: sanao.com

C:\Test>_
```

FIGURE 11.70 Output of "ADSI List ADSystemInfo.vbs"

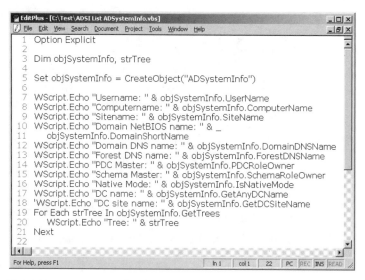

FIGURE 11.71 ADSI List ADSystemInfo.vbs

ACCESS CONTROL LISTS

ADSI enables you to list and modify the access control lists of Active Directory objects by using three security interfaces. In this section, we first explain the interfaces and then show the sample scripts.

NOTE   Unfortunately, the security interfaces don't allow you to access file and folder ACLs. However, you can use the ADsSecurity component, as demonstrated in the last example in this section.

Security Interfaces

Active Directory uses security descriptors, ACLs, and ACEs to control who has access to each object and what kind of access he has. We explain them all in detail at the end of Chapter 4, so you might want to refresh your memory by reading those pages again.

The three security interfaces are as follows:

- IADsSecurityDescriptor gives you access to the fields of a security descriptor, the most interesting one being the discretionary ACL.

- `IADsAccessControlList` gives you access to ACLs, whether they are discretionary or system ACLs. This interface enables you to enumerate all ACEs.
- `IADsAccessControlEntry` gives you access to the fields of an individual ACE.

Figure 11.72 shows how the interfaces work.

NOTE   We have drawn several `objACE` variables in Figure 11.72. In practice, however, there is usually only one of them and it represents different entries one at a time.

The Access Control List Sample Scripts

We present the following examples in this section:

- CH11-33 ADSI List ACEs—Short.vbs
- CH11-34 ADSI List ACEs to Excel—Short.vbs

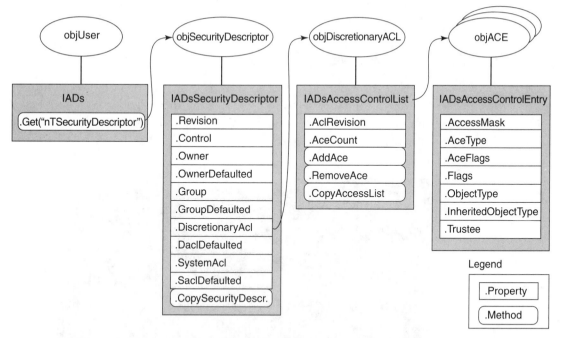

FIGURE 11.72 By reading the `nTSecurityDescriptor` attribute of an Active Directory object, you can create an object variable to be used with the `IADsSecurityDescriptor` interface. This way, you will get your hands on the discretionary ACL and the individual ACEs.

- CH11-35 ADSI List Binary GUIDs.vbs
- CH11-36 ADSI List ACEs—Long.vbs
- CH11-37 ADSI Add ACEs.vbs
- CH11-38 ADSI Add ACEs to a Folder.vbs

We start with a short example as an introduction and then present a long script that is probably more useful in practice.

List ACEs—Short.vbs

We start with a short script that lists all (discretionary) ACEs of a given Active Directory object. You can enter the object name into an input box.

Figure 11.73 shows part of the script's output for the CN=Users container. We interpret something of the output with the next sample, where we have the same output in Excel. Here we just say that the access mask "&HF01FF" is the same as Full Control.

Figure 11.74 shows the script's contents.

If you like to see only some of the ACEs, you can put an If statement inside the loop to filter out unwanted ACEs.

List ACEs to Excel—Short.vbs

This script is nearly identical to the previous one, except this time we dump the ACEs into Excel. You have the knowledge to write this script on your own based on the samples we have provided so far, but we wanted to show a complete script because the output format is so nice.

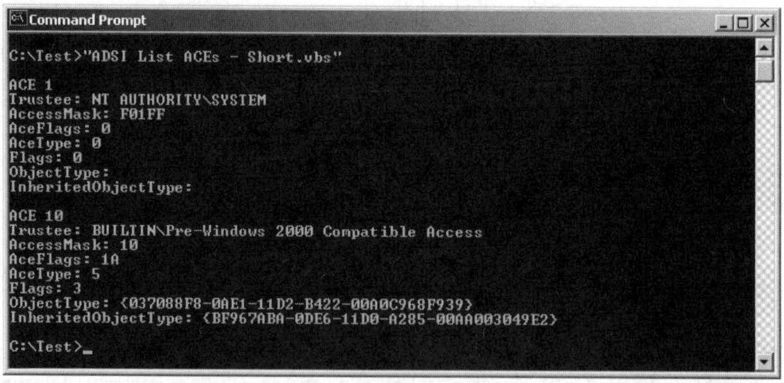

FIGURE 11.73 Output of "ADSI List ACEs—Short.vbs"

```
 1  Option Explicit
 2
 3  Dim objDSE, strDefaultDN, strDN, objADObject, i
 4  Dim objSecDesc, objDACL, objACE
 5
 6  Set objDSE = GetObject("LDAP://rootDSE")
 7  strDefaultDN = "CN=Users," & objDSE.Get("defaultNamingContext")
 8
 9  strDN = InputBox("Enter the distinguished name of an object" & _
10      vbCrLf & "(e.g. " & strDefaultDN & ")", , strDefaultDN)
11
12  If strDN = "" Then WScript.Quit(0)   'user clicked Cancel
13
14  Set objADObject = GetObject("LDAP://" & strDN)
15
16  Set objSecDesc = objADObject.Get("ntSecurityDescriptor")
17  Set objDACL = objSecDesc.DiscretionaryAcl
18
19  WScript.Echo "Number of ACEs: " & objDACL.AceCount
20
21  i = 0
22  For Each objACE In objDACL
23      i = i + 1
24      WScript.Echo ""
25      WScript.Echo "ACE " & i
26      WScript.Echo "Trustee: " & objACE.Trustee
27      WScript.Echo "AccessMask: " & Hex(objACE.AccessMask)
28      WScript.Echo "AceFlags: " & Hex(objACE.AceFlags)
29      WScript.Echo "AceType: " & Hex(objACE.AceType)
30      WScript.Echo "Flags: " & Hex(objACE.Flags)
31      WScript.Echo "ObjectType: " & objACE.ObjectType
32      WScript.Echo "InheritedObjectType: " & objACE.InheritedObjectType
33  Next
34
```

FIGURE 11.74 ADSI List ACEs—Short.vbs

Figure 11.75 shows the resulting spreadsheet for the CN=Users container.

We are not going to repeat the ten-page discussion that we presented about the access control architecture in Chapter 4. However, we will provide you with some short comments on the output.

- AccessMask "F01FF" (hex) is the same as Full Control, and "20094" (hex) is the same as Read + List Object.

- AceFlags "12" (hex) means that the ACE was inherited from above and it applies to "This object and all child objects."

- The GUIDs starting with "BF967ABA" refer to the user objects (i.e., those ACEs somehow apply to user objects).

You can open up the list of permission entries for CN=Users (i.e., ACL Editor) using the Users and Computers snap-in. This way, you can compare those entries to the ones shown here.

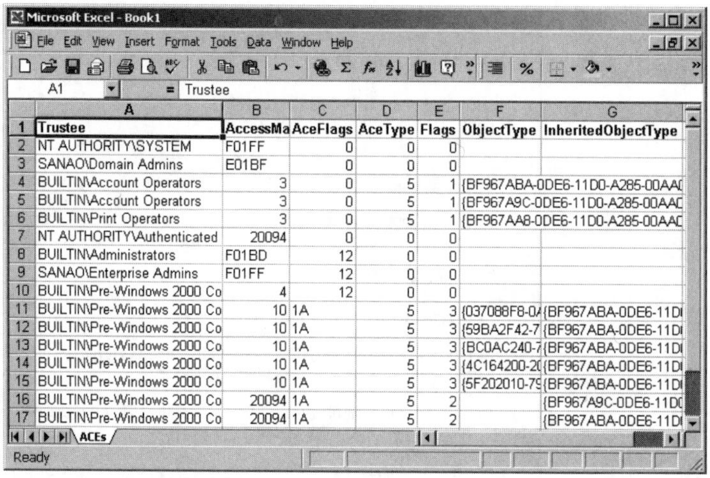

	Trustee	AccessMa	AceFlags	AceType	Flags	ObjectType	InheritedObjectType
2	NT AUTHORITY\SYSTEM	F01FF	0	0	0		
3	SANAO\Domain Admins	E01BF	0	0	0		
4	BUILTIN\Account Operators	3	0	5	1	{BF967ABA-0DE6-11D0-A285-00AA	
5	BUILTIN\Account Operators	3	0	5	1	{BF967A9C-0DE6-11D0-A285-00AA	
6	BUILTIN\Print Operators	3	0	5	1	{BF967AA8-0DE6-11D0-A285-00AA	
7	NT AUTHORITY\Authenticated	20094	0	0	0		
8	BUILTIN\Administrators	F01BD	12	0	0		
9	SANAO\Enterprise Admins	F01FF	12	0	0		
10	BUILTIN\Pre-Windows 2000 Co	4	12	0	0		
11	BUILTIN\Pre-Windows 2000 Co	10	1A	5	3	{037088F8-0	{BF967ABA-0DE6-11D
12	BUILTIN\Pre-Windows 2000 Co	10	1A	5	3	{59BA2F42-7	{BF967ABA-0DE6-11D
13	BUILTIN\Pre-Windows 2000 Co	10	1A	5	3	{BC0AC240-7	{BF967ABA-0DE6-11D
14	BUILTIN\Pre-Windows 2000 Co	10	1A	5	3	{4C164200-2	{BF967ABA-0DE6-11D
15	BUILTIN\Pre-Windows 2000 Co	10	1A	5	3	{5F202010-7	{BF967ABA-0DE6-11D
16	BUILTIN\Pre-Windows 2000 Co	20094	1A	5	2		{BF967A9C-0DE6-11D
17	BUILTIN\Pre-Windows 2000 Co	20094	1A	5	2		{BF967ABA-0DE6-11D

FIGURE 11.75 Output of "ADSI List ACEs to Excel—Short.vbs"

NOTE If you compare what you see in ACL Editor to the output in Figure 11.75, you'll notice that the script lists five ACEs that are not visible in the user interface of the snap-in (lines 11 through 15 in the Excel spreadsheet). Those five ACEs are read permissions to various property sets applying to user objects, but because line 17 is a read permission to all properties, those first five are redundant. It is logical that the user interface doesn't show them, but it is a slight bug that those redundant ACEs are part of the default permissions.

The script is as follows:

```
Option Explicit

Dim objDSE, strDefaultDN, strDN, objADObject, i
Dim objSecDesc, objDACL, objACE, objExcel

Set objDSE = GetObject("LDAP://rootDSE")
strDefaultDN = "CN=Users," & objDSE.Get("defaultNamingContext")

strDN = InputBox("Enter the distinguished name of an object" & _
   vbCrLf & "(e.g. " & strDefaultDN & ")", , strDefaultDN)

If strDN = "" Then WScript.Quit(0)  'user clicked Cancel

Set objADObject = GetObject("LDAP://" & strDN)

Set objSecDesc = objADObject.Get("ntSecurityDescriptor")
Set objDACL = objSecDesc.DiscretionaryAcl
```

```
Set objExcel = WScript.CreateObject("Excel.Application")
objExcel.Visible = True
objExcel.Workbooks.Add
objExcel.ActiveSheet.Name = "ACEs"

objExcel.ActiveSheet.Range("A1").Activate
objExcel.ActiveCell.Value = "Trustee"
objExcel.ActiveCell.Offset(0,1).Value = "AccessMask"
objExcel.ActiveCell.Offset(0,2).Value = "AceFlags"
objExcel.ActiveCell.Offset(0,3).Value = "AceType"
objExcel.ActiveCell.Offset(0,4).Value = "Flags"
objExcel.ActiveCell.Offset(0,5).Value = "ObjectType"
objExcel.ActiveCell.Offset(0,6).Value = "InheritedObjectType"
objExcel.ActiveCell.Offset(1,0).Activate  'goto next line

i = 0
For Each objACE In objDACL
   objExcel.ActiveCell.Value = objACE.Trustee
   objExcel.ActiveCell.Offset(0,1).Value = Hex(objACE.AccessMask)
   objExcel.ActiveCell.Offset(0,2).Value = Hex(objACE.AceFlags)
   objExcel.ActiveCell.Offset(0,3).Value = Hex(objACE.AceType)
   objExcel.ActiveCell.Offset(0,4).Value = Hex(objACE.Flags)
   objExcel.ActiveCell.Offset(0,5).Value = objACE.ObjectType
   objExcel.ActiveCell.Offset(0,6).Value = _
      objACE.InheritedObjectType
   objExcel.ActiveCell.Offset(1,0).Activate  'goto next line
Next
```

The script should be self-explanatory.

List Binary GUIDs.vbs

This example shows how to list values of binary GUIDs. We have placed this sample in the middle of the access control samples because you mainly need to access binary GUIDs when listing or modifying ACLs.

GUIDs in ACEs and the `rightsGuid` attribute use the string representation of GUIDs. The binary format in turn is in use with `objectGUID`, `schemaIDGUID`, and `attributeSecurityGUID`.

Figure 11.76 shows some lines of the output of the script when it displays the `schemaIDGUID` for all classes and attributes.

The script shows `schemaIDGUID` for the `user` class to be

```
BA7A96BFE60DD011A28500AA003049E2
```

If we need to compare this to a string format GUID used in ACEs, we must first convert it. As we add curly braces and some dashes, we get

```
{BA7A96BF-E60D-D011-A285-00AA003049E2}
```

FIGURE 11.76 Some lines of output of "ADSI List Binary GUIDs.vbs"

Then we swap bytes 1, 2, 3, and 4 to be 4, 3, 2, and 1 (and also bytes 5, 6, 7, and 8) to get the final result:

```
{BF967ABA-0DE6-11D0-A285-00AA003049E2}
```

Our next sample script (List ACEs—Long.vbs) is a complete solution and in it we include lines to automate this conversion process.

NOTE   The Guid property method of the IADs interfaces returns the objectGUID for any Active Directory object. Note that even though the value is of the string data type, there are no dashes or curly braces and the bytes are in the same order as in binary GUIDs.

Figure 11.77 shows the script's contents.

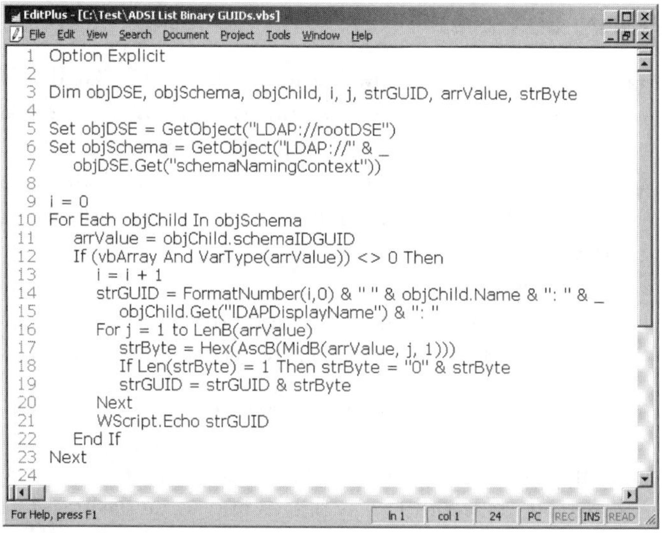

```
1   Option Explicit
2
3   Dim objDSE, objSchema, objChild, i, j, strGUID, arrValue, strByte
4
5   Set objDSE = GetObject("LDAP://rootDSE")
6   Set objSchema = GetObject("LDAP://" & _
7       objDSE.Get("schemaNamingContext"))
8
9   i = 0
10  For Each objChild In objSchema
11      arrValue = objChild.schemaIDGUID
12      If (vbArray And VarType(arrValue)) <> 0 Then
13          i = i + 1
14          strGUID = FormatNumber(i,0) & " " & objChild.Name & ": " & _
15              objChild.Get("lDAPDisplayName") & ": "
16          For j = 1 to LenB(arrValue)
17              strByte = Hex(AscB(MidB(arrValue, j, 1)))
18              If Len(strByte) = 1 Then strByte = "0" & strByte
19              strGUID = strGUID & strByte
20          Next
21          WScript.Echo strGUID
22      End If
23  Next
24
```

FIGURE 11.77 ADSI List Binary GUIDs.vbs

If an attribute has no value, `objChild.schemaIDGUID` returns a `vbEmpty` variable. The `VarType` check filters out these entries, so that we examine GUIDs only when they exist. There is actually only one object, `CN=Aggregate`, that doesn't have this attribute set.

List ACEs—Long.vbs

In two earlier examples you saw all the ACEs, but the contents were just hex numbers. In this script, we interpret the numbers and display the results in (more or less) plain English.

Unfortunately, interpreting the numbers makes the script quite long. We need to define all the bit values and bit names for the ACE fields and that alone takes 80 lines, which is about one-third of the total length of 250 lines.

We define all ACE "constants" in arrays and use `For` loops to go through them. This approach makes the script slightly more cryptic, but the alternative would have been a 30 percent longer script (320 lines).

NOTE   The array approach works only when you go through all values. If you need to use certain values, it is better to have traditional constant definitions, such as `Const ADS_RIGHTS_DS_WRITE_PROP = &H20`.

NOTE   In the constant definitions (such as `ADS_RIGHTS_DS_WRITE_PROP`) permissions are called "rights."

Figure 11.78 shows part of the script's output for the `CN=Users` container. The access mask "&HF01FF" contains 13 set bits and now you see which 13 permissions they correspond to. As we mentioned earlier, this list of 13 permissions is the same as Full Control.

It would seem that ACE flags and flags are not interpreted for ACE 1. However, because the value for both is "0," it means that they have no bits (and, consequently, no flags) set, so there is nothing to interpret. An ACE flag "0" means that the ACE was not inherited and it does not inherit. On the other hand, ACE 10 has the value "1A," which means that it is inherited and it inherits to children.

ACE type "0" we have interpreted. It is not a bitfield like the others, so the value "0" means something (it means "access allowed").

NOTE   As with the two previous examples, ACE 10 is something that you won't see in the user interface due to a slight bug in Active Directory default permissions.

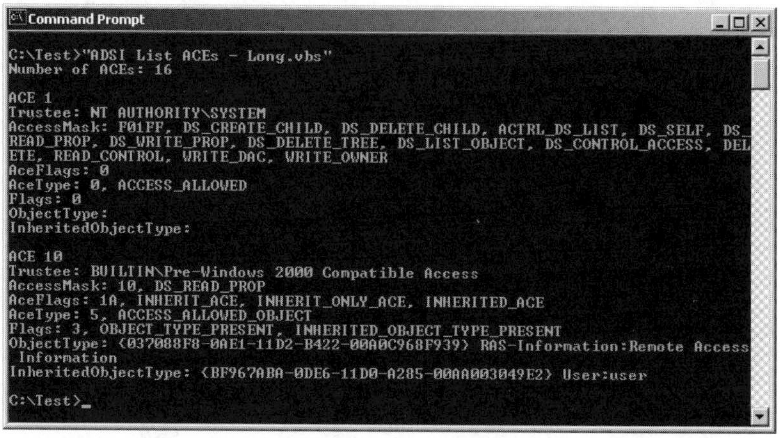

FIGURE 11.78 Part of the output of "ADSI List ACEs—Long.vbs"

The script is as follows:

```
Option Explicit

'AccessMask Bits
'Constants would be like ADS_RIGHT_DS_CREATE_CHILD
Dim arrADSRights(18,1)  '19 value pairs, name and bit in each
arrADSRights(0,0) = "DS_CREATE_CHILD"
arrADSRights(0,1) = &H1
arrADSRights(1,0) = "DS_DELETE_CHILD"
arrADSRights(1,1) = &H2
arrADSRights(2,0) = "ACTRL_DS_LIST"
arrADSRights(2,1) = &H4
arrADSRights(3,0) = "DS_SELF"
arrADSRights(3,1) = &H8
arrADSRights(4,0) = "DS_READ_PROP"
arrADSRights(4,1) = &H10
arrADSRights(5,0) = "DS_WRITE_PROP"
arrADSRights(5,1) = &H20
arrADSRights(6,0) = "DS_DELETE_TREE"
arrADSRights(6,1) = &H40
arrADSRights(7,0) = "DS_LIST_OBJECT"
arrADSRights(7,1) = &H80
arrADSRights(8,0) = "DS_CONTROL_ACCESS"
arrADSRights(8,1) = &H100
arrADSRights(9,0) = "DELETE"
arrADSRights(9,1) = &H10000
arrADSRights(10,0) = "READ_CONTROL"
arrADSRights(10,1) = &H20000
arrADSRights(11,0) = "WRITE_DAC"
arrADSRights(11,1) = &H40000
arrADSRights(12,0) = "WRITE_OWNER"
```

```
        arrADSRights(12,1) = &H80000
        arrADSRights(13,0) = "SYNCHRONIZE"
        arrADSRights(13,1) = &H100000
        arrADSRights(14,0) = "ACCESS_SYSTEM_SECURITY"
        arrADSRights(14,1) = &H1000000
        arrADSRights(15,0) = "GENERIC_ALL"
        arrADSRights(15,1) = &H10000000
        arrADSRights(16,0) = "GENERIC_EXECUTE"
        arrADSRights(16,1) = &H20000000
        arrADSRights(17,0) = "GENERIC_WRITE"
        arrADSRights(17,1) = &H40000000
        arrADSRights(18,0) = "GENERIC_READ"
        arrADSRights(18,1) = &H80000000

        'AceFlags Bits
        'Constants would be like ADS_ACEFLAG_INHERIT_ACE
        Dim arrADSACEFlags(5,1)   '6 value pairs, name and bit in each
        arrADSACEFlags(0,0) = "INHERIT_ACE"
        arrADSACEFlags(0,1) = &H2
        arrADSACEFlags(1,0) = "NO_PROPAGATE_INHERIT_ACE"
        arrADSACEFlags(1,1) = &H4
        arrADSACEFlags(2,0) = "INHERIT_ONLY_ACE"
        arrADSACEFlags(2,1) = &H8
        arrADSACEFlags(3,0) = "INHERITED_ACE"
        arrADSACEFlags(3,1) = &H10
        arrADSACEFlags(4,0) = "SUCCESSFUL_ACCESS"
        arrADSACEFlags(4,1) = &H40
        arrADSACEFlags(5,0) = "FAILED_ACCESS"
        arrADSACEFlags(5,1) = &H80

        'AceTypes
        'Constants would be like ADS_ACETYPE_ACCESS_ALLOWED
        Dim arrADSACETypes(5,1)   '6 value pairs, name and value in each
        arrADSACETypes(0,0) = "ACCESS_ALLOWED"
        arrADSACETypes(0,1) = 0
        arrADSACETypes(1,0) = "ACCESS_DENIED"
        arrADSACETypes(1,1) = &H1
        arrADSACETypes(2,0) = "SYSTEM_AUDIT"
        arrADSACETypes(2,1) = &H2
        arrADSACETypes(3,0) = "ACCESS_ALLOWED_OBJECT"
        arrADSACETypes(3,1) = &H5
        arrADSACETypes(4,0) = "ACCESS_DENIED_OBJECT"
        arrADSACETypes(4,1) = &H6
        arrADSACETypes(5,0) = "SYSTEM_AUDIT_OBJECT"
        arrADSACETypes(5,1) = &H7

        'Flags Bits
        'Constants would be like ADS_FLAG_OBJECT_TYPE_PRESENT
        Dim arrADSFlags(1,1)   '2 value pairs, name and bit in each
        arrADSFlags(0,0) = "OBJECT_TYPE_PRESENT"
        arrADSFlags(0,1) = &H1
        arrADSFlags(1,0) = "INHERITED_OBJECT_TYPE_PRESENT"
        arrADSFlags(1,1) = &H2
```

```
Dim objDSE, strDefaultDN, strDN, objADObject, i
Dim objSecDesc, objDACL, objACE

'===The Main Program===

Set objDSE = GetObject("LDAP://rootDSE")
strDefaultDN = "CN=Users," & objDSE.Get("defaultNamingContext")

strDN = InputBox("Enter the distinguished name of an object" & _
    vbCrLf & "(e.g. " & strDefaultDN & ")", , strDefaultDN)

If strDN = "" Then WScript.Quit(0)  'user clicked Cancel

Set objADObject = GetObject("LDAP://" & strDN)

Set objSecDesc = objADObject.Get("ntSecurityDescriptor")
Set objDACL = objSecDesc.DiscretionaryAcl

WScript.Echo "Number of ACEs: " & objDACL.AceCount

i = 0
For Each objACE In objDACL
    i = i + 1
    WScript.Echo ""
    WScript.Echo "ACE " & i
    WScript.Echo "Trustee: " & objACE.Trustee
    WScript.Echo GetStringBits("AccessMask", _
        objACE.AccessMask, arrADSRights)
    WScript.Echo GetStringBits("AceFlags", _
        objACE.AceFlags, arrADSACEFlags)
    WScript.Echo GetStringAceType(objACE.AceType)
    WScript.Echo GetStringBits("Flags", _
        objACE.Flags, arrADSFlags)
    WScript.Echo GetObjectType(objACE.ObjectType)
    WScript.Echo GetInheritedObjectType(objACE.InheritedObjectType)
Next

'===End of the Main Program===
'=============================

Function GetStringBits(strName, intBitfield, arrBits)
    Dim strOut, i

    strOut = strName & ": " & Hex(intBitfield)

    For i = LBound(arrBits) To UBound(arrBits)
        If intBitfield And arrBits(i,1) Then
            strOut = strOut & ", " & arrBits(i,0)
        End If
    Next

    GetStringBits = strOut
End Function
```

```
'==============================

Function GetStringAceType(intACEType)
   Dim strOut, i

   strOut = "unknown ACE type"
   For i = LBound(arrADSACETypes) To UBound(arrADSACETypes)
      If intACEType = arrADSACETypes(i,1) Then
         strOut = arrADSACETypes(i,0)
      End If
   Next

   GetStringAceType = "AceType: " & Hex(intACEType) & ", " & _
      strOut
End Function

'==============================

Function GetObjectType(strGUID)
   GetObjectType = "ObjectType: " & _
      strGUID & " " & MapGUIDToMatchingName(strGUID)
End Function

'==============================

Function GetInheritedObjectType(strGUID)
   GetInheritedObjectType = "InheritedObjectType: " & _
      strGUID & " " & MapGUIDToMatchingName(strGUID)
End Function

'==============================

Function MapGUIDToMatchingName(strGUIDAsString)
   Dim strOut, objExtRights, objChild, objSchema

   If strGUIDAsString = "" Then Exit Function

   strOut = ""

   Set objExtRights = GetObject("LDAP://CN=Extended-Rights," & _
      objDSE.Get("configurationNamingContext"))

   For Each objChild In objExtRights
      'Actually all should be of the same class
      If objChild.Class = "controlAccessRight" Then
         If UCase("{" & objChild.Get("rightsGuid") & "}") = _
            UCase(strGUIDAsString) Then
            strOut = objChild.Get("cn") & ":" & _
               objChild.Get("displayName")
            Exit For
         End If
      End If
   Next
```

```
   If strOut = "" Then  'Didn't find a match in extended rights
      Set objSchema = GetObject("LDAP://" & _
         objDSE.Get("schemaNamingContext"))

      For Each objChild In objSchema
         If objChild.Class = "classSchema" Or _
            objChild.Class = "attributeSchema" Then
            If  UCase(GetSchemaIDGUID(objChild)) = _
               UCase(strGUIDAsString) Then
               strOut = objChild.Get("cn") & ":" & _
                  objChild.Get("lDAPDisplayName")
               Exit For
            End If
         End If
      Next
   End If


   MapGUIDToMatchingName = strOut
End Function


'===============================


Function GetSchemaIDGUID(objSchemaObj)
   Dim arrValue, i, strByte, strGUID

   arrValue = objSchemaObj.Get("schemaIDGUID")
   strGUID = ""
   For i = 1 to LenB(arrValue)
      strByte = Hex(AscB(MidB(arrValue, i, 1)))
      If Len(strByte) = 1 Then strByte = "0" & strByte
      strGUID = strGUID & strByte
   Next
   GetSchemaIDGUID = GuidBinFormatToStrFormat(strGUID)
End Function


'===============================


Function GUIDBinFormatToStrFormat(strGUIDBin)
   Dim i, strDest
   Dim arrBytes(16)              'We will use elements 1 to 16 but not 0

   For i = 1 To 16    'A GUID has 16 bytes
      arrBytes(i) = Mid(strGUIDBin, 2 * i - 1, 2)
   Next

   strDest = "{"
   For i = 1 To 4 : strDest = strDest & arrBytes(5 - i) : Next
   strDest = strDest & "-"
   For i = 1 To 2 : strDest = strDest & arrBytes(7 - i) : Next
   strDest = strDest & "-"
   For i = 1 To 2 : strDest = strDest & arrBytes(9 - i) : Next
```

```
        strDest = strDest & "-"
        For i = 1 To 2 : strDest = strDest & arrBytes(8 + i) : Next
        strDest = strDest & "-"
        For i = 1 To 6 : strDest = strDest & arrBytes(10 + i) : Next
        strDest = strDest & "}"

        GuidBinFormatToStrFormat = strDest
End Function
```

As with previous examples, if you like to see only some of the ACEs, you can put various `If` statements inside the loop to filter out unwanted ACEs.

The `GetStringBits` function can handle all ACE fields that are bitfields. ACE type is not a bitfield, so it needs a separate function.

In `MapGUIDToMatchingName` we find the extended right name (including property sets) that corresponds to the GUID in the ACE. If there is no match, we next check all the `classSchema` and `attributeSchema` objects and compare the GUID to their `schemaIDGUID` attribute.

The latter comparison requires converting the binary GUID to a string format. In `GetSchemaIDGUID` we convert the binary attribute to a string value and then in `GUIDBinFormatToStrFormat` we finally convert it to a string format.

NOTE ACEs contain both "ACE flags" (containing mainly inheritance information) and "flags" (indicating whether ObjectType or InheritedObjectType is present). Don't get confused.

USING REGULAR EXPRESSIONS TO CONVERT THE GUID

VBScript includes a feature called *regular expressions* (regexp), which should be familiar to anyone who has used UNIX sed (streaming editor). Regular expressions enable you to perform complex search/replace functions and other string manipulation. Therefore, we could use them to convert the GUID format.

The following lines show `GUIDBinFormatToStrFormat` implemented using regular expressions:

```
Function GUIDBinFormatToStrFormat(strGUIDBin)
    Dim objRegExp, strRearranged

    Set objRegExp = New RegExp

    objRegExp.Pattern = _
        "(.{2})(.{2})(.{2})(.{2})(.{2})(.{2})(.{2})(.{2})(.{16})"
    strRearranged = objRegExp.Replace(strGUIDBin, _
        "$4$3$2$1$6$5$8$7$9")
```

```
objRegExp.Pattern = "(.{8})(.{4})(.{4})(.{4})(.{12})"
GUIDBinFormatToStrFormat = objRegExp.Replace(strRearranged, _
    "{$1-$2-$3-$4-$5}")
End Function
```

Each (.{2}) means "take two characters and remember them for later use." This means that we first chop the 32 hex characters to 2+2+2+2+2+2+2+2+9 characters and then rearrange the chops again as 4-3-2-1-6-5-8-7-9. After rearranging, we chop the result again so that we can add curly braces and dashes. If we tried both steps together, we would get ten chops, but VBScript regular expressions support only nine chops ($1–$9).

This latter implementation uses fewer script lines, but it is 30 percent slower, so we opted to use a traditional approach in our long script. However, we wanted to introduce regular expressions to you.

Add ACEs.vbs

This script demonstrates how to add new ACEs to Active Directory objects. The script shows the order of events and the appropriate lines that will get the job done. However, we don't explain which ACE flags and other settings you should use in various scenarios. There are two reasons for this.

- We already explained the ACE contents thoroughly in Chapter 4.
- There is an easy way to get the right ACE contents for any scenario you could imagine, as explained in the next subsection.

After presenting the sample script, we have two subsections at the end of this section about how to use trustees and how to use the generic permissions.

KNOWING WHAT TO ADD

To find out which inheritance and other flags and settings you should apply to your various ACEs you can take the following steps:

1. Create a test target object and a test user, who will become the trustee in the ACE.
2. Using ACL Editor in the Users and Computers snap-in (or perhaps the Delegation of Control wizard), add any necessary ACEs to your test trustee and for your test target object.
3. List the ACEs using the "List ACEs—Long.vbs" script presented earlier in this section and redirect the output to a text file with the greater-than sign (>).
4. Open the text file in Notepad and remove ACEs other than to your test trustee.

Now you have an exact documentation of what settings you need to put in your ADSI script. For example, you might notice that you need to apply `INHERIT_ACE` and `NO_PROPAGATE_INHERIT_ACE` together if you want to apply the ACE to children in this container only.

NOTE
The "List ACEs—Long.vbs" script lists both the hex values and their interpretations, such as the value "20094" would correspond to four different permissions (i.e., access mask bits). If you are a little lazy, you can just use the number "20094" without even knowing which permissions it contains. A better way, however, is to use the actual constants, such as `ACTRL_DS_LIST` + `DS_READ_PROP` + `DS_LIST_OBJECT` + `READ_CONTROL`.

THE ADD ACES SAMPLE SCRIPT

We have about 40 lines of constant definitions in the script, because we want to define all access mask, ACE flag, ACE type, and flag constants, whether we use them or not (because you may want to use any of them in your scripts).

For your convenience, we have also added the `schemaIDGUIDs` for the `user`, `group`, `computer`, `contact`, `organizationalUnit`, and `printQueue` classes.

We create an OU ACEDemo for which the ACEs will be added. As a trustee, we use RedBaron (`Red.Baron@sanao.com`), which must be created manually beforehand. The reason that we create the OU automatically, but not the user, is that we want to delete the OU between each run of the script and this way clean the table for the next test.

We add the following three ACEs:

- ACE 1: Write all properties of this OU.
- ACE 2: Full Control to user objects in the subtree. With this ACE, we define the user class in the `InheritedObjectType`, because `user` is where the permissions will be inherited.
- ACE 3: Create/delete user objects in the subtree. With this ACE, we define the `user` class in the `ObjectType`, because `user` is the target of the permission.

The last two ACEs are the same ones that the Delegation of Control wizard adds if you select the "Create, delete and manage user accounts" option.

Both ACEs 2 and 3 use the ACE flag "inherit ACE." ACE 2 also uses "inherit only," because we don't want Full Control to apply to the OU itself.

Here is the script:

```
Option Explicit

'AccessMask
Const ADS_RIGHT_DS_CREATE_CHILD          = &H1
Const ADS_RIGHT_DS_DELETE_CHILD          = &H2
Const ADS_RIGHT_ACTRL_DS_LIST            = &H4
Const ADS_RIGHT_DS_SELF                  = &H8
Const ADS_RIGHT_DS_READ_PROP             = &H10
Const ADS_RIGHT_DS_WRITE_PROP            = &H20
Const ADS_RIGHT_DS_DELETE_TREE           = &H40
Const ADS_RIGHT_DS_LIST_OBJECT           = &H80
Const ADS_RIGHT_DS_CONTROL_ACCESS        = &H100
Const ADS_RIGHT_DELETE                   = &H10000
Const ADS_RIGHT_READ_CONTROL             = &H20000
Const ADS_RIGHT_WRITE_DAC                = &H40000
Const ADS_RIGHT_WRITE_OWNER              = &H80000
Const ADS_RIGHT_SYNCHRONIZE              = &H100000
Const ADS_RIGHT_ACCESS_SYSTEM_SECURITY   = &H1000000
Const ADS_RIGHT_GENERIC_ALL              = &H10000000
Const ADS_RIGHT_GENERIC_EXECUTE          = &H20000000
Const ADS_RIGHT_GENERIC_WRITE            = &H40000000
Const ADS_RIGHT_GENERIC_READ             = &H80000000

Const ADS_RIGHT_FULL_CONTROL             = &HF01FF

'ACE flags
Const ADS_ACEFLAG_INHERIT_ACE               = &H2
Const ADS_ACEFLAG_NO_PROPAGATE_INHERIT_ACE  = &H4
Const ADS_ACEFLAG_INHERIT_ONLY_ACE          = &H8
Const ADS_ACEFLAG_INHERITED_ACE             = &H10
Const ADS_ACEFLAG_SUCCESSFUL_ACCESS         = &H40
Const ADS_ACEFLAG_FAILED_ACCESS             = &H80

'ACE types
Const ADS_ACETYPE_ACCESS_ALLOWED            = 0
Const ADS_ACETYPE_ACCESS_DENIED             = &H1
Const ADS_ACETYPE_SYSTEM_AUDIT              = &H2
Const ADS_ACETYPE_ACCESS_ALLOWED_OBJECT     = &H5
Const ADS_ACETYPE_ACCESS_DENIED_OBJECT      = &H6
Const ADS_ACETYPE_SYSTEM_AUDIT_OBJECT       = &H7

'Flags
Const ADS_FLAG_OBJECT_TYPE_PRESENT             = &H1
Const ADS_FLAG_INHERITED_OBJECT_TYPE_PRESENT   = &H2

'Some schemaIDGUIDs
Const SCHEMAIDGUID_USER     = "{BF967ABA-0DE6-11D0-A285-00AA003049E2}"
Const SCHEMAIDGUID_GROUP    = "{BF967A9C-0DE6-11D0-A285-00AA003049E2}"
Const SCHEMAIDGUID_COMPUTER = "{BF967A86-0DE6-11D0-A285-00AA003049E2}"
Const SCHEMAIDGUID_CONTACT  = "{5CB41ED0-0E4C-11D0-A286-00AA003049E2}"
Const SCHEMAIDGUID_OU       = "{BF967AA5-0DE6-11D0-A285-00AA003049E2}"
Const SCHEMAIDGUID_PRINTER  = "{BF967AA8-0DE6-11D0-A285-00AA003049E2}"
```

```
Dim objDSE, objDom, objOU, objSecDesc, objDACL
Dim objACE1, objACE2, objACE3


'=====================

'Create the OU
'-------------
Set objDSE = GetObject("LDAP://rootDSE")
Set objDom = GetObject("LDAP://" & objDSE.Get("defaultNamingContext"))
Set objOU = objDom.Create("organizationalUnit", "OU=ACEDemo")
objOU.SetInfo

'Create the first ACE - write all properties of the OU
'-----------------------------------------------------
Set objACE1 = CreateObject("AccessControlEntry")
objACE1.Trustee      = "Red.Baron@sanao.com"
objACE1.AccessMask   = ADS_RIGHT_DS_WRITE_PROP
objACE1.AceFlags     = 0  'no inheritance from up or to below
objACE1.AceType      = ADS_ACETYPE_ACCESS_ALLOWED
objACE1.Flags        = 0  'no object types present
'objACE1.ObjectType = not used
'objACE1.InheritedObjectType = not used


'Create the second ACE - Full Control to user objects in the subtree
'-------------------------------------------------------------------
Set objACE2 = CreateObject("AccessControlEntry")
objACE2.Trustee      = "Red.Baron@sanao.com"
objACE2.AccessMask   = ADS_RIGHT_FULL_CONTROL   'all 13 bits
objACE2.AceFlags     = ADS_ACEFLAG_INHERIT_ACE + _
                       ADS_ACEFLAG_INHERIT_ONLY_ACE
objACE2.AceType      = ADS_ACETYPE_ACCESS_ALLOWED_OBJECT
objACE2.Flags        = ADS_FLAG_INHERITED_OBJECT_TYPE_PRESENT
'objACE2.ObjectType = not used
objACE2.InheritedObjectType = SCHEMAIDGUID_USER


'Create the third ACE - Create/Delete user objects in the subtree
'----------------------------------------------------------------
Set objACE3 = CreateObject("AccessControlEntry")
objACE3.Trustee      = "Red.Baron@sanao.com"
objACE3.AccessMask = ADS_RIGHT_DS_CREATE_CHILD + _
                     ADS_RIGHT_DS_DELETE_CHILD
objACE3.AceFlags     = ADS_ACEFLAG_INHERIT_ACE
objACE3.AceType      = ADS_ACETYPE_ACCESS_ALLOWED_OBJECT
objACE3.Flags        = ADS_FLAG_OBJECT_TYPE_PRESENT
objACE3.ObjectType = SCHEMAIDGUID_USER
'objACE3.InheritedObjectType = not used


'Add the ACEs
'------------
Set objSecDesc = objOU.Get("ntSecurityDescriptor")
Set objDACL = objSecDesc.DiscretionaryAcl
```

```
Call objDACL.AddAce(objACE1)
Call objDACL.AddAce(objACE2)
Call objDACL.AddAce(objACE3)

objSecDesc.DiscretionaryAcl = objDACL
Call objOU.Put("ntSecurityDescriptor", objSecDesc)
objOU.SetInfo

WScript.Echo "Number of ACEs after: " & objDACL.AceCount
```

We could have used just one objACE variable if we had arranged the lines a little differently. However, we wanted to get the "Add the ACEs" lines together, so that you could see in a compact way how we first retrieve the current discretionary ACL from nTSecurityDescriptor, add the ACEs to the list, and then put the new list back.

The order of the ACEs in an ACL is important, because the same ACEs may have a different effect depending on the order. We explain this in the next subsection.

ORDER OF ACEs

When a securable object (such as an Active Directory object or a file) is opened, Windows 2000 must evaluate the ACEs in the object's DACL to determine whether or not to allow access. Windows 2000 starts from the beginning of the list and goes through the list of ACEs as long as needed to find enough permissions either to grant or deny the access. Also, if the list runs out before enough permissions are found, Windows 2000 will deny the access.

If a certain access-denied ACE applies to Jack, he will be denied access if the ACE is at the beginning of the list. On the other hand, if the ACE is at the end of the list, Jack might be allowed access (depending on if there are appropriate access-allowed ACEs for him).

Because the effect of ACEs in a DACL depends on the order, Microsoft has defined a preferred order for the ACEs. All inherited ACEs should be after noninherited ACEs, and within these categories all access-allowed ACEs should be after access-denied ACEs. The following hierarchical list illustrates the preferred order:

```
Noninherited ACEs
    Access-denied ACEs
        ACEs with ACE type ADS_ACETYPE_ACCESS_DENIED
        ACEs with ACE type ADS_ACETYPE_ACCESS_DENIED_OBJECT
    Access-allowed ACEs
        ACEs with ACE type ADS_ACETYPE_ACCESS_ALLOWED
        ACEs with ACE type ADS_ACETYPE_ACCESS_ALLOWED_OBJECT
Inherited ACEs
    Access-denied ACEs
        ACEs with ACE type ADS_ACETYPE_ACCESS_DENIED
        ACEs with ACE type ADS_ACETYPE_ACCESS_DENIED_OBJECT
```

```
Access-allowed ACEs
    ACEs with ACE type ADS_ACETYPE_ACCESS_ALLOWED
    ACEs with ACE type ADS_ACETYPE_ACCESS_ALLOWED_OBJECT
```

Remember from Chapter 4 that the ACE types that end with "_OBJECT" indicate that either ObjectType or InheritedObjectType is not empty, so the corresponding ACE is for some particular object class, property, property set, or extended right.

If the order of the access-denied ACEs is not correct when you open the ACL Editor, you will see the error message shown in Figure 11.79.

The `AddAce` method doesn't allow you to specify where in the list the new ACE will go. The three levels of hierarchies in the preceding list will be handled as follows:

- *Noninherited versus inherited.* You shouldn't add any inherited ACEs because they will appear automatically where and when appropriate. As you add noninherited ACEs with the method, it will automatically place them after any existing noninherited ACEs and before any inherited ACEs. Consequently, the outcome is just right.

- *Access denied versus access allowed.* If you add an access-denied ACE, the `AddAce` method doesn't put the ACE at the beginning of the list as it should. If you need to add such ACEs, you can use the `ReorderDacl` subprogram listed in Microsoft Knowledge Base article Q279682. That subprogram divides the ACEs in an ACL into five pools and rebuilds the ACL in the correct order. Without reordering, you will get the warning shown in Figure 11.79.

- *Apply to the object versus apply to the "subobject."* The `AddAce` method doesn't perform the correct ordering in this case either. However, you don't get any error message when opening the ACL Editor. Also, the wrong order is not likely to hurt you—even some Active Directory default permissions use a different ACE order than this third level of the hierarchy indicates.

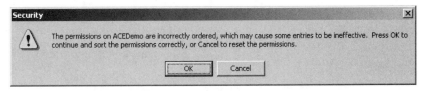

FIGURE 11.79 If you add access-denied ACEs with the AddAce method, you will get the error shown in this figure once you go to the security page of the object. If you click OK on the error message and then click OK on the security page, the ACL Editor will sort the ACEs in the correct order. Note that the Apply button is grayed out in that case, which might lead you to think that there is nothing to be saved if you click OK. However, the reordering will take place when you click OK.

DEFINING TRUSTEES

You already know that trustees can be users, security groups, computers, or well-known security principals. In Table 11.4 we list the name formats that you can use in the `Trustee` property of the `IADsAccessControlEntry` interface. Note that you cannot use the common name, such as `CN=Red Baron`, or the distinguished name, such as `CN=Red Baron, CN=Users, DC=sanao, DC=com`.

USING THE GENERIC PERMISSIONS

We listed 19 access mask bits as constants in the script. Active Directory uses the first 13 of them; therefore, we discussed those 13 in Chapter 4. We called those 13 permissions "special permissions," and you probably remember that there were also standard permissions, each of which mapped to a certain set of special permissions.

The generic permissions discussed here are like standard permissions, because they also map to a set of certain special permissions. The only difference is that the generic permissions are used in the programming interface and the

TABLE 11.4 Name Formats to Use in the `Trustee` Property

Name Format	Examples
SAM name (pre–Windows 2000 name)*	RedBaron
	Authenticated Users
	Users
SAM name with domain** NetBIOS name	SANAO\RedBaron
	NT AUTHORITY\Authenticated Users
	BUILTIN\Users
User principal name	red.baron@sanao.com
SID (string representation)	S-1-5-21-1718597718-1078345429-1030254238-1143 (same as RedBaron)
	S-1-5-11 (same as Authenticated Users)
	S-1-5-32-545 (same as Users)

*Computers have a dollar sign ($) as the last character in the SAM name. If you have a computer DC1, you must use the name DC1$ in the `Trustee` property.
**Whether the "domain" name is SANAO, NT AUTHORITY, or BUILTIN depends on in which category the corresponding SID belongs. See the discussion of SIDs in Chapter 4.

standard permissions are used in the user interface. And as you would guess, the list of generic permissions is not the same as the list of standard permissions.

Even though Active Directory doesn't use the remaining 6 permissions (of the 19) in ACEs, the 6 include the 4 generic permissions, which you can use when setting permissions programmatically.

NOTE   Don't use the remaining two permissions (i.e., `ADS_RIGHT_SYNCHRONIZE` and `ADS_RIGHT_ACCESS_SYSTEM_SECURITY`).

Each generic permission maps to some of those first 13 permissions. If you give someone the `ADS_RIGHT_GENERIC_ALL` permission, he will actually get all the 13 permissions, meaning that he just got Full Control. Table 11.5 lists the generic permission mappings.

NOTE   When you read ACEs, you never see generic permissions. Even if you wrote them, they were converted to corresponding permissions from the set of the first 13.

As you can see in Table 11.5, the generic write and read are not quite the same as the standard permissions Write and Read in the graphical user interface

TABLE 11.5 Generic Permission Mappings to Special Permissions

Generic Right	Maps to Access Mask	Access Mask Contains	Maps to the User Interface*
`ADS_RIGHT_GENERIC_ALL`	F01FF (13 are set)	All 13	Full Control
`ADS_RIGHT_GENERIC_EXECUTE`	20004 (2 are set)	`ACTRL_DS_LIST`, `READ_CONTROL`	List Contents, Read Permissions
`DS_RIGHT_GENERIC_WRITE`	20028 (3 are set)	`DS_SELF`, `DS_WRITE_PROP`, `READ_CONTROL`	Write, Read Permissions
`ADS_RIGHT_GENERIC_READ`	20094 (4 are set)	`ACTRL_DS_LIST`, `DS_READ_PROP`, `DS_LIST_OBJECT`, `READ_CONTROL`	Read, List Object

*We have both standard permissions and special permissions in this column. For example, Write is a standard permission but Read Permissions is a special permission.

(i.e., ACL Editor). Both these generic permissions map to one more special permission than their standard permission counterparts.

We explained in Chapter 4 that in a prerelease version of Windows 2000 the standard permission Read corresponded to four special permissions, but in the final release List Object was dropped out, so Read now corresponds to three special permissions. As you see in Table 11.5, the generic read permission is equal to standard Read + special List Object. Consequently, the generic read permission is the same as the prerelease definition of the standard permission Read.

Now that we have added ACEs to an Active Directory object, we will show the same process for a folder on disk.

Add ACEs to a Folder.vbs

Adding ACEs to a folder is quite similar to adding ACEs to an Active Directory object. There are, however, the following differences.

- You read and write security descriptors with the ADsSecurity component, which is part of the ADSI Resource Kit. You would need to register this component as described in the example "List the Operations Masters with ADsFSMO.vbs."

- The meanings of access mask bits, as well as the other flags in the ACEs, are somewhat different. Also, if some meaning is the same, it may have a different constant name, because these constants are defined in two different header files (WinNT.h versus IADs.h).

The following sample script creates a folder and adds one ACE for it. The ACE grants Modify permissions, which apply to the whole subtree. The script wouldn't be that long if we hadn't added all the constant definitions for the ACE contents.

```
Option Explicit

'AccessMask
Const FILE_READ_DATA            = &H1     'file & pipe
Const FILE_LIST_DIRECTORY       = &H1     'folder
Const FILE_WRITE_DATA           = &H2     'file & pipe
Const FILE_ADD_FILE             = &H2     'folder
Const FILE_APPEND_DATA          = &H4     'file
Const FILE_ADD_SUBDIRECTORY     = &H4     'folder
Const FILE_CREATE_PIPE_INSTANCE = &H4     'named pipe
Const FILE_READ_EA              = &H8     'file & folder
Const FILE_WRITE_EA             = &H10    'file & folder
Const FILE_EXECUTE              = &H20    'file
Const FILE_TRAVERSE             = &H20    'folder
Const FILE_DELETE_CHILD         = &H40    'folder
Const FILE_READ_ATTRIBUTES      = &H80    'all
Const FILE_WRITE_ATTRIBUTES     = &H100   'all
```

```
Const DELETE                        = &H10000
Const READ_CONTROL                  = &H20000
Const WRITE_DAC                     = &H40000
Const WRITE_OWNER                   = &H80000
Const SYNCHRONIZE                   = &H100000
Const ACCESS_SYSTEM_SECURITY        = &H1000000
Const GENERIC_ALL                   = &H10000000
Const GENERIC_EXECUTE               = &H20000000
Const GENERIC_WRITE                 = &H40000000
Const GENERIC_READ                  = &H80000000

Const FULL_CONTROL = &H1F01FF   '14 permissions
Const MODIFY = &H1301BF         '11 permissions

'ACE flags
Const OBJECT_INHERIT_ACE            = &H1
Const CONTAINER_INHERIT_ACE         = &H2
Const NO_PROPAGATE_INHERIT_ACE      = &H4
Const INHERIT_ONLY_ACE              = &H8
Const INHERITED_ACE                 = &H10
Const SUCCESSFUL_ACCESS_ACE_FLAG    = &H40
Const FAILED_ACCESS_ACE_FLAG        = &H80

'ACE types
Const ACCESS_ALLOWED_ACE_TYPE           = &H0
Const ACCESS_DENIED_ACE_TYPE            = &H1
Const SYSTEM_AUDIT_ACE_TYPE             = &H2
Const SYSTEM_ALARM_ACE_TYPE             = &H3
Const ACCESS_ALLOWED_COMPOUND_ACE_TYPE  = &H4
Const ACCESS_ALLOWED_OBJECT_ACE_TYPE    = &H5
Const ACCESS_DENIED_OBJECT_ACE_TYPE     = &H6
Const SYSTEM_AUDIT_OBJECT_ACE_TYPE      = &H7
Const SYSTEM_ALARM_OBJECT_ACE_TYPE      = &H8

'Flags
Const ADS_OBJECT_TYPE_PRESENT           = &H1
Const ADS_INHERITED_OBJECT_TYPE_PRESENT = &H2

Dim objFS, objSecDesc, objDACL, objACE, objADsSec

'Create the Folder
'--------------------
Set objFS = CreateObject("Scripting.FileSystemObject")
Call objFS.CreateFolder("D:\ACEDemo")

'Create the ACE - modify permission for a the subtree
'-----------------------------------------------------
Set objACE = CreateObject("AccessControlEntry")
objACE.Trustee      = "Red.Baron@sanao.com"
objACE.AccessMask   = MODIFY
objACE.AceFlags     = OBJECT_INHERIT_ACE + _
                      CONTAINER_INHERIT_ACE
objACE.AceType      = ACCESS_ALLOWED_ACE_TYPE
```

```
'Add the ACE
'---------------
Set objADsSec = CreateObject("ADsSecurity")

Set objSecDesc = objADsSec.GetSecurityDescriptor("FILE://D:\ACEDemo")
Set objDACL = objSecDesc.DiscretionaryAcl

Call objDACL.AddAce(objACE)
objSecDesc.DiscretionaryAcl = objDACL
Call objADsSec.SetSecurityDescriptor(objSecDesc)
```

The AddAce method of the ADsSecurity component doesn't order the access-denied ACEs to exist before any access-allowed ACEs. Consequently, if you check the permissions with the ACL Editor after having added access-denied ACEs, you will get the ACE ordering error message that we discussed in the "Order of ACEs" section (see Figure 11.79). If you need to add such ACEs, you can use the ReorderDacl subprogram listed in Microsoft Knowledge Base article Q279682.

OU, GROUP, AND COMPUTER MANAGEMENT

In this section, we show how to manage OUs, groups, and computer objects. With OUs, we use just a few line clips instead of complete, independent scripts. With groups, we show two complete scripts and one clip, and with computers, we show a full, working script. We present the following independent scripts in this section:

- CH11-39 ADSI Create a Group.vbs
- CH11-40 ADSI Add Users of One OU to a Group.vbs
- CH11-41 ADSI Create a Computer Object.vbs

We start with managing OUs.

OU Management

In this section, we'll cover the following OU management tasks:

- Creating an OU
- Deleting an OU
- Moving users of one OU to another
- Deleting objects of one OU

We've already shown how to list users of one OU in the "User Management" section.

CREATING AN OU

You create an OU just like any other object by using the `Create` method of `IADs-Container`. The following lines create an OU under a domain root:

```
Set objContainer = GetObject("LDAP://DC=sanao,DC=com")
Set objOU = objContainer.Create("organizationalUnit", "OU=Sales")
objOU.SetInfo
```

As usual, you need to call `SetInfo` to save the new object to Active Directory.

DELETING AN OU

Before you can delete an OU (or any other container) that object must be empty of any child objects. You use the `Delete` method of `IADsContainer`. The following lines delete an OU under a domain root:

```
Set objContainer = GetObject("LDAP://DC=sanao,DC=com")
Call objContainer.Delete("organizationalUnit", "OU=Sales")
```

Note that this time you don't need to call `SetInfo`.

MOVING USERS OF ONE OU TO ANOTHER

The third `IADsContainer` method that you might use is `MoveHere`. The following lines show how you can move all users (and computers) of one container to another:

```
Set objSourceContainer = GetObject("LDAP://OU=RD,DC=sanao,DC=com")
Set objTargetContainer = GetObject("LDAP://OU=Sales,DC=sanao,DC=com")

objSourceContainer.Filter = Array("user")
For Each objUser in objSourceContainer
    Call objTargetContainer.MoveHere(objUser.ADsPath, objUser.Name)
Next
```

NOTE As we mentioned earlier, the `user` filter also includes `computer` class objects, because `computer` is a subclass of user.

DELETING OBJECTS OF ONE OU

If you want to delete all objects in one container, you can use the following lines:

```
Set objContainer = GetObject("LDAP://OU=Sales,DC=sanao,DC=com")
For Each objADObject in objContainer
    Call objContainer.Delete(objADObject.Class, objADObject.Name)
Next
```

Needless to say, you should be careful with a script like this.

Group Management

Next, we'll cover the following group management tasks:

* Creating a group
* Deleting a group
* Adding users of one OU to a group

In addition, in Chapter 10 we showed how to list members of a group or groups of a user.

CREATE A GROUP.VBS

When you create a group, you must specify sAMAccountName, just as when you create a user. You may also define the groupType attribute, which defines both group scope (global, universal, or local) and type (security or distribution).

The lines shown in Figure 11.80 create a group.

If you don't specify groupType, the default is scope "global" and type "security," which is actually what we just specified in the example. However, we wanted to include setting the groupType to show you how to do it.

There is no flag for distribution groups. If you want a distribution group, you just don't include the "security enabled" flag, but you do include some scope flag so that the default doesn't kick in.

```
EditPlus - [C:\Test\ADSI Create a Group.vbs]
 File  Edit  View  Search  Document  Project  Tools  Window  Help

 1   Option Explicit
 2
 3   Dim objContainer, objGroup
 4
 5   Const ADS_GROUP_TYPE_GLOBAL_GROUP        = &H2
 6   Const ADS_GROUP_TYPE_DOMAIN_LOCAL_GROUP  = &H4
 7   Const ADS_GROUP_TYPE_LOCAL_GROUP         = &H4
 8   Const ADS_GROUP_TYPE_UNIVERSAL_GROUP     = &H8
 9   Const ADS_GROUP_TYPE_SECURITY_ENABLED    = &H80000000
10
11   Set objContainer = GetObject("LDAP://OU=Sales,DC=sanao,DC=com")
12   Set objGroup = objContainer.Create("group", "CN=Salesmen")
13   Call objGroup.Put("sAMAccountName", "Salesmen")
14   Call objGroup.Put("groupType", ADS_GROUP_TYPE_GLOBAL_GROUP + _
15                                 ADS_GROUP_TYPE_SECURITY_ENABLED)
16   objGroup.SetInfo
17

For Help, press F1                        ln 1    col 1    17    PC  REC  INS  READ
```

FIGURE 11.80 ADSI Create a Group.vbs

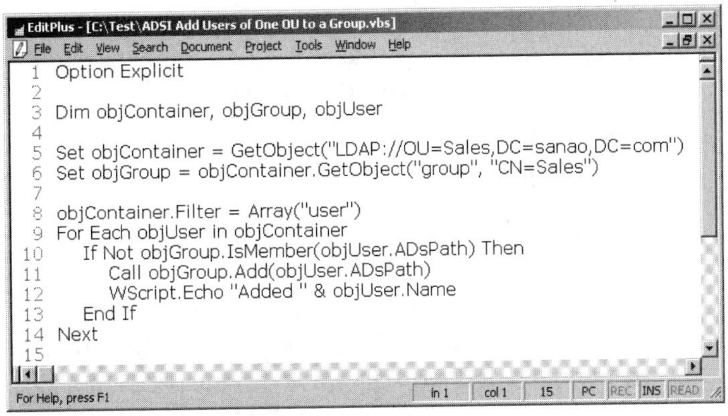

FIGURE 11.81 ADSI Add Users of One OU to a Group.vbs

DELETING A GROUP

You delete a group just like you would delete any other object type. The following lines delete a group:

```
Set objContainer = GetObject("LDAP://OU=Sales,DC=sanao,DC=com")
Call objContainer.Delete("group", "CN=Salesmen")
```

You don't need to remove any members from a group before you delete it.

ADD USERS OF ONE OU TO A GROUP.VBS

As you know, you cannot give permissions to an OU. Therefore, you may want to have a security group that has all the users of an OU as members. The little script in Figure 11.81 browses through the users of OU=Sales and adds them to the group CN=Sales, unless they are already members.

If you need to remove group members, the Remove method works like the Add method. There is one argument, which is the ADSI path.

Create a Computer Object.vbs

You saw earlier that you could create an OU with just two lines of code (Create and SetInfo). Creating a computer object requires almost 100 lines, because you need to specify a number of settings that ADSI doesn't specify for you.

- As with users and groups, you need to specify the SAM name. It should be the same as the common name, but with a dollar sign ($) appended as the last character.

- You need to specify that the account type of the object is UF_WORKSTATION_ TRUST_ACCOUNT (workstation or member server account) instead of UF_ NORMAL_ACCOUNT (user account).

- You must enable the account.

- You must not require a password.

- You could set the initial password to "computername$". However, the script works also with an empty password.

- You must give the following four permissions for the computer object to the user or group who will join the computer to a domain: Write Account Restrictions, Validated write to service principal name, Validated write to DNS host name, and Reset Password.

NOTE   The previous list contains the settings that the Users and Computers snap-in applies when you create a computer object. We haven't tested whether or not you could skip some of them, but obviously the safest path is to create similar settings to the snap-in's.

The following is the script that does all the listed things and creates a computer called PC17:

```
Option Explicit

Const UF_ACCOUNTDISABLE                   = &H0002
Const UF_PASSWD_NOTREQD                   = &H0020
Const UF_WORKSTATION_TRUST_ACCOUNT        = &H1000 'ws or ms computer

Const ADS_RIGHT_DS_SELF                   = &H8
Const ADS_RIGHT_DS_WRITE_PROP             = &H20
Const ADS_RIGHT_DS_CONTROL_ACCESS         = &H100
Const ADS_ACETYPE_ACCESS_ALLOWED_OBJECT   = &H5
Const ADS_FLAG_OBJECT_TYPE_PRESENT        = &H1

Const GUID_ACCOUNT_RESTRICTIONS = _
    "{4C164200-20C0-11D0-A768-00AA006E0529}"
Const GUID_VALIDATED_SPN        = _
    "{F3A64788-5306-11D1-A9C5-0000F80367C1}"
Const GUID_VALIDATED_DNSHOST    = _
    "{72E39547-7B18-11D1-ADEF-00C04FD8D5CD}"
Const GUID_RESET_PASSWORD       = _
    "{00299570-246D-11D0-A768-00AA006E0529}"

Call CreateComputer("PC17", "Red.Baron@sanao.com")

'===================================
```

```
Sub CreateComputer(strComputerName, strWhoCanJoin)
   Dim objDSE, objComputersContainer, objComputer, objSecDesc
   Dim objDACL, objACE1, objACE2, objACE3, objACE4

   Set objDSE = GetObject("LDAP://rootDSE")
   Set objComputersContainer = GetObject("LDAP://CN=Computers," & _
      objDSE.Get("defaultNamingContext"))

   Set objComputer = objComputersContainer.Create("computer", _
      "CN=" & strComputerName)
   Call objComputer.Put("sAMAccountName", strComputerName & "$")
   Call objComputer.Put("userAccountControl", _
      UF_PASSWD_NOTREQD _
      Or UF_WORKSTATION_TRUST_ACCOUNT _
      ) 'Or UF_ACCOUNTDISABLE   We want to enable, not disable

   objComputer.SetInfo

   Set objACE1 = CreateObject("AccessControlEntry")
   objACE1.Trustee    = strWhoCanJoin
   objACE1.AccessMask = ADS_RIGHT_DS_WRITE_PROP
   objACE1.AceFlags   = 0  'no inheritance from up or to below
   objACE1.AceType    = ADS_ACETYPE_ACCESS_ALLOWED_OBJECT
   objACE1.Flags      = ADS_FLAG_OBJECT_TYPE_PRESENT
   objACE1.ObjectType = GUID_ACCOUNT_RESTRICTIONS
   'objACE1.InheritedObjectType = not used

   Set objACE2 = CreateObject("AccessControlEntry")
   objACE2.Trustee    = strWhoCanJoin
   objACE2.AccessMask = ADS_RIGHT_DS_SELF
   objACE2.AceFlags   = 0  'no inheritance from up or to below
   objACE2.AceType    = ADS_ACETYPE_ACCESS_ALLOWED_OBJECT
   objACE2.Flags      = ADS_FLAG_OBJECT_TYPE_PRESENT
   objACE2.ObjectType = GUID_VALIDATED_SPN
   'objACE2.InheritedObjectType = not used

   Set objACE3 = CreateObject("AccessControlEntry")
   objACE3.Trustee    = strWhoCanJoin
   objACE3.AccessMask = ADS_RIGHT_DS_SELF
   objACE3.AceFlags   = 0  'no inheritance from up or to below
   objACE3.AceType    = ADS_ACETYPE_ACCESS_ALLOWED_OBJECT
   objACE3.Flags      = ADS_FLAG_OBJECT_TYPE_PRESENT
   objACE3.ObjectType = GUID_VALIDATED_DNSHOST
   'objACE3.InheritedObjectType = not used

   Set objACE4 = CreateObject("AccessControlEntry")
   objACE4.Trustee    = strWhoCanJoin
   objACE4.AccessMask = ADS_RIGHT_DS_CONTROL_ACCESS
   objACE4.AceFlags   = 0  'no inheritance from up or to below
   objACE4.AceType    = ADS_ACETYPE_ACCESS_ALLOWED_OBJECT
   objACE4.Flags      = ADS_FLAG_OBJECT_TYPE_PRESENT
   objACE4.ObjectType = GUID_RESET_PASSWORD
   'objACE4.InheritedObjectType = not used
```

```
Set objSecDesc = objComputer.Get("ntSecurityDescriptor")
Set objDACL = objSecDesc.DiscretionaryAcl

Call objDACL.AddAce(objACE1)
Call objDACL.AddAce(objACE2)
Call objDACL.AddAce(objACE3)
Call objDACL.AddAce(objACE4)

objSecDesc.DiscretionaryAcl = objDACL
Call objComputer.Put("ntSecurityDescriptor", objSecDesc)
objComputer.SetInfo

    WScript.Echo "Created computer " & strComputerName
End Sub
```

The script is implemented as a subprogram so that you can easily adapt it to create several computer accounts. Currently, the script creates computer objects always in CN=Computers, but you can change this if you'd like.

ADSI WITHOUT ACTIVE DIRECTORY

Recall from Chapter 10 that even though the WinNT provider is primarily for Windows NT, you could use it also with Windows 2000 computers for the following tasks:

- Managing some server services, such as file shares, print queues, user sessions, and so on (even on domain controllers)
- Managing users and groups of Windows 2000 workstations and stand-alone/ member servers

We don't cover the preceding tasks extensively in this Active Directory book, but we do give you the following short examples to provide you with a taste of these functions:

- CH11-42 ADSI List Services.vbs
- CH11-43 ADSI List Shares.vbs
- CH11-44 ADSI Create a Share.vbs
- CH11-45 ADSI List WinNT Properties of User Class.vbs
- CH11-46 ADSI Create a User in a Workstation.vbs

You can apply the "List Services.vbs" script also to list users, groups, and print queues.

When we create a share, we also publish it in Active Directory, so we do use Active Directory a little.

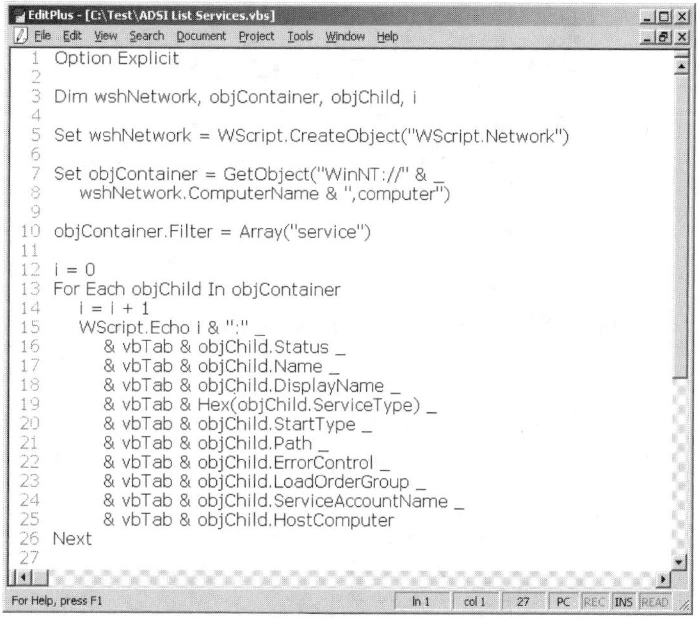

```
Option Explicit

Dim wshNetwork, objContainer, objChild, i

Set wshNetwork = WScript.CreateObject("WScript.Network")

Set objContainer = GetObject("WinNT://" & _
   wshNetwork.ComputerName & ",computer")

objContainer.Filter = Array("service")

i = 0
For Each objChild In objContainer
   i = i + 1
   WScript.Echo i & ":" _
      & vbTab & objChild.Status _
      & vbTab & objChild.Name _
      & vbTab & objChild.DisplayName _
      & vbTab & Hex(objChild.ServiceType) _
      & vbTab & objChild.StartType _
      & vbTab & objChild.Path _
      & vbTab & objChild.ErrorControl _
      & vbTab & objChild.LoadOrderGroup _
      & vbTab & objChild.ServiceAccountName _
      & vbTab & objChild.HostComputer
Next
```

FIGURE 11.82 ADSI List Services.vbs

List Services.vbs

This script lists the Win32 services in a computer, whether they are running or not. The script has the lines shown in Figure 11.82.

We read the local computer name from the WSH Network object. We also need to add `,computer` to the binding string so that ADSI knows to find a computer DC1 instead of a domain DC1.

Because the same computer container also contains the users, groups, and print queues of the computer, we need to apply a filter to include just the services. With Active Directory, the filter used to refer to a class LDAP name, but this time "service" in the filter is an "internal ADSI class name."

In the `For` loop, we browse through all services and list a number of properties for each service. Note that the `Status` property is from a dynamic ADSI interface, `IADsServiceOperations`, while the remaining properties are from a persistent ADSI interface, `IADsService`. (We listed the persistent and dynamic ADSI interfaces in Chapter 10.)

Because each line of output contains 11 elements, it is pretty ugly to read. However, because of the tab characters between the elements, it is easy to redirect the output to a text file and open it up in Excel. Figure 11.83 shows the first lines of the output.

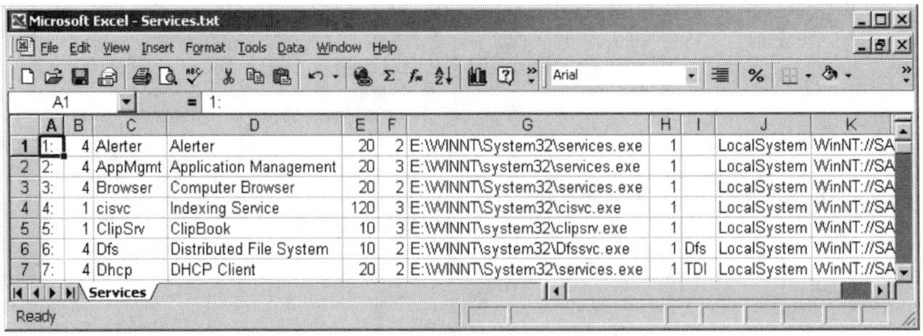

	A	B	C	D	E	F	G	H	I	J	K
1	1:	4	Alerter	Alerter	20	2	E:\WINNT\System32\services.exe	1		LocalSystem	WinNT://SA
2	2:	4	AppMgmt	Application Management	20	3	E:\WINNT\system32\services.exe	1		LocalSystem	WinNT://SA
3	3:	4	Browser	Computer Browser	20	2	E:\WINNT\System32\services.exe	1		LocalSystem	WinNT://SA
4	4:	1	cisvc	Indexing Service	120	3	E:\WINNT\System32\cisvc.exe	1		LocalSystem	WinNT://SA
5	5:	1	ClipSrv	ClipBook	10	3	E:\WINNT\system32\clipsrv.exe	1		LocalSystem	WinNT://SA
6	6:	4	Dfs	Distributed File System	10	2	E:\WINNT\system32\Dfssvc.exe	1	Dfs	LocalSystem	WinNT://SA
7	7:	4	Dhcp	DHCP Client	20	2	E:\WINNT\System32\services.exe	1	TDI	LocalSystem	WinNT://SA

FIGURE 11.83 Part of the output of "ADSI List Services.vbs"

Column B contains the status code of each service. The value "4" means "running" and value "1" means "stopped," as you can see from the following constants:

```
Const ADS_SERVICE_STOPPED          = 1
Const ADS_SERVICE_START_PENDING    = 2
Const ADS_SERVICE_STOP_PENDING     = 3
Const ADS_SERVICE_RUNNING          = 4
Const ADS_SERVICE_CONTINUE_PENDING = 5
Const ADS_SERVICE_PAUSE_PENDING    = 6
Const ADS_SERVICE_PAUSED           = 7
Const ADS_SERVICE_ERROR            = 8
```

If you already know how services are defined in Windows NT or Windows 2000, the output looks pretty familiar. Explaining all the options is outside the scope of this book, but we cannot resist the temptation to give a few hints.

- Column E contains the service type as a hexadecimal number, because the type is a bitfield. "&H10" means that the service is running in its own process, such as Distributed File System is running in Dfssvc.exe.
- Service type "&H20" means that the service is running in a process with other services, such as Alerter, and many others are running in services.exe.
- Column F contains the start type and value "2" means "Automatic," whereas value "3" means "Manual" (or "Load on Demand").

Column K contains the name of the computer that contains the service as an ADSI path (e.g., WinNT://SANAO/DC1).

You can list the services and processes of a computer in the following ways.

- To see all running processes, start the Task Manager by simultaneously pressing Ctrl-Shift-Esc. Then choose the Processes tab.
- To see all running services, start Command Prompt (click the Start button and select Programs, Accessories, Command Prompt), type NET START, and press Enter.

You can see more information on each service in two places of Computer Management (My Computer, Manage). The first node is System Tools, System Information, Software Environment, Services, and the other node is Services and Applications, Services.

List Users, Groups, and Print Queues

You can also use the previous script to list users, groups, and print queues. Just replace the `service` filter with `user`, `group`, or `printQueue`, respectively.

Obviously, you also need to change which properties you read from these other "classes."

List Shares.vbs

Our next example lists the file shares of a computer. The script has the lines shown in Figure 11.84.

This script is similar to the previous one in many ways, but there are also the following differences between them.

- The file shares are contained not in the computer, but in its Server service. However, that is only a display name. The internal name of the service is `lanmanserver` and that is the name we need to append to the binding string (internal service names are the same as their key names in the registry).

```
     EditPlus - [C:\Test\ADSI List Shares.vbs]
     File  Edit  View  Search  Document  Project  Tools  Window  Help
 1   Option Explicit
 2
 3   Dim wshNetwork, objServerService, objFileShare, i
 4
 5   Set wshNetwork = WScript.CreateObject("WScript.Network")
 6
 7   Set objServerService = GetObject("WinNT://" & _
 8      wshNetwork.ComputerName & "/lanmanserver")
 9
10   i = 0
11   For Each objFileShare In objServerService
12      If VarType(objFileShare) <> vbEmpty Then
13         i = i + 1
14         WScript.Echo i & ":" _
15             & vbTab & objFileShare.Name _
16             & vbTab & objFileShare.Path _
17             & vbTab & objFileShare.Description _
18             & vbTab & objFileShare.CurrentUserCount _
19             & vbTab & objFileShare.MaxUserCount _
20             & vbTab & objFileShare.HostComputer
21      End If
22   Next
23
```

FIGURE 11.84 ADSI List Shares.vbs

"Lanman" refers to LAN Manager, which we have already mentioned in this book several times.

- Now that we append /lanmanserver to the binding string, our target is not a computer anymore and, consequently, the text ,computer doesn't work. ADSI will still find the target computer, but you must wait 20 seconds, because ADSI first tries if the name is a domain name. If you don't want to wait, you can hard-code the domain name (in NetBIOS format) to your binding string. You could also use the UserDomain property of the WSH Network object. However, this method works only if the user logged on to the same domain that the computer is a member of.

- We don't need the filter anymore, because lanmanserver contains only shares.

When we browse the children of lanmanserver, we get all the file shares as object variables. However, for some reason after the file shares we get one extra vbEmpty when running the script on a Windows 2000 server (but not on a Windows 2000 workstation). Therefore, we have included the If VarType(objFile-Share) <> vbEmpty statement.

Again, it is best to redirect the output to a text file and open it in Excel. Figure 11.85 shows the result. Value "–1" in column F means that there is no limit on how many users may connect to the share at the same time.

NOTE   The IADsFileShare interface, which we use in this script, returns only those file shares (normal or hidden) that are defined in the lanmanserver key of the registry. Consequently, the shares that the Server service creates each time it is started are not listed. These automatically created shares include IPC$, ADMIN$, C$, D$, and so on. You can see them with the NET SHARE command.

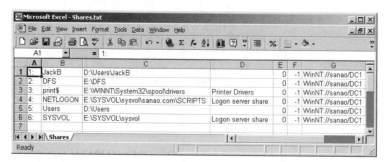

FIGURE 11.85 Output of "ADSI List Shares.vbs"

FIGURE 11.86 ADSI Create a Share.vbs

Create a Share.vbs

The script shown in Figure 11.86 creates a new folder and shares it. At the end we include lines that publish the new share in Active Directory.

You probably want to change the target container CN=Users to something else. We are using it so that this demo script will work in any domain. Without the MaxUserCount setting on line 18, only one user at a time could connect to the share.

Note that the published share in Active Directory refers to a UNC path (\\server\ShareDemo) instead of a physical path (such as C:\ShareDemo).

NOTE   Normally you don't need to set any file share permissions, because NTFS permissions are enough. If you do, however, you will find out that ADSI doesn't allow you to manage share permissions, nor does it allow you to manage the caching settings of file shares. For the former task, you can use RMTSHARE.EXE from the Windows NT 4 Resource Kit, and for the latter task, you can use the NET SHARE command. You can call both from a script using the Run method, as we demonstrated in the example "Create a Home Folder for a User—ver 2.vbs" earlier in this chapter.

List WinNT Properties of User Class.vbs

The WinNT provider has somewhat different and much fewer properties for user objects than LDAP. WinNT has only 25 user properties whereas Active Directory has over 200.

Even though there is no real schema in Windows 2000 workstations or Windows NT, the WinNT provider exposes a fake schema. You can read it just like the abstract schema of LDAP to find out which classes and properties are supported.

The script in Figure 11.87 reads the fake schema and lists all optional properties of the user "class." We didn't include lines for mandatory properties because there wouldn't be any.

NOTE   If your test computer is a domain controller, you can still run this script, even though it is meant for workstations and stand-alone/member servers.

Unlike with the LDAP provider, we now have to include a domain or computer name in the path, so the path becomes something like `WinNT://pc17/schema/user` instead of just `WinNT://schema/user`.

The list of optional properties includes one empty name and that is why we have one extra `If` statement inside the `For` loop.

Figure 11.88 shows most of the output of the script. We dropped four lines out (password minimum length and so on), because they are actually per-domain

```
1   Option Explicit
2
3   Dim wshNetwork, objClass, objAttribute, strPropName, i
4
5   Set wshNetwork = WScript.CreateObject("WScript.Network")
6
7   Set objClass = GetObject("WinNT://" & _
8       wshNetwork.ComputerName & "/schema/user")
9
10  i = 0
11  For Each strPropName In objClass.OptionalProperties
12      If strPropName <> "" Then
13          i = i + 1
14          Set objAttribute = GetObject("WinNT://" & _
15              wshNetwork.ComputerName & "/schema/" & strPropName)
16          WScript.Echo i & ": " & strPropName & _
17              " (" & objAttribute.Syntax & ")"
18      End If
19  Next
20
```

FIGURE 11.87 ADSI List WinNT Properties of User Class.vbs

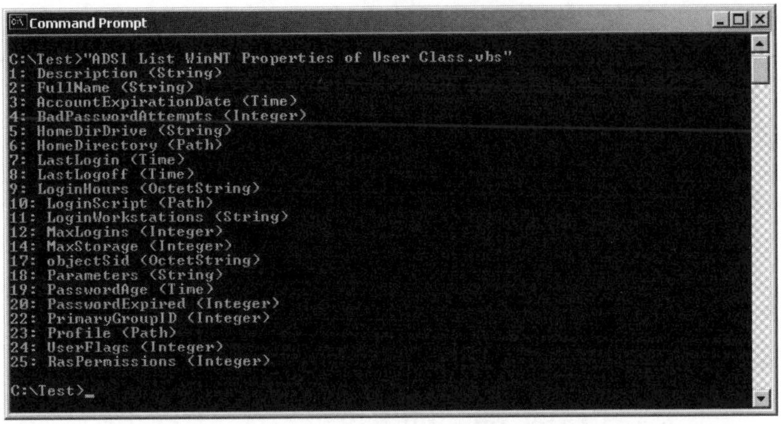

FIGURE 11.88 Most of the output of "ADSI List WinNT Properties of User Class.vbs"

(or per-computer) settings instead of per-user. The `PasswordAge` property indicates how old the user password is in seconds.

NOTE   In addition to the properties shown in Figure 11.88, you can use the following `IADsUser` static property methods: `AccountDisabled`, `IsAccountLocked`, `PasswordRequired`, and `PasswordExpirationDate`. The fake schema doesn't list them.

NOTE   `UserFlags` in Figure 11.88 corresponds to `userAccountControl` with the LDAP provider. Both have the same bits, except that `UserFlags` doesn't support the smart card requirement and some other new settings. Also, `UserFlags` uses `UF_PASSWD_CANT_CHANGE`, while `userAccountControl` does not (because Active Directory implements that feature using ACLs).

Create a User in a Workstation.vbs

Now that you know which properties you can use with WinNT users, we'll show how to create a user. The lines in Figure 11.89 create the user Jack on the local computer. Note that the name to be created is just "Jack," not "CN=Jack."

This time we don't use the explicit `Put` method, because there are no attribute LDAP names that we would want to emphasize. You can choose whether or not to use explicit `Get` and `Put` except with the four static property methods we listed. Because they are already methods, you cannot put them inside a `Put`.

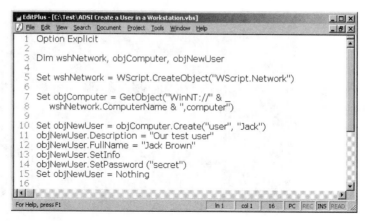

```
Option Explicit

Dim wshNetwork, objComputer, objNewUser

Set wshNetwork = WScript.CreateObject("WScript.Network")

Set objComputer = GetObject("WinNT://" & _
    wshNetwork.ComputerName & ",computer")

Set objNewUser = objComputer.Create("user", "Jack")
objNewUser.Description = "Our test user"
objNewUser.FullName = "Jack Brown"
objNewUser.SetInfo
objNewUser.SetPassword ("secret")
Set objNewUser = Nothing
```

FIGURE 11.89 ADSI Create a User in a Workstation.vbs

ADDITIONAL TECHNIQUES

In this section, we briefly explain some additional techniques that you can use in your scripts. The techniques are as follows:

- Binding with credentials
- Binding with WKGUIDs and binding rename-safely to other objects
- Binding to the global catalog
- Listing objects of a subtree
- Error checking
- Scripts as command-line tools

We show some example lines of each technique. In addition, we present the following complete scripts in this section:

- CH11-47 ADSI Bind to a WKGUID.vbs
- CH11-48 ADSI List the Users of a Subtree.vbs
- CH11-49 VBS Error Checking.vbs
- CH11-50 CmdTool.vbs

We start by explaining how to bind with credentials.

Binding with Credentials

So far, all the scripts we have shown have used the credentials of the logged-on user, because it is usually most convenient to log on as an administrator and then run any appropriate scripts.

Occasionally there may be a need to run a script with alternate credentials. One way is, of course, to use the RunAs feature of Windows 2000, but ADSI also allows specifying the credentials.

When you bind without credentials (the traditional way), you use the following lines:

```
Set objDSE = GetObject("LDAP://rootDSE")
Set objContainer = GetObject("LDAP://CN=Users," & _
    objDSE.Get("defaultNamingContext"))
```

When credentials are added to the picture you must use OpenDSObject instead of GetObject. In this case, you use the following lines:

```
Const ADS_SECURE_AUTHENTICATION = 1
Set objDSE = GetObject("LDAP://rootDSE")
Set objLDAP = GetObject("LDAP:")
Set objUser = objLDAP.OpenDSObject( _
  "LDAP://CN=Guest,CN=Users," & objDSE.Get("defaultNaming-Context"), _
  "red.baron@sanao.com", "somesecret", ADS_SECURE_AUTHENTICATION)
```

You need one extra step, because you first need to bind to the LDAP namespace ("LDAP:") and only then can you call OpenDSObject. In addition to the same ADsPath as with GetObject, there are three other arguments: username, password, and authentication method.

The following usernames are valid:

- UPN (user principal name), such as red.baron@sanao.com
- SAM name, such as "RedBaron"
- SAM name with domain NetBIOS name, such as "SANAO\RedBaron"
- Distinguished name, such as CN=Red Baron, CN=Users, DC=sanao, DC=com

If you use a constant vbNullStrin both as the username and password, you will authenticate with the credentials of the logged-on user, so the result is actually the same as if you used plain old GetObject.

For the authentication method, you can use the following constants:

```
Const ADS_SECURE_AUTHENTICATION   = &H1
Const ADS_USE_ENCRYPTION          = &H2
Const ADS_USE_SSL                 = &H2
Const ADS_READONLY_SERVER         = &H4
Const ADS_PROMPT_CREDENTIALS      = &H8
Const ADS_NO_AUTHENTICATION       = &H10
Const ADS_FAST_BIND               = &H20
Const ADS_USE_SIGNING             = &H40
Const ADS_USE_SEALING             = &H80
```

Some of the authentication methods can (or must) be used together using the "+" operator. For example, the sealing option requires also the secure authentication option. ADS_SECURE_AUTHENTICATION, which we showed in the example, means a normal authentication that any Windows 2000 does when a user logs on to Active Directory. The underlying protocol would be Kerberos (or NTLM, if there were Windows NT computers involved).

Using the option ADS_NO_AUTHENTICATION would result in using the anonymous access option, or "null session." In this case, the username and password must be empty strings—that is, two consecutive quotation marks (""). Note that we cannot use vbNullString with ADS_NO_AUTHENTICATION, even though we are talking about a null session.

NOTE   Whether anonymous access is allowed at all and what an anonymous logon may do is explained in Chapter 4.

For information about the other authentication options, refer to the ADSI documentation.

ADSI caches the credentials supplied in OpenDSObject, so you need to define the password only in the first call. In subsequent calls you can use just vbNullString instead of the real password. However, this works only if the following conditions are true:

- You use exactly the same username in all OpenDSObject calls.
- You use serverless binding or specify the same server name in all OpenDS-Object calls.
- You keep the session open by keeping at least one object in use all the time from one of the OpenDSObject calls.

Needless to say, you should avoid storing administrative passwords in your clear-text scripts. You should at least download Microsoft Script Encoder and use it to encode those scripts.

Binding with WKGUIDs

WKGUID means a GUID for a well-known object. ADSI has a special syntax that specifies how you can use WKGUIDs in your scripts.

The reason behind WKGUIDs is that if you bind to CN=Users, for example, your script is not *rename-safe*. It works only if that container is still using its default name. If you use the WKGUID for CN=Users, the script will always work because the corresponding GUID will always be the same.

NOTE Active Directory doesn't allow you to change the name of CN=Users or any of the other default containers. Therefore, it should be quite safe to bind with a name, but because Microsoft recommends WKGUIDs, we'll introduce them. Besides, you also need to learn to read scripts that you download, and some of them might use WKGUIDs.

The syntax for using a WKGUID is as follows:

```
Set objCont = GetObject("LDAP://<WKGUID=someGUID,parentContainer-DN>")
```

WKGUIDs don't use any curly braces or dashes, even though you use them as strings inside the binding string. They just have 32 hexadecimal characters, which results in a 128-bit value.

In this section, we first show a script that binds using a WKGUID and then we explain how to create new WKGUIDs.

BIND TO A WKGUID.VBS

The following lines show a script that binds to CN=Users using a WKGUID and lists all objects in that container:

```
Option Explicit

Const GUID_USERS_CONTAINER                = _
    "a9d1ca15768811d1aded00c04fd8d5cd"
Const GUID_COMPUTRS_CONTAINER             = _
    "aa312825768811d1aded00c04fd8d5cd"
Const GUID_SYSTEMS_CONTAINER              = _
    "ab1d30f3768811d1aded00c04fd8d5cd"
Const GUID_DOMAIN_CONTROLLERS_CONTAINER = _
    "a361b2ffffd211d1aa4b00c04fd7d83a"
Const GUID_INFRASTRUCTURE_CONTAINER       = _
    "2fbac1870ade11d297c400c04fd8d5cd"
Const GUID_DELETED_OBJECTS_CONTAINER      = _
    "18e2ea80684f11d2b9aa00c04f79f805"
Const GUID_LOSTANDFOUND_CONTAINER         = _
    "ab8153b7768811d1aded00c04fd8d5cd"

Dim objContainer, objChild, strContainerDN

Set objContainer = GetObject("LDAP://<WKGUID=" & _
    GUID_USERS_CONTAINER  & _
    ",DC=sanao,DC=com>")
strContainerDN = objContainer.Get("distinguishedName")
Set objContainer = GetObject("LDAP://" & strContainerDN)
```

```
For Each objChild In objContainer
   WScript.Echo objChild.Name & vbTab & objChild.Description
Next
```

We didn't use `rootDSE` this time so that you could better see how the binding string is formed.

If you right away start to use an object that was bound with a GUID, you will have only part of the properties and interfaces available. Therefore, we get the distinguished name of the container and perform a second bind right after the first one. Without the second bind you would see only the child object names in the list and not their other attributes, such as descriptions.

NOTE   We use `objChild.Description` instead of `objChild.Get("Description")` to avoid "property not found" errors.

We took the WKGUID names and values from the NtDsAPI.h file, which is part of the Platform SDK. Note that `GUID_SYSTEMS_CONTAINER` refers to `CN=System` despite of the extra "S" and that the `GUID_INFRASTRUCTURE_ CONTAINER` name is a little misleading because `CN=Infrastructure` is a leaf object.

NOTE   `GUID_LOSTANDFOUND_CONTAINER` and `GUID_DELETED_OBJECTS_CONTAINER` can also be used in the Configuration container—not that you are likely to do so.

RENAME-SAFE BINDING TO OTHER OBJECTS

WKGUIDs are not the same as `objectGUIDs` of the corresponding containers. Instead, the values are stored in the `wellKnownObjects` attribute of the parent container. That attribute uses the `DN with binary` data type, which is so exotic that even ADSI Edit cannot show the contents to you.

To see the values, you can use LDIFDE with the following command:

```
ldifde -f wellKnownObjects.txt -p base -l wellKnownObjects
```

The `-p base` option specifies that we don't want any child objects and the `-l` option lists the attributes that we are interested in. Figure 11.90 shows the resulting file.

The benefit of using `DN with binary` is that should an object name change, Active Directory will update the distinguished name part of the value pair and, consequently, the name will be always current.

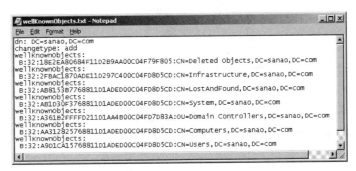

FIGURE 11.90 Each domain object contains a `wellKnownObjects` attribute, which lists the default object distinguished names and corresponding GUID values.

The `wellKnownObjects` attribute is "system only," which means that even administrators cannot modify it. There is also an `otherWellKnownObjects` attribute, which works like `wellKnownObjects`. This other attribute is not "system only"; therefore, it allows administrators and developers to specify new rename-safe objects in addition to the few default ones.

Handling `DN with binary` attributes with VBScript is difficult. ADSI does contain an interface `IADsDNWithBinary`, but it seems not to work when the attribute has multiple values. With a single value, the binary component is returned as a byte array, which is somewhat laborious to digest in VBScript. Therefore, it is best to use LDIFDE again.

To create your own WKGUID for `OU=Sales` (in domain root), perform the following steps:

1. Run UUIDGen from the Platform SDK to generate a new GUID. You will get a GUID such as "aa63b9fc-e8bb-4e8a-b235-cf3556517d32."

2. Because that GUID is using the string representation of a GUID (even though curly braces are missing), swap some bytes to get a binary representation (even though WKGUIDs are strings). We explained in the example "List Binary GUIDs.vbs" how you need to swap bytes 1-2-3-4 to 4-3-2-1, 5-6 to 6-5, and 7-8 to 8-7. When you also remove the dashes, you will get "fcb963aabbe88a4eb235cf3556517d32."

3. Create an LDIF file that specifies that you want to add one new value to the `otherWellKnownObjects` attribute of the `DC=sanao,DC=com` object. The file should look like the one in Figure 11.91.

4. Import the LDIF file with the following command:

```
ldifde -i -f addotherwk.ldf
```

FIGURE 11.91   This LDIF file modifies the domain object by adding a new value to the
`otherWellKnownObject` attribute.

Now you have a new WKGUID, and you could use the following line to bind to
`OU=Sales`:

```
Set objOU = _
      GetObject("LDAP://<WKGUID=FCB963AABBE88A4EB235CF3556517D32" & _
      ",DC=sanao,DC=com>")
```

If you later use LDIFDE to export the contents of `otherWellKnown-`
`Objects`, you will get a similar text file to the one you just saw about `well-`
`KnownObjects`.

NOTE   If the common name of your object contains characters other than "safe UTF8
characters," LDIFDE will show the name in base64 encoding, as RFC 2849 man-
dates. An example of an "unsafe" character is the European "ä" (a-umlaut). Also, if
you delete the target object, it will get a distinguished name with some special
characters, and again base64 encoding kicks in. Base64 encoding looks like this:
QjozMjpGQ0I5.

Binding to the Global Catalog

You can replace "LDAP:" with "GC:" in a binding string, in which case you bind to
the global catalog in a global catalog server. Just as with the LDAP choice, you can
either specify a server name or do a serverless binding.

As you probably know, the global catalog has the following characteristics and
they naturally apply also when you use it with ADSI:

• The global catalog is read-only. You cannot create or modify objects.

• The global catalog contains all the objects of a forest. You can search the
  whole enterprise forest using a single server.

• The global catalog contains only part of the attributes (in the base schema,
  138 out of 863).

The first and third items in the list limit your options, but the second item is an advantage. You can bind to objects in other domains and still communicate with a server that is located on your local site—provided, of course, that you have designated a global catalog server for each location.

NOTE   We don't show a sample script of binding to the global catalog (using a path such as `GC://CN=Users,DC=sanao,DC=com`) because the only difference from using "LDAP:" is a couple of letters.

You get the biggest benefits from binding to the global catalog when you perform searches. However, when using VBScript, searches require ADO and therefore we show any related examples in the ADO section later in this chapter.

When you later perform ADO searches, binding to any "GC:" container enables you to enumerate all the objects in the tree below that target of binding. For example:

- If you bind to the root domain of a domain tree, you can enumerate all the objects in the domain tree.
- If you bind to any domain, you can enumerate not only all objects in that domain, but also all objects in its child domains.

NOTE   There is also an option to bind to just "GC:" without any distinguished name, but that option is for C programmers. You don't need it in your VBScript scripts.

NOTE   We explained in Chapter 6 that when searching the global catalog, you can use `DC=com` or just an empty string as the DN of the base object. This includes several domain trees of a forest in a query. Unfortunately, this option seems not to work with ADSI/ADO scripts, so you can search only one domain tree at a time.

List the Users of a Subtree.vbs

So far when we have enumerated children of a container, we have done so for a single container only. In this example script, we show how it is also possible to include the whole subtree in the enumeration.

In the sample script, we use *recursion*. This means that we perform the enumeration of a single container in a subprogram and each time our enumeration notices an OU or another container, the subprogram will call itself to enumerate that target also.

If we have a domain where we have added a couple of users in the CN=Users container and two more in OU=Sales, our script would produce the output shown in Figure 11.92. The script's contents are shown in Figure 11.93.

We start the recursion by calling the ListUsers subprogram the first time. After that, we call the same subprogram from itself every time we find an OU or another container.

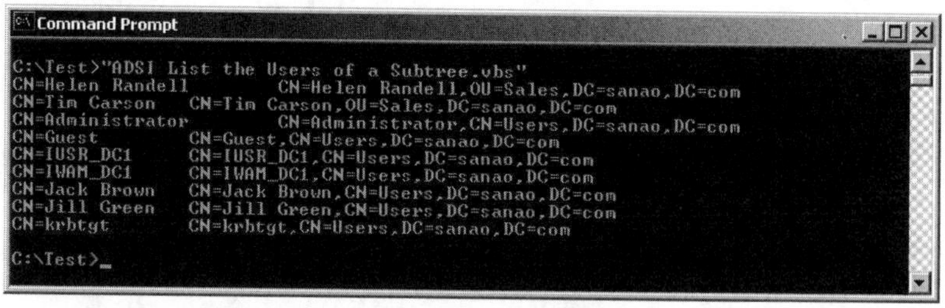

FIGURE 11.92 Output of "ADSI List the Users of a Subtree.vbs"

```
1   Option Explicit
2
3   Dim objDSE, strDefaultDN, strDN, objContainer, objChild
4
5   Set objDSE = GetObject("LDAP://rootDSE")
6   strDefaultDN = objDSE.Get("defaultNamingContext")
7
8   strDN = InputBox("Enter the distinguished name of a container" & _
9       vbCrLf & "(e.g. " & strDefaultDN & ")", , strDefaultDN)
10
11  If strDN = "" Then WScript.Quit(1)    'user clicked Cancel
12
13  Set objContainer = GetObject("LDAP://" & strDN)
14  Call ListUsers(objContainer)
15
16  Sub ListUsers(objADObject)
17      Dim objChild
18      For Each objChild in objADObject
19          Select Case objChild.Class
20              Case "user"
21                  WScript.Echo objChild.Name & vbTab & _
22                      objChild.Get("distinguishedName")
23              Case "organizationalUnit" , "container"
24                  Call ListUsers(objChild)
25          End select
26      Next
27  End Sub
28
```

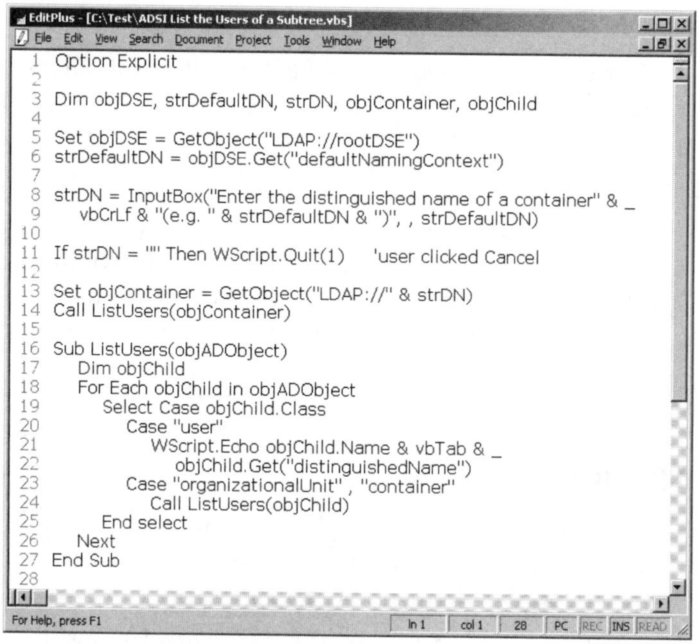

FIGURE 11.93 ADSI List the Users of a Subtree.vbs

Error Checking.vbs

We have occasionally done some error checking in the scripts of this chapter. In those cases, we have wanted to react to some expected situations and not to actual unexpected errors. Consequently, the error code we may have received is not an indication of a traditional error. Instead, the error code has told us, for example, that a certain attribute is not set.

If you want to write complete scripts, you should prepare for unexpected real errors. The need for error checking increases if other people in various environments will run your scripts.

In this section, we say a few words about error mechanics, introduce the various error categories, and finally give an example of an error-checking script.

ERROR MECHANICS

As we explained in the example "List User Properties with Get.vbs," VBScript has an `Err` object that has a `Number` property. Because `Number` is the default property of `Err`, you can refer to it with just "Err" instead of "Err.Number." You can clear a possible old error code with `Err.Clear` (or `Err = 0`) and then retrieve the new error code by reading the value of `Err` (`.Number`).

A successful ADSI call doesn't clear the error code. If you make two ADSI calls and the first one fails, you will get its error code also if you read it after the second call. The consequence is that you will probably get confused trying to find an error in the second call without knowing that the error code is from the first call.

Any error code is cleared automatically when one of the following statements is executed:

- `On Error Resume Next`
- `Exit Sub`
- `Exit Function`

However, it may be easier to add some extra `Err.Clear` lines than to try to remember when it was already called automatically.

Normally any error will terminate the script execution, but you can take error handling into your own hands by adding an `On Error Resume Next` statement either to the beginning of the script or some other location, such as the beginning of a subprogram. You can reverse the effect by adding an `On Error Goto 0` statement.

NOTE If you handle errors yourself, perhaps the biggest drawback to this is that you no longer see the line number where the error occurred.

NOTE   Depending on your needs, you may do perfectly fine by relying on the default error handling of VBScript.

ERROR CATEGORIES

Your ADSI VBScript script could run into the following kinds of errors:

- VBScript syntax errors (or compilation errors), such as "Expected identifier." These errors are easy to notice and locate because the script doesn't run at all. It just displays the error message and the line it appears on. Using `On Error Resume Next` won't hide these errors.

- VBScript runtime errors, such as code "438" (decimal): "Object doesn't support this property or method."

- Generic COM errors, such as code "80004001" (hex): `E_NOTIMPL` ("Not implemented").

- Generic ADSI errors, such as code "8000500D" (hex): `E_ADS_PROPERTY_ NOT_FOUND`.

- Standard Win32 errors, such as code "80072030" (hex): `ERROR_DS_ NO_SUCH_OBJECT`. You can get some help on the error by taking the last four digits (2030), converting them to decimal (8240), and then typing "NET HELPMSG 8240" (without quotes) on the command line. That command has been around since the 1988 launch of LAN Manager. This category includes the traditional errors dating back to MS-DOS, such as code "5": "Access denied." Only this time it is "80070005." The LDAP provider maps also any LDAP errors to this "8007" format. The example in the beginning of the paragraph is the same as the LDAP error `LDAP_NO_SUCH_OBJECT`.

Of course, your script may also have errors that don't produce error codes or messages, but are just logical errors in what the script is doing.

Though there are quite a few possible error sources, try not to fall into despair. You can find more information about the two VBScript error categories in the VBScript Help and more information about the three last categories in the ADSI documentation.

The first two categories are something that you don't want to prepare for in your scripts. They are just plain programming errors and there is no point in writing code in your script to test if you forgot to declare some variable, for example.

THE ERROR CHECKING SAMPLE SCRIPT

This sample script checks for errors after each ADSI operation. It doesn't have any fancy logic to evaluate if it continues running after some corrective action. It just displays the error code and quits.

You might wonder why you should write lines for this, because VBScript would do this automatically for you. Well, there are two reasons.

- You can give better feedback to the user by handling the errors yourself.
- For the functionality of your script, you may be forced to use On Error Resume Next. This means that you should probably also handle the unexpected (real) errors.

However, we don't want to tell you that you must write your scripts like this. We just want to demonstrate the option.

The following lines show the sample script. They create user Jack in OU=Sales.

```
Option Explicit

Const ERROR_OBJECT_ALREADY_EXISTS = &H80071392
Const ERROR_DS_NO_SUCH_OBJECT     = &H80072030

Dim strName, objContainer, objNewUser

On Error Resume Next

strName = "Jack"

Err.Clear
Set objContainer = _
    GetObject("LDAP://OU=Sales,DC=sanao,DC=com")
Call CheckIfError("Bind to OU=Sales")

Err.Clear
Set objNewUser = objContainer.Create("user", "CN=" & strName)
objNewUser.sAMAccountName = strName
objNewUser.userAccountControl = &H200
objNewUser.userPrincipalName = strName & "@sanao.com"
objNewUser.SetInfo
Call CheckIfError("Create user " & strName)

Err.Clear
WScript.Echo "Last name " & objNewUser.Get("sn")
Call CheckIfError("Read the last name of " & strName)

Err.Clear
objNewUser.SetPassword ("secret")
Call CheckIfError("Set password for user " & strName)
```

```
Sub CheckIfError(strOperation)
   Dim strMessage, intErrCode

   If Err = 0 Then Exit Sub

   strMessage = "Attempted operation: " & strOperation & vbCrLf

   Select Case Err
      Case ERROR_OBJECT_ALREADY_EXISTS
         strMessage = strMessage & _
            "Unfortunately the object to be created already exists."
      Case ERROR_DS_NO_SUCH_OBJECT
         strMessage = strMessage & _
            "Unfortunately couldn't find that object."
      Case Else
         strMessage = strMessage & _
            "Error code: " & Hex(Err) & " (hex)" & vbCrLf & _
            Err.Description
         If (Err And &HFFFF0000) = &H80070000 Then
            intErrCode = (Err And 65535)  '65535 = &HFFFF
            strMessage = strMessage & vbCrLf & _
               "You can get more help on the error by typing" & _
               vbCrLf & _
               "on the command line: NET HELPMSG " & intErrCode
         End If
   End Select

   MsgBox strMessage & vbCrLf & vbCrLf & _
      "Click OK to terminate the script.", _
      vbOKOnly + vbCritical, "Error"

   WScript.Quit(1) 'there was an error so we set the errorlevel
End Sub
```

We call `Err.Clear` before each ADSI operation to make sure that there is no previous error code. Immediately after each operation, we call the subprogram `CheckIfError` and pass the operation description as a text argument.

If there was no error, we immediately return from the subprogram. Otherwise, we build an error message string, which reports the attempted operation and what went wrong. After the user clicks OK, we terminate the script with an errorlevel set.

Setting the errorlevel is useful for the following reason: If the script was launched from another application or batch file, that other party will know about the error if it only checks the errorlevel.

NOTE It wouldn't make much difference if we omitted the `Err.Clear` calls. Because we quit in case of an error, it is highly unlikely that any old error code was already there. Anyway, we play it safe and use plenty of `Err.Clear` calls. This way, we make sure that the correct error code and operation name appear in the message box.

We expect that a couple of errors are more likely to occur than any others, so we want to dedicate a `Case` option to handle these particular errors. Another reason for this dedication is that Win32 errors (i.e., "8007xxxx") don't include `Err.Description` texts, so this way we can type our own error description. Figure 11.94 shows one of the error messages that we created.

We handle all other errors in the `Case Else` option. We include the error code (in hexadecimal because the ADSI documentation lists them in that format) and a possible error description. Figure 11.95 shows one such error.

NOTE   The VBScript documentation lists errors as decimal values, so if you get any of those errors, you need to convert them back to decimal before looking them up in the documentation.

In the last `If` statement, we check if the error code is of type "8007xxxx." These errors don't have a built-in error description, but you can get it with the command NET HELPMSG *errnumber*. Therefore, we want to give a hint of that in the message, including the right decimal value to enter. Figure 11.96 shows the resulting message box. If you type the suggested command, you will see that the description is as follows: "A referral was returned from the server." This description means that you specified an unknown forest name in the binding string.

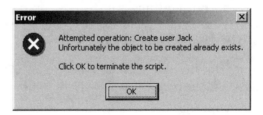

FIGURE 11.94 In case of ADSI error "80071392," we build up a description text for it and display the bad news to the user.

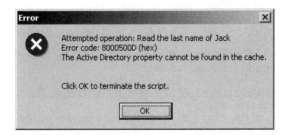

FIGURE 11.95 For the majority of errors, we display the error code (line 2) and "built-in" description (line 3).

FIGURE 11.96 In case of "8007xxxx" errors, we want to give a hint of the command that offers the error description.

It would be logical to use "&HFFFF" in the latter And expression to get the lower 16 bits (or four digits) of the error code. However, it doesn't give the desired result, so we use "65535" instead.

Scripts as Command-Line Tools

Most traditional command-line commands and tools enable you to specify options that determine which kind of operation or operations should be performed this time. For example, you can use the /S option with XCOPY to specify that you want to copy the subfolders also.

You can do the same with your scripts by examining the command-line options (i.e., arguments) and changing the script behavior accordingly. There are two slightly different approaches.

- The script has one basic purpose (e.g., XCOPY's basic purpose is to copy files), and the options somewhat adjust how the mission is accomplished.

- The script includes various functions that are related to some degree. By specifying an option, you choose which function should be performed. For example, the Resource Kit includes REG.EXE, which you can use to manipulate the registry. You can use it with options such as REG QUERY, REG ADD, and REG SAVE to perform the functions you want.

In this section, we show a sample script that is a skeleton of the latter case. It doesn't do anything yet, but once you add your own functions, you will have a command-line tool ready for use.

NOTE   If you want to implement the former case (the one with one basic purpose and modifying options) with five options that the user can specify in random order, you can create a Boolean variable for each of them. In the beginning, you set the values to False, and then you browse through all arguments (For Each str-Argument in objArguments) and set to True those variables that have a corresponding option in the list of arguments.

CMDTOOL.VBS

The help screen of the sample script is displayed in Figure 11.97. The script shows the help screen because the user entered one argument too few.

The script is as follows:

```
Option Explicit

Const ERROR_NOT_CSCRIPT    = 1    'wrong WSH environment
Const ERROR_NO_OPTIONS     = 2    'wrong number of options or requested
                                   help
Const ERROR_COULDNT_ADD    = 3
Const ERROR_COULDNT_DELETE = 4

Dim objArguments, intResult
Dim strObjectDN, strObjectRDN, strParentDN

Call CheckWSHEnvironment    'we want CScript and not WScript

Set objArguments = WScript.Arguments
If objArguments.Count < 1 Then Call ShowHelp

Select Case UCase(objArguments.Item(0))
   Case "?", "/?", "H", "/H", "HELP"
      Call ShowHelp
   Case "ADD"
      If objArguments.Count <> 3 Then ShowHelp
      strObjectRDN = objArguments.Item(1)
```

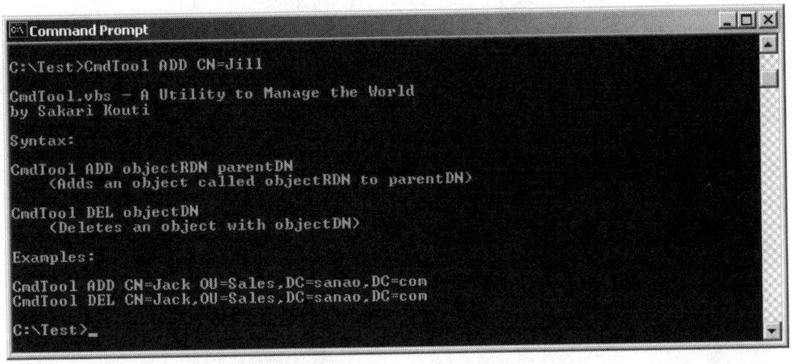

FIGURE 11.97 If used with the "ADD" option, the tool requires two more arguments. However, the user entered only one (CN=Jill), so the script just shows the help screen and terminates.

```
         strParentDN = objArguments.Item(2)
         intResult = AddObject(strObjectRDN, strParentDN)
      Case "DEL"
         If objArguments.Count <> 2 Then ShowHelp
         strObjectDN = objArguments.Item(1)
         intResult = DeleteObject(strObjectDN)
      Case Else
         Call ShowHelp
End Select
WScript.Quit(intResult)    'the program end


'==========================


Function AddObject(strObjectRDN, strParentDN)
   WScript.Echo "Object RDN: " & strObjectRDN
   WScript.Echo "Parent DN: " & strParentDN
   AddObject = 0   'and not ERROR_COULDNT_ADD
End Function


'==========================


Function DeleteObject(strObjectDN)
   WScript.Echo "Object DN: " & strObjectDN
   DeleteObject = 0   'and not ERROR_COULDNT_DELETE
End Function


'==========================


Sub CheckWSHEnvironment()
   Dim strScriptHostName

   strScriptHostName = WScript.FullName
   strScriptHostName = _
      Right(strScriptHostName, Len(strScriptHostName) _
      - InStrRev(strScriptHostName,"\"))
   If UCase(strScriptHostName) <> "CSCRIPT.EXE" Then
      MsgBox "You should run this script in the CScript" & vbCrLf & _
         "command line environment. Either type CSCRIPT" & vbCrLf & _
         "before the script name or change CScript as" & vbCrLf & _
         "the default environment with the command" & vbCrLf & _
         "CSCRIPT //H:CSCRIPT", _
         vbOKOnly + vbCritical, "Error"
      WScript.Quit(ERROR_NOT_CSCRIPT)
   End If
End Sub


'==========================
```

```
Sub ShowHelp()
   WScript.Echo _
      vbCrLf & _
      "CmdTool.vbs - A Utility to Manage the World" & vbCrLf & _
      "by Sakari Kouti" & vbCrLf & _
      vbCrLf & _
      "Syntax:" & vbCrLf & _
      vbCrLf & _
      "CmdTool ADD objectRDN parentDN" & vbCrLf & _
      "      (Adds an object called objectRDN to parentDN)" & vbCrLf & _
      vbCrLf & _
      "CmdTool DEL objectDN" & vbCrLf & _
      "      (Deletes an object with objectDN)" & vbCrLf & _
      vbCrLf & _
      "Examples:" & vbCrLf & _
      vbCrLf & _
      "CmdTool ADD CN=Jack OU=Sales,DC=sanao,DC=com" & vbCrLf & _
      "CmdTool DEL CN=Jack,OU=Sales,DC=sanao,DC=com"
   WScript.Quit(ERROR_NO_OPTIONS)
End Sub
```

First we check that we are running the script in the CScript environment instead of WScript. This is not that important if we just add or delete an object, but because this is a skeleton, you could use the script for displaying a long list, in which case WScript would mean tens or hundreds of message boxes.

NOTE Of course, we could add the environment check to all our sample scripts, but we don't want to repeat the same 20 lines in all scripts.

We implement the help screen as a subprogram, so that we can call it from here and there if we find anything wrong with the arguments.

We define a number of error constants and return them outside the script to indicate what went wrong, if anything. Because this is a command-line tool, chances are that you are calling it from a batch file (or another script) and by returning a descriptive value from the script the calling application knows what happened.

The main program includes a `Select` statement and almost nothing else. It is then up to that `Select` statement to call the appropriate function based on the command-line option.

The next (and last) section in the chapter describes how to use ADO to enhance Active Directory searches.

USING ADO

ActiveX Data Objects (ADO) is a programmatic interface to any database or data source that has implemented an *OLE-DB provider;* that is, a driver component between ADO and the data source. Examples of such data sources are SQL Server, Oracle database server, and Active Directory.

In this section, we describe ADO concepts and then provide a few examples of how you can use ADO in your administration scripts. Note that you can use ADO in one script either together with ADSI or in place of ADSI.

We offer the following examples in this section:

- CH11-51 ADO Basic Example.vbs
- CH11-52 ADO Basic Example with SQL.vbs
- CH11-53 ADO Modifying Objects.vbs
- CH11-54 ADO List Objects That Have Blocked ACL Inheritance.vbs

We also describe how you can pass partition boundaries by using the global catalog or turning on referral chasing.

We discuss only a subset of ADO features—the ones that you need to successfully use ADO with Active Directory.

ADO Concepts

ADO is a COM-based programming interface that Microsoft has designed to be used with relational databases, such as SQL Server, but also with other data sources, such as other databases and Active Directory (or rather, any LDAP directory).

Figure 11.98 presents the ADO architecture and how it relates to ADSI. As you can see from the figure, you can use ADSI in your script or ADO, or both. Whether you choose to use just ADO for some script or to complement ADSI with ADO depends on what you are doing with your script.

One analogy for ADSI versus ADO is that using ADSI is like opening a Web page by typing its URL (Uniform Resource Locator) and using ADO is like searching Web pages using a search engine.

ADSI VERSUS ADO

In Table 11.6 we compare ADSI and ADO, so you can see the different nature of ADO as well as its pros and cons.

You could use ADO for two slightly different purposes, or should we say, usage philosophies:

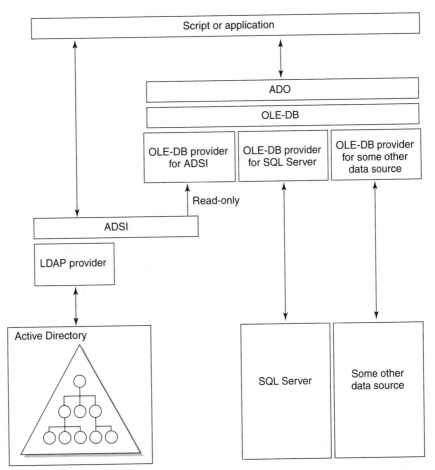

FIGURE 11.98 ADO is another COM-based programming interface that can be used on top of ADSI. However, this provider is read-only, so you cannot change any Active Directory data using ADO.

- *Searching.* For example, you could use ADO to locate a certain user or if you don't remember which objects have the fSMORoleOwner attribute.
- *Filtering.* For example, if you want to copy a file to every user's home folder, you could use ADO to filter all those user objects from different OUs that have a home folder attribute set. Then you would perform the copy operation on all found users. You could also print out a report of all those users that don't have their phone number set and ask someone to fill in the missing phone numbers.

The latter purpose is probably more common in administration.

TABLE 11.6 ADSI and ADO Comparison

Feature	ADSI	ADO	ADO Pro/Con
Binding	To one object based on its name and path in the directory	Cannot bind; instead returns a set of all objects that match the search criteria (zero, one, or several objects)	+ −
Enumerating objects	Need to use recursion if you want to numerate from several containers	Easily from several containers	+
Filtering of objects	Limited to class name	Full power of LDAP search filters and some other search settings	+
Reading other domains	Can do with default settings	Requires nondefault settings	−
Available attributes	All	Only those that were listed in the search	−
Authentication	Use the credentials of the logged-on user or specify others	Use the credentials of the logged-on user or specify others	
Can modify object	Yes	No	−

NOTE   It doesn't really hurt that ADO over ADSI is read-only. You could use ADO to retrieve the distinguished names or ADSI paths of 137 particular users, bind to each one using ADSI, and then modify the objects. We show an example of this later.

ADO MECHANICS

ADO has an object model that includes among others *connection, command,* and *recordset* objects. These three objects have certain properties and methods.

There are at least three ways to use various properties and methods when reading Active Directory with these objects. Also, you could specify many settings either as properties before calling a method or as arguments in the method call. This introduces variety to the scripts that you will see if you read scripts from different sources.

Because you need only one way to access Active Directory with ADO, we present only one in this book. Also, we are not very interested in all possible options and settings, so we explain only those relevant when working with Active Directory (most of them appear later in this section, however).

The three objects we mentioned work as follows:

- *A connection object* represents a connection from your script to a data source, such as Active Directory. Using this object, we can specify a username and password (although usually we don't) and open the connection.

- *A command object* represents a search command and by specifying this object's properties we can specify what kind of query we want to perform. We perform the query with the `Execute` method.

- *A recordset object* represents the returned data. You can think of it as a two-dimensional array, where each row corresponds to one returned Active Directory object and each column to one attribute.

Next, we show the first example and continue the discussion based on it.

Basic Example.vbs

This script picks up all users and contacts in your default domain (no matter what container they are in) that have a last name starting with *A*. Then it lists the distinguished names of all those people. Figure 11.99 shows the script's output and Figure 11.100 displays the script's contents.

On lines 7 through 9 we create a connection object, and then tell it to use the OLE-DB provider for ADSI and open the connection. Because we didn't specify a username or password, the connection is made with the logged-on user's credentials.

On lines 11 and 12 we create a command object and tell it to use our just-opened connection.

On lines 14 through 18 we have the LDAP search string, which specifies what objects and attributes should be read from Active Directory. We describe the string contents in the next subsection.

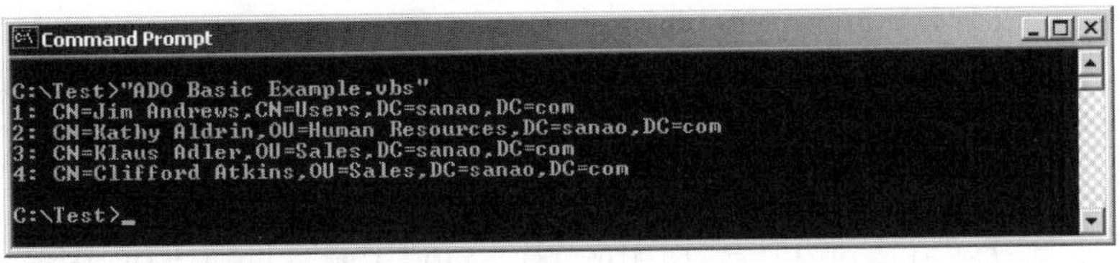

FIGURE 11.99 Output of "ADO Basic Example.vbs"

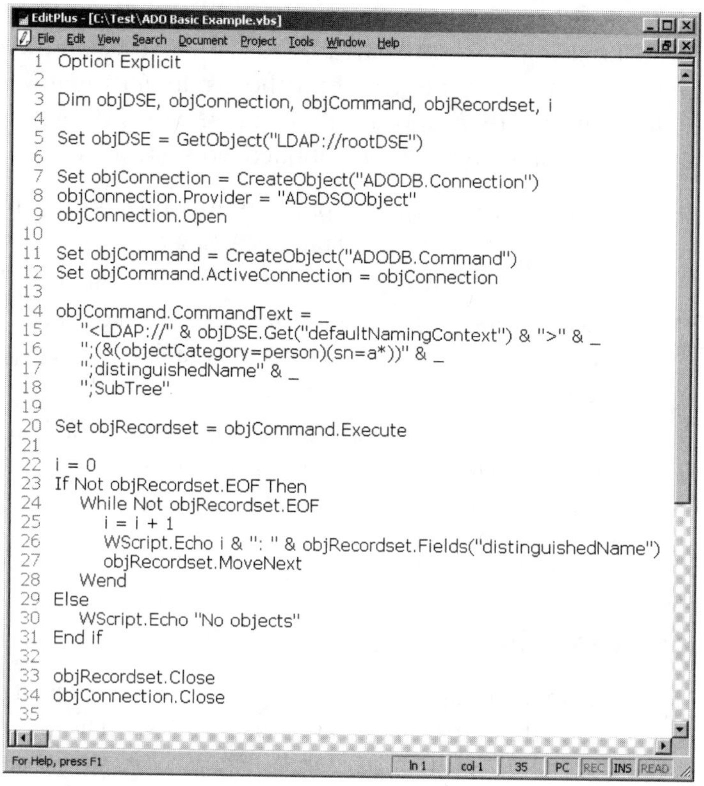
EditPlus - [C:\Test\ADO Basic Example.vbs]
File Edit View Search Document Project Tools Window Help
```
1  Option Explicit
2
3  Dim objDSE, objConnection, objCommand, objRecordset, i
4
5  Set objDSE = GetObject("LDAP://rootDSE")
6
7  Set objConnection = CreateObject("ADODB.Connection")
8  objConnection.Provider = "ADsDSOObject"
9  objConnection.Open
10
11 Set objCommand = CreateObject("ADODB.Command")
12 Set objCommand.ActiveConnection = objConnection
13
14 objCommand.CommandText = _
15    "<LDAP://" & objDSE.Get("defaultNamingContext") & ">" & _
16    ";(&(objectCategory=person)(sn=a*))" & _
17    ";distinguishedName" & _
18    ";SubTree"
19
20 Set objRecordset = objCommand.Execute
21
22 i = 0
23 If Not objRecordset.EOF Then
24    While Not objRecordset.EOF
25       i = i + 1
26       WScript.Echo i & ": " & objRecordset.Fields("distinguishedName")
27       objRecordset.MoveNext
28    Wend
29 Else
30    WScript.Echo "No objects"
31 End if
32
33 objRecordset.Close
34 objConnection.Close
35
```
For Help, press F1
ln 1 col 1 35 PC REC INS READ

FIGURE 11.100 ADO Basic Example.vbs

Now we are ready to perform the query. We do it on line 20, and on the same line we get the read data in a recordset.

A recordset has a *cursor,* which specifies the line (or *record*) that we can currently read. Because we want to read every line, we start from the beginning of the recordset and with each loop we read one line and then move the cursor to the next line.

We could first call the method `objRecordset.MoveFirst` to move the cursor to the first line, but because it is already there, we don't bother. When the cursor is after the last line, the EOF property becomes True. EOF stands for "end of file," and the acronym has been used with computers since the 1960s. It was chosen also for ADO, even though we don't have a "file" this time.

NOTE For the purposes of this book and the skills it covers, it's quite sufficient to read the recordset just from the beginning to the end. If you get more into ADO programming, you can start learning how to move around the recordset, perhaps with help from bookmarks.

On line 23, we first test that EOF is not already True. This would indicate that the query didn't return any objects from Active Directory, as we display on line 30.

Usually the recordset contains data, so we can browse through it on lines 24 through 28. We can read the attribute value from the recordset by specifying the attribute LDAP name as an argument to `Fields`.

NOTE   We could also read the value using an index number instead of an attribute name. The first retrieved attribute would be `objRecordset.Fields(0)`, the next one would use index "1," and so on. However, Microsoft is not committed to this syntax in the long run and they recommend using the attribute names.

THE LDAP SEARCH STRING

When you study the script, you'll notice that lines 1 through 14 are always the same, no matter what you search. The same goes for lines 19 through 34, perhaps with some slight variance around line 26. Therefore, lines 15 through 18 contain the "beef" of the script—they define what the search is actually like. The rest is just mandatory dressing.

Lines 15 through 18 contain an LDAP search string. It consists of four parts separated by semicolons. The string has the following syntax:

```
<LDAP-path-to-base-object>;LDAP-filter;list-of-attributes;scope
```

These four parts correspond to the four main parameters of an LDAP search, which are described in Table 6.8 in Chapter 6. We show a brief summary in Table 11.7.

NOTE   Because the essence of an ADO query is in the LDAP search string, you could say that in the case of Active Directory, ADO is just a wrapper that enables you to perform LDAP queries in a script.

NOTE   By default, even with the `SubTree` keyword, the scope of the query doesn't cross partition (or naming context) boundaries, such as from one domain to another. Later in the "Multipartition Queries" section we explain how to reach multiple partitions in one query.

TABLE 11.7 The LDAP Search String Contents

Part	Example	Comments
LDAP path to base object	`LDAP://DC=sanao,DC=com`	The ADSI path (i.e., LDAP path) to the base object of the query.
LDAP filter	`(&(objectCategory=person)(sn=a*))`	Specifies the criteria that each object must meet to be included in the search result set.
List of attributes	`distinguishedName, givenName, sn`	The list of attribute LDAP names that are to be returned in the query.
Scope	`SubTree`	The value is `Base`, `OneLevel`, or `SubTree`; if you omit this fourth part, `SubTree` is the default.

When you use an LDAP search string with ADO, it is called the *LDAP dialect*. Another dialect you could use is the *SQL dialect*, which we introduce next.

Basic Example with SQL.vbs

The Structured Query Language, or SQL (pronounced "sequel"), is used to read, write, and manage data in relational databases, such as SQL Server. Because the roots of ADO are in databases, Microsoft implemented also the SQL dialect to the OLE-DB provider for ADSI.

If you don't already know how to use SQL, you shouldn't learn it just because of ADO. We do not teach SQL in this book, but we present the previous script modified to use the SQL dialect, so that if you do know SQL, you can easily catch on from this example.

The only thing that has changed from the previous example is the "beef" part of the script. Therefore, we show only lines 14 through 18 in Figure 11.101. You can see the familiar elements in a different order and with different surroundings. Note that the strings on lines 15 through 17 have a space as the last character so that there is a space before the first word on the next line. Note also that there is an apostrophe (') at the end of line 16 between the quotation marks.

You cannot specify the search scope with this dialect, so the default `SubTree` is used unless you change it with the command object parameters, as described later.

There is also one new element. We now sort by the last name (`sn`). When using the LDAP dialect, you can define the sort order with those command object parameters that we describe later. You must use indexed attributes for sorting; otherwise, it doesn't work.

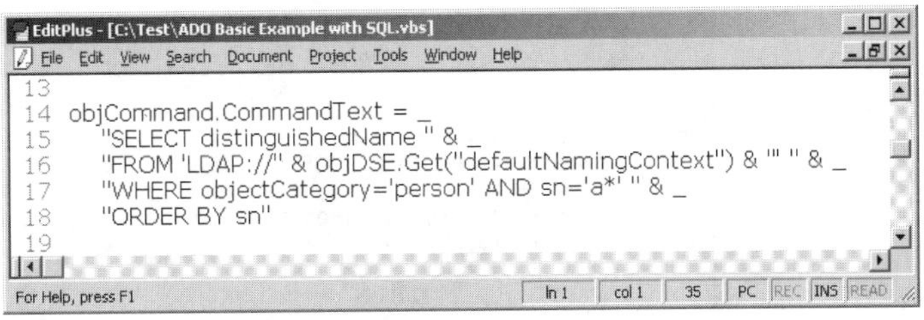

```
13
14 objCommand.CommandText = _
15     "SELECT distinguishedName " & _
16     "FROM 'LDAP://" & objDSE.Get("defaultNamingContext") & "' " & _
17     "WHERE objectCategory='person' AND sn='a*' " & _
18     "ORDER BY sn"
19
```

FIGURE 11.101 Part of the script lines of "ADO Basic Example with SQL.vbs." The lines not shown are identical to the previous example.

Modifying Objects.vbs

An easy way to circumvent the read-only restriction of ADO over ADSI is to get just the object names with ADO, bind to each one using ADSI, and finally modify them as needed. This script demonstrates the technique. It finds all users of the domain that don't have a home folder set and sets this attribute for them.

We show the contents in two parts: part A in Figure 11.102 and part B in Figure 11.103. The latter part handles the returned set of users.

Once again, the only changed lines are the LDAP search string on lines 15 through 19. The best way to filter user objects is to use both the conditions on line 16. The first attribute is indexed, which makes it efficient, and if it alone would also return contact objects, the latter condition makes sure that only user objects

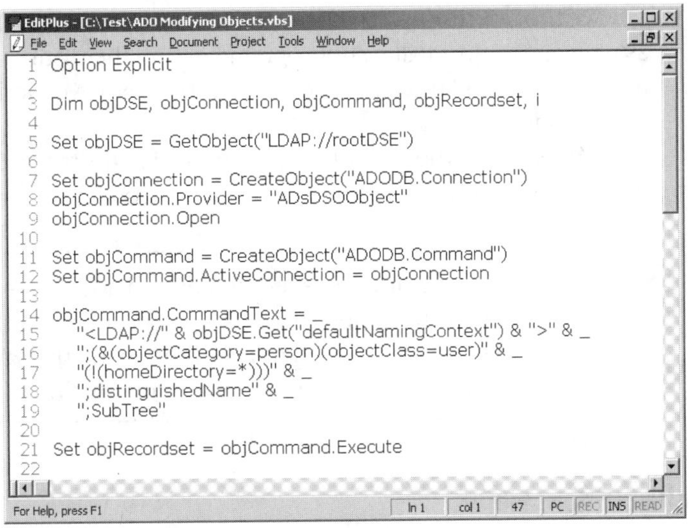

```
1  Option Explicit
2
3  Dim objDSE, objConnection, objCommand, objRecordset, i
4
5  Set objDSE = GetObject("LDAP://rootDSE")
6
7  Set objConnection = CreateObject("ADODB.Connection")
8  objConnection.Provider = "ADsDSOObject"
9  objConnection.Open
10
11 Set objCommand = CreateObject("ADODB.Command")
12 Set objCommand.ActiveConnection = objConnection
13
14 objCommand.CommandText = _
15     "<LDAP://" & objDSE.Get("defaultNamingContext") & ">" & _
16     ";(&(objectCategory=person)(objectClass=user)" & _
17     "(!(homeDirectory=*)))" & _
18     ";distinguishedName" & _
19     ";SubTree"
20
21 Set objRecordset = objCommand.Execute
22
```

FIGURE 11.102 Part A of "ADO Modifying Objects.vbs"

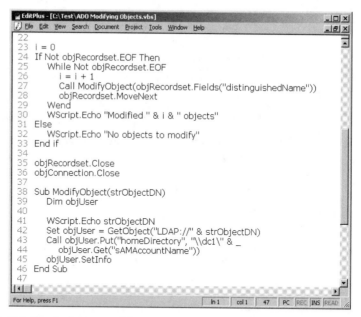

```
22
23  i = 0
24  If Not objRecordset.EOF Then
25      While Not objRecordset.EOF
26          i = i + 1
27          Call ModifyObject(objRecordset.Fields("distinguishedName"))
28          objRecordset.MoveNext
29      Wend
30      WScript.Echo "Modified " & i & " objects"
31  Else
32      WScript.Echo "No objects to modify"
33  End if
34
35  objRecordset.Close
36  objConnection.Close
37
38  Sub ModifyObject(strObjectDN)
39      Dim objUser
40
41      WScript.Echo strObjectDN
42      Set objUser = GetObject("LDAP://" & strObjectDN)
43      Call objUser.Put("homeDirectory", "\\dc1\" & _
44          objUser.Get("sAMAccountName"))
45      objUser.SetInfo
46  End Sub
47
```

FIGURE 11.103 Part B of "ADO Modifying Objects.vbs"

are returned. In addition, as you know, if we used only the latter condition, we would get all computer objects.

The =* on line 17 means "attribute value exists," and the exclamation point in the beginning negates the effect.

We browse through the recordset in a loop in Figure 11.103 (lines 25 through 29), where we just call a subprogram passing the distinguished name as an argument. On lines 42 through 45 of this subprogram, we bind to one user and set her home folder.

We also want the script to report on which users it is changing and how many users there are. These output commands are on lines 30, 32, and 41.

NOTE   Now we retrieve the distinguished names and add LDAP:// on line 42. Another approach would be to retrieve the ADsPath properties, which already contain the LDAP://. However, we wanted to avoid retrieving the same seven characters for each user over the network, although we admit that this is not a big deal.

Multipartition Queries

All the ADO examples so far have used the SubTree scope, but as we mentioned, they were still limited to a single partition only (or naming context).

There are two ways to include several partitions, such as several domains or the configuration and schema partitions, in one query:

- Use the global catalog
- Turn on referral chasing

We discuss both options in the following subsections.

USING THE GLOBAL CATALOG

You can direct a search to the global catalog by specifying "GC:" instead of "LDAP:" in the base object path.

Using the global catalog is easy, because all you need to do is change a couple of letters. It is also efficient in terms of network utilization and search performance, as long as you have a decent communication link to the nearest global catalog server.

An obvious limitation to this approach is that you can search on and retrieve only those attributes that are part of the global catalog.

A SubTree query to the global catalog will automatically include any child domains, and if targeted to the forest root domain, the query will include the configuration partition, which in turn will include the schema partition. Figure 11.104 should help you visualize the tree and the partitions.

Next we describe the other option: referral chasing.

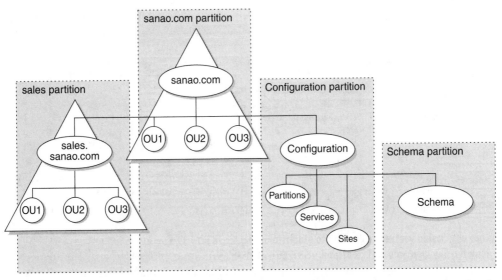

FIGURE 11.104 Configuration, schema, and every child domain is an independent partition, but together they form a logical tree where each one is a child to another.

REFERRAL CHASING

By default, referral chasing is off, which means that an LDAP query (wrapped in ADO) is limited to only one partition. In addition, that one partition must exist on the domain controller that you are communicating with. This results in two limitations.

- Even though the configuration and schema partitions are on your server, they are not included if you target the read to the domain partition.

- If you want to read just one domain, but that domain is not the home domain of your domain controller, you need to specify in the LDAP path a domain controller name that is a member of the wanted domain.

You can turn on referral chasing with one of the command object parameters. When you do this, the WLDAP32.DLL component of your computer starts chasing referrals for you. If a server doesn't contain the requested object, the server returns a *referral* to the client that points to another server, so WLDAP32.DLL can contact that server to get the needed information.

This description of referrals suggests that the configuration and schema partitions should be included, because they already are on the first domain controller. However, as stated earlier, they are not included because they are different partitions.

WARNING Using referral chasing in a large network could mean that your computer starts gathering the information from ten domain controllers all over the world. Consider using the global catalog instead.

To turn on referral chasing, you could add the following lines to your script:

```
Const   ADS_CHASE_REFERRALS_NEVER        = 0
Const   ADS_CHASE_REFERRALS_SUBORDINATE  = &H20
Const   ADS_CHASE_REFERRALS_EXTERNAL     = &H40
Const   ADS_CHASE_REFERRALS_ALWAYS       = &H60  '&H20 + &H40
objCommand.Properties("Chase referrals") = ADS_CHASE_REFERRALS_ALWAYS
```

As we mentioned, the default is Never, so there is no point in adding that choice to your script (unless you explicitly want to show that Never is in use). We explain the other choices in the following list:

- *Subordinate*. Specifying this option includes those other partitions that have the base object's distinguished name as part of their distinguished name. In other words, it will include all child domains (not just immediate), and if the base object is the forest root domain, it will include also the configuration and schema partitions.

- *External*. Specifying this option returns referrals to objects in other directory trees as well as the other domain trees in the forest.
- *Always*. Specifying this option includes both Subordinate and External.

NOTE   If your default domain controller belongs to sanao.com and you specify an LDAP path LDAP://DC=sales,DC=sanao,DC=com, your query won't return any objects with the Subordinate option. You need to use External instead, which may seem a little confusing.

Referrals are returned based on crossRef objects, which reside in the CN=Partitions container of the configuration partition. If you are interested, you can check them with ADSI Edit. Notice in particular the attributes dnsRoot, nCName, and trustParent.

Additional Settings

You can specify some settings with either the connection object or command object properties, as explained in the next two subsections.

THE CONNECTION OBJECT PROPERTIES

Before opening the connection, you can specify a username and password with the following properties:

```
objConnection.Properties("User ID") = _
   "CN=Jack Brown,OU=Sales, DC=sanao,DC=com"
objConnection.Properties("Password") = "somesecret"
objConnection.Properties("Encrypt Password") = True
```

In addition, you can use the ADSI Flag property to specify any of the authentication flags that we listed in the discussion about binding to ADSI with credentials (such as ADS_SECURE_AUTHENTICATION).

SEARCH OPTIONS AS COMMAND OBJECT PARAMETERS

You can specify a number of search options as command object properties. Even though they are properties of an ADO object, they are actually general LDAP search options. Table 11.8 explains these options.

For example, to set the Page size to 500, you would use the following line:

```
objCommand.Properties("Page Size") = 500
```

TABLE 11.8 Search Options

Option	Default	Description
Asynchronous	False	Setting this option to True specifies that control should return to the program after the first row of the search results is available (instead of waiting for all rows or at least the first page). This option has no meaning in VBScript scripts.
Deref Aliases	0	If Active Directory supported alias objects, you could use this option to specify that when either the base object of a search (or some of its subordinates) is an alias, it will be dereferenced to get the target object.
Size Limit	0 (i.e., no limit)	Setting this option specifies how many objects you want back. Unlike the later Page size option, this one doesn't return more than the specified number of objects. If you sort the returned objects based on some attribute, you may want to retrieve only the first ones on the list.
Server Time Limit	0 (i.e., no limit)	Setting this option specifies the number of seconds the server should use to fulfill your query. Unlike the later Time limit option, this one will fail if the specified time is not enough.
Column Names only	False	Setting this option to True returns only the attribute names and not their values. In LDAP searches you could use this option to determine which attributes are present, but in ADO scripts you probably don't have any use for it.
SearchScope	2 (i.e., SubTree)	This option has the same three choices as the fourth part of an LDAP search string (Base, OneLevel, and SubTree).
Timeout	0 (i.e., no timeout)	Setting this option specifies how many seconds the client is willing to wait for the query results.
Page size	0 (i.e., no size)	With the default value "0" there is no paging, which means that if a query contains 15,000 objects, the server sends them all to the client. By specifying the page size (i.e., the number of objects returned in one chunk), you can lessen the burden of your client, the network, and the server. You don't have to add lines to the script to read the next page. ADSI takes care of this automatically when the objects of the previous page run out.
Time limit	0 (i.e., no limit)	Like Page size, this option turns on paging. However, instead of the number of objects, this one specifies how many seconds the server can spend gathering the objects. After the time is up, it must return the objects found so far to the client.

(continued)

TABLE 11.8 (*continued*)

Option	Default	Description
Chase referrals	0 (i.e., never chase)	We described this option in the "Referral Chasing" subsection.
Sort On	(none)	If you specify an attribute LDAP name, the returned objects are sorted on this attribute. However, the attribute must be indexed in Active Directory for this option to work.
Cache Results	True	The default setting True means that the results are cached on the client. This is beneficial if you want to move back and forth in the recordset. If you just browse through the set once, the default setting only consumes more memory.

NOTE   It is a good idea to set a `Page size` for all your ADO scripts to avoid overloading the client, network, or server.

You can use the following constants for `SearchScope`:

```
Const ADS_SCOPE_BASE     = 0
Const ADS_SCOPE_ONELEVEL = 1
Const ADS_SCOPE_SUBTREE  = 2
```

Before we conclude our ADO discussion, we present one more example.

List Objects That Have Blocked ACL Inheritance.vbs

This last example lists all (visible) objects of the default domain that have blocked inheritance of ACEs. You might want to list these objects, because they are exceptions to the general access control strategy. However, if blocking the inheritance means that your permissions are also blocked, you obviously won't get a complete list.

Because the search is based on one bit in the `nTSecurityDescriptor`, we cannot use an LDAP filter for the job. Instead, we need to read all the objects and then inspect them individually.

We use the LDAP filter just to narrow the field a little by excluding all those objects that are set to "show in advanced view only." They are likely to be system objects, which we don't manage.

We show the script in two parts. Figure 11.105 displays part A and Figure 11.106 shows part B.

```
 1  Option Explicit
 2
 3  Const ADS_SD_CONTROL_SE_DACL_PROTECTED = &H1000
 4
 5  Dim objDSE, objConnection, objCommand, objRecordset, i
 6
 7  Set objDSE = GetObject("LDAP://rootDSE")
 8
 9  Set objConnection = CreateObject("ADODB.Connection")
10  objConnection.Provider = "ADsDSOObject"
11  objConnection.Open
12
13  Set objCommand = CreateObject("ADODB.Command")
14  Set objCommand.ActiveConnection = objConnection
15  objCommand.Properties("Page Size") = 500
16
17  objCommand.CommandText = _
18    "<LDAP://" & objDSE.Get("defaultNamingContext") & ">" & _
19    ";(!(showInAdvancedViewOnly=TRUE))" & _
20    ";distinguishedName" & _
21    ";SubTree"
22
23  Set objRecordset = objCommand.Execute
24
```

FIGURE 11.105 Part A of "ADO List Objects That Have Blocked ACL Inheritance.vbs"

```
24
25  If Not objRecordset.EOF Then
26     i = 0
27     While Not objRecordset.EOF
28        Call ShowBlocked(i, objRecordset.Fields("distinguishedName"))
29        objRecordset.MoveNext
30     Wend
31  Else
32     WScript.Echo "No objects to check"
33  End if
34
35  objRecordset.Close
36  objConnection.Close
37
38  Sub ShowBlocked(i, strObjectDN)
39     Dim objADObject, objSecDesc, intSDControl
40
41     Set objADObject = GetObject("LDAP://" & strObjectDN)
42     Set objSecDesc = objADObject.Get("ntSecurityDescriptor")
43     intSDControl = objSecDesc.Control
44
45     If intSDControl And ADS_SD_CONTROL_SE_DACL_PROTECTED Then
46        i = i + 1
47        WScript.Echo "Blocked " & i & ": " & strObjectDN
48     End If
49  End Sub
50
```

FIGURE 11.106 Part B of "ADO List Objects That Have Blocked ACL Inheritance.vbs"

On line 15 we set the `Page size`, because we recommended that you should always set it.

On line 19 is the LDAP filter. We must use "not true" instead of "false," because many objects are missing that attribute. Without this syntax, we wouldn't get those objects.

In the subprogram (lines 38 through 49 in Figure 11.106) we bind to the given object and read the `Control` property of its security descriptor. If that integer property has a certain bit set, it means that the corresponding object won't inherit any ACEs from above.

Note that we pass the value of the `i` variable as an argument and then change the value in the subprogram. By default, the argument was passed "by ref," which means that the changed value can get back to the calling program. This way, the incremented value is available in the next call. We could also have not passed it as an argument, which would have given us the same result.

CONCLUSION

After having read this chapter and studied some or all of the sample scripts, you should have sound knowledge and skills to administer your Active Directory network with scripts. At the same time, you have probably also learned quite a few things about the Active Directory architecture.

Bibliography

BOOKS

Howard, Michael, with Marc Levy and Richard Waymire. *Designing Secure Web-Based Applications for Microsoft Windows 2000.* Redmond, Wash.: Microsoft Press, 2000.

Howes, Timothy A., Mark C. Smith, and Gordon S. Good. *Understanding and Deploying LDAP Directory Services.* Indianapolis: New Riders Publishing, 1999.

Iseminger, David. *Active Directory Developer's Reference Library.* Redmond, Wash.: Microsoft Press, 2000.

Iseminger, David. *Active Directory Services for Microsoft Windows 2000 Technical Reference.* Redmond, Wash.: Microsoft Press, 2000.

Microsoft Consulting Services. *Building Enterprise Active Directory Services—Notes from the Field.* Redmond, Wash.: Microsoft Press, 2000.

Microsoft Windows 2000 Server Resource Kit. Redmond, Wash.: Microsoft Press, 2000.

WEB SITES, ONLINE WHITE PAPERS

Active Directory Programmer's Guide. http://msdn.microsoft.com/library/default.asp?url=/library/en-us/netdir/adsi/active_directory_start_page.asp

Active Directory Schema Site. http://msdn.microsoft.com/certification/schema/

Implementing Common Desktop Management Scenarios White Paper. http://www.microsoft.com/windows2000/techinfo/howitworks/management/grouppolicy.asp

Windows 2000 Group Policy White Paper. http://www.microsoft.com/windows2000/techinfo/howitworks/management/grouppolwp.asp

Windows 2000 Home Page. http://www.microsoft.com/windows2000/

Index

Also from Addison-Wesley

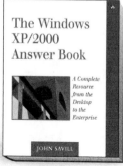

The Windows
XP/2000
Answer Book

A Complete
Resource
from the
Desktop
to the
Enterprise

JOHN SAVILL

0-321-11357-8

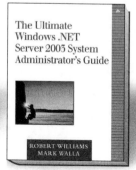

The Ultimate
Windows .NET
Server 2003 System
Administrator's Guide

ROBERT WILLIAMS
MARK WALLA

0-201-79106-4

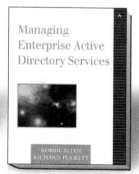

Managing
Enterprise Active
Directory Services

ROBBIE ALLEN
RICHARD PUCKETT

0-672-32125-4

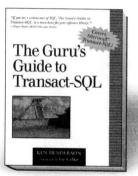

The Guru's
Guide to
Transact-SQL

Covers Microsoft Transact-SQL

KEN HENDERSON

0-201-61576-2

The Guru's Guide
to SQL Server
Stored Procedures,
XML, and HTML

Covers .NET?

KEN HENDERSON

0-201-70046-8

Essential
SQL
Server
2000

An
Administration
Handbook

Buck Woody

0-201-74203-9

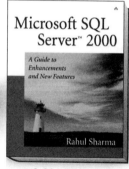

Microsoft SQL
Server 2000

A Guide to
Enhancements
and New Features

Rahul Sharma

0-201-75283-2

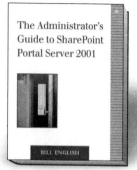

The Administrator's
Guide to SharePoint
Portal Server 2001

BILL ENGLISH

0-201-77574-3

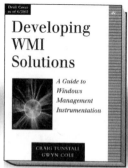

Developing
WMI
Solutions

A Guide to
Windows
Management
Instrumentation

CRAIG TUNSTALL
GWYN COLE

0-201-61613-0

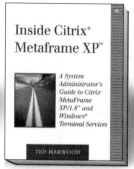

Inside Citrix®
Metaframe XP™

A System
Administrator's
Guide to Citrix
MetaFrame
XP/1.8™ and
Windows®
Terminal Services

TED HARWOOD

0-7357-1192-5

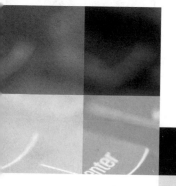